IT Auditing
A Practical Guide to the CISA Exam

Second Edition

IT Auditing
A Practical Guide to the CISA Exam
Second Edition

Trony Clifton CISA, CISM, CPA

Edited by Jerome Hill CISSP, CISA, CISM

Mandem Publishing ® Inc.

Mandem Publishing
Mandem Inc.
East Brunswick, NJ 08816

ISBN:0-9706741-04

IT Auditing
Copyright © 2007 by Mandem Inc. and Trony Clifton
All rights reserved. No part of this book may be reproduced or transmitted in any form or by any means, electronic or mechanical, including photocopy, recording or any information storage and retrieval systems without permission in writing from the publisher. Requests for permission to make copies of any part of this publication should be mailed to :

Mandem Publishing
Mandem Inc.
East Brunswick, NJ 088816

ISBN: 0=9706741-0-4 0-9706741-7-1
Second Edition

Printed in the United States of America

The publisher offers discounts on this book when ordered in bulk quantities. For more information, please contact:

Mandem Corporate Sales Department
197 State Route 18 South
East Brunswick, NJ 08816
info@mandem.com

Many of the names, acronyms and other designations used by standards and accrediting bodies, manufacturers and vendors to distinguish their products are claimed as trademarks. Where those designations appear in this book, and we were aware of a trademark claim, the designations have been printed in initial capital letters or in all capitals. Any failure, perceived or otherwise to acknowledge trademarked designations is purely accidental. Neither Trony Clifton, Mandem Inc. or any contributor to this text has any intent to infringe upon, slight or ignore copyrights, trademarks or any of the privilieges enjoyed by the holders of these marks.

About the Author

Trony Clifton, CISA, CISM, CPA is one of the country's leading professional trainers and educators, specializing in Audit and the CISA/CISM certifications. Trony has a long-standing tradition of excellence through his educational courses and has taught thousands of CISA and CISM candidates over the past 13 years both for ISACA International, Local ISACA Chapters and many Fortune 500 organizations. Trony is currently a professor at the New Jersey Institute of Technology (NJIT).

In addition to holding the Certified Information Systems Auditor designation, Trony is an active member of the New Jersey ISACA Chapter, and has taught the Chicago ISACA CISA Review course from 1995-1998 as well as the CISA review course for the North America CACS conference from 1996-1998. Trony currently teaches the Atlanta Chapter (1997 to present), New Jersey Chapter (1999 to 2006), the Mexico City Chapter (1997 to 2001), Beijing China (2001-2003) chapters, Pittsburgh Chapter (2004-Present), Philadelphia Chapter (2005-Present) and Seattle Chapter (2006-Present).

In his tenure as a CISA Instructor, Trony's passing rate has ranged from 72 to 80 percent. In 2002, two of his students, one from Atlanta and one from New Jersey used his study and training techniques to obtain the highest CISA scores in their respective states.

Acknowledgements

I would like to thank Jerome Hill for his hard work as an editor. He waded through many pages of text over several months making many valued suggestions and modifications. His efforts are greatly appreciated. Without his dedication and hard work this book would not have been completed.

Jerome is a Senior Auditor for Mandem Consulting who performs IT Audits for various Fortune 100 clients as well as not-for-profit organizations. Jerome has over 9 years of professional IT experience including four years as an IT Auditor. His expertise includes performing IT audits and Network evaluations and assessing IT controls in very large IT infrastructures. Companies Jerome worked for or consulted with include Mandem Inc., Bergen County Technical Schools, EMTEC, and Exodus Communications. Jerome is also an adjunct professor at New Jersey Institute of Technology (NJIT) and Essex County College in NJ.

Jerome is a Certified Information Security System Professional, Certified Information Systems Auditor, and Certified Information Security Manager. He has received extensive training in audit and security. He earned a Master's degree in Information Systems from NJIT and received his Bachelor's degree in Computer Science from Nyack College in NY.

In addition, I would like to thank all of the staff members, students, and colleagues whose feedback has influenced this book directly and indirectly. Your comments and suggestions were meaningful, insightful and assisted me in designing a text that I hope will be useful to the profession of IT Audit as well as assist those seeking the designation of CISA.

I would also like to extend a special thanks to ISACA. This is an organization that I hold in high regard and dear to my heart. I was introduced to ISACA very early in my career and my affiliation with the organization has taught me many lessons professionally and personally. There is no doubt that my association with ISACA has provided both the spark and the fuel for my passion for IT Auditing. I am grateful for the background and framework for practice offered by ISACA. I believe that the approaches to management and security recommended by this group are sound and worthy of careful review. I encourage everyone currently in the audit field and all those considering a career here to familiarize themselves with the material offered by ITGI and ISACA. I am fortunate to have this body of work available for use in teaching IT Audit principles and introducing others to the perspective and role of the auditor in the workplace.

Dedication

For Amanda, Nina, Trony Jr. and of course the most important person who keeps everything all together, my wife Michelle -

Without your deep understanding and patience with me during a seemingly endless commitment of time and effort, I would not have had the time or the courage to put pen to paper. To my family,

I THANK YOU.

Foreword

Trony has proven himself to be loyal and trustworthy person to many clients and friends around the world. His professional services and gentle personality are respected by all that work with him. I am grateful for the opportunity to express my respect and thanks for the dedication, and enthusiasm Trony has brought to the people that he has encountered.

Over the years, Trony has proven himself to be an outstanding advisor and educator to his clients and students. During this time, I have had the opportunity to get to know Trony on a personal level. He has surprised me with his wealth of knowledge and understanding of the audit space. We share common interests in travel, auditing, and information technology.

Information Technology audit and security are the strong pillars Trony Clifton embodies. His work in these areas has contributed to the implementation and improvement of these activities at many dozens of companies and in the day-to-day lives of hundreds of individual IT audit and security personnel.

I have personally witnessed many occasions on which Trony has gone over and above his responsibilities to ensure a quality result for clients and students alike. I am convinced of his commitment to teamwork and the building of strong partnerships. He is a highly valued member of the Information System Audit and Control Association (ISACA®) and a strong advocate of the audit and security framework with the clients he serves.

Trony has developed effective techniques to educate individuals in the practice of IT audit and security. His concise and focused study materials have assisted numerous ISACA® candidates pass their certification exams. His subject matter expertise helps students build the confidence needed to sit for the CISA and CISM examinations. He has a unique ability to convey complex information technology concepts into an easy to understand lessons.

This book delivers a rich array of information technology audit and security best practices that can give its readers a greater appreciation for security management and strategy. Be aware that the ultimate responsibility for tailoring the material in this text to each unique environment lies with the professionals tasked with administering or advising on risk and controls. That group of professionals now includes you.

Peter Duranti, CISA, CISM
President, ISACA Philadelphia Chapter

Table of Contents

INTRODUCTION 1
   IT Audit Related Positions: 1
   History of ISACA 1
   Benefits of becoming a CISA 2
   Certification Requirements 2
   How to use this book 6
   The most important things to focus on during your studies 7
   Exam Results 8
   Exam Grading 8

CHAPTER 1   INFORMATION SYSTEMS AUDIT PROCESS 9
   ISACA Professional Standards 9
      Tasks 9
      Knowledge Statements 9
   Standards, Guidelines and Procedures 10
   ISACA Auditing Standards 11
   Corporate Governance of Information Systems 14
   Studying any regulatory reports or regulations 18
   Reviewing prior reports 18
   Audit Charter 19
   Planning the IS Audit 19
   Audit Program Development 21
   Evaluation 23
   REPORTING 23
   CAATs – Audit Tools 24
   Recommendations/Remediation 24
   ETHICS 25
   THE CONTROL OBJECTIVES 25
   OTHER LAWS AND REGULATIONS 26
   Audit Risk and Materiality 26
   Risk Assessment Techniques 28
   General Audit Procedures 30
      Compliance vs. Substantive Testing 31
   Rules of Evidence 32
   Audit Resource Scheduling 33
   Project Management Techniques 33
   Applying Sampling Techniques 35
   Computer Assisted Audit Techniques 37
   Presentation Techniques 41
   Continuous Audit Approach 41
   Control Self-Assessment 43
   The COSO Framework 43
      CHAPTER 1 PRACTICE QUESTIONS 44
      CHAPTER 1 ANSWERS TO PRACTICE QUESTIONS 46

CHAPTER 2   IT GOVERNANCE 49
   INFORMATION SYSTEMS ORGANIZATION AND MANAGEMENT 49
      Corporate Governance 51

IT Audit and IT Governance	51
IT Security Governance	52
Corporate-Level Roles and Responsibilities	52
IS Strategy	53
The Information Security Policy	*53*
Risk Management	56
Types of Risk Analysis	*57*
Qualitative Risk Analysis	*60*
Quantitative Risk Analysis	*62*
Management Tasks	65
Audit/Security Concerns of Outsourcing	68
Organizational Structure	71
Project Management	72
Separation of Duties	78
Auditing of IT Governance	80
CHAPTER 2 PRACTICE QUESTIONS	81
CHAPTER 2 ANSWERS TO PRACTICE QUESTIONS	83
CHAPTER 3 SYSTEMS AND INFRASTRUCTURE LIFECYCLE MANAGEMENT	**85**
INFORMATION SYSTEMS MANAGEMENT PROCESS	85
Business Realization	*86*
System Development Methodologies	*88*
TRADITIONAL SYSTEM DEVELOPMENT LIFE CYCLE	89
Alternative Application Development Approaches	114
Incremental or progressive development	*114*
Iterative development	*114*
Prototyping	*115*
Rapid Application Development (RAD)	*116*
Agile development	*117*
Data-Oriented System Development (DOSD)	*118*
Object-Oriented System Development	*118*
Spiral Development	*118*
Component-Based Development	*119*
Web-Based Application Development	*120*
Reengineering	*120*
Reverse Engineering	*120*
Project Management	122
Project Organizational Forms	129
The Work Breakdown Structure (WBS)	*130*
Systems Development Methodology	*133*
Critical Path Methodology (CPM)	*134*
Gantt Charts	*137*
Program Evaluation Review Technique (PERT)	*138*
General Project Management Tools and Techniques	139
Decision support systems	*139*
Auditing Project Management	139
Implementation and Change Control Procedures	141
Other System Development Controls	150
Input/Origination Controls	*151*
Input Batch Controls	*152*
Input Error Reporting	*153*
Processing Procedures and Controls	*154*

Output Controls *155*
    Data Validation Controls *156*
    Data File Control Procedures *157*
APPLICATION TYPES *159*
    Electronic Commerce *159*
    Electronic Data Interchange *162*
    E-Mail *166*
    Electronic Banking *167*
    Electronic Funds Transfer (EFT) *169*
    Automated Teller Machine *170*
    Image Processing *171*
    Artificial Intelligence and Expert Systems *172*
    Business Intelligence *174*
    Decision Support System (DSS) *177*
    Customer Relationship Management (CRM) *179*
    Supply Chain Management (SCM) *180*

    Software Capability Maturity Model (CMMI *181*
CHAPTER 3 PRACTICE QUESTIONS *183*
CHAPTER 3 ANSWERS TO PRACTICE QUESTIONS *185*

CHAPTER 4 IT SERVICE DELIVERY AND SUPPORT *187*

INFORMATION SYSTEMS OPERATIONS *187*
    Service Levels *189*
    Infrastructure Operations *189*
    Lights-Out Operations *189*
    Input-Output Controls *190*
    Job Scheduling *190*
RESOURCE MONITORING *190*
    Incident Management *190*
    Problem Management *190*
    Error Handling *191*
    Help Desk/Technical Support *191*
    Change Management *192*
    Library Management *192*
    Release Management *192*
    Information Security Management *192*
INFORMATION SYSTEMS HARDWARE *193*
    Server Functions and Processing *193*
    Processing Types *194*
    Common Storage Devices *195*
COMPUTER OPERATING SYSTEMS AND ARCHITECTURE *196*
DATABASE MANAGEMENT SYSTEM (DBMS) SOFTWARE *197*
NETWORK ARCHITECTURES *199*
THE INTERNET *200*
REMOTE ACCESS *207*
LAN TOPOLOGIES *209*
WIRELESS TECHNOLOGY *210*
    Basic Wireless Security Methods *211*
NETWORK MANAGEMENT *212*
INFRASTRUCTURE DEVELOPMENT/ACQUISITION PRACTICES *212*
AUDITING THE ACQUISITION PLAN *216*

	xi
AUDITING THE IT INFRASTRUCTURE	217
AUDITING SOFTWARE	219
CHAPTER 4 PRACTICE QUESTIONS	222
CHAPTER 4 ANSWERS TO PRACTICE QUESTIONS	224

CHAPTER 5   PROTECTION OF INFORMATION ASSETS 227

- INFORMATION SYSTEMS INTEGRITY, CONFIDENTIALITY AND AVAILABILITY ... 227
- COMPONENTS OF A GOOD SECURITY POLICY ... 232
- SECURITY PROGRAM DETAILS ... 233
  - Security Lifecycle ... 233
- HARDWARE AND SOFTWARE INVENTORY CONTROL ... 236
- LOGICAL ACCESS CONTROLS ... 238
  - Access Permissions ... 238
  - Access Control Methods ... 239
  - Paths of Logical Access ... 239
- COMPUTER CRIMES AND CRIMINALS ... 240
  - Types of Computer Criminals ... 241
  - Logical Access Exposures ... 242
  - Auditing Logical Access Controls ... 249
- NETWORK INFRASTRUCTURE SECURITY ... 250
  - LANS (Local Area Networks ... 250
  - Internet Threats and Security ... 252
- FIREWALLS ... 254
  - Firewall Services and Configuration ... 257
  - Firewall Policies ... 258
  - Firewall. and Gateway. Architecture ... 259
- REMOTE ACCESS—VIRTUAL PRIVATE NETWORK (VPN) ... 264
  - IPSec Overview ... 265
  - PPTP Overview ... 266
  - L2TP Overview ... 266
  - VPN Architecture ... 266
- REMOTE ACCESS SECURITY RISKS ... 267
- REMOTE ACCESS SECURITY RISK COUNTERMEASURES ... 268
- INTRUSION DETECTION ... 269
- TECHNOLOGY OVERVIEW ... 274
  - Wireless Networking ... 274
  - Controls for Wireless Networking ... 276
- SECURITY FOR VOICE OVER INTERNET PROTOCOL (VoIP) ... 278
- ENCRYPTION ... 284
  - Private Key Cryptography ... 284
  - Public Key Cryptography ... 284
- PUBLIC KEY INFRASTRUCTURE (PKI) ... 287
- AUDITING APPLICATIONS ... 288
- AUDITING DEVICES ... 289
- PRIVACY IN THE ORGANIZATION ... 290
- DISPOSAL OR DESTRUCTION OF PII ... 291
- PHYSICAL ACCESS SECURITY ... 291
- ENVIRONMENTAL CONTROLS AND PROTECTION OF ASSETS ... 293
- CHAPTER 5 PRACTICE QUESTIONS ... 295
- CHAPTER 5 ANSWERS TO PRACTICE QUESTIONS ... 297

CHAPTER 6 BUSINESS CONTINUITY AND DISASTER RECOVERY 299

Business Continuity Planning 299
Components of an Effective BCP 299
Develop Contingency Planning Policy Statement 301
The Business Impact Analysis 301
Recovery Point Objective and Recovery Time Objective *302*
Alternate/Backup Processing Facilities 304
Development of Recovery Strategies 307
The Risk Assessment Process 307
Acquisition of Equipment *308*
Documentation 309
Testing of BCP/DR plans 310
Plan Updates and Evaluation 310
Backups 314
Hard Drive Redundancy 316
Insurance Coverage 317
Telecommunications 318
Disposal or Destruction of PII 318
Auditing Business Continuity and Disaster Recovery 318
CHAPTER 6 PRACTICE QUESTIONS 320
CHAPTER 6 ANSWERS TO PRACTICE QUESTIONS 322

Glossary 325
Index 391
References 401

INTRODUCTION

Profession

Information Systems Auditing is one of the fastest growing fields in the world today. As the world's reliance upon technology and digital communications increases, new issues and challenges regarding these operations are being discovered. The newer issues include the following: information privacy, information availability, authentication and reliability concerns, and protection of information assets. In addition, regulatory requirements at the state and federal levels are increasing in number and complexity. To add to the chaos, the market for technology-based solutions for these issues is experiencing an overload of new offerings and variations on older themes. The level of knowledge and experience needed to chart clear paths through the maze of competing concerns is increasing at a steady pace. As a result, the role of the Information Systems Auditor within the organization should also increase in both size and importance.

IT Audit Related Positions:
- IS Auditors
- Consultants
- Educators
- Security Consultant/Technician
- Regulators
- Chief Information Officer
- Chief Technical/Security Officer
- Audit Manager
- Internal Auditors
- IT Security Compliance Manager

History of ISACA and the CISA

The Information Systems Audit and Control Association (ISACA) was created in 1967, when a small group of individuals with similar jobs -- auditing controls in computer systems, became critical in organizations. In 1969, the group formalized the EPA Auditors Association. In 1976, the association formed an education foundation to expand the knowledge and value of IT governance and control. In 1978, the Certified Information Systems Auditor (CISA) program was established to develop and maintain a testing instrument that could be used to evaluate an auditor's practical knowledge in conducting IS audits.

ISACA currently has approximately 65,000 members in over 140 countries. Percentages of professionals by geographical regions are estimated as follows: North America has 52 percent of all current CISA professionals, Asia/Mid-East has 22 percent, Europe has 21 percent, Oceania has 3 percent and Europe/Africa has 2 percent. In the near term, it is believed that the Oceania and Asia/Middle East regions will be those that experience the largest percentage of growth in CISA candidates. The members of this group come from many different career fields; CISA professionals have a broad base of knowledge in several areas within information technology. There are currently over 50,000 CISA professionals and over 6500 CISM professionals worldwide.[1] It can be said of many qualified CISA professionals that they are "experienced in all, but master of none". On the other hand, every CISA should develop a high level of competency in the areas of Risk and Control.

ISACA wants to encourage IS Auditors in general to maintain and even expand upon their core competencies by means of continuing education. To promote this activity, ISACA requires those that obtain the CISA certification to obtain a minimum of 120 CPE hours during the three year period that the certification is valid. In addition, each CISA must earn no less than 20 CPE hours in any one of those three years. These requirements benefit the CISA professional in two ways: First, each CISA is forced to maintain a steady exposure to current trends. Second, the certification establishes a baseline criterion by which executives and senior managers within government, business, education and other areas may judge the overall competence of candidates for auditing positions.

The first CISA exam was given in 1981. 659 candidates took the exam and 417 of them passed. Over time, the usefulness and popularity of the exam have increased. In June 2005, over 14,000 individuals took the exam worldwide, but only 7,581 passed. This amounts to a pass rate of approximately 51%. However, only 60% of those who did pass were successful on their first attempt. The pass rate is low for two reasons. First, based on my experience, I am certain that many people do not devote sufficient time to study for this exam. Second, many of those that devote time to study for the exam don't focus on the right areas. Many of the study materials and review courses for the CISA exam fail to properly emphasize the importance of a significant investment of study time. In addition, even the most thorough of these guides does not clearly focus on those topics that are most critical.

Benefits of becoming a CISA

CISA certification brings with it a great number of personal and organizational benefits. An individual that obtains this certification demonstrates that an above average understanding of IS audit theory and practice has been achieved. Those that have the ability to provide effective guidance on IS audit security and control practices should be in high demand for many years to come. Finally, according to Foote Partners LLC (May 29, 2007), obtaining the CISA certification helped those that responded to the survey to earn premiums of 10% to 14% of their base pay.[2]

Certification Requirements

To earn the CISA designation, candidates are required to:

- Successfully pass the CISA exam, which consists of 200 multiple choice questions and lasts 4 hours. A score of 450 or more is necessary to pass this exam. The exam is graded on a curve. Therefore, in order to pass the exam you will need to answer approximately 125 to 150 questions correctly.
    - Submit evidence of a minimum of 5 years of professional IS Audit, control and security experience.
    - Substitution and waivers of experience may be allowed as follows:
    - A maximum of one year of information systems, operating, financial or programming experience, or one year of auditing experience can be substituted for 1 year of IS auditing experience.
    - An Associates or Bachelors degree (the equivalent of 60 or 120 completed college credits) can be substituted for one or two years, respectively, of information systems auditing.
    - Each two years of experience as a full-time university instructor in a related field (i.e. computer science, accounting, information systems auditing) may be substituted for 1 year of information systems audit experience.
    - Experience may be gained:
        - Within a 10 year period proceeding the date of the application for certification or,
        - Within 5 years from the date of initially passing the exam.

These requirements may be confusing to some. The following is an example of one individual's experience:

- College graduate with BBA in accounting
- Worked for a bank as a financial auditor
- Has 7 years of audit experience

The way this person fills out the application will obviously influence any decision regarding acceptance. Filling out the application is like filing out a job application. A candidate must supply the relevant educational and employment histories and at least 3 job references. In the example above one can assume that the person has at least 3 years of experience that can be applied against the 5 years required.

- If this person's employer affirms that this employee performed general control reviews, logical security access reviews, and disaster recovery testing for the past 2 years, that the person will be certified.
- However, if the individual has only performed such reviews for approximately 1 year, then an additional 1500 hours worth of itemized work experience would be necessary to reach the level experience ISACA requires.

Taking additional classes related to IS Auditing may also be helpful. My recommendation is that those who pass the CISA apply for certification as soon as possible. The application submission process is free of charge. Have ISACA tell you exactly what you need based on your current job situation or experience in order to become a CISA. Many people choose to take the CISA exam prior to meeting the experience requirements. ISACA does not state or imply that a lack of audit experience is a valid reason to avoid taking the exam. The following requirements for certification are common to both the CISA and CISM (Certified Information Systems Manager):

- Successful completion of the requisite exam
- Experience as an information systems auditor, with a minimum of five years professional experience in an area of direct interest to the certification
- Agreement to the ISACA Code of Professional Ethics
- Continuing education policy that requires maintenance fees and a minimum of 20 contact hours of continuing education each year and a minimum of 120 contact hours over the three-year certification period

The Information Systems Audit and Control Association (ISACA) currently offers the CISA certification for auditing, networking, and security professionals and the CISM certification for information security management professionals. A new certification in IT Governance will soon be released. The CISA certification is open to those who have passed the CISA exam. Both exams are currently offered twice a year (June and December) worldwide, and it covers the following areas of information systems auditing:

- The IS Audit process (10%)
- IT Governance (15%)
- Systems and Infrastructure Lifecycle (16%)
- IT Service Delivery and Support (14%)
- Protection of Information Assets (31%)
- Business Continuity and Disaster Recovery (14%)

The CISM has a higher emphasis on the roles and responsibilities of those who manage information systems. This certificate is open to those who pass the CISM exam. This exam includes the following areas:
- Information Security Governance (23%)
- Information Risk Management (22%)
- Information Security Program Development (17%)
- Information Security Program Management (24%)
- Incident Management and Response (14%)

Individuals that took the exam prior to 2005 should familiarize themselves with the changes in the focus areas appearing on the exam. These changes are documented in the table below. Every 5 years ISACA conducts a practice analysis study of the work performed by CISA professionals. This is done to ensure that the focus areas and the topics included within each area accurately reflect current standards, guidelines and practices. The study also includes a forecast of current trends in organizational activity, with an emphasis on anticipating the skills CISA candidates will need in the future. This review and update process helps maintain the practical relevance and value of the CISA certification for those that obtain it and for the organizations that employ them. The most recent practice analysis study was completed in January 2005 and applies to CISA exams beginning in June 2006.

This review and update process helps maintain the practical relevance and value of the CISA certification for those that obtain it and for the organizations that employ them. The most recent practice analysis study was completed in January 2005 and applies to CISA exams beginning in June 2006. As a result, major changes in exam content or emphasis should not occur before the next review. However, due to the breadth of material covered by these exams, suitable questions may appear in a wide variety of forms. The amount of study required for a successful exam experience should not be underestimated. The following table provides brief explanations about the prior and current exam emphases. There is significant overlap in the presentation of the older and newer chapter material.

2000-2005 CISA Job Analysis	New 2006 CISA Job Analysis	Difference between 2005 and 2006	Changes
The IS Audit Process (10%)	The IS Audit Process (10%)	Same as Chapter 1	This area does not materially change
Management, Planning and Organization of IS (11%)	IT Governance (15%)	Same as Chapter 2	IT governance is recognized as an area that requires more attention from IS auditors; therefore, topics related to management, planning and organization of IS become part of the IT governance content area
Business Process Evaluation and Risk Management (15%)	Rolled into Chapter 3	Same as Chapter 2	These areas are combined in the Risk Management area in Chapter 2
Business Application System Development, Acquisition, Implementation and Maintenance (16%)	Systems and Infrastructure Life Cycle Management (16%)	Same as Chapter 3	The new systems and infrastructure life cycle management area is integrated with the previous content of the technical infrastructure and operational practices and the business application system development, acquisition, implementation and maintenance areas.
Technical Infrastructure and Operational Practices (13%)	IT Service Delivery and Support (14%)	Same as Chapter 4	Approximately 4 additional questions are added to this area.
Protection of Information Assets (25%)	Protection of Information Assets (31%)	Same as Chapter 5	More attention is given to Logical Security
Disaster Recovery and Business Continuity (10%)	Business Continuity and Disaster Recovery (14%)	Same as Chapters 4 and 6	This area combines both technology and system development

Whether a candidate has taken the exam before or not, time and attention should be focused on chapters 3, 5, 4, 6, 2 and then chapter 1, in that order. The reason this order is important may be derived from the chart below:

2006 CISA Exam Questions By Chapters			
CHAPTERS	Percentage Weighting	Approximate Number of Questions	Recommended Minimum Study Time (in hours)
1	10	20	10
2	15	30	25
3	16	32	30
4	14	28	20
5	31	62	60
6	14	28	20
Total	100	200	165

Chapter 3 explains the use of the traditional SDLC (Systems Development Lifecycle) and other frameworks for managing the development and/or purchase of new systems. Another area to watch in chapter 3 involves the various types of tests that can be run against data and systems to verify their integrity. Chapters 5 and 4 are the most "tech" oriented and they require a strong familiarity with networking theory, architecture, hardware and technologies. Those with significant experience or strength in these areas should skim the relevant chapters in this book as a guide and strengthen their knowledge of any weak areas and but focus most of their time on the remaining chapters.

In general, candidates with strong technical backgrounds should have an easier time than others. The questions related to topics in chapters 3 though 6 that require some technical knowledge should account for 50% to approximately 65% of the total number offered. Those with financial, managerial or other non-technical backgrounds should be prepared to spend more time on the material in these chapters.

Chapters 1 and 2 differ in their emphasis. Chapter 1 deals with the audit process, while chapter 2 covers IT governance, introduces various organizational roles and explains their relationship to the audit process. There is some unavoidable overlap in these two chapters. Finally, regarding chapter 6 "Disaster Recovery and Business Continuity", you either know it or you don't. If you have not been exposed to this type of planning before, be prepared to spend some time here.

According to ISACA, the Percentage Weighting and Number of Questions are approximations. The recommendations included here are based on those approximations. As the table shows, chapter 5, Protection of Assets, has been given the highest level of importance by ISACA. It is essential that every candidate understands the theory and practice behind logical security controls. Without this knowledge, it will be extremely difficult to pass the CISA exam. Weakness in chapter 5 topics may also indicate some weakness in parts of chapter 4 as well. More importantly, a candidate that is weak in this area will find it difficult to properly gauge and report on the effectiveness of controls actually deployed in live environments.

Exam Tip: Chapter 3 contains information that is echoed in different forms in chapters 4, 2, 1 and 6. It is strongly recommended that exam candidates become familiar with the various SDLCs and look for situations in other chapters and in questions where they might be referred to, either directly or indirectly.

ISACA does not expect IS Auditors to become computer technicians or administrators. In addition, it is not necessary for CISA candidates to have extensive technical work experience prior to obtaining the certification. However, it is reasonable to require IS auditors to understand the vulnerabilities and threats applicable to IS assets. It is also expected that IS Auditors will be able to assess risk levels and be able to suggest appropriate preventative, detective and corrective controls, in both mainframe and client/server environments.

How to use this book
This book has been designed to meet the following needs:
- It may be used as an introductory textbook for Information Systems Auditing.
- It may be used as a study guide for those seeking to obtain CISA certification.
- It may function as a high-level overview of the IS/IT audit process for management personnel or those that may lack a strong technical background.

I (Trony) have held the CISA certification for 15 years and taught CISA review courses for 12 years. I know that the CISA exam has been successfully taken by individuals with no experience and individuals with over 20 years of IT experience. On the other hand, I know that people with significant IT experience have sat for and failed this exam. This book outlines areas that have been tested in the past and allows each candidate to concentrate on the areas of the exam in which they need the most improvement. The candidate using this material will also benefit from my recommendations about those topics that might be considered critical for success on the exam. In addition, the book offers study tips and recommendations about the amount of time and effort that should be devoted to each area.

It is strongly recommended that all candidates read through the entire book at least once at the time they are about to begin their studies. Ideally, this initial reading will occur at the start of the candidate's 165+ hour journey. This will give the candidate a better idea of all the sub-topics involved in each area and enable each person to more precisely allocate study time to the areas that require the most attention. It is also strongly recommended that each candidate perform this reading with pen in hand. While doing this, keep the following questions and objectives in mind:

- What are the major topics and subtopics within each area?
- What are the terms or concepts that I am unfamiliar with?
- Have I reviewed any ISACA documentation, including the COBIT framework, which covers my weak areas?

One of the goals set for the production of this text is a complete coverage of exam objectives. However, it should not be assumed that this book provides an in-depth discussion of all of the areas covered. Consider that ISACA requires each candidate to have 5 years of experience or its equivalent in order to actually receive the CISA certification. No single book could provide that much information. A search of any of the popular online bookstores will reveal that entire volumes have been written that cover the material of each of the chapters in this study guide. Also, many of the subtopics within these chapters such as risk management, project management, firewalls, encryption, etc. are sufficiently complex that additional texts, study guides and certifications exist that focus solely on these areas. As a result, every candidate is encouraged to identify the areas or topics that are least clear and devote the time to become familiar with them.

The most important things to focus on during your studies

Candidates often ask questions about the "best" way to study or the "most important topics" for the exam. It is very difficult to provide a precise answer to these questions for each candidate. Overall, I recommend that each candidate spend a minimum of 165 to 200 hours of study time for this exam. On the other hand, since each person is unique, several factors must be taken into account for each individual. These factors include:

- An individual's optimal learning and communication styles.
- Affinities or tendencies to exhibit or prefer either a more logical or a more artistic viewpoint.
- An individual's overall level of intelligence or ability to absorb and apply new material.
- Each individual's unique combination of educational and work experiences.

The CISA exam has proven to be difficult to pass even for highly skilled and competent people from inside and outside of the audit profession. Time has shown that the wording of many of the questions require the candidate to apply reasoning skills in very specific ways. For this reason, I also recommend that each candidate obtain practice questions from one or more sources and practice reasoning through as many of them as possible. Practice questions should not be used to simply memorize answers. Instead, each candidate should attempt to understand how to eliminate incorrect answers and explain why the answer supplied is the correct one. In particular, each successful CISA candidate must be able to do the following:

- Read each question as many times as necessary to determine what is really being asked
- Eliminate as many obviously incorrect answers as possible early in the process. Hopefully, this will amount to at least two of the four possible answers.
- Select from the remaining choices either:
    - The answer which *most accurately* reflects the ideas found in the framework ISACA has established.
    - The answer that is *most* consistent with technical or established industry standards or practices.
    - The answer that might be considered the least bad or least awkward of the two or more remaining answers.

The time allotted for the exam is 4 hours. There are 200 questions on the exam. This gives each candidate approximately 1.2 minutes (1min. 12sec.) on average to complete each question. As a result, unless one's test taking style demands it, I do not recommend that candidates answer the questions in a linear form. Instead, it is recommended that each candidate proceed as follows:

1) Immediately after being allowed to begin the exam, the candidate should work through the entire exam and only answer those questions that can be answered very easily and without multiple readings of the question and answer sets. Every question that requires *any* serious effort should be skipped during this first pass through the exam. If there is any doubt at all about which of the choices is the correct answer, then the question should be skipped. Hopefully, each candidate will be able to complete *at least* 30 questions (15% of 200) during this first pass.
2) The candidate should then start from the beginning again and work through all the questions. On this second pass, the candidate should have two new advantages:
    a. The questions and answer sets that appear later in the booklet could jog some useful memories and/or provide other clues about questions that appeared earlier in the exam.
    b. By focusing on getting through the easier questions on the first pass, the candidate should feel a bit more confident and get through any initial anxiety a bit sooner.
3) On this second pass, repeat number "1" above; again, only answering those questions that can be done easily. After this pass, the candidate should have a minimum of 40 to 70 questions done (20% to 35% of 200) and approximately 2.5 to 3 hours left. The key benefit of this approach is that the candidate is so certain about the answers selected for these questions that it may be assumed that at least 90% to 95% of them are correct. Since approximately 125 to 150 correct answers will be needed to pass the exam, the candidate may assume that approximately 30% to 50% of all the correct answers needed for success have all ready been marked on the answer sheet.

4) By the time the third pass begins, most of the questions that remain will require a lot of time, meaning multiple readings of the question and answer sets or struggles with definitions of terms. This phase of the exam will be much easier for those candidates that took the time to memorize the terms they were unfamiliar with. The practice of working through hundreds of questions prior to the exam will also be a huge benefit at this stage.

Exam Results

ISACA estimates that results of the exam will be available approximately 8 weeks after the exam date. During registration for the exam, candidates may choose to receive their results by email or by regular mail.

Exam Grading

The ISACA organization does not release detailed information about how it grades each item on an exam. However, ISACA does provide some general information about the grading process:[3]

1) ISACA has begun using a scoring method with a point range of 200 to 800. At present, 450 is the passing grade.

2) Candidates will also receive information about their scores for each of the six subject areas. This score report will not include a list of exactly which questions were answered correctly or incorrectly.

3) According to the CISM Exam Candidates Guide, "Questions identified as being ambiguous or having technical flaws will either not be used in the grading process or will be given multiple correct answer keys. Raw scores then will be mathematically converted to scaled scores."[4] It may be assumed that a similar process occurs for the CISA grading. Specific details about questions that may have been removed or had the number of correct answers increased is not available.

4) As noted above, after the initial grading is complete, ISACA converts all final test scores to a "scaled" score. This amounts to a grading curve. As a result, adding the scores received in each sub-area will not provide the candidate with the exact final grade for the exam. Specifics regarding the calculation of the scale or curve are not available.

Not If a candidate normally watches approximately 2 hours of television per day, the weekly total would be approximately 14 hours. That adds up to 52 hours in one month if only 28 days per month are counted. In three months time, this adds up to 156 hours. If a full 30 days per month are counted, this becomes 180 hours. At this pace, a candidate could fulfill the minimum study time suggested without making any other lifestyle changes.

These recommendations bear repeating:
- Spend a *minimum of 165 to 200 hours in preparation* for this exam.
- *Memorize* as many *unfamiliar terms* as possible
- *Work through as many practice questions as possible* as part in your overall study plan.

Chapter 1 INFORMATION SYSTEMS AUDIT PROCESS

ISACA Professional Standards

Information systems (IS) auditing is defined as an audit whose focus is the review and evaluation of any or all aspects of information processing systems, including any of the related and non-automated processes and the interfaces between them. Since the Internet was made available for general public use, there has been a phenomenal increase in the skill sets needed to perform IS audits. As an organization, the Information Systems Audit and Control Association (ISACA) tries to keep abreast of the changes in the IS auditing arena. One of the contributions ISACA has made to the auditing field is a set of standards, guidelines and procedures that applies specifically to IS auditing.

A primary objective of ISACA is to inform auditors of the minimum level of knowledge and performance required to reach the professional level of responsibilities set forth in the Code of Professional Ethics. Another objective is to inform management and other interested parties of the profession's expectations concerning the work of practitioners. The standards promoted by ISACA apply to information systems auditing work performed by those individuals that are members of ISACA and by holders of the Certified Information Systems Auditor (CISA) designation.

The information in this chapter represents approximately 10 percent of the CISA examination (approximately 20 questions).

Tasks
There are several tasks within this area that the CISA candidate must understand and be able to perform:
- Develop and implement a risk-based IS audit strategy for the organization in compliance with IS audit standards, guidelines and best practices.
- Plan specific audits to ensure that IT and business systems are protected and controlled.
- Conduct audits in accordance with IS audit standards, guidelines and best practices to meet planned audit objectives.
- Communicate emerging issues, potential risks, and audit results to key stakeholders.
- Advise on the implementation of risk management and control practices within the organization, while maintaining independence.

Knowledge Statements
The following statements describe specific topics a CISA candidate should be familiar with and use as guidance in the fulfillment of the tasks outlined above:

- Knowledge of ISACA IS Auditing Standards, Guidelines and Procedures and Code of Professional Ethics
- Knowledge of IS auditing practices and techniques
- Knowledge of techniques used to gather information and preserve evidence (e.g., observation, inquiry, interview, CAATs, electronic media)
- Knowledge of the evidence life cycle (e.g., the collection, protection, chain of custody)
- Knowledge of control objectives and controls related to IS (e.g., COBIT)
- Knowledge of risk assessment in an audit context
- Knowledge of audit planning and management techniques
- Knowledge of reporting and communication techniques (e.g., facilitation, negotiation, conflict resolution)
- Knowledge of control self-assessment (CSA)
- Knowledge of continuous audit techniques

Exam Tip: ISACA provides a very high-level overview of the contents of each chapter via the Task and Knowledge statements it supplies. The scope of the exam questions, in broad strokes, is offered through these statements. Each CISA candidate should examine these statements and mark any that are unfamiliar for additional research.

The purpose of this subject area is to provide an IS auditor knowledge of generally accepted information systems audit standards, guidelines and practices in accordance with COBIT (Control Objectives for Information and related Technology). The CISA candidate must understand and be able to explain the various procedures and techniques involved in the planning, performance and completion of an audit. In particular, the interpretation and performance of these actions should be in compliance with the framework described in the Information Systems Audit and Control Association's Standards for IS Auditing, ISACA Auditing Guidelines, the Code of Ethics and COBIT.

In addition, a candidate is required to understand the objectives and methods of audit testing and evidence gathering. This includes a broad knowledge of sampling, computer-assisted audit techniques and their usage in an IT Audit. The candidate must also be able to identify and explain various types of risk and the controls used to mitigate these risks as well.

An outline of the stages of an IS Audit should include the following:

- Audit Plan
    - Reaching an agreement on an audit charter that clearly defines the audit objectives and scope, preparing the audit program and scheduling resources. If necessary, a follow up review of prior audit findings may also be arranged.
- Documentation
    - Review of documentation supplied by the organization regarding policies and procedures.
    - Obtaining and documenting evidence of the controls in use within the audit area according to accepted policies and procedures and/or any means or format agreed upon in the audit charter.
- Evaluation
    - Analyzing the evidence obtained and drawing conclusions based on that evidence and a comparison with the stated business objectives of the organization.
- Reporting
    - Composing a report that will provide its readers with findings, conclusions and recommendations regarding the audited areas in a clear and useful format. This also includes presenting this report and/or any findings that demand immediate attention to those parties agreed upon in the audit charter.
- Recommendations/Remediation
    - Assessing actions taken by management regarding the implementation of the audit report's recommendations by using appropriate follow-up and reporting techniques.
- Ethics
    - Adhering to the Association's Code of Ethics and Auditing Guidelines to ensure quality and consistency of audit work.

Standards, Guidelines and Procedures

ISACA assigns specific definitions to these terms[1]

1) **Standards** define mandatory requirements for IS auditing and reporting
2) **Guidelines** provide guidance in applying IS auditing standards. Auditors must use professional judgment when considering the implementation of guidelines.
3) **Procedures** provide further information on how to comply with and meet the standards when performing IS auditing work. Procedures do not set requirements.

Exam Tip: ISACA has created a document entitled "IS Standards, Guidelines and Procedures for Auditing and Control Professionals". As of June 2007, this document may be downloaded at no cost and without the need of a membership or registration from ISACA's website. This document will prove to be of immense value to a candidate for any of ISACA's certifications. It will also benefit any manager or technical implementer currently working in the audit field.

ISACA Auditing Standards[2]

S1 Audit Charter:
- The purpose, responsibility, authority and accountability of the information systems audit function or information systems audit assignments should be appropriately documented in an audit charter or engagement letter.
- The audit charter or engagement letter should be agreed and approved at an appropriate level within the organization(s).

S2 Independence
- Professional Independence - In all matters related to the audit, the IS auditor should be independent of the auditee in both attitude and appearance.
- Organizational Independence - The IS audit function should be independent of the area or activity being reviewed to permit objective completion of the audit assignment.

S3 Professional Ethics and Standards
- The IS auditor should adhere to the ISACA Code of Professional Ethics in conducting audit assignments.
- The IS auditor should exercise due professional care, including observance of applicable professional auditing standards, in conducting the audit assignments.

S4 Professional Competence
- The IS auditor should be professionally competent, having the skills and knowledge to conduct the audit assignment.
- The IS auditor should maintain professional competence through appropriate continuing professional education and training.

S5 Planning
- The IS auditor should plan the information systems audit coverage to address the audit objectives and comply with applicable laws and professional auditing standards.
- The IS auditor should develop and document a risk-based audit approach.
- The IS auditor should develop and document an audit plan that lists the audit detailing the nature and objectives, timing and extent, objectives and resources required.
- The IS auditor should develop an audit program and/or plan and detailing the nature, timing and extent of the audit procedures required to complete the audit.

S6 Performance of Audit Work
- Supervision — IS audit staff should be supervised to provide reasonable assurance that audit objectives are accomplished and applicable professional auditing standards are met.
- Evidence — during the course of the audit, the IS auditor should obtain sufficient, reliable and relevant evidence to achieve the audit objectives. The audit findings and conclusions are to be supported by appropriate analysis and interpretation of this evidence.
- Documentation — the audit process should be documented, describing the audit work performed and the audit evidence that supports supporting the IS auditor's findings and conclusions.

S7 Reporting
- The IS auditor should provide a report, in an appropriate form, upon completion of the audit. The report should identify the organization, the intended recipients and any restrictions on circulation.
- The audit report should state the scope, objectives, period of coverage and the nature, timing and extent of the audit work performed.
- The report should state the findings, conclusions and recommendations and any reservations, qualifications or limitations in scope that the IS auditor has with respect to the audit.
- The IS auditor should have sufficient and appropriate audit evidence to support the results reported.
- When issued, the IS auditor's report should be signed, dated and distributed according to the terms of the audit charter or engagement letter.

S8 Follow-Up Activities
- After the reporting of findings and recommendations, the IS auditor should request and evaluate relevant information to conclude whether appropriate action has been taken by management in a timely manner.

S9 Irregularities and Illegal Acts
- In planning and performing the audit to reduce audit risk to a low level, the IS auditor should consider the risk of irregularities and illegal acts.
- The IS auditor should maintain an attitude of professional skepticism during the audit, recognizing the possibility that material misstatements due to irregularities and illegal acts could exist, irrespective of his/her evaluation of the risk of irregularities and illegal acts.
- The IS auditor should obtain an understanding of the organization and its environment, including internal controls.
- The IS auditor should obtain sufficient and appropriate audit evidence to determine whether management or others within the organization have knowledge of any actual, suspected or alleged irregularities and illegal acts.
- When performing audit procedures to obtain an understanding of the organization and its environment, the IS auditor should consider unusual or unexpected relationships that may indicate a risk of material misstatements due to irregularities and illegal acts.
- The IS auditor should design and perform procedures to test the appropriateness of internal control and the risk of management override of controls.
- When the IS auditor identifies a misstatement, the IS auditor should assess whether such a misstatement may be indicative of an irregularity or illegal act. If there is such an indication, the IS auditor should consider the implications in relation to other aspects of the audit and in particular the representations of management.
- The IS auditor should obtain written representations from management at least annually or more often depending on the audit engagement. It should:
    - Acknowledge its responsibility for the design and implementation of internal controls to prevent and detect irregularities or illegal acts
    - Disclose to the IS auditor the results of the risk assessment that a material misstatement may exist as a result of an irregularity or illegal act
    - Disclose to the IS auditor its knowledge of irregularities or illegal acts affecting the organization in relation to:
        - Management
        - Employees who have significant roles in internal control
    - Disclose to the IS auditor its knowledge of any allegations of irregularities or illegal acts, or suspected irregularities or illegal acts affecting the organization as communicated by employees, former employees, regulators and others
- If the IS auditor has identified a material irregularity or illegal act, or obtains information that a material irregularity or illegal act may exist, the IS auditor should communicate these matters to the appropriate level of management in a timely manner.
- If the IS auditor has identified a material irregularity or illegal act involving management or employees who have significant roles in internal control, the IS auditor should communicate these matters in a timely manner to those charged with governance.
- The IS auditor should advise the appropriate level of management and those charged with governance of material weaknesses in the design and implementation of internal control to prevent and detect irregularities and illegal acts that may have come to the IS auditor's attention during the audit.
- If the IS auditor encounters exceptional circumstances that affect the IS auditor's ability to continue performing the audit because of a material misstatement or illegal act, the IS auditor should consider the legal and professional responsibilities applicable in the circumstances, including whether there is a requirement for the IS auditor to report to those who entered into the engagement or in some cases those charged with governance or regulatory authorities or consider withdrawing from the engagement.
- The IS auditor should document all communications, planning, results, evaluations and conclusions relating to material irregularities and illegal acts that have been reported to management, those charged with governance, regulators and others.

S10 IT Governance
- The IS auditor should review and assess whether the IS function aligns with the organization's mission, vision, values, objectives and strategies.
- The IS auditor should review whether the IS function has a clear statement about the performance expected by the business (effectiveness and efficiency) and assess its achievement.
- The IS auditor should review and assess the effectiveness of IS resource and performance management processes.
- The IS auditor should review and assess compliance with legal, environmental and information quality, and fiduciary and security requirements.
- A risk-based approach should be used by the IS auditor to evaluate the IS function.
- The IS auditor should review and assess the control environment of the organization.
- The IS auditor should review and assess the risks that may adversely effect the IS environment.

S11 Use of Risk Assessment in Audit Planning
- The IS auditor should use an appropriate risk assessment technique or approach in developing the overall IS audit plan and in determining priorities for the effective allocation of IS audit resources.
- When planning individual reviews, the IS auditor should identify and assess risks relevant to the area under review.

S12 Audit Materiality
- The IS auditor should consider audit materiality and its relationship to audit risk while determining the nature, timing and extent of audit procedures.
- While planning for audit, the IS auditor should consider potential weakness or absence of controls and whether such weakness or absence of control could result into significant deficiency or a material weakness in the information system.
- The IS auditor should consider the cumulative effect of minor control deficiencies or weaknesses and absence of controls to translate into significant deficiency or material weakness in the information system.
- The report of the IS auditor should disclose ineffective controls or absence of controls and the significance of the control deficiencies and possibility of these weaknesses resulting in a significant deficiency or material weakness.

S13 Using the Work of Other Experts
- The IS auditor should, where appropriate, consider using the work of other experts for the audit.
- The IS auditor should assess and be satisfied with the professional qualifications, competencies, relevant experience, resources, independence and quality control processes of other experts, prior to engagement.
- The IS auditor should assess, review and evaluate the work of other experts as part of the audit and conclude the extent of use and reliance on expert's work.
- The IS auditor should determine and conclude whether the work of other experts is adequate and complete to enable the IS auditor to conclude on the current audit objectives. These conclusions should be clearly documented.
- The IS auditor should apply additional test procedures to gain sufficient and appropriate audit evidence in circumstances where the work of other experts does not provide sufficient and appropriate audit evidence.
- The IS auditor should provide appropriate audit opinion and include scope limitation where required evidence is not obtained through additional test procedures.

S14 Audit Evidence
- The IS auditor should obtain sufficient and appropriate audit evidence to draw reasonable conclusions on which to base the audit results.
- The IS auditor should evaluate the sufficiency of audit evidence obtained during the audit.

Exam Tip: As stated previously, ISACA defines standards as mandatory activities. Any candidate for an ISACA exam would do well to become familiar with the official list from the original documentation.

Corporate Governance of Information Systems

High profile problems experienced by a variety of organizations in recent years have focused attention on corporate governance issues. One of the responsibilities of upper management is to establish an effective system of internal control over the organization's operational and financial activities. The policies and procedures used by management in fulfillment of this responsibility are now subject to increasing public scrutiny and often form part of the audit scope for both internal and external auditors. This guideline sets out how IS Auditors should comply with Standards S7, S9, S12 and S14[3] of the Standards for Information Systems Auditing when they are reporting on corporate governance where information systems are concerned. In addition, an overview of the planning process is provided in Standard S5 of the Standards for Information Systems Auditing. Its purpose is to enable IS Auditors to identify the necessary levels of planning and documentation needed to accomplish their objectives. This guideline sets out how the IS Auditor should comply with the above standard.

Understanding the Business and Its Environment

When planning for any audit, the IS auditor should have a reasonable understanding of the environment under review. In this case, "reasonable" should include, at a minimum, the following:

- Having a general understanding of the various business practices and functions relating to the audit subject
- Awareness of the long and short term goals and objectives of the organization
- Knowing the types, intended functions and controls applied to the information systems deployed by the organization.

The IS Auditor should also understand the various laws and statutes applicable to the organization and the products and services it provides. For example, a financial institution might be subject to information systems integrity and control requirements that are not found or required in other industries. Steps an IS Auditor could take to gain an understanding of the business include:

- Taking a tour of key facilities
- Reading background material including industry publications, annual reports and independent financial analysis reports
- Reviewing the organization's long-term strategic plans
- Interviewing key managers to obtain a clear view of business issues
- Studying any documents containing relevant regulatory information or guidance.
- Reviewing prior reports

Touring facilities

While touring key organization facilities such as data centers or business units, an auditor can see the implementation of policy through various procedures via direct observation and interviews. No one-to-one interviews or reviews of written documentation, no matter how thorough, can be as revealing and objective as actual visits to the physical sites included in the audit scope.

The use of background material

It is important for an IS auditor to have a sound understanding of the business units, systems and organizations being audited. Although an organization may appear to be honest and forthcoming with its documentation and other information, no auditor may rely upon this alone. It is essential that any information regarding financials and controls be verified by some combination of direct observation and testing. In addition, the auditor should perform any research necessary to gain an understanding of guidance or findings disclosed by experts in related industries. Some sources of information are:

- The internet
- Whitepapers
- Industry publications

Review of long term strategic plans

An auditor should obtain and evaluate the long term strategic plans of the organization under review. From this, the auditor will learn about upper management's ideas and plans regarding its business goals, strategies for growth and its use of technology. This will enable the auditor to tailor the audit plan to focus more accurately on Business/IT alignment and add increased value to the audit findings and recommendations. Examples of long term goals might include:

Business Goals	Audit Objectives that may be derived from the stated Business Goals
Expanding product lines	Review SLA (Service Level Agreements) Review physical and logical access controls at distribution facilities.
Going Public	Coordinate with accounting to review application controls with accounting software, and discuss possible SOX issues. Identify budget and resources.
Initiating a new CRM system	Review any relevant business cases and process re-engineering reports. Review/Audit software development project plan. Review relevant application audit
Closing the New York and Atlanta locations	Review change controls, termination policies, access privileges, etc.

Each of the activities described in these examples presents its own set of potential problems. An IS auditor should be aware the problems that may result from each activity and plan the audit to allow for a review of possible problem areas.

Interviewing key managers to understand business issues

It is important that management understands the importance of the IS auditor's role within the organization. In order to effectively communicate IS audit's purpose as well as understand the various business sectors that may be within an organization the IS auditor or audit committee should understand and focus on the following six factors:

1. An understanding of business risks

Knowing the inherent risks of your organizations strategic business model is critical. The auditor should communicate directly with department heads and other members of senior management and familiarize them with the risks associated with their industry in general and with their own assets in particular. Areas of concentration should include:

- Internal and external auditor findings
- Control environment
- Legal and regulatory issues
- Emerging business and fraud risks

2. An understanding of internal controls

Internal controls may be defined as "any policies, procedures, guidelines or organizational processes established for the purpose of managing risk". Often, the term "internal controls" is used in a very broad sense. This makes it difficult to determine which level of the control program a speaker is referring to. In general:

- **Internal Control Objectives** refer to higher level, long-term initiatives such as policies or strategies. Objectives and policies define what must be accomplished at lower levels in the organization. Examples of high-level objectives include:
    o Maintaining the integrity of I/O functions in transaction driven environments.
    o Establishment and maintenance of strong change and configuration management programs
    o Protection of all IS/IT assets
    o Control Objectives may be divided into three categories:
        - **Internal accounting controls:** These are primarily directed at accounting operations. They concern the safeguarding of the assets and the reliability of financial records.
        - **Operational controls:** These controls focus on the day-to-day operations, functions and activities and ensure the operation is meeting the business objectives.
        - **Administrative controls:** These controls promote operational efficiency in a functional area and adherence to management policies, including operational controls. The administrative controls can be described as supporting the operational controls specifically concerned with operating efficiency and adherence to the organization's policies.
- **Internal Control Activities or General Control Procedures** refer to lower-level operations such as guidelines and procedures. The procedures and guidelines should be implemented in such a way that they fulfill the requirements specified by statements in higher-level documents.
- **General Controls** are interdependent IS controls which apply to all areas of the organization.
- **Control procedures** include policies and practices established by management to provide reasonable assurance that specific objectives will be achieved. The following are examples of general control procedures:
    o Logical security policies and procedures to ensure proper authorization of transactions and activities
    o Overall policies for the design and use of documents and records to help ensure proper recording of transactions, such as transactional audit trail
    o Procedures and features to ensure adequate safeguards over access to and use of assets and facilities and adequate procedures to ensure service quality and continuity of operations and service
    o Physical security policies which apply to all data centers
- Lower-level control processes are usually divided into three classes:
    o Preventive: Designed to stop or deter specified actions before they become problems. Doors with Biometric locks, internal security cameras, motion detectors and segregation of duties all qualify as preventive controls.
    o Detective: Logging and review of access attempts to critical areas or assets, multiple checks on transaction totals and the audit function itself are examples of detective controls.
    o Corrective: These controls are designed to fix problems after they have occurred. Restoring information from backups, computer forensics/incident management and the creation and testing of a disaster recovery plan are corrective in nature.
- **General Audit Objectives:** The term "**control objective**" refers to how an internal control should function, whereas the term "**audit objectives**" describes the specific goals of the audit. Audit objectives often focus on substantiating that internal controls exist to minimize business risks. Management may give the IS auditor a general objective to follow when performing an audit. For example, they may ask the auditor to evaluate overall internal controls in a given area or they may request that the auditor test the tape inventory. In the former case, the IS auditor might do a general review consisting of observations, interviews and reviews of documentation. There may not be detailed testing. In the latter case, the IS Auditor might perform detailed tests of the tapes inventory including user access reconciliations. Determination of the objectives of an audit is a critical step in planning an Information Systems audit.

- **Information Systems Audit Objectives:** A key step in the planning of an Information Systems audit is the translation of general audit objectives into specific Information Systems audit objectives. For example, in a financial/operational audit, an internal control objective could be to assure that transactions are properly posted to the general ledger accounts. However in the Information Systems audit, the objective could be extended to include ensuring that editing features are in place to detect errors in the coding of these transactions that may impact the account posting activities. The IS Auditor should have an understanding of how general audit objectives can be translated into specific information systems control objectives.

3. Understanding oversight of the financial reporting process

This is one of the most difficult and important responsibilities of the audit committee; it is generally performed by personnel from the organization's financial or operational audit groups. The objective is the creation of a set of financial statements and disclosure documents that provide a transparent review of the results of the risk management process to any user of those statements. To accomplish this, the committee should know the major drivers of the organization's revenue and the critical accounting policies used to record transactions. They must also understand:
- Significant balance sheet changes
- Changes in trends in financial statement account relationships
- Accounting principles and relationship to industry norms
- Issues that may impact financial reporting
- Related-party transactions
- Off-balance sheet activity
- Fraud risk factors
- Impact of new or proposed accounting rules

In addition, the audit committee, with management and the external auditor, should review the actual accounting policies that have the greatest impact on the financial statements.

4. Understanding the audit function

When evaluating the internal IS audit function, the committee should determine the appropriate types and levels of resources allocated to each task. They must also review the quality, experience and objectivity of the internal IS auditors. If any internal IS audit services have been outsourced, the committee should examine the qualifications of the provider and regularly review the scope of the outsourced audit coverage.

The appointment or replacement of the external IS audit firm also requires audit committee involvement. However, because management works closely with external IS auditors, the managers are usually better suited to evaluate an external firm's overall quality of service Therefore, it is suggested that management make the initial recommendations regarding any selection of an external firm to the committee. The committee may then perform any additional reviews and make recommendations to the board of directors.

5. Proper staffing of the audit committee

The size of the audit committee is related to the size of the organization. In many cases, this committee may be composed of three to six members. These individuals are selected because of their backgrounds and experience with regard to the operations of the organization. As a whole, this group should possess sufficient financial literacy, decision-making and leadership skills, independent thinking, technology expertise and strategic thinking to enable it to properly fulfill its role within the organization.

6. Understand the audit committee charter
In general, the audit committee operates with a formal charter that outlines:
- Its responsibilities (assumed and not assumed) and composition
- Minimum number of meetings
- Its ability to retain outside advisors, conduct investigations and discuss issues with legal counsel
- Its role in the oversight of risk management
- Its duties regarding the review and approval of external audit firms and related fees

The primary duty of the audit committee is the oversight of the audit function. The committee should be granted the authority to request and obtain from management and the internal and external auditors any information that will help it better perform its duties. To avoid any conflict of interest and promote separation of duties, committee members should not be involved in day-to-day management or with the details of the IS audit process.

Studying any regulatory reports or regulations
It is essential that each organization bring itself into compliance with any laws or regulations that are relevant to the nature of its industry or any other work it performs. These regulations may be issued at the federal, state or local levels. They may apply to physical plant, individual health and safety, financial processes and reporting, security and privacy issues and any other aspect of the organization's processes or service and product offerings. The audit team must familiarize itself with every aspect of the organization's day-to-day activities. The team should then research and document any regulatory concerns applicable to the organization's activities. Cooperation between the audit team and the organization's legal counsel should be encouraged. The team should then provide relevant guidance to the organization based on those regulations. Finally, the team must create a schedule for regular reviews of the regulatory climate and guidance from expert sources.

Reviewing prior reports
A review of prior audits will provide the auditor with the following useful information:
- The auditor will be able to identify which areas within the scope of the current audit have been subject to previous audits.
- The auditor will be able to document areas in which weaknesses may have been identified earlier.
- The auditor will be able to document the controls discovered during previous audits and see reports regarding their effectiveness.

The auditor can review past findings and recommendations and evaluate the status of any remedial actions taken. The auditor can be better equipped to estimate the types and amount of audit resources needed for the current audit as a result of the review of prior audits.

Audit Charter

Before the planning phase of the audit, the following questions must be asked and answered:

Audit Questions	Examples of Audit Answer
Who are we auditing? This question should address what departments or business units will be subjected to the audit process.	**Payroll**
What are we auditing? This may include systems, physical environments, financial records or transactions, processes, controls, compliance, etc.	**UNIX, PEOPLE SOFT, application controls, etc.**
Where are we auditing? This includes the exact location of systems and where data or applications will be accessed.	**Data warehouse in Phoenix**
When are we auditing? A specific time frame should be given and allocated accordingly Any procedure for a request of additional time should also be documented.	**April 20th – 25th 2009**
Why are we auditing? Possible reasons may include, but are not limited to: materiality, previous audit, business unit request, possible or known exposure.	**Rollout of a New Application**
How are we going to audit? There should be sufficient evidence or documentation to support the need for the audit and the budget and resources it will require.	**We will allocate two auditors** who specialize in ERP solutions. They will review policies, procedures and controls, conduct interviews as necessary and review relevant documentation. These auditors will be allotted 120 hours to complete the assignment.

In essence, the audit charter is a contract between the auditor/audit team and the management of the organization. Its purpose is to outline the following:
- The authority, scope and responsibilities of the auditor
- Management's responsibility and objectives for, and delegation of authority to the auditor.

Planning the IS Audit

An audit plan should be developed by the auditor and management and agreed upon by the audit committee prior to the beginning of the audit work. Audit planning and the audit process cannot be properly performed and should not be attempted until the details of this document have been agreed upon. The plan should:
- Define the scope and objectives for the audit
- Provide timelines for the audit
- Identify where and when the audit will take place
- Identify requirements to be audited against
- Identify groups and areas to be audited
- List documents and records to be studied
- List responsible people whose functions will be audited
- Clarify who will get the final report and when it will be ready

A diagram explaining the creation of audit areas and carrying out the overall audit process can be seen below:

Understanding the Business Environment in Creating an Audit Schedule

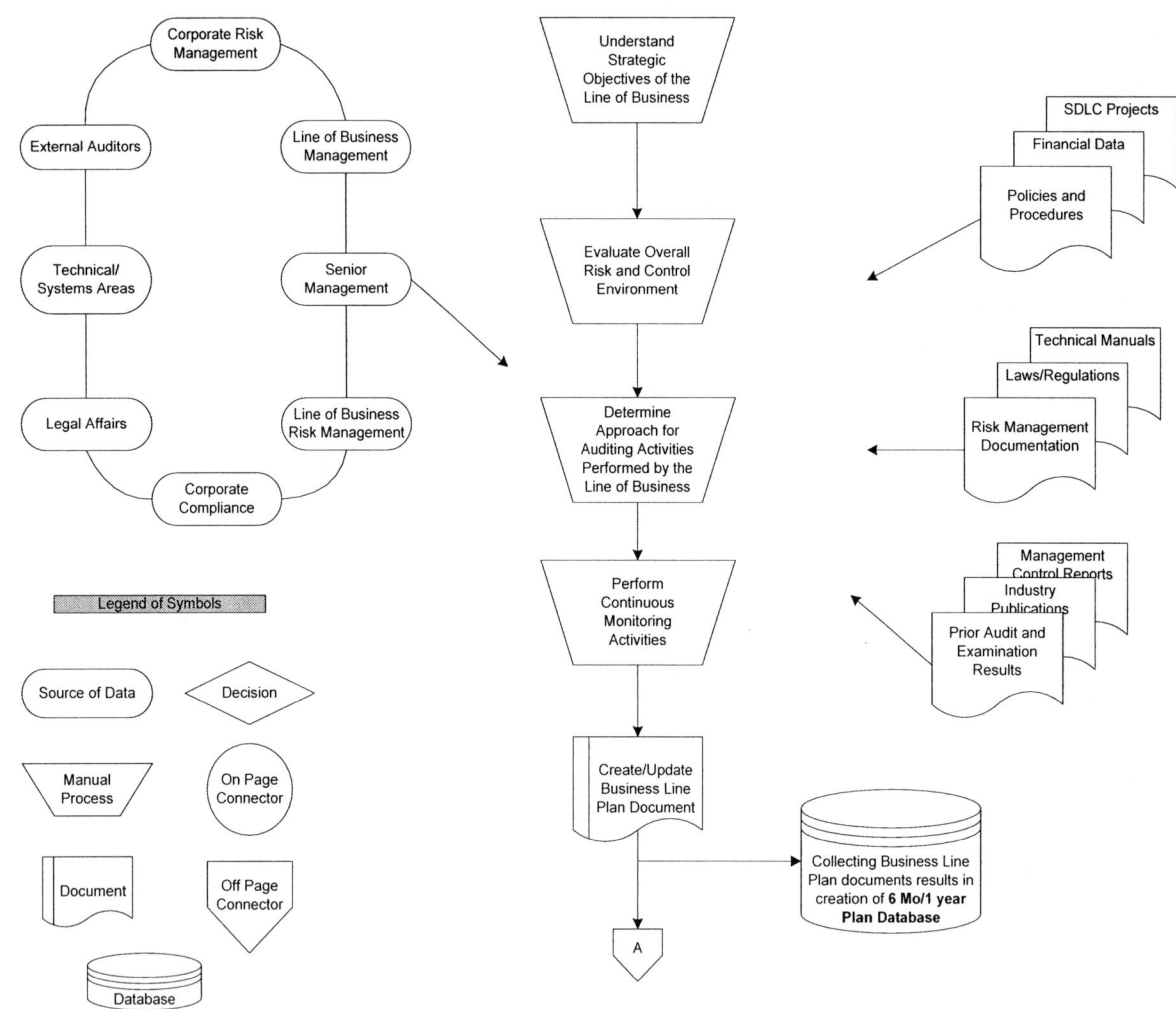

Performing an IS Audit

There are several steps involved in the performance of an IS audit. The IS Auditor must assess the overall risks and then develop an audit program which consists of control objectives and audit procedures which should satisfy those objectives. The audit process requires the IS Auditor to gather evidence, to evaluate the strengths and weaknesses of controls based upon the evidence gathered and to prepare an audit report which presents those audit issues in an objective manner to management.

In addition, audit management must ensure adequate audit resource availability and scheduling for both the performance of the audit and for any follow-up reviews focused on corrective actions taken by management. IS Auditors also must have good knowledge of both the Association's Code of Ethics and the Professional Standards which were described earlier in this chapter. Careful planning is a necessary first step in performing effective IS audits. A high level diagram of the audit process is shown below. Details about the various tasks and subtasks will be provided later.

Key Tasks within the Audit Process

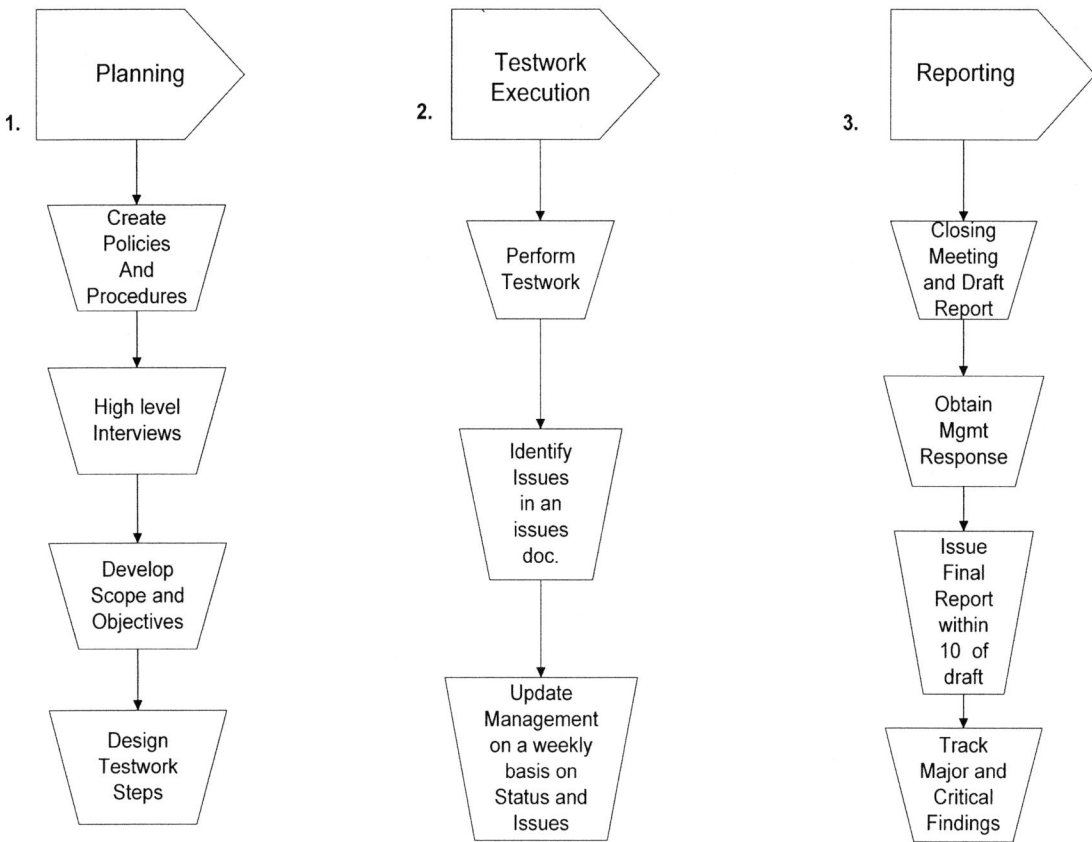

Other Planning Criteria and Considerations

The IS Auditor should understand that other considerations may impact the overall approach to the audit and should be taken into consideration, such as:
- System implementation/upgrade deadlines
- Current and future technologies
- IS resource limitations

Audit Program Development

An **audit program** is a set of documented audit procedures designed to achieve planned audit objectives. The chart below describes the phases of a typical program. A candidate is required to understand the steps and techniques necessary to plan, perform and complete an audit.

Audit Program Structure and Phases	
Audit subject	- Identify the area to be audited.
Audit objective	- Identify the purpose of the audit. For example, an objective might be to determine that program source code changes occur in a well-defined and controlled environment.
Audit scope	- Identify the specific systems, function or unit of the organization to be included in the review. For example, in the above program changes example, the scope statement might limit the review to a single application system or to a limited period of time.
Pre-audit planning	- Identify technical skills and resources needed. - Identify the sources of information for test or review such as functional flow-charts, policies, standards, procedures and prior audit work-papers. - Identify locations or facilities to be audited.
Audit procedures and steps for data gathering	- Identify and select the audit approach to verify and test the controls. - Identify a list of auditees to interview. - Identify and obtain departmental policies, standards and guidelines for review. - Develop audit tools and methodology to test and verify control.
Procedures for evaluating the test or review results	Organization specific
Procedures for communication with management	Organization specific
Audit report preparation	- Follow-up review procedures - Procedures to evaluate/test operational efficiency and effectiveness. - Procedures to test controls. - Review and evaluate the soundness of documents, policies and procedures.

The audit program becomes a guide for documenting the various audit steps performed and the extent and types of evidential matter reviewed. It also provides a trail of the process used to perform the audit as well as accountability of performance. Although an audit program does not necessarily follow a specific set of steps, the IS Auditor would typically follow sequential program steps to gain an understanding of the entity under audit, evaluate the control structure and then test the controls.

Documentation
Using the Work of Other Auditors and Experts
The interdependency of customers' and suppliers' processing and the outsourcing of non-core activities mean that an IS Auditor (internal or external) will often find that parts of the environment being audited are controlled and audited by other independent functions or organizations. This guideline sets out how the IS Auditor should comply with the above standard in these circumstances.

The Audit Processes
This is the most intensive part of any audit process because it is the period during which information is assessed and recorded. Steps in this process include:

- Interviewing personnel
- Reading documents
- Reviewing manuals
- Studying records
- Reading reports
- Analyzing data
- Observing activity
- Examining conditions
- Confirming interview evidence
- Documenting observations

Listed below are steps an information systems control practitioner should perform to determine the level of compliance by an organization regarding external requirements:

- Conduct appropriate research and document all relevant laws, regulations, etc.
- Identify government or other relevant external requirements dealing with computer system practices and controls
- The manner in which computers, programs and data are stored
- The organization and activities of the IS Department
- Assess whether the management of the organization and the Information Systems function have considered the relevant external requirements in making plans and in setting policies, standards and procedures.
- Review internal Information Systems department/function/activity documents that address adherence to laws applicable to the industry.
- Determine adherence to established procedures that address these requirements.

Exam Tip: At present, CISA candidates will not be required to answer questions about any specific laws or regulations such as California's SB 1386[4], but may be questioned about how one would audit for compliance with laws and regulations.

Evaluation
Audit Evidence Requirement
The purpose of this section is to define the word "evidence" as used in Standard S14 and Guideline G2 of ISACA's IS Standards and Guidelines (ISSG) document. It also addresses the type and sufficiency of audit evidence used in information systems auditing. These sections also provide assistance in applying IS auditing standards. The IS Auditor should consider them in determining how to derive appropriate implementation of the above. The IS Auditor must use professional judgment in any application of these principles and be prepared to justify any departure.

Develop conclusions
Once the review and observational tasks have been completed, the auditor must process and analyze the data to define conclusions and preliminary recommendations. The auditor will:
- List nonconformities supported by evidence
- Cross-reference with regulatory requirements

REPORTING
Report Content and Form
The purpose of this Guideline is to describe the recommended practices for preparing and issuing an IS audit report. The Guideline provides a framework and direction in the application of IS auditing standards. This guidance should be applied in using CAATs regardless of whether the auditor concerned is an IS Auditor. The IS Auditor should consider it in determining how to achieve implementation of the above standard, use professional judgment in its application and be prepared to justify any departure. If management requires extra reports or reports containing significant variances from the recommended content and format, then the Audit Charter may be used to specify the changes required and the rationale for those changes.

CAATs – Audit Tools
Use of Computer Assisted Audit Techniques

Computer Assisted Audit Techniques (CAATs) are software-based tools and techniques, such as generalized audit software, utility software, test data, application software tracing and mapping and audit expert systems. They are important tools for the IS Auditor in performing audits. CAATs include many types of CAATs may be used in performing various audit procedures including:

- Tests of details of transactions and balances
- Analytical review procedures
- Compliance tests of IS general controls
- Compliance tests of IS application controls
- Vulnerability and/or Penetration testing

CAATs may produce a large proportion of the audit evidence developed in IS audits and, as a result, the IS Auditor should carefully plan for and exhibit due professional care in the use of CAATs.

Recommendations/Remediation
Discuss results
The auditor will arrange a closing meeting to discuss the compiled evidence, observations, conclusions, recommendations or nonconformities. This is an interim measure to suggest an outcome but should not be viewed as the final and complete results of the audit.

Final audit report
Over a specified period from initial audit, the auditor will review the gathered information and compile a final report, which will be disseminated to Senior Management. The report will include:

- The detailed audit plan
- A review of the evidence collected
- A discussion of any conclusions drawn from the audit
- A list of identified nonconformities, threats, or weaknesses
- An assessment of how well regulatory requirements, and controls have been met
- Recommendations for change in practice to conform to regulations or strengthen controls
- A timescale for corrective action
- A date for recommended review

Follow-up actions
It is the auditor's responsibility to document any actions taken to correct and prevent nonconformities. This will be in the form of a re-audit of the identified nonconformities and should occur within a clearly specified time period (generally 6 months after the final report is issued). This gives the organization time to ensure appropriate corrective action has been taken.

Exam Tip: CAATs are a very important part of an auditor's toolkit. Candidates should expect several exam questions related to CAATs, however, some of these questions may address the types of tests or checks that CAATs can perform. Additional information about these tests and checks is provided in chapter 3

ETHICS

The ethical integrity of an auditor possessing the CISA certification auditor is expected to be of the highest standard. ISACA has created a Code of Professional Ethics to guide the professional and personal conduct of members of the association and/or its certification holders. ISACA Members and certification holders shall:[5]

- Support the implementation of, and encourage compliance with, appropriate standards, procedures and controls for information systems.
- Perform their duties with objectivity, due diligence and professional care, in accordance with professional standards and best practices.
- Serve in the interest of stakeholders in a lawful and honest manner, while maintaining high standards of conduct and character, and not engage in acts discreditable to the profession.
- Maintain the privacy and confidentiality of information obtained in the course of their duties unless disclosure is required by legal authority. Such information shall not be used for personal benefit or released to inappropriate parties.
- Maintain competency in their respective fields and agree to undertake only those activities, which they can reasonably expect to complete with professional competence.
- Inform appropriate parties of the results of work performed; revealing all significant facts known to them.
- Support the professional education of stakeholders in enhancing their understanding of information systems security and control.

An ISACA member or certification holder that fails to comply with this Code of Professional Ethics may be subject to an investigation, and ultimately, in disciplinary measures.

THE CONTROL OBJECTIVES

The Control Objectives for Information and Related Technology (COBIT) may be considered the cornerstone of ISACA's audit initiatives. Please note that ITGI (the IT Governance Institute) is credited for the creation of this document. ISACA and ITGI are affiliated organizations. The latest version of this document (version 4.1) includes four sections:
- Executive Overview
- Framework
- Control Objectives, Management Guidelines and Maturity Models (the "Core Content")
- Appendices

Audit Guidelines are mentioned throughout the Control Objectives section, but those new to ISACA's terminology and structures may be able to identify these guidelines more easily by comparing COBIT to the related Standards and Guidelines in the IS Standards and Guidelines (ISSG) document. The Framework focuses on linking business requirements to good practices and objectives for IT governance. The Control Objectives aid managers in providing effective controls for their IT processes by offering a set of high-level requirements targeted to each of those processes. For each for the 34 IT processes of the Framework, there are from 3 to 34 detailed control objectives. The section on Control Objectives aligns the overall Framework with detailed control objectives from 36 primary sources. These sources supply the de facto and de jure international standards and regulations relating to IT. This section contains descriptions statements of the results desired or purposes to be achieved by implementing specific control procedures within an IT process. In doing so, it provides both clear policy and good practice for IT control throughout the industry worldwide.

COBIT is directed to the management and staff of the information services, controllers of audit functions and also to the business process owners. The various standards and guidelines discussed in COBIT provide a working blueprint for these individuals. An outline and delineation of the minimum set of controls to ensure effectiveness, efficiency and economy of resource utilization is supplied. For each process, detailed are provided concerning the minimum number or type of controls that need to be implemented. The controls described there are those that an audit or compliance specialist will seek to identify and assess for effectiveness. There are over 300 detailed control objectives that provide an overview of the domain/process/control objective relationships. COBIT provides a translation of concepts presented in the *Framework* into specific controls applicable for each IT process.

Exam Tip: A candidate will not be asked to identify specific control objectives from COBIT, but rather to understand how each is applied in practice. As of July 2007, ISACA offered a complimentary download of COBIT 4.1. Note that official access to the full COBIT document requires a registration process on ISACA's website. This process can be initiated by attempting to log in.

OTHER LAWS AND REGULATIONS

Each organization, regardless of its size or the industry within which it operates, will need to comply with a number of government and external requirements related to computer system practices and controls and to the manner in which computers, programs and data are used.[6, 7] Special attention should be given to these issues in those industries that historically have been regulated closely. For example, the banking industry worldwide has severe penalties for companies and its officers should the company not be able to provide an adequate level of service because of sub-standard backup and recovery procedures. In addition, because of the world's growing dependency on Information Systems and related technology, several countries are making efforts to establish added layers of regulatory requirements concerning IS audit. The contents of these regulations include:

- Establishment
- Organization
- Responsibilities
- Correlation to financial and operational audit functions

Audit Risk and Materiality

According to ISACA, the term "**material**", when used in association with risk concepts, "refers to an error that should be considered significant to any party concerned with the item in question".[8] Material issues are those issues that, based on the auditor's judgment, should be reported to the appropriate mangers or other personnel within the organization. Clearly, an IS Auditor must have sufficient knowledge and/or experience with the systems being reviewed to be able to make informed judgements.

Many organizations are moving to a risk-based audit approach adapted to develop and improve the continuous audit process. This approach is used to assess risk and determine an auditor's decisions regarding the use and extent of compliance and/or substantive testing. Within this concept, inherent risk, control risk or detection risk might not be assessed as high despite the documented presence of some weaknesses. In a risk based audit approach, auditors also factor in the presence of internal and operational controls as well as knowledge of the organization and related industries.[9] This type of risk assessment decision can help relate the cost/benefit analysis of the control to the known risk, allowing the organization to implement controls suited to the perceived risk.

By understanding the nature of the business, auditors can identify and categorize the types of risks that will better determine the risk model or approach in conducting the audit. The risk model assessment can be as simple as creating weights for the types of risks associated with the business and identifying the risk in an equation. For example: Total Audit Risk = 2 (Inherent Risk) x (Control Risk) x (1/2 Detection Risk). On the other hand, risk assessment can be a scheme where risks have been given elaborate weights based on the nature of the business or the significance of the risk. The following is an overview of the steps taken in a risk-based audit approach:

- **Auditor's Gathering of Information**
    - Knowledge of business and industry
    - Regulatory statutes
    - Prior year's audit results
    - Inherent risk assessments
    - Recent financial information

- **Auditor's Understanding of Internal Controls**
    - Control environment
    - Control risk assessment
    - Control procedures
    - Equate total risk
    - Detection risk assessment

- **Perform Test Controls**
    - Test policies and procedures
    - Test segregation of duties

- **Perform Substantive Tests**
    - Analytical procedures
    - Detailed tests of account balances
    - Other substantive audit procedures

- **Finalize the Audit**
    - Create recommendations
    - Write audit report

Audit risk may be defined as the risk that the information/financial report may contain material error or that the IS Auditor may not detect an error that has occurred. The types of audit risk are:

- **Inherent Risk:** The risk that an error exists which could be material or significant when combined with other errors encountered during the audit, assuming that there are no related compensating controls. Inherent risk can also be categorized as the susceptibility to a material misstatement in the absence of related controls. As examples of this, complex calculations are more likely to be misstated than simple ones and cash is more likely to be stolen than an inventory of coal. Inherent risks exist independent of an audit and can occur because of the nature of the business.
- **Control Risk:** The risk that a material error exists which will not be prevented or detected on a timely basis by the system of internal controls.
- **Detection Risk:** The risk that an IS Auditor uses an inadequate test procedure and concludes that material errors do not exist when, in fact, they do. Detection of an error would not be determined during the risk assessment phase of an audit, however, identifying detection risk would better evaluate and assess the auditor's ability to test and identify correct assessments of material errors of a test.
- **Overall Audit Risk:** Overall audit risk is the combination of the individual categories of audit risks assessed for each individual specific control objective. An objective in formulating the audit approach is to limit the audit risk in the area under scrutiny so that overall audit risk is at a sufficiently low level at the completion of the examination. Another objective is to assess and control those risks to achieve the desired level of assurance as efficiently as possible. The term "audit risk" is also used to describe the level of risk that the auditor is prepared to accept during an audit engagement. The auditor may set a target level of risk and adjust the amount of detailed audit work to minimize the overall audit risk. An auditor that lacks the knowledge and/or experience necessary to test certain systems may unintentionally increase the overall audit risk by failing to properly test or assess the controls present in a given environment.
- **Statistical sampling risk:** This is the risk that incorrect assumptions are made about the characteristics of a population from which a sample is performed. This is not the same as audit risk. See below for further information regarding sampling.
- **Business Risk:** This is the risk that the likely consequences of an event that may occur will produce results that will have a negative impact on one or more stated business objectives. These risks may be financial, regulatory or operational and they may impact the long-term viability of the entire organization or one or more divisions within the organization.

The IS Auditor should have a good understanding of the types of audit risk when planning an audit. For example, an audit sample may not detect every potential error in a population. However, by using proper statistical sampling procedures or a strong quality control process, the probability of detection risk could be minimized. Similarly, when evaluating internal controls, the IS Auditor should realize that a given system may not detect a minor error, but that error, combined with others, could become material to the overall system.

The concept of materiality requires strong IS Auditor judgment. The IS Auditor may detect a small error which should be considered significant at an operational level but may not be viewed as significant to upper management. Materiality considerations, combined with an understanding of audit risk, are essential when planning audits of a given area and deciding which tests should be used in the examination of an area.

Risk Assessment Techniques

During the course of an audit, the IS auditor may identify a large number of potential audit subjects. Each of these may represent different types of audit risks. The IS Auditor should evaluate these various risk candidates to determine which are the high-risk areas and therefore should be audited. There are five reasons for using risk assessment techniques[10, 11]:

- To determine which areas should be audited.
- Enables management to effectively allocate limited audit resources.
- Ensures that relevant information has been obtained from all levels of management, including the board of directors, IS auditors and functional area management. Generally, the information includes items that will assist management to effectively fulfill its responsibilities and provide assurance that the resources of the audit function maintain a focus on the high priority risk areas for the business. This adds value to the results provided by the audit function to management.
- Establishes a basis for effectively managing the audit department.
- Summarizes the relationship between the audit subject, the organization as a whole and the long term goals of the organization.

There are several methods currently employed to perform risk assessments. One approach is a scoring system that is useful in prioritizing audits based on an evaluation of risk factors that consider variables such as technical complexity, level of control procedures in place and level of financial loss. These variables may or may not be weighted. These risk values are then compared to each other and audits are scheduled accordingly. Another form of risk assessment is judgmental. This method is more subjective; calling for decisions to be made based upon the directives of executive management, historical perspectives, business climate, etc.

Evaluation of Business Risk Management Processes

Auditors are often asked to assess the risk assessment process that management has used to identify, evaluate and manage the risks that they face. The process of security risk assessment used by management may start with an identification of information assets and the underlying systems which generate, store, use or manipulate the assets. Any vulnerability the assets might be subject to would be documented next. Threats to those vulnerabilities are identified and assigned weights depending on the likelihood of their occurrence. After this, the potential impact of a compromised asset would be assessed. Now the risks may be delineated in terms of CIA (Confidentiality, Integrity and Availability). The next step is to identify and evaluate the current and/or proposed controls and security measures. These measures may seek to prevent or reduce the likelihood of a risk occurring, detect the occurrence of a risk and minimize the impact or transfer the risk to another organization. This can be achieved by:

- Identifying all existing controls used to minimise risk
- Determining and evaluating any new or additional controls identified during the analysis of business risk
- Prioritizing all the identified risk and identifying those controls that provide the most effective and efficient countermeasures and that are commensurate with the business risks.
- Appropriate and cost-effective countermeasures to address those risks that are not considered to be adequately controlled can then be selected. The selection of appropriate countermeasures will depend on:
    - The cost of the control compared to the benefit of minimising the risk.
    - Management's appetite for risk (the level of risk that management is prepared to accept)
    - Preferred risk reduction methods (terminate the risk, minimise probability of occurrence, minimise impact, transfer/insurance)

There are risk assessment processes that begin with an identification of threats, rather than assets. It is important for the auditor to understand that there are a wide variety of formal and informal approaches to risk assessment and management. The auditor should not be concerned about which approach is adopted. Instead the auditor should be able to critically appraise the thought process that management has employed to identify and evaluate risks and come to a decision about which risks to minimize. An example of a risk assessment template is supplied below.

Exam Tip: One of the key themes or foundations of ISACA's framework is the need for the integration of a risk-based approach to decision making processes. Candidates should expect several exam questions that relate to risk directly or indirectly.

Risk Assessment Workplan Template

Steps	Estimated Days	Estimated Cost	Deliverable	Timeframe (Weeks) 1-15
Risk Assessment				
Process 2.1 - Plan the Risk Assessment				
1 Prepare Preliminary Plan				
2 Identify Project Team, Agree Responsibilities, Finalize Risk Assessment Workplan				
a) Identify Project Team				
b) Conduct Planning Meeting				
c) Document Risk Assessment Plan				
d) Update Workplan				
Total Estimated Days			Updated Risk Assessment Workplan	
Process 2.2 - Understand the Auditee's Business				
1 Assess the Control Environment				
a) Preliminarily Complete the ICQ				
b) Document and Analyze Control Environment Issues				
c) Raise Control Environment issues with Auditee Management				
2 Develop and Confirm Audit's Understanding of the Processes				
a) Arrange Meetings with Process Owners				
b) Explore Auditee's Business with Process Owners				
c) Identify Significant Risks Inherent in Achievement of Business Objectives				
3 Understand the IT Environment				
Total Estimated Days			ICQ updated	
Process 2.3 - Map Processes to the Internal Audit Focus				
1 Map Business Processes to the Internal Audit Focus				
2 Analyze and Agree Most Critical Processes with Client				
3 Re-visit Risk Assessment Workplan				
Total Estimated Days			Map of Processes to Internal Audit focus	
Process 2.4 - Identify Risks and Related High Level Controls				
1 Develop Process Understandings (Analytical Review)				
2 Identify Business Risks				
3 Identify High-Level Controls				
4 Agree Risks and Controls Identified with Management				
Total Estimated Days				
Process 2.5 - Assess Risks				
1 Assess Individual Risks				
a) Determine the initial risk assessment				
b) Determine the initial evaluation of high level controls				
2 Assess Overall Risk of Each Process				
3 Assess Risk across the Organization Structure				
4 Agree Assessment with Process Management				
Total Estimated Days			Updated Risk Assessment Workplan	
Process 2.6 - Report and Agree Risk Assessment				
1 Discuss and Preliminarily Agree the Risk Assessment with the Internal Audit Liaison or Auditee				
2 Finalize and Report Risk Assessment in Accordance with Auditee Protocols				
a) Prepare the presentation in the format as agreed with the client				
b) Update the Control Environment				
Total Estimated Days				
Total Estimated Days - Cumulative Project Cost	-	-		

General Audit Procedures

General audit procedures are the basic steps in the performance of an audit and usually include the following:

- Annual risk assessment and audit planning
- Individual audit planning
- Preliminary review of audit area/subject
- Obtaining and recording an understanding of audit area/subject
- Evaluating audit area/subject
- Compliance testing (often referred to as "tests of controls")
- Substantive testing
- Follow-up

Information Systems Control Procedures

Each general control procedure can be translated into an information systems specific control general procedure. The IS Auditor should understand how general control procedures can be translated into more specific information systems control procedures. This understanding is important in planning an audit. For example, the IS Auditor can translate the general procedure on adequate safeguards over access to assets and facilities to an information systems related set of control procedures covering access safeguards over computer programs, data and computer equipment. Information control procedures can be categorized into the following areas:

- General Organization Control Procedures
- Access to Data and Programs
- System Development Methodologies
- Data Processing Operations
- Systems Programming and technical support Functions
- Data Processing Quality Assurance Procedures

Information Systems audits follow the same general audit procedures as those outlined earlier. However, the IS Auditor should then apply unique techniques to these efforts. For example, in order to obtain an understanding of a given area, the IS Auditor may need to review technical documentation and to document application controls which include:

- Reviewing technical systems documentation
- Interviewing technical specialists

Information Systems Audit Procedures

The IS Auditor must understand the procedures for testing and evaluating information systems controls. These procedures include:

- The use of generalized audit software to survey the contents of data files
- The use of specialized software to assess the contents of operating systems parameter files
- Flow-charting techniques for documenting automated applications
- The use of audit reports available in operation systems

The IS Auditor should have a sufficient understanding of these procedures to allow for the planning of appropriate audit tests.

Planning Criteria

Short and long term planning criteria and considerations should be analyzed and evaluated regularly, at least annually. This is necessary to take into account new control issues, changing technologies and enhanced evaluation techniques. And, as usual, the resulting planning methodologies should be reviewed and approved by the audit committee, if available and communicated to relevant levels of management.

Compliance vs. Substantive Testing

There is a difference between evidence gathering for the purpose of testing an organization's compliance with control procedures and evidence gathering to evaluate the fairness of amounts and disclosures in the financial records. The former procedures are called tests of compliance and the latter are called substantive tests.[12]

Compliance tests determine if controls are being applied in a manner that "complies with" management policies and procedures. For example, if the IS Auditor is concerned whether program library controls are working properly, the IS Auditor might select a sample of programs to determine if the source and object versions are the same. Stated somewhat differently, the broad objective of any compliance test is to provide auditors with reasonable assurance that a particular control on which the auditor plans to rely on is operating as the auditor perceived it in the preliminary evaluation. It is important that the IS Auditor understand the specific objective of a compliance test and the control being tested. In most cases, compliance tests will be used when there is a trail of documentary evidence, such as written authorization to implement a modified program.

Substantive tests verify or "substantiate" the integrity of actual processing. They provide evidence of the validity and propriety of the balances in the financial statements and the transactions that support these balances. Auditors would use substantive tests to test for monetary errors directly affecting financial statement balances. An IS auditor might develop a substantive test to determine if the tape library inventory records are correctly stated. To perform this test, the auditor might take a 100 per cent inventory or might use a statistical sample which will allow the auditor to develop a conclusion regarding the accuracy of the entire inventory.

There is a direct correlation between the level of internal controls and the amount of substantive testing required. If the results of testing controls reveal the presence of adequate internal controls then IS Auditor is justified in minimizing the substantive procedures. Conversely, if the testing of controls reveals weaknesses that may raise doubts about the completeness, accuracy or validity of the accounts, substantive testing can alleviate those doubts. The chart below shows the relationship between substantive and compliance tests and describes the two categories of substantive tests.[13]

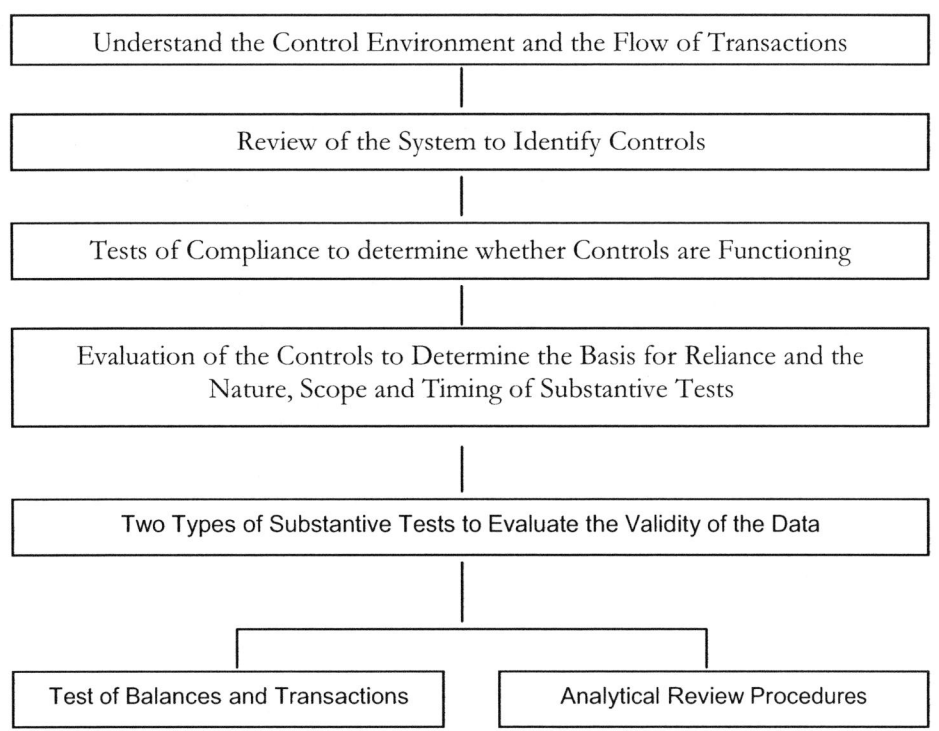

Key Controls

A basic purpose of any IS audit is to identify control objectives and the related preventive, detective and corrective controls that address the objective. The IS Auditor would then perform compliance tests of these controls. Generally, it is not efficient to try to evaluate all controls; therefore, audit programs should be designed to focus on identifying and evaluating key controls.

Financial, Operational and Comprehensive Audits

An IS Auditor should understand the various types of audits and the associated audit procedures for each. Three types of audits are Financial, Operational and Comprehensive. Audit programs for financial, operational and comprehensive audits should be based on the objective and scope of the particular assignment. IS Auditors may evaluate systems from different perspectives such as quality, service, efficiency, reliability and capacity.

- **Financial Audits** - The purpose of a financial audit is to assess the correctness of financial statements or records. A financial audit will often invoke detailed, substantive testing. External auditors are often responsible for financial audits. The IS Auditor will often use computer assisted procedures to support financial auditors in these types of audits.
- **Operational Audits** - An operational audit is designed to evaluate the internal control structure in a given area. Internal auditors are associated most often with operational audits. Many IS audits, including reviews of application controls or of logical security systems, are operational in nature.
- **Comprehensive Audits** - A comprehensive audit combines both financial and operational audit steps. The planning phase should be a joint venture involving IS, financial and operational auditors. A comprehensive audit would include both compliance and substantive audit steps.

Rules of Evidence

Evidence is any information used by the IS Auditor to determine whether the entity or data being audited follow the established audit criteria or objectives. Audit evidence may include the IS Auditor's observations, notes taken from interviews, material extracted from correspondence or internal documentation or the results of audit test procedures. While all evidence will assist the IS Auditor in developing audit conclusions, some evidence is more reliable than others. Important factors involved in an evaluation of the reliability of audit evidence include:

Independence of the provider of the evidence - Evidence obtained from outside sources is more reliable than from within the organization. This is why External Auditors send out confirmation letters for verification of accounts receivable balances.

Qualification of the individual providing the information or evidence - Whether the providers of information or evidence are inside or outside of the organization, the IS Auditor should always consider the qualifications of the persons providing the information. This also can be true of the IS Auditor. If an Information Systems Auditor does not, for example, have a good understanding of the technical area under review, the information gathered from testing that area may not be reliable, especially if the IS Auditor does not fully understand the test.

Objectivity of the evidence - Objective evidence is much better than evidence that requires considerable judgment or interpretation. An auditor's count of a cash fund is direct, objective evidence. An auditor's analysis of the efficiency of an application, based upon discussions with certain personnel, may not be objective audit evidence. Both the quality and quantity of evidence must be assessed by the IS Auditor. These two characteristics are referred to by The International Federation of Accountants (IFAC) as competent (Quality) and sufficient (Quantity).

Evidential matter is competent when it is both valid and relevant. Audit judgment is used to determine when sufficiency is achieved in the same manner that is used to determine the competency of evidential matter.
Individual nations may require compliance with their own "rules of evidence" when any criminal proceedings might be involved. An understanding of the rules of evidence is important for the IS Auditor who may encounter a variety of evidence types.

Exam Tip: The exam will only test for knowledge of generally accepted, global practices.

Audit Resource Scheduling

Staffing Resources

In most organizations, IS Auditors are a limited resource and their time should be appropriately planned and scheduled. This means that IS audit management should have an understanding of resources available within the organization to perform audits. IS Auditors may come from varied backgrounds, having been former programmers, former financial auditors and college graduates with various degrees. Their levels of experience could range from inexperienced auditors to experienced, CISA qualified auditors. The IS Auditor should understand techniques for managing audit projects with appropriately trained members of the audit staff. Skill and knowledge should be taken into consideration when planning audits and assigning staff to specific audit assignments.

Constraints on the Conduct of the Audit

Although an audit organization may be staffed with people who have an appropriate mix of required skills, constraints may limit the availability of this staff. These constraints may range from summer holidays to time off for professional conferences to conflicts with other audit projects. For example, IS Auditors may be asked to support the financial auditors with computer assisted procedures at year-end. Thus, these IS Auditors may not be available during this period for other audit projects. Auditee constraints may include the following:

- Recent employee turnover or unavailability
- Infringement on deadline dates or cyclical processing dates
- Overall lack of knowledge or documentation

In many cases, these constraints can be avoided by adequate planning. In order to understand and adapt properly to the constraints on the conduct of a given audit, the IS Auditor should have a good understanding of overall project management techniques.

Project Management Techniques

Numerous project management techniques have been developed or can be purchased to administer audit projects. Some are automated, some are manual. They all incorporate the following basic steps:[14]

- **Develop a Detailed Plan:** The plan should spread the necessary audit steps across a time line. Realistic estimates should be made of the time requirements for each task with proper consideration given to the availability of the auditee.
- **Report Project Activity against the Plan:** There should be some type of reporting system in place such that IS Auditors can report their actual progress against planned audit steps.
- **Adjust the Plan and Take Corrective Action as Required:** Actual accomplishments should be measured against the established plan on a continuous basis. Changes should be made in IS Auditor assignments or in planned schedules, as required.
- **Matching Available Resources to Requirements:** A basic component of good planning is the matching of available audit resources to the tasks as defined in the audit plan. This is often a delicate balancing job for the IS Auditor preparing the plan. There will be a mixture of resource skills that should be balanced against audit project requirements. The IS Auditor preparing the plan should consider the requirements of the audit project, staffing resources and other constraints. This matching exercise should consider the needs of individual audit projects as well as the overall needs of the audit department.
- **Defining, Organizing and Monitoring Audit Tasks:** Project management tasks generally follow the project management tasks briefly discussed in Chapter 3. The IS Auditor should follow good management techniques in reviewing the progress over IS audit projects.
- **Training of Personnel:** Information systems technology is constantly changing. It is important that an IS Auditor maintain his/her competency through updates of existing skills as well as training directed towards new audit techniques and technological areas. In fact, in order to maintain such competency, CISAs are required to comply with a continuing education policy.

Exam Tip: Project Management Theory and Techniques are another important focus of ISACA's approach. Candidates should expect to see questions and/or answer choices that deal with this on the exam.

Evidence Gathering Techniques

The collection or gathering of evidential matter is a key step in the audit process.[15] The IS Auditor should be aware of the various forms of audit evidence and how they can be gathered and reviewed. The IS Auditor should understand Information Systems Audit and Control Association General Standard S14, Audit Evidence and should obtain evidence of a nature and sufficiency to support audit findings.

Reviewing Information Systems Organization Structures

A strong plan of organization with an adequate separation or segregation of duties is a key general control in an information systems function. The IS Auditor should understand general organizational controls and be able to evaluate these controls in the organization under audit. Information systems functions, where there is a heavy emphasis on cooperative distributed processing or on end-user computing, may be organized somewhat differently than the "classic" information systems organization consisting of separate system and operations functions.[16] The IS Auditor should be able to review these organizational structures and assess their organizational controls.

Reviewing Information Systems Documentation Standards

A first step in reviewing the documentation for an information system is to understand the existing documentation standards in place within the organization. The IS Auditor should look for a minimum level of information systems documentation which may include:

- Systems development initiating documents
- Functional design specifications
- Program change histories
- User documentation manuals

IS Auditors should recognize that with systems development techniques such as CASE, prototyping, etc., traditional systems documentation will not be required or the documentation will be in a digital format rather than on paper. However, the IS Auditor should look for and evaluate documentation standards and practices within the information systems organization.

Reviewing Systems Documentation

The IS Auditor should be able to review documentation for a given system and determine whether it follows the organization's documentation standards. In addition, the IS Auditor should understand the less traditional approaches to developing systems, such as CASE or prototyping and how the documentation is constructed. The IS Auditor should recognize other components of information systems documentation such as database specifications, file layouts or self-documented program listings.

Interviewing Appropriate Personnel

Although the IS Auditing literature does not stress audit interview techniques, this is an important skill for the IS Auditor. Interviews should be organized in advance, should follow a fixed outline and should be documented through interview notes. An IS Auditor-prepared interview form or checklist is a good approach. The IS Auditor must realize that the purpose of such an interview is to gather audit evidence. Personnel interviews are discovery in nature and should never be accusatory.[17]

Observing Operations and Employee Performance

Observation of operations is a key audit technique for many types of reviews. The IS Auditor should be unobtrusive while making observations and should document everything in sufficient detail to be able to present it as audit evidence at a later date, if required.

Audit Documentation Techniques

The IS Auditor should understand techniques for documenting an information system as well as documenting the understanding of the information systems environment. The IS Auditor should be able to prepare adequate and understandable systems flowcharts. Other documentation techniques involve the creation and/or use of workpapers, narratives and completed interview questionnaires.[18]

Selecting and Testing Key Controls

The IS Auditor's initial review of an information system should identify key controls. The IS Auditor will then decide to test these controls through substantive or compliance verification methods as discussed previously. The IS Auditor should identify key application controls after developing an understanding of and documenting the various functions of the application. With that understanding, the IS Auditor should be able to identify the key control points. The identification of control points will then allow the IS Auditor to develop a preliminary understanding through compliance tests of those controls to determine if they are working as expected. The results of these compliance tests will allow the IS Auditor to design more extensive compliance or substantive testing.

Applying Sampling Techniques

Sampling is used when time and cost considerations preclude a 100 per cent verification of all transactions or events in a predefined population. The population consists of the entire group of items that need to be examined. The subset of population members is called a sample. Sampling is used to infer characteristics about a population, based on the results of examining the characteristics of a sample of the population. There are two general approaches to audit sampling - statistical and non-statistical:[19]

Statistical Sampling: is an objective method of determining the sample size and selection criteria. With statistical sampling, the auditor quantitatively decides how closely the sample should represent the population (assessing sample precision), and the number of times in 100 the sample should represent the population (the reliability or confidence level). This assessment will be represented as a percentage.

Non-Statistical Sampling: (often referred to as judgmental sampling) uses auditor judgment to determine the following:

- The method of sampling
- The number of items that will be examined from a population (sample size)
- Which items to select (sample selection).

Both the statistical and non-statistical sampling techniques require the auditor to use some amount of subjective judgment when defining the population characteristics, which items/transactions are the most material, most risky, etc. This means that both methods are, in fact, subject to the risk that the auditor will draw the wrong conclusion from the sample (**sampling risk**). However, statistical sampling permits the auditor to quantify the probability of error (**confidence coefficient**). To be a statistical sample, each item in the population should have an equal opportunity of being selected.

Within these two general approaches to audit sampling, there are two primary sampling techniques: attribute sampling and variable sampling. **Attribute sampling** is generally applied in compliance testing situations and deals with the presence or absence of the attribute and provides conclusions that are expressed in rates of incidence. **Variable sampling** is generally applied in substantive testing situations and deals with population characteristics that vary, such as dollars and weights and provides conclusions related to deviations from the norm. Attribute sampling refers to three different, but related types of proportional sampling:

- **Attribute Sampling** - (or fixed sample-size attribute sampling or frequency estimating sampling) is a sampling model that is used to estimate the rate (percent) of occurrence of a specific quality (attribute) in a population. It answers the question of "how many." An example of an attribute that might be tested is approval signatures on computer access request forms.
- **Stop-or-Go Sampling** - is a sampling model that helps prevent over sampling of an attribute by allowing an audit test to be stopped at the earliest possible moment. It is used when the IS Auditor believes that relatively few errors are expected to be found in a population.
- **Discovery Sampling** - is a sampling model that can be used when the expected occurrence rate is extremely low. Discovery sampling is most often used when the objective of the audit is to seek out (discover) fraud, circumvention of regulations or other irregularities.
- **Formula:** For Attribute sampling, $S = (C^2 * P * Q) / (PRE^2)$

Variable sampling, also known as dollar estimation or mean estimation sampling, is a technique used to estimate the dollar value or some other unit of measure, such as weight, of a population from a sample portion of it. An example of variable sampling would be a review of an organization's balance sheet for material transactions and an application review of the program that would have produced the balance sheet. Variable sampling refers to a number of different types of quantitative sampling models:

- **Stratified Mean per Unit:** is a statistical model in which the population is divided into groups and samples are drawn from the various groups. Stratified mean sampling is used to produce a smaller overall sample size, relative to unstratified mean per unit.
- **Unstratified Mean per Unit:** is a statistical model whereby a sample mean is calculated and projected as an estimated total.
- **Difference Estimation:** this is a statistical model used to estimate the total difference between audited values and book (unaudited) values based on differences obtained from observations of samples.
- **Formula:** Variable Sampling: $S=(C^2 * S^2)/(PRE^2)$

To perform either attribute or variable sampling, the following statistical sampling terms need to be understood:

- **Confidence Coefficient: (c)** (also referred to as confidence level or reliability factor) this figure is a percentage expression (90 percent, 95 percent, 99 percent, etc.) of the probability that the characteristics of the sample are a true representation of the population. Generally, a 95 percent confidence coefficient is considered a high degree of comfort. If the auditor knows internal controls are strong, the confidence coefficient may be lowered. The larger the sample size is, the greater the confidence coefficient will be.
- **Level of Risk:** This figure is equal to 1 minus the Confidence Coefficient. For example, if the Confidence Coefficient is 95 percent, the Level of Risk is 5 percent (100 percent-95 percent).
- **Precision:** This figure, set by the auditor, represents the acceptable range difference between the sample and the actual population. For attribute sampling this figure is stated as a percentage, for variable sampling this figure is stated as a "dollar" amount or a number. The higher the Precision amount, the smaller the sample size, and the greater the risk of fairly large total error amounts going undetected. The greater the sample size is, the smaller the precision will be. A very low precision level may lead to an unnecessarily large sample size.
- **Expected Error Rate:** This value is an estimate of the errors that may exist. It is usually stated as a percentage. The greater the sample size is, the greater the expected error rate should be. This figure is applied to attribute sampling formulas, but not to variable sampling formulas.
- **Sample Mean: ($\bar{x}$)** The sample mean is the sum of all sample values, divided by the size of the sample. It measures the average size of the sample.
- **Sample Standard Deviation: (SD)** Computes the variance of the sample values from the mean of the sample. It measures the spread(s) or dispersion of the sample values.
- **Tolerable Error Rate: (E)** This is used to describe the maximum misstatement or number of errors that can exist without an account being materially misstated. Tolerable rate is used for the planned upper limit of the precision range for compliance testing. The term is expressed as a percentage. Precision range or precision mean the same thing when used in substantive testing.
- **Population Standard Deviation: (σ)** This figure is a mathematical concept that measures the relationship to the "normal distribution". The larger the sample size is, the greater the standard deviation will be. This figure is applied to variable sampling formulas, but not to attribute sampling formulas.

Key steps to perform when conducting an audit sampling test include:
- Determine the objectives of the test.
- Define the population to be sampled.
- Determine the sampling method, such as attribute versus variable sampling.
- Calculate the sample size.
- Select the sample.
- Evaluate the sample from an audit perspective.

Exam Tip: Candidates will not be expected to perform calculations regarding attribute or variable sampling. However, they may be expected to know the effects of increases or decreases to individual variables such as the confidence coefficient on the total figure.

Computer Assisted Audit Techniques

The IS Auditor should have a thorough understanding of computer assisted techniques. This understanding should include knowledge of how each test type is used and also which tests are most effective for different circumstances. In addition, the auditor's understanding should include both the use of generalized audit software and other techniques such as test data generators and integrated test facility techniques. In addition to selecting the appropriate technique, the IS Auditor should understand the importance of documenting the results of such tests for audit evidence purposes. Examples of various types of Computer Assisted Audit Techniques (CAATs) are as follows:[20, 21]

- **Test Data Generators:** Prepare a computerized test data file for use in testing and verify the logic of application programs.
- **Expert Systems:** Software applications developed to hold a base of expert knowledge and logic provided by experts in a given field. Such a software application permits the computerized use of the decision-making processes of these experts.
- **Standard Utilities:** Resident in software packages that specify the status of parameters used to install the package
- **Software Library Packages:** Verify the integrity and appropriateness of program changes.
- **Integrated Test Facilities:** Involves setting up dummy entities on an application system and processing test or production data against the entity as a means of verifying processing accuracy.
- **Snapshot:** This technique involves taking "pictures" of a transaction as it flows through the computer system. Audit software routines are embedded at different points in the processing logic to capture images of the transaction as it progresses through the various stages of processing. Such a technique permits the auditor to track data and evaluate the computer processes applied to this data throughout the various stages of processing.
- **System Control Audit Review File:** Involves embedding audit software modules within an application system to provide continuous monitoring of the system's transactions. The information is collected into a special computer file that can be examined by the auditors.
- **Specialized Audit Software:** Used to perform specific audit steps for the IS Auditor, such as sampling, footing and matching.

CAATs offer the following advantages:
- Reduced level of audit risk
- Greater independence from the auditee
- Broader and more consistent audit coverage
- Faster availability of information
- Improved exception identification
- Greater flexibility of run times
- Greater opportunity to quantify internal control weaknesses
- Enhanced sampling
- Cost savings over time

An IS Auditor should weigh the cost/benefit of CAATs before going through the effort, time and expense of purchasing or developing CAATs. Issues to consider include:

- Ease of use, both for existing audit staff and future staff
- Training requirements
- Complexity of coding and maintenance
- Flexibility of uses
- Installation requirements
- Processing efficiencies (especially with a microcomputer-based CAAT)
- Effort required to bring the source data into the CAATs for analysis

When developing CAATs, the following documentation should be retained:
- Program listings
- Flowcharts, both detailed and overview
- Sample reports
- Record and file layouts
- Field definitions
- Operating instructions
- Description of source documents

The documentation derived from a CAAT should directly reference the audit program and clearly identify the audit procedures and objectives being served. When requesting access to production data for testing via CAATs, the IS Auditor should request read-only access. Any data manipulation done by the auditor should be done to copies of production files in a controlled environment that ensures production data are not exposed to unauthorized updating.

Evaluation of Audit Strengths and Weaknesses

After developing an audit program and gathering audit evidence, the next step is evaluating the information gathered in order to develop an audit opinion. The IS Auditor must enumerate and weigh strengths and weaknesses and then develop audit opinions and recommendations. These steps require good IS Auditor judgment which is often gained from experience, rather than from reference materials. While it is applied throughout the Information Systems audit process, the Information Systems Audit and Control Association Guideline G7, Due Professional Care, is particularly important to the IS Auditor in evaluating audit strengths and weaknesses.

Assessing Control Requirements

The IS Auditor should assess the results of the evidence gathered for compliance with the control requirements or objectives established during the planning stage of the audit. This requires a considerable amount of judgment, as controls are often unclear. In essence, controls should be in place to remove or minimize every perceived risk or threat to the entity being audited. A control matrix is often utilized in assessing the proper level of controls. The matrix works by placing known types of errors that can occur in the area under review on the top axis and known controls to detect or correct errors on the side axis. Then, using a ranking method, the matrix is filled in with appropriate measurements. When completed, the matrix will illustrate areas where controls are weak or lacking.

Relevant and Peripheral Information

The IS Auditor may gather a wide variety of evidence during the audit. Some may be relevant to the objectives of the audit while other evidence may be considered peripheral. The IS Auditor should focus on the overall objectives of the review and not the nature of the evidential matter gathered. Good judgment should be applied to determine which material is directly appropriate to the objectives of the audit and which is not specifically relevant.

Compensating and Overlapping Controls

As part of the information systems review, the IS Auditor may discover a variety of strong and weak controls. All should be considered when evaluating the overall control structure. In some instances, one strong control may compensate for a weak control in another area. For example, if the IS auditor finds weaknesses in a systems transaction error report, the auditor may find that a detailed manual balancing process over all transactions compensates for the weaknesses in the error report. The auditor should be aware of compensating controls in areas where controls have been identified as weak.

As an example of a compensating control, the IS Auditor might find that the tape management system at a data center has a control weakness in that some parameters are set to bypass or ignore the labels written on tape header records. This is a control weakness. However, if the IS Auditor finds very strong staging and job set-up procedures that are considered to be adequate, the IS Auditor may conclude that this control compensates for the control weakness over tape label controls.

A **compensating control** situation occurs when one stronger control supports a weaker one. On the other hand, **overlapping controls** exist when two strong controls are applied to a given asset. For example, a data center may employ a card key system to control physical access. If there was also a guard inside the door who requires employees to also show their card key or badge, that would be overlapping control. Each control on its own would be adequate to restrict access and the two complement each other.

The Interrelationships of Controls
A control objective will not normally be achieved because one control has been deemed adequate. Rather, the IS auditor will perform a variety of testing procedures and evaluate how these relate to one another. An auditor should always review for compensating controls prior to reporting a control weakness. The auditor may not find each control procedure to be in place but should evaluate the totality of control by considering the strengths and weaknesses of control procedures.

Determining the Nature of Efficient and Effective Operations
The IS auditor should review evidence gathered during the audit in order to determine if the operations are well controlled and effective. The IS Auditor should assess the strengths and weaknesses of the controls evaluated and then determine if they are effective in meeting the control objectives established as part of the audit planning process.

Techniques used to Analyze Evidence
The IS Auditor should have an understanding of the techniques used to analyze the evidence gathered from the review. For example, the IS auditor may wish to analyze findings based in statistical trends, either in terms of overall rates during a review or as period to period comparisons. Regression analysis is another powerful tool for this type of analysis that allows the IS Auditor to analyze a variety of random data and determine if they represent a trend. The nature of the analysis technique will depend upon the evidence under review.

Judging the Materiality of Findings
Materiality is a key issue when deciding which findings to bring forward in an audit report to management. The key to determining the materiality of audit findings is to understand the business environment well enough to know which issues might be significant to different levels and areas of management. This assessment requires judgment of the potential effect of the finding if corrective action is not taken. For example, a weakness in computer security physical access controls at a remote distributed computer site may be significant to management at the site, but will not necessarily be material to upper management at headquarters. However, there may be other matters at the remote site which would be material to upper management.

In another case, the IS auditor may find that the transmittal form for delivering tapes to the off-site storage location is not properly initialed by management as required by established procedures. If the auditor finds that management otherwise pays attention to this process and that there have been no problems in this area, the auditor may decide that this failure to initial transmittal documents is not material enough to bring to the attention of upper management. The auditor might decide to only discuss this with local operations management. However, if other control problems exist in the same area, creating a cumulative effect which would be material, the auditor may choose to report the existence of the entire set of weaknesses to upper management. The auditor should always judge which findings are material to various levels of management and should report them accordingly.

Audit Reports
Audit reports are the end product of the IS audit work. This is the vehicle that the IS Auditor uses to report findings and recommendations to management. The exact format of an audit report will vary by organization. However, the skilled IS Auditor should understand the basic components of an audit report and how it properly communicates audit findings to management.[22] The IS Auditor should understand Information Systems Audit and Control Association Standards S7, Reporting and S8, Follow-up Activities.

Report Structure and Contents

There is no single, industry-wide format for an IS audit report and each organization's audit standards will generally dictate the format. However, audit reports will usually have the following structure and content:
- Introduction to the report, including a statement of audit objectives and scope, the period of audit coverage and a general statement on the nature and extent of audit procedures examined during the audit.
- The IS Auditor's overall conclusion rendering an opinion on the adequacy of controls and procedures examined during the audit.
- Detailed audit findings and recommendations.
- Management responses to the findings, stating corrective actions to be taken and timing for implementing these anticipated corrective actions. Some organizations may wish to issue a summary report with detailed findings communicated separately. Others may issue the report without responses.

Criteria for Inclusion of Findings in Audit Reports

The decision to include or not include findings in an audit report should be based on the materiality of the audit findings and the intended recipient of the audit report. An audit report directed to the Audit Committee of the Board of Directors, for example, may not include findings that are important to local management but have little control significance to the overall organization. This decision also depends upon the guidance provided by upper management. However, the IS auditor should make the final decision of what to include or exclude from the audit report. The auditor should understand Information Systems Audit and Control Association General Standard S2, Independence and exercise independence in reporting.

Constraints on Implementing Recommendations

The IS auditor should recognize that management may not be able to implement all audit recommendations immediately. For example, the auditor may recommend changes to an information system which is all ready undergoing other changes or enhancements. The auditor should not necessarily expect that the other changes will be suspended until the auditor's recommendations are installed. Both may be installed together or the recommended changes may be implemented after a change management review has been performed.

The IS Auditor should discuss the recommendations and any planned implementation dates while in the process of releasing the audit report. While the auditor should realize that various constraints, such as staff limitations, budgets or other projects, may limit immediate implementation, management should develop a firm program for corrective action. If appropriate, the auditor may want to report to upper management on the progress of implementing these recommendations.

Relative Importance of Weaknesses

An audit report may include a variety of findings, some of which may be quite material while others are minor in nature. In following up on management's program for implementing recommendations, the IS Auditor should consider their relative importance to the overall internal control structure of the entity.

Communicating Results to Management and Audit Committee

IS Auditors should be aware that their ultimate responsibility is to senior management and to the Audit Committee of the Board of Directors. IS Auditors should feel free to communicate issues or concerns to such management. An attempt by less senior management to deny the access would limit the independence of the audit function. Audit Committees typically are composed of individuals who do not work directly for the organization and thus provide the auditors with an independent route to report sensitive audit findings. As a result of their increased numbers and use, audit committees also are coming under greater scrutiny from outside investors interested in ensuring fair representation.[23]

Conclusions and Opinion Statements

The audit report should include an opinion statement regarding the IS Auditor's findings. As defined in Information Systems Audit and Control Association Standard S7, Reporting, the IS Auditor also should communicate any reservations or qualifications with respect to the audit. This may take the form of the controls or procedures examined were found to be adequate or inadequate. The balance of the audit report should support that conclusion and the overall evidence gathered during the audit should provide an even greater level of support.

Exit Interview

The exit interview, conducted at the end of the audit, provides the IS Auditor with the means to discuss the findings and recommendations with management. The objectives and scope of the audit can be discussed and the IS audit process can be explained further. During the exit interview, the IS Auditor can also ensure that the facts presented in the report are correct; ensure recommendations are realistic and cost effective and if not, seek alternatives through negotiation with the audit area; and seek out implementation dates for agreed recommendations. The exit interview should/could be based upon a draft of the audit report.

Presentation Techniques

The IS Auditor will frequently be asked to present the results of audit work to various levels of management. The IS Auditor should have a thorough understanding of the presentation techniques necessary to communicate these results. Presentation techniques could include the following:

- **Executive Summary:** An easy to read, grammatically correct and concise report that presents findings to management in an understandable manner. Many executive managers are not well versed in computer jargon; therefore, executive summary reports should be free of terminology. Detailed attachments can be more technical in nature since operations management will require the detail to correct the reported situations.
- **Visual Presentation:** This could include overhead transparencies, 35mm slides or computer graphics.

Management Actions to Implement Recommendations

IS Auditors should realize that auditing is an ongoing process. The IS Auditor is not effective if audits are performed and reports issued, but no follow up occurs to determine if management has taken appropriate corrective actions. Auditors should have a follow-up program to determine if promised corrective actions have been taken on audit recommendations. The timing of follow-up will depend upon the criticality of the findings and would be subject to the auditor's judgment. The results of follow-up should be communicated to appropriate levels of management. The level of the auditor's follow-up review will depend upon several factors. In some instances, the auditor may merely need to inquire as to the current status. In other instances, such as technical information systems review, the auditor may have to perform certain audit steps to determine if the corrective actions agreed to by management have been implemented.

Continuous Audit Approach

To improve audit efficiency, IS Auditors must develop audit techniques that are appropriate for use with advanced computerized systems. In addition, they must be involved in the creation of advanced systems at the very early stages of development and implementation and they must make greater use of automated tools that are suitable for use with their organization's automated environment. This is the form of the continuous audit approach.

The **continuous audit approach** requires an IS auditor to collect evidence on system reliability while processing takes place to evaluate the system on a timely basis. The approach allows auditors to monitor the operation of systems on a continuous basis and to gather selective audit evidence through the computer. If the information collected by the computer technique is not deemed serious or material enough to warrant immediate action, it is stored in separate audit files for verification by the auditor at a later time. The continuous audit approach cuts down on paperwork and promotes the performance of paperless audits. In this type of setting, an auditor can report directly through the microcomputer on significant errors or other irregularities that may require immediate management action. This approach reduces both audit cost and time.

Continuous audit techniques are important IS audit tools, particularly when they are used in time-sharing environments that process a large number of transactions but leave a scarce paper audit trail. By permitting auditors to evaluate operating controls on a continuous basis without disrupting the organization's usual operations, continuous audit techniques improve the security of a system. For example, when a system is misused by someone withdrawing money from an inoperative account, a continuous audit technique will report this withdrawal in a timely fashion to the IS auditor. Thus, the time lag between the misuse of the system and the detection of that misuse is reduced. For both auditors and management, the realization that failures, improper manipulation and lack of controls will be detected on a timely basis by the use of continuous audit procedures gives greater confidence in a system's reliability. There are five types of continuous audit techniques available:

- **Systems control audit review file and embedded audit modules (SCARF/EAM):** The use of this technique involves embedding specially written audit software in the organization's host application system so that the application systems are monitored on a selective basis.
- **Snapshots:** Involves taking what might be termed pictures of the processing path that a transaction follows from the input to the output stage. With the use of this technique, transactions are tagged by applying identifiers to input data and recording selected information about what occurs for the auditor's subsequent review.
- **Audit Hooks:** Embedded in application systems to function as red flags and to induce IS Auditors to act before an error or irregularity gets out of hand.
- **Integrated Test Facilities (ITF):** Also known as dummy companies, include records of the dummy entities in an auditee's production files. The IS Auditor can make the system process either live transactions or test transactions during regular processing runs and have these transactions update the records of the dummy entity. The operator enters the test transactions simultaneously with live transactions that are entered for processing. The auditor then compares the output with the data that have been independently calculated previously to verify the validity of the computer processed data.
- **Continuous and Intermittent Simulation (CIS)** – The computer system, during a process run of a transaction, simulates the instruction execution of the application. As each transaction is entered, the simulator decides whether the transaction meets with certain predetermined criteria and if so, audits the transaction. If not, the simulator waits until it encounters the next transaction that meets the criteria.

The use of each of the continuous audit techniques has advantages and disadvantages. The selection and implementation of any one of them depends to a large extent on the complexity of an organization's computer systems and the IS Auditor's ability to understand and evaluate the system with and without the use of continuous audit techniques. In addition, IS Auditors must recognize that continuous audit techniques are not a cure all for all control problems and that use of these techniques provides only limited assurance that the information processing systems examined are operating as they were intended to function. In the exhibit below, the relative advantages and disadvantages of the various concurrent audit tools are presented.

	SCARF/EAM	ITF	Snapshots	CIS	Audit Hooks
Complexity	**Very High**	**High**	**Medium**	**Medium**	**Low**
Useful when	Regular processing cannot be interrupted.	It is not beneficial to use test data.	An audit trail is required.	Transactions meeting certain criteria need to be examined.	Select transactions or processes only need be examined.

Exam Tip: The candidate should be aware that CAATs are used to implement testing via the continuous audit approach. Any tests applicable to this approach may be listed alongside other test types listed in chapter 3. in questions or in the answers supplied for those questions. It is the responsibility of each candidate to be able to distinguish each type of test, control or check of data.

Control Self-Assessment

Control Self-Assessment (CSA) is a process in which management and/or work teams are directly involved in judging and monitoring the effectiveness of existing controls. Auditors serve as control professionals and assessment facilitators. In practice, CSA can be conducted using many different methods ranging from simple questionnaires completed by line management and personnel, to facilitated workshops involving line management, line staff and internal audit. When employing a CSA program, measures of success for each phase (planning, implementation and monitoring) should be developed to determine the value derived from CSA and its future use. Several objectives are associated with a CSA program including:

- An enhancement of audit responsibilities (not a replacement)
- An education for line management in control responsibility and monitoring
- A concentration by all on areas of high risk

Auditors need more than a list of controls to assess how management deals with risks. Some best practices for internal auditors to adopt are monitoring business activities and key performance indicators continuously, coordinating with other risk management functions, developing the audit plan based on risk priorities and getting involved in technology projects. Business units profit from ongoing risk monitoring and the information exchange internal audit teams provide. The auditors can track progress, identify new opportunities, or ask questions without waiting for the formal audit to take place.

The COSO Framework

In 1992 the Committee of Sponsoring Organizations of the Treadway Commission (COSO) issued a document called "*Internal Control—Integrated Framework*".[24] The primary objectives of this document were to:

- Establish a common definition of internal control
- Provide a standard to help auditing professionals assess control systems
- Determine how control systems might be improved

COSO defines **internal control** as "a process, effected by an entity's board of directors, management and other personnel, designed to provide reasonable assurance regarding the achievement of objectives in the following categories: effectiveness and efficiency of operations, reliability of financial reporting [and] compliance with applicable laws and regulations."[25] COSO says internal control consists of five interrelated components that are derived from the way management runs a business and are integrated into the management process:[26]

- **Control environment:** The tone of the organization influences the control consciousness of its people. Examples include the integrity, ethical values and competence of employees; management's philosophy; and input provided by the board of directors.
- **Risk assessment:** Identification and analysis of risks relevant to achieving corporate goals, determination of how such risks should be managed and implementation of a process to address risks associated with change.
- **Control activities:** Policies, procedures and processes that help ensure a company carries out management directives. Examples include approvals, verifications, reconciliations, reviews of operating performance, security of assets and segregation of duties.
- **Information and communication:** Communication within the company and with external parties such as customers, regulators and shareholders. For example, reports that contain operational, compliance or financial data or that share ideas or events across lines of business are generated from a company's information systems
- **Monitoring:** Assessing the quality of a company's internal control systems. This is done through ongoing monitoring of activities within the business unit and an independent evaluation of existing controls by auditors.

CHAPTER 1 PRACTICE QUESTIONS

1) Which of the following should be the FIRST step of an IS audit?
    A. Create a flowchart of the decision branches.
    B. Gain an understanding of the environment under review.
    C. Perform a risk assessment.
    D. Develop the audit plan.

2) An audit charter should:
    A. be dynamic and change often to coincide with the changing nature of technology and the audit profession.
    B. clearly state audit objectives for the delegation of authority for the maintenance and review of internal controls.
    C. document the audit procedures designed to achieve the planned audit objectives.
    D. outline the overall authority, scope and responsibilities of the audit function.

3) The initial step in establishing an information security program is the:
    A. development and implementation of an information security standards manual.
    B. performance of a comprehensive security control review by the IS auditor.
    C. adoption of a corporate information security policy statement.
    D. purchase of security access control software.

4) In sampling, which of the following is a measure of central tendency?
    A. Variance
    B. Range
    C. Mode
    D. Standard deviation

5) A long-term IS employee with a strong technical background and broad managerial experience has applied for a vacant position in the IS audit department. Determining whether to hire this individual for this position should be based on the individual's experience and:
    A. ability, as an IS auditor, to be independent of existing IS relationships.
    B. age as training in audit techniques may be impractical.
    C. the length of service since this will help ensure technical competence.
    D. IS knowledge since this will bring enhanced credibility to the audit function.

6) Each of the following is a general control concern EXCEPT:
    A. documentation procedures within the IS Department.
    B. physical access controls and security measures.
    C. organization of the IS Department.
    D. balancing of daily control totals.

CHAPTER 1 PRACTICE QUESTIONS (CONT.)

7) Which of the following online auditing techniques is most effective for the early detection of errors or irregularities?
   A. Embedded audit module
   B. Audit hooks
   C. Integrated test facility
   D. Snapshots

8) In a review of the IS resource management function, the IS Auditor finds that no computer routines were developed or acquired to read and take extracts from the mainframe system's job accounting software facility. Instead, the complete log record of system activity is printed out on a daily basis and distributed to several responsible managers in the IS department. The most reasonable interpretation of this situation by the IS Auditor is that:
   A. Management's review of systems activity is unusually thorough; control in this area is probably strong.
   B. IS management makes little real use of this system facility; control in this area is probably weak.
   C. IS Management is probably concerned over the high cost of developing or acquiring programs of this type.
   D. Operations management has decided to take this approach in the interest of maximizing systems efficiency.

9) Which of the following would an Information Systems Auditor consider most important in selecting an application for audit?
   A. the IS Auditor's level of experience.
   B. The application's degree of exposure.
   C. The results of previous audits.
   D. Whether or not the system is a financial one.

10) The primary purpose of an audit charter is to:
    A. describe the authority and responsibilities of the audit department.
    B. formally document the audit department's plan of action.
    C. document a code of professional conduct for the auditor.
    D. document the audit process used by the enterprise.

CHAPTER 1 ANSWERS TO PRACTICE QUESTIONS

1) Answer: B

   An auditor needs to gain an understanding of the processes prior to creating a flowchart. Based on the scope of the audit, the IS auditor should gain an understanding of the environment under review, and then carry out a risk assessment. Finally, on the basis of understanding the environment under review and the risk assessment, the IS auditor should prepare an audit plan.

2) Answer: D

   An audit charter should state management's objectives for, and delegation of authority to, IS audit. This charter should not significantly change over time and should be approved at the highest level of management. The audit charter would not be at a detail level and therefore would not include specific audit objectives or procedures.

3) Answer: C

   A policy statement reflects the intent and support provided by executive management for proper security and establishes a starting point for developing the security program.

4) Answer: C

   Answer "C" is correct. Mode identifies the number of times a particular number is duplicated more than once. For example, in the following list of numbers find the mode: 01483873263. The mode is 3.

5) Answer: A

   Independence should be continually assessed by the auditor and management. This assessment should consider such factors as changes in personal relationships, financial interests and prior job assignments and responsibilities. The fact that the employee has worked in IS for many years may not in itself ensure credibility. The audit department's needs should be defined and any candidate should be evaluated against those requirements. In addition, the length of service will not ensure technical competency, and evaluating an individual's qualifications based on the age of the individual is not a good criterion and is illegal in many parts of the world.

6) Answer: D

   Answer "D" is the BEST answer because balancing of daily control totals relates to specific applications and is not considered an overall general control concern. Answer "A" is NOT the best answer since documentation procedures within the IS Department is an important general control concern. Answer "B" is NOT the best answer since organization of the IS Department is an important general control concern. Answer "C" is NOT the best answer since physical access controls and security measures are important general control concerns.

CHAPTER 1 ANSWERS TO PRACTICE QUESTIONS (CONT.)

7) Answer: B

   The audit hook technique involves embedding code in application systems for the examination of selected transactions. This helps the IS auditor to act before an error or an irregularity gets out of hand. An embedded audit module involves embedding specially written software in the organization's host application system so that application systems are monitored on a selective basis. An integrated test facility is used when it is not practical to use test data, and snapshots are used when an audit trail is required.

8) Answer: B

   Answer "B" is correct. The system log from any moderately used computer will be abundant and labor intensive to interpret at a meaningful level. It could be reasonable to assume and easy to verify that management "makes little real use of this system." It would be prudent of the IS Auditor to recommend the development of programs to summarize and provide management with meaningful reports.

9) Answer: B

   Answer" B" is correct. The degree of exposure or audit risk should always be the key criteria for selecting candidates for an audit.

10) Answer: A

   The audit charter typically sets out the role and responsibility of the internal audit department. It should state management's objectives for and delegation of authority to the audit department. It is rarely changed and does not contain the audit plan or audit process which is usually part of annual audit planning, nor does it describe a code of professional conduct since such conduct is set by the profession and not by management.

Chapter 2 IT GOVERNANCE

INFORMATION SYSTEMS ORGANIZATION AND MANAGEMENT

One objective of this chapter is to ensure that an IS Auditor understands policy and procedure regarding monitoring and control of IT systems. In addition an IS Auditor should understand the organizational structures, job roles and management practices that govern Information Systems Departments. Within this chapter there are six tasks that specifically address this. The student will be expected to understand how each of the six tasks/categories contributes to the Information Systems Department's ability to effectively, efficiently and economically support an organization's business objectives. Within each task the candidate may be asked questions about the structure, advantages and disadvantages of the specific techniques.

This chapter will represent approximately 15 percent of the CISA examination (approximately 30 questions).

The nine tasks that a CISA is expected to understand and be able to perform are as follows:

- Evaluate the effectiveness of IT governance structure to ensure adequate board control over the decisions, directions, and performance of IT so that it supports the organization's strategies and objectives.
- Evaluate IT organizational structure and human resources (personnel) management to ensure that they support the organization's strategies and objectives.
- Evaluate the IT strategy and the process for its development, approval, implementation, and maintenance to ensure that it supports the organization's strategies and objectives.
- Evaluate the organization's IT policies, standards, and procedures; and the processes for their development, approval, implementation, and maintenance to ensure that they support the IT strategy and comply with regulatory and legal requirements.
- Evaluate management practices to ensure compliance with the organization's IT strategy, policies, standards, and procedures.
- Evaluate IT resource investment, use, and allocation practices to ensure alignment with the organization's strategies and objectives.
- Evaluate IT contracting strategies and policies, and contract management practices to ensure that they support the organization's strategies and objectives.
- Evaluate risk management practices to ensure that the organization's IT related risks are properly managed.
- Evaluate monitoring and assurance practices to ensure that the board and executive management receive sufficient and timely information about IT performance.

Knowledge Statements
The following statements describe specific topics a CISA candidate should be familiar with and use as guidance in the fulfillment of the tasks outlined above:

- Knowledge of the purpose of IT strategies, policies, standards and procedures for an organization and the essential elements of each
- Knowledge of IT governance frameworks
- Knowledge of the processes for the development, implementation and maintenance of IT strategies, policies, standards and procedures (e.g., protection of information assets, business continuity and disaster recovery, systems and infrastructure lifecycle management, IT service delivery and support)
- Knowledge of quality management strategies and policies
- Knowledge of organizational structure, roles and responsibilities related to the use and management of IT
- Knowledge of generally accepted international IT standards and guidelines
- Knowledge of enterprise IT architecture and its implications for setting long-term strategic directions
- Knowledge of risk management methodologies and tools

- Knowledge of the use of control frameworks (e.g., COBIT, COSO, ISO 17799)
- Knowledge of the use of maturity and process improvement models (e.g., CMM, COBIT)
- Knowledge of contracting strategies, processes and contract management practices
- Knowledge of practices for monitoring and reporting of IT performance (e.g., balanced scorecards, key performance indicators [KPI])
- Knowledge of relevant legislative and regulatory issues (e.g., privacy, intellectual property, corporate governance requirements)
- Knowledge of IT human resources (personnel) management
- Knowledge of IT resource investment and allocation practices (e.g., portfolio management return on investment {ROI})

To fulfill the task objectives as stated above, the IS Auditor should seek to complete the following five generalized audit objectives:

- Obtain the overall business strategies and policies, identify the areas concerning information processing and gain an understanding of the business practices and functions.
- Identify the significant functional areas, tasks and reporting responsibilities of IS departments to gain an understanding of the organization's information processing environment through local review of relevant documentation, inquiry and observation.
- Evaluate management's practices, procedures and the organizational structure of IS departments to assess their adequacy by determining whether they are efficient and effective and include appropriate controls.
- Test the controls to determine compliance with appropriate standards by applying suitable audit techniques.
- Assess the organizational control environment to determine that control objectives were achieved by analyzing test results and other audit evidence.

Access to the Internet and its vast stores of freely available data is changing the planet, making it a much smaller place. Communications that took days via the fastest shippers now take seconds. The internet is also changing the way that individuals and other businesses conduct business. Entrepreneurs are able to start new businesses more easily, with smaller upfront investment requirements, by accessing the Internet's worldwide network of customers.

The benefits that Internet access and Internet-based commerce (or "e-commerce") offer to an organization are accompanied by new challenges in the areas of administration, infrastructure and security. One result of new regulations such as Sarbanes-Oxley (SOX) and California's SB 1386 is that the executives and other managers of both public and privately held companies may be held personally liable for certain acts of fraud or fiscal misconduct. In addition, the organizations may be held liable for any demonstrable losses their customers or employees experience as a consequence of any unauthorized exposure of their PII (Personally Identifiable Information) due to security breaches.

Theft of physical items has always been a risk. However, certain types of data are now considered valuable commodities, especially by those that trade in stolen PII. The methods used to keep people from stealing PCs or other tangibles offer little or no protection to digital assets. The safeguards that might have been effective in a paper-based storage system could be completely useless for digital storage systems. Controlling the bits and bytes that move into and out of an organization is an enormous task. A new subset of Corporate Governance is known as IT Governance. The security of an organization's digital assets and other IT resources falls under IT Governance. It is the responsibility of an organization's executives and board of directors to ensure that a comprehensive and systematic approach to IT Governance and security is designed, implemented and maintained.

Corporate Governance

Corporate governance is defined as ethical corporate behavior by directors or others charged with governance in the creation and preservation of wealth for all stakeholders.[1] Corporate governance includes a set of responsibilities and practices used by an organization's management to provide strategic direction. Its aim is to ensure that goals are achievable, risks are properly addressed and organizational resources are properly utilized. IT Governance is a subset of corporate governance. **IT governance** may be defined as management's involvement in the implementation and review of the use of IT in attaining the goals and objectives set by the organization. Given the increasing importance of Internet-based technologies, the IT subset should continue to grow in importance within most organizations. It may be argued that IT governance begins when an organization realizes that it is a part of a larger, even global, commercial picture.

Some believe that organizations are governed by generally accepted good or best practices, the assurance of which is guaranteed by certain controls. IT Governance is concerned with the ideas of risk management, business alignment, and appropriate use of resources. These three objectives may be condensed into two, namely:
- The development of a Value-oriented approach to IT management
- The use of a comprehensive Risk Management approach throughout the IS/IT infrastructure

Within IT governance, information security governance should become a focused activity with specific value drivers (Better known as the **CIA** principle):
- Protection of information assets   (**C**onfidentiality)
- Accuracy and validity of information   (**I**ntegrity)
- Continuity of services   (**A**vailability)

One result of connecting organizations to the global network is that security is emerging as a significant governance issue. The information security function should become an important and integral part of IT governance. Negligence in this regard will diminish an organization's capacity to take advantage of IT opportunities for business process improvement. Ultimately, IT governance is the responsibility of the board of directors and executive management. Corporate-level management must ensure that the organization's IT sustains and extends the organization's strategy and objectives.

IT Audit and IT Governance

The IT auditor and IT management must review regulatory requirements to ensure that the organizations activities do not cause it to violate local laws. This practice is even more important for multi-national corporations. The transfer of data across national boundaries can present many challenges to an organization. The use of risk management techniques to guide security expenditures and even the pursuit of certain business opportunities has increased dramatically. The huge variety of legal constraints and the never-ending changes in technology increase the importance of the IS/IT auditor in the organization. As risk and control specialists, IT auditors are uniquely positioned to help organizations maneuver through the various regulatory and information security hurdles they currently face.

As long as these factors remain a part of business, there will be a need for effective, interdependent systems of enterprise and IT governance. IT auditors have an important role in this process. There are several popular sets of standards and best practices that deal with various aspects of IT Governance and Security. The following is a list of several of these standards:
- AS8015-2005 (Australian Standard for Corporate Governance of Information and Communication Technology)
- ISO 17799 (International Organization for Standardization); ISO 27001
- NIST (National Institute of Standards and Technology) 800 Series
- ISM3 (Information Security Management Maturity Model)
- COBIT (Control Objectives for Information and related Technology)
- ITIL (IT Infrastructure Library)
- CMMI (Capability Maturity Model Integration)
- ISF (Information Security Forum) Standard of Good Practice for Information Security

This text focuses on IT Governance and security as it is described in the COBIT framework. COBIT is derived from many sets of standards and best practices and has a strong emphasis on management concerns. COBIT can be downloaded by ISACA members on a complimentary basis from www.isaca.org. It includes a publication containing detailed management guidelines to bridge the gaps among business risks, control needs and technical issues. These new tools help businesses monitor processes by using critical success factors (CSFs), key goal indicators (KGIs), key performance indicators (KPIs) and maturity models (MMs). Additional resources and information are available at www.itgi.org.

IT Security Governance

Chapter 4 deals with IT Service Management (ITSM). It therefore contains a broader set of objectives for the oversight of Information Systems as a whole. In this chapter, the focus is on a subset of IT Governance known as Information Security Governance. Infosec (Information Security):

- Deals with every facet of the Information System
- Should be applied at every point of the life cycle of a system
- Should also apply to people and the processes they use when interacting with software or physical devices.
- Addresses security concerns from a corporate-level perspective (CIO, CSO, CISO)

Information Security Governance provides value to the organization in several ways:

- It minimizes risk to the businesses' reputation
- It enhances newer, Internet-based business methods by increasing the security of transactions
- It offers assurance to stakeholders that regulatory concerns are adequately managed
- The improved levels of data integrity allow managers to have greater reliance upon the decisions or conclusions based on that data.
- It provides a means by which critical business functions can be maintained in the event of a disaster or unexpected business event.
- It involves the consideration and adoption of one or more layers of policy and procedure designed to further business objectives while improving security

In general, Information Security Governance will play an integral role in each of the following:

- **Performance Measurement**: Monitoring and auditing of various OS, application, hardware and other metrics that may bear on security.
- **Resource Management:** Appropriate use, maintenance, storage and tracking of IS data and physical resources.
- **Risk Management:** Policies and procedures aimed at lowering operational risks to tolerable levels
- **Business/Strategic/IT Alignment:** Ensuring that IT purchases, implementation and maintenance all serve the needs of the business
- **Value Delivery:** Focused on maximizing the ROI (Return on Investment) for any IT or Security related expenditure.

Corporate-Level Roles and Responsibilities

The responsibility for the objectives, design, implementation, maintenance and improvement of an InfoSec program is in the hands of corporate executives and the board of directors.

- CIO (Chief Information Officer): Recent legislation in the U.S. has weakened or removed the "corporate shield" from corporate executives. This means that corporate level personnel can now be held personally liable for certain types of fraud, financial misconduct or security breaches. Even if an organization does not have a person possessing the job title of "CIO", (or CISO – Chief Information Security Officer, CSO – Chief Security Officer, CTO – Chief Technical Officer, etc.) it would be assumed that someone at the corporate level should be functioning in that capacity.
- Executive Management: The CEO, CFO and others in the corporate-level arena must lend their support to security initiatives. Even the most diligent CIO will have to get funding approved for various initiatives. In addition, without some universal system of consequences or punishment for failure to follow security rules, it is unlikely that security objectives will be realized.

- Board of Directors: Depending on the size of the organization, one or more Board member may be involved in oversight or monitoring of the audit, value delivery, risk management or other key security areas. The Board must echo any corporate sentiments in favor of improving and enforcing Information Security.
- Steering Committee(s): Again, depending on the size of the organization, one or more committees will be manned by appropriate staff from the departments needed. Steering committees may perform or delegate a wide variety of tasks including:
    - Development of the overall Information Security Policy
    - Development of lower-level policy, procedures and guidelines
    - Development of training modules appropriate for each level of staff
    - IT Purchasing/Procurement
    - IT Audit/Process Improvement

    Committees of this type should be headed by a corporate-level executive with the power to ensure:
    - Alignment/compliance with business objectives (upward).
    - Compliance with/Adherence to stated security procedures (downward).

Information Systems (Enterprise) Architecture

An Information Systems or Enterprise Architecture is a relatively new area in IS management. It involves the use of a structured approach, such as an SDLC, for the requirements, design, implementation and day-to-day operation of an IS Infrastructure. Chapter 4 offers a more detailed look at the key or common components of modern IS Architectures. However, it is important to know that best practices for IT Governance are now beginning to include references to one or more suggested frameworks as baselines for Infrastructure development. Examples of these frameworks include:
- The Zachman Framework (Most popular)[2]
- The FEA (Federal Enterprise Architecture) Reference Models[3]
- TOGAF (The Open Group Architecture Framework)[4]

IS Strategy

Information Systems Strategy is concerned with the long-term goals and objectives of the organization. An outline of these goals might be made publicly available in the form of a Mission Statement or similar document. The following are characteristics of strategic planning:
- These tend to be high-level objectives
- They are clear and fairly specific in nature, specifying "what" needs to be done and even "why" things need to be done, but not "how"
- Strategy is usually expressed in high-level documents such as an information security policy or other policy document
- Strategies may change for several valid reasons. However, part of the development of long-term goals is a process wherein predictions about the future business climate are discussed. In theory, if the strategic planning was carefully done, then the overall plan will not change too often or endure radical changes

The Information Security Policy

This document is the cornerstone of an Information Security program and Architecture. This should be the highest level security policy document in the organization. It may address all, but it is not limited to the following:
- It defines the high-level business objectives of the organization.
- It states security goals and objectives that support the stated business objectives
- It defines the organization's risk tolerance
- It outlines the organization's stances on Employee education, Disaster Recovery, Business Continuity, Punishment for Security Violations, and Appointment of Committees/Assignment of Responsibility for IT Governance Tasks
- Acceptance of one or more Security or Management Frameworks or Guidelines
- It suggests a schedule by which management should perform any review and update of security documents, including the Information Security Policy itself.

The approach described above is called a "top-down approach". This is because the control and guidance for projects and other business activities is defined at the top and all subsequent documents and activities must be brought into line with this top-level document. Business drivers are normally the reason for the use of a top-down approach. Upper management has the most effective influence on lower-level activities this way. In a top-down approach, operational control is prioritized in terms of a risk assessment. These policy statements are implemented throughout the organization as generally accepted requirements.

Some organizations may focus on operations level policy statements as their immediate priority, in a bottom-up manner. Organizations that perform product or application development have determined that the use of a bottom-up approach can accelerate the delivery of products by eliminating one or more bureaucratic layers. Controls must be present in a bottom-up approach, but these a greater percentage of these controls are implemented by project or line management. The following diagram illustrates the flow of each approach:

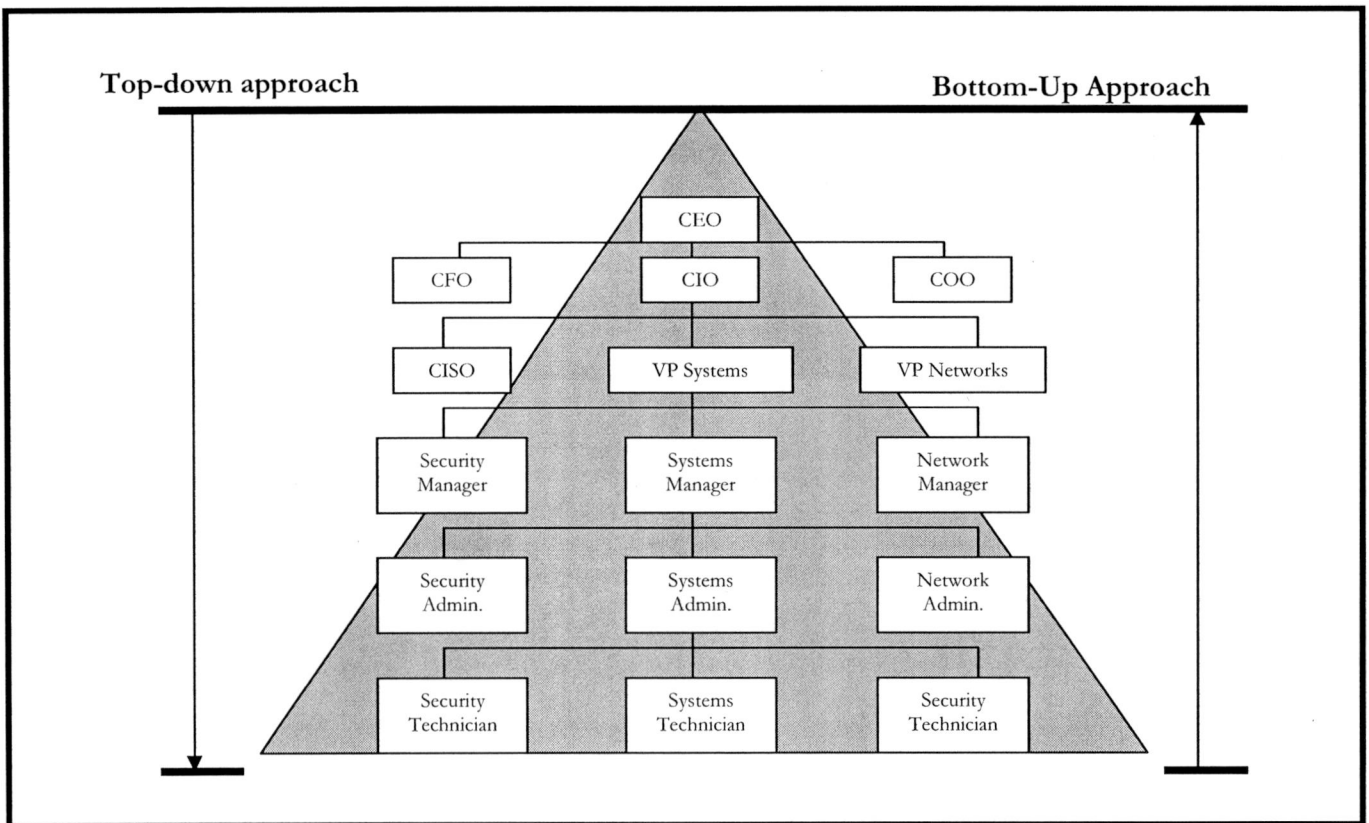

Acceptable Use Policies

Organizations spend large sums of money to provide its employees with access to PCs and other technology with the idea that doing so will promote productivity. Recently, issues of privacy, productivity and employee rights have been merged in battles over Internet, IM (Instant Messaging) and email usage. Many organizations have been sued by employees that claim they have been harassed, offended or otherwise harmed as the result of the viewing or reading of material sent by *other* employees of the organization.

The role of the auditor is to be aware of the risks inherent in "free" systems and to make management aware of steps that can be taken to mitigate or avoid those risks. Some organizations, especially those in financial services, have regulatory requirements that define the types of electronic transmissions that must be maintained and how long they should be stored. However, the best approach for any organization is a proactive response to the problem.

Acceptable use policies can be structured to define the following:
- The owner and provider of the system (namely, the organization) and its right to set policy
- They types of communication that are acceptable and unacceptable
- The penalties for failure to use any or all IS/It resources according to the policies set forth.

The following is an example of an Acceptable Use policy:

ABC INC.
INFORMATION SYSTEM USAGE POLICY

Voice mail, email, and Internet usage assigned to an employee's computer or telephone extensions are solely for the purpose of conducting Company business. Some job responsibilities at the Company require access to the Internet and the use of software in addition to the Microsoft Office suite of products. Only people appropriately authorized, for Company purposes, may use the Internet or access additional software.

Software Access Procedure
Software needed, in addition to the Microsoft Office suite of products, must be authorized by your supervisor and downloaded by the IT department. If you need access to software, not currently on the Company network, talk with your supervisor and consult with the IT department.

Internet Usage
Internet use, on Company time, is authorized to conduct Company business only. Internet use brings the possibility of breaches to the security of confidential Company information. Internet use also creates the possibility of contamination to our system via viruses or spy-ware. Spy-ware allows unauthorized people, outside the Company, potential access to Company passwords and other confidential information.

Removing such programs from the Company network requires IT staff to invest time and attention that is better devoted to progress. For this reason, and to assure the use of work time appropriately for work, we ask staff members to limit Internet use.

Additionally, under no circumstances may Company computers or other electronic equipment be used to obtain, view, or reach any pornographic, or otherwise immoral, unethical, or non-business-related Internet sites. Doing so can lead to disciplinary action up to and including termination of employment.

Email Usage at Company
Email is also to be used for Company business only. Company confidential information must not be shared outside of the Company, without authorization, at any time. You are also not to conduct personal business using the Company computer or email.

Please keep this in mind, also, as you consider forwarding non-business emails to associates, family or friends. Non-business related emails waste company time and attention.

Viewing pornography, or sending pornographic jokes or stories via email, is considered sexual harassment and will be addressed according to our sexual harassment policy.

Emails That Discriminate
Any emails that discriminate against employees by virtue of any protected classification including race, gender, nationality, religion, and so forth, will be dealt with according to the harassment policy.

These emails are prohibited at the Company. Sending or forwarding non-business emails will result in disciplinary action that may lead to employment termination.

Company Owns Employee Email
Keep in mind that the Company owns any communication sent via email or that is stored on company equipment. Management and other authorized staff have the right to access any material in your email or on your computer at any time. Please do not consider your electronic communication, storage or access to be private if it is created or stored at work.

Procedures
These documents are developed from higher-level policies such as the Information Security Policy. These documents are usually directed at middle to low-level processes. In contrast to policies, procedures should be:
- Highly Detailed
- Fairly narrow in scope
- Aimed at explaining "how" more than "what" or "why"
- Tailored to accommodate specific job functions or staff levels.
- The focus of most Security Education efforts

RISK MANAGEMENT

Risk management may be defined as a set of processes used to assess any threats or vulnerabilities applicable to a given asset and then determine how to best mitigate or eliminate the risk level identified, based on the value of the asset in question and the business goals of the organization.

There are many formulas used to calculate risk. Many organizations use proprietary schemes with weights on different metrics depending on the criticality of the resource and its location. In general, the IS Auditor is not concerned which risk assessment techniques an organization uses. Instead, the auditor is concerned with consistency in the risk assessment approach and the adequacy or relevance of the approach to the business goals and IT resources in question. A very simple formula for calculating risk is:

Total Risk = (k* Threat Potential) x (l* Vulnerability1 + m* Vulnerability2...) x (n* Stated Value of Asset or Resource) where k, l, m and n are weights assigned to each of the metrics

Risk may be handled in five different ways:
- **Acceptance:** Performing the assessment and determining that implementing additional controls is not a cost effective move.
- **Avoidance:** Cease the performance of the activity that is generating the risk
- **Eliminate:** Completely remove the threat or vulnerability, effectively reducing risk to zero (or very near zero)
- **Mitigate:** Implement various controls to minimize the chances of a successful exploit
- **Transfer:** Shift the risk to a third party, such as an outsourcing firm or an insurance company.

As stated earlier, there are many formulas used to calculate risk. However, each of the more comprehensive schemes includes some aspect of the following six steps (Note that the order of events is important here):
- Perform Physical Inventory of all resources
- Classify/Categorize all resources using a consistent naming convention
- Analyze resources and processes and assign values to each process and component of the process, whether that component is hardware, software, etc. (This process can be quite difficult and time-consuming, but doing it during risk management pays dividends later)
- Assess the vulnerabilities that each resource or process currently carries
- Assess the threat potential to each resource or process identified. (Since the threat potential is usually related to the value of the asset, it is extremely difficult to calculate that potential without having calculated a value for that resource.)
- Calculate the overall risk based on some formula that utilizes the metrics you have developed.

Note that BIAs (Business Impact Analyses) and BCP (Business Continuity Planning) processes both rely on the outputs generated during a comprehensive risk assessment. Also, BIAs are used to determine the processes that must be duplicated in a BCP or DR (Disaster Recovery) Plan. Therefore, an auditor that is aware of a client's desire or need to implement a BCP/DR process will strongly suggest that the time and effort be spent to perform a good risk assessment first. These issues are discussed at greater length in Chapter 6.

After the organization has done all that is feasible in terms of handling its risk, some risk will still remain. The risk that remains after all justifiable means have been employed to deal with it is called **residual risk**. It is normally impossible to reduce **all** risk within an organization to zero. The reason for this is that most organizations have some kind of data or resources that have value. As long as there is value present, there is usually some threat potential, and therefore, some amount of risk.

Types of Risk Analysis
Although there are many ways to perform risk analysis, they all tend to fall into one of three categories:
- Qualitative Analysis: This type of analysis is based on verbal or semantic distinctions rather than crunched numbers. Although this type of assessment is very popular and easy to perform, those with financial responsibilities prefer a more rigorous approach.
- Quantitative Analysis: These methods rely heavily upon the use of numbers in the generation of results. Whether the information is obtained from internal or external sources, trend analyses or just logs of past events, all of the inputs selected are thrown into the mix
    - ALE (Annual Loss Expectancy): This is a quantitative method that can simplify the process by which probability (p) and value (v) are obtained.
    - Probability and Expectancy: This is another quantitative method that relies upon the use of more stringent statistical methods for calculating loss and gain.
- Semi-quantitative: These methods combine the verbal rankings of the qualitative schemes with one or more numeric components from the quantitative camp.

Other Considerations Regarding Risk
As is the case with every other aspect of IS Management, risk management is ultimately the responsibility of Executive (Corporate) level management. Quantitative methods tend to be easier to defend than Qualitative methods. Although Quantitative methods may offer more objectivity than qualitative methods, there is no such thing as a purely objective quantitative method. This is true because at multiple points in the risk management process, one or more humans used some type of subjective judgment or criteria when determining:
- Which metrics to use
- What values to assign to different resources in the same process.
- What values to assign to identical resources that support different processes
- What weights (if any) to assign to different metrics (Note that choosing **not** to use weights in the calculation of risk is also a subjective decision)

It is impossible to completely remove subjectivity from calculations of this type because each organization is unique. The goals and objectives, financial resources, regulatory and business environments are all variable. The most experienced of IT security managers would not choose the exact set of controls and metrics for a large data center and a local bank branch. There is no "one size fits all" template or framework for information security. It is important that audit professionals understand the background of the organizations they review and the actual processes and motivations behind the controls they find in place.

To develop a risk management program:
- Establish the purpose of the risk management program-The first step is to determine the organization's purpose for creating a risk management program. The program's purpose may be to reduce the cost of insurance or to reduce the number of program-related injuries. By determining its intention before initiating risk management planning, the organization can evaluate the results to determine its effectiveness. Typically, the executive director, with the board of directors, sets the tone for the risk management program.
- Assign responsibility for the risk management plan-The second step is to designate an individual or team responsible for developing and implementing the organization's risk management program. While the team primarily is responsible for the risk management plan, a successful program requires the integration of risk management within all levels of the organization. Operations staff and board members should assist the risk management committee in identifying risks and developing suitable loss control and intervention strategies.

A Risk Management Plan
In the following graphic, Section 2 provides a graphical representation of the risk management processes and the tool that will be utilized to track risk status. Sections 3 through 7 of the plan describe how risk identification, qualitative and quantitative analysis, response planning, and monitoring and control will be structured and performed throughout the transition program life cycle. Throughout the sections 3 through 7 roles and responsibilities, timings of action throughout the program life cycle, risk scoring and interpretation, risk response thresholds, reporting formats, and utilization of the risk-tracking tool are defined. The plan does not address the actual responses to individual risks – this is accomplished in the actual risk response plans.

Following the flow of decisions through the graphic may prove initially to be a difficult task. However, patience with the flow and the descriptions of the various group activities that follow can be quite helpful.

Risk Management Process Flow
The following diagrams depict the risk management process flow.

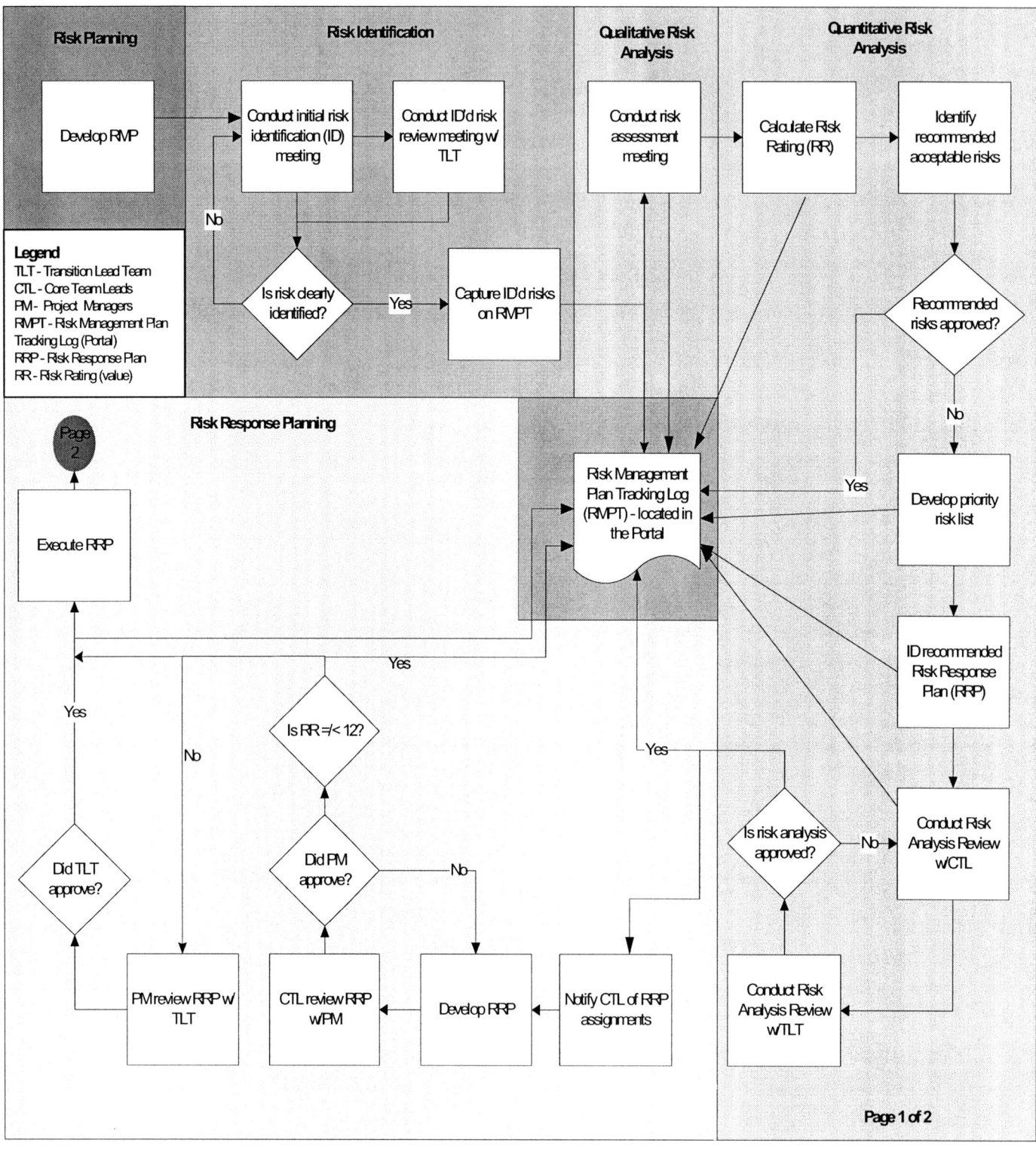

RMP Tool
This tool is used to track progress and resolution of all project risks.

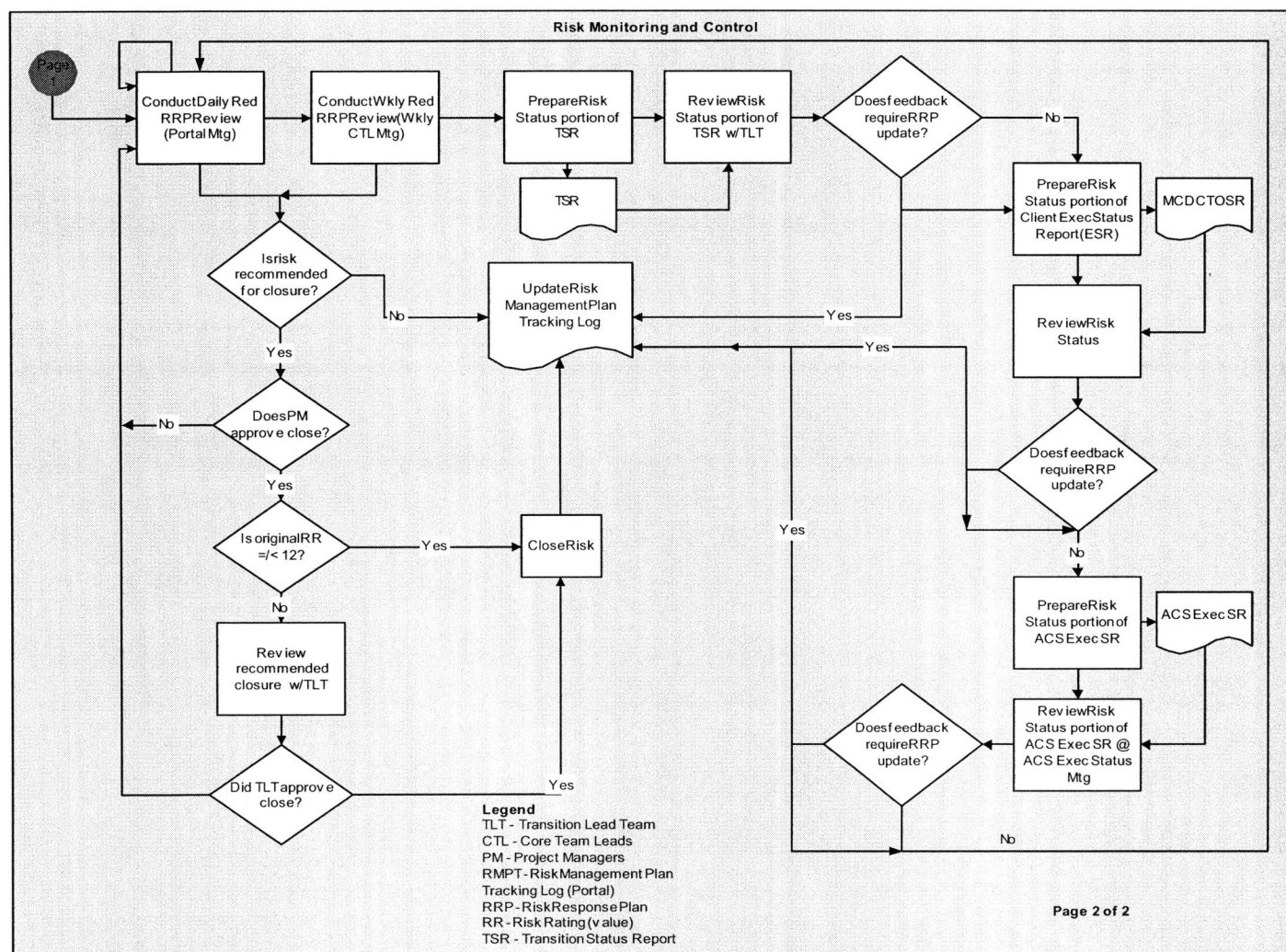

Risk Identification
Risk identification is the process of identifying and determining which risks might affect the project and documenting their characteristics.

Identify and Document Risk
During the program planning phase, the transition manager conducts an initial risk identification brainstorming session with Core Team Leads, Tower Leads, and other appropriate subject matter experts (SMEs). The purpose of the session is to identify any potential risks to the program goals and objectives established by the Transition Sponsors. During the brainstorming session, the Transition Manager captures the identified risk and also identifies individuals that should participate in the initial risk assessment (Qualitative Risk Analysis) meeting for the identified risks.

Throughout project execution, all project team members are responsible for being aware of potential risks to the project, and forwarding information about those risks to their Core Team Lead. Identified risks need to be clear and unambiguous to include the identification of specific project activities that are at risk. All clearly identified risks move forward for qualitative and quantitative analysis. The purpose of risk identification brainstorming sessions is to identify potential risks. Scoring and interpretation evaluation should not occur during the conduct of risk identification brainstorming sessions.

Roles and Responsibilities

Role	Responsibility
Transition Sponsors	- Establish program goals and objectives
Transition Lead Team	- Review identified risks and provide the Transition Manager with any areas requiring further risk identification
Transition Manager	- Schedule and facilitate review of identified risks with the Transition Lead Team
Project Managers	- Schedule and facilitate risk identification sessions for each assigned project - Log identified risk in the RMPT
Core Team Leads	- Participate in risk identification sessions - Submit newly identified risks throughout the project life cycle to the Transition Manager
Tower Leads	- Participate in risk identification sessions - Submit to Core Teal Lead newly identified risks throughout the project life cycle
Project Team Members	- Participate in risk identification sessions - Submit to Core Teal Lead newly identified risks throughout the project life cycle

Timing
Initial risk identification brainstorming sessions are completed prior to finalizing the project schedule.

Reporting Formats and Tracking
The RMPT tab of the Program Portal is utilized to capture identified risks. As risks are identified in the risk identification brainstorming sessions or throughout the course of the project, the project manager captures the risk on the RMPT tab of the Program Portal.

The following information is captured during risk identification:
- Risk Number
- Track
- Movement
- Risk Description
- Potential Impact
- Related Actions/Issues/WBS UID
- Comments

Qualitative Risk Analysis
In Qualitative Risk Analysis, an analysis of risks and conditions is performed with the goal of prioritizing their potential effects on project objectives.

Risk Assessment Scoring: Probability and Impact
The assignment of Likelihood Probability and Impact to identified risk is a point-in-time evaluation. After initial risk identification, the Transition Manager schedules a Risk Assessment meeting with the Core Teams Leads and pertinent Subject Matter Experts. At the risk assessment meeting, the probability and impact of each identified risk is assessed.

Probability Rating
A "likelihood" rating that represents the likelihood that the identified risk will occur is assigned to each identified risk.
- Rating 1 - Very unlikely to occur
- Rating 2 - Less likely to occur
- Rating 3 - 50/50 chance of occurring
- Rating 4 - More likely to occur than not
- Rating 5 - Certain, Already Observed

Impact Rating
A rating that represents the importance of the impact the risk realization would have on the Project and assigned to each identified risk.
- Rating 0 - No impact
- Rating 1 - Insignificant changes, re-planning may be required
- Rating 2 - Small delay, small increased cost, but absorbable
- Rating 3 - Delay, increased cost in excess of tolerance
- Rating 4 - Substantial delay, key deliverable not met, increase costs
- Rating 5 - Inability to deliver, business case/objective not viable

The Transition Manager enters the probability and impact ratings on the RMPT along with any clarifying risk description and potential impact information obtain during the assessment.

Roles and Responsibilities

Role	Responsibility
Transition Manager	- Participate in the risk assessment meeting
Project Managers	- Schedule and facilitate risk assessment meeting for assigned projects - Update RMPT
Core Team Leads	- Participate in the risk assessment meeting
Tower Leads	- Participate in risk assessment meeting
Project Team Members	- Participate in the risk assessment meeting

Timing
The initial risk assessment meetings should be completed within one week of the initial risk identification session.

Reporting Formats and Tracking
The RMPT tab of the Program Portal is utilized to capture updated risk information. As risks are assessed during the risk assessment meeting, the Transition Manager updates the RMPT tab of the Program Portal. The following information is captured during risk assessment scoring for probability and impact:
- Risk Description
- Potential Impact
- Date of Risk Assessment
- Probability
- Impact
- Comments

Quantitative Risk Analysis

Quantitative Risk Analysis involves the estimation of the probability and consequences of risks and their implications for project objectives. The quantitative risk analysis process aims to analyze numerically the probability of each risk and its consequence on project objectives.

Risk Assessment Scoring, Interpretation, and Thresholds: Risk Rating

After completing qualitative risk analysis, the Transition Manager calculates the Risk Rating. The Risk Rating represents the overall "assessment" of the risk to the project, and is the product of the probability and Impact ratings. The risk rating provides an index that is used to understand the relative importance of risks to the project, and hence the amount of attention that needs to be paid to risk response planning. Once the Risk Rating is calculated for each identified risk, the following actions are taken:

- The Transition Manager develops a prioritized list of quantified risks recommended for risk response plans. The Transition Manager also identifies a recommended Core Team Lead to lead development and execution the Risk Response Plan for each risk. The Transition Manager then conducts a review of the prioritized list and recommended risk response plan leads with the Core Team Leads.
- A review of the risk analysis and recommendations is then conducted with the Transition Lead Team. The Transition Manager schedules the review with the Transition Lead Team at a Transition Lead Team meeting. The Transition Lead Team reviews and approves the prioritized list of risks recommended for risk response planning and the list of risks identified as acceptable.

The following guideline is used to assist with developing risk response plan recommendations.

Risk Condition	Risk Rating	Risk Response Plan Recommendation Guideline
Green	Less than 8	Causes little disruption; manageable through issues management.
Yellow	8 – 12	Causes some disruption – potential cost of risk response plan evaluated against potential impact to determine risk response plan recommendation. Requires Transition Lead Team approval to deem acceptable.
Red	Greater than 12	Significant potential to disrupt project schedule, increase costs, impact services – Risk response plan is required.

Roles and Responsibilities

Role	Responsibility
Transition Lead Team	• Review and approve risk rating, prioritized list of risks for Risk Response Planning, and lists of risks assessed as acceptable
Transition Manager	• Schedule risk analysis review with the Transition Lead Team
Project Managers	• Calculate risk rating • Develop prioritized list of quantified risks recommended for risk response plans • Develop recommended Core Team Lead to lead development and execution of Risk Response Plan • Conduct review of prioritized risk list and recommended risk response leads with the Core Team Leads • Present recommendations to Transition Lead Team • Update RMPT

Role	Responsibility
Core Team Leads	• Review and provide feedback to the Transition Manager on the prioritized risk list and the recommended risk response plan leads.

Timing
Calculation of the risk rating, development of the prioritized risk list, and the recommended risk response plan lead is completed with 3 business days of the Risk Assessment meeting. The review of the quantitative analysis with the Transition Lead Team is then scheduled for the next Transition Lead Team meeting.

Reporting Formats and Tracking
The RMPT tab of the Program Portal is utilized to capture updated risk information. The following information is updated by the Transition Manager during quantitative risk analysis:
- Owner
- Risk Rating
- Date of Closure
- Comments

Risk Response Planning
Risk Response Planning is developing the action plan to enhance opportunities and reduce threats to the project's objectives.

Create Risk Response Plan
After the completion of the quantitative risk analysis review with the Transition Lead Team, the Transition Manager notifies the Core Team Leads of their assigned risk response plans. The assigned Core Team Leads then lead the development of the risk response plans. The Risk Response Plan describes the activities that are being performed currently or in the very near term to prevent the identified risk from occurring or to reduce the risk's impact if it does occur. Since these activities are to be performed, they are immediately identified as tasks in the project schedule. The Risk Response Plan also includes the activities that will be implemented if the identified risk does occur. This is especially important when actions can't be identified to reduce the risk probability rating below 3. Since these activities will occur only once the risk has become reality, they are not placed in the project schedule.

The Core Team Lead submits the developed risk response plan to the Transition Manager for approval. The Transition Manager may approve risk Response Plans for risks with a risk rating of 12 or below. Risk Response Plans for risks with a risk rating above 12 are scheduled for review with the Transition Leadership Team. The Transition Manager schedules the review of the risk response plan at the next Transition lead Team Meeting. Once the plan is approved, the Core Team Lead leads execution of the risk response plan.

Roles and Responsibilities

Role	Responsibility
Transition Lead Team	Review and approve risk response plans for risk with a risk rating above 12
Transition Manager	Schedule risk response plan reviews with the Transition Lead Team
Project Managers	Notify Core Team Leads of Risk Response Plan assignments Review and approve risk response plans with a risk rating of 12 or below Present risk response plans for risk with a risk rating above 12 to the Transition Lead Team for approval
Core Team Leads	Lead the development of assigned risk response plans Execute approved risk response plans

Role	Responsibility
Tower Leads	Participate in risk response plan **development** as assigned by Core Team Lead Participate in risk response plan **execution** as assigned by Core Team Lead
Project Team Members	Participate in risk response plan **development** as assigned by Core Team/Tower Lead Participate in risk response plan **execution** as assigned by Core/Tower Team Lead

Reporting Formats and Tracking

The RMPT tab of the Program Portal is utilized to capture updated risk information. The following information is updated by the Transition Manager during risk response planning:
- Risk Response Plan
- RRP Approval Date
- Comments

Risk Monitoring and Control

Risk Monitoring and Control is monitoring residual risks, identifying new risks, executing risk reduction plans, evaluating their effectiveness throughout the project life cycle, and reporting on the status and progress of the risk management actions.

Risk Status and Escalation

Core Team Meetings

The RMPT is reviewed and updated during Core Team Meetings. Each risk is reviewed by the Risk Response Plan owner to determine:
- if the risk is still valid
- if the probability of occurrence or impact has changed
- if Risk Response Plan mitigation efforts are effective
- if Risk Response Plan contingency plan is still valid

In addition, the current trend risk rating is discussed and captured to determine whether the risk is more likely to occur, less likely to occur, or no change. New risks are also identified and added to the RMPT during the meeting.

Portal Red / Yellow Review Meetings

Risks with a Probability Rating above 12 are reviewed to determine if any immediate action is necessary. Again, new risks are also identified and added to the RMPT during the meeting.

Risk Closure

Closure of a risk with an original risk rating of 12 or below requires approval from the Transition Manager. Based on the effectiveness of the Risk Response Plan or changing project conditions, the risk owner may recommend closure of the risk to the Transition Manager. Closure of a risk with an original risk rating of above 12 requires Transition Lead Team approval. Based on the effectiveness of the Risk Response Plan or changing project conditions, the risk owner and Transition Manager may recommend closure of the Risk to the Transition Lead Team. Upon recommendation, the Transition Manager schedules a review of the recommendation for closure with the Transition Lead Team at the next Transition lead Team meeting. The status of a risk will be changed to Closed if the project management team determines the risk is no longer valid.

Risk Escalation

The escalation path for risks is documented in the Mellon Transition Program Communications Management Plan.

Roles and Responsibilities

Role	Responsibility
Transition Lead Team	1. Approve closure of risks with an original risk rating above 12
Transition Manager	2. Schedule recommended closure review for risk with an original rating above 12 with the Transition Lead team
Project Managers	3. Review and approve closure recommendations for risks with an original rating of 12 or below with the Transition Lead team 4. Make risk closure recommendations to the Transition Lead Team for risks with an original rating above 12 5. Maintain the RMPT
Core Team Leads	6. Report Risk Response Plan status 7. Submit RMPT updates to the Transition Manager during Core Team meetings and Daily Red ./ Yellow Portal Reviews

Timing

Monitoring and Control of risks with a risk rating above 12 is done daily. Monitoring and control of risks with a risk rating of 12 or below is done weekly.

Reporting Formats and Tracking

Throughout monitoring and control risks status is maintained in the RMPT

Risk assessment is a complicated topic and it cannot be given the attention it deserves in a text of this type. However, risk and controls should be considered the areas specialization for audit professionals. Therefore, given the increasing importance of IS to modern organizations, the value of experienced IS Auditors to those organizations should also increase over time.

Exam Tip: Questions that deal with risk-related issues or that have risk related topics as potential answers can be found anywhere on the exam However, chapters 1, 2, 3 and 6 are the most likely areas to find this area discussed. Risk Management is an important focus for ISACA; therefore it should be an area on which the CISA candidate focuses a great deal of attention.

Management Tasks

Human Resources/Staff Management

Staffing concerns have traditionally been performed by in-house HR personnel or contracted out (in part) to recruitment firms. As many organizations have discovered, the tasks involved in acquiring and retaining qualified IS/IT staff are more expensive and time consuming than those for non-technical staff. In addition, the expanded presence of technology in the workplace has increased the costs of training for all employees, including those in job roles that are considered non-technical. In short, the addition of technological resources to the workplace adds cost and complexity to the HR function. The following are common to corporate and IS-related HR activity:

- Hiring
- Training
- Employee performance evaluation and promotion
- Employee time recording/task or project scheduling
- Termination procedures

Each of the areas involved may include sub-areas or procedures that should be reviewed by an auditor for control strengths and weaknesses. For example, the hiring process may not include background checks or require appropriate non-compete and confidentiality agreements from staff. The controls on the way that employee attendance is recorded may be subject to fraudulent entries. Also, termination procedures may not be comprehensive in scope or depth, which could allow former employees to retain access to internal resources via the Internet or a login accomplished from an internal workstation. Management should not consider its HR functions to be low priority targets. In fact, the resources that HR usually controls may be of great value to malicious parties; therefore, these resources should be subject to very strong controls.

Job Rotation/Cross Training and Forced Vacations
Both of these activities provide benefits to employees. Job rotation enables employees to gain experience in different duties or job roles within the same department or perhaps even in different departments. In this way, the company provides on the job training and increases the breadth of skills in each member of its IT workforce. Forced vacations may help decrease the odds that employees will become too stressed or "burned out" by the rigors and/or routine of the role they normally work in. Employees that experience less stress are more likely to be regular in attendance, perform at high levels of efficiency and remain with the company longer.

The organization also derives security-related benefits from these practices. During the time that an employee is away from the regular job role or work area, another employee or security person can fill in. Any abnormalities in processing or fulfillment of established procedures are more likely to be discovered during this time than they would while the regular employee is at work. This type of control can be effective as a preventative if employees are aware of its purpose and it can be a detective control whether they are aware of its purpose or not.

Provisioning
The provisioning or sourcing process for IS/IT functions is becoming a critical area for many organizations. Provisioning and sourcing is not limited to the acquisition of telecommunications links. In recent years, the acquisition or contracting out of entire processes, such as payroll services, customer service/call centers, programming teams, etc have all been subject to review by many organizations. The growth of the Internet and the abundance of alternatives for telecommunications links have given many organizations the ability to decrease in-house staff by outsourcing functions that can be easily automated. The following is a brief set of motives or justifications for the outsourcing of processes:
- The vast majority of accounting and payroll functions are now computerized
- Most IS/IT work (by definition) is related to the use of computer systems
- Many manufacturing processes can be performed by less expensive labor pools outside of the U.S. or in developing nations
- Labor Unions are virtually non-existent in "third world" or developing nations
- Government regulations regarding health, safety, unemployment, retirement and other types of benefits and insurance are less strict or non-existent in developing nations
- Secure connections between different geographic areas may be:
    - Purchased (i.e. dedicated lines or trunks)
    - Configured (via one or more types of VPN or other secure transmission technology)

The combination of one or more of the above may provide compelling reasons for many organizations to pursue stable outsourcing relationships for some of their in-house processes. The availability of the Internet and fast shipping methods has forced many organizations to compete based on price. This means that finding ways to cut costs is just as important, if not more so, than offering a quality product.

The idea that a product can be envisioned and designed by a management team in the U.S., coded and/or manufactured by groups in two or more countries and then sold in the EU (European Union) and the U.S. is not new. There are currently many websites that offer advice on managing this type of development team. There are several names that have been ascribed to this kind of organizational structure, including: Virtual or Geographically Dispersed Teams, Organizations or Enterprises.[5,6,7]

There are several varieties of outsourcing arrangements. The classifications depend on the location of the home or main office of the firm and the percentage of the original process that is performed by staff at the main office or in the same nation as the main office. The following are some of the more common varieties of outsourcing relationships:

- Hybrid: The main office or primary firm continues to perform some of the work involved in the process
- Outsourced: The main office or primary firm contracts the entire process out to another provider
- Onshore (or Offsite): The outside provider of services is located in the same nation as the primary firm
- Offshore: The outside provider is located in a different country than the primary firm

Any outsourcing agreement requires special and intensive consideration and research. This is especially true when the party that will be providing the service is in a different country and is therefore subject to a different set of laws and regulations. If the service provided include verbal or other kinds of contact with customers of the primary firm, language, culture and other concerns also become important.

The contract is perhaps the most critical part of any outsourcing arrangement, regardless of its particular variety. Only in the contact can the primary firm specify its requirements for security, expected service levels, material and product quality, product costs and penalties, bail-out or cancellation clauses, options for resolution of legal disputes, etc. All of the research, risk analysis and number crunching engaged in by a parent firm will be wasted if the chosen provider cannot meet deadlines, provides poor customer care or delivers flawed or inferior products to the marketplace. The cost of monitoring service levels, customer satisfaction and the performance of the provider must also be included into the calculations.

Another area that should be covered by contract is the audit of the service provider's facilities. The type, frequency and scope of audits must be agreed upon in advance. Depending on the nature of the work being outsourced, any or all of the audit and monitoring techniques specified in Chapters 3 and 4 regarding the SDLC (Systems Development Lifecycle) and the IS infrastructure have to be applied to the provider's environment. This can be extremely difficult when the regulatory climate in the provider's country does not support the same types of legal redress that might be available in the nation where the primary firm is headquartered.

Language and cultural differences can also create problems for organizations that are looking at outsourcing alternatives. If call centers or other customer contact is a part of the outsourced process, the provider has to ensure that its staff can:

- Speak and/or read and write the language(s) of the majority of the primary firm's customers
- Speak read and write the languages in question with enough fluency to avoid errors in understanding
- Speak the language **without** an accent strong enough to offend or annoy the customers of the primary firm

The issue of language differences is very important to firms that want to outsource customer service functions. Since many of the firms that want to outsource are based in the U.S., this means that English must be spoken fluently by the staff of the outsourcing firm. The concern of the U.S. companies is that significant cost savings is usually not achieved when the outsourcing firm is located in Europe or other countries where English might be widely spoken. The type of savings desired may normally be found in nations considered to be "third world" or "developing" nations. When political stability and educational requirements are factored in, Asian nations such as India have proven to be the most popular sites for outsourcing arrangements.

Auditors should be expected to review any outsourcing contracts with due professional care. However, contracts involving parties in other countries can be extremely difficult to manage. Security of customer PII and the primary firm's intellectual property are paramount concerns. The auditor should ensure that the primary firm is aware of the risks related to lawsuits that might arise as the result of the disclosure of sensitive information from an offshore site. It is unlikely that a service provider located in a favorable developing nation will absorb the judgments of any lawsuits against the parent firm. Therefore, the risk associated with outsourcing arrangements of any kind must be considered carefully and mitigated appropriately.

Audit/Security Concerns of Outsourcing

Contract protection: Does the contract adequately protect the company?
- **Audit Rights:** right to audit vendor operations
- **Continuity of operations:** Continued service in the event of a disaster
- **Integrity, confidentiality and availability** of company owned data
- **Personnel (Organization):** The remaining employees of the organization may be disgruntled over the outsourcing arrangement. Morale and loyalty to the organization may suffer.
- **Personnel (Vendor):** The employees of the outsourcing vendor may display little if any loyalty to the organization's customers or, in the case of many offshore arrangements, be unable to communicate clearly to customers
- **Access control/security administration:** vendor controlled
- **Violation reporting and follow-up:** vendor controlled
- **Change control and testing:** vendor controlled
- **Network controls:** vendor controlled
- **Early contract termination:** Under *exactly* what circumstances may the organization, either with or without penalty, end its business relationship with the vendor?

In recent years, it has become more common for IS auditors to encounter situations in which some percentage of the information technology activities in an enterprise have been outsourced, i.e., performed by an external entity for a fee. In such a situation, how does the IS auditor carry out the audit? The objective of carrying out an audit of an outsourced function or process would be to determine whether:

- The risks associated with outsourcing, such as continued availability of services, acceptable levels of services and security of information, are adequately and effectively mitigated through appropriate controls that are implemented and functioning
- The objectives of outsourcing are being achieved
- The IT strategy has been suitably modified to make best use of outsourcing

These objectives are critical to the organization and it is important for the organization to have a fair assessment of these areas for the success of the outsourcing arrangement. An IS audit of outsourcing involves all elements of IS audit, including: application security, network security, physical and environmental security, system administration and business continuity planning. An IS auditor who is carrying out an audit of an outsourcing arrangement must plan to make important conclusions in each of these areas. A few typical areas of the audit are detailed below. The IS auditor can develop an audit program around these points for use during an audit of outsourcing whether it is onshore or offshore.

- **Contract:** Most outsourcing arrangements are put in place after a detailed process of evaluations, due diligence and negotiations, with exchange of communications between the company and the service provider over a period of time. In addition to this, it is important for all parties to have a legally enforceable contract document that details the agreed expectations on all the various facets of the arrangement. For the IS auditor, a good starting point should be the outsourcing contract. The IS auditor should make a thorough scrutiny of the contract, as would be done for any major commercial contract, and evaluate all risks as done in any contract audit.
- **Statement of work:** The next important information from the contract should be the statement of work that lists the work to be done by the service provider. The work may fall into one or more of the categories described above. The auditor should ascertain from the activities at the company's IT department what activities have been outsourced and what are being done in-house. The auditor should examine whether the work projects actually performed by the service provider and those mentioned in the contract are the same. Also in this area, the auditor should ensure that the statement of work agrees with the operational areas that are using the outsourced facilities and that it meets their control expectations.
- **Project monitoring and governance:** The IS auditor should check if monitoring and governance processes as described in the contract document have actually been set up and are functioning as intended. The IS auditor should verify the performance measurement reports for a number of sample months, verify the methodology and calculations for compliance with service level agreements and ensure the calculation of incentives and penalties. The IS auditor should verify samples of the bills and their payments from a performance measurement perspective. A review of the performance at various levels is important and can be completed by scrutinizing periodic reports and minutes of the review meetings and noting the frequency and participant lists.

- **The auditor should verify:** that the security policy and processes of the service provider are in sync with those of the company. This is generally done prior to the engagement by exchange of policies and due diligence, identification of gaps and implementation of the required measures to ensure security at both ends is uniformly strong.
- **High-level monitoring:** The service provider's financial status and standing in business should be assessed formally using a defined procedure at periodic intervals, and results documented and communicated. This should also cover important developments in the service provider's country, area of operations, quarterly results, press briefings and analyst reports. The auditor should check whether this activity is being done by the company through a duly designated person/department with due care as well as due diligence.
- **Connectivity and network security:** Communications between the company and the service provider are important to the success of the outsourcing arrangement. In certain limited engagements, the service provider merely delivers completed work to the company. However, in the case of larger engagements such as application support or infrastructure management from offshore locations, dedicated connectivity is a primary requirement. In all cases, dedicated communication links should be established between the company and the service provider through leased lines, international private leased circuits (IPLCs) or a virtual private network (VPN) over the Internet or private VPN through other agencies. In such cases, the service provider's offshore location becomes an extended part of the company's internal network.
- **Data security:** Varying degrees of access to applications and systems have to be provided to the personnel of the service provider to enable them to carry out the work. Proper procedures should be defined that specify how such access is granted and maintained. Security is concerned with maintaining confidentiality, integrity and availability of information. In an outsourcing scenario, events and environment at both the company and the service provider can impact any of these.
- **The auditor should check for mechanisms:** that have been established for ongoing monitoring of security and the related processes at both ends. The auditor should also evaluate the adequacy of the business continuity plans and the results of the tests and drills. In some cases, depending on the nature of work outsourced, the personnel from the service provider may even be required to have super-user access to some systems. In all such cases, suitable monitoring processes may be set up, including writing of logs on remote systems depending on the risk assessment associated with the system. The auditor should evaluate the existence and efficacy of such processes.
- **Compliance with regulatory requirements:** Privacy laws that have been enacted by many countries and states impact data processing in many ways. Some of these laws could also impact export of data to other countries for processing. The IS auditor should examine the applicability of such laws to the outsourcing arrangement and verify whether the safeguards have been implemented and are complied with. The auditor should also evaluate the confidentiality and nondisclosure agreements.
- **Benefit measurement:** Outsourcing is used for specific reasons and with expectation of benefits. The realization of those gains is an important part of the outsourcing arrangement. The IS auditor should verify whether suitable procedures and ownership for these measurements have been instituted by the company. The IS auditor should also check and evaluate the measurement methodology to ensure that it is approved by management and includes quantitative and qualitative factors and is measured in monetary and non-monetary terms.
- **Customer satisfaction:** In an outsourcing arrangement there is a change in the entity that provides the IT services to the end users and customers. A focused outsourcing service provider with expert skills could deliver better service, but there could also be gaps due to culture and other business or domain-related factors. Even in a situation where the benefits of outsourcing are being realized, it is a good idea to ascertain the level of customer satisfaction from the end users through well-designed feedback processes and administered surveys, as a means toward continuous improvement in the outsourced services. The auditor should check for the existence and results of these exercises and evaluate the methodology and action taken on the feedback received.
- **Impact on IT strategy:** IT outsourcing is often strategic and done on a fairly large scale. Outsourcing needs to be incorporated into the business and IT strategy of the company. In the process of outsourcing, the company should not lose sight of the significance that its IT processes have on its overall business goals. Even outsourced IT functions must be implemented and judged according to the principles of business alignment. The IS auditor should perform a check of the overall IT scenario of the company after outsourcing, to ensure that key IT management activities have not been neglected due to lack of clarity on the ownership of these activities due to outsourcing.

Management of Change

Many people are resistant to change. Some perceive change as threatening or a burden of some kind. Others simply prefer the known to the unknown. A significant percentage of personnel may be technically illiterate or even technophobes. Organizational psychology is another subject that is beyond the scope of this text. However, the effect that change has on an organization's employees cannot be overlooked by an auditor.

Most descriptions of the traditional SDLC do not mention the effect that change has on employees. In recent decades, the introduction of new technology into the workplace has often been the warning that layoffs would soon follow. In fact, a significant percentage BPR (Business Process Re-engineering) projects are driven by a pursuit of cost reduction. The addition of the Internet marketplace and the increased ability of consumers to shop by price concerns alone have only increased this trend in BPR. Many employees in today's workplaces either know someone that has been laid off or "downsized" due to technological advances or they have personal experience with that trend.

A problem for many organizations is that the fear of change may actually result in the failure of IT projects. Due to the public's knowledge of this trend, these failures may occur where layoffs are actually planned or not. Unless the employees that have to use the new software or other technologies "buy in" to the project and make it work, the funds spent in research, development and implementation of the new products may be wasted. Even middle or upper level managers that believe a new product will cause them to lose budget money, personnel, power or other perks might become obstacles to the success of a project.

Auditors involved in the SDLC should inform management about the risks related to change. It is possible that training or other communications of the intentions of executive managers may decrease or eliminate the fears of staff members. For example, if layoffs are not intended after the rollout of a new application, management may inform personnel about this through email or other means. Training programs that would have been needed for the new application could reinforce this. The organization could also offer incentives, financial or otherwise, to those employees that show the highest levels of performance improvement with the new application. Since the objective of the auditor is to advise on risks and controls, it is perfectly appropriate for the auditor to inform management about any risk of failure that might be related to issues of fear or distrust within the organization.

Service and Product Quality

In general, a quality is a characteristic or attribute of a given item. When the word "quality" is used in reference to a product or service, it usually refers to a level of excellence or functionality that the product or service possesses. Although many organizations must now adapt to competition based on price, it is understood that price alone cannot be the only concern in product development.

It is possible to get people to buy a product once based on price. However, unsatisfied customers seldom become repeat customers. In addition, unsatisfied customers often tell others about their experience with a product perceived as having poor quality. Finally, poor quality in certain service or product areas such as food or drug manufacturing, automobile and even home appliance manufacturing can cause harm or even death to those that use the product. Lawsuits and bad publicity translate to financial losses and loss of reputation. If perceptions about an organization are that it produces low-quality or even dangerous products, then potential profits from products it markets months or even years later may be adversely affected.

Managing quality involves the monitoring, control and improvement of any and all processes related to the production or provision of a product or service. There are several popular standards and methodologies that focus on quality management and improvement including:
- The Shewhart Cycle: Plan – Do – Check – Act (PDCA)
- ISO 9001:2000; ISO 9004:2000; ISO 9126:2001-2004; ISO 25000:2005
- NIST/Baldridge Criteria for Performance Excellence
- EFQM (European Foundation for Quality Management) Excellence Model
- The TQM (Total Quality Management) Strategy
- Six Sigma
- CMMI (Capability Maturity Model Integration)

Although this may be disputed by some, the terms Quality Control (QC) and Quality Assurance (QA) are nearly synonymous in common usage. The clearest distinction between the terms might be that QC focuses on the design and development areas of a project or process (what is built into a product), while QA-related processes may be utilized across the entire product life cycle (what is built in **and** how the construction occurs at each stage of the process). Most of the popular quality management schemes share certain characteristics:

- They are iterative in nature; improvement is a continuous, never-ending process
- Most, if not all of the newer models, include variations of or expansions upon the PDCA scheme
- Most emphasize the importance of setting goals and planning as first steps even if their acronyms use terms such as Define, Conceptualize or Identify.
- In practice, most require extensive organizational changes and require many months or years for a full implementation

Quality models usually cover the following practices associated with systems development:

Management

- Internal Quality Audits (including follow-up)
- Corrective Action
- Technical
- Contract review
- Standards of acceptability for product features and requirements
- Design control (including product verification)
- Design changes (including review and approval)
- Process control (work instructions and standards)
- Purchase – supplier product (verification, storage and maintenance)
- Inspection and testing (receiving, in-process and final)
- Control of non-conforming product (including review and rework)
- Inspection, measuring and test equipment
- Product handling, storage, packaging and delivery
- Servicing

Support

- Document control
- Training (in particular, in areas of need)
- Product identification and traceability
- Quality records
- Statistical techniques (verification of process capability and product effectiveness)

Organizational Structure

Organization and management controls include those controls providing protection for the actual or tangible physical environment, as well as staffing and operation of the Information Processing Facility (IPF). Organization and management controls provide effective and efficient operation staffed with qualified and dependable personnel. Proper levels of responsibilities should be clearly defined and provide for adequate separation of duties. Organizational and management controls surrounding the IPF encompass the following:[8]

- Sound personnel policies and management practices
- Separation of duties between the information processing environment and other organizational environments or functions
- Separation of duties within the information processing environment
- Methods to assess effective and efficient operations

Management Structures

Two distinct types of management should be noted: line management and project management.[9] Line management in an organization is concerned with routine day to day decisions external to projects. A project is normally a one-time effort, with a specific objective or deliverable with specific start and end dates and is divisible into explicit phases (see Systems Development Life Cycle - "SDLC"). Project managers and staff for projects are drawn from within the resources controlled by the line management. Some organizations also set up project steering committees to facilitate the decision making process.

Line Management

Management structure will vary among organizations due to size, platforms and maturity. Modern IT environments may have positions such as Customer Service Manager. Traditionally the data processing department consists of an IS Director with the following managers reporting to him/her:

- **Systems Development Manager** – responsible for programmers and analysts who implement new systems and maintain existing systems
- **End-User Support Manager** – responsible for liaison between the IS department and the end-users
- **Data Management** – responsible for the data architecture in larger IT environments and tasked with managing data as a corporate asset
- **Database Administrator** – responsible for maintenance and integrity of the organization's database systems
- **Technical Support Manager** – responsible for system programmers who maintain the system software
- **Security Administrator** – responsible for providing adequate physical and logical security for IS programs, data and equipment
- **Operations Manager** – responsible for computer operations personnel, including computer operators, librarians, schedulers and data control personnel. These individuals keep the computer operational.
- **Quality Assurance Manager** – responsible for negotiating and facilitating quality activities in all areas of information technology, although most frequently quality initiatives are focused on systems development activities.

Project Management

IS projects may be initiated from within any part of the organization, including the IS department. In some organizations, project requests are submitted to and prioritized by, the IS Steering Committee. In a pure project model, the project manager should be given complete operational control of the project and be allocated the appropriate resources for the successful completion of the project. IS Auditors may be included in the project team so they can recommend controls throughout the project life. They may also provide an independent, objective review for purposes of ensuring that the level of involvement (commitment) of the responsible parties is appropriate.

Note that the principles and techniques of Project Management can be applied to analysis of management functions. An auditor assigned to review management processes should be aware of project management techniques. Assessments and recommendations made concerning the management function that are acquired by use of accepted project principles are more likely to be accepted and implemented.

Job Description and Organizational Structure Charts

Job descriptions and organizational structure charts are important items for all employees to have as they provide a clear definition of their job, responsibilities and authority. It is also important for an IS Auditor to obtain this information so that the relationship between various job functions, responsibilities and authorities can be assessed for adequate segregation of duties. Segregation of duties is an important means by which fraudulent and or malicious acts can be discouraged and prevented. Time should be spent in an auditee's area observing and ensuring that the job description and structures are adequate in this way. Eexamples of generic organizational charts follow:

Generic IS Organizational Charts

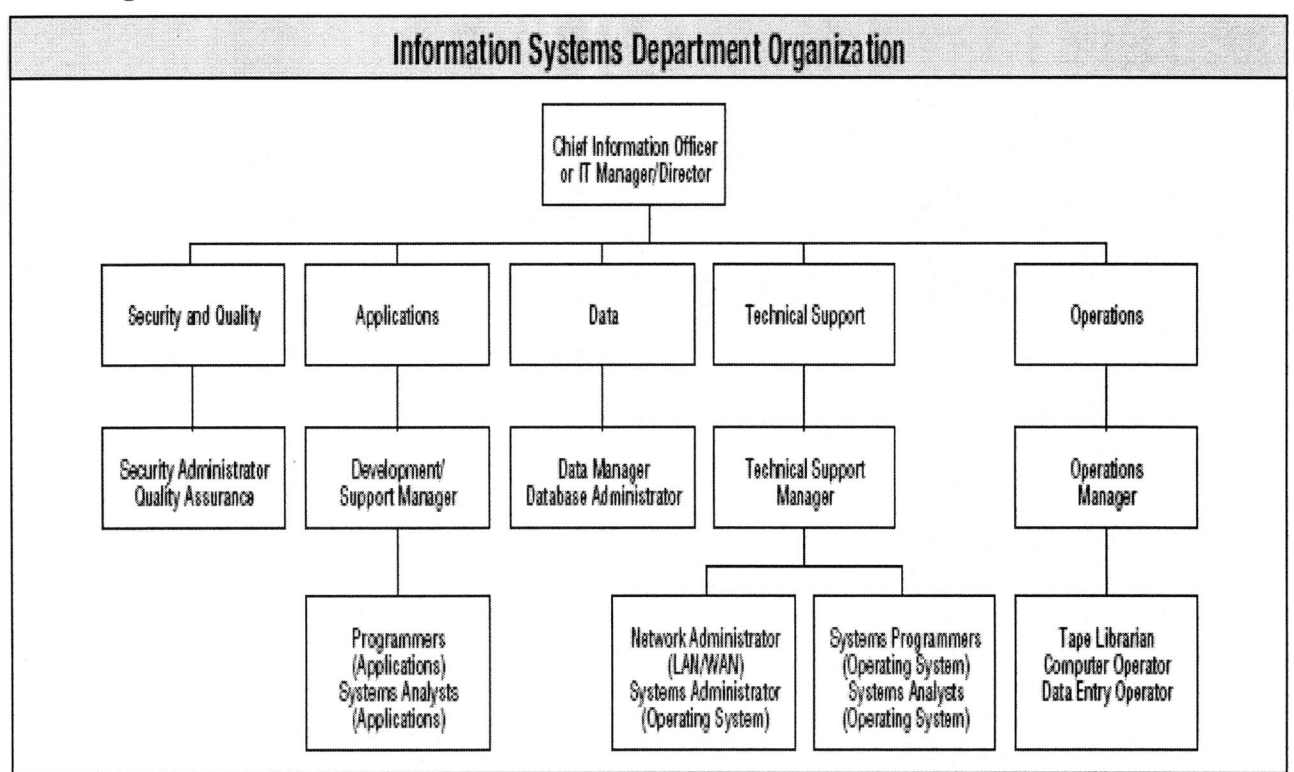

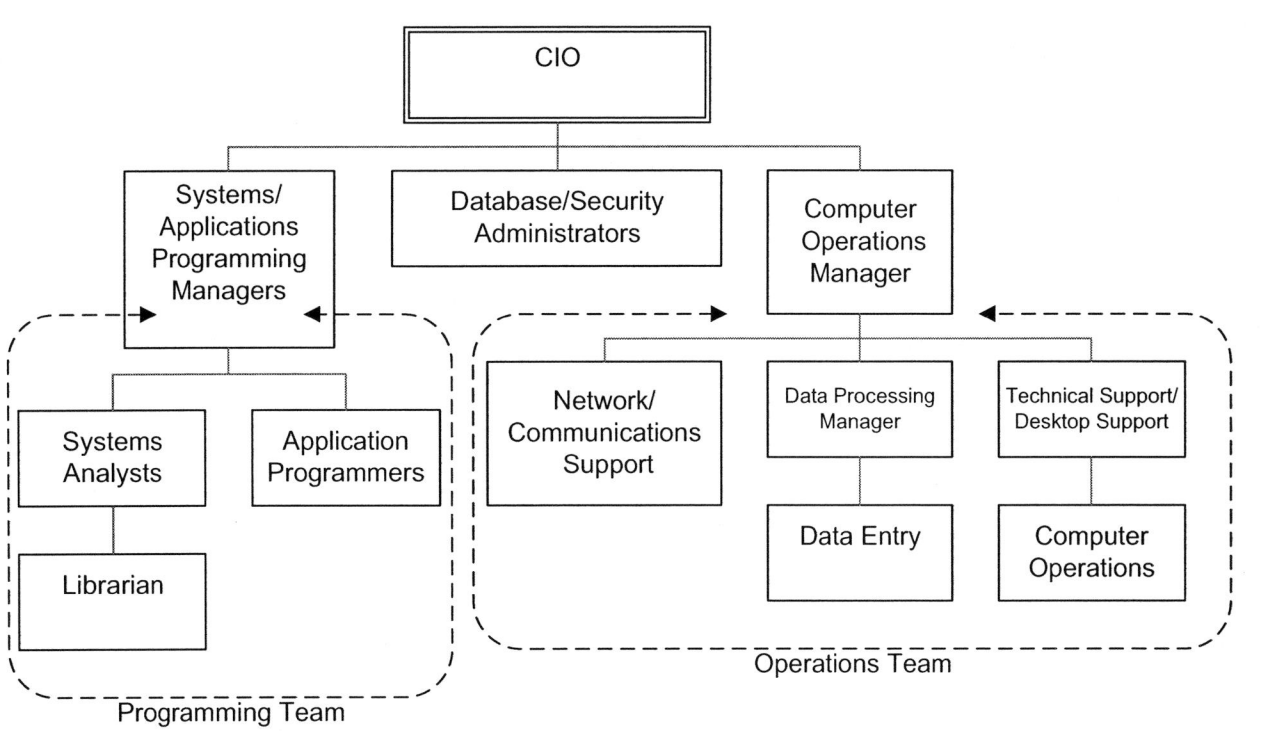

Job descriptions should be suitable for use in performance evaluations. In addition, there should be a published code of conduct for the organization, which specifies all employees' responsibilities to the company particularly in regard to conflicts of interest and non-disclosure/confidentiality. Although the exact job titles listed below will not be found in every organization, the responsibilities listed along with each job title are very common and are normally assigned to one or more IT staff members.

ROLES	DESCRIPTION	JOB FUNCTION
Data Entry	In the early days of information systems, data were gathered from various departments and then entered via batches. Today, in online environments, data entry is generally performed by personnel in the user departments or is initiated by the customer.	The separation of duties will be different within the two environments and the responsibilities to ensure the maintenance of data integrity are listed below.
Online Data Entry	If data entry is online and controlled in the originating department, the data must be protected and properly edited by the system. It would then be the responsibility of that particular department manager to ensure that data are authorized, accurate and complete when entered into the system.	An online system provides various screen edits to perform basic input verification of the data entered, such as range checks, alpha-numeric checks, limit checks, valid predefined value checks from an internal table. The department manager or supervisor would be required to provide for an adequate separation of duties by being responsible for overrides and resubmission of errors or rejected entries. All reentered transactions should go through the same edits as first-time data. Data entry personnel should be prohibited from accessing and updating software and sensitive data files.
Batch Data Entry	The batch data control department should be staffed with adequate, authorized personnel to process work in a timely manner. A supervisor should be assigned to ensure that the work is properly prepared and submitted for processing. This individual should also ensure that all exceptions and rejected input are brought to the attention of the originating department and resubmitted in a timely fashion	Data entry within the typical information systems department is often the responsibility of the data control department. This area performs the following tasks: • Receives source documents from various departments and ensures proper safekeeping of such until processing is complete and source documents and output are returned • Prepares batches of source documents with accurate control totals • Schedules and sets up the jobs to process input • Verifies, logs and distributes output to the appropriate department with special care to confidential information
Librarian	The Librarian should be a full-time individual who usually reports to the data control manager. In some smaller organizations, however, a member of the data control section may perform this function.	The librarian is required to record, issue, receive and safeguard all program and data files that are maintained on computer tapes and/or disks in an IPF. Most organizations use an automated tape management system to assist in maintaining inventory and movement of the tape reels and cartridges. Library control software is used to automate program change control by controlling program versions.
Systems Analysis	Systems Analysts are specialists who design systems based on the needs of the user. They are usually involved during the initial phase of the Systems Development Life Cycle (SDLC).	The functions of a Systems Analyst are similar to those of a project leader. This individual is responsible for interpreting the needs of the user and determining the programs and the programmers necessary to create the particular application.

ROLES	DESCRIPTION	JOB FUNCTION
Control Group	The input/output control group should be in a separate area where only authorized personnel are permitted. The supervisor of the Control Group usually reports to the IPF Operations Manager.	The Control Group is often responsible for the collection, conversion and control of input and the balancing and distribution of output to the user community.
Operations	Operations is synonymous with the information processing facility. It includes all the staff required to run the computer efficiently and effectively. The computer room area should be secured and only authorized personnel should have access. No one except operations personnel should have access to the IPF.	The responsibility for the IPF is the operations manager(s), who reports directly to the Director of the IPF. Within computer operations, management controls can be sub-divided into three categories:
Operations Physical Security	Physical security defines the various measures or controls that protect an organization from a loss of computer processing capabilities caused by theft, fire, flood, malicious destruction and mechanical and power failures. Physical security measures must be sufficient to deal with any losses that may occur.	the IPF, including the computer, peripherals, magnetic media and the data stored on the media, constitutes a major investment in both asset value and its impact on the organization's ability to function effectively
Operations Data Security	Data security programs must effectively integrate: ♦ Physical security such as safeguarding hardware used during the processing of data and the media on which the data are stored ♦ Employee education that encompasses the need for data security and privacy. Employees also must understand that disciplinary action will be taken against anyone who violates corporate guidelines in this area. Logical security such as software or hardware controls built into the system to prevent and detect unauthorized access to data.	Includes the standards and procedures designed to protect data against accidental or intentional unauthorized disclosure, modification or destruction. A critical part of the management control exercised by the IPF is providing an adequate level of data security. Data security covers many aspects of security and must be continually modified and expanded to cover IS technological advances that are taking place.
Applications Programming	The application programming area is made of the Applications Programmers who are responsible for maintaining systems in production.	They should work in a test environment only and should not move test versions into the production environment. Application Programmers should not have access to system program libraries.

ROLES	DESCRIPTION	JOB FUNCTION
Operations Processing Controls	Necessary to ensure that the organization receives timely, complete, accurate and secure processing of data	These controls are particularly pertinent to the work performed by the computer operations groups that include: ♦ Data control is often responsible for all the data necessary to run various systems and for checking to ensure that output information received is complete. Adequate, up-to-date control manuals are essential for each system. Manuals should state the source of the various forms of input, the media involved and the time frame in which such input should be available. ♦ Production control is often responsible for job scheduling, job submission and media management. Job scheduling may be done manually or with an automated scheduling package. Effective scheduling is essential if the computer resources are to be used at optimum efficiency. Computer operations should be responsible for monitoring the execution of various tasks operating in the computer, providing resources such as tapes, disks and special stationery and correcting any problems during execution of those systems.
Security Administration	Security Administration must begin with management's commitment. Management must understand and evaluate security risks. Upper management should develop and enforce a written policy that clearly states the standards and procedures to be followed. The duties of the security administrator should be defined in the policy. This individual should be a full-time employee who reports directly to the Director of the IPF to provide adequate separation of duties. However, if it is a small shop it may not be practical to hire an individual for this position. Common sense should prevail.	The individual performing the function should ensure that the various users are complying with the corporate security policy and that controls are adequate to prevent unauthorized access to the company assets (including data, programs and equipment). The security administrator's functions usually include: ♦ Maintaining access rules to files and resources ♦ Maintaining security and confidentiality over the issuance and proper maintenance of authorized user IDs and passwords ♦ Monitoring security violations and taking corrective action to ensure that adequate security is provided ♦ Periodically reviewing and evaluating the security policy and suggesting any necessary changes to management
Quality Assurance	The QA group also can assist by periodically checking the accuracy and authenticity of the input, processing and output of various applications.	The Quality Assurance (QA) group usually performs testing and verification to ensure that programs, program changes and documentation adhere to standards and naming conventions before the programs are moved into production. In some organizations this group may be a part of data control but under no circumstances should it be a function of the programming staff.
Systems Programming	Systems Programmers are responsible for maintaining the systems software including the operating system.	This function may allow for unrestricted access to the entire system. They should keep logs of their work and only have access to the system libraries of the specific software that they maintain.

ROLES	DESCRIPTION	JOB FUNCTION
Database Administration	The Database Administrator (DBA) usually reports directly to the director of the IPF. This position is responsible for the security and information classification of the shared data stored on large database systems. The DBA is responsible for the actual design, definition and proper maintenance of the corporate databases. Since the DBA should have no application programming or end user responsibilities, he/she should be prohibited from accessing the production data within the databases the DBA administers. A DBA is a person who defines and maintains the data structures in the database system. To be effective, a DBA must understand the organization and user data and data relationship (structure) requirements.	The DBA's role includes: • Specifying physical (computer orientated) data definition • Changing physical data definition to improve performance • Determining database optimization tools • Testing and evaluating programmer and optimization tools • Answering programmer queries and educating programmers in the database structures • Implementing database definition controls, access controls, update controls, concurrence controls, etc. • Monitoring database usage, collecting performance statistics and tuning the database • Defining and initiating backup and recovery procedures The DBA has the tools to establish controls required over the database and the ability to override these controls. The DBA also has the capability of obtaining user passwords and gaining access to data. Controls over Database Administration should include: • Separation of duties • Management approval of DBA activities • Supervisor review of access logs • Detective controls over the use of database tools
Local Area Networks (LANs) Administration	The Local Area Networks (LAN) Administrator can report to the director of the IPF or, if in a decentralized operation, can report to the end-user manager.	This position is responsible for technical and administrative control over the local area network. This includes ensuring transmission links are functioning correctly, backups of the system are occurring and software/hardware purchases are authorized and properly installed. In smaller installations, this person also may be responsible for security administration over the LAN. The LAN Administrator should have no application programming responsibilities, but may have end-user responsibilities.
Help Desk Administration	In today's IS environment more and more companies find it important to have a technical administration help desk function that specializes in operating system enhancement techniques used by systems programming.	The help desk function usually monitors, improves and controls system performance in mainframe and client server hardware and software.

Separation of Duties

A proven method to ensure that transactions are properly authorized and recorded and that the company's assets are protected is called **separation (or segregation) of duties**. When duties within a process are divided and assigned to different personnel, opportunities for successful fraud or other misconduct are less likely to succeed. For example, access to the production servers, the production data library, the production programs, the programming documentation and the operating system and associated utilities can be limited. Potential damage from the actions of any one person is therefore reduced. Organization of the IPF should be structured such that the highest possible separation of duties is achieved. See the Separation of Duties Control Matrix for the job responsibilities that should not be combined.

SEPARATION OF DUTIES CONTROL MATRIX[10]

	Control Group	Systems Analyst	Application Programming	Data Entry	Computer Operator	Database Admin.	Security Admin.	Tape Librarian	Systems Programming	Quality Assurance
Control Group	▓	X	X	X	X	X			X	
Systems Analyst	X	▓			X		X	X	X	X
Application Programming	X		▓	X	X	X	X	X	X	X
Data Entry	X		X	▓	X	X	X		X	
Computer Operator	X	X	X	X	▓	X	X		X	
Database Administrator	X		X	X	X	▓	X		X	
Security Administrator		X	X	X	X	X	▓	X	X	
Tape Librarian		X	X				X	▓	X	
Systems Programming	X	X	X	X	X	X	X	X	▓	X
Quality Assurance		X	X						X	▓

X - Functions should not be combined since no compensating controls can mitigate the separation of duties risk.

Note: The Segregation of Duties Control Matrix shown above is not an industry standard, but a guideline indicating which positions should be separated in a mainframe environment. In a small business client/server environment where the MIS department may only consist of four to five people, strong compensating controls must exist in order to mitigate the risk or loss of production data.

Controls and Techniques to Facilitate Adequate Separation of Duties

The implementation of a separation of duties scheme is a control in itself. However, a layered or overlapping approach offers even more assurance about security to managers and audit personnel. The following controls should be implemented along with a separation of duties program.

- **Use of Authorization Forms:** Authorization forms (either hard copy or electronic), state who should have access to what. Authorization forms must be properly evidenced with management level approval. Generally, all users should be authorized to specific system access via written request of management. In large companies or those with remote sites, signature authorization logs should be maintained and written requests should be compared to the signature log to ensure that management periodically reviews access privileges to ensure that they are current and appropriate to the users' job functions.
- **Use of Password Authorization Tables:** Password authorization tables define who is authorized to update, modify, delete and/or view data. These privileges are provided by the system, transaction or field level. In addition, password authorization tables should be secured against unauthorized access, with additional password protection or data encryption. A control log should record all user activity and appropriate management should review this log. All exception items should be investigated.
- **Supervision:** Supervision provides a higher tier of responsibility for the tasks performed by employees. At this level, specific functions can be performed based on a higher level of authority and responsibility. Some typical examples are approvals for high dollar transactions, review and handling of exceptions and overriding the system defaults.
- **Exception Reporting:** Exception reporting should be handled at the supervisory level and require evidence, such as initials on a report, noting that the exception has been properly handled. Management also should ensure that exceptions are being resolved in a timely manner.
- **Controls over Access to Data:** Controls over access to data are provided by a combination of adequate physical, system and application security in both the user area and the IPF. The physical environment must be secured to prevent unauthorized personnel from access to the various tangible devices connected to the central processing unit and thereby permitting access to data. System and application securities are additional layers of security that may prevent unauthorized individuals from gaining access to corporate data. Access to data from external connections is a growing concern.
- **Compensating Controls** Compensating controls are internal controls that are intended to reduce the risk of an existing or potential control weakness.
    - **Audit Trails:** Audit trails provide the IS Auditor with a map to retrace the flow of a transaction. They enable the IS Auditor to recreate the actual transaction flow from the point of origination to its existence on an updated file. Good audit trails may be acceptable compensating controls in the absence of adequate separation of duties resulting from having a limited staff. The IS Auditor should be able to determine who initiated the transaction, the time of day and date of entry, the type of entry, what fields of information it contained and what files it updated.
    - **Transaction Logs:** A transaction log may be manual or automated. An example of a manual log is a record of transactions (grouped or batched) before they are submitted for processing. An automated transaction log or journal provides a record of all transactions processed in batch production and is maintained by the computer system.
    - **Batch Control Total Reconciliations:** Batch control totals represent a count of the number of transactions and total dollar amounts (where applicable) of source documents that are maintained by the computer and/or manually for reconciliation purposes. Control total reconciliations are often performed by the data control group and are independent of the user area.
    - **Independent Review:** An independent review is necessary to ensure that policies and procedures have been properly understood and executed. The reviewer should maintain independence at all times and not be influenced or instructed by anyone in the group being reviewed. Evidence of work performed should be adequate and provide the reviewer with a level of confidence that the work was performed in compliance with established policies and procedures.

Auditing of IT Governance

In spite of their importance, both Corporate Governance and IT Governance are still classified as business processes. They can and should be subjected to analysis and modified periodically to improve their performance and overall quality. Improvement in the quality of management should be pursued as vigorously as the organization pursues ways to cut costs.

An auditor attempting to review the IT Governance function should begin by trying to understand the nature and process of the business as a whole. The following are all valid techniques in this regard:
- Study of the business and regulatory climate
- Review of the company's current organizational and functional charts and current job descriptions and responsibilities
- Analysis of any outsourcing arrangements related to IT functions (contracts, audit results, SLAs, recorded performance metrics, etc.)
- Reports generated by steering or other internal committees that bear on the IT function
- Long-term goals and objectives of the organization
- Training manuals, Employees handbooks and other procedural documents
- Review of industry best practices relevant to the work performed by the organization
- Change, Problem and Incident Management procedures along with help desk statistics
- Analysis of the organization's security policy and/or results of the latest IS and security audits

Although the task of reviewing all of the documentation above may be enormous, the auditor may narrow the search to approximately a dozen metrics that can indicate problems with the IT Governance function or issues that simply require further study. The metrics in question include, but are not limited to the following:
- Low staff morale/motivation
- Slow/Poor handling of incidents and exceptions
- Poor customer satisfaction ratings
- Few or no ongoing training programs
- High percentage of projects considered as "failures" internally, in spite of statements issued to the media
- High or increasing rates of software/hardware downtime or errors
- High turnover rates
- Slow help desk response times
- Inadequate or no monitoring of key performance or security metrics
- Dependence on a small group of personnel who are needed to ensure that any work gets done
- High CPU, bandwidth utilization rates/slow network response times

CHAPTER 2 PRACTICE QUESTIONS

1) An internal audit department that organizationally reports exclusively to the chief financial officer (CFO) rather than to an audit committee, is MOST likely to:
    A. have its audit independence questioned.
    B. report more business-oriented and relevant findings.
    C. enhance the implementation of the auditor's recommendations.
    D. result in more effective action being taken on the recommendations.

2) A strength of an implemented quality system based on ISO 9001 is that it:
    A. guarantees quality solutions to business problems.
    B. enhances improvements in software life cycle activities
    C. provides clear answers to questions concerning cost-effectiveness.
    D. does not depend on the maturity of the implemented quality system.

3) The use of a GANTT chart can:
    A. aid in scheduling project tasks.
    B. determine project checkpoints.
    C. ensure documentation standards.
    D. direct the post-implementation review.

4) An IS auditor reviewing the key roles and responsibilities of the database administrator (DBA) is LEAST likely to expect the job description of the DBA to include:
    A. defining the conceptual schema.
    B. defining security and integrity checks.
    C. liaising with users in developing data model.
    D. mapping data model with the internal schema.

5) A data administrator is responsible for:
    A. maintaining database system software.
    B. defining data elements, data names and their relationship.
    C. developing physical database structures.
    D. developing data dictionary system software.

6) Which of the following audit techniques is not included in an evaluation of a firm's IS strategy?
    A. Review of prior year audit reports
    B. Review both the short and long-term IS plans
    C. Interview appropriate personnel from corporate management
    D. Assess the procedures for IS security

7) In the course of performing a risk analysis, an IS auditor has identified threats and potential impacts. Next, an IS auditor should:
    A. identify and assess the risk assessment process used by management.
    B. disclose the threats and impacts to management.
    C. identify and evaluate the existing controls.
    D. identify information assets and the underlying systems.

CHAPTER 2 PRACTICE QUESTIONS (CONT.)

8) A probable advantage to an organization that has outsourced its data processing services is that:
   A. needed IS expertise can be obtained from the outside.
   B. greater user involvement is required to communicate user needs.
   C. greater control can be exercised over processing.
   D. processing priorities can be established and enforced internally.

9) In order to maintain independence, the data base administrator should report to:
   A. a user department manager.
   B. the data processing manager.
   C. the operations manager.
   D. the systems and programming manager.

10) While reviewing helpdesk performance, the IS auditor observed that in a few cases, problems were getting solved only after long delays. The reasons attributed were lack of expertise of the junior computer service engineers, lack of authority to buy costly spares or gaps in inter-departmental coordination. The BEST recommendation to correct the situation would be to:
    A. Define qualifications and experience criteria for help desk staff.
    B. Setup minimum levels of service and benchmark time limits for solving the problems.
    C. Implement suitable problem escalation procedures.
    D. Increase the inventory of critical spares that are required for carrying out repairs.

CHAPTER 2 ANSWERS TO PRACTICE QUESTIONS

1) Answer: A

   According to a recent ISACA benchmarking survey most internal audit departments report directly to an audit committee. However, many organizations also choose to have the internal audit department either jointly or solely report to the chief financial officer (CFO). In this same survey, the IS audit function almost exclusively reports directly to the director of internal audit. The IS auditor who reports to the head of an operational department would have the appearance of a compromised independence. Generally, an IS auditor should report one level above the reporting level of the auditee. Reporting to the CFO may not have an impact on the content of audit findings, which should normally be business-oriented and relevant as an auditor is expected to understand the business being audited. Taking effective action on an audit's recommendations should be the responsibility of senior management and will not be enhanced by the fact that the audit department reports to the CFO. Follow-up of the implementation of audit recommendations is conducted by the auditor and/or by the administration department and would not be enhanced by reporting to the CFO.

2) Answer: B

   A strength of an implemented quality system based on ISO 9001 is that it enhances improvements in software life cycle activities, quality assurance and quality control. Weaknesses of the system include that it can fail to provide clear answers to questions concerning productivity, reliability or cost-effectiveness of the system. A quality system is not a guarantee of quality solutions to business problems since poorly defined user requirements will adversely affect the design of the software. Depending on the maturity of the implemented quality system stages can vary from not implemented to fully implemented procedures.

3) Answer: A

   A GANTT chart is used in project control. It may aid in the identification of needed checkpoints but its primary use is in scheduling. It will not ensure the completion of documentation nor will it provide direction for the post-implementation review.

4) Answer: D

   A DBA only in rare instances should be mapping data elements from the data model to the internal schema (physical data storage definitions). To do so would eliminate data independence for application systems. Mapping of the data model occurs with the conceptual schema since the conceptual schema represents the enterprise wide view of data within an organization and is the basis for deriving an end-user department data model.

5) Answer: B

   A data administrator is responsible for defining data elements, data names and their relationship. Choices A, C and D are functions of a database administrator (DBA)

6) Answer: D

   This would be considered a detailed audit procedure in evaluating either general controls or application controls. All other answers should be included in the evaluation of a firm's IS strategy.

7) Answer: C

   It is important for an IS auditor to identify and evaluate the existing controls and security once the potential threats and possible impacts are identified. Upon completion of an audit an IS auditor should describe and discuss with management the threats and potential impacts on the assets.

CHAPTER 2 ANSWERS TO PRACTICE QUESTIONS (CONT.)

8) Answer: A

Outsourcing is a contractual arrangement whereby the organization relinquishes control over part or all of the information processing to an external party. This is frequently done to acquire additional resources or expertise that is not obtainable from inside the organization.

9) Answer: B

Having the data base administrator report directly to the data processing manager provides more independence than the other individuals listed. Answer "C" is NOT the best answer because the operations manager would not be independent. Answer "a" is NOT the best answer because the systems and programming manager would not be independent. Answer "d" is NOT the best answer because a user department manager would not be independent.

10) Answer: C

Answer c is correct. Answer a, and b address only part of the problem but does not encompass the solution for all problems. A proper escalation process would set priority as far as which technician would work of which PC problem as well as setting priority to PC problems. Answer d would only increase PC inventory and spare parts which is not a suitable alternative.

Chapter 3 Systems and Infrastructure Lifecycle Management

INFORMATION SYSTEMS MANAGEMENT PROCESS
The CISA candidate must understand the ten tasks within this chapter and be able to identify, test and assess how each contributes to the effective, efficient and economic use of resources. In addition, the Candidate should be able to evaluate the implementation and delivery of services to support the IS organization as defined in chapter 2 with an emphasis on meeting business objectives.

This chapter represents approximately 16 percent of the CISA examination (approximately 32 questions).

There are ten tasks within this area that the CISA candidate must understand and be able to perform:
- Evaluate the business case for the proposed system development/acquisition to ensure that it meets the organization's business goals.
- Evaluate the project management framework and project governance practices to ensure that business objectives are achieved in a cost-effective manner while managing risks to the organization.
- Perform reviews to ensure that a project is progressing in accordance with project plans, is adequately supported by documentation and status reporting is accurate.
- Evaluate proposed control mechanisms for systems and/or infrastructure during specification, development/acquisition, and testing to ensure that they will provide safeguards and comply with the organization's policies and other requirements.
- Evaluate the processes by which systems and/or infrastructure are developed or acquired and tested to ensure that the deliverables meet the organization's objectives.
- Evaluate the readiness of the system and/or infrastructure for implementation and migration into production.
- Perform post-implementation review of systems and/or infrastructure to ensure that they meet the organization's objectives and are subject to effective internal control.
- Perform periodic reviews of systems and/or infrastructure to ensure that they continue to meet the organization's objectives and are subject to effective internal control.
- Evaluate the process by which systems and/or infrastructure are maintained to ensure the continued support of the organization's objectives and are subject to effective internal control.
- Evaluate the process by which systems and/or infrastructure are disposed of to ensure that they comply with the organization's policies and procedures.

Knowledge Statements
The following 18 statements describe specific topics a CISA candidate should be familiar with and use as guidance in the fulfillment of the tasks outlined above:
- Knowledge of benefits management practices, (e.g., feasibility studies, business cases)
- Knowledge of project governance mechanisms (e.g., steering committee, project oversight board)
- Knowledge of project management practices, tools, and control frameworks
- Knowledge of risk management practices applied to projects
- Knowledge of project success criteria and risks
- Knowledge of configuration, change and release management in relation to development and maintenance of systems and/or infrastructure
- Knowledge of control objectives and techniques that ensure the completeness, accuracy, validity, and authorization of transactions and data within IT systems applications
- Knowledge of enterprise architecture related to data, applications, and technology (e.g., distributed applications, web-based applications, web services, n-tier applications)
- Knowledge of requirements analysis and management practices (e.g., requirements verification, traceability, gap analysis)
- Knowledge of acquisition and contract management processes (e.g., evaluation of vendors, preparation of contracts, vendor management, escrow)
- Knowledge of system development methodologies and tools and an understanding of their strengths and weaknesses (e.g., agile development practices, prototyping, rapid application development [RAD], object-oriented design techniques)
- Knowledge of quality assurance methods

- Knowledge of the management of testing processes (e.g., test strategies, test plans, test environments, entry and exit criteria)
- Knowledge of data conversion tools, techniques, and procedures
- Knowledge of system and/or infrastructure disposal procedures
- Knowledge of software and hardware certification and accreditation practices
- Knowledge of post-implementation review objectives and methods (e.g., project closure, benefits realization, performance measurement)
- Knowledge of system migration and infrastructure deployment practices

Business Realization

Information Systems programs are logical groupings of projects and/or other related tasks. These activities may be managed as a group because their objectives, resource requirements, financial allocations and intended outcomes are considered to be closely related. In general, projects are less complex, of shorter duration and less costly than programs. Multiple projects may be managed under the umbrella of a single program. Projects always have a limit to their duration. Programs may run indefinitely if the activities conducted within them are considered vital to the ongoing success of an organization. For example, an organization may grow to the point where it is no longer possible to manage it properly without ongoing configuration, problem and change management programs. By their nature, programs are usually designed to handle processes that are of high strategic value to the organization.

Program management is similar to project management in many ways. The same types of questions, calculations and problem solving techniques are present in both areas. When a program is designed to manage the activities of multiple projects simultaneously, the term **portfolio management** is sometimes used to describe the process. In other organizations, the **project portfolio** describes the sum of all active projects whether they are managed within a program or not. Examples of technology-related programs that require project management techniques might include: the implementation of a large-scale ERP system, IT infrastructure maintenance and software development and acquisition.

Program and project management techniques are not limited in scope to information systems. These techniques may also be applied successfully to the operations or business side of the organization. Non-IT processes that may be managed in this way could include: BPR (Business Process Reengineering), employee training and development and even M&A (Mergers and Acquisitions). Successful program management includes but is not limited to management of:
- Program scope, program financials (costs, resources, cash-flow, etc.), program schedules, and program objectives and deliverables
- Program context and environment
- Program communication and culture
- Program organization

To make autonomous projects possible, yet provide for any synergies between projects, a specific program organization is required. Typical roles in a program management environment are:
- Program owner
- Program manager
- Program team
- Program office

The role of a program owner is not the same as that of a project owner. Program team meetings may not include all of the staff assigned to each project within the program. As stated earlier, program management and project management are distinct, but they utilize similar techniques. To start a program, some form of written assignment from the program sponsor (owner) to the program manager and program team is absolutely necessary. A critical aspect of program development is the establishment of:

- A clear and logical management hierarchy
- Rules governing the chain of command and communication
- Project team expectations and boundaries.

The creation of a PMO (Program Management Office) is a wise initial step for organizations that want to manage their current projects more efficiently. One huge benefit of developing a PMO is that it allows an organization to apply well-defined project management principles to its current project management processes. Over time, this should improve the management of all projects run within the organization. The following actions are usually asociated with the creation of a program management office:

- The identification of SMEs (Subject Matter Experts) to populate expert pools
- Project management experts to focus on the new "project" of managing other projects
- Appropriate updates to all financial, change, configuration, problem and incident management
- Changes in the organization's hierarchical structures that will allow for:
    - Efficient horizontal communcations between project groups
    - Clear and unabiguous assignments of responsibility and authority that are relevant for the newer management model
    - New reporting structures, policies and procedures to ensure that stakeholers and other relevant parties have access to the information they need when they need it.

The PMO (Program/Project Management Office) is usually the owner of the project management and program management processes. It must be a permanent structure within the organization and adequately staffed and funded. This makes the PMO itself to be an example of a program with an indefinite duration. One of its roles is to ensure that adequate professional support is always available to maintain current procedures and standards and develop new ones. Another objective of the PMO is to manage and improve its own processes. This means that the PMO is responsible for adopting and iterative self-improvement process. Functions that the PMO should NOT undertake are:

- The creation of new projects or obtaining approval for new projects
- Obtaining Initial funding for new projects.

By avoiding these activities, the PMO can maintain independence from the departments that may want certain projects done. The PMO should be allowed to focus its efforts on the efficient management of projects, rather than taking part in getting new projects started. This approach allows for fewer conflicts of interest between those that championed the approval of the project and those that have to manage it. The PMO should be able to maintain objectivity at later stages of project management when difficult decisions about continuing a project might have to be made.

The objectives of program management/project portfolio management are:

- Ensuring that projects are completed on time and within the budget specified
- Optimization of the results of the project portfolio (not of the individual projects)
- Prioritizing and scheduling projects
- Resource coordination (internal and external)
- Knowledge transfer throughout the projects

Program, project portfolio or project management processes should be database driven. This enables the most efficient means of aggregating data from multiple projects including information about the owner, schedules, objectives, deliverables, project type, status, cost, etc. A properly managed database will also facilitate report generation in a variety of formats such as: bar chart, a profit vs. risk matrix, a progress graphs, etc. The PMO must be able to supply the organization's stakeholders and other relevant parties with the information they need to be able to assess the status of any or all projects that it manages.

System Development Methodologies

In many organizations, the creation of a business case is necessary for any kind of IT project or expenditure. The output of the business case should be information that justifies the allocation of funds and other resources to the proposed project. Depending on the culture, structure and policies of the organization, a business case will be developed prior to project approval or as the first step in a mandatory process.

A feasibility study is an organized set of research results and calculations that help determine the probability or success for a proposed project, expenditure or other activity. The business case should include or be linked to the results of a feasibility study. The concept of **Business Alignment** (or IT Alignment) specifies that IT or other technology-related expenditures must promote or fulfill a valid business goal or objective. One objective of **IT Governance** is to ensure Business Alignment.[1] Therefore, either the feasibility study or the business case or both should state the business goal that the proposed project will address. In general, the feasibility study should define the business objective that needs to be addressed and the scope of two or more possible solutions. Business cases should be developed for each solution suggested in the feasibility study. The solution which has the highest likelihood of success and the greatest degree of alignment with the stated business objective(s) should be adopted. Together, the feasibility study and business case should ask and answer the following questions:

- What business objectives are being considered?
- What options are available for meeting this objective?
- What are the costs associated with each possible solution?
- What are the best case, worst case and most likely scenarios that might occur with each possible solution?
- Which solution is most likely to succeed given the resources available?
- Which solution most closely fulfills the business need in question?
- At what points in the expected duration of each proposed solution is it wise to review the project status and determine whether the project should continue?

During a periodic review, if changes in circumstances show that the results of the business case are no longer valid, procedures for deciding on project termination should be considered. The points in time that these reviews should be scheduled are called "stage gates" or "kill points". On the other hand, if the results of the review show that the business need or objective continues to be a priority, the project is on track and no other circumstances negate the information obtained earlier, then continued funding and effort for the project should be approved.

Companies often commit significant information technology resources (e.g., people, applications, facilities, technology, etc.) to develop, acquire and maintain application systems that are critical to the effective functioning of key business processes. These systems become IS/IT assets that contain and/or control critical data assets or access to other resources. As information assets, the new systems need to be effectively managed and controlled. The processes used in the development/acquisition, management and control of these IT resources are part of yet another process called a life cycle. The system's life cycle should include policies and procedures that govern its development/acquisition, deployment, maintenance and retirement. Each step or phase in the life cycle is an incremental step that lays the foundation for the next phase for effective management control in building and operating business application systems.

The implementation process for business applications commonly referred to as a SDLC Systems Development Life Cycle), often begins when a project is initiated as a result of one or more of the following situations:

- An opportunity that relates to a new or existing business process
- A problem that relates to an existing business process
- A new opportunity that will enable the organization to take advantage of technology
- A problem with the current technology

The primary purpose of any SDLC is to facilitate the management of the development processes in question at each possible stage. Proper and consistent use of a SDLC may help minimize **business risk** associated with systems development. This is the risk that the finished product will not meet the stated business objectives or requirements. Organizations have several well known life cycle models to choose from. In addition, there are models that are hybrids or other variations on the well known versions. The choice of a model should reflect the needs and resources of the organization and the type of system being considered. In most cases, the primary criterion for the selection of a life cycle model should be its usefulness in enabling the organization to adequately monitor and manage the progress of the project and its status at any point in time. Failure to choose an appropriate model or to thoroughly manage each of its stages may result in the failure of the project.

The traditional SDLC or **"waterfall model"** and its variants, normally involve a life cycle verification approach that helps identify potential problems as early as possible. In general, the earlier a problem is detected, the less expensive it is to correct. The verification and validation model, sometimes called the v- model, also emphasizes the relationship between development phases and testing levels.[2] The most granular testing, the **unit test**, occurs immediately after programs have been written. Following this model, testing occurs to validate the detailed design. **System testing** attempts to measure how well the application meets the requirements of the system, while **user-acceptance testing** is performed by the end-user or client to determine whether to accept the product. A more detailed understanding of all tests that an auditor might use will be provided later.

TRADITIONAL SYSTEM DEVELOPMENT LIFE CYCLE

Business application development occurs largely through the use of the traditional SDLC phases shown in figure 3.1 or figure 3.2. Also referred to as the waterfall technique, this life cycle approach is the oldest and most widely used for developing business applications. The approach is based on a systematic, sequential approach to software development (usually business applications) that begins with a feasibility study and progresses through requirements definition, design, development, implementation and post-implementation. Each step or phase in the traditional SDLC has a well-known set of goals and activities that are designed to achieve those goals. This approach works best when a project's requirements are likely to be stable and well defined. It is least effective when rapid development is required. In general, the SDLC causes work on the development of the system architecture fairly early in the process. As purchased packages have become more common, the design and development phases of the traditional life cycle have become replaceable with the selection/acquisition and configuration phases.

Figure 3.1
Traditional Systems Development Life Cycle Approach[3]

SDLC Phase	General Description	Users Involved
Phase 1- Feasibility	Identify the strategic benefits of implementing the system either in productivity gains or in future cost avoidance identify and quantify the cost savings of a new system, and estimate a payback schedule for costs incurred in implementing the system (determining the Return on Investment). This business case provides the justification for proceeding to the next phase.	System Development Board, C-Level Management, Data Owner, Project Manager, Audit
Phase 2- Requirements	Define the problem or need that requires resolution and define the functional and quality requirements of the solution system. This can be either a customized approach or vendor supplied software package that would entail following a defined and documented acquisition process. In either case the user needs to be actively involved. Also, this phase identifies the user functional requirements that are needed in order to perform the job function. In this phase detail documentation as well as outlined controls should exist.	Business Management, Project Manager, Audit, Systems Analyst, Security Manager, Risk Management

SDLC Phase	General Description	Users Involved
Phase 3A- Design	Based on the requirements defined, establish a baseline of system and subsystem specifications, that describe the parts of the system, how they interface and how the system will be implemented using the chosen hardware, software and network facilities. Generally, the design also includes both the program and database specifications and a security plan. This would entail part of the functional specifications. Additionally, the formal control process is established to prevent uncontrolled entry of the new requirements into the development process.	Application Programmer, System Analyst, Security, QA, Project Manager, Audit
Phase 3B- Selection	Based on the requirements defined, prepare a proposal from suppliers or packaged systems. In addition to the functionality requirements, there will be operational, support and technical requirements, and these together with considerations of the suppliers' financial viability and provision for escrow will be used to select the packaged system that best meets the organization's total requirements.	Vendor, Business Management, Project Manager, Risk Management, Security Manager, QA, Legal
Phase 4A- Development	If the organization decides to develop the application in-house, the Applications management will use the design specifications to begin programming and formalizing supporting operational processes of the system.	Application Programmer, Project Manager, Security Manager
Phase 4B- Configuration	Configure the system, if it is a packaged system, tailor it to the organization's requirements. This is best done through the configuration of system control parameters, rather than changing program code. Modern software packages are extremely flexible, making it possible for one package to suit many organizations simply by switching functionality on and off parameters in tables. There may be a need to build interface programs that will connect the acquired system with the existing programs and databases.	Vendor, QA, IT Operations, Risk Management, Security, Audit
Phase 5- Testing	Various levels of testing also occur in this phase to verify and validate what has bee developed. This would generally include all unit and system testing, as well as several iterations of user acceptance testing.	Application Programmer, Users, QA, Security, Project Manager, Audit
Phase 6- Certification	Prior to implementing the system into production, individual workgroups or departments involved in the development should certify or attest that the work performed has been done with appropriate controls and due diligence in place. This accreditation process is used to assess the effectiveness of the business application in mitigating risks to an appropriate level and providing management accountability over the effectiveness of the system in meeting its intended objectives and in establishing an appropriate level of internal control.	Business Management, Users, Application Programmer, Vendors, QA, Project Management
Phase 7- Implementation	Establish the actual operation of the new information system, with final iteration of use acceptance testing and user sign-off conducted in this phase.	Business Management, Project Management, QA, IT Operations
Phase 8-Post Implementation	Following the successful implementation of a new or extensively modified system, implement a formal process that assesses the adequacy of the system and projected cost-benefit or return on investment (ROI) measurements. In so doing, IS project and end-user management can provide lessons learned and /or plans for addressing system deficiencies as well as recommendations for future projects regarding system development and project management processes followed.	Project Management, Risk Management, Audit, Security

The primary advantage of this approach is that it provides a very clear and highly structured template into which methods for the requirements (i.e., definition, design, programming, etc.) can be placed. However, some of the problems encountered with this approach include:
- Unanticipated events: Real projects usually don't proceed in an orderly fashion from one programmed step to the next. Unless procedures in place that help address problems, this approach can be difficult to manage
- End user requirements that have not been defined in detail or described adequately to the development staff
- Since the traditional SDLC is highly structured, it is also slower than some newer models. Pressure for a fast result may come from the client, internal management or both.
- The customer may want to alter the stated set of requirements due to changes in the circumstances in the business climate, regulatory issues, etc. This will increase the amount of time, effort and costs associated with the project.

Roles and Responsibilities of Groups and Individuals

Involving the audit function in the SDLC as early as possible may increase the likelihood that the project will be completed, delivered and implemented successfully. In particular, IS auditors may be able to eensure that controls related to privacy, security, monitoring, fraud ,etc are considered early and built into every component of the system. Other roles in the SDLC include:

ROLE	RESPONSIBILITIES
Project Steering Committee	Provides overall direction and ensures appropriate representation of the affected parties. The project steering committee is ultimately responsible for all costs and timetables. This committee should be comprised of a senior representative from each function that will be significantly affected by the proposed new system or system modification. Each member must be authorized to make decisions relating to system designs that will affect their respective departments. Generally, a project sponsor who would assume the overall ownership and accountability of the project will chair the steering committee. The project manager must also be a member of this committee and in some cases may serve as its chair. The project steering committee should perform the following functions: • Review project progress regularly (for example, semi-monthly or monthly) and hold emergency meetings when required. • Serve as coordinator and advisor. Members of the committee should be available to answer questions and make user-related decisions about system and program design. • Take corrective action. The committee should evaluate progress and take action or make recommendations regarding personnel changes on the project team, re-planning budgets or schedules, changes in project objectives, and the need for redesign. The committee should be available to deal with risks and issues that cannot be dealt with at the project level. The project manager should feel free to escalate such matters. In the worst case, the committee may recommend that the project be halted.
Senior Management	Commits to the project and approves the necessary resources to complete the project. This commitment from senior management helps ensure involvement by those needed to complete the project.
User Management	Assumes ownership of the project and resulting system, allocates qualified representatives to the team, and actively participates in system requirements definition, acceptance testing and user training. User management should review and approve system deliverables as they are defined and accomplished. It is concerned particularly with the following questions: • Are the required functions available in the software? • How reliable is the software? • How efficient is the software? • Is the software easy to use? • How easy is it to transfer the software to another environment?

ROLE	RESPONSIBILITIES
Project Sponsor	Provides funding for the project and works closely with the project manager to define the success measurement for the project. It is crucial that success is translated to measurable and quantifiable terms. Data and application ownership are assigned to a project sponsor. A project sponsor is typically the senior manager in charge of the primary business function the application will support.
Systems Development Management	Provides technical support for hardware and software environments by developing, installing and operating the requested system. This component also provides assurance that the system is compatible with the organization's computing environment and strategic direction, and assumes operating support and maintenance activities after installation.
Project Manager	Provides day-to-day management of the project, ensuring that it remains in line with the overall direction, ensures appropriate representation of the affected departments, ensures the project adheres to local standards, ensures that deliverables are quality products, resolves interdepartmental conflicts, and monitors and controls costs and the project timetable. This person can be an actual end user, a member of the systems development team or a professional project manager. Where projects are staffed by personnel dedicated to the project, the project manager will have a line responsibility for such personnel.
Systems Development Project Team	Completes assigned tasks, communicates effectively with users by actively involving them in the development process, works according to local standards, and advises the project manager of necessary project plan deviations
User Project Team	Completes assigned tasks, appropriately allocates user resources where needed, communicates effectively with the systems developers by actively involving themselves in the development process, works according to local standards, and advises the project manager of expected and actual project plan deviations
Security Officer-	Ensures that system controls and supporting processes provide an effective level of protection, based on the data classification set in accordance with corporate security policies and procedures as well as regulatory requirements; consults throughout the life cycle on appropriate security measures that should be incorporated into the system; reviews security test plans and reports prior to implementation; evaluates security-related documents developed in reporting the system's security effectiveness for accreditation; and periodically monitors the security system's effectiveness during its operational life. The security officer also becomes part of the data conversion or migration to ensure that data elements are not touched removed or viewed by any unauthorized individual part of the development process.
IS Auditor	It is essential for the IS auditor to understand the systems development, acquisition and maintenance methodology in use, and to identify potential vulnerabilities and points requiring control. If controls are lacking (either as a result of the organizational structure or of the software methods used) or the process is disorderly, it is the IS auditor's role to advise the project team and senior management of the deficiencies. It may also be necessary to advise those engaged in development and acquisition activities of appropriate controls or processes to implement and follow.

ROLE	RESPONSIBILITIES
Quality Assurance (QA)	Reviews results and deliverables within each phrase and at the end of each phase confirm compliance with requirements. The points where reviews occur depend on the systems development life cycle (SDLC) methodology used, the structure and magnitude of the system, and the impact of potential deviations. Additionally, QA's focus may include a review of appropriate process-based activities, related to either project management or the use of specific software engineering processes within a particular life cycle phase. Such a focus is crucial to completing a project on schedule and within budget and in achieving a given software process maturity level. Specific objectives of the quality assurance function include: • Ensuring the active and coordinated participation by all relevant parties in the revision, evaluation and dissemination of standards, management guidelines and procedures • Maintaining the agreed upon systems development methodology • Reviewing and evaluating large system projects at significant development milestones and making appropriate recommendations for improvement • Establishing, enhancing and maintaining a stable, controlled environment for the implementation of changes within the production software environment • Defining, establishing and maintaining a standard, consistent and well-defined testing methodology for computer systems • Evaluating test cases and verifying that the cases have been successfully completed and signed off by appropriate management • Reviewing and overseeing the data conversion process • Reporting to management on systems that are not performing as defined or designed

Description of the Traditional SDLC Phases

The traditional SDLC contains eight distinct phases, each with a defined set of activities and outcomes. The "S" in SDLC actually refers to the Systems Development Life Cycle. The structure of this model does not apply to software or application development. Over time, the principles developed within this model have been adapted to development of many different types of systems and product. It has also been adapted to aid in business management.

An example of the latter adaptation exists in the field of project management. The idea is that all of the people, processes and technology allocated to complete a project form a "system". As stated earlier, the purpose of an SDLC is to aid in the management of systems development processes. Therefore, project management is the application of an SDLC to the business goal of project delivery or completion. The principles of the SDLC can be found in many areas of business and technology. The next diagram and the sections immediately following it describe the traditional SDLC in detail:

Exam Tip: IS auditors should become very familiar with the various types of SDLCs, and especially with the strengths and weaknesses (advantages/disadvantages) of each type.

Figure 3.2

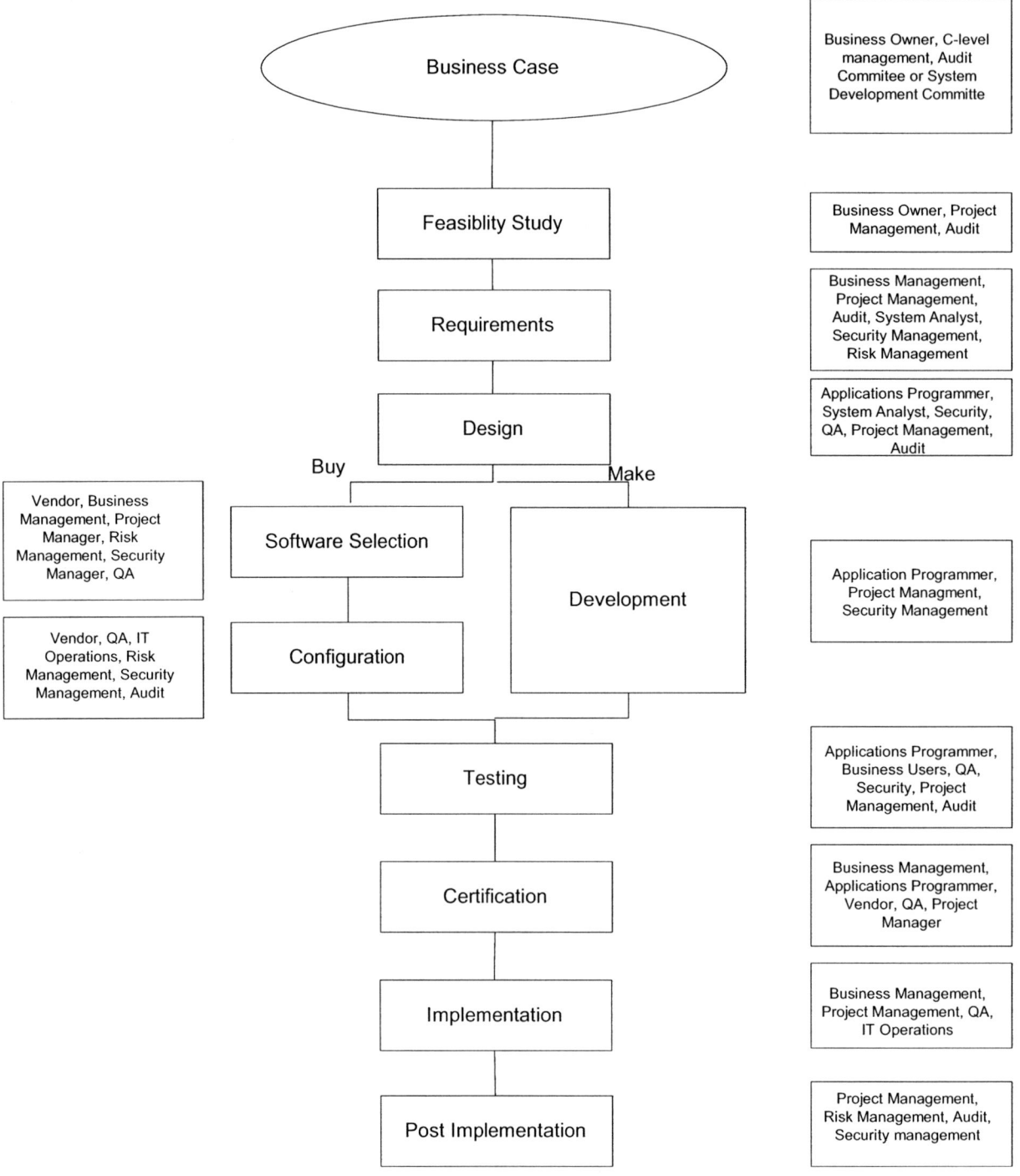

Feasibility Study

Once the decision has been made to move forward with a project, an analysis begins. This analysis is used to define the need and to identify alternatives for addressing the need. This analysis is known as the feasibility study. A **feasibility study** is concerned with analyzing the benefits and solutions for the identified problem area. It includes development of a business case, which determines the strategic benefits of implementing the system, either in productivity gains or in future cost avoidance. It may predict costs, savings or other consequences related to the solutions suggested. It may outline or estimate a payback schedule for the cost incurred in implementing the system or offer a projection about the return on investment (ROI). Within the feasibility study, the following typically are addressed:

- Define a time frame for the implementation of the required solution.
- Determine an optimum alternative risk-based solution for meeting business needs and general information resource requirements (e.g., whether to develop or acquire a system).
- Information resources, as defined in COBIT, include people, applications, technology, facilities and data organized and managed through a given set of IT processes (e.g., SDLC, RAD, etc. for the acquisition and implementation domain).
- Determine if an existing system can correct the situation with slight or no modification (e.g., work around).
- Determine if a vendor product offers a solution to the problem.
- Determine the approximate cost to develop the system to correct the situation.
- Determine if the solution fits the business strategy.

Factors that influence the decision to develop or acquire a system include:
- The date the system needs to be functional
- The cost to develop the system, as opposed to buying it
- The resources, staff and hardware, required to develop the system or to implement a vendor solution
- Compatibility and/or migration issues with existing systems that are needed to supply information to or use information from the new system
- Compatibility with strategic business plans
- Compatibility with the organization's IT infrastructure
- Likely future requirements or changes to functionality offered by the system

The result of the completed feasibility study should be some type of a comparative report, including all alternatives and solutions and shows the results of criteria analyzed (e.g., costs, benefits, risks, resources required and organizational impact). The IS auditor should perform the following functions within the feasibility study:
- Review the documentation produced in this phase for reasonableness.
- Determine whether all cost justifications/benefits are verifiable, and present them showing the anticipated benefits to be realized.
- Identify and determine the criticality of the need.
- Assess if a solution can be achieved with systems already in place. If not, review the evaluation of alternative solutions for reasonableness.
- Verify the reasonableness of the chosen solution.

If the organization's policies call for a business case to made and approved before the feasibility study is done, then the objectives and activities undertaken within the feasibility study are in line with those shown above. In other SDLCs the activities and objectives of the business case and feasibility study may be combined. In practice, the only "wrong" way to do things is to avoid seeking business alignment, fail to propose multiple solutions to the problem and become inconsistent in following the procedures mandated for the organization's system.

Requirements Definition

The **requirements definition** is concerned with identifying and specifying the business requirements of the system chosen for development during the feasibility study. Requirements include descriptions of what a system should do, how users will interact with a system, conditions under which the system will operate, and the information criteria the system should meet. COBIT's framework of principles for information criteria shows that this includes issues associated with effectiveness, efficiency, confidentiality, integrity, availability, compliance and reliability. The requirements definition phase deals with these issues, which are sometimes called nonfunctional requirements. To accomplish the above in the requirements definition phase, management must:

- Identify and consult stakeholders to determine their expectations.
- Analyze requirements to detect and correct conflicts and determine priorities.
- Identify system bounds and how the system should interact with its environment.
- Convert user requirements into system requirements (e.g., an interactive user interface prototype that demonstrates screen look and feel).
- Record requirements in a structured format. Historically, requirements have been recorded in a written requirements specification, possibly supplemented by some schematic models. Commercial requirements management tools now are available that allow requirements and related information to be stored in a multi-user database.
- Verify that requirements are complete, consistent, unambiguous, verifiable, modifiable, testable and traceable. Because of the high cost of rectifying requirements problems in downstream development phases, effective requirements reviews have a large payoff.
- Resolve conflicts between stakeholders.
- Resolve conflicts between the requirements set and the resources that are available.

During this phase, process owners, data owners and users specify their information resource needs, non-automated as well as automated, and how they wish to have them addressed by the system (e.g., access controls, regulatory requirements, management information needs, and interface requirements). Often, the data owner for the primary business area or process involved will aggregate sign-off on and submit the proposed business requirements for processing at the next phase. During this phase, a preliminary design of the system may be developed and presented to user management for their review, modification, approval, and endorsement. A project schedule is created for developing, testing and implementing the system. Also, commitments are obtained from the systems developers and affected user departments to contribute the necessary resources to complete the project. An important tool in the creation of a general preliminary design is the use of entity relationship diagrams. In the requirements phase the IS auditor should perform the following functions:

- Obtain the detailed requirements definition document, and verify its accuracy through interviews with the relevant user departments.
- Identify the key team members on the project team, and verify that all affected user groups have appropriate representation.
- Verify that project initiation and cost have received proper management approval.
- Review the conceptual design specifications (transforms, data descriptions) to ensure they address the needs of the client/data owner/end user..
- Review the conceptual design to ensure that all relevant control specifications have been defined.
- Determine whether a reasonable number of vendors received a proposal covering the project scope and user requirements.
- Review the user acceptance testing (UAT) specification that has been agreed upon..
- Determine whether the application is a candidate for the use of embedded monitoring or audit routine(s). If so, request that the appropriate modules be incorporated in the conceptual design of the system.

Software Acquisition

Software acquisition is not a phase in the standard system development life cycle. It is an alternate path related to the result of the "make or buy" determination from the feasibility study. If a the end result of the feasibility study and/or business case was that it is in the organization's best interest to buy, rather than make, then the appropriate alternate set of procedures should be invoked. The decision is generally based upon various factors such as the cost differential between development and acquisition, availability of generic software, and time gap between development and acquisition. The feasibility study should contain the documentation that supports the decision to acquire the software. There are three possible outcomes of a feasibility study that favors acquisition. The end result depends on the stated requirements and the flexibility or capabilities of the vendor's product.

- Software is required for generic business process for which vendor(s) are available and software can be implemented as-is (out of the box).
- No out of the box solution will work, a vendor's software needs to be customized to suit to business processes.
- A new software product needs to be developed by the vendor.

A project team, with participation by technical support staff and key users, should be created to write a **request for proposal** (RFP) or **invitation to tender** (ITT). An RFP needs to be prepared separately for each case referred to previously. The RFP should be sent to a variety of vendors (i.e. long list of vendors) to determine which of their products offers the best solution at the most cost-effective price. The RFP should include the areas shown in figure 3.3. There are times that an ITT is to be preferred to an RFP. An ITT is the preferred vendor contact method when the end product or objective and related services are well known in advance. The use of the ITT enables the organization to submit the same set of very detailed requirements to multiple vendors simultaneously. Since the type and levels of service have all ready been narrowly defined by the organization, the vendors will then compete against each other, primarily on price. ITTs are most often used when the organization concludes that a hardware-related solution or an off the shelf software package is their best choice.

RFPs are generally preferred when:
- The requirement calls for an application solution with related support and maintenance
- The solution requires a significant amount of modification and/or configuration by the vendor before it can be implemented.
- The solution sought involves the purchase and implementation of system integration packages, such as enterprise resource planning (ERP) and supply chain management (SCM), that involve extensive customization and delivery or escrowing of source code.

Prior to the development of an RFP, organizations may choose to develop a request for information (RFI) document, using it to solicit software development vendors for advice in addressing problems with existing systems. Information obtained in this manner may be used to develop an RFP. The project team needs to carefully examine and compare the vendors' responses to the RFP. After the RFP responses have been examined, the project team may be able to identify a single vendor who stands out from all the rest. In other cases, the team may narrow the list to two or three acceptable candidates (i.e., the short list). A benefit of adopting a well known SDLC process is that methods and procedures for the evaluation of vendor solutions may all ready be present in the model.

Any methodology used should ensure objective, equitable and fair comparison of the products/vendors (e.g., a gap analysis to find out the differences between requirements and software, the parameters required to modify, etc.). Often, it is likely that more than one product/vendor fits the requirements with advantages and disadvantages with respect to each other. To resolve this situation, agenda-based presentations should be requested from the short-listed vendors. The agenda-based presentations are pre-scripted business scenarios that are designed to show how the vendor will perform certain critical business functions.

At this point, the project team can assess certain intangibles such as:

- The vendor's knowledge of the product
- The vendor's ability to understand the business issues at hand
- The flexibility the vendor displays (if any) by offering multiple solutions or techniques to address the issues presented.

This also enables the project team to evaluate and finalize the product/vendor with knowledge and objectivity built into the process. The finalist vendor candidate is then requested to organize site visits to confirm the findings from the agenda-based presentations and to check the system in a live environment. Once the finalist is confirmed, a conference room pilot needs to be conducted. A conference room pilot will enable the project team to understand the system with a hands-on session and identify the areas that need certain customizations or workarounds.

It is strongly recommended that those in charge of the procurement process consider the needs and concerns of the end user whenever possible during the SDLC. This phase is no exception. It is still early in the overall process and it is important to invite participation from various user groups when evaluating the product/vendor fit and the system's ease of use. The end user is important for the success of the project for the following reasons:

- Lack of end user support for the new system
    - People are resistant to change
    - The final result doesn't meet their needs
    - People don't want to do the "extra" work of learning something new or doing more work for the same rate of pay.
- Some end users are aware from past events that a new implementation may result in layoffs (being automated out of job).

Additionally, for the short list of vendors remaining, it can be very beneficial for the project team to talk to one or more current users/clients of each of the potential products. If it can be arranged and the cost can be justified, an onsite visit can be even more beneficial. Whenever possible, the companies chosen should be those that use the products in a manner similar to the way the company will use the products. The IS auditor should encourage the project team to contact current users. The information obtained from these discussions or visits validates statements made in the vendor's proposal and can determine which vendor is selected. The discussions should concentrate on each vendor's:

- Reliability- Are the vendor's deliverables (enhancements or fixes) dependable?
- Commitment to service-Is the vendor responsive to problems with its product? Does the vendor deliver on time?
- Commitment to providing training and documentation for its product-What is the level of customer satisfaction?

One weakness of the above approach is that the vendor is likely to provide information about clients with which its project result was very successful. It may be useful to develop and utilize another agenda-based set of questions about projects that have not been considered successful. The vendor's responses to questions of this type may be very instructive.

After completion of the activities mentioned previously, including vendor presentations and final evaluations, the project team can make a product selection. The rationale for any choices made should be documented. The last step in the acquisition process is to negotiate and sign a contract for the chosen product. Appropriate legal counsel should review the contract prior to its signing. The contract should contain the following items:

- Specific description of deliverables and their costs
- Commitment dates for deliverables
- Commitments for delivery of documentation, fixes, upgrades, new release notifications and training
- Allowance for a software escrow agreement, if the deliverables do not include source code
- Description of the support to be provided during installation/customization
- Criteria for user acceptance
- Provision for a reasonable acceptance testing period, before the commitment to purchase is made
- Allowance for changes to be made by the purchasing company
- Maintenance agreement
- Allowance for copying software for use in business continuity efforts and for test purposes
- Payment schedule linked to actual delivery dates

If the decision to buy is approved, then all subsequent steps will include interaction with one or more vendors. The software acquisition team must handle the contract management process carefully, ensuring that all audit and legal concerns are addressed. In addition, the software acquisition team must take steps to assure that the deployment/implementation efforts are planned, documented, controlled, measured and improved upon, where appropriate. This may include regular status reporting requirements. Additionally, the milestones and metrics to be reported against should be agreed to with the vendor.

IS auditors can play an important role in this process into the Design phase. At this level, the auditor should be quite active, verifying that adequate security and monitoring controls are built into the propsed system wherever possible. The auditor should be able to confirm that the vendor understands the issues involved with security and that the vendor has the expertise to make sure that security measures will function as expected. If security controls are inadequate or non-existent, the confidentiality and integrity of the organization's data may be more easily compromised. This is especially true in the case where a new and unfamiliar system is being implemented by IT staff and the vendor. Some risks that may occur with new software packages include, but are not limited to:

- Inadequate or non-existent monitoring and audit capability
- Weak or non-existent password (access) controls
- Insecure transfers of data between applications
- Overall security of the application, including vendor awareness of hacking techniques and defenses against them.

There may also be risks involved with the use of vendor software within the organization's environment. Because of these risks, the IS Auditor should perform the following:

- Ensure that adequate controls are built into the software application.
- Analyze the documentation from the feasibility study to determine whether the decision to acquire a solution was appropriate.
- Review the RFP to ensure it covers the items listed in this section.
- Determine whether the rationale for the choice of vendor is supported by RFP documentation.
- Attend agenda based presentations and conference room pilots to ensure that the system matches the vendor's response to the RFP.
- Review the vendor contract prior to its signing to ensure it includes the items listed.
- Require that vendor testing be done with hardened devices and anti-virus scans run on any software introduced into the organization's environment
- Require that the vendor clearly document any backdoor/trapdoor code introduced during the development stage and ensure that it is removed, disabled or password protected before the full implementation begins.
- Ensure the contract is reviewed by legal counsel before it is signed.

Figure 3.3 RFP Request for Proposal Contents Table

Item	Description
Product vs. system requirements	The chosen vendor's product should come as close as possible to meeting the defined system. If the vendor's product does not meet the defined requirements, the project team especially the users, will have to decide whether to accept the deficiencies. An alternative to living with a product's deficiencies is for the vendor or the purchaser to make customized changes to the product. This becomes a risk since in most cases customizing changes by passes automated controls that the business relied on.
Customer references	Project management should check vendor references to validate the vendor's claim of product performance and completion of work by the vendor.
Vendor viability/financial stability	The vendor supplying or supporting the product should be reputable and therefore, should be able to provide evidence of financial stability. New vendors may not be able to prove financial stability; they, especially if the product is new and/or you are the first customer, present a substantially higher risk to the organization.
Availability of complete and reliable documentation	The vendor should be willing and be able to provide a complete set of system documentation for review prior to acquisition. The level of detail and precision found in the documentation may be an indicator of the detail and precision utilized within the design and programming of the system itself.
Vendor support	The vendor should have available a complete line of support products for the software package. This may include a 24-hour, seven-day-a-week help line, onsite training during implementation, product upgrades, automatic new version notification and onsite maintenance, if requested.
Source code availability	The source code should either be received from the vendor initially or there should be provisions for the acquiring the source code in the event that the vendor goes out of business. Usually, these clauses are part of a software escrow agreement in which a third party holds the software in escrow such an event occur. The acquiring company should ensure that the product updates and program fixes are included in the escrow agreement.
Number of years of experience in offering the product	More years indicates stability and familiarity with the business the product supports.
A list of recent or planned enhancements to the product, with dates	A short list suggests the product is not being kept current.
Number of client sites using the product with a list of current users	A larger number suggests wide acceptance of the product in the market place.
Acceptance testing of the product	Such testing is crucial in determining whether the product really satisfies your system requirements. This is allowed before a purchasing commitment is made.

Design

Based on the general preliminary design and user requirements as defined in the requirements definition phase, a detailed design can be developed. Generally, a programming and systems analysis team is assigned the tasks of defining the software architecture depicting a general blueprint of the system and then detailing or decomposing the system into its constituent parts, such as modules and components. This approach assists in an effective allocation of resources for both the design work and for ensuring that the new system will satisfy all of its information requirements. Depending on the complexity of the system, several iterations in defining system level specifications may be needed to get down to the level of detail necessary to start development activities, such as coding.

Users need not be continually involved during the design process. Participation in the review of detailed design work products is normally not appropriate, as end users will have little understanding of what is being discussed. However, developers should be able to explain how the software architecture will satisfy system requirements and outline the rationale for key design decisions. Choices of particular hardware and software configurations may have cost implications that stakeholders need to be aware of, and control implications that are of interest to the IS auditor. Key design phase activities include:

- Developing system flowcharts and entity relationship models to illustrate how information will flow through the system
- Determining the use of structured design techniques, which are processes to define applications through a series of data or process flow diagrams, showing various relationships from the top level down to the detail
- Describing inputs and outputs, such as screen designs and reports. If a prototyping tool is going to be used, they most often are used in the screen design and presentation process, via online programming facilities, as part of an integrated development environment.
- Determining processing steps and computation rules, when addressing functional requirement needs
- Determining data file or database system file design
- Preparing program specifications for the various types of requirements or information criteria defined
- Developing test plans for the various levels of testing, which may include some or all of the following:
    - Unit (program)
    - Subsystem (module)
    - Integration (system)
    - Interface with other systems
    - Loading and initializing files
    - Stress
    - Security
    - Backup and recovery
- Developing data conversion plans to convert data and manual procedures from the old system to the new system. Detailed conversion plans will alleviate implementation problems that arise due to incompatible data, insufficient resources or staff that are unfamiliar with the operations of the new system.

The software design phase represents the optimum point for software baselining to occur. The term **software baseline** refers to the cut-off point in the design and is also referred to as design freeze. User requirements are reviewed item-by-item and considered in terms of time and cost. Changes are undertaken only after taking into account various risks, and change does not occur without undergoing formal strict procedures for approval, based on a cost-benefit impact analysis. Failure to adequately manage the requirements for a system through baselining can result in a number of risks.

Foremost among these risks is **scope creep**, the process through which requirements change during development. Empirical studies have shown that a typical project can experience at least a 25 percent change in requirements throughout development, resulting in an increase in the effort and costs required for development. Software baselining also relates to the point when formal establishment of the software configuration management process occurs. At this point, software work products are established as configuration baselines with version numbers. This would include for example functional requirements, specifications and test plans.

All of these work products are "configuration items" and are identified and brought under formal change management control. This process will be used throughout the application system's life cycle, where SDLC procedures for analysis, design, development, testing and deployment are enforced on new requirements or changes to existing requirements. After the detailed design has been completed, including user approvals and software baselining, the design is then distributed to the system developers for coding. In the detailed design phase the IS auditor should perform the following functions:

- Review the system flowcharts for adherence to the general design. Verify that appropriate approvals were obtained for any changes and all changes were discussed and approved by appropriate user management.
- Review the input, processing and output controls designed into the system for appropriateness.
- Interview the key users of the system to determine their understanding of how the system will operate, and assess their level of input into the design of screen formats and output reports.
- Assess the adequacy of audit trails to provide traceability and accountability of system transactions.
- Verify the integrity of key calculations and processes.
- Verify that the system can identify and process erroneous data correctly.
- Review the quality assurance results of the programs developed during this phase.
- Verify that all recommended corrections to programming errors were made and that the recommended audit trails or embedded audit modules were coded into the appropriate programs.

The IS auditor's involvement in the SDLC is primarily focused on researching and recommending an adequate system of controls for the system and testing to ensure that the necessary controls are incorporated into system specifications. The auditor should also verify that test plans and continuous online auditing functions are built into the system (particularly for e-commerce applications and other types of paperless environments). The key documents coming out of this phase include system, subsystem, program and database specifications, test plans, and a defined and documented formal software change control process. The auditor may review:
- The use of structured design techniques
- Any prototyping and test plans
- Software baselining
- Change management, particularly any limits placed on changes/additions to the requirements previously submitted (scope creep)

Development

The development phase uses the detailed design that was developed in the previous step to begin coding, moving the system one step closer to a final physical software product. Responsibilities in this phase rest primarily with programmers and systems analysts who are building the system. In general, auditors are not involved with the development of a product. Becoming part of a development team would compromise the objectivity of an auditor if that auditor also had to evaluate the finished product. Key activities performed in a test/development environment include:
- Coding and developing program and system-level documents
- Debugging and testing programs developed
- Developing programs to convert data from the old system for use on the new system
- Creating user procedures to handle transition to the new system
- Training selected users on the new system since their participation will be needed
- Ensuring modifications are documented and applied accurately and completely to vendor acquired software to ensure that future updated versions of the vendor's code can be applied

Programming Languages

Some programming or scripting languages are better suited than others for different types of applications. Languages control the actions of computers and peripherals. Based on the type of program needed, applications must first be coded in statements, instructions, a programming language or source code that is easy for a programmer to write and that can be understood by a compiler program that is specific to the language and opertaing system in use. The **compiler** converts the source code into **object code** or machine code. Finally, a **linker** combines all the object code and any additional code stored in code libraries and combines these into a single executable file that an operating system and CPU can directly work upon.[4] Older languages such as C and C++ are often chosen for back-end applications that require stability and extensive strong data manipulation. Programming languages that are easy for programmers to write in pseudo English are called **fourth generation languages** (4GL). Examples of languages with 4GL characteristics are: SQL, ColdFusion, Windows Forms and Borland Delphi.

Exam Tip: Although the hands-on role of the auditor should decrease during the development and implementation phases, it is important for auditors to understand the controls that should be employed during these phases. Auditors should also know the strengths and weaknesses of different coding languages and know which might be more appropriate in different situations.

Programming Methods and Techniques

To improve the quality of programming and ease future maintenance efforts, program coding standards should be applied. Program coding standards are essential to reading and understanding code simply and clearly, without having to refer back to design specifications. Elements of program coding standards may include methods and techniques for internal (source code level) documentation, methods for data declaration, an approach to statement construction and techniques. Programming standards are an essential control, since they serve as a method of communicating among members of the program team and between the team and users during system development. Program coding standards minimize system development setbacks resulting from personnel turnover, provide the documentation needed to use the system effectively, and are required for program maintenance and modifications.

Structured programming techniques are a natural progression from the top-down structuring design techniques previously described. Like the design specifications, structured application programs are easier to develop, understand and maintain, since they are divided into subsystems, components, modules, programs, subroutines and units. In coding terminology, **cohesion** is the extent to which each software item described is optimized to perform a single dedicated function. High cohesion is considered desirable. **Coupling** refers to the extent to which each software item or unit can function on its own, retaining independence from similar code items. Low or loose coupling translates to low dependence upon other code units. One of the goals of good software design is that for each software unit or method, cohesion should be maximized (high) while coupling for the same unit is minimzed (low). Designing application methods, modules, objects or units in this way promotes the concept of **code reusability**, which can save development time on future projects. In addition, this approach can minimize any adverse effects that might result from making changes to any given code method or unit.

Exam Tip: The relationship between code reuse, coupling and cohesion may be easily confused. Additional study by all candidates is warranted here, especially by candidates possessing stronger financial than technical skills.

An online programming facility that offers an IDE (**integrated development environment**) may be implemented to allow an organization to enforce the use of structured programming methods and techniques. This allows programmers to code and compile programs interactively with a remote computer or server from a terminal or a client's PC workstation. Through this facility, programmers can enter, modify, and delete programming codes, as well as compile and store programs (source and object) on the computer and list programs. The online facilities also can be used by non-IS staff to update and retrieve data directly from computer files. In general, an online programming facility allows faster program development and the application of standards and structured programming techniques. Lead programmers may set mandatory or global changes in the programming interface that compel the other programmers to comply with certain standards. The standardization of techniques may also serve to improve each programmer's problem-solving abilities.

This approach can lower the development costs, maintain rapid response time and increase access to the programming resources and aids available (e.g., editing tools, programming languages, debugging aids). The downside is that this approach may introduce the following control weaknesses:
- The proliferation of multiple versions of programs
- Reduced program and processing integrity through the increased potential for unauthorized access and updating
- The possibility that valid changes could be overwritten by other valid or even unauthorized changes

However, online systems create opportunities for security issues and errors resulting from unauthorized or uncontrolled accesses. Library Access control software such as ClearCase, StarTeam or Visual Studio Team System Can help form the foundation of change and configuration management processes in development environments. Software of this type or some other compensating controls should be implemented to help reduce the risks associated with online programming facilities.

Program Debugging

Many programming bugs are detected during the system development process, after a programmer runs a program in the test environment. The purpose of debugging programs during system development is to ensure that all program **abends** (unscheduled termination of a program's execution) and program coding flaws are detected and corrected before the final program goes into production. A debugging tool is a program that will assist a programmer in fine tuning, fixing or debugging the program under development. Compilers have some potential to provide feedback to a programmer, but they are not considered debugging tools. Debugging tools fall into three main categories:

- **Logic path monitors** that report on the sequence of events achieved by the program, thus providing the programmer with clues on logic errors
- **Memory dumps** that provide a picture of the contents of internal memory at a single point in time. This is often produced at the point where the program is aborted, providing the programmer with clues on inconsistencies in data or parameter values. A variant, called a trace, will do the same at different stages in the program execution to show tile evolution of such things as counters and registers.
- **Output analyzers** that help check results of program execution for accuracy. This is achieved by comparing expected results with the actual results.

Cost Budgets

A system development project should be analyzed with a view toward estimating the amount of effort that will be required to carry out each task. Individual tasks may consume human effort and/or machine time. The estimates for each task should contain some or all of the following elements:

- Personnel hours by type (e.g., system analyst, programmer, clerical)
- Machine hours (predominantly computer time as well as duplication facilities, office equipment, and communication equipment)
- Other external costs, such as third-party software, licensing of tools for the project, consultant or contractor fees, training costs, certification costs (if required) and occupation costs (if extra space is required for the project).

Once a best estimate of expected work efforts by task (i.e., actual hours, minimum/maximum) for personnel costs has been established, budgeting now becomes a two-step process which includes:

- Obtaining a phase-by-phase estimate of human and machine effort by summing the expected effort for the tasks within each phase.
- Extending the summation of effort expressed in hours by the appropriate hourly rate to obtain a phase-by-phase estimate of systems development expenditure. Other costs may require tenders or vendor quotes. Cost estimation can be reasonably performed only after the size estimation is completed. This is a necessary step in properly scoping a project. There are automated techniques for cost estimation of projects at each phase of system development. To use these products, a system is usually divided into main components, and a set of cost drivers is defined. Once all the drivers are defined, the program will develop cost estimates of the system and total project.
- Components of this estimate may include:
    - Source code language
    - Execution time constraints
    - Main storage constraints
    - Data storage constraints
    - Computer access
    - Target machine used for development
    - Security environment
    - Staff experience

Lines of source code

One of the ealiest, simplest, and most widely-used methods is measuring size just by counting the number of lines of source code, measured in **source lines of code** (SLOC), and usually reported in thousands, referred to as KLOC. The 1999 US average software production was around 9 KLOCs per person-year. An alternative but similar metric is based on **thousands of delivered source instructions** (KDSI). The problem with SLOC is that it is very rough, using just a one-factor metric (the code length). Several multifactor methods for estimating application size have also been developed. The importance of all of these methods stems from the need of program or project managers to deliver the most accurate cost predictions possible. Since the size of the application development project is directly proportional to the cost, size has become a critical metric.

Another technique used to address these issues is function point analysis, which was developed in the late 1970s and has become widely used for estimating complexity in the development of large business applications. FPA (**function point analysis**) is a more refined and useful **five-factor method** based on the number and complexity of inputs, outputs, inquiries, files and interfaces with which a sophisticated user (programmer, systems analyst) might interact. The Function Point (FP) is also an indirect measurement of the overall size of the application or information system. Function points (FPs) are computed by first completing a table (see *figure* 3.4) for determining whether a particular entry is simple, average or complex. All five FP count values must be included. Organizations that use FPA often develop proprietary criteria for determining whether a particular entry is simple, average or complex.

Computing Function Point Metrics (figure 3.4)

Measurement Parameter	Count	Weighing Factor			
		Simple	Average	Complex	Results
Number of inputs		*3	4	6	=
Number of user outputs		*4	5	7	=
Number of user inquiries		*3	4	6	=
Number of files		*7	10	15	=
Number of external interfaces		*5	7	10	=
Count total					

Upon completion of the table entries, the count total in deriving the function point is computed through an algorithm that takes into account complexity adjustment values (i.e., weights or rating factors) based on responses to questions related to issues such as reliability, criticality, complexity, reusability, changeability and portability. Function points derived from this equation are then used in a manner analogous to SLOC counts as a measure for cost, schedule, productivity and quality metrics (e.g., productivity = FP/person-month, quality = defects/FP, and cost = $/FP).

In most standard applications, lists of functions are identified and corresponding effort is estimated. In web-enabled applications, the development effort depends upon the number of screens (forms), features to be enabled, interfaces and cross referencing that is required. Thus, from the point of view of web applications, the effort would include all the metrics used in standard function point calculations, plus the features that need to be enabled for different types of user groups. The measurement would involve identification or listing of features, access rules, links, storage, etc. FPA behaves reasonably well in estimating business applications, but not as well for other types of software (i.e. OS, process control, communications, engineering, etc.).

Exam Tip: Candidates may have to answer questions about software size estimation or handle questions that use terms related to software size estimation in their answer sets.

Testing

Testing is an essential part of the development process. Testing proves that a program, subsystem or application performs the functions for which it has been designed. Testing also determines whether the units being tested operate without any malfunction or adverse effect on other components of the system. The variety of development methodologies and organizational requirements provide for a large range of testing schemes or levels. Each set of tests is performed with a different set of data and under the responsibility of different people or functions. After the system staff has modified the program, it must be thoroughly tested prior to implementation.[5]

To guide the testing process and help ensure that all facets of the system function as expected, it is helpful to develop and document a formal test plan. Such a plan identifies the specific portions of the system to be tested and documents the actual versus expected results of the test. The test plan and results should be retained as part of the system's permanent documentation. The IS auditor can play a preventive or detective role in the testing process. To guide the testing process and help ensure that all facets of the system function as expected, basic elements for application software testing activities have been defined that include the following:

1. **Test plan:** Developed early in the life cycle and incrementally refined until the actual testing phase, test plans identify the specific portions of the system to be tested. This includes identifying test approaches to apply such as the two reciprocal approaches to software testing:

Bottom up testing	Top down testing
Begin testing of atomic units, such as programs or modules, and work upwards until a complete system test has taken place.	Follow the opposite path, either in depth-first or breadth-first search order.
The advantages are: • No need for stubs or drivers • Can be started before all programs are complete • Errors in critical modules are found early	The advantages are: • Tests of major functions and processing are conducted early. • Interface errors can be detected sooner. Raises confidence in the system, as programmers and users actually see a working system

   Most application tests of large systems follow a bottom-up approach involving several levels of testing (e.g., unit or program, subsystem/integration, system, etc.)

2. **Conduct and report test results:** Describe resources needed for testing, including personnel involved and information resources/facilities used during the test as well as actual versus expected test results. Results reported, along with the test plan, should be retained as part of the system's permanent documentation.

3. **Address outstanding issues:** Errors and irregularities are identified from the actual tests conducted. When such problems occur, the specific tests in question have to be redesigned in the test plan until acceptable conditions occur when the tests are re-done.

General Testing Levels

The following tests relate, to varying degrees, to the above approaches that can be performed, based on the size and complexity of the modified system:

Unit testing	This focuses on tests of single modules, objects or programs. The objective is to ensure that the smaller units perform as expected.
Interface or integration testing	This type of tests focuses of the transfer of data from one application to another. Data integrity and confidentiality must be maintained when it moves into a module or an application for processing and when it moves out to another module or application.
System testing	A Test battery, executed in a safe environment, whose purpose is to ensure that a new, integrated system performs according to requirements. This battery may include: [6] - **Recovery testing**-Checking the system's ability to recover after a software or hardware failure - **Security testing**-Malting sure the modified/new system includes appropriate access controls and does not introduce any security holes that might compromise other systems - **Stress/volume testing**-Testing an application with large quantities of data in order to evaluate its performance during peak hours - **Performance testing**-Comparing the system's performance to other equivalent systems, using well-defined benchmarks
Final acceptance testing	Two distinct types of test should be scheduled during the implementation phase: - **QAT (Quality Assurance Testing)**: This is done in-house by the IT staff and focuses on ensuring that all project deliverables are present and that they work as specified in the requirements. - **UAT (User Acceptance Testing)**: this type of testing involves various end user groups and focuses on the end user's perspective and the functionality of the end product. Both test types should be performed in secure (non-production) areas. Any last-minute updates or changes should be tested. Any additional hardware or software that was purchased or developed to accommodate the new package should also be tested here. The organization should use either sanitized production data, made-up data or both are used to ensure that processing works as expected. The IT Department should be able to simulate enough of the production environment in a safe, test-bed area to perform stress tests on the new application. It is important that assurance be provided about the ability of the new application to handle all expected workloads without the generation of errors or delays in processing. In addition, vulnerability and/or penetration testing should be done in the test-bed before the application gets approval for implementation. After all security tests have been run, a determination may be made regarding the safety of the new application. If the IT department is satisfied that the application is free of malicious code, then the vendor should no longer be able to make any changes before implementation.

Other Test Types:

Pilot Testing	Similar to unit testing, this type of test is a trial run of a subset of the new system.
Regression Testing	This type of test is run after changes have been made to the code in the software. It requires use of the original data. It verifies that the changes made to the code do not create any additional errors.
Parallel Testing	This type of test involves running the same data through both the current and the new systems and monitoring the results generated by each.
White box testing	A test of the internal logic or processing stages within a module or program. This test type is similar to unit and integration tests.
Black box testing	A test of a module or program based on an "external" perspective. This test is more focused on "Does it work?" rather than how it might work.
Sociability testing	This type of test is used to verify that the introduction of the new software will not adversely affect any existing systems, whether they are servers, user workstations or any other device that might receive information or send information to the new application.
Functional Testing	Helps to ensure a system functions in a manner consistent with requirements. Functional tests assess how a system meets the functional, security, monitoring, and reporting requirements specified by end users and business owners. Functional tests are process focused, and seek to establish if a system can adequately support business needs. Functional Testing Tools provide the following functionality: •Rapid development of testing scripts •Capture / Replay & Design functionality •Test across platforms and technologies •Identification of errors in test or data •Multiple verification techniques at various levels •Functional and regression testing •Reporting
Operational Testing	Helps to ensure that systems can support current and forecasted resource demand. In other words, this test component verifies that a system operates as required or mandated by end users, members, and business owners. In addition, this test component helps to validate risk mitigation strategies related to failure recovery activities. Operational Testing Tools provide the following functionality: •Leverage of functional scripts •Data driven scripting •Scenario driven tests of multiple scripts •System monitoring, benchmarking, and reporting •Real-time or Scheduled execution of tests
Alpha and beta testing	These tests involve early, unfinished versions of the software product. Normally, alpha testing is done by the development team or other staff internal to the vendor. After updates or improvements are made from the results of alpha testing, the beta test stage is performed. Beta tests are usually done by a select group of end users. As a result, it should be considered as a type of end user testing. Feedback from these end users can be quite valuable, since the size and variety of IS environments the software will be tested in will be far greater than the vendor could possibly obtain on its own.

After this point, the IS auditor should be able to make a judgment about the application's fitness for implementation/rollout into production. Although the auditor may not administer or perform all of these tests, arrangements should have been made to allow the following:

- Collection of meaningful performance indicators and observations during testing
- Generation of highly detailed and comprehensive reports of test results in formats useful to relevant decision makers.

As a result of the evidence provided by the testing, any risks and adverse findings should be clearly noted by the auditor in the recommendation. The following concerns should be addressed by the auditor:
- Review the test plan for completeness, indicate evidence of user participation, such as user development of test scenarios and/or user sign-off of results, and consider rerunning critical tests.
- Reconcile control totals and converted data.
- Review error reports for their precision in recognizing erroneous data and for resolution of errors.
- Verify cyclical processing for correctness (month-end, year-end processing, etc.).
- Interview end users of the system for their understanding of new methods, procedures and operating instructions.
- Review system and end-user documentation to determine its completeness, and verify its accuracy during the test phase.
- Review parallel testing results for accuracy.
- Verify that system security is functioning as designed by developing and executing access tests.
- Review unit and system test plans to determine whether tests for internal controls are planned and performed.
- Review the user acceptance testing and ensure that the accepted software has been delivered to the implementation team. The vendor should not be able to replace this version.
- Review procedures used for recording and following through error reports.

An Example of the Testing Process

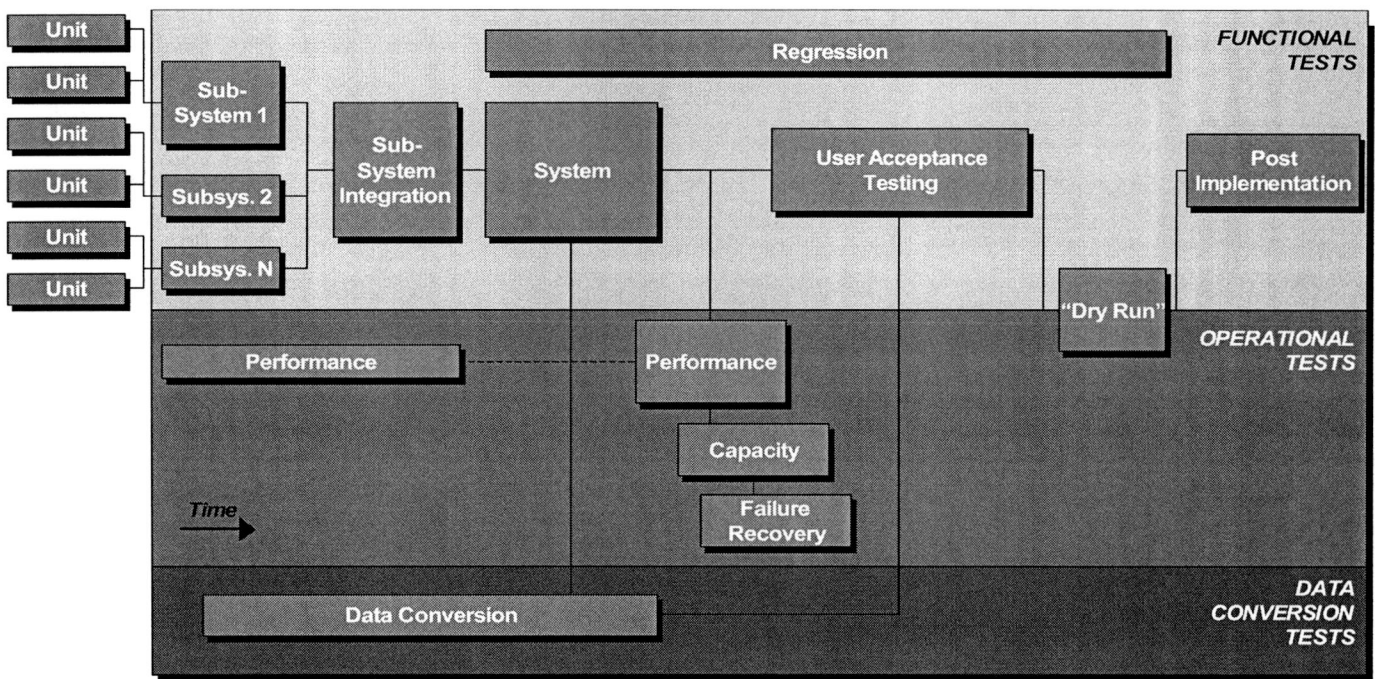

Certification and Accreditation

Upon completion of user acceptance testing, the final step is usually a certification and accreditation process if the organization has this process as part of their system development policy and procedures. This process includes evaluating program documentation and testing effectiveness. It will result in a final decision for deploying the business application system. For information security issues, the evaluation process includes reviewing security plans, the risk assessments performed and test plans, and it results in an assessment of the effectiveness of the security controls and processes to be deployed. **Certification** is that set of processes by which a product is tested and proved to meet or exceed baselines for performance, quality, etc. described within a given set of standards, requirements or legal regulations.

This process provides some degree of accountability to the business owner regarding the state of the system that he/she will accept for deployment. If this process is performed by in-house staff, it generally involves the security staff and the business owner of the application. When the tests are completed, the IS auditor should issue an opinion to management as to whether the system should be put into production. This report should specify the deficiencies in the system that need to be corrected and should identify and explain any risk(s) that the organization is taking by implementing the new system.

There are certification and accreditation processes that involve external parties and tests of performance or compliance standards developed by other organizations. These certification steps are similar to those descibed above. **Accreditation** is the process of recognizing that a certifiying agency has met the standards required by an accreditation body and is competent to determine whether another organization, product or service is compliant with standards and requirements set forth in the accreditation/certification program. Accreditation allows the certifying agency to sign certificates issued to the customer/clients. The permission to make endorsements on behalf of an accreditation body is provided only after evaluating the certifying agency's ability to examine and assess the level of compliance required to meet the requirements of a certification standard using measurable metrics. Certification can be performed on hardware devices, applications, processes, business systems, etc. A product such as a laptop may require certification by an accredited certification body.

An example of this process is as follows: Organization "A" has spent a great deal of time and effort implementing a new transaction processing application. The organization wants to inform potential clients about this via advertising, but believes the message would carry more weight if it could also state that its transaction processing met a standard for security and performance that is recognized throughout their industry. The standard in question was created by Accreditation Body "B". Many organizations want their processes to be examined and certified, but Accreditation Body "B" has a limited number of field staff to handle this type of work. In order to meet the needs of the many organizations that might otherwise forego the certification process (and also to enhance certification-related revenue), Accreditation Body "B" farms out some of the field work to Certifying Agency "C". Body "B" charges Agency "C" some set fees for training and testing then authorizes Agency "C" to send its staff into the field to test organizations such as "A" for compliance. At this point, field staff that work directly for "B" or "C" may perform the evaluation of an organization's processes. Staff from "B" and "C" are now equally capable of declaring that an organzation's process is "certified".

A **seal of approval** provides an assurance to the user of the system that the product or its process of creating product has gone through an assessor's examination or audit/review by a certification agency that has been endorsed by an accreditation agency or body. This provides assurance to the consumer of the software service that the process used by the software company meets the criteria required by the respective level of the company's certification.

Implementation
During the implementation phase, operation of the new information system is initialized and tested. Final **user-acceptance testing** is conducted in this environment. Any certification and accreditation process the organization chooses to submit to can also be performed during this phase. The certification process should also provide assurance to management regarding:

- The effectiveness of the system in meeting its intended business objectives
- Confirmation that adequate levels of internal controls have been implemented and are working as planned.

After a successful test of the full-system, the system is ready to be migrated to the production environment. The programs have been tested and refined; program procedures and production schedules are in place; all necessary data have been successfully converted and loaded into the new system; and the users have developed procedures and been fully trained in the use of the new system. Date(s) for system migration/rollout are determined and the production turnover takes place.

Planning for the implementation should commence well in advance of the actual implementation date. This plan should be constructed in the design phase and revised as needed while development progresses. Each step in the setup of the production environment should be described, including:
- Who will be responsible for which tasks
- How each step will be verified
- How the back-out procedure(s) should be implemented if problems are experienced.

If the new system will interface with other systems or is distributed across multiple platforms, additional tests of data transfers within the production environment may be desirable to prove end-to-end connectivity and data integrity across the platforms. If such tests are run, care will be needed to ensure test transactions do not remain in production databases or files.

When dealing with purchased applications, avoiding changes that could adversely affect security is vital. Both the IS and User Management teams should consider this task to be a joint effort during implementation. The IS auditor should ensure that all parties responsible for verifying the implementation and possible rollback have completed their tasks and provided attestations regarding this. The IS auditor should also carry out the following tasks:

- Verify any batch programs or other automated activities to ensure that they match production environment expectations.
- Verify the status of the documentation generated during this process and ensure that all relevant updates have been entered
- Confirm the status of the data conversion effort and review test procedures before recommending that the new system be brought online.

Post Implementation Review
After going live with the new system, the IT department should be closely monitoring and documenting any problems that the new system might be causing. Planning for the post-implementation should have begun during design phase and been incrementally revised throughout subsequent stages. The time that the new system would be allowed to run before the post-implementation review should have been fixed prior to the implementation if possible. In any event, it is recommended that the new system be allowed to run long enough so that any issues it might cause can be identified and addressed. The following activities should be considered central to the post-implementation process:
- From the user's (subjective) viewpoint, determine whether the system as is meets the specified requirements. Document any areas of dispute.
- Review the initial feasibility study and compare it with the current cost estimations. Determine whether the costs or savings projected during the feasibility study are accurate.
- Check all requests for changes to the system to determine if there is any pattern to them or if any items stand out in terms of urgency or frequency.
- Audit the system controls to ensure that they function as expected. Verify that any monitoring or test functions built into the system are working properly.
- Check helpdesk requests, system maintenance logs and any other documentation regarding work performed on the system to ensure that requirements and functionality as delivered are in line with what was specified.
- Run any tests deemed necessary to confirm that data integrity and confidentiality are being maintained throughout all expected paths and data interfaces.

Depending on the organization's post-implementation procedure, the project development team and appropriate end users may perform reviews jointly. Typically, the focus of this type of internal review is to assess and critique the project process. Alternatively, an independent group not associated with the project implementation (internal or external audit) may perform a post-implementation review. The IS auditors performing this review must be independent of the system development process. Therefore, IS auditors involved in consulting with the project team on the development of the system should not perform this review. Unlike internal project team reviews, post-implementation reviews performed by IS auditors have a tendency to concentrate on the control aspects of the system development and implementation processes.

Data Conversion

Data conversion includes the analysis, design, planning and implementation of the translation of data from the formats used by the current system into the formats required by the new system. This can be a huge and complex process, especially if the core functionality of the databases and data stores are being upgraded. The objective of data conversion is to convert the existing data controls and transactions to the new system while ensuring that the meaning of the data and its integrity is maintained. In many cases, there is a business need for additional functionality driving the upgrade to the new system. This means that the increased capabilities must be carefully configured within the new system, using the old data and testing for errors at each step along the way.

The steps necessary for a successful data conversion may include:
- Deciding which translations can safely be scripted and which translations must be done manually.
- Verifying data by cleansing prior to the start of the translation process.
- Selecting the tests best suited for verifying data integrity. These may include: automated file comparisons, comparing record counts and control totals, comparing accounting balances, and comparing individual data items on a sample basis
- Defining the goal of "success". What are the indicators that will allow the appropriate parties to categorize the conversion effort as successful? Ensuring that these parameters are monitored and recorded for analysis.
- Scheduling the sequence of conversion tasks
- Logging and monitoring the status of each aspect of the translation process.
- Ensuring that scripted translations provide meaningful alerts in the event of any failures
- Verifying the parties deemed responsible for the various parts of the conversion process. Obtaining sign-offs from them regarding the completion of their tasks.
- Developing and testing conversion programs, including functionality and performance
- Operating one or more practice runs of various phases of the conversion process to familiarize all parties with the procedures.
- If necessary, creating any SLAs and non-disclosure agreements for an outsourced conversion effort.
- Ensuring that all key personnel are available in case of an emergency when the translation process is scheduled.

Once operations are established, the next step is to perform **site acceptance testing**, which is a full-system test conducted on the actual operations environment. User acceptance testing supports the process of ensuring that the system is production-ready and satisfies all documented requirements. Details on UAT methods and procedures were discussed in the Testing Phase section of this chapter.

The scripts used for data translation must be created by the development team. In general, computers are used to help with complex and repetitive tasks. In the case of data conversion, the more complex the conversion is, the more likely it is to be assigned to the manual process. For those data elements that can be more easily fitted to an automated conversion, scripts will be created and tested on selected subsets of the group. **This is referred to as program or unit testing**. Test data is run through the scripts after the developers sign off on it. The scripts themselves are tested and refined through several iterations of data tests. After testing has been completed the next step is to promote the converted database to production. The following should be considered during the translation process:[7]

- **Completeness** of data conversion, i.e., the total number of records from the source database is transferred to the new database assuming the number of field is the same
- **Integrity** of data, i.e., the data are not altered manually, mechanically or electronically by person, program, substitution or overwriting in the new system. Integrity thus includes error creep due to transposition, transcription, trans-record, trans-field, trans-file, trans-library, etc.
- **Confidentiality** of data under conversion, i.e., data is backed up before conversion for future reference or any emergency that might arise out of data conversion program management. Unauthorized copy or too many copies can lead to misuse, abuse or theft of data from the system.
- **Consistency** of data i.e., the find/record called for from the new application should be consistent with that of the original application. This should enable consistency in repeatability of the testing exercise.
- **Continuity**, i.e., the new application should be able to continue with newer records as addition (append) and helps ensuring seamless business continuity.
- That a latest copy of the data before conversion from the old platform and the first copy of the data after conversion on the new platform should be maintained separately in the archival for any reference in future.

Training

If the end user cannot use the new system properly, the project may end up considered as a failure. Training of all staff that must interact with the new system is a very important tool for the organization in this regard. The earlier that planning for the training sessions begins, the more likely it is that those sessions will be of use to the various user groups that receive it. A primary objective of the training effort is that the end users become capable of working productively, without assistance, as soon as possible.

The **shadowing** and **relay-baton** method is considered to be most appropriate for accomplishing a knowledge transfer from instructor to student. The information is condensed, prepared by the instructor and handed off to the student during the training sessions. The instructor must then step out of the activity and allow the student to move forward with the information received. This overview is accurately summed up by the relay-baton metaphor. All training should be tailored to the job roles of the end users that will be receiving the training. For example, it is unlikely that end users will need to know various steps in creating and deleting accounts or troubleshooting the system if they are not functioning in an IT role. Training at any level usually contains the following elements:
- Who: (Instructor, end users)
- What: (Content/information regarding the new system and how to use it)
- Where: (Online? In a classroom?)
- When: (What session(s) should be attended? How long is each session?)
- Why: (The new system is a reality and the organization wants it to succeed)

Responsibility for the development and implementation of training programs cannot be placed on a single set of shoulders. The people who will be training all of the others should obviously be trained first. The questions they present and the problems they discover can be very helpful for those that are tasked with the design of the curriculum. After the trainers have been trained, they should be monitored as they train selected groups of end users from a variety of departments in the organization. The lessons learned from this phase of the training process will help in the tailoring of classes to each job function. Even the types of course format and material may be altered to facilitate the most rapid handoff of information.

The alpha and beta tests of the course format and material (with the trainers and cross-section of end users, respectively) should help the training coordinator to produce a set of solid training products. The training must be timed to allow maximum retention for the end user, while being initiated early enough so that adequate feedback and adjustments to the content may be introduced. Any of the following may be used to help provide the most effective sessions:

- Case studies
- Role-based training
- Lecture and breakout sessions
- Modules at different experience levels
- Practical sessions on how to use the system
- Remedial computer training (if needed)
- Online sessions on the web or on a CD-ROM

Alternative Application Development Approaches

SDLCs in general are primarily tools for management and control of the systems development process. The phases discussed previously do not directly improve the skills of individual programmers, although continued practice with structured analysis, design and development techniques should produce this result. The SDLC introduces a great deal of structure and procedural activity into the systems development process. One drawback of the additional structure is that it can slow the overall process down significantly.

As globalization of the marketplace seems to be continuing without resistance, competition is being increasingly driven by price concerns. Products have to be approved and completed much faster and at lower cost in order to remain viable in this new arena. As a result, developers have created alternative development strategies to reduce development time, maintenance costs and hopefully, improve the quality of software. Several of the more well-known alternative methods may be used to complement or even replace the traditional life cycle management approach in some organizations.

Bottom-up development strategies can benefit from the use of some of these alternative SDLCs. The newer approaches compress or eliminate a significant amount of the bureaucracy that is associated with the traditional model. Auditors need to remember that the use of an alternative strategy does not imply a lack of adequate controls. Instead, the auditor must examine the controls in use to determine their adequacy for the environment in which they are employed. The following are descriptions of some of the newer methods:

Method	Description
Incremental or progressive development	This type of SDLC calls for the delivery of the product in measured stages, usually in line with a long-term plan. The first deliverable is perhaps the most comprehensive. It includes the core system architecture and the basic functionality. All subsequent releases add functionality and/or expand upon the core of the system.
Iterative development	This model is similar to the incremental SDLC since it delivers the product in stages. However, this model relies more heavily upon information derived from prior stages and changes in system requirements to determine the plans for subsequent releases. This model has become very popular and has been adopted by many developers as part of a best practice solution. It allows a great deal of flexibility in situations where the requirements or other circumstances are unknown or expected to change. Some of the variables that may be subject to change include: • Type and/or functionality of GUI web interface; • Which OS and/or web server platforms will be used. • What type of security mechanisms, such as firewalls, proxy or application servers, etc will be used. • Will a two or three tier solution be needed • Which middleware and back-end databases must be supported This SDLC has been adapted to suit the requirements of various types of medium to large scale development projects including: e-business, CRM, supply-chain integration, online transaction processing and online analytical processing.

Method	Description
Prototyping	Prototyping involves the creation of small, fully operational systems that are used to test functionality and adherence to specified requirements. It is similar to iterative development because it uses information from previous stages to refine or enhance the work planned during later stages. In contrast to the iterative model, the initial design must be a fully operational model. Any changes to requirements or other circumstances are built, tested as modules, added to the main system and tested again. At some point, the system is tested for security issues, hardened and moved into production. This type of model allows developers to obtain fairly high levels of assurance regarding the functionality and reliability of the finished product at each testing stage, since the product being tested is a full working model. It also allows for changes in requirements to be added at pre-determined stages in the evolution of the product. An additional advantage of prototyping is that some implementations of this model use newer 4GL development platforms to speed the coding process. A 4GL platform has the ability to translate the code input to forms that are considered more localized or robust (such as Java) for deployment into production. Examples of this type of programming platform include PowerBuilder and the OpenEdge suite of products. Even with coding "middleware" platforms such as these, it is important to maintain control over the planning of each development stage. In spite of the prototyping emphasis on a working model, some larger stages, including the development of the initial model, may still require development in stages to facilitate management efforts. Any development plan must account for scope creep as well and the prototyping model is no exception to this.

Method	Description
Rapid Application Development (RAD)	**Rapid Application Development** is another hybrid development model. As its name implies, its goal is to facilitate rapid solutions to application development efforts. RAD is a hybrid because it uses iterative development, prototypes and/or 4GL development platforms as necessary to produce its finished product. In addition, RAD environments may also employ: • Small, well-trained development teams • A central repository • Interactive requirements and design workshop • Rigid limits on development time frames RAD differs from the models mentioned previously in several ways. First, approved projects need not involve representatives from across the entire organization to add input to the process. Either the requirements or planning are geared toward the needs of a smaller subset of the organization, or it has been decided that the need for a rapid solution outweighs the advantages that might be gained from a more comprehensive, but slower traditional approach. Second, code reuse via a library or central repository is highly emphasized in RAD. The RAD methodology has four major stages: **Concept Definition:** Here, the scope, data interface requirements and practical business functions are determined. In general, this is what has been approved as the result of a business case. **Functional Design:** During this stage, prototypes are built and tested in environments called **workshops**. **Development Stage:** The final database infrastructure is completed, data conversion is also completed and the application is prepared for testing and deployment. **Deployment Stage**: Data conversion, training efforts and final-user testing are performed. Any errors or inconsistencies are documented and decisions made regarding a go-ahead on deployment as planned and/or a rollout of fixes for the problems encountered.

Method	Description
Agile development	Agile development is another hybrid with an emphasis on decreasing development time. It is similar to RAD in that it uses both the prototyping and iterative models as a foundation. It emphasizes the idea that each iteration or evolutionary stage should produce a fully working model for testing and analysis. This type of approach allows the developers to have a high level of confidence that the architecture, data reliability and functionality requirements are met ate every stage. The fact that development is planned in stages allows for new requirements to be added and/or changes to existing requirements to be introduced during subsequent stages. The term agile development refers to a nontraditional way of developing complex systems. One of the first agile processes to emerge in the early 1990s was Scrum. Scrum is not an acronym. In the game of rugby, a scrum is a way of getting the game restarted if any kind of accidental infringement takes place. The Scrum methodology was developed over time by several different teams, although they were not working in unison. Scrum's usefulness may extend beyond system development to project management as a whole since its viewpoint may be considered more philosophical and comprehensive in scope. One objective of Scrum aims is to change the role of project manager to project facilitator or **Scrum Master**, meaning that this person will now act to ensure that any obstacles to development are eliminated. The tasks of planning and controlling development activities are shifted downward into the hands of development team (**Scrum Team**) members. There are several popular implementations of Scrum that have been utilized and documented. Some of the shared ideas or processes include: - An emphasis on the creation of fully working, test-ready products at each stage of development. A complete architecture is tested at each stage so that the development team is always working on a proven core. In theory, problems with the development observed at one stage will be corrected in the next stage, so that the cost of correct problems is minimized. - Each stage or "**sprint**" of development should be completed within a specified time frame. - Each iteration is planned based on the results obtained from the testing of the previous working model. - The role of the client or customer is increased in this model, allowing the client greater access to the testing process and increasing their input and ability to suggest changes. One objective is that changes to requirements may be decreased and also rapidly implemented due to the increased client interaction. Little or no management of a requirements baseline is necessary in this model. - To speed development, teams are kept small, teams work within a close proximity to each other, coders tend to work in pairs within these smaller teams and written documentation is de-emphasized. Instead, the primary day-to-day method of sharing information is through regular (daily, if necessary), highly structured meetings. in favor of promoting the sharing of tacit knowledge within the teams. - Agile development only plans for the next iteration of development in detail, rather than planning subsequent development phases far out in time. Agile development does not rely upon a set of documented and repeatable processes to achieve its goals. It is more results oriented, using test results as a means by which its progress and success may be measured.
Agile development	

Method	Description
DATA-ORIENTED SYSTEM DEVELOPMENT (DOSD)	Data-oriented system development is a method for representing software requirements by focusing on data and its structure. It is a philosophy that emphasizes customized data collection, modeling, mining and analysis for each client. This is a subset of systems development that may be included with any SDLC, but it is more likely to be used in conjunction with one of the alternative models.
OBJECT-ORIENTED SYSTEM DEVELOPMENT	**Object-oriented system development** is normally associated with software development. It redefines an application's data processing tasks by the implementation of objects, which are code groups containing both data and procedures. The Traditional SDLC follows older programming techniques in which the application's processing and data are managed separately. OOP (Object-Oriented Programming) is an attempt to code applications in a manner similar to the way humans think of things. Some key concepts in OOP include: **Classes:** These are the general outlines or templates that contain the basic features of objects. **Encapsulation:** allows programmers to hide the details of the attributes of a class by defining it using terms that limit access to the code inside the class. Examples of these terms are: "private", "protected" and "internal"; the choice of which is used depends on the language involved and the level of access permitted. **Inheritance:** Objects inherit characteristics from the class (called a parent class or superclass) used to create them. **Instantiation:** is the creation of a specific object from a class. **Constructors:** are code that allow for the creation of an object from a class. **Methods:** are the functions performed upon data within a class. **Polymorphism:** is a term whose meaning is heavily debated in programming circles. It is not utilized in all programming languages and its usage has not been standardized across OOP languages. Polymorphism is the manipulation of data or function via a set of code called an interface. One type of polymorphism requires the programmer to specifically define the types of data or functions that may be manipulated; another kind of polymorphism does not. This means that two or more different objects can use a set of data or group of functions in different ways. Obviously this will be an area that requires extensive documentation to avoid problems during code maintenance. Object oriented programming concepts are very popular and OOP is also implemented in 4GLs. Many types of applications including web interfaces, business applications, artificial intelligence and other commonly known programs are coded based on OOP principles. JAVA, C++, Python, Ruby, Perl, JavaScript, PHP, C# and Visual Basic.Net are examples of programming and scripting languages that allow the use of object oriented techniques.
Spiral development	This model is a hybrid of the iterative and prototyping models. Ideally, it is begun with a working model and subsequent additions are made in highly controlled stages. Its primary difference involves an increased emphasis on testing and risk analysis at each evolutionary stage encountered.

Method	Description
COMPONENT-BASED DEVELOPMENT	Component-based development is a combination of object oriented development and advanced code reuse principles. It relies upon the development of applications from large blocks or libraries of software that have known properties and interfaces. This type of coding is very popular, especially with development projects that call for extensive communication between database, ecommerce and/or web technologies. Some of the types of components that are most often used include • **In-process client components**-These components must run from within a container of some kind, such as a web-browser; they cannot run on their own. • **Stand-alone client components**-Applications that expose services to other software can be used as components. Well-known examples are Microsoft's Excel and Word. • **Stand-alone server components**-Processes running on servers that provide services in standardized ways can be components. These are initiated by remote procedure calls or some other kind of network call. Technologies supporting this include Microsoft's Distributed Component Object Model (DCOM), Object Management Group's Common Object Request Broker Architecture (CORBA) and Sun's Java through Remote Method Invocation (RMI). • **In-process server components**-These run on servers within containers. Examples include Microsoft's Transaction Server (MTS) and Sun's Enterprise Java Beans (EJB).
COMPONENT-BASED DEVELOPMENT (cont.)	*Note*: COM, DCOM, CORBA (itself a standard not a specific product) and RMI are sometimes referred to as distributed object technologies. As the name suggests, this is because they allow objects on distributed platforms to interact. Middleware has a few definitions, and the technologies described above qualify as middleware. They facilitate interaction provision of services or data communication between two or more distinct applications. Component development offers many of the benefits of OOP and code reuse. It can improve the overall quality of applications, since the components are usually well known and thoroughly tested entities. The purchase and use of components may significantly reduce development times, which should lower costs and increase profits. In many cases, the purchase of a programming platform or IDE includes a large library of these standardized components. This can reduce costs a greater degree. Finally, the use of these components can reduce the training time for new and seasoned programmers, since the components themselves may be used as trusted "black boxes". The programmers usually don't need to change how the components work; they simply need to know how to integrate them into the new application being created.

Method	Description
WEB-BASED APPLICATION DEVELOPMENT	Web-based application development is similar to component-based application development in that it is often facilitated by the use of standardized and well-tested components. In recent years, the introduction of several languages and standards by the W3C (World Wide Web Consortium) have greatly facilitated the development of web applications. Some of these languages and standards include: XML (Extensible Markup Language), XSLT (Extensible Stylesheet Language Transformations), SOAP (Simple Object Access Protocol), SAX (Simple API for XML), and WSDL (Web Services Description Language).

All of these standards and others help speed the development of standardized components which allow greater ease and security for those that offer and those that access Web Services. Web Services are usually client/server interfaces created over a network such as the Internet. The use of components offers all the advantages mentioned above. The introduction of web-specific standards can improve the way in which applications that enable the sharing of information across the Internet are developed.

The use of XML-based technologies is all ready making changes in the way e-commerce is conducted. XML-based EDI applications, with proprietary security methods, are replacing the traditional EDI (Electronic Data Interchange) applications used by many organizations. Decreased costs and greater control over each aspect of the data flow arrangements are significant advantages. On the other hand, the use of the public Internet as a communications medium requires a careful implementation of security controls to safeguard transaction data. |
| **REENGINEERING** | In general, reengineering is a process involving the restructuring of existing business processes in order to achieve cost savings and/or greater efficiency. In practical terms, reengineering usually creates huge changes in the way an organization creates its products and services. A large percentage of reengineering projects involve a significant amount of employee layoffs. Since changing the processes usually removes the existing controls or lowers their effectiveness, it is important to have an auditor review the planned changes before they are introduced. A comparison of the existing controls with those planned for the new processes should serve as a good foundation for this type of controls review. |
| **REVERSE ENGINEERING** | Reverse engineering is the process of decompiling or otherwise removing protections on existing code in order to examine the code and reuse its functions or methods in other applications. This is done by some individuals and organizations for the following reasons:
    To achieve savings in time and cost on current and future development within their own firm by: decreasing the staff needed to complete a given project and/or decreasing the testing needed on a project that uses the proven, existing code
    Malicious intentions, such as: hacking a system or network, redirecting traffic to unauthorized locations or making unauthorized transactions or copies of data

Reverse engineering is prohibited by the agreements attached to most retail software. There are also open source agreements that limit how the code may be used and what types of use require some form of financial payment. IS auditors should be aware of this type of risk and be prepared to document and report this activity if it can be substantiated. |

When considering alternative approaches, attention should be given to software integration issues early and continuously during the development process. No matter how efficient component-based development, if system requirements are poorly defined or the system fails to adequately address business needs; the project will not be successful. For example, an OOP development methodology can be executed using any of the Life Cycle Models (e.g., waterfall, spiral, RAD). Whatever Life Cycle Model is chosen, OOP development will require some iteration within and across development phases, as shown in the figure below and do this to a greater extent than structured methodologies. The extent of such iteration will depend both on the specific methodology chosen and the scope of the problem.

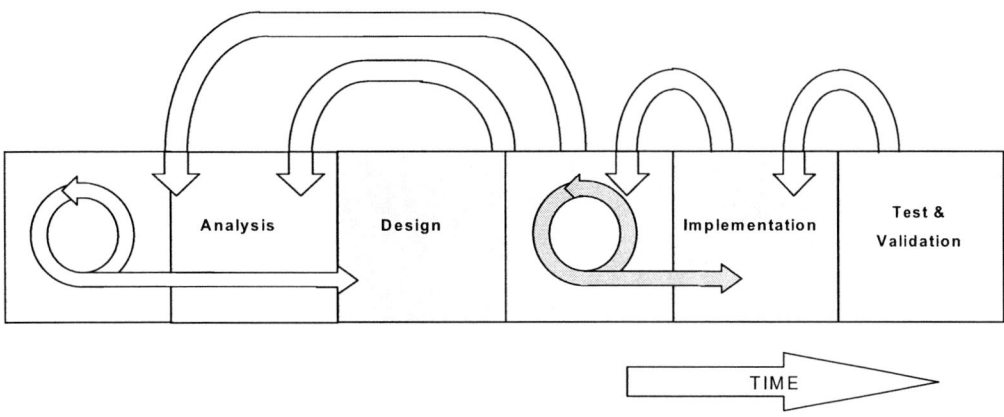

Iterative Nature of OOP Phases

Spiral development can be viewed as a series of incremental developments. The system is built in a series of cycles and the goal is to start from smaller modules and end with a complete system. Spiral development may be justified when a project is known to be fairly large in size and its requirements are unknown or subject to change. Risk definition and management is an important step to review if success is desired using this approach. The first diagram below shows the foundation for the Spiral Model.

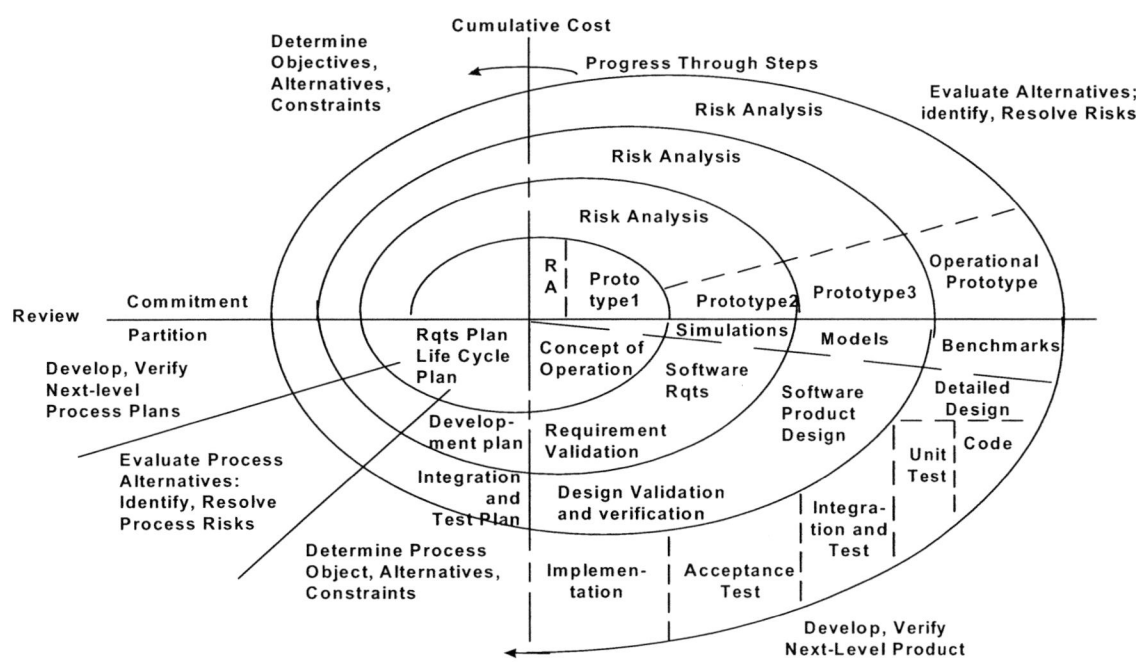

The second graphic shows that package developments are both domain-based and sequentially produced. In this model, internally tested packages are dropped into the verification environment before the start of each new package development. Multiple packages may be introduced at each stage or increment depending time constrints and the overall size of the project. Concurrent development may be used for packages to decrease production time, but a waterfall model is generally used for the design of individual packages.

Rapid Application Development Life Cycle (RADL) Model

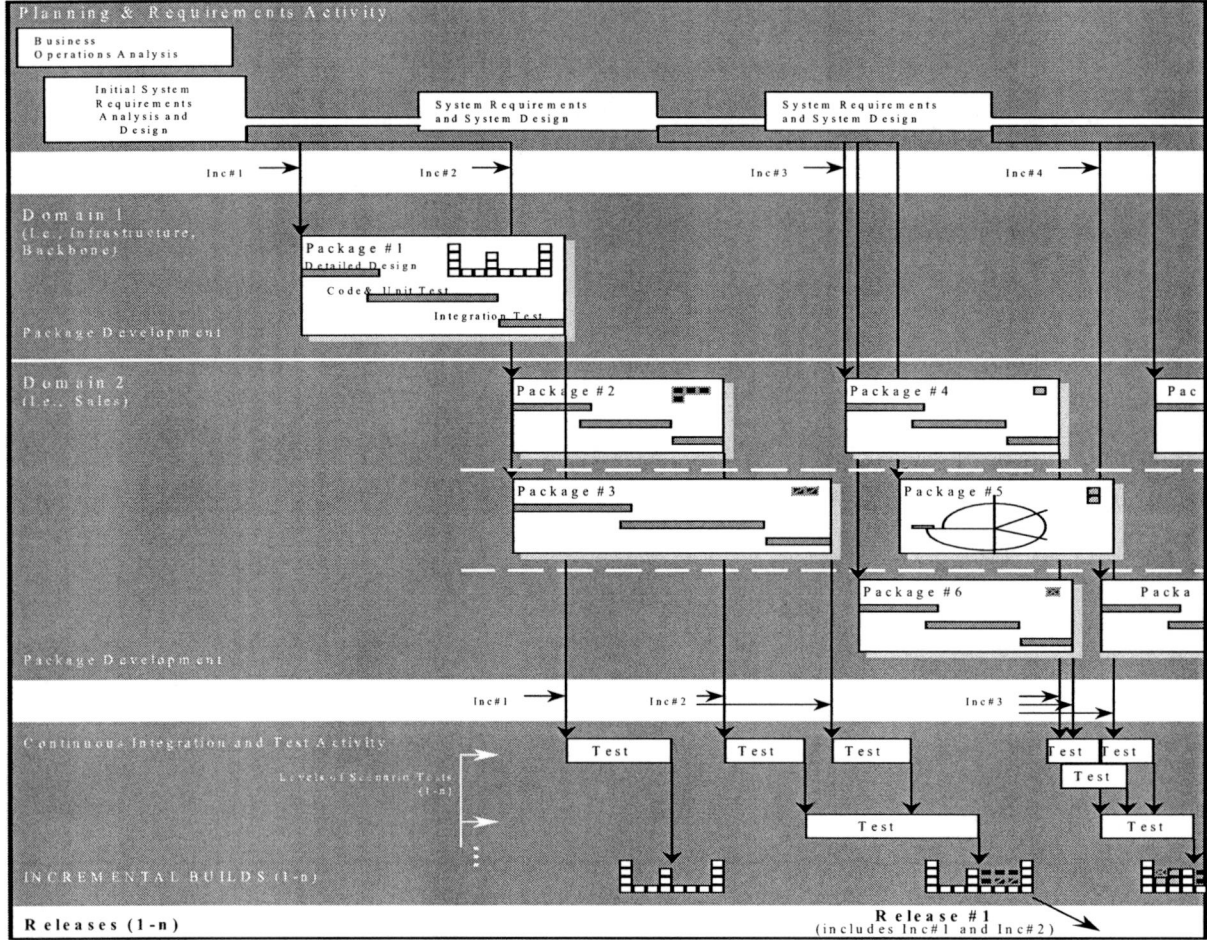

Project Management

IS projects may be initiated from within any part of the organization, including the IS department. A project is normally a one-time effort. It can be complex; involves an element of risk, with a specific objective, deliverable, and start and end dates; and is divisible into explicit phases (see the description of an SDLC in this chapter). It can be perceived not only as a group of complex tasks but also as a social system and/or a temporary organization (in contrast to the relatively stable structures of the permanent organization).

PM (Project Management) should be an established business process of any organization that delivers products or services for profit. The project management process begins with the project assignment and ends with approval of a completed project. It contains sub-processes such as project initiation, project coordination, project controlling, project discontinuity management (including the management of stage boundaries) and project closing. These sub-processes of project management are related to one another, and their objectives are to consider the project's goal, scope, schedule, resources, costs, organization, culture and context (i.e., pre- and post-project phases, project environments, other projects, etc.).

The project management process is, by definition, a process. Therefore, it can benefit from being subjected to the very principles that it applies to the management of systems development, infrastructure changes, etc. Any design lessons or issues applicable to the management of other projects may be applied to the project management process itself. There are many approaches to project management. While some are focused on software development, others have a more general approach. Some concentrate on a holistic and systematic view, others provide a very detailed workflow including templates for document creation. Some organizations use a hybrid model to fit their unique needs. A few of the most prominent *de facto* project management standards organizations are:

- PMBOK (Project Management Body of Knowledge as defined by the Project Management Institute - PMI)
- PRINCE2 (*PRojects IN a Controlled Environment*-- The APM Group [APMG])
- IPMA (International Project Management Association – Levels D through A).

Since there are significant differences in the scope, content and wording of the various standards, an auditor must become familiar with the standard used in the organization prior to getting involved in a review of the PM (this type of effort. The project managers are responsible for the timely execution of project activities, and the overall quality of project deliverables. In order to fulfill these responsibilities, project managers must take an active role in:

- Analyzing metrics and status reports to uncover trends and deviations, and working with project team members to develop corrective action plans,
- Developing and managing deliverable/milestone schedules,
- Monitoring the quality review of deliverables both internally and by the client,
- Risk monitoring and management,
- Managing changes in project scope with the client and with the project team, and
- Communicating information flows and issue resolutions between the client, the project team, and senior management.

Project managers are not responsible for working on each of the tasks described above. Instead, they are responsible for ensuring that these tasks get done, by scheduling them with their team leaders and client counterparts, by monitoring their completion, and by formally recording the results in the project archive. The following diagram depicts an example of a Project Management Framework. There are four project phases (Initiate, Plan, Execute, and Close), with project monitoring and control activities occurring throughout. The diagram outlines the major activities, deliverables, and goals of each project phase.

- **Phase 1 - Initiate:** Primarily owned by sales, business owner or manager, though the project manager should be working to define the initial project charter and management plans.
    - **Activities:** proposals, due diligence, contract negotiations, charter development
    - **Goals:** signed contract, project manager identified and on board, initial charter defined
- **Phase 2 - Plan:** Owned by the project manager
    - **Activities:** all management plans are completed and agreed to with the project team and client; project teams are on-board and have completed their planning activities; project manager is working with all project teams to establish the controlling and reporting activities and tools
    - **Goals:** project team is ready to begin work on deliverables; project manager is ready to monitor and control execution
- **Phase 3 – Execute:** Owned by the project management and project teams
    - **Activities**: project teams are working on deliverables and milestones; quality reviews ensure that work is appropriate for use; project execution activities complete as project is implemented; project manager is controlling quality, risk, issues, communications, schedule, changes to contractual scope etc. and is regularly reporting status of all activities
    - **Goals:** project execution activities are completed on schedule at the required levels of quality
- **Phase 4 - Close:** Owned by project manager and business manager
    - **Activities:** open project activities transition to business manager; operations begin; project assessment completed and archived
    - **Goals:** operations begin in a seamless handoff from the project team

Identify and define project opportunities	Identify, define, and plan project details	Prepare, build, test, document, implement, and deliver project service or products

Initiate	Plan	Execute	Close
Owner: Business	**Owner: Project Manager**		
	Project Definition	**Project Monitoring and Control**	
•Opportunity identified •Project recommended •Scope defined •Proposal submitted •Due diligence conducted •Best and Final submitted •Approval received •Project manager on-board •Project Repository established •Deliverables: cost model, proposal, contract, draft charter •Goals: contract signed, project manager on-board, charter drafted	•Project Notebook completed 　•Charter agreed 　•Deliverables agreed 　•Schedule & mgmt. plan agreed 　•Quality mgmt plan agreed 　•Risk mgmt plan agreed 　•Communication mgmt plan and other templates agreed 　•Change mgmt plan agreed •Project teams identified and on-board •Project kick-off held •Deliverables: project notebook •Goals: project team ready to begin work on deliverables; project manager ready to monitor and control execution	•Facilities acquired, built-out, equipped •Hardware identified, acquired, installed •Software defined, designed, developed, tested, implemented •Connectivity designed, built out, tested •New employees acquired, trained •Employees transitioned •Desktop (operational) procedures defined, developed, tested •New business processes designed, developed, tested, trained, implemented •Policies and procedures defined, developed, reviewed, accepted •Deliverables: facility, connectivity, hardware, software, processes, employees •Goals: project activities are completed on schedule at the required levels of quality	•Project acceptance sign-off performed •Operations team on-board •Production/operations turnover conducted •Project assessment completed •In-progress project activities transitioned •SLAs operational •Project team recognized •Satisfaction Surveys performed •Deliverables: project assessment •Goals: operations begin in a seamless handoff from the project team

Analysis/Design	Construction/Development	Implementation

•Technical architecture and solution designed
•Software requirements and general designs
•Implementation, test approaches
•Knowledge transfer, data cleansing defined
•Employee and facilities plans defined

•Hardware, software, network, infrastructure built and tested
•Facilities completed
•Resources acquired and trained
•Implementation plans completed
•Employee staffing plan executed
•Processes/procedures finalized

•Implementation plans executed
•Integration testing completed
•Final data migration
•New processes/procedures implemented
•Go Live decision made
•Production turnover completed

The following section describes the management various project management roles and responsibilities.

Project Management Responsibilities: Project Charter:	Implementation Process	Tools
Develop Project Charter: Introduce the business case for the project. Have a single source, agreed between all parties, for project goals, scope, objectives, success criteria, milestones and deliverables **To Do List:** ☑ Set boundaries for in-scope and out-of-scope activities and deliverables ☑ Establish project mission statement ☑ Determine criteria for measures of project success and completion ☑ Define project assumptions and constraints ☑ Define project objectives ☑ Document high-level project milestones and major deliverables. ☑ Document client agreement with all of the above actions by achieving sign-off on the charter	**Timing:** Work commences on the Project Charter at time of contract negotiations. The document is complete at the time of contract signing and project kick-off with approval of project governance teams. It is critical that the client project sponsor signs the Charter to signify acceptance. **Template Summary:** The Project Charter should define and set the boundaries for the project. Once this document is completed, all readers should have a clear understanding of the project purpose, scope, activities, and structure. The template allows a project manager to introduce the project, and to summarize the background, context, and purpose of the project. It addresses the business value, and sets the boundaries for scope by defining both inclusions and exclusions at a high level. Measures of success, including both client business objectives and project objectives, are clearly stated. Dependencies, assumptions, and constraints further define the project boundaries.	**Sources:** • RFP • Proposal • Due Diligence Reports and Findings • Cost Model • Contract Documents • Statements of Work • Letters of Intent • Vendor Agreements • Project Plan **Output:** Project Charter Deliverables Inventory

Project Management Responsibilities: Risk Management	Implementation Process	Tools
Develop Risk Management Plan to: - Identify events that are most likely to negatively impact the successful delivery of the project. - Document steps to prevent events from happening, and prepare plans to lessen the impact **To Do List:** ☑ Work with business management, team leads and client stakeholders to develop initial risk list. ☑ Agree on impact assessment methodology (Low, Medium, or High for both probability and impact). ☑ Determine impact for each risk, using above methodology. Classify each risk according to impact, project (scope, schedule, quality, etc.) impact, likelihood of occurrence, and severity. Define trigger events for each risk (optional). ☑ Develop risk mitigation strategies (and potentially contingency plans) for each risk, taking into account the risk impacts, likelihood, and severity. ☑ Develop and implement project risk measurement and reporting tools. *Monitor and Control:* - Risk Identification – determining which risks might affect the project and defining their characteristics. - Risk Logging – capturing the characteristics of the identified risks in a defined tracking mechanism. - Risk Assessment – performing an analysis of identified risks to determine their potential impact to the project and to prioritize their effects on the project's success. - Risk Reaction Planning – developing procedures and techniques to reduce the risk to the project's success (mitigation planning) and to respond to risks that become realities (contingency planning). - Risk Tracking – monitoring identified risks, identifying new risks, reviewing risk mitigation/contingency plans, evaluating exposure to identified risks through the project life cycle.	**Timing:** Work commences on the Risk Management Plan at time of proposal. The document is complete at project kick-off with approval of project teams. Risk tracking and management continues throughout the duration of the project. **Template Summary: The Risk Management Plan defines the project strategy for identifying and managing project risks. Risk Management is defined as risk identification, risk assessment, development of mitigation efforts and contingency plans, with continuing risk monitoring and control. The plan is used to ensure that all risks are communicated to senior management and other project stakeholders as appropriate and in a timely manner.**	**Sources:** - Contract - Statements of Work - Proposal - Due Diligence Reports and Findings - Vendor Agreements - Cost Model - Project Charter **Output:** Risk Management Plan Project Log

Project Management Responsibilities: Change Management	Implementation Process	Tools
Develop Change Management Plan to: - Define change control process for changes to the contractually-agreed scope, schedule, quality, and cost. - Define, develop and implement required roles, responsibilities and procedures for Change Control. **To Do List:** ☑ Develop and implement required tracking and reporting tools to manage the change control process. ☑ Review the management plan, change control processes and procedures, and reporting with the client. Address their concerns, and modify processes, procedures, tools, and reports as required. ☑ Add new change requests (CR): work with tower managers to estimate level of effort, assess schedule and cost impacts, develop recommendation, present to change control board, update change log. ☑ Review open change requests: work with vendors/tower managers to assess progress, review checkpoints, acquire sign-offs, update levels of effort, update schedule and cost impacts, update change log, update master project plan. ☑ Close existing change requests: update change log with reason for closure (i.e., not approved, completed, cancelled), work with vendors/business managers to close the CR, update master project plan. **Monitor and Control:** o Add new change requests: work with team leads/tower managers to estimate level of effort, assess schedule and cost impacts, develop recommendation, present to change control board, update change log. o Review open change requests: work with vendors/tower managers to assess progress, review checkpoints, acquire sign-offs, update levels of effort, update schedule and cost impacts, update change log, update master project plan. o Close existing change requests: update change log with reason for closure (i.e., not approved, completed, cancelled), work with vendors/tower managers to close the CR, update master project plan. o Review change requests weekly with vendors/tower managers to ensure that project plans are updated.	**Timing:** Work commences on the Change Management Plan at contract signing. The document is complete at project kick-off with approval of project teams. Change management continues throughout the duration of the project. **Template Summary:** The Change Management Plan defines the process for initiating, assessing and controlling modifications to a project. It defines the required documentation, review process and management approvals to implement changes to baseline deliverables and schedules. This plan provides a tracking mechanism to be used throughout the project. The objectives of the change management plan are to: - Provide a process that clearly defines how project modifications – scope, deliverables, timelines, resources, execution strategy – are initiated and documented; - Provide a guideline fore analyzing and evaluating proposed changes; - Provide a process for review and approval of requests; - Provide a process for implementation of changes to the project.	**Sources:** Proposal Contract Statements of Work Vendor Agreements Project Governance Model Operations and Engineering Standards Project Charter **Output:** Change Management Plan Project Log

Project Management Responsibilities: Schedule Management	Implementation Process	Tools
Develop Schedule Management Plan to: • Define team deliverables with established completion dates • Track and report progress in relation to project schedule **To Do List:** ☑ Work with project managers/team leads and client stakeholders to decompose key deliverables and milestones into team deliverables and schedules. ☑ Work with project managers/team leads to define the required level of detail and information for their component of the master project plan. ☑ Integrate all vendor plan components into the master project plan. ☑ Synchronize all vendor components within the master project plan, resolving date discrepancies as required. Insert cross-tower dependencies. ☑ Define and document process and procedures for updating and re-synchronizing the master project plan with vendor/tower components (when and how are updates sent, to whom, how). ☑ Work with project managers, business management, team leads and client stakeholders to define and schedule all required reports. *Monitor and Control:* • Review progress against team schedules. • Assess team schedule changes against the master plan and against other team schedules to discover dependencies. • Work with client project manager on changes that affect client deliverables and schedules. • Review schedules and progress weekly with vendors/tower managers to ensure that their project plans are updated.	**Timing:** Work commences on the Schedule Management Plan at contract signing. The document is complete at project kick-off with approval of project teams. Schedule management continues throughout the duration of the project. **Template Summary:** The Schedule Management Plan defines the process for confirming key deliverables and establishing key milestones with completion dates and assigned resources, decomposing these key deliverables and milestones into team deliverables and team schedules, and tracking and reporting progress, The plan defines the required documentation, review process and management approvals to implement changes to the baseline schedule and deliverables. This plan provides a tracking mechanism to be used throughout the project. The objectives of the schedule management plan are to: • Confirm key deliverables • Confirm critical milestones and completion dates • Decompose key deliverables and milestones into team deliverables • Confirm project team resources – matrix organization structure • Establish process for how progress is tracked and reported	**Sources:** Proposal Contract Statements of Work Vendor Agreements Project Governance Model Project Charter **Output:** Schedule Management Plan Deliverables Inventory Team Status Reporting Template

Project Management Responsibilities: Project Close	Implementation Process	Tools
Develop Assessment to: • Document the closure of project activities and client acceptance of completed tasks and deliverables. • Formally transition any remaining project activities to the business manager. **To Do List:** • Prepare project close assessment	**Timing:** Work commences on the Project Close Assessment at contract signing by reviewing the template and confirming the acceptance and close process with the client. Completion of project close activities continues throughout the project until all components are complete and accepted by the client and operations begin. **Template Summary: The Project Close Assessment documents the end of the project and the transition of ongoing project activities to the business manager.**	Sources: Proposal Contract Statements of Work Deliverables Inventory Output: Project Close Assessment Template

Project Organizational Forms

There are three major forms of organizational alignment for the project management function:
- Influence project organization
- Pure project organization
- Matrix project organization

Influence project organization - The project manager may only advise team members and peers about the activities that should be completed. No formal authority is assigned to the position of Project Manager.

Pure project organization – The project manager has authority over those taking part in the project. This authority may be emphasized by the designation of separated office space for the PMO.

Matrix Project Organization --Management authority is shared between the project manager and the department managers in a matrix project organization. The organizational and reporting hierarchy may be very complex in this type of arrangement. If an auditor is assigned to review the project management process, then a clear and unambiguous statement regarding the organization's reporting needs should be obtained from a corporate-level officer with authority over the audit process before proceeding with reviews or reporting on project-related issues. Without a clear understanding of the organizational strucure, it is extremely difficult to evaluate controls over the PM process.

The IS steering committee, or a similar group should:
- Receive submissions for major project requests
- Prioritize project requests
- Appoint a program/project manager.
- Determine the scope of the authority of the program/project manager

The role of IS auditors on a project team may include:
- SME (Subject Matter Expert) in risk and controls
- Objective reviewer of the project management process as implemented by the organization
- Objective reviewer of the roles played and processes employed by team members as developers of a specific project

The latter role involves auditing the development process for a project. Either of the actions below could compromise the objectivity of an auditor assigned to review controls for a *specific* project. Care should be taken by the auditor to maintain objectivity if there is any possibility that:
- The auditor may be asked to participate in the development of the project
- The auditor may be asked to review the PMO and its effectiveness.

Project Objectives

A project needs clearly defined results that are **SMART** (specific, measurable, achievable, and relevant and time bound). A holistic project view calls for maintaining a perspective that includes the needs of the entire business. This expanded perspective will include the following:

Main objectives are those that are related to meeting business goals or objectives.

Additional objectives are secondary objectives whose implementation may contribute to the success of the project, in spite of their lack of direct relationship to any of the stated business goals.

Non-objectives provide guidance and aid all relevant parties in understanding the details of the project and the contributions expected from each person or group.

Some general strengths of modern project management are:
- It is iterative in nature.
- It emphasizes a risk-based approach to project implementation.
- There are many methods available for use in calculating essential metrics and indicators such as productivity, resource allocation, project size and duration, etc.
- Either quantitative or qualitative methods or both may be used to provide the greatest amount of clarity regarding the measurement of metrics.

One method used to define project objectives calls for the creation of an OBS (**object breakdown structure**) and a supporting WBS (**work breakdown structure**) The OBS forms an outline used to display the various parts of a solution and the ways that they relate to each other. The WBS expands upon each part of the solution by describing the WPs (work packages) or work units necessary to complete a package. This approach offers the following advantages:
- It allows a process-oriented approach to be used in the management of projects.
- It may help minimize the omission of necessary objectives from the overall process.
- The use of well-defined packages of work facilitates detailed assignments of responsibility and leadership for each aspect of the package and for the package as a whole.

The Work Breakdown Structure (WBS)

The WBS is a framework that allows complex work assignments to be broken down into smaller and more manageable WPs. The WBS utilizes a top-down approach to project management. This enables the PM to view the project as a whole (project scope) and also maintain a focus on the status of individual parts or deliverables. A well-defined set of WPs can aid in scheduling, resource allocation and cost estimation. Using a WBS for planning may save a great deal of time and expanse by avoiding the need to re-plan or re-evaluate the work necessary for project success. Each level should represent exactly 100% of the amount of work needed to be done. This means that if a level contains exactly three elements, the sum of the percentages of work included in each of the three elements should be 100%.

Note that delegating operational control to a project manager or office can be useful in any organization. However, this is especially true when a bottom-up strategy is employed. The PMO can act as an additional control at the operational level when upper layers of management are removed from the process for the sake of decreasing development time. If an organization uses a bottom-up approach, the need for speed should have all ready been established as a business driver. The alternative SDLCs discussed later can make good use of a bottom-up approach. The following diagrams illustrate some very basic high-level views of a project and represent possible variations on work breakdown structures:

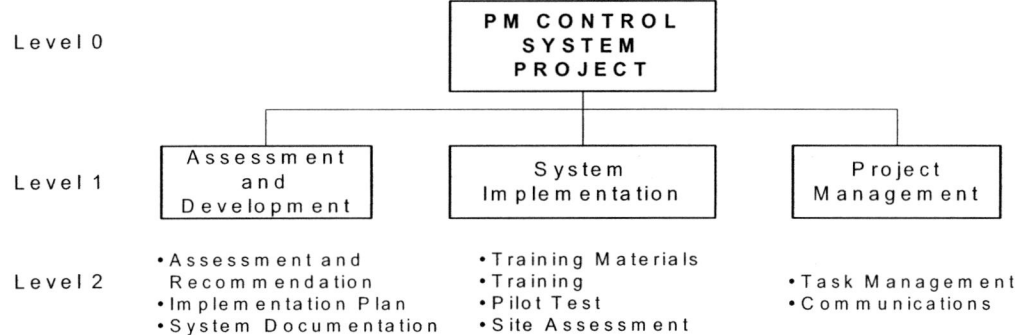

Top-Level Work Breakdown Structure

Level 0 is the total project. Level 1 is the subdivision into the final products (for example, an assessment, set of recommendations and an implemented and operational system) as well as complementary work needed for the project, such as the project management function. The total scope of the project is represented, in this example, by the sum of the work in the three Level 1 elements.

1) Define the project's objective (this will be used as the Project Summary Task in Microsoft Project).

The next step is:

2) **Define the major summary tasks.**

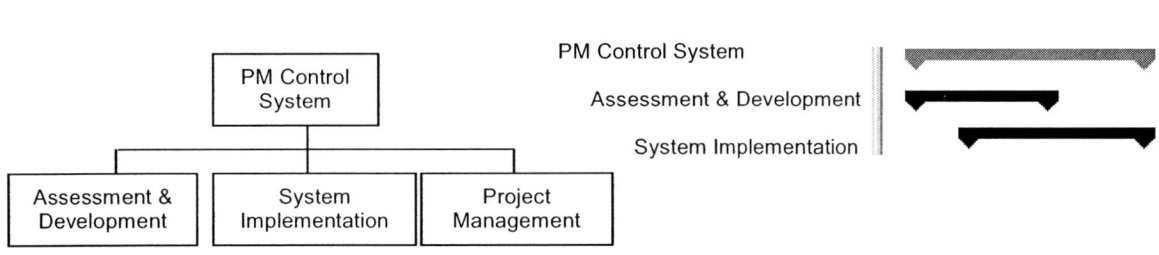

Adding lower levels of detail

The major summary tasks have now been defined and they need to be systematically broken down into lower levels of detail until quantifiable tasks are at the bottom of the outline structure:

3) Take each major summary task (phase) and break it down into appropriate summary tasks:

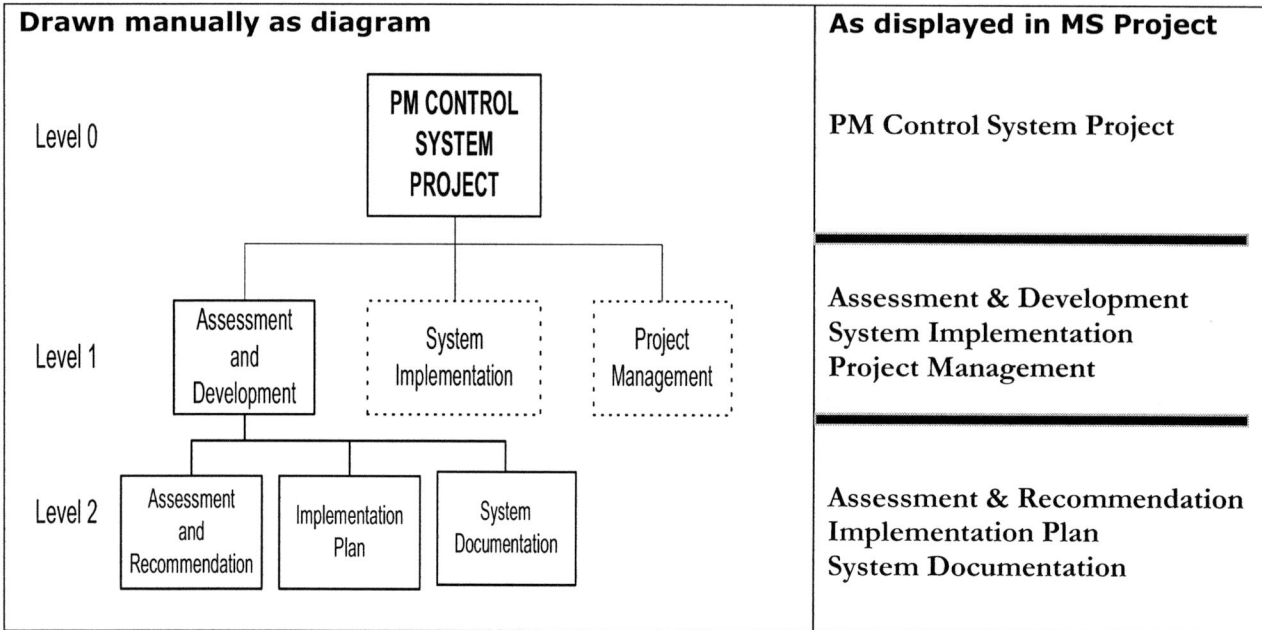

Hints:
- Try to keep each sub-objective (Summary task) similar in size (work / cost).
- Major summary tasks may relate to: products, functions, disciplines, cost areas.
- Major summary tasks should be listed within the project's documentation.
- Remember that work breakdown structures do not usually allow for clear representations of time and size relationships.

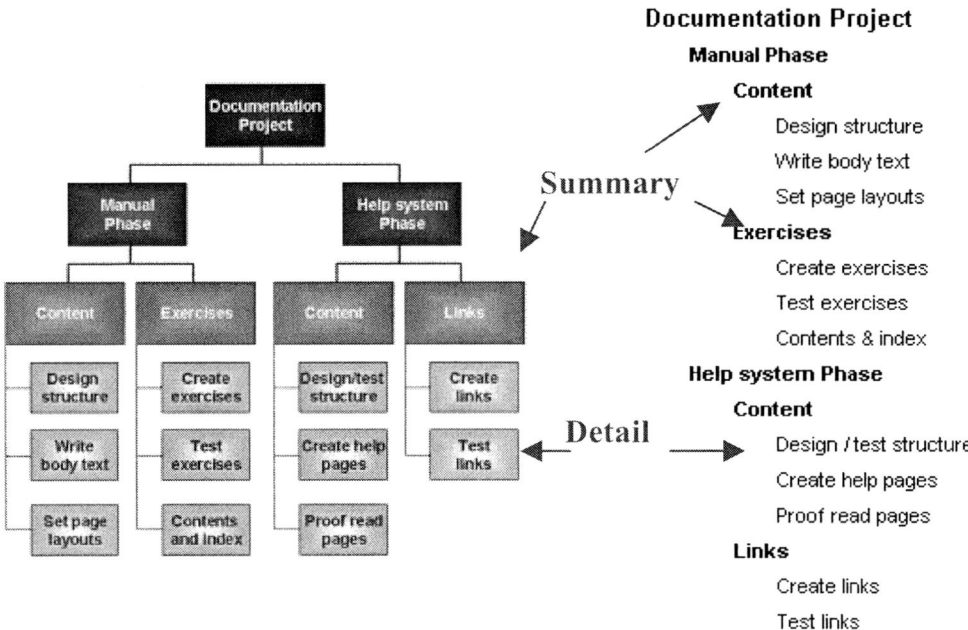

Hints:
- Enlist the project team's assistance when listing the tasks that comprise the project. This facilitates accuracy on scope definition and increases team motivation and commitment.
- The smaller the task, the more accurately it can be estimated (8-40hrs). Aim to have tasks that can be attributed to one individual or team for completion.

Systems Development Methodology

When planning the WBS, it is critical the project subtasks be clearly identified and mapped in logical groups to ensure the project scope and deliverables are accurately depicted. To support this front end planning, a Systems Development Methodology should be followed throughout the planning process.

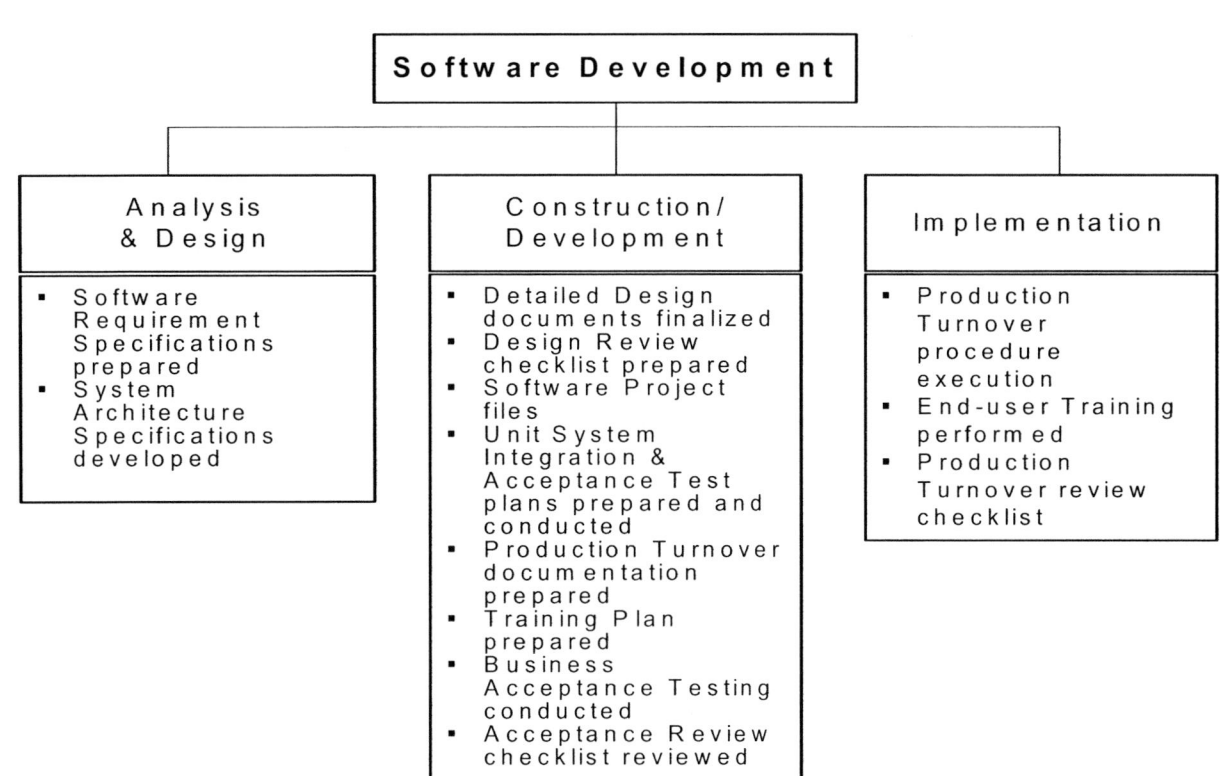

There are techniques that are useful in creating this plan, and in monitoring its achievement:

> **System Development Methodology – Example**
> Software (SW) development/acquisition or maintenance projects have to be planned and controlled. The project manager needs to determine:
> - What tasks need to be performed to produce the expected system
> - How long each task will take
> - Which order the tasks need to be performed in
> - What resources are available to perform the tasks
> - How much each task will cost, and how it will be funded

Scheduling And Establishing The Time Frame
While budgeting involves totaling the human and machine effort involved in each task, scheduling involves establishing the sequential relationship among task. This is achieved by arranging task according to:
- Earliest start date, by considering the logical sequential relationship among task and attempting to perform tasks in parallel wherever possible
- Latest expected finish date, by considering the estimate of hours per the budget and the expected availability of personnel or other resources and allowing for known elapsed time considerations (holidays, recruitment time, full-time/part-time employees)

Either Gantt or PERT charts may be used to create graphical representations of a schedule. At key points or milestones within the project, the budget and schedule should be revisited to verify compliance and identify variances. Any changes to the budget and schedule should be analyzed to determine the cause and corrective action to take in minimizing or eliminating the total project variance. Variances and the variance analysis should be reported to management on a timely basis.

Critical Path Methodology (CPM)
The **Critical Path** is the longest continuous sequence of tasks through the project with no slack. This path is important because, if everything goes according to schedule, its length gives the shortest possible completion time of the overall project. The tasks on the Critical Path are not necessarily more important or more difficult than other project activities, but the lack of slack means that slippage on any of these tasks could delay project completion.

Slack time is a calculation concerning the excess of any time or resources that may be devoted to a given activity. It refers to the amount of delay in start time an activity can stand before it results in delays to the entire project. Slack is also known as "**float**". By default, activities on the critical path have a slack of zero. A **negative slack** means the activity is behind schedule. **Zero slack** means that the activity is on schedule. **Positive slack** means the activity is ahead of schedule. Negative slack on the CPM may result in delays for completion of the overall project. Delays on the CPM must be montiored and acted upon with all possible speed to avoid cost overruns.

Since a project consists of an ordered set of independent activities, it can be represented as a network where activities are shown as branches connected at nodes immediately preceding and immediately following activities. **A path** through the network is any set of successive activities that may be followed from the beginning to the end of a given project. In a CPM diagram, a single number is associated with each activity in the network. This number represents an estimate of the time that activity needs to be completed from start to finish. Differences in the way this number is obtained distinguish the major variants of the technique.

The critical path and associated slack times for a project are found by simply working forward through the network, computing the earliest possible completion time for each activity, until the earliest possible completion time for the total project is found. Then, by working backward through the network, the latest completion time for each activity is found, the slack time computed and the critical path identified. This procedure is usually programmed into a computer for easy calculation and what-if scenarios.

Computation of the critical path proceeds by first arranging activities by "paths" based on any required order of completion, from the beginning to the end of a project. An activity may be included in multiple paths. Next, a number representing a measure of time should be assigned to each activity. This number should reflect the estimated duration of the activity. The critical path may be calculated at this point by tracing through each path from beginning to end and identifying the path with the longest duration. This is the critical path.

Crashing, or shortening the estimated duration of activities on the critical path should decrease the overall project time. However, such decreases in time usually result in an increase in the cost of those activities. Software packages that allow for CPM-related calculations usually offer the ability to add estimated times and costs and perform what-if scenarios regarding resource utilization and leveling.

Task Name	Start	Finish	Late Start	Late Finish	Free Slack	Total Slack
⊟ **Manual Project**	Feb 2 '04	Mar 24 '04	Feb 2 '04	Mar 24 '04	0 days	0 days
⊞ **Weekly meetings**	Feb 2 '04	Mar 22 '04	Feb 2 '04	Mar 24 '04	2.75 days	2.75 days
⊟ **Content**	Feb 2 '04	Mar 19 '04	Feb 2 '04	Mar 18 '04	0 days	-1 day
Design structure	Feb 2 '04	Feb 6 '04	Feb 2 '04	Feb 6 '04	0 days	0 days
Write body text	Feb 9 '04	Mar 13 '04	Feb 9 '04	Mar 13 '04	0 days	0 days
Set page layouts	Mar 15 '04	Mar 19 '04	Mar 15 '04	Mar 18 '04	0 days	-1 day
⊟ **Exercises**	Feb 11 '04	Mar 24 '04	Feb 11 '04	Mar 23 '04	0 days	-1 day
Create exercises	Feb 11 '04	Feb 20 '04	Feb 11 '04	Feb 20 '04	0 days	0 days
Test exercises	Feb 23 '04	Feb 27 '04	Feb 23 '04	Feb 27 '04	0 days	0 days
Create contents & index	Mar 18 '04	Mar 24 '04	Mar 17 '04	Mar 23 '04	0 days	-1 day
Manual completed	Mar 23 '04	Mar 23 '04	Mar 23 '04	Mar 23 '04	0 days	-1 day

- **Free Slack** or free float is the amount of time a task can slip before it delays any other task.
    - If tasks are completed or are critical, their total slack value will be 0.
    - If any tasks can be delayed without affecting the project finish date or a task with an inflexible constraint, their total slack value will be positive.
    - If a **scheduling conflict** exists, tasks will have a negative total slack value.

Where negative slack values are displayed against tasks, the sequence of tasks needs to be performed quicker (possibly at higher cost) in order to meet the project finish date. In the example above, a saving of one day on EITHER "Set page layouts" OR "Create contents & index" would be enough to bring the project back on schedule and reduce the total slack to 0 days.

PERT/CPM

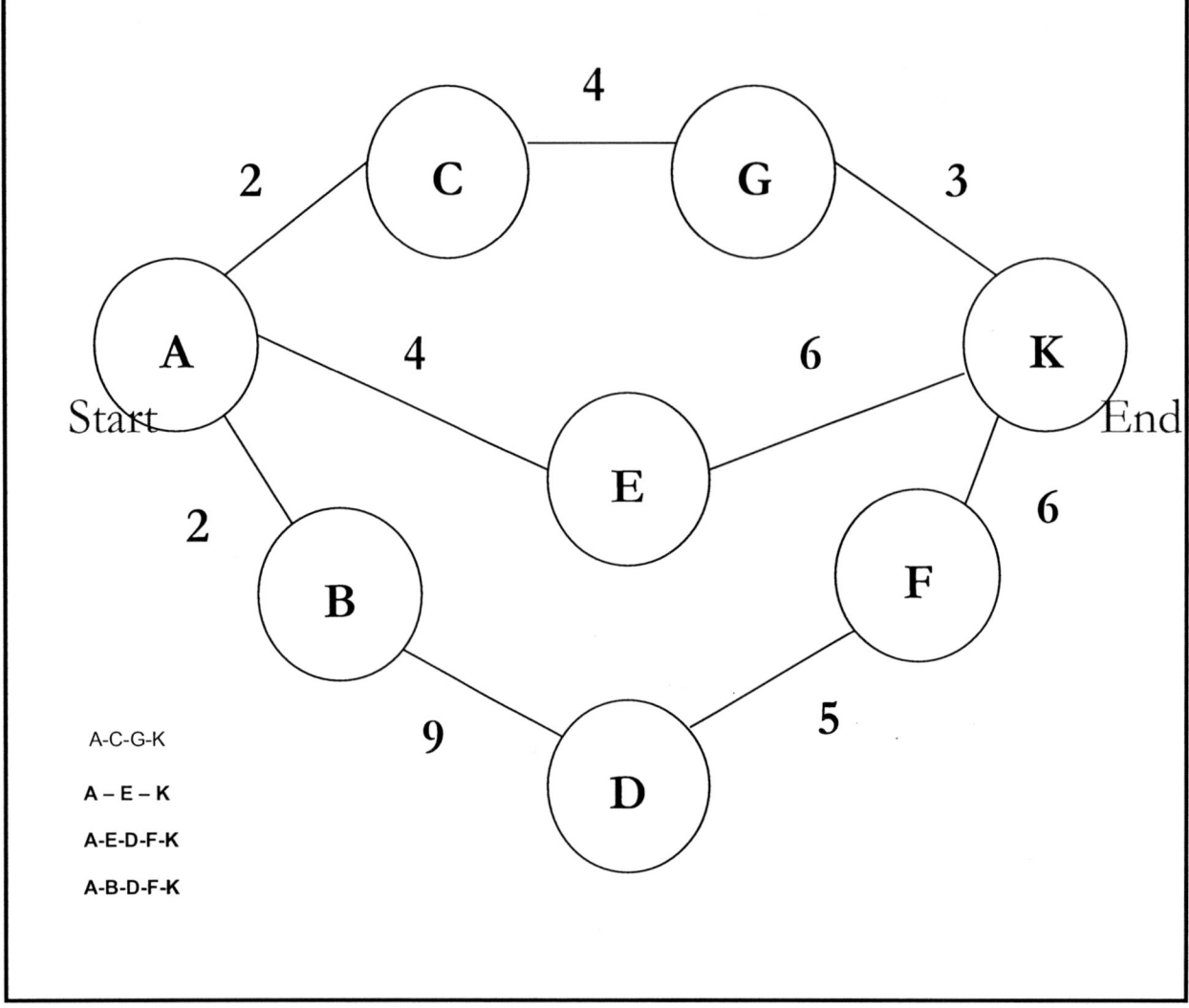

Example: Based on the information given in the diagram:
1. Find the critical path.
2. Find the highest amount of slack time.

The answer to question 1 would be D since the longest time for A to K is A-B-D-F-K which is 22 days. All other tasks must be complete before the 22 day period. The other tasks C, G, and E can start at any time, but must be completed before F is completed in the time line.

The answer to question 2 would be A since A-C-G-K = 9, and when you subtract 9-22 you get 13 (9 – 22 = 13). 13 days is the highest number of slack time when evaluating all other tasks (paths).

Exam Tip: In general, the CISA exams have not included any calculations requiring calculators. However, it is possible that candidates will be asked to calculate the critical path, given a diagram containing a set of activities.

Gantt Charts

Another way that progress can be measured is by the addition of progress lines to the Gantt chart. These progress lines can be used for a graphical representation of task slippage. Use the following instructions to apply progress lines:

- From the **Tools** menu, select **Tracking** and then select **Progress Lines**.
- To show a progress line based upon the project's status date check "**Always display current progress line**" and select "**At project status date**".
- Confirm with **OK** to display:

The "Progress Lines" form

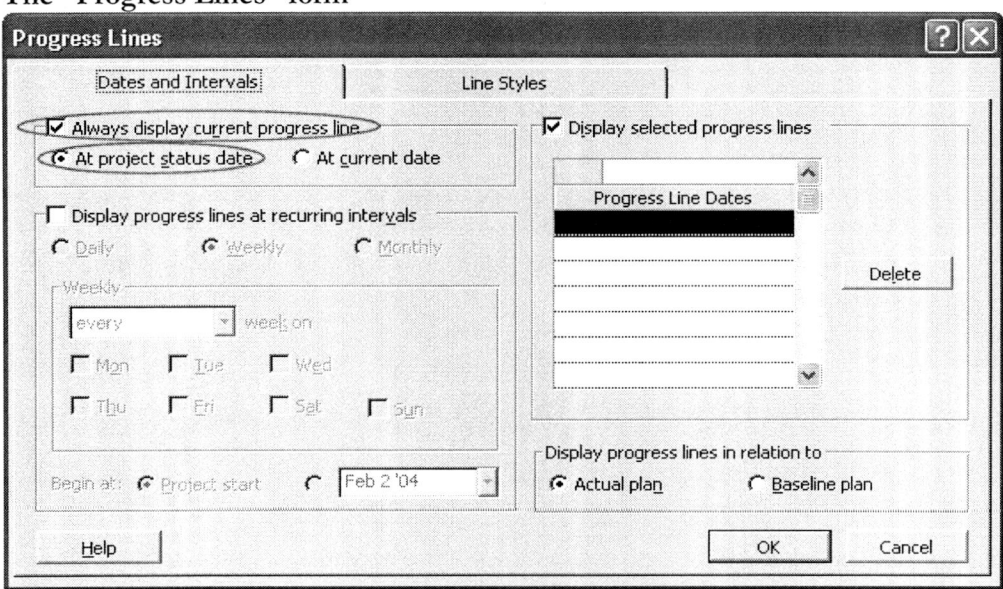

Progress Lines view

The progress line for "**Write body text**" below has been drawn back behind the **Status Date**. This indicates that the task is behind schedule. The progress against the two summary tasks is rolled up from their subtasks. The summary tasks are described as being ahead of schedule.

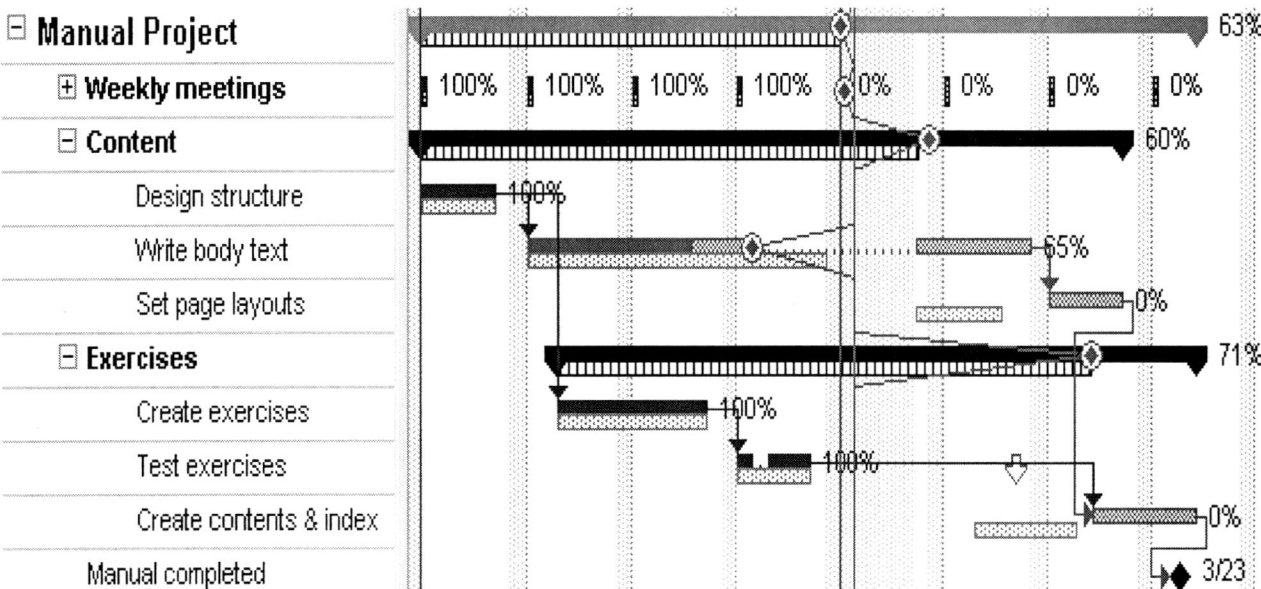

Gantt charts can be constructed to aid in scheduling the activities (tasks) needed to complete a project. The charts show when an activity should begin and when it should end. The charts will also show which activities can be in progress concurrently and which activities must move ahead serially. The charts can also reflect the resources assigned to each task and by what percent of allocation. Gantt charts aid in identifying what will happen if an activity is either completed early or late. The progress of a project can be shown on the charts and, thereby, show if the project is behind, ahead or on schedule.

Project management may be thought of in terms of a "**project management triangle**" or "**triple constraints**". Two popular variations of this triangle have sides representing **time, cost and scope** or **time cost and deliverables**. Gantt charts focus on scheduling (time) but are generally weaker in their representations of cost, scope and deliverables. Depending on the nature of the project and the needs of the project management team, the Gantt chart may be useful, but it may need to be supplemented by methods that allow for a more comprehensive view of the project.

Program Evaluation Review Technique (PERT)
The Program Evaluation Review Technique is a network management technique often used in system development projects that are based on well-defined events and activities for specific project management tasks. **Events** are specific points in time that mark the beginning or ending of one or more activities. Events relate to a specification of time and do not absorb resources. **Activities** are the work that needs to be done. Activities consume resources such as time, material, man-hours, etc.

PERT uses up to four distinct measures for the duration of an activity:
- Optimistic (O): If everything goes very well and ahead of schedule.
- Pessimistic (P): Worst case scenario. The second is the most likely scenario. This estimate is based on experience
- Most Likely Time (M): If all proceeds according to estimated schedules (on time).
- Expected Time (T_E): Derived from the following formula assuming the average of the times it would take for the same project to be performed if it were repeated multiple times: attained from projects similar in size and scope.

To calculate the PERT time estimate for each given task, the following calculation is applied:
$$(T_E) = (4M + O + P)/6$$

The development of a PERT network requires a detailed list of all project activities, a list of any time constraints on deliverables or activities and a list of any activities that require the completion of other activities in order to be initiated. The creation of a WBS with its work packages and a critical path chart would be very helpful for this. The project manager or analyst might utilize several diagrams representing different project stages in order to fully develop a PERT network for a given project.

Timebox Management
Timebox management is an emerging and highly regarded project management technique. Its strength lies in facilitating the development of projects with limited resources, in a short time frame and with little margin for error, replanning or iteration. Timebox management is not suitable for all types of projects. It is contraindicated for medium to large scale projects, projects whose scope spans a large part of the client's organization and projects where quality and security concerns are paramount.

Exam Tip: Candidates should understand the strengths and weaknesses of any project management methodology such as Gantt or PERT charting,

General Project Management Tools and Techniques

Decision support systems

DSSs (Decision Support Systems): These are software packages designed to aid in decision making processes. They are also known as digital or executive dashboards. They rely on installed or imported knowledge bases and may perform either pre-programmed or user-configurable calculations to provide results. One of their chief strengths is that they aggregate all relevant decision and monitoring tools in one application. These packages may use or require: database integration, artificial intelligence, what-if scenarios and business modeling techniques to help generate its results. Due to the complexity of these packages, they are usually expensive and they require a steep learning curve in addition to an intermediate knowledge of business-related mathematics. Many of these packages include routines for project management calculations.

Document Management Systems

DMS (Document Management Systems) are also known as (Enterprise) Content Management Systems or Digital Asset Software. These are specialized database products optimized for storage, retrieval and access management functions related to digital documents. Many of these packages allow the generation and dissemination of reports, copies and other collections of the documents it contains. When connected to a data mining application, the information contained in these documents may be used to help search for new business advantages or opportunities.

Office Automation

Some of the tools in this category such as email are considered vital parts of an organization's communcation network. Other tools such as time and contact management software, voicemail systems and now workflow and forms management are now commonplace. In the rush to increase productivity while decreasing the size of the workforce, tools like these are rapidly becoming essential parts of a company's infrastructure.

Project Control

Project Control is actually a combination of a group of activities related to project management including risk analysis, time and resource allocation, change management processes, etc. Project scope and costs must also be carefully managed. Without adequate control over every stage of a project, the likelihood of cost overruns and delayed deliverables increases while overall quality and chances of the client's approval of the project will decrease.

Closing A Project

Project planning must include the close of a project. The end of a long series of activities cannot be left to chance. Project closing may include, but is not limited to:

- Final contract management tasks
- End User Tests
- Training of users
- Compliation of all relevant documentation/escrow items
- Comparison of product functionality against stated requirements/project approval procedures and sign-offs

Responsibility for the completion of all of these tasks must be clearly and unambiguously assigned and results of these efforts must be recorded and archived. Any infomration from post-mortems or lessons learned should be documented and supplied to the apprpriate change, configuration or problem management personnel for consideration in other projects.

Auditing Project Management

An auditor may be called upon to audit the development of a project or audit the project management process. If reviewing the latter, the auditor should analyze the way that the PMO handles risk and controls at each stage of a development process. The goal of an auditor in this scenario is to observe the management process and provide guidance on the status of its current methods and/or how those methods may be improved.

The organizational hierarchy may be complex and understanding the roles and responsibilities of all the managers and team members may be a tremendous task. However, the organization itself may derive significant cost savings or quality improvements or both from even minor enhancements to its management processes. The role the auditor plays as a risk and control expert may be invaluable to an organization if the result of the audit work results in a competitive advantage. The following represent some of the areas an auditor might review in this type of audit:

- Change, configuration and problem management and control
- Planning and cost/resource/time estimation and control
- Involvement/oversight by senior management, board of directors, IS Steering or Project Management committee
- Risk management methods
- Reporting processes

Documentation of every phase of the SDLC should be planned and implemented This documentation may include:

- List of client requirements; RFP or ITT replies
- List of project deliverables
- Clear and unambiguous assignment of responsibility for each work activity (total amount of work assigned must equal 100%)
- Outline of project objectives divided by project phase:
- A project schedule mapped to economic forecasts/cost and resource allocations.
- Sign-offs from all relevant parties regarding project cost and resource allocations and reporting and authority structures.

Architecture Assessment and Planning

This is a critical stage because it lays the groundwork for the architecture and delivery plan. Three major activities are performed during Stage 2 (Design Phase); information gathering, problem analysis and partitioning, and solution definition, as illustrated in the following figure.

The Phases of Stage 2

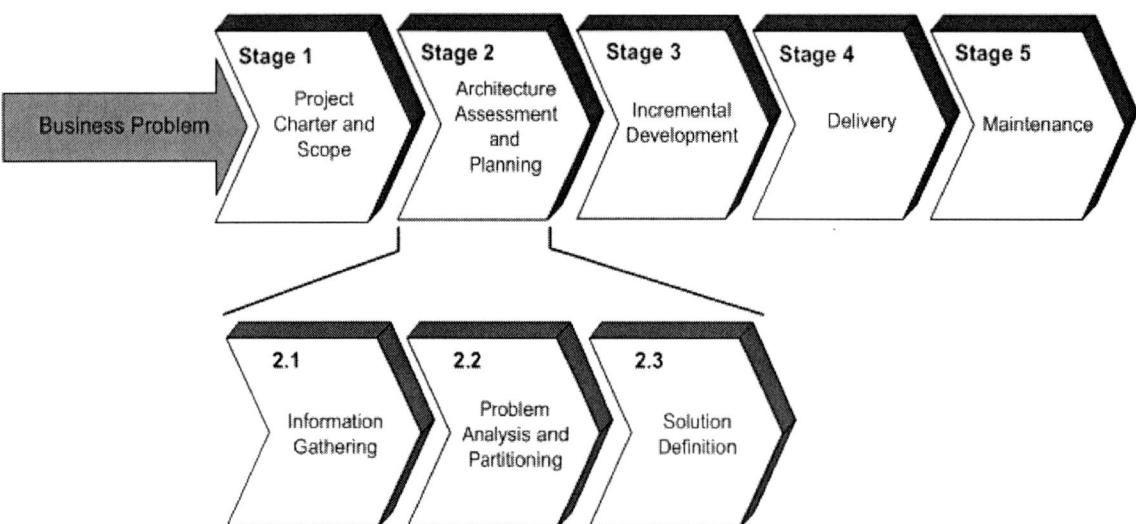

The objective of Stage 2 is to plan the architecture of the system, the inclusion of client requirements and begin the planning for the development and implementation phases (or equivalent phases) of the SDLC in use. The design of the system architecture begins with a bird's eye view of the client's stated business goals and objectives for this project. The requirements supplied by the client area primary concern here and their fulfillment must be carefully planned. Various documentation is usually generated as a result of the design process, which may include the items in the following chart:

Specification Type	Name of Distributed Document
Business Requirements Specification	Use Cases
Technical Requirements Specification	System Requirement Document
System Architecture Specification	Detail Design Document
Information Architecture Specification	Functional Design Document
Integration Architecture Specification	Interface Control Document
Technical Architecture Specification	Technology Architecture
Project Plan	Project Notebook

Information Gathering
Joint Application Design (JAD) is a gathering of people from the IT/development and also tech-savvy representatives of the customer or the business/financial sides of the process. Together, at highly structured workshop sessions these groups translate the high-level requirements submitted by the client into specific work activities or packages. Immediate feedback and focused workshop agendas enhance the usefulness of each session. In addition, a choice of SDLC or other methodologies may be made by this group. A significant savings of both time and money may result from obtaining clear definitions of the stated requirements and expected outcomes of the project at this early phase. At the end of this phase, we can produce:
- **A Use Cases Document --** that provides business requirements specifications
- **A System Requirements Document --** that specifies technical requirements

Problem Analysis and Partition
The design of the architecture may well become an iterative process. This will depend on the stability of the requirements specification and the stability of the business needs and economic climate in which the project must progress. The processes associated with this phase are:
- System Design:
  - A Functional Design Document that embodies the information architecture specification
  - An Interface Control Document that embodies the integration architecture specification
- Solution Definition: The Solution Definition phase is the final phase of Stage 2. It provides the technical foundation for next stage, Incremental Development

Performance Engineering (Development Phase)
The documentation produced during this phase includes:
- A Detailed Design Document that embodies the system architecture specification
- A Technical Architecture Specification that defines the technology architecture
- A more detailed Project Plan that provides the timeline and milestones for project management

Implementation and Change Control Procedures
A Change Management program is an essential part of any development environment. It ensures that:
- Some type of formal change request process exists.
- Any proposed changes mustbe reviewed and properly authorized before implementation of the change may take place.
- All change requests and all approved or denied requests are documented.
- A risk management process is invoked for major issues, at a minimum.
- Changes that affect configuration management or any other processes are documented and any relevant parties in those areas are informed of the change and any potentialproblems that may occur.
- Procedures exist for the handling of emergencies that allow for rapid responses, but still provide for subsequent documentation and review of actions taken.

Authorization for all changes, even "safe" changes, should still be obtained from appropriate levels of management.[8] Updates and patches supplied by product vendors should be subject to the change process; updates to improve one area of functionality have been known to create new problems in other areas. Without testing and a risk analysis, the rollout of some updates may indefinitely "break" the functionality of a vital application.

A formaized change request may include any of the following:
- Submission of an electronic form via a change database.
- Calculations of risk/reward analysis
- The requestor's ID and approval from the requestor's supervisor
- Information regarding the urgency or business need for the proposed change
- Information about security concerns or controls that may be needed if the change is implemented.
- Information about any adverse effects the change may have on other applications or processes.

The manager of the change management program should be responsible for tracking change requests and the results of those requests. In environments where segregation of duties may be difficult to maintain, a strong change management process is a necessary compensating control. In the event that approved changes need to be verified and reversed at a later date, the documentation generated by the approval process should provide a rollback method or at least specifics about what updates or parameters may have been changed.

Change Management Process
The change management process is composed of the following major processes.

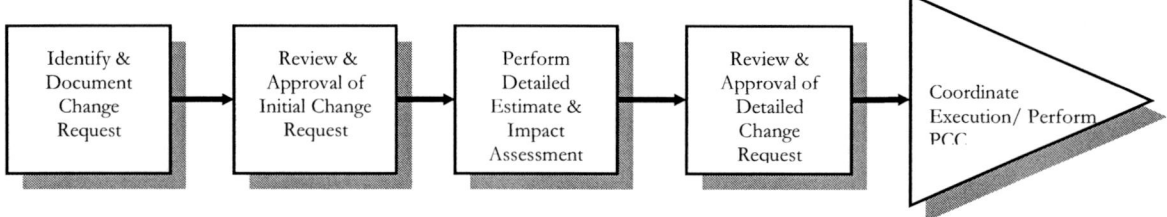

Change Management Detailed Process Flow

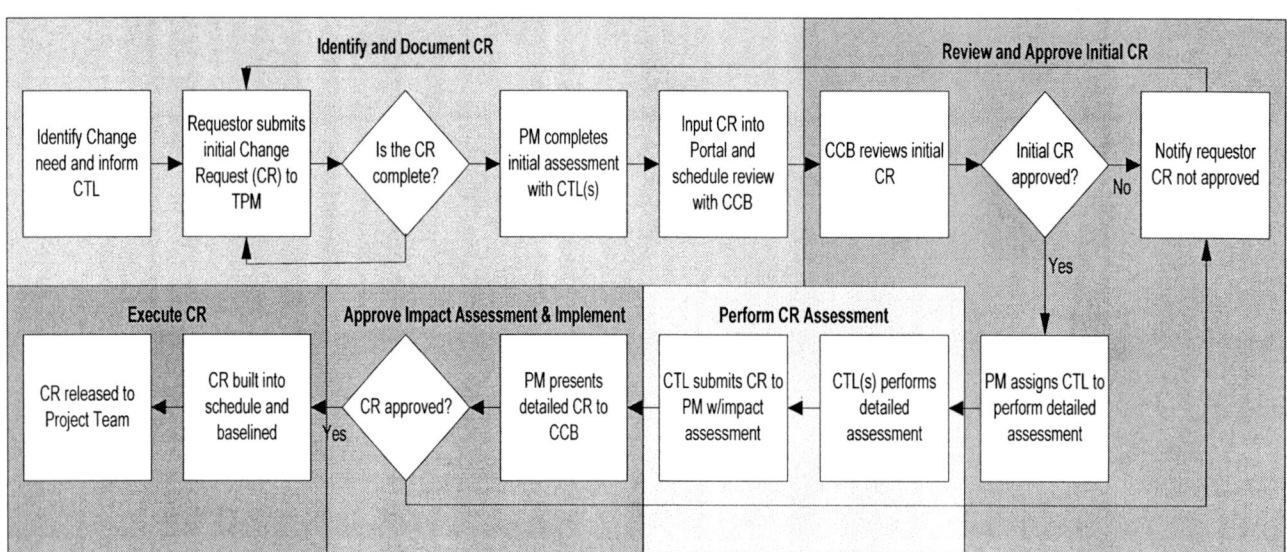

Legend
CCB - Change Control Board
CR - Change Request
CTL - Core Team Lead
PM - Project Manager

Change Management Plan Tracking (CMPT)

The change management process may require that the following items be documented on a change management request form. (See Sample Change Request form below)

- Change Request #
- Track
- Change Request Title
- Requested by
- Date Submitted
- UID
- Initial CCB Review Date
- Assigned To
- Detailed CCB Review Date
- Master Schedule Baseline Version
- Current Disposition Code
- Comments

Identify and Document Change Requests

Document Change Request

Any stakeholder/team member associated with the business management team can initiate a change request (CR). The stakeholder who identifies the need for a change will be responsible for documenting section 1A of the Change Request Form (see the sample Change Request Form below). The change requestor must complete all required section 1A fields. The CR is submitted to the applicable Project Manager. The Project Manager reviews the form to ensure that section 1A is complete.

If section 1A is complete, the Project Manager completes section 1B and then contacts the responsible impacted Core Team Lead(s) to work out an estimated assessment for the Change Control Board. Once the initial assessment is complete, the Project Manager completes section 2A of the CR and schedules a review of the CR with the Change Control Board – CCB (Transition Lead Team). The Project Manager also enters the CR into the CMPT tab of the Program Portal. If section 1A is not complete, the Project Manager returns the CR to the requestor.

Roles and Responsibilities

Role	Responsibility
Project Manager	Review section 1 of the Change Request for completeness Complete initial estimated assessment with impacted team Leads Complete sections 1B and 2A of the Change Request Form Schedule change request for Initial CCB review Enter change request data into the CMPT
Team Leads	Assist the Project Manager with completing the initial estimated assessment
Project Team Members	Assist the Project Manager with completing the initial estimated assessment
Change Requestor	Document section 1 of the Change Request Form and submit to the Project Manager

Timing

The identification of change requests occurs throughout the program life cycle. The Project Manager completes the review and initial assessment of submitted change requests.

Sample Change Request Form

Section 1: Initial Scope Change Request Data			
Section 1 A: Completed by <Requestor>			
Submitted By			
Requestor Company			
Change Request Title			
Description of Proposed CR			
Business Justification for CR			
Date Required By			
Section 1 B: Completed by <Project Manager>			
Change Request #		Track	
Date Submitted		Project Manager	
Section 2: Initial Change Request Assessment			
Section 2A: Completed by <Project Manager>			
Impacted UID # and Task Name			
Initial Impact Assessment			
Initial CCB Review Date			
Section 2B: Completed by <Project Manager>			
Initial CCB Review Disposition	❑ Additional Info Required ❑ Approved ❑ Deferred ❑ Rejected		
Disposition Comments			
Detailed Change Impact Assessment Assignments			

Change Request Form (cont.)

Section 3: Detailed Change Request Assessment
Section 3: Completed by assigned Core Team Lead(s)

Project Milestones Impacts

Milestone Level	UID	Task Name	Current Baseline Finish Date	New Finish Date

Cost Impacts

Incremental Costs	
Incremental Costs	

Incremental Risk Impacts

Risk Description	Impact Description	Probability Rating	Impact Rating	Risk Rating

Section 4: CCB Detailed CR Approvals

Name	Signature	Approval	Date
Transition Executive		☐ Approved ☐ Disapproved	
Transition Manager		☐ Approved ☐ Disapproved	
Business Manager		☐ Approved ☐ Disapproved	
Transition Manager		☐ Approved ☐ Disapproved	

Section 5: CR Execution
Section 5: Completed by <Project Manager>

Master Schedule Baseline Version		Baseline Date	

Program Change Control

Program Change Control (PCC) procedures, often referred to as change control, are established by IS management to control the movement of applications (composed of jobs or programs) from the test environment, where development occurs, to the staging environment, where through testing occurs and then to the production environment. That portion of the PCC mechanism that describes the actions to be performed by IS operations personnel after a job or program has passed user acceptance testing and is to be moved from the staging environment to the production environment is usually referred to as formal job turnover procedures. The procedures associated with this turnover process include ensuring that:

- System, operations and program documentation are complete, up-to-date and in compliance with the established standards.
- Job preparation, scheduling and operating instructions have been established.
- System and program test results have been reviewed and approved by user and project management.
- Data file conversion, if necessary, has occurred accurately and completely as evidenced by review and approval by user management.
- System conversion has occurred accurately and completely as evidenced by review and approval by user management.
- All aspects of jobs turned over have been tested, reviewed and approved by control/operations personnel.

Programmers should not have write, modify or delete access to production data. In addition, they should not have physical access to production machines or user accounts that will enable them to log into production machines. If customer/client PII (Personally Identifiable Information: credit card, social security numbers, etc.) is in use on production machines, it may be necessary to deny even read access to programmers. System software implementation controls include:

- Controls over the design and testing of new software
- Controls over how approved software is placed into production
- Controls to ensure that all impacted system and application software and data are properly converted and verified prior to implementation.

Siftware testing should begin after the completion of design and development and be performed in the following stages:

- Program testing to check the logic of individual programs
- System testing to ensure program and file consistency as they are linked together and that they meet system requirements
- Parallel testing of the new software simultaneously with the existing software. In some cases it will not be possible to perform parallel testing due to resource constraints (such as lack of alternative processing facilities). In such circumstances careful monitoring of the live system should be undertaken during the initial period of live operation. In addition, care must be taken to ensure that the new software can be backed out and the old system restored.

All test results should be documented, reviewed and approved by technically qualified subject area experts prior to production use.

Information Systems Maintenance Practices

	Developer's Library	Test Library	Staging Area	Production Environment
Access				
Change Control	Application Programmer	Application Programmer QA and User	QA Computer Operator	Computer Operator
Change Management	Request is made For a Change	QA User	Owner Acceptance	

Information Systems Maintenance Practices

	Developer Library /Version Control	Production Environment
Access		
Change Control	Programmer takes out a Version of the program	QA or Computer Ops Moves change to prod
Change Management	QA reviews request and accepts Change and performs config mgmt	PMO or Owner accepts change

IN

Information Systems Maintenance Practices

The only constant in a production system is change. Change may occur because of on user preferences, business needs, gain or loss of business opportunities and many other events. **System maintenance controls** refer to the process of modifying application programs, based on organizational needs, while maintaining the integrity of both the production source and executable code. The IS Auditor's tasks include the following:[9]

- Evaluate system maintenance standards and procedures to ensure their adequacy through review of appropriate documentation, discussion with key personnel and observation.
- Test system maintenance procedures to ensure that they are being applied as described in the standards through discussion and examination of supporting records.
- Evaluate the system maintenance process to determine that control objectives were achieved by analyzing test results and other audit evidence.
- Determine the adequacy of production library security to ensure the integrity of the production resources by identifying and testing existing controls.

Deploying Changes

After the end user is satisfied with the system test results and the adequacy of the system documentation, approval should be obtained from user management. User approval should be documented on the original change request via signoffs and possibly by email using digital signatures to provide assurance about the identity of the requestor and the details of the change requested.

Documentation

To ensure the effective utilization and future maintenance of a system, it is important that all relevant system documentation be updated. Due to tight time constraints and limited resources, thorough updates to documentation are often neglected. Documentation requiring revision may consist of program and/or system flowcharts, program narratives, data dictionaries, entity-relationship modules, data flow diagrams (DFDs), operator run books and end-user procedural manuals.[10] Procedures should be in place to ensure documentation stored off-site for disaster recovery purposes are also updated. This documentation is often overlooked and if required during a disaster situation, may be out of date.

Testing of Program Changes

When reviewing program change requests, the IS Auditor should also evaluate the controls on the production and library or backup versions of the applications. The following control objectives should be addressed:

- Whenever possible, electronic forms submission should be used. Verification of data fields on the form may be programmed to check for:
- Blank fields
- Missing approvals and dates
- Missing or inadequate attachments to provide additional information such as risk and cost/benefit analyses, security reviews and impact statements
- Access to program libraries should be restricted.
- Supervisory reviews should be conducted.
- Personnel assigned to implement and verify the change should be noted. Verification of the time and dates of changes and signoffs on that verification should be added.
- Whenever possible, before and after copies of the changed application and copies of the exact code modifications should be made and archived.
- If errors or fraud were introduced into the system, procedures for immediate rollback should exist.

A review of changes may reveal errors or new inconsistencies that were not anticipated. If the verification process did not reveal these errors, the auditor should obtain proof of the findings before reporting them. If proof has been offered and the problem has been confirmed, either a rollback or a change to the change may be required. When segregation of duties is difficult, testing of changes prior to deployment may not be possible. The following list includes control or security exposures that may exist in production environments:

- The programmer has access to production libraries containing programs and data including object code.
- The user responsible for the application was not aware of the change (no user signed the maintenance change request approving the start of the work).
- A change request form and procedures were not formally established.
- The appropriate management official did not sign the change form approving the start of the work.
- The user did not sign the change form signifying acceptance before the change was updated.
- The changed source code was not properly reviewed by the appropriate programming personnel.
- The appropriate management official did not sign the change form approving the program for update to production.
- The programmer put in extra code for personal benefit (i.e., committed fraud).
- Changes received from the acquired software vendor were not tested or the vendor was allowed to load the changes directly into production/site. This particularly happens when in cases of distributed processing sites, such as point-of-sale, banking applications, ATM networks, etc.

Program/Change Migration: Deploying changes into production
In general, programmers should not have access to production data, code or machines. This means that other personnel must be tasked with deploying changes. Oversight of this process should also fall under the umbrella of change management. It is best that documentation regarding testing (if any), deployment, verification of deployment and additional data integrity testing be compiled by a single group. Strong access controls should exist on machines deployed in the production environment and all available auditing or monitoring facilities should be utilized.

Configuration Management
In brief, Configuration management is responsible for tracking and maintaining lists of configuration items, their properties and locations. An example of a CI (Configuration Item) is a user workstation. Any serial numbers, part numbers or other uniquely identifying codes on or within the workstation's case, monitor or peripherals is documented. In addition, the Operating system version, installed patch list and another list of installed applications with their version and patch or release numbers would be included. The amount and type of RAM installed, hard disk size and manufacturer and even the brand of CD-ROM installed would be noted. Finally, the building, room number and even the desk or cubicle number may be included.

A database program or module optimized for use as a configuration database may be purchased and deployed to store and organize all of this information. In theory, once a CI has been properly set up and documented in the database, the only way changes should occur to it are though the change management process or through normal wear and tear. The list of approved CIs is called the **baseline**. Software of this type usually allows the addition of detailed change records for any CI it maintains. New versions of system (or builds) should only be built from the baselined items. Some configuration management software can automate release management tasks to minimize human error and decrease the costs of deploying changes throughout the organization.

Checking in is the process of moving a CI into the controlled environment. When a change is required and supported by a change control form, the item will be checked out by the configuration manager. Once the change is made, it can be checked using a different version number. The process of checking out also prevents or manages simultaneous code edits. As part of the software configuration management task, the maintainer performs the following task steps:
- Develop the configuration management plan.
- Baseline the code and associated documents.
- Analyze and report on the results of configuration control.
- Develop the reports that provide configuration status information.
- Develop release procedures.
- Perform configuration control activities, such as identification and recording of the request.
- Update the configuration status accounting database.

Software Control Features or Parameters
Various operating system software products provide parameters and options for the tailoring of the system and activation of features such as activity logging. Parameters are important in determining how a system runs. Parameter selections should be appropriate to the organization's work load and control environment structure. The most effective means of determining how controls are functioning within an operating system is to review the software control features and/or parameters. Some of the software control parameters deal with:
- Data management
- Resource management
- Job management
- Priority Setting

Activity Logging and Reporting Options
Logging of various computer-related activities may be enabled to create a digital audit trail. The following is a long list of actions that may be logged, audited or monitored. However, this list is not an exhaustive one. Please recall that one of the recommendations an auditor will make during the design phase of a software development product is the addition of this type of functionality to any applications being created:

Success or failure of access attempts to:
- Critical OS files
- Databases/records
- Payroll or other HR information
- Backups/Archived data
- Source or Production code libraries
- Production machines
- Routers, switches, firewalls and other network control devices

- Additions, Modifications to or Deletions of:
  - Any data files deemed critical
  - Log files
  - Production or source code
  - System documentation
  - Payroll or other HR information
  - Program checksums
  - Organizational Policies and procedures

Other System Development Controls
Executable and Source Code Integrity

The applications used to process business transactions must be free of errors or inconsistencies in calculations. In addition, the code must be kept free from malicious tampering. Errors may cause some embarrassment to an organization, but customers may be compensated for losses due to errors with minimal press. However, if fraud can be proven, the organization faces losses due to a loss of reputation in the marketplace. The loss of reputation is not as easy to regain.

Library Management software may be used to facilitate the process of securing access to software. Any accesses or changes to the library or the code it contains can be logged and reported to one or multiple people in the organization. This type of software may be deployed for use by any organization that develops or purchases software used for the purpose of conducting financial or other business-related transactions.

In some environments, financial or other constraints may prohibit the purchase of this type of application, therefore adequate compensating controls must be implemented to provide a similar level of assurance. Physical controls such as doors with biometric locks, security guards and magnetic ID key cards or smart cards may be used to control access to areas where sensitive data and equipment are housed. Logical controls such as access lists applied within the Network OS, the database, the production or code storage machines and within the production applications will form a layered approach to security. The implementation of overlapping security methods is considered an industry best practice and it is strongly recommended for use in production environments.
Library management software usually provides most if not all of the following functionality:
- Denying programmers access to production source and object libraries.
- Enforcing read-only access to library code.
- Requiring strict naming conventions that facilitate the application of access controls.
- Limit update and modification access privilege to a small set of operators or other IT staff.
- Implement access controls that limit the code that may be run by any individual
- Implement time-based constraints on the user accounts allowed to run programs
- Prohibit automated or scripted updates of code within libraries or in production.
- Enforce policies regarding transfer of code to and from programmer access areas.
- Require reviews or verification of any modifications to software be performed by appropriate lead programmers of other supervisory personnel.

Coding Standard Requirements
Coding standards have been mentioned previously as a valid control over the development process. The use of library management software will also help in the implementation and enforcement of these standards. Coding standards do not merely apply to the way that code is entered and compiled. These standards apply to every phase of development including access to test code and data, changes to code or test data, etc. These standards may include:

- A change management process for development code
- Controls over access to libraries and additions or modifications of code revisions
- Controls over test data, scope and even the types of tests that may be performed.
- Documentation and fixes for abends and review of system logs related to these events

Source Code Comparison

Either library management software or other standalone products may be used to document and verify the status of code verified as free of errors or malicious entries. Even the use of digital signatures, when aplied to code, can supply a means by which changes can be identified. The IS auditor may research and suggest options that will provide an organization with a reasonable level of assurance that unauthorized changes may be detected rapidly. Other options include decreasing access to the files and devices where the code is stored or run, storing the code in an encrypted format that may only be unlocked and viewed by authorized personnel and verification procedures for all updates to code in storage or prodcution.

Business Application Systems

Application controls are designed to test the integrity of data and transactions occurring within applications and the validity of transfers of data between applications or program interfaces. The nature of automated transactions makes audit and review efforts very difficult. As a result, application controls can be built into new systems or CAATs (Computer Assisted Audit Techniques) may be run against the data and transactions performed by existing applications. The goal of both efforts is the same, namely, to obtain assurance that data processing efforts are proceed as planned, without error or malicious tampering in place.

An auditor may conclude that the controls in the processing environment are adequate if the results of both automated controls and manual verifications are free of incidents. Application controls include a variety of tests designed to confirm totals, compare inputs and outputs, test the results of calculations, etc. Auditors of automated processing environments need to be aware of the nature of the applications and which tests are best suited to confirm the validity of the data and the results of processing.

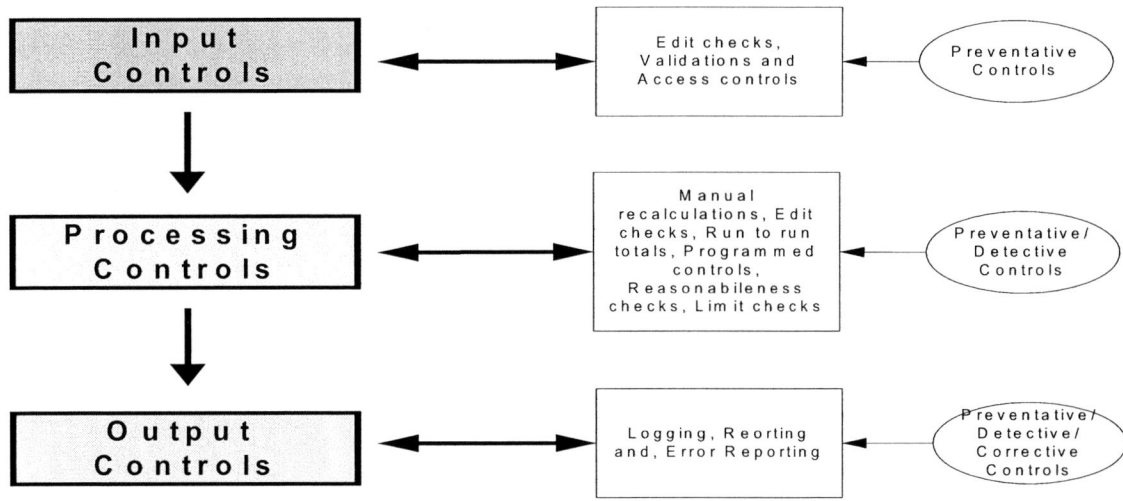

Input/Origination Controls

In general, the types of tests that are most appropriate for use as input controls are edit checks, validations and access controls. If the data that enters the system is incorrect in any way, then it is unlikely that the problem will be caught during subsequent tests if all the calculations are performed properly. If it is possible, the applications should provide means by which tests of this type might be performed automatically. Alternatives would include the purchase of additional software that would perform the input security tests or additional verification and authorization procedures applied to data while it is considered an "output" from another application or storage media.

Authorization Control Type	Description
Signatures on batch forms or source documents	Provide evidence of proper authorization
Online access controls	Ensure that only authorized individuals may access data or perform sensitive functions
Unique passwords	Necessary to ensure that access authorization cannot be compromised through use of another individual's authorized data access. Individual passwords also provide accountability for data changes.
Terminal or workstation identification	Used to limit input to specific terminals or workstations as well as to individuals. Terminals or client workstations in a network can be configured with a unique form of identification, such as serial number or computer name that is authenticated by the system.
Source documents	The forms used to record data. A source document may be a piece of paper, a turnaround document or an image displayed for online data input. A well designed source document achieves several purposes. It increases the speed and accuracy with which data can be recorded, controls work flow, facilitates preparation of the data in machine readable form for pattern recognition devices, increases the speed and accuracy with which data can be read and facilitates subsequent reference checking. Ideally, source documents should be preprinted forms, to provide consistency, accuracy and legibility. Source documents should include standard headings, titles, notes and instructions. Source document layouts should: • Emphasize ease of use and readability • Group similar fields together to facilitate input • Provide predetermined input codes to reduce errors • Contain appropriate cross reference numbers or a comparable identifier to facilitate research and tracing • Use boxes to identify field size errors • Include an appropriate area for management to document authorization All source documents should be appropriately controlled. If source documents are not pre-numbered, procedures should be established to ensure that all source documents have been input and accounted for.

Input Batch Controls

Batch controls group input transactions to provide control totals. The batch control can be based on total monetary amount, total items, total documents or hash totals. Batch header forms are a data preparation control. The goal of this type of control is to confirm that some type of number representing an approved set of transactions is the same as a number representing the set of transactions received for processing. Forms or digital files containing transaction codes with these totals should be used to provide accurate comparisons Types of batch controls include:

Authorization Control Type	Description
Total monetary amount	Verification that the total monetary value of items processed equals the total monetary value of the batch documents. For example, the total monetary value of the sales invoices in the batch agrees with the total monetary value of the sales invoices processed.
Total items	Verification that the total number of items included on each document in the batch agrees to the total number of items processed. For example, the total number of units ordered in the batch of invoices agrees with the total number of units processed.
Total documents	Verification that the total number of documents in the batch equals the total number of documents processed. For example, the total number of invoices in a batch agrees with tile total number of invoices processed.
Hash totals	Verification that the total (albeit meaningless in itself) for a predetermined numeric field that exists for all documents in a batch agrees with the total calculated by the system. For example, a total of customer account numbers is meaningless, but can be manually calculated and compared to the system calculated value.

Batch balancing is used to track the integrity of verified batches of transactions throughout the various stages of processing. Balancing controls are used in conjucntion with controls on batch totals. Types of batch balancing include:

Authorization Control Type	Description
Batch registers	These registers enable manual recording of batch totals and subsequent comparison with system reported totals.
Control accounts	Control account use is performed through an initial edit file to determine batch totals. The data are then processed to the master file and reconciliation is performed between the totals processed during the initial edit file and the master file.
Computer agreement	Computer agreement with batch totals is performed through the input of batch header details that record the batch totals; the system compares these to calculated totals, either accepting or rejecting the batch.

Input Error Reporting

Input errors may result from a variety of events involving changes in electrical voltage, duplicated transactions, mistakes in manual inputs, and calculation/conversion errors. Controls that handle this type of error include the following:

Authorization Control Type	Description
Rejecting only transactions with errors	Only transactions containing errors would be rejected; the rest of the batch would be processed.
Rejecting the whole batch of transactions	Any batch containing errors would be rejected for correction prior to processing
Holding batch in suspense	Any batches containing errors would not be rejected; however, the batch would be held in suspense pending correction.
Accepting batch and flagging error transactions	Any batch containing errors would be processed; however, those transactions containing errors would be flagged for identification enabling subsequent error correction.

Authorization Control Type	Description
Transaction log	Contains a detailed list of all updates. The log can be either manually maintained or provided through automatic computer logging. A transaction log can be reconciled to the number of source documents received to verify that all transactions have been input.
Reconciliation of data	Controls whether all data received are properly recorded and processed
Documentation	Written evidence of user, data entry and data control procedures
Error correction procedures	These include: • Logging of errors Timely corrections • Upstream resubmission • Approval of corrections • Suspense file • Error file • Validity of corrections
Cancellation of source documents	Procedures to cancel source documents, for example, by punching with holes or marking them to avoid duplicate entry.

Processing Procedures and Controls

One way of conducting an audit of data transactions is to view those transactions as a series of inputs and outputs. In fact, the data that is the output of one stage of a transaction or calculation will become an input of the next processing stage. Auditors should become familiar with data flow diagrams in order to better understand the nature of the input/output sequences involved. Whenever possible, tests and controls of data should be performed as soon as possible after the data has moved past an origination point (output). These controls include the types mentioned before and also checks of data format and structure. These controls should:

- Confirm that data conforms to predetermined standards or falls within specified parameter values.
- Establish Identify the procedures for aggregating and forwarding accurate information on control totals at each stage of processing
- Provide a means of verifying valid transaction in the event of a loss of power or other major event.
- Provide a means to verify that data is accepted only from approved sources, processed securely and forwarded only to approved destination files or applications
- Confirm the accuracy of validation routines and assure that the audit trail is complete from the beginning to the end of the processing effort.

The following are processing control techniques that can be used to address the issues of completeness and accuracy of accumulated data:

Control Type	Description
Manual recalculations	A sample of transactions may be recalculated manually to ensure that processing is accomplishing the anticipated task.
Editing	An edit check is a program instruction or subroutine that tests the accuracy, completeness and validity of data. It may be used to control input or later processing of data.
Run-to-run totals	Run-to-run totals provide the ability to verify data values through the stages of application processing. Run-to-run total verification ensures that data read into the computer was accepted and then applied to the updating process.
Programmed controls	Software can be used to detect and initiate corrective action for errors in data and processing. For example, if the incorrect file or file version is provided for processing, the application program could display messages instructing that the proper file and version be used.
Reasonableness verification of calculated amounts	Application programs can verity the reasonableness of calculated amounts. Tile reasonableness can be tested to ensure appropriateness to predetermined criteria. Any transaction that is determined to be unreasonable may be rejected pending further review.
Limit checks on calculated amounts	An edit check can provide assurance, through the use of predetermined limits, that calculated amounts have not been keyed incorrectly. Any transaction exceeding the limit may be rejected for further investigation.
Reconciliation of file totals	Reconciliation of file totals should be performed on a routine basis. Reconciliations may be performed through the use of a manually maintained account, a file control record or an independent control file.
Exception reports	An exception report is generated by a program that identifies transactions or data that appear to be incorrect. These items may be outside a predetermined range or may not conform to specified criteria.

Output Controls

Output controls should help an auditor to:
- Identify and view the procedures for ensuring completeness of output
- Confirm that all expected output is appears as expected and falls within reasonable value ranges
- Confirm that output serves a useful purpose and that its confidentiality is maintained
- Verify that output is only used for approved purposes
- Confirm that error handling procedures are adequate
- Verify the completeness of the audit trail through the output cycle
- Provide assurance that the data delivered to users will be presented, formatted and delivered in a consistent and secure manner

Output controls include the following:

Control Type	Description
Logging and storage of negotiable, sensitive and critical forms in a secure place	Negotiable, sensitive or critical forms should be properly logged and secured to provide adequate safeguards against theft or damage. The form log should he routinely reconciled to have inventory on hand, and any discrepancies should he properly researched.
Computer generation of negotiable instruments, forms and signatures	The computer generation of negotiable instruments forms and signatures should be properly controlled. A detailed listing of generated forms should be compared to the physical forms received. All exceptions, rejections and mutilations should be accounted for properly.
Report distribution	Output reports should be distributed according to authorized distribution parameters, which may be automated or manual. Operations personnel should verify that output reports are complete and that they are delivered according to schedule. All reports should be logged prior to distribution. In most environments, processing output is spooled to a buffer or print spool upon completion of job processing, where it waits for an available printer. Controls over access to the print spools are important to prevent reports from being deleted accidentally from print spools or directed to a different printer. In addition, changes to the output print priority can delay printing of critical jobs.

Access to distributed reports can compromise confidentiality. Therefore, physical distribution of reports should be controlled adequately. Reports containing sensitive data should be printed under secured, controlled conditions. Secured output drop-off points should be established. Output disposal also should be secured adequately to ensure that no unauthorized access can occur. Reports that are distributed electronically through the computer system also need to be considered.

Logical access to these reports also should be controlled carefully and subject to authorization. When distributed manually, assurance should be provided that sensitive reports are properly distributed. Such assurance should include the recipient signing a log as evidence of receipt of output. |
Balancing and reconciling	Data processing applicationError! Bookmark not defined. program output should be balanced routinely to the control totals. Audit trails should be provided to facilitate the tracking of transaction processing and the reconciliation of data.
Output error handling	Procedures for reporting and controlling errors contained in tile application program output should be established. The error report should be timely and delivered to the originating department for review and error correction.
Output report retention	A record retention schedule should be adhered to firmly. Any governing legal regulations should be included in the retention policy.
Verification of receipt of reports	To provide assurance that sensitive reports are properly distributed the recipient should sign a log as evidence of receipt of output.

Data Validation Controls

Data validation identifies data errors, incomplete or missing data and inconsistencies among related data items. Front-end data editing and validation can be performed if intelligent terminals are used. Edit controls are preventive controls that are used in a program, before data are processed. If the edit control is not in place or does not work effectively, the preventive control measures do not work effectively. This may cause processing of inaccurate data.

Edit Control	Description
Sequence Checks	The control number follows sequentially and any out of sequence or duplicated control numbers are rejected or noted on an exception report for follow-up purposes. For example, invoices are numbered sequentially. The day's invoices begin with 12001 and end with 15045. If any invoice larger than 15045 is encountered during processing, that invoice would be rejected as an invalid invoice number.
Limit check	Data should not exceed a predetermined amount. For example, payroll checks should not exceed US $4,000. If a check exceeds US $4,000, the data would be rejected for further verification/authorization.
Range check	Data should be within a predetermined range of values. For example, product type codes range from 100 to 250. Any code outside this range should be rejected as an invalid product type.
Validity check	Programmed checking of the data validity in accordance with predetermined criteria. For example, a payroll record contains a field for marital status and the acceptable status codes are M or S. If any other code is entered the record should be rejected.
Reasonableness check	Input data are matched to predetermined reasonable limits or occurrence rates. For example, in most instances, a widget manufacturer usually receives orders for no more than 20 widgets. If an order for more than 20 widgets is received, the computer program should be designed to print the record with a warning indicating the order appears unreasonable.
Table look-ups	Input data complies with predetermined criteriaError! Bookmark not defined. in a computerized table of possible values. For example, the input clerk enters a city code of 1 to 10. This number corresponds with a computerized table that matches the code to city name.
Existence check	Data are entered correctly and agree with valid predetermined criteria. Or example, a valid transaction code must be entered in the transaction field.
Key Verification	Keying-in process is repeated by separate individual using a machine that compares the original keystrokes to the repeated keyed input. For example, the worker number is keyed twice and compared to verify the keying process.
Check Edit	A numerical value that has been calculated numerically is added to data to ensure that the original data have not been altered or that an incorrect but valid value substituted. This control is effective in detecting transposition and transcription errors. For example, a check edit is added to an account number so it can be checked for accuracy when it is used.
Completeness check	A field should always contain data and not zeroes or blanks. A check of each byte of that field should be performed to determine that some form of data, not blanks or zeros, is present. For example, a worker number on anew employee record is left blank. This is identified as a key field and the record would be rejected, with a request that the field be completed before the record is accepted for processing.
Duplicate check	New transactions are matched to those previously input to ensure that they have not already been entered. For example, a vendor invoice agrees with previously recorded invoices to ensure that the current order is not a duplicate and therefore, the vendor will not be paid twice.
Logical relationship check	If a particular condition is true, then one or more additional conditions or data input relationships may be required to be true and consider the input valid. Or example, the hire date of an employee may be required to be more than sixteen years past his or her date of birth.

Data File Control Procedures

File controls should ensure that only authorized processing occurs to stored data. Types of controls over data files are:

Method	Description
Before and after image reporting	Computer data on a file prior to and after a transaction is processed can be reported. The before and after images make it possible to trace the impact of the transaction.
Maintenance error reporting and handling	Control procedures should be in place to ensure that all error reports are properly reconciled and the corrections are submitted on a timely basis. To ensure segregation of duties, error corrections should be reviewed properly and authorized by personnel who did not initiate the transaction.
Source documentation retention	Source documentation should be retained for an adequate time period to enable retrieval, reconstruction or verification of data. Polices regarding the retention of source documentation should be enforced. Originating departments should maintain copies of source documentation and ensure that only authorized personnel have access. When appropriate, source documentation should be destroyed in a secure, controlled environment.
Internal and external labeling	Internal and external labeling of removable storage media is imperative that the proper data are loaded for processing. External labels provide the basic level of assurance that the correct data medium is loaded for processing. Internal labels, including file header records, provide the proper data files are used and allow for automated checking.
Version usage	It is critical that the proper version of a file be used as well as the correct file, for processing to be correct. For example, transactions should be applied to the most current database, while restart procedures should use earlier versions.
Data file security	Data file security controls prevent unauthorized access by unauthorized users that may have access to the application to alter data files. These controls do not provide assurances relating to the validity of data, but ensure that the unauthorized users, who may have access to the application, cannot alter stored data improperly.
One-for-one checking	Individual documents agree with a detailed listing of documents processed by the computer. It is necessary to ensure that all documents have been received for processing.
Prerecorded input	Certain information fields are preprinted on blank input forms to reduce initial input errors.
Transaction logs	All transaction input activity is recorded by the computer. A detailed listing, including date of input, user ID and terminal location, can then be generated to provide an audit trail. It also permits operations present to determine which transactions have been posted. This will help to decrease the research time needed to investigate exceptions and to decrease recovery time, if a system failure occurs.
File updating and maintenance authorization	Proper authorization for file updating and maintenance is necessary to ensure that stored data are safeguarded adequately, correct and up-to-date. Application programs may contain access restrictions in addition to the overall system access restrictions. The additional security may provide levels of authorization as well as an audit trail of file maintenance.
Parity checking	Data transfers in a computer system are expected to be made in a relatively error-free environment. However, when programs or vital data are transmitted, additional controls are needed. Transmission errors are controlled primarily by error detecting or correcting codes. The former is used more often because error-correcting codes are costly to implement and are unable to correct all errors. Generally error detection methods such as a check bit and redundant transmission are adequate redundancy checking is a common error-detection routine. A transmitted block of data containing one or more records or messages is checked for the number of characters or patterns of bits contained in it. If the numbers or patterns do not confirm to predetermined parameters, the receiving device ignores the transmitted data and instructs the user to retransmit. Check bits are often added to the transmitted data by the telecommunications control unit and may be applied either horizontally or vertically. These checks are similar to the parity checks normally applied to data characters within on-premises equipment. A parity check on a single character is normally referred to as a vertical or column check; and a parity check on all the equivalent bits is known as horizontal, longitudinal or row check. Use of both checks greatly improves the possibilities of detecting a transmission error, which may be missed when either of those checks is used alone.

Exam Tip: Any of the application tests and controls listed above or in subsequent sections may appear on an exam. Information relating to one or more of these tests may appear in test questions, in the proposed answers or both. CISA candidates should be familiar with the broad categories of test types and the specific purposes of individual tests as well.

The IS auditor's tasks in application control review include the following:
- Identifying the significant application components and the flow of transactions through the system, and gaining a detailed understanding of the application by reviewing the available documentation and interviewing appropriate personnel
- Identifying the application control strengths, and evaluating the impact of the control weaknesses on the development of a testing strategy by analyzing the accumulated information
- Testing the controls to ensure their functionality and effectiveness by applying appropriate audit procedures
- Evaluating the control environment to determine that control objectives were achieved through analyzing the test results and other audit evidence
- Considering the operational aspects of the application to ensure its efficiency and effectiveness by comparing the system with efficient programming standards, analyzing procedures used and comparing them to management's objectives for the system

Application Types
Electronic Commerce
Electronic Commerce (e-commerce) refers to the sale and purchase of goods and services via the Internet or other digital media. Typically, a web site will advertise goods and services, and a buyer will fill in a form on the site to select the items to be purchased, enter personally identifiable information (PII) and provide delivery and payment details. The web site may gather details about customers and offer other items that may be of interest. The costs associated with brick and mortar establishments may be avoided altogether and some of the savings may be passed on to customers, which increases the likelihood of repeat business.

The term e-business includes buying and selling online as well as other aspects of online business, such as customer support or relationships between businesses. E-commerce, as a general model, is achieved by the use of technology to enhance the processes of commercial transactions among a company, its customers and business partners. The technology in use may include the Internet, streaming media, web browsers, proprietary networks, ATMs and home banking. In addition, for many business-to-business (B2B) transactions, the traditional approach to EDI is still heavily favored. At this time, the primary cause of growth in e-commerce is the increasing use of the Internet as an enabling technology.

There are many choices to be made when attempting to implement an appropriate e-commerce architecture. Initially, e-commerce architectures were either two tiered (i.e., client browser and web server), or three tiered (i.e., client browser, web server and database server). With increasing emphasis on integrating the web channel with a business' internal legacy systems and the systems of its business partners, company systems now typically will run on different platforms, using different software, and centered on different databases. In addition to supporting browser connections, companies eventually may move in the direction of supporting connections from active content clients, mobile phones or other wireless devices, and host-to-host connections.

The challenge of integrating diverse technologies within and beyond the walls of the business has caused many companies to move to component-based systems. In general, these systems utilize a three-tier infrastructure, utilizing a back-end database or application server, a middleware layer and a presentation layer or interface. This supports current trends in the evolution of software development, namely, building systems from components with proven quality and functionality. An example of an e-commerce infrastructure is shown below:

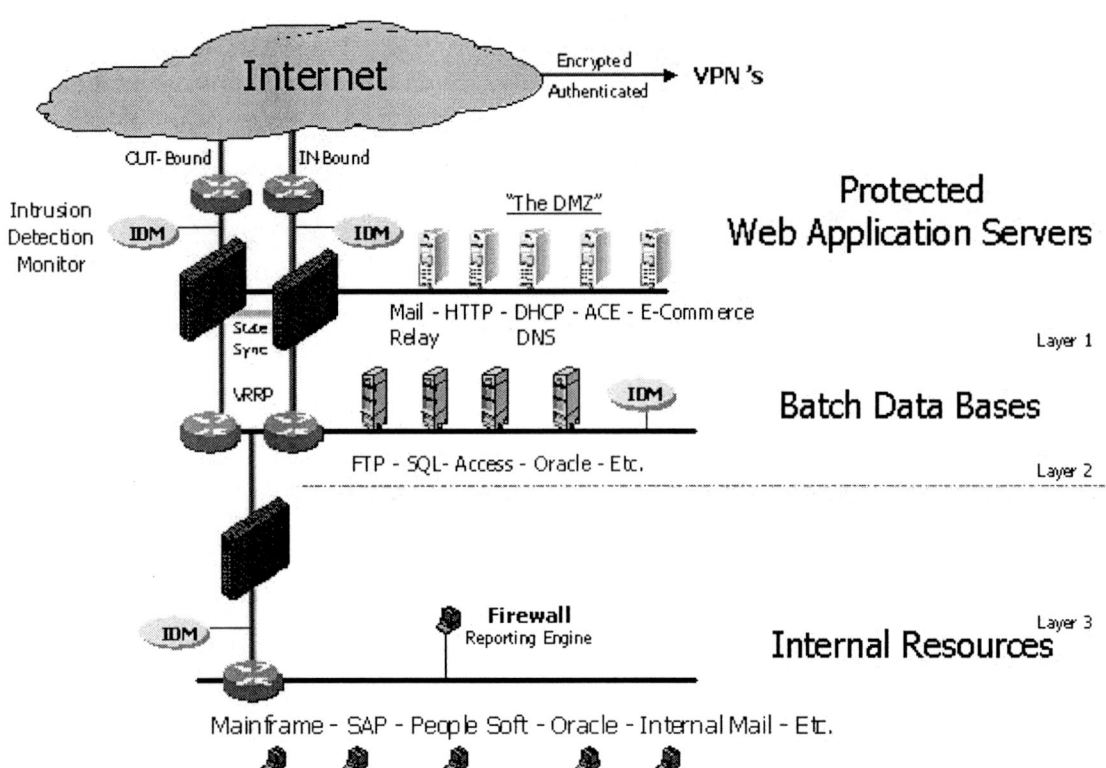

Application servers normally support a particular component model and provide services, such as data management, security and transaction management, either directly or through connection to another service or middleware product, such as MQSeries. A number of major software vendors, including BEA, IBM, Oracle, Sybase and others, now offer application servers. Microsoft offers their version of an application server, Distributed Transaction Coordinator as a standard part of the Windows 2003 server operating system. Application servers in conjunction with other middleware products allow development of multi-tiered systems. This type of application architecture allows the user interface to remain separate from the details of back-end processing and vice-versa. Either end may be changed without necessitating a change on the other end.

Databases play a key role in most e-commerce systems. They maintain data for web pages, accumulate customer information, store click-stream data for analyzing web site usage, allow searches of product catalogs and provide many other services. To provide full functionality and achieve back-end efficiencies, an e-commerce system may require connections to in-house legacy systems, including accounting, inventory management, an ERP (Enterprise Resource Planning) or a BI (Business Intelligence)/data mining system. As a result, additional business logic and data persistence tiers are added.

Extensible Markup Language (XML) is also likely to form an important part of an organization's overall e-commerce architecture. XML was originally conceived as a technique to facilitate electronic publishing, but was quickly seized upon as a medium that could store any kind of structured information and could enclose information so that it could be passed between different computing systems. XML has emerged as a key means of exchanging a wide variety of data on the web and elsewhere. In addition to basic XML, a variety of associated standards is continuing to be developed. Some of these standards include:
- Extensible Stylesheet Language (XSL)-Used to define Row an XML document is to be presented, e.g., on a web page
- XML Query (XQuery)-Deals with querying XML format data
- XML Encryption-Deals with encrypting and decrypting and digitally signing XML documents

As mentioned previously, XML and its related standards help to facilitate access to Web Services (APIs or Application Programming Interfaces related to Internet servers and applications). Web Services represent a way of using XML format information to remotely invoke processing. Web Services messages can contain both an XML document and a corresponding schema defining the document. This means that they are self-describing which lines up well with the development goal of "loose coupling." If the format of a Web Services message changes, the receiving Web Services will still work provided the accompanying schema is updated. This advantage, combined with the support for Web Services that has emerged from major software industry players, e.g. IBM, Microsoft and SUN, means Web Services may soon become the key middleware technology used to connect distributed web systems. Cooperation between the W3C (World Wide Web Consortium) and the different software vendors means that Web Services can communicate in spite of differences in hardware, operating system and programming languages that may be used. Development environments such as Microsoft's.NET and Sun's ONE (Open Net Environment) support Web Services.

E-Commerce Control Issues

The use of a public medium such as the Internet to carry private transaction information provides many security challenges to an organization and its IT staff. Many controls are needed to provide assurance of data integrity and confidentiality in this type of scenario. Various technologies have been developed that attempt to address some or all of the security issues that the Internet presents. Regardless of the technology chosen, IS auditors should carefully review all of the following when making an assessment of any e-business solutions:

- The security mechanisms and procedures implemented as a security architecture for e-commerce (e.g., Internet firewalls, PKI, encryption, certificates and password management)
- The firewall, remote access and IDS/IPS (Intrusion Detection/Intrusion Prevention Systems) that protect an organization's private network from whatever may occur on the public network (the Internet)
- The procedures in place to control changes to an e-commerce presence
- A process whereby participants in an e-commerce transaction can be identified uniquely and positively (e.g., process of using some combination of public and private key encryption and certifying key pairs)
- Digital signatures, so the initiator of an e-commerce transaction can be uniquely associated with it. Attributes of digital signatures include:
    - The digital signature is unique to the person using it.
    - It can be verified.
    - The mechanism for generating and affixing the signature is under the sole control of the person using it.
    - It is mathematically linked to data (or a web site/server) in such a manner that if the data (or device information) is changed, the digital signature is invalidated.
- An infrastructure to manage and control public key pairs (i.e., public key infrastructure-PKI) and their corresponding certificates which include:
    - **Certificate authority (CA)** Attests, as trusted provider of the public/private key pairs, to the authenticity of the owner (entity or individual) to whom a public/private key pair has been given. The process involves a CA trusting the verification of the recipient provided by the RA. When the RA provides the information, the CA issues a certificate to the requestor. End users trust the certificate of the CA, the CA trusts the verification provided by the RA and the RA verifies the information provided by the requestor. Therefore a PKI utilizes a web of trust to perform its functions..
    - **Registration authority (RA)** An optional entity separate from a CA that would be used by a CA with a very large customer base. CAs use RAs to handle the verification of a user's information. In this arrangement, the CA still retains sole responsibility for signing either digital certificates or CRLs.
    - **Certification revocation list (CRL)**-Instrument for checking the continued validity of the certificates. If a certificate is compromised, if the holder is no longer authorized to use the certificate or if there is a fault in binding the certificate to the holder, then that certificate must be revoked and taken out of circulation immediately. The CRL is usually a highly controlled online database through which subscribers and administrators may determine the status of a target partner's certificate.
    - **Certification practice statement (CPS)**-A CPS is a detailed set of rules governing the certificate authority's operations. It provides an understanding of the value and trustworthiness of certificates issued by a given CA, the terms of the controls that an organization observes, the method it uses to validate the authenticity of certificate applicants and the CA's expectations of how its certificates may be used.

- Logs of e-commerce applications, which should be monitored by responsible personnel includes operating system logs and console messages, network management messages, firewall logs and alerts, router management messages, intrusion detection alarms, application and server statistics, and system integrity checks
- Transaction logging and disaster recovery methods built into databases and other critical applications.
- Hardware failover and telecommunications redundancy mechanisms
- The privacy policies and procedures implemented by the organization.
- The means to ensure confidentiality of data communicated between customers and vendors (safeguarding resources such as through encrypted secure sockets layer-SSL)
- Anti-virus anti-spyware and other hacking prevention methods.
- An Information Security Policy
- Industry standards for security implemented by the organization and communicated to external parties.
- An iterative and regular program of security program audit and assessment

Electronic Data Interchange

Electronic data interchange (EDI) has been in use for more than 20 years. It was one of the first e-commerce applications that allowed organizations with different computer systems to securely conduct business transactions over a public medium. It involves the exchange and transmittal of business documents, such as invoices, purchase orders and shipping notices, in a standardized, machine-processable format. Even the record types and field definitions have been standardized.

General Requirements

An EDI system requires communications software, translation software and access to standards. Communications software moves data from one point to another, flags the start and end of an EDI transmission, and determines how acknowledgements are transmitted and reconciled. Translation software helps build a map and shows how the data fields from the application correspond to elements of an EDI standard. Later, it uses this map to convert data back and forth between the application and EDI formats. To build a map, an EDI standard appropriate for the kind of EDI data to be transmitted is selected. For example, there are specific standards for invoices, purchase orders, advance shipping notices, etc. The final step is to write a partner profile that tells the system where to send each transaction and how to handle errors and exceptions.

To sum up, the components of an EDI process include system software and application systems. EDI system software includes transmission, translation and storage of transactions initiated by or destined for application processing. EDI is also an application system in that the functions it performs are based on business needs and activities. The applications, transactions and trading partners supported will change over time. Changes in the mixture of transactions, purchase orders, shipping notices, invoices and payments in the EDI process makes it necessary to include application processing procedures and controls in the EDI process. In reviewing EDI, IS auditors need to be aware of the two approaches related to EDI, the traditional proprietary version of EDI used by large companies and the development of Web-based EDI facilitated by newer standards for cross-platform communications

Traditional EDI

Moving data in a batch transmission process through the traditional EDI process generally involves three functions within each trading partner's computer system:

Function	Description
1. Communications handler	Process for transmitting and receiving electronic documents between trading partners via dial-up lines, public switched network, multiple dedicated lines or a **value added network** (VAN). VANS use computerized message switching and storage capabilities to provide electronic mail box services similar to a post office. The VAN receives all the outbound transactions from an organization, sorts them by destination and passes them to recipients when they login to check their mail box and receive transmissions. VANS may also perform translation and verification services. VANS specializing in EDI applications also provide technical support; help desk, and troubleshooting assistance for EDI and telecommunication problems. VANS help in configuration of software, offer upgrades to telecommunications connectivity, provide data and computer security, audit and trace transactions, recover lost data, and confirm service reliability and availability.
2. EDI Interface	This function manipulates and routes data between the application system and the communications handler. The interface consists of two components: • **EDI** translator-This device translates the data between the standard formats (ANSI X12) and a trading partner's proprietary format. • **Application interface**-This interface moves electronic transactions to or from the application systems and performs data mapping. **Data mapping** is the process by which data are extracted from the EDI translation process and integrated with the data or processes of the receiving company. The EDI interface may generate and send functional acknowledgments, verify the identity of partners and check the validity of transactions by checking transmission information against a trading partner master file. **Functional acknowledgments** are standard EDI transactions that tell the trading partners that their electronic documents were received. Different types of functional acknowledgments provide various levels of detail and can therefore act as an audit trail for EDI transactions.
3. Application system	The programs that process the data sent to, or received from, the trading partner. Although new controls should be developed for the EDI interface, the controls for existing applications, if left unchanged, are usually unaffected.

Application-initiated transactions, such as purchase orders from the purchasing system, are passed to a common application interface for storage and interpretation. All outbound transactions are formatted according to an accepted EDI standard and batched by destination and transaction type by the translator. The batches of transactions, like functional groups, are routed to the communications processor for transmission. The process is reversed for inbound transactions, including invoices destined for purchasing and accounts payable systems. A well-designed and well-managed EDI implementation will have adequate controls for error handling and reporting.

Web-Based EDI
Web-based EDI is becoming the most common type of EDI process because of the following:
- **Internet Service Providers** (ISPs) offer generic network access (i.e., not specific to EDI) for all computers connected to the Internet, whereas VAN services have typically used a proprietary network or a network gateway linked with a specific set of proprietary networks. Web-based EDI allows for a substantial reduction is costs.
- The Internet's is an open marketplace, allowing large or small firms to interact with each other without concerns about maintaining equivalent hardware and software to facilitate transactions.
- Security products that handle issues of confidentiality, authentication, data integrity and non-repudiation of origin and return are constantly being improved.
- Improvements in the x.12 EDI formatting standard

EDI Risks and Controls

The nature of EDI is subject to the same security issues as other e-commerce transactions. In addition, there are issues and risks unique to EDI. Transaction authorization is a huge problem due to the fact that many current systems have no built-in authentication for these electronic transactions. Traditional EDI arrangements utilize trading partner agreements which clearly define the responsibilities of both parties in the event of problems with transactions. Due to the reputational risk that may exist if the integrity or confidentiality of transactions is compromised, agreements between Internet based trading partners require additional consideration.

A **trading partner agreement** should define the format and types of transactions to be used, responsibilities of both parties in handling and processing the transactions as well as the written business terms and conditions associated with the transactions. The following issues must also be specifically addressed:
- Unauthorized access to electronic transactions
- Deletion or manipulation of transactions prior to or after establishment of application controls
- Loss or duplication of EDI transmissions
- Loss of confidentiality and improper distribution of EDI transactions while in the possession of third parties

Auditing Controls in EDI Environments

Security risks can be addressed by enforcing general controls and establishing an added layer of application control procedures over the EDI process that can take over where traditional application controls leave off. These controls need to secure the current EDI activity as well as historical activities that may be called on to substantiate business transactions should a dispute arise.

Controls for Outbound Transactions
Standards should be set to indicate the message format and content are valid to avoid transmission errors.
Controls should be in place to ensure standard transmissions are properly converted for the application software by the translation application.
The receiving organization must have controls in place to test the reasonableness of messages received. This should be based upon a trading partner's transaction history or documentation received that substantiates special situations.
Controls should be established to guard against manipulation of data in active transactions, files and archives. Attempts to change records should be recorded by the system for management review and attention.
Procedures should be established to determine messages are only from authorized parties and that transactions are properly authorized.
If possible, dedicated lines should be created between the parties to reduce the risks related to tapped lines.
Data should be encrypted using algorithms agreed to by the parties involved.
Electronic signatures should be in the transmissions to identify the source and destination
Message authentication codes should exist to ensure that what is sent is received.
Logging outbound transactions in a secure temporary file until authorized and due for transmission
Requiring paperless authorization, which would establish special access to authorization fields (probably two levels, requiring the intervention of different users) within the computer system

Receipt Of Inbound Transactions
Use of encryption when the Internet is the means of communication
Edit checks to identify erroneous, unusual or invalid transactions prior to updating applications
Perform additional computerized checking to assess transaction reasonableness, validity, etc. (consider expert system front ends for complex comparisons)
Logging of each inbound transaction upon receipt
Use control totals on receipt of transactions to verify the number and value of transactions to be passed to each application; reconcile totals between applications and with trading partners
Segment count totals built into transaction set trailer by the sender
Control techniques in the processing of individual transactions, such as check digits on control fields, loop or repeat counts
Ensure the exchange of control totals of transactions sent and received between trading partners at predefined intervals
Maintain the number of messages received/sent and validating with the trading partners from time to time
Arrange for security over temporary files and data transfer to ensure that inbound transactions are not altered or erased between time of transaction receipt and application updates

The controls listed above are designed to either facilitate or achieve the following objectives:
- Controlling the set up and change of trading partner details
- Comparing transactions with trading partner transaction profiles
- Matching the trading partner number to the trading master file, prior to transmission
- Limiting the authority of users within the organization to initiate specific EDI transactions
- Segregating initiation and transmission responsibilities for high-risk transactions
- Documenting management sign-off on programmed procedures and subsequent changes
- Logging all payment transactions to a separate file which is reviewed for authorization before transmission
- Segregating duties within the transaction cycle, particularly where transactions are automatically generated by the system
- Segregating access to different authorization processes in a transaction cycle
- Reporting large (value) or unusual transactions for review prior to or after transmission

The Web-based EDI process must be able to detect and handle transactions that do not conform to the standard format or are from/to unauthorized parties. Options for handling detected errors include requesting retransmissions or manually changing the data. The critical nature of many EDI transactions, such as orders and payments, requires that there be positive assurances that the transmissions were complete. The transactions need to be successfully passed from the originating computer application to the destination organization. Methods for providing these assurances include internal batch total checking, run-to-run and transmission record count balancing, and use of special acknowledgment transactions for functional acknowledgments.

The sender should then match this against a file/log of EDI messages sent. EDI audits may also involve:
- **Audit monitors**-Devices can be installed at EDI workstations to capture transactions as they are received. Such transactions can be stored in a protected file for use by the auditor. Consideration should be given to storage requirements for voluminous amounts of data.
- **Expert systems**-Within the context of utilizing the computer system for internal control checks, consideration should be given to have audit monitors evaluate the transactions received. Based upon judgmental rules, the system can determine the audit significance of such transactions and provide a report for the auditor's use.

Other Types of Critical Applications
E- Mail
Electronic mail may be the most popular application within most organizations and across the Internet. In general, e-mail communication is made possible by the use of two types of applications:
- E-Mail servers, such as qmail, sendmail and Exchange. These applications deliver, forward and store mail
- E-Mail clients, such as Eudora, Thunderbird and Outlook. These applications enable end users to send mail to and retrieve mail from e-mail servers.

E-mail messages are sent in the same way as most Internet data. When a user sends an e-mail message, it is first broken down into packets. Those packets are examined by the server to determine if the recipient is actually on the same server or in the same email domain. If so, the server uses internal methods to route the email to the recipient. If the recipient is not on the same email domain, the email server forwards the email out to a router, which forwards the message to the Internet based on the IP address of the recipient's domain.

After several **hops**, or trips through other routers or switches, the email message finally reaches the recipient's domain (network). At this point, the message may pas through one or more additional routers, firewalls or switches before it gets to the recipient's mail server. That mail server will verify the presence of a user with that email address and forward the message to a storage area known to the user as the Inbox.

A sender may also can attach binary files, such as pictures, videos, sounds and executable files to the e-mail message. To do this, the user must encode the file in a way that will allow it to be sent across the network. The recipient's mail server will have to decode the file once it is received. There are a variety of encoding schemes that can be used. Encryption and digital signatures may also be applied to an email and its attachments. Most e-mail servers transparently handle the encoding for the sender and the decoding for the recipient.

Text in an email message is usally encoded in formats known as ASCII or Unicode. **ASCII** (American Standard Code for Information Interchange), is an older standard that allows any computer, regardless of its operating system or hardware, to read the text. ASCII assigns numerical equivalents to the letter and numbers typed into an email. The numerical equivalents are translated back into letters and numbers on the recipient's computer. ASCII has a limit of 256 possible character combinations, which makes it impossible to represent languages such as Cyrillic, Hebrew, and most Asian languages that do not use Latin character sets.

Email Security Issues
Some e-mail-related security issues are:
- Configuration flaws on the mail server application may be used as the means of compromising the underlying server and the attached network.
- Denial-of-service (DoS) attacks may be directed to the mail server denying or hindering valid users an ability to use the mail server.
- Different types of configuration flaws may allow the mail server to function as an **open relay**. This will allow a hacker who can compromise the system to configure that mail server for use as a spam server. If a mail domain gets added to an internet blacklist for spam, it may take a while to get the problem resolved[11]. In the meantime, many email antivirus programs update themselves based on information from Internet blacklists. This may cause the Email servers from other organizations to automatically discard even legitimate emails that arrive from a blacklisted domain. The loss of reputation and also potential business losses that may result from this situation could be huge.
- Sensitive information transmitted unencrypted between mail server and e-mail client may be intercepted
- Information within the e-mail may be altered at some point between the sender and recipient.
- Viruses and other types of malicious code may be distributed throughout an organization via e-mail.
- Users may send inappropriate, proprietary or other sensitive information via e-mail leading to a legal exposure.

Standards for E-Mail Security

To improve e-mail security, organizations should:
- Address the security aspects of the deployment of a mail server through maintenance and administration standards
- Ensure that the mail server application is deployed, configured and managed to meet the security policy and guidelines laid down by management
- Consider the implementation of encryption technologies to protect user authentication and mail data

In e-mail security, a digital signature authenticates a transmission from a user in an untrusted network environment. A digital signature is a sequence of bits appended to a digital document. Like a handwritten signature, its authenticity can be verified. But unlike a handwritten signature, it is unique to the document being signed. Digital signatures are another application of public key cryptography. Digital signatures are a good method of securing e-mail transmissions in that:

- The signature can not be forged.
- The signature is authentic and encrypted.
- The signature cannot be reused (a signature on one document cannot be transferred to another document).
- The signed document cannot be altered; any alteration to the document (whether or not it has been encrypted) renders the signature invalid.

The receiver of the message needs the sender's public key to verify the digital signature. The public key may be obtained at no cost from the CA that issued the key to the sender. The receiver uses a software program installed into his email client to verify the key and decrypt the message. The process is mostly transparent. received from the Certification Authority (CA) to decrypt the message. Digital signatures also use are based on a procedure called hashing to create a message digest, which is a short fixed length number mathematically derived from the contents of the message. This is a one-way process, meaning that possession of the digest will not enable a party to reconstruct the original message.

A digest is similar to a checksum in that it compactly represents the message and is used to detect changes in the message. One also can think of the message digest as a fingerprint of the message. The message digest authenticates the user's message in such a way that if it were altered, then the message would be considered corrupted and in some cases unreadable. In using digital signatures for securing e-mail messages, there are two different types of encryption techniques used to ensure secured messages. Messages can be secured using a symmetric (secret key) key management system, using AES (Advanced Encryption Standard), or a public key (asymmetric) management, using RSA. Organizations should employ their network infrastructure to protect their mail server (s) through appropriate use of firewalls, routers and intrusion detection systems.

Electronic Banking

Banking organizations have been delivering electronic services to consumers and businesses remotely for years. Electronic funds transfers, including include small payments, corporate cash management systems, publicly accessible automated machines for currency withdrawal and retail account management, are ubiquitous.

Major risks associated with banking activities are strategic, operational (including security-sometimes called transactional-and legal risks), credit, price, foreign exchange, interest rate and liquidity. Another major risk is that the company's reputation might be damaged by any serious security breach. Electronic banking adds some of the risks involved with e-commerce, since the Internet is now used as the medium by which most people perform these transactions.

Banks are more likely to rely upon well-documented control structures similar to those developed for use in mainframe environments. In fact, the primary driver of client/server implementations for banks has been the need to keep up with demand for online access to bank accounts and transactions. Overall, a bank's core business functions and its IT infrastructure are tightly linked. This helps decrease the risk profile associated with electronic banking. Often, the most serious weakness in the transaction process is the computer or workstation used by the banking customer to connect to the bank's network. If the account holder's machine has been compromised, a malicious user may be able to impersonate the account holder and initiate unauthorized actions from that account.

Banks should have a risk management process to enable them to identify measure, monitor and control their technology risk exposure. At a high-level, risk management for the new technologies has three essential elements:

- Risk management is the responsibility of the board of directors and senior management. They are responsible for developing the bank's business strategy and establishing an effective risk management methodology. They need to possess the knowledge and skills to manage the bank's use of electronic banking and all related risks. The board should take an explicit, informed and documented strategic decision as to whether and how the bank is to provide electronic banking services. The initial decision should include the specific accountabilities, policies and controls to address risks, including those arising in a cross-border context. The board should review, approve and monitor electronic banking technology-related projects that have a significant impact on the bank's risk profile and ensure that adequate controls are identified, planned and implemented.
- Implementing technology is the responsibility of information technology senior management. They should have the skills to effectively evaluate electronic banking technologies and products and to ensure that they are appropriately installed and documented.
- Measuring and monitoring risk is the responsibility of operational management. They should have the skills to effectively identify, measure, monitor and control risks associated with electronic banking. The board of directors should receive regular reports on the technologies employed, the risks assumed and how those risks are managed.

Risk Management Challenges in Electronic Banking

Electronic banking presents a number of risk management challenges:

- Banks are under pressure to provide access to new services to all customers as soon as possible to remain competitive. There is always a temptation to compromise security in order to have a product out on the market. The challenge is to maintain focus and offer a secure, quality driven experience in spite of business pressures.
- Transactional electronic banking web sites and associated retail and wholesale business applications are typically integrated as much as possible with legacy computer systems to allow more straight-through processing of electronic transactions. Such straight through automated processing reduces opportunities for human error and fraud inherent in manual processes, but it also increases dependence on sound systems design and architecture as well as system interoperability and operational scalability.
- Electronic banking increases banks' dependence on information technology. This increases the technical complexity of many operational and security issues and fuels a trend towards more partnerships, alliances and outsourcing arrangements with third parties, such as Internet service providers, telecommunication companies and other technology firms.
- The Internet is ubiquitous and global by nature. It is an open network accessible from anywhere in the world by unknown parties. Messages are routed through unknown locations and via fast evolving wireless devices. Therefore, the Internet significantly magnifies the importance of security controls, customer authentication techniques, data protection, audit trail procedures and customer privacy standards.

Risk Management Controls for Electronic Banking

Effective risk management controls for electronic banking include the following 14 controls divided among three categories:

- **Board and management oversight:**
    - Effective management oversight of e-banking activities
    - Establishment of a comprehensive security control process
    - Comprehensive due diligence and management oversight process for outsourcing relationships and other third-party dependencies
- **Security controls:**
    - Authentication of e-banking customers
    - Session encryption, non-repudiation and accountability for e-banking transactions
    - Appropriate measures to ensure segregation of duties
    - Proper authorization controls within e-banking systems, databases and applications
    - Data integrity of e-banking transactions, records and information
    - Establishment of clear audit trails for e-banking transactions
    - Confidentiality of key bank information

- **Legal and reputational risk management:**
    o Appropriate disclosures for e-banking services
    o Privacy of customer information
    o Capacity, business continuity and contingency planning to ensure availability of E-banking systems and services
    o Incident response planning

Electronic Funds Transfer (EFT)

Electronic funds transfer is the exchange of money via authorized digital transfers without currency actually changing hands. In other words, EFT is the electronic transfer of funds between a buyer's financial institution and a seller's financial institution. EFT refers to any financial transaction that transfers a sum of money from one account to another electronically. EFT allows parties to move money from one account to another account, replacing traditional check writing and cash collection procedures. EFT services have been available for two decades, but with the increased interest in Internet business, more and more consumers and businesses have begun to utilize them. In the settlement between parties, EFT transactions usually function via an internal bank transfer from one party's account to another or via a clearing house network.

Transactions generally originate from a computer at one institution (location) and are transmitted to a computer at another institution (location) with the monetary amount recorded in the respective organization's accounts. Because of the potential high volume of money being exchanged, these systems may be in an extremely high-risk category. Therefore, access security and authorization of processing are important controls. Regarding EFT transactions, central bank requirements should be reviewed for applicability in these processes.

Controls in an EFT Environment

Security should focus on the methods used by the customer to gain access to the system, the communications network and the host or application processing site. Individual consumer access to the EFT system is generally controlled by a plastic card and a personal identification number (PIN). Both items are required to initiate a transaction. The IS auditor should review the physical security of un-issued plastic cards, the procedures used to generate PINs, the procedures used to issue cards and PINs and the conditions under which the consumer uses the access devices.

Security in an EFT environment ensures that:
- All of the equipment and communication linkages are tested to effectively and reliably transmit and receive data.
- Each party uses security procedures that are reasonably sufficient for effecting the authorized transmission of data and for protecting business records and data from improper access.
- There are guidelines set for the receipt of data and to ensure that the receipt date and time for data transmitted are the date and time the data has been received.
- Upon receipt of data, the receiving party will immediately transmit an acknowledgment or notification to communicate to the sender that a successful transmission occurred.
- Data encryption standards are set.
- Standards for unintelligible transmissions are set.
- Regulatory requirements for enforceability of electronic data transmitted and received are explicitly stated.

Access to commercial EFT systems generally does not require a plastic card, but the IS auditor should ensure that reasonable identification methods are required. The communications network should be designed to provide maximum security. Data encryption is recommended for all transactions; however, the IS auditor should determine any conditions under which the PIN might be accessible in a clear mode. An EFT switch involved in the network is also an audit concern. An EFT switch is the facility that provides the communication linkage for all equipment in the network. The IS auditor should review the contract with the switch and the third-party audit of the switch operations. If a third party audit has not been performed, the auditor should consider visiting the switch location. At the application processing level, the IS auditor should review the interface between the EFT system and the application systems that process the accounts from which funds are transferred.

Availability of funds or adequacy of credit limits should be verified *before* funds are transferred. This, unfortunately, is not always the case. Because of the penalties for failure to make a timely transfer, the IS auditor should review backup arrangements or other methods used to ensure continuity of operations. Since EFT reduces the flow of paper and consequently reduces normal audit trails, the IS auditor should determine that alternative audit trails are available.

AUTOMATED TELLER MACHINE (ATM)

An **automated teller machine** is a specialized form of a **point-of-sale** (POS) terminal that is designed for unattended use by a banking customer. ATMs offer users a range of banking and debit operations, but the primary operations are deposits and cash withdrawals. Banks usually charge a fee for use of the ATMs they support to those that are customers of other institutions. They may also charge their own customers a fee for ATM use if their account balances do not meet certain levels. ATMs are usually located in uncontrolled areas to facilitate easy access to customers after hours. They may be found in the outer lobbies of many banks. They are also known as retail EFT (electronic funds transfer) networks, transferring information and money over communication lines. Therefore, the system must provide high levels of logical and physical security for both the customer and the machinery. The ATM architecture has a physical network layer, a switch and a communication layer connecting the various ATM POS terminals.

Recommended internal control guidelines for ATMs, apart from what has been provided for any EFT, include the following:
- Written policies and procedures covering personnel, security controls, operations, disaster recovery credit and check authorization, floor limits, override, settlement, and balancing
- Reconciliation of all general ledger accounts related to retail EFTs review of exception items and suspense accounts
- Procedures for PIN issuance and protection during storage
- Procedures for the security of PINs during delivery and the restriction of access to a customer's account after a small number of unsuccessful attempts
- Systems should be designed, tested and controlled to preclude retrieval of stored PINs in any non-encrypted form. Application programs and other software containing formulas, algorithms and data used to calculate PINs must be subject to the highest level of access for security purposes.
- Controls over plastic card procurement should be adequate with a written agreement between the card manufacturer and the bank that details control procedures and methods of resolution to be followed if problems occur.
- Controls and audit trails of the transactions that have been made in the ATM. This should include internal registration in the ATM, either in internal paper or digital media depending on regulation or laws in each country, and on the hosts that are involved in the transaction.

Audit of ATMs
To perform an audit of automated teller machines, the IS auditor should:
- Review measures to establish proper customer identification and maintenance of their confidentiality.
- Review files maintenance and retention system to trace transactions.
- Review exception reports to provide an audit trail.
- Review daily reconciliation of ATM machine transactions, including:
- Review segregation of duties in the opening of ATM and recount of deposit.
- Review the procedures made for the retained cards.
- Review encryption key change management procedures.

Exam Tip: There is an ATM (Asynchronous Transfer Mode) that is a high-speed telecommunications protocol. Candidates should be careful to read the context of any question mentioning "ATM" to avoid confusing the two.

Image Processing

Image processing is computer manipulation of images. Some of the many algorithms used in image processing include convolution (on which many others are based), PFT, DCT, thinning (or skeletonization), edge detection and contrast enhancement. These are usually implemented in software but may also use special-purpose hardware for speed. Image processing may be used in specialized applications, such as document management, product catalog databases architectural or graphic design firms; television, magazines, newspapers and other media that relay heavily on visual data or any other applications or environments designed to offer users graphical representations of various items.

Imaging systems may digitize, process store and retrieve many types of graphic data, such as pictures, charts and graphs, instead of or in addition to text data. The storage capacities must be enormous and most image systems include optical disk storage. In addition to optical disks, the systems include high-speed scanning, high-resolution displays, rapid and powerful compression, communications functions and laser printing. The systems include techniques that can identify levels of shades and colors that cannot be differentiated by the human eye. These systems are expensive and companies do not invest in them lightly. Most businesses that perform large-scale image processing only do so because they derive some significant business benefit by doing so.

Examples of potential benefits are:
- Item processing (e.g., signature storage and retrieval)
- More appealing product views for prospective customers.
- Immediate retrieval via secure optical storage medium
- Increased productivity
- Improved control over paper files
- Reduced deterioration due to handling
- Enhanced disaster recovery procedures

Imaging systems represent one of the fastest growing areas of the graphics industry. They are an outgrowth of microfilm and microfiche, which have in the past been heavily used in paper intensive fields, such as insurance and banking. Not surprisingly, these same fields were the first to incorporate imaging systems into their standard operations. The replacement of paper documents with electronic images can have a significant impact on the way that an institution does business. Many of the traditional audit and security controls for paper-based systems may be reduced or discarded altogether in environments that have converted all their systems to electronic documentation workflow. Controls implemented in these situations must focus on access and modification restrictions and backup/recovery concerns.

Risk areas that management should address when installing imaging systems and that IS auditors should be aware of when reviewing an institution's controls over imaging systems include:

- **Planning**-The lack of careful planning in selecting and converting paper systems to document imaging systems can result in excessive installation costs, the destruction of original documents and the failure to achieve expected benefits. Critical issues include converting existing paper storage files and integration of the imaging system into the organization workflow and electronic media storage to meet audit and document retention legal requirements.
- **Audit**-Imaging systems may change or eliminate the traditional controls as well as the checks and balances inherent in paper-based systems. Audit procedures may have to be redesigned and new controls designed into the automated process.
- **Redesign of workflow**-Institutions generally redesign or reengineer workflow processes to benefit from imaging technology.
- **Scanning devices**-Scanning devices are the entry point for image documents and a significant risk area in imaging systems. Scanning operations can disrupt workflow if the scanning equipment is not adequate to handle the volume of documents or the equipment breaks down. The absence of controls over the scanning process can result in poor quality images, improper indexing and incomplete or forged documents being entered into the system. Factors that should be considered in an imaging system are: quality control over the scanning and indexing process, the scanning rate of the equipment, the storage of images, equipment backup and the experience level of personnel scanning the document. Procedures should be in place to ensure original documents are not destroyed before it has been determined that a good image has been captured.
- **Software security**-Security controls over image system documents are critical to protect institutions and customer information from unauthorized access and modifications. The integrity and reliability of the imaging system database is related directly to the quality of controls over access to the system.
- **Training**-Inadequate training of personnel scanning the documents can result in poor quality document images and indexes and the early destruction of original documents.

The installation and use of imaging systems can be a major change for department personnel. They must be trained adequately to ensure quality control over the scanning and storage of imaging documents, as well as the use of the system to maximize the benefits of converting to imaging systems.

Artificial Intelligence and Expert Systems

AI (Artificial intelligence is the study and application of computing techniques to the principles by which:

- Knowledge is acquired and analyzed
- Decisions are made
- Goals are generated and achieved
- Information is communicated
- Collaboration is achieved
- Concepts are formed
- Languages are developed

LISP and Prolog are examples of programming language developed for use in handling AI-related tasks.

Some of the specialty areas within the field of Artificial Intelligence are:

- Expert systems
- Natural and artificial (such as programming) languages
- Neural networks
- Intelligent text management
- Theorem proving
- Abstract reasoning
- Pattern recognition
- Voice recognition
- Problem solving
- Machine translation of foreign languages

Expert systems are in an area of artificial intelligence that is becoming increasingly popular. They perform a specific function and are prevalent in certain industries, especially business and investing. An **expert system** allows the user to specify certain basic assumptions or formulas and then uses these assumptions or formulas to analyze arbitrary events. Based on the information used as input to the system, a conclusion is produced. The use of expert systems has many potential benefits within an organization including:

- Capturing the knowledge and experience of individuals before they leave the organization
- Sharing knowledge and experience in areas where there is Limited expertise
- Facilitating consistent and efficient quality decisions
- Enhancing personnel productivity and performance
- Automating highly (statistically) repetitive tasks (help desk, score credits, etc.)
- Operating in environments where a human expert is not available (e.g., medical assistance on board of a ship, satellites, etc.)

The **knowledge base** (KB), which contains specific information, verified results or other relevant fact patterns associated with a particular subject. It may also contain rules for interpreting these facts. The KB is usually built upon a specialized database type designed to group items of this type in meaningful units. The information in the KB can be expressed in several ways:

An **inference engine** is a separate program that uses the KB and may include its own built-in set of rules and queries. It can accept rules or calculations that the user creates as well. The combination of KB and inference engine usually includes the following proprietary items:

- **Knowledge interface**: Allows the expert to enter knowledge into the system without the traditional mediation of a software engineer
- **Data interface:** Enables the expert system to collect data from non-human sources, such as measurement instruments in a power plant
- **Decision trees**-Using questionnaires to lead the user though a series of choices, until a conclusion is reached. Flexibility is compromised, because the user must answer the questions in an exact sequence.
- **Rules**-Expressing declarative knowledge through the use of if-their relationships. For example, *if* a patient's body temperature Is over 39°C (102.2"F) and their pulse is under 60, then they might be suffering from a certain disease.
- **Semantic nets**-Consist of a graph in which the nodes represent physical or conceptual objects and the arcs describe the relationship between the nodes. Semantic nets resemble a data flow diagram and make use of an inheritance mechanism to prevent duplication of data.

Expert systems are gaining acceptance and popularity as audit tools. Expert systems for IS Auditing facilitate the audit process in areas such as operating systems, online software environments, access control products and microcomputer environments. These tools can take the form of a series of well-designed questionnaires or actual software that integrates and reports on system parameters and datasets. Other accounting and auditing related applications for expert systems include audit planning, internal control analysis, and account attribute analysis, quality review, accounting decisions, tax planning and user training. Consistent with standard systems development methodologies, stringent change control procedures should be followed as the basic assumptions and formulas may need to be changed as more expertise is gained. As with other systems, access should be on a need-to-know basis.

AUDITING AI

IS auditors should be knowledgeable about any applications that use AI in the organization. As the business increasingly relies upon the results of these applications to determine business direction and planning, the data and methods employed in the generation of these results must be subject to strict controls. The IS auditor should begin review of AI in the following ways:

- Understand the purpose and functionality of the system
- Assess the system's significance to the organization and related businesses processes as well as the associated potential risks
- Review the adherence of the system to corporate policies and procedures
- Review the decision logic built into the system to ensure that the expert knowledge or intelligence in the system is sound and accurate. The IS auditor should ensure that the proper level of expertise was used in developing the basic assumptions and formulas.
- Review procedures for updating information in the knowledge base
- Review security access over the system, specifically the knowledge base
- Review procedures to ensure that qualified resources are available for maintenance and upgrading

Business Intelligence

Business intelligence is an expanding area in IT that encompasses the collection, analysis and dissemination of information to assist decision-making and assess organizational performance. Investments in BI technology can be applied to enhance understanding of a wide range of business questions. Some typical areas in which BI is applied for measurement and analysis purposes include:

- Process cost, efficiency and quality
- Customer satisfaction with product and service offerings
- Customer profitability, including determination of which attributes are useful predictors of customer profitability
- Staff and business unit achievement of key performance indicators
- Risk management, e.g., by identifying unusual transaction patterns and accumulation of incident and loss statistics
- Project scheduling, resource allocation

The interest in BI as a distinct field of IT activity is being spurred by a number of factors:

- **The increasing size and complexity of modern organizations**: The result of this is that even fundamental business questions cannot be properly answered without establishing serious BI capability.
- **Pursuit of competitive advantage**: Most organizations have automated their basic, high-volume activities. Significant organization wide IT investment, such as ERP systems are now common place. Many companies have begun investment in secure Internet technology as a means of distributing product service and supply chain integration. However, utilization of IT to maintain and extend a firm's knowledge capital represents a new opportunity to use technology to gain an advantage over competitors
- **Legal requirements:** Legislation such as Sarbanes-Oxley and the US Patriot Act, enforce the need for companies to have an understanding of the "whole of business."
- Financial institutions must now be able to report on all accounts/instruments that their customers have and all transactions against those accounts/instruments, including any suspicious transaction patterns.

To deliver effective BI, organizations need to design and implement complex data architectures. This type of data architecture consists of two components:

- The enterprise data flow architecture (EDFA)
- A logical data architecture

The components of an optimized, enterprise data flow architecture are identified as follows:

- **Presentation/desktop access layer**: This is where end users directly deal with information. This layer may utilize familiar desktop tools such as Microsoft Access and Excel, direct querying tools, reporting and analysis suites offered by vendors, such as COGNOS and Business Objects, and even applications such as balanced scorecards and digital dashboards. Power users will have the ability to build their own queries and reports while other users will interact with the data in predefined ways.
- **Data source layer**-Enterprise information derives from a number of sources:
- **Operational data**-Data captured and maintained by an organizations existing systems, usually held in system-specific databases or possibly flat files
- **External data**-Data provided to an organization by external sources. This could include data, such as customer demographics and market share information.
- **Non-operational** data-Information needed by end users that is not currently maintained in a computer accessible format.
- **Core data warehouse**-This is where all the data of interest to an organization is captured and organized to assist reporting and analysis. Data warehouses are normally instituted as large relational databases. While there is not unanimous agreement, many suggest the warehouse should hold fully normalized data to give it the flexibility to deal with complex and changing business structures. A properly constituted data warehouse should support three basics forms of inquiry:

    o **Drilling up and drilling down**-Using dimensions of interest to the business, it should be possible to aggregate data (e.g., sum store sales to get region sales and ultimately national sales), as well as drill down (e.g., break store sales down to counter sales). Attributes available at the more granular levels of the warehouse can also be used to refine the analysis (e.g., analyze sales by product).
    o **Drill across**-Use common attributes to access to a cross-section of information in the warehouse, e.g., sum sales across all product lines by customer and groups of customers according to length of association with the company (and/or other attribute of interest)
    o **Historical analysis-**The warehouse should support this by holding historical, time variant data. An example of historical analysis would be to report monthly store sales and then repeat the analysis using only customers who were preexisting at the start of the year, to separate the effect of new customers from the ability to generate repeat business with existing customers.

- **Data mart layer-** Data marts represent subsets of information from the core data warehouse selected and organized to meet the needs of a particular business unit or business line. Data marts may be relational databases or some form of online analytical processing (OLAP) data structure (also known as a data cube). OLAP technologies and some variants, e.g., relational OLAP (ROLAP), allow users to "slice and dice" data presented in terms of standardized measures (i.e., numerical facts) and dimensions (i.e., business hierarchies). Data marts have a simplified structure compared to the normalized data warehouse. If using a relational database, a popular structure is the star schema, which involves a fact table connected to de-normalized dimension tables. A simplified structure assists the business user's understanding of the data and relationships. If data is held in relational tables, less joins (connections between tables) are necessary when querying, and the need to become familiar with a large number of code values is avoided if full text descriptions are used instead.

- **Data staging and quality layer**-This layer is responsible for data copying, transformation into data warehouse format and quality control. It is particularly important that only reliable data gets loaded to the core data warehouse. This layer needs to be able to deal with problems periodically thrown up by operational systems, e.g., changes to account number formats and reuse of old account and customer numbers (when the data warehouse still holds information on the original entity).

- **Data access layer**-This layer operates to connect the data storage and quality layer with data stores in the data source layer and, in the process, avoiding the need to know exactly how these data stores are organized. Technology now permits SQL access to data even if it is not stored in a relational database.

- **Data preparation layer:** This layer is concerned with the assembly and preparation of data for loading to data marts. The usual practice is to pre-calculate the values that are loaded into OLAP data repositories to increase access speed. Specialized data mining also normally requires preparation of data. Data mining is concerned with exploring large volumes of data to determine patterns and trends of information. Data mining often identifies patterns that are counter-intuitive due to the number and complexity of data relationships. Data quality needs to be very high to not corrupt the results.
- **Metadata repository layer**-Metadata is data about data. The information held in the metadata layer needs to extend beyond data structure names and formats to provide detail on business purpose and context. The metadata layer should be comprehensive in scope, covering data as it flows between the various layers including documenting transformation and validation rules. Ideally information in the metadata layer can be directly sourced by software operating in the other layers as required.
- **Warehouse management layer**-The function of this layer is the scheduling of the tasks necessary to build and maintain the data warehouse and populate data marts. This layer is also involved in the administration of security.
- **Application messaging layer**-This layer is concerned with transporting of information between the various layers. In addition to business data, this layer encompasses generation, storage and targeted communication of control messages.
- **Internet/intranet layer**-This layer is concerned with basic data communication. Included here are browser-based user interfaces and TCPIP networking.

The construction of the logical data architecture for an enterprise is a major task that would normally be undertaken in stages. One reason for separating logical, data model determination by business domain is that different parts of large business organizations will often deal with different transaction sets, customers and products. Ultimately, the data architecture will need to be structured to accommodate the needs of the organization in the most efficient manner. Factors to consider include the types of transactions in which the organization engages; the entities that participate in or form part of these transactions, such as customers, products, staff and communication channels; and the dimensions (hierarchies) that are important to the business, such as product and organization hierarchies. Multi-tier data delivery architectures are probably the best solution.

With modern data warehouses storage capacity is not really an issue. Hence, the goal should be to obtain the most granular or atomic data possible. The lowest level data will most likely have attributes that can be used for analysis purposes that would be lost if summarized data is loaded. Various analysis models used by data architects/analysts follow:

- **Context diagrams**-Outline the major processes of an organization and the external parties with which the business interacts
- **Activity or swim-lane diagrams**-Deconstruct business processes
- **Entity relationship diagrams**-Depict data entities and how they relate. These data analysis methods obviously play an important part in developing an enterprise data model. However, it is also crucial that knowledgeable business operatives are involved in the process. This way proper understanding can be obtained of data's business purpose and context. This also mitigates the risk of the replication of suboptimal data configurations from existing systems and databases into the data warehouse.

Business Intelligence Governance

A **BI Governance** program helps organizations maximize the returns on its BI-related investments. Data Governance establishes controls over the way in data is obtained, cleansed, converted, reconciled and accessed. At some point, an organization will have to utilize the results obtained from BI applications it purchases or develops. The manner in which analyses are performed, the format and content of the results, the research done to verify results and the extent to which the firm incorporates the results are all valid topics for BI Governance. The capability of computers to generate results is undeniable. However, the extent to which those results may be trusted and relied upon is a matter of great speculation. Many would argue for the usefulness of BI, but how many will stake their employment on the validity of the results obtained? One of the purposes of BI Governance is to adopt a controlled response to these results to protect the company from flaws in the assumptions made, incomplete data, inaccurate calculations or any of the other variables that could skew the results of BI queries.

Decision Support System (DSS)

A **decision support system** (DSS) is an interactive system that provides the user with easy access to decision models and data from a wide range of sources, to support semi-structured decision-making tasks typically for business purposes. It is an **informational application** designed to assist an organization in making decisions through data provided by business intelligent tools (in contrast to an **operational application** which collects the data in the course of normal business operations). Typical information that a decision support application might gather and present would be:
- Comparative sales figures between one week and the next
- Projected revenue figures based on new product sales assumptions
- The consequences of different decision alternatives, given past experience in the described context

A decision support system may present information graphically and may include an expert system or artificial intelligence. Further, it may be aimed at business executives or some other group of knowledge workers. Characteristics of a DSS are:
- Aims at solving less structured, under-specified problems that senior managers face
- Combines the use of models or analytic techniques with traditional data access and retrieval functions
- Emphasizes flexibility and adaptability to accommodate changes in the environment and the decision-making approach of the users

A principle of DSS design is to concentrate less on efficiency (i.e., performing tasks quickly and reducing costs) and more on effectiveness (i.e., performing the right task). Therefore, DSSs are often developed using 4GL tools that are less efficient, but allow for flexible and easily modified systems. DSSs are often developed with a specific decision or well-defined class of decisions to solve; therefore, some commercial software packages that claim to be DSSs are nothing more than DSS generators (tools with which to construct DSSs).

Frameworks are generalizations about a field or area of interest that can help put many specific cases and ideas into perspective (COBIT is an Information Security Management framework). The G. Gorry-M.S. Morton framework[12] is the most complete knowledge and system-control-related information system model, and it is based on problem classification into structured and unstructured types, as well as the time-horizon of the decisions. According to this framework, the degree to which a problem or decision is structured corresponds roughly to the extent to which it can be automated or programmed. This framework characterizes DSS activities along two dimensions:
- The degree of structure in the decision process being supported
- The management level at which the decision-making takes place

The management-level dimension is broken into three parts:
- Operational control
- Management control
- Strategic planning

The decision-structure dimension is also broken into three parts:
- Structured
- Semi-structured
- Unstructured

Another DSS framework is the Spraye-Carson framework that began with an effort to create family trees, which are a generalization of the structure of a decision support system. This framework suggests that every DSS has a data, a model and a dialogue generator subsystem. This framework emphasizes the importance of data management in DSS work. This framework also stresses the importance of interactive user interfaces in DSS systems. The generation and management of these interfaces require appropriate software and hardware: the dialogue management system. In general, a system must offer more than one interface and might need to provide a tailored interface for each user.

Prototyping is the most popular approach to DSS design and development. Prototyping usually bypasses the requirement definition. System requirements evolve through the user's learning process. The benefits of prototyping include the following:

- Learning is explicitly incorporated into the design process, because of the iterative nature of the system design.
- Feedback from design iterations is rapid, to maintain an effective learning process for the user.
- The user's expertise in the problem area helps the user suggest system improvements.
- The initial prototype must be inexpensive to create.

DSSs are difficult to implement because of their discretionary nature. Using a DSS to solve a problem represents a change in the behavior of the user in regard to the way in which the user normally interacts with software. In addition, DSSs may generate results that could influence the behavior of the organization as a whole. As mentioned previously, the processes used to create these results need to be monitored and carefully controlled. The following are the steps involved in changing behavior:[13]

- **Unfreezing**-This step alters the forces acting on individuals such that the individuals are distracted sufficiently to change. Unfreezing is accomplished either through increasing the pressure for change or by reducing some of the threats of, or resistance to, change.
- **Transitioning**-This step presents a direction of change and the actual process of learning new attitudes.
- **Refreezing**-This step integrates the changed attitudes into the individual's personality.

Risk Factors

Developers should be prepared for eight implementation risk factors:

1. Nonexistent or unwilling users
2. Multiple users or implementers
3. Disappearing users, implementers or maintainers
4. Inability to specify purpose or usage patterns in advance
5. Inability to predict and cushion impact on all parties
6. Lack or loss of support
7. Lack of experience with similar systems
8. Technical problems and cost-effectiveness issues

Implementation Strategies

To plan for the risks and prevent them from occurring:

- Divide the project into manageable pieces.
- Keep the solution simple.
- Develop a satisfactory support base.
- Meet user needs and institutionalize the system.

Assessment and Evaluation

The true test of a DSS lies in whether it improves a manager's decision-making, which is something not easily measured. There are no standardized methods for making this type of evaluation. Also, DSS systems rarely result in cost displacements like a reduction in staff or other expenses. In addition, because DSS systems are evolutionary in nature, they lack neatly defined completion dates. Using an incremental approach to DSS development reduces the need for evaluation. By developing one step at a time and achieving tangible results at the end of each step, the user does not need to make extensive commitments of time and money at the beginning of the development process. The DSS designer and user should use broad evaluation criteria. These criteria should include:

- Traditional cost-benefit analysis
- Procedural changes, more alternatives examined, less time consumed in making the decision
- Evidence of improvement in decision malting
- Changes in the decision process

Corporate Executives, Boards of Directors and auditors need to develop some type of assurance that DSSs and the results they generate are not used to shift the consequences of decision-making from any user of these systems to the software, the software manufacturer or the organization itself for approving the purchase and use of the system. Under Sarbanes-Oxley, stakeholders are held accountable for certain adverse end results regardless of the source of the decisions that led to those results. Therefore, results obtained from DSSs or any other AI driven application should be tested and subjected to separate risk analysis methods before they are implemented. Some common trends and issues with DSS usage include:

- The need for more accurate information by managers is an important motivator for DSS development.
- Gradual improvement and sharpening of skills in the development and implementation of traditional DSS systems
- Advances in database and graphics capabilities for microcomputers
- Exploratory work in such fields as expert systems, DSS systems to support group decision making and visual interactive modeling
- Few DSS evaluations use the traditional cost/benefit analysis.
- End users are usually the motivators in developing a DSS.
- Development staff members are drawn largely from functional area staff or the planning department, not from the IS department.
- Users perceive flexibility as the most important factor influencing the system's success.
- Few DSS systems are being developed today for third-generation software facilities; user-oriented fourth-generation languages and planning languages predominate.
- Planning, evaluation and training for DSS projects traditionally have been performed quite poorly.

What if (refers to scenario modeling, i.e., determining the results of changes in variables)
- Sensitivity analysis
- Goal-seeking
- Excellent graphic presentations
- Dynamic graphic, data editing
- Simulation

Customer Relationship Management (CRM)

The most recent business initiatives have become heavily customer-focused. Access to the Internet and fast delivery services means that businesses that once relied upon a captive customer base have seen declines in revenues due to online comparison shopping. CRM software is yet another database-driven application with an emphasis on maintaining information about each customer's personal and account information, purchase history, technical support or other support issues and any other interaction deemed relevant to the business implementers.

Customer expectations are increasing, and thanks to the Internet, they can choose from a variety of products that may meet their needs and make their buying decisions based solely on price. As businesses are becoming aware of this trend, they are struggling to improve service levels in the hope of offsetting price considerations by offering better customer service. CRM applications are the norm in modern call centers, where all of the operators, associates, service representatives, etc. interact with the customer on the basis of the functionality offered through the applications on their desktop.

A benefit of CRM systems is that the databases upon which they are built often have BI modules built in for use by higher-level managers. Information about new customer purchases and other interactions may be analyzed for trends based on weekly, daily and even hourly updates. New business models will have an integration of telephony, web and database technologies, and inter-enterprise integration capabilities. Also, it spreads to the other business partners who can share information, communicate and collaborate with the organization with the seamless integration of web-enabled applications and without bothering their local network and other configuration.

Supply Chain Management (SCM)

Supply chain management enables computer-driven links between customer orders, business transactions and order fulfillment and various product delivery methods. Many companies that ship tangible products utilize applications and consulting services from shippers such as UPS or Federal Express to help streamline their order fulfillment processes. The link is provided to all the connected areas, such as managing logistics, exchange of information, services and goods between supplier, consumer, warehouse, wholesale/retail distributors, and the manufacturer of goods.

SCM has become a focal point and is seen as a new area in strategic management. SCM is growing in importance because of the shift in business processes driven by global competition, the proliferation of the Internet, the instantaneous transmission of information, and a web presence in all spheres of business activities. SCM can help decrease the costs associated with managing the flow of goods, services and information between suppliers, manufacturers, wholesalers, distributors, stores, consumers and end users. SCM can also improve the buying experience of the customer by reducing the time necessary to receive goods and services, increasing the variety of payment options and even offer an online shopping experience that provides more product choices, yet remains easy to navigate, even for non-technical users.

Continuous Online Auditing

The focus of **continuous online auditing** is the use of audit tools that may be utilized during regular production times and upon production machines and data. The tests used provide a method for the IS auditor to collect evidence on system reliability, while normal processing takes place. If the selective information collected by the computer technique is not deemed serious or material enough to warrant immediate action, it is stored in separate audit files for verification by the IS auditor at a later time. The continuous audit approach cuts down on needless paperwork and leads to a reduction in the paperwork generated by audit processes.

Using these tools, an auditor or other security professional can observe, verify and report errors and/or suspicious activities in real time, or within minutes of their occurrence. This reduction in detection time can help the organization catch and prosecute malicious users or locate and fix processing errors before they affect too many transactions. The overall impact is an improvement in security and a reduction in audit costs.

Online Auditing Techniques

There are five types of automated evaluation techniques applicable to continuous online auditing:

- **Systems control audit review file and embedded audit modules (SCARF/EAM)-**The use of this technique involves embedding specially written audit software in the organization's host application system so that the application systems are monitored on a selective basis.
- **Snapshots-**This technique involves taking what might be termed pictures of the processing path that a transaction follows from the input to the output stage. With the use of this technique, transactions are tagged by applying identifiers to input data and recording selected information about what occurs for the auditor's subsequent review.
- **Audit hooks-**This technique involves embedding hooks in application systems to function as red flags and to induce IS auditors to act before an error or irregularity gets out of hand.
- **Integrated test facilities (ITF)-**In this technique, dummy facilities are set up and included in an auditee's production files. The IS auditor can make the system either process live transactions or test transactions during regular processing runs, and have these transactions update the records of the dummy entity. The operator enters the test transactions simultaneously with the live transactions that are entered for processing. The auditor then compares the output with the data that have been independently calculated to verily the correctness of the computer processed data.
- **Continuous and intermittent simulation (CIS)-**The computer system, during a process run of a transaction, simulates the instruction execution of the application. As each transaction is entered, the simulator decides whether the transaction meets certain predetermined criteria and if so, audits the transaction. If not, the simulator waits until it encounters the next transaction that meets the criteria.

The use of each of the continuous audit techniques has advantages and disadvantages. Their selection and implementation depends, to a large extent, on the complexity of an organization's computer systems and applications, and the IS auditor's ability to understand and evaluate the system with and without the use of continuous audit techniques. In addition, IS auditors must recognize that continuous audit techniques are not a cure for all control problems and that the use of these techniques provides only limited assurance that the information processing systems examined are operating as they were intended to function. In the exhibit below, the relative advantages and disadvantages of the various concurrent audit tools are presented.

Concurrent Audit Tools - Advantages and Disadvantages

	SCARF/EAM	ITF	Snapshots	CIS	Audit Hooks
Complexity	Very high	High	Medium	Medium	Low
Useful when:	Regular proceeding cannot be interrupted	It is not beneficial to use test data	An audit trail is required	Transactions meeting certain criteria need to be examined	Only select transactions of processes need to be examined

Exam Tip: CISA candidates should be familiar with each of the online auditing techniques mentioned and be able to make judgments about the optimal conditions for their use.

ISO 9126

IS0 9126[14] and the updated version, ISO/IEC 25000:2005 (SQuaRE), provide definitions and recommendations about software quality and associated quality evaluation processes to be used during the product life cycle. Attributes evaluated include the following:
- **Functionality**-The set of attributes that bear on the existence of a set of functions and their specified properties. The functions are those that satisfy stated or implied needs.
- **Reliability**-The set of attributes that defines the capability of software to maintain its level of performance under stated conditions for a stated period of time.
- **Usability**-The set of attributes that measures the effort needed for use and on the individual assessment of such use by a stated or implied set of users.
- **Efficiency**-The set of attributes that bears on the relationship between the level of performance of the software and the amount of resources used, under stated conditions.
- **Maintainability**-The set of attributes that bears on the effort needed to make specified modifications.
- **Portability**-The set of attributes that describes the ability of software to be transferred from one environment to another.

Software Capability Maturity Model (CMMI)

The software CMMI, developed by Carnegie Mellon's Software Engineering Institute and various industry and government affiliates in the early 1990s, is a process maturity model or framework that helps organizations improve their software life cycle processes. The model is particularly adept at enabling organizations to prevent excessive project schedule delays and cost overruns by providing the appropriate infrastructure and support necessary to help projects avoid these problems.

The CMMI has five **maturity** levels ranging from one through five.[15] The CMM was designed to guide software organizations in selecting process improvement strategies by determining current process maturity and identifying the few issues most critical to software quality and process improvement. This enables organizations to focus on a limited set of activities to steadily improve software process capability. COBIT recognizes a sixth **maturity** level, level zero, representing "non-existent".[16] Non-existent means that incidents are dealt with as they arise; there is no formal policy or procedure in place regarding this area and no intention to assess the need for internal controls is present.

Level	Continuous Representation Capability Levels	Staged Representation Maturity Levels
Level 0	Incomplete	N/A
Level 1	Performed	Initial
Level 2	Managed	Managed
Level 3	Defined	Defined
Level 4	Quantitatively Managed	Quantitatively Managed
Level 5	Optimizing	Optimizing

The five CMMI maturity levels attainable by software organizations include:

- **Initial**-Characterized as *ad hoc,* where success depends solely on individual effort.
- **Repeatable-**Disciplined management processes are established to plan and track cost, schedule and functionality, and provide oversight over a software project. This creates a learning environment where successfully defined and applied processes can be repeated successfully on other projects of similar size and scope.
- **Defined-**Lessons learned from the prior phase provide the impetus to develop a standard software process across the organization. This includes both management and software engineering activities, documented, standardized and integrated into an institutionalized standard software process applicable to all software development projects.
- **Managed-**Once processes are well-defined and applied, the organization has reached a point where it can develop and apply quantitative managed control over its software development processes. This provides a greater degree of precision and control over software projects for improving software productivity and reaching zero-defect goals.
- **Optimizing-**When an organization has attained the ability to quantitatively and successfully control its software projects; it is in a position to use continuous process improvement strategies in applying innovative solutions and state-of-the-art technologies to its software processes.

ISO 15504

ISO/IEC TR 15504,[17] also known as SPICE (Software Process Improvement and Capability Determination) is based on CMMI. Instead of than implementing a new set of standards, SPICE utilizes existing standards as references. SPICE is a framework of management and development capabilities. Auditors using SPICE as their framework must be aware of the different standards that SPICE uses and make determinations about an organization's management (process improvement) and development capabilities (process capability) in the light of those standards. An overall rating may be derived based on some combination of the scores or compliance ratings obtained by the organization from each reference standard used by SPICE. Reference models for SPICE include:

- **Software life cycle processes**-Through ISO/IEC 12207 AMD1/2
- **System life cycle processes**-Through ISO/IEC 15288
- **Human-centered life cycle processes**-Through ISO 18529
- **Component-based development processes**-Through the OOSPICE project
- **IT service management processes**-Through a SPICE user group initiative
- **Quality management system processes**-Through SPICE for 9000 (S9K)
- **Automotive embedded software**-Through Automotive SPICE (an initiative of The Procurement Forum and The Spice User Group with major European car manufacturers) and
- **Medical device software**-Through the Medi SPICE initiative

CHAPTER 3 PRACTICE QUESTIONS

1) Which of the following is a dynamic analysis tool for the purpose of testing software modules?
    A. Black box test
    B. Desk checking
    C. Structured walk-through
    D. Design and code

2) Which of the following would be the BEST method for ensuring that critical fields in a master record have been updated properly?
    A. Field checks
    B. Control totals
    C. Reasonableness checks
    D. A before-and-after maintenance report

3) IS management has decided to rewrite a legacy customer relations system using fourth generation languages (4GLs). Which of the following risks is MOST often associated with system development using 4GLs?
    A. Inadequate screen/report design facilities
    B. Complex programming language subsets
    C. Lack of portability across operating systems
    D. Inability to perform data intensive operations

4) Which of the following data validation edits is effective in detecting transposition and transcription errors?
    A. Range check
    B. Check digit
    C. Validity check
    D. Duplicate check

5) A number of system failures are occurring when corrections to previously detected errors are resubmitted for acceptance testing. This would indicate that the maintenance team is probably not adequate1yperforming which of the following types of testing?
    A. Unit testing
    B. Integration testing
    C. Design walk-throughs
    D. Configuration management

6) Which of the following BEST describes the necessary documentation for an enterprise product reengineering (EPR) software installation?
    A. Specific developments only
    B. Business requirements only
    C. All phases of the installation must be documented
    D. No need to develop a customer specific documentation

CHAPTER 3 PRACTICE QUESTIONS (CONT.)

7) The use of a GANTT chart can:
   A. aid in scheduling project tasks.
   B. determine project checkpoints.
   C. ensure documentation standards.
   D. direct the post-implementation review.

8) Which of the following audit tools is MOST useful to an IS auditor when an audit trail is required?
   A. Integrated test facility (ITF)
   B. Continuous and intermittent simulation (CIS)
   C. Audit hooks
   D. Snapshots

9) A strength of an implemented quality system based on ISO 9001 is that it:
   A. guarantees quality solutions to business problems.
   B. enhances improvements in software life cycle activities
   C. provides clear answers to questions concerning cost-effectiveness.
   D. does not depend on the maturity of the implemented quality system.

10) An organization is developing a new business system. Which of the following will provide the MOST assurance that the system provides the required functionality?
    A. Unit testing
    B. Regression testing
    C. Acceptance testing
    D. Integration testing

CHAPTER 3 ANSWERS TO PRACTICE QUESTIONS

1) Answer: A

   A black box test is a dynamic analysis tool for testing software modules. During the testing of software modules a black box test works first in a cohesive manner as one single unit/entity, consisting of numerous modules and second, with the user data that flows across software modules. In some cases, this even drives the software behavior. In choices B, C and D, the software (design or code) remains static and somebody simply closely examines it by applying his/her mind, without actually activating the software. Hence, these cannot be referred to as dynamic analysis tools.

2) Answer: D

   A before-and-after maintenance report is the best answer because a visual review would provide the most positive verification that update was accurate.

3) Answer: D

   4GLs are usually not suitable for data intensive operations. Instead, they are used mainly for graphic user interface (GUI) design or as simple query/report generators. Screen/report design facilities are one of the main advantages of 4GLs, and 4GLs have simple programming language subsets. Portability is also one of the main advantages of
   4GLs.

4) Answer: B

   A check digit is a numeric value that is calculated mathematically and is appended to data to ensure that the original data have not been altered or an incorrect but valid, value substituted. This control is effective in detecting transposition and transcription errors. A range check is checking data that matches a predetermined range of values. A validity check is programmed checking of the data validity in accordance with predetermined criteria. In a duplicate check, new or fresh transactions are matched to those previously entered to ensure that they are not already in the system.

5) Answer: B

   A common system maintenance problem is that errors are often corrected quickly (especially when deadlines are tight), units are tested by the programmer, and then transferred to the acceptance test area. This often results in system problems that should have been detected during integration or system testing. Integration testing aims at ensuring that the major components of the system interface correctly.

6) Answer: C

   A global enterprise product reengineering (EPR) software package can be applied to a business to replace, simplify and improve the quality of IS processing. Documentation is intended to help understand how, why and which solutions that have been selected and implemented, and therefore must be specific to the project. Documentation is also intended to support quality assurance and must be comprehensive.

CHAPTER 3 ANSWERS TO PRACTICE QUESTIONS (CONT.)

7) Answer: A

A GANTT chart is used in project control. It may aid in the identification of needed checkpoints but its primary use is in scheduling. It will not ensure the completion of documentation nor will it provide direction for the post-implementation review.

8) Answer: D

A snapshot tool is most useful when an audit trail is required. ITF can be used to incorporate test transactions into a normal production run of a system. CIS is useful when transactions meeting certain criteria need to be examined. Audit hooks are useful when only select transactions or processes need to be examined.

9) Answer: B

A strength of an implemented quality system based on ISO 9001 is that it enhances improvements in software life cycle activities, quality assurance and quality control. Weaknesses of the system include that it can fail to provide clear answers to questions concerning productivity, reliability or cost-effectiveness of the system. A quality system is not a guarantee of quality solutions to business problems since poorly defined user requirements will adversely affect the design of the software. Depending on the maturity of the implemented quality system stages can vary from not implemented to fully implemented procedures.

10) Answer: C

Acceptance testing is primarily conducted by the users before sign-off. It is performed from the perspective of the users to confirm that the system has the required functionality. Unit testing is used for testing the basic functionality of a program. Regression testing is used to compare changes to an application to ensure that the programs are working the same after a change as before the change. Integration testing is used to ensure that all of the programs in an application are working correctly and that information is flowing correctly.

Chapter 4 IT Service Delivery and Support

Information Systems Operations

The objective of this chapter is to ensure that the CISA candidate is able to describe, evaluate and test methodologies and practices used in the development, acquisition and maintenance of both information systems (business applications) and system architectures.[1]

This chapter represents approximately 14 percent of the CISA examination (approximately 28 questions).

There are seven tasks within this area that the CISA candidate must understand and be able to perform:
- Evaluate service level management practices to ensure that the level of service from internal and external service providers is defined and managed.
- Evaluate operations management to ensure that IT support functions effectively meet business needs.
- Evaluate data administration practices to ensure the integrity and optimization of databases.
- Evaluate the use of capacity and performance monitoring tools and techniques to ensure that IT services meet the organization's objectives.
- Evaluate change, configuration, and release management practices to ensure that changes made to the organization's production environment are adequately controlled and documented.
- Evaluate problem and incident management practices to ensure that incidents, problems, or errors are recorded, analyzed, and resolved in a timely manner.
- Evaluate the functionality of the IT infrastructure (e.g., network components, hardware, system software) to ensure that it supports the organization's objectives.

Knowledge Statements
The following statements describe specific topics a CISA candidate should be familiar with and use as guidance in the fulfillment of the tasks outlined above:
- Knowledge of service level management practices
- Knowledge of operations management best practices (e.g., workload scheduling, network services management, preventive maintenance)
- Knowledge of systems performance monitoring processes, tools, and techniques (e.g., network analyzers, system utilization reports, load balancing)
- Knowledge of the functionality of hardware and network components (e.g., routers, switches, firewalls, peripherals)
- Knowledge of database administration practices
- Knowledge of the functionality of system software including operating systems, utilities, and database management systems
- Knowledge of capacity planning and monitoring techniques
- Knowledge of processes for managing scheduled and emergency changes to the production systems and/or infrastructure including change, configuration, release, and patch management practices
- Knowledge of incident/problem management practices (e.g., help desk, escalation procedures, tracking)
- Knowledge of software licensing and inventory practices
- Knowledge of system resiliency tools and techniques (e.g., fault tolerant hardware, elimination of single point of failure, clustering)

IS Operations Management
In most modern organizations, information systems have all ready become an accepted part of doing business. Internet connections, email systems, e-banking and e-business functions are as common today as manual typewriters were three decades ago or more. With each investment in e-business innovation, management and controls must be adapted or implemented to allow the organization to derive the maximum possible return on those investments. There are many possible ways that businesses use technology; the following are some of the areas of common concern:

- Problem management and Incident management
- Physical plant and security management
- Technical/Customer support and Internal Help desk functions
- Project management: Time and resource allocation
- Data processing, collection and storage
- IT Infrastructure
- Change and configuration management
- Audit and monitoring of resource usage

Management utilizes controls as tools to aid in the administration of the areas mentioned above. Operational and Administrative control objectives and procedures were discussed at length in Chapter 1. However, several points bear repeating here:

- **Internal controls** may be defined as "any policies, procedures, guidelines or organizational processes established for the purpose of managing risk"
- **Operational controls:** These controls focus on the day-to-day operations, functions and activities and ensure the operation is meeting the business objectives.
- **Administrative controls:** These controls promote operational efficiency in a functional area and adherence to management policies, including operational controls. The administrative controls can be described as supporting the operational controls specifically concerned with operating efficiency and adherence to the organization's policies.
- **Internal Control Activities or General Control Procedures** refer to lower-level operations such as guidelines and procedures. The procedures and guidelines should be implemented in such a way that they fulfill the requirements specified by statements in higher-level documents.

Control Objectives are higher-level statements that correspond to overall policy. Control Procedures are lower-level activities that provide detailed methods for use in achieving the stated objectives.

IT Service Management
(ITSM) IT Service Management represents another high-level objective. Its business goal is the adoption, control, configuration and improvement of IT processes in such a way that:

- Other business-oriented objectives may be achieved or facilitated
- IT investments, resources and assets serve the business (business or IT alignment) and are not acquired for the sake of keeping up with the activities of competitors.

The originator and primary source for most of the ITSM concepts is the ITIL (IT Infrastructure Library)[2]. The ITIL was developed by the British Government as a set of best practices for IT Services Management. In the ITILv3 (its latest update), the areas of focus include:

- **Service Strategy:** This area covers Financial Management and Service Portfolio Management and. is concerned with the identification of market opportunities for which services could be developed in order to meet a requirement on the part of internal or external customers.
- **Service Design:** This area covers Security Management, Capacity Management, Availability Management and Continuity Management. It focuses on the methods by which business goals and objectives may be translated into infrastructure design requirements.
- **Service Transition:** This area includes Release Management, Service-Knowledge Management and Change and Configuration Management. It focuses on the creation or modification of production or other existing IT services and the implementation of infrastructure design requirements as they may be specified from Service Design principles.
- **Service Operation:** This area covers Request Fulfillment, Problem Management and Incident Management. It is concerned with the management and maintenance of day-to-day operations and maintaining SLA (Service Level Agreements) as contracted with customers.
- **Continual Service Improvement:** This area focuses on Service Level Management, Service Measurement and Service Reporting. It is concerned with the development and implementation of regular, incremental improvements in service standards and quality across the IT area.

Service Levels

In general, **Service Levels** may be defined as targets for availability, performance or quality of IT services contracted by a customer from a service provider. SLAs (Service Level Agreements) are the contracts that specify these targets in detail and provide information regarding service definitions, guarantees, consequences for violation of the agreement, etc. One function of ITSM is to ensure that SLAs are maintained.

Service Providers may implement various technologies to enable redundancy for service availability, monitoring of performance levels, security controls and any other items agreed upon with the customer. The responsibility of management is to ensure that the controls regarding availability, performance levels, etc. are adequate and that procedures covering maintenance, upgrades, capacity improvement and other areas are properly documented and observed by IT staff.

An example of the management responsibilities here would be the creation of policy and procedure regarding logging of critical events. Extensive logging, reviews of those logs for potential problems and reporting of any problems are essential detective and administrative controls that service providers should utilize. Yet another function is **job accounting**, which involves monitoring of services or resources supplied to enable accurate billing of customers and may alert IT staff to usage trends that require system upgrades or other configuration changes.

In contrast, customers of service providers may develop, purchase or outsource any testing and monitoring of agreed upon services. For example, customers may hire a third party to perform regular checks on the availability/uptime of a hosted website. If the availability over a 365 day period is measured to be less than the current standard of "five nines" (99.999% uptime), then the service provider may be required to offer discounts on future services or refunds of fees all ready paid.

Infrastructure Operations

Management's responsibility is to ensure that internal performance levels and general operations tasks are maintained. To accomplish this, detailed procedures for maintenance and other duties must be created and training of employees on those procedures must be implemented where appropriate. These procedures may include, but are not limited to, the following activities:

- Backup and Restore operations
- Troubleshooting and reporting of system abends and other incidents
- Help desk request fulfillment
- Code/Software library maintenance tasks

The role of computer operator is very important in environments that rely upon mainframe and/or client/server systems to provide services. Although the job title of "computer operator" is becoming less common, the responsibilities of those hired to fulfill those duties are crucial to the organization. Some of the job responsibilities include the following:

- Monitoring of operating system, application and network device performance.
- Performing scheduled backups/changing media on various machines
- Performing basic troubleshooting tasks
- Monitoring exits and entries into the processing facility
- Creating and disseminating reports to appropriate personnel
- Following problem escalation procedures for significant events.
- Creating, modifying and running batch files

Lights-Out Operations

This class of operation includes any set of tasks that may be scripted (automated) and run without human intervention. Advantages of this type of operation include: a decrease in the number of errors or failure of jobs to initialize and decreased operating costs. However, some IT staff should be available 24/7 to start or restart tasks that fail to run properly and to report on any trouble with automated processes.

Input-Output Controls

Transaction processing was discussed at length in Chapter 3. Management has a responsibility to ensure that controls exist that will enable the detection, reporting and perhaps even the correction of data processing errors. Malicious use of the processing system should also be a concern and should be included in the testing that is performed. The nature of computerized transactions limits the ability of humans to review and validate every transaction that occurs. This is especially true in high-volume environments. As a result, automated controls that check the transactions for inconsistencies must be implemented. In an environment where orders may only be taken from 9am to 5pm, it might be expected that most or all of the key staff members would be present if any problems were detected. In an automated, 24/7 environment, specialized software must be added to the processing that allows for detailed reporting of these events. The computer operator on duty should be notified, but in addition, separate notifications by email or pop-up windows should be sent to the database or application administrators. These staff members are the best qualified to troubleshoot processing errors and implement fixes to the system

Job Scheduling

This task is most applicable to automated and/or lights-out functions. Many maintenance tasks require that certain functions be performed on a regular basis, whether this is daily, weekly or some other schedule. Modern operating systems include some functionality that enables the scheduling of automated tasks. The scheduling functions need not be limited to operating system maintenance. It is possible to use job scheduling functions built into the OS to start or stop nearly any application that runs on a given server. Some of these built-in schedulers will even permit the scheduling of tasks on other network machines if the connections and permissions are properly configured.

Many applications, such as databases, include their own scheduling functions. Specialized job scheduling software also exists to manage network backups, anti-virus scans and other tasks whose functions might require a standardized solution. This is especially important in environments that utilize multiple computing platforms or are so large that efficient management of automated tasks merits a specialized solution.

Resource Monitoring

Incident Management is a business function whose focus is to handle events that occur within the IT framework that are outside of normal operations. The objectives are to anticipate, plan for, classify, respond to and document these events. This means that managers must develop procedures that describe the handling of expected and unexpected occurrences. These occurrences should be prioritized according to some meaningful system or metric and the response should result in a timely and adequate resolution for the event. Finally, documentation should be created to allow management to track incident handling and possibly contribute to improvements on the procedures that have been created.

Problem Management is very similar to Incident Management because one of its goals is a timely and adequate resolution to an event that affects the IT environment. Problem management may be indistinguishable from Incident Management in many organizations. A key difference is that Problem Management has an additional goal of system, quality or process improvement. While Incident Management is primarily focused on getting the issue resolved, problem management requires some kind of **root-cause analysis** or **post-mortem** to be performed. Information obtained from this process will be used to make improvements or changes to the IT infrastructure or process that was affected by the event. The end result should be a process or environment that is less vulnerable to that type of event in the future.

The types of events that are classified as Incidents or Problems have not been standardized. Each organization makes its own judgments regarding this. Many organizations include all of these activities under the umbrella of just one of the two management areas. The important issue for auditors is not whether an organization maintains distinct IT groups and policies for this type of issue. Instead the auditor should focus on the presence of adequate preventive and detective controls and the existence and adequacy of procedures to deal with whatever might produce a disturbance or risk concern to the organization (corrective controls).

Error Handling
System, application and even security errors and alerts may occur on workstations and servers at any time after the power is turned on. Most end users and many IT personnel do not look at error logs on their machines. They respond to critical errors that cause their devices or software to stop working and usually end up restarting the application, the machine or both to return everything to "normal". IS management must take a more proactive approach to error handling. Logs are an important detective control and in some cases, especially with certain hacking incidents, the initial logs generated may be the only clue that an intrusion or other unauthorized activity has taken place. The following is a brief list of procedures that could prove very useful:

- Logging should be enabled on every server and workstation. This should include the logging of security events.
- The servers and workstations should be configured to send information about critical or security errors across the network to a logging server.
- The organization should invest in software, workstations and storage devices that can be configured to capture, filter, report on and store the log data. Depending on the size of the network and the overall amount of traffic occurring on it, the storage capacity needed might easily amount to terabytes of data within a very short period. Special consideration should be given to the purchase and implementation of storage devices that can handle this load.
- Specialized logging software may allow very granular filtering of the logs for important issues. This type of application may also allow several types of alerts to be sent to various IT personnel for follow-up action.

The output of this type of application might easily be the start of an incident or problem management event.

Help Desk/Technical Support
Requests for assistance with technical issues may originate from an organization's staff or from its customers or others that use its resources. Management of this function usually involves action in three areas: problem identification, problem resolution and problem documentation.

Problem identification is usually performed by first or second level IT staff members that specialize in this area. They may follow scripts designed to help with troubleshooting and root-cause isolation. They may walk remote users through troubleshooting steps or they may respond in person to address the concerns of internal staff. They may escalate issues that they cannot resolve to IT staff with greater expertise. Procedures usually require first level staff to document every request and its disposition, including those involving escalations.

Problem resolution involves isolating the root cause of the issue and applying an appropriate solution to it. If a first-tier technician can fix the problem, then one-call resolution has been achieved. If that technician must escalate the issue, the task of documenting the actual root cause and its resolution fall upon the technicians who receive the escalated problem.

In recent years, the initial documentation of these requests has been likely to occur in a CRM application. One area this type of application has been optimized for is the documentation of each customer call or contact. Management may periodically review problem resolutions to determine if any trends may be detected. This can facilitate posting of a "known issue" and its solution on a publicly accessible site, which may reduce costs related to incoming calls about that issue.

Change Management

This topic was also covered at length in Chapter 3. The basic idea behind change management is to implement controls on changes that ensure the following:

- Changes only occur for valid (business) reasons
- Proposed changes must go through an approval process.
- Risk analysis should be performed when changes may adversely impact normal business functioning
- Procedures exist to ensure that any parties affected by a proposed change are notified in advance.
- All change requests are documented, whether they are approved or not.
- Only authorized personnel can implement changes.
- Procedures for rolling a system back to its previous state are documented and ready to be implemented if the proposed change creates any unstable conditions.
- All changes are verified; especially changes made to code destined for production environments, transaction processing or other critical tasks.
- A separate configuration database is updated so that an accurate and detailed list of all deployed IT resources and their configurations is maintained.

Library Management

The goal of Library Management is to ensure that adequate controls over access to the organization's software assets are implemented and enforced. Library management software provides an interface that offers several services to its administrators. It protects the integrity of the code it manages by allowing implementation of granular access controls. It also allows logging of any accesses, additions, modifications or deletions that occur within the library. The software may also be configured to generate alerts based on the occurrence of unauthorized activities. This software may also allow detailed comparisons of code versions to determine the exact location and extent of any changes made.

Release Management

In some organizations, this term may include or be synonymous with **"Patch Management"**. It involves the rollout of authorized updates or upgrades to firmware, operating systems and/or applications that have all ready been installed on workstations or other machines in the network. Since the scope of this action may be the entire organization, it is imperative that product release go through the same change management process used for internal change requests. Unfortunately, some useful updates, especially operating system updates, can cause unexpected problems in one or more vital applications. If the update cannot be rolled back, the organization may have a serious problem to correct. Therefore, release management should be a subset of change management and carefully controlled to maximize the stability of IS Operations.

Information Security Management

From ISACA's perspective, this topic is so important that an entire chapter has been devoted to it. In addition, the weight, emphasis or number of questions devoted to this topic is approximately twice that of any other topic in ISACA's auditing framework. Chapter 5 will cover this topic at length; however, it emphasizes the use or implementation of:

- Risk Assessments
- BIA (Business Impact Analyses)
- Security Reviews or Assessments
- A Vulnerability Management process.

Information Systems Hardware

At the core of every IS infrastructure is a collection of servers and workstations. Over time, the definitions applied to the various types and capabilities of these devices have changed. It is said that the average desktop computer sold today has more usable computing power than NASA had available when it enabled a man to walk on the moon. The following is a list of the most common or recognizable types of computing devices today:

- **Supercomputers**: These are expensive, specialized devices that run proprietary hardware and software to perform extremely rapid calculations on complex problems or data sets.
- **Mainframes:** These devices have the longest history in business usage and also have the most extensive and thoroughly tested sets of security controls. They may have standardized or proprietary Operating systems and they may also run specialized applications. Their primary strength has been data and transaction processing and they are still widely utilized for that purpose on the back-end of many processing-intensive environments.
- **Mini-computers/Midrange computers**: The technical distinctions between these classes of hardware are becoming blurred over time. These tend to be single purpose servers offered in tower or blade configurations for rack mounting. A vendor may prepare a device of this type in a hardened or other pre-configured state for use by a client or a client may purchase these devices and configure them internally. They still fall beneath the mainframes in capacity, yet they remain too powerful and costly to justify for purchase as end-user workstations.
- **Workstations/PCs/Microcomputers:** This is the category into which the vast majority of end-user devices fall. They may be configured to offer as much computing power as mini or midrange devices, but this is not the usual case. In general, organizations purchase this type of device in bulk and they order standardized configurations to allow for easier maintenance and upgrades. The Intel/AMD compatible versions of these devices may run variants of UNIX, Linux, Windows and most new Macintosh operating systems.
- **Thin Clients:** These are specialized microcomputers that possess minimal computing functionality when compared to "normal" PCs. These devices are usually purchased and implemented in carefully planned environments, since they only allow contact to a remote server on which the real applications reside. Depending on their configuration, they may be more secure devices for use by salespeople or others that are granted remote access. They can be more secure simply because they offer so little that a hacker might compromise.
- **Notebooks/Laptops:** These are usually lightweight, small footprint PCs. They are primarily designed for use by mobile personnel that need the full computing power of a PC wherever they may travel. Each vendor usually builds in enough proprietary features and software sets so that customers are locked in to the same vendor for upgrades or replacements to hardware and peripherals such as keyboards, batteries, display screens, AC power cords, etc. Because these devices run full operating systems and application sets, they are subject to the same security issues as PCs within an organization's physical infrastructure. Unfortunately, the fact that these devices may be issued to employees that work outside and connect remotely means that the organization's firewalls, IDS, content filtering and other controls will not be available to remote users.
- **PDAs/Blackberry devices/High-end Internet-capable phones**: These devices are usually offered only to personnel whose job functions or influence within the organization enable them to justify a request. Other employees may be free to purchase them for personal use, however, these employees may not be allowed to access internal resources with these devices. The various interfaces, email integration procedures and generally weak security controls on these devices cause them to be considered as administrative challenges at best or administrative nightmares at worst.

Server Functions and Processing

Many information systems resources and key functions in organizations are offered through client/server configurations. This usually requires the following steps:

- The installation of an operating system of some kind on a hardware platform
- The installation and configuration of one or more applications that will run on that operating system.
- The configuration of the network's directory and/or access services to monitor and control traffic or access to and from the application or hardware device.

There are many types of services or functions that may be implemented within an organization. The following are some of the more common types:

- **Applications:** These may include databases, software development systems, payroll systems, intranets, clustering (if the application offers that functionality) and many other services that must allow access to multiple users.
- **Networking Functions:** These services are normally offered through specialized hardware devices configured with proprietary operating systems and application functions. Please note that depending on the vendor from which these devices are purchased, one or more of these functions may be combined in a single device or application. These functions/devices include:
    - Routers
    - Switches
    - Application Gateways
    - Load Balancers
    - IDS/IPS (Intrusion Detection/Prevention Systems)
    - VPN Concentrators
    - Firewalls
- **Specialized Servers:** These devices and the applications run on them usually require special configuration, tuning and hardware to perform at optimal efficiency. The following types of servers are common:
- **Database Servers:** (These will be discussed later in this chapter)
- **E-Commerce/EDI/Transaction Processing Servers:** (See chapter 3 for more details)
- **Web Servers:**
    - Internet (Facing the public)
    - Intranet (For internal use only)
    - Extranet (For use by business partners and clients; this may be part of an ERM (Enterprise Relationship Management), CRM (Customer Relationship Management) or SCM (Supply Chain Management) setup.
- **Proxy/Content Filtering Servers:** This type of server is implemented to add to network security by acting as a go-between or middleman for web requests from internal users and the actual web sites on the Internet. When this type of service is used, no end user device connects directly to any external sources.
- **File and Print Servers**

Processing Types

The manner in which a hardware platform/OS/application combination handles the data that flows through it can have a huge effect on the overall speed of data flow and the availability or number of connections to resources that may be obtained through that device. The following are some technologies in current use on server-type systems:

- **Multi-Using:** Nearly all client/server environments work this way. Multiple workstations may access resources on a server at the same time. Each request is handled in a series of steps by the server's CPU and a certain number of CPU cycles are allotted to these stages. This is equivalent to "**timesharing**", because the operating system determines how these cycles are allotted to each workstation's requests.
- **Multi-tasking:** In general, this refers to the ability of an operating system to allow multiple applications to be opened and "running" at the same time. In practice, the operating system allots CPU cycles to each application in order depending on the algorithms built into that OS. In the case of single CPU systems, the various stages of application requests are only processed one instruction at a time, so it is not technically correct to say that two tasks can be performed at once (see Multi-processing below).
- **Multi-threading:** Some applications may be developed in such a way that they can make multiple requests for system resources simultaneously. However, the same problem or limitation exists with this type of application as exists with "multi-tasking" as explained above.
- **Distributed or Grid Processing:** This type of application has been designed to access hundreds or even thousands of machines simultaneously. The various processing requests are divided up across spare CPU cycles of all of these machines. The SETI@home project is probably the most famous of all such systems.[3]
- **Multi-processing:** Some motherboard configurations are equipped to allow two or more CPUs (Central Processing Units) to be installed simultaneously. If (and only if) the operating system and the applications installed have been developed to take advantage of this type of configuration, then it is possible for very high data throughput rates to be achieved. Only when two or more CPUs are present is it possible to allow processing of two or more requests at the same time. Note that the term "support" when used in connection with multiple processor platforms is not equivalent to "optimization" for use on multi-processing systems.

Common Storage Devices

Several types of storage devices and media are available for use by the organization, end users or both. The following types of storage are very common today:

- **Hard Disks:** These devices are usually the primary long-term storage media for servers and workstations. Their balance of speed and storage capacity has kept the technology alive. These devices come in internal and external formats. "External" usually refers to hard drives that are:
    - Not permanently installed within the PCs case. Some configurations allow a drive to be slid into a PC for temporary use, and then removed via a handle for portability and/or security reasons.
    - Encased in a shell that allows the use of external AC power and connection of USB or IDE cables.
    - MP3/Music Players: Many of these devices are actually small hard drives encased in attractive cases that are accompanied by software that facilitates the recording and playback of music in various file formats. Some of these portable players can store up to 40GB of data.
- **USB Flash Drives and Memory Cards**
    - The USB 2.0 (Universal Serial Bus) connector is standard on nearly every PC and laptop sold today. Even devices that are marketed as servers often have one or more built-in USB ports. These drives are small, rewritable and easily concealed. At the time this chapter was written, USB drives with capacities of up to 16GB might be purchased for less than $200.
    - Memory cards come in several formats including SD (Secure Digital), MiniSD, MicroSD, XD Picture cards Memory Sticks and CF (Compact Flash Cards). Depending on the card type, these rewriteables may hold 64 MB to 16GB of data. Memory cards are most commonly used in PDAs, phones, cameras and music players.
- **DVD-R, DVD-RW, CD-R, CD-RW, HD-DVD, Blu-Ray:** These devices also come in internal and external configurations. CDs may store up 700MB of uncompressed data. Single and Dual-layer DVDs may store 4.7GB to 8.5GB of uncompressed data. Individual HD-DVD and Blu-Ray discs may hold up to 30GB and 50GB, respectively. The external versions of these devices are usually connected to PCs by means of a USB cable.

Unfortunately, many organizations do not implement adequate security measures in regard to devices that may be connected via USB to internal machines. As a result, it might be possible for someone on the inside to copy huge amounts of data onto one of these media and simply carry it out of the building. Also, the **use of compression** on files that are to be copied may increase the total amount of data that can be stored on any of the media mentioned above by 25% or more.

Infrastructure Monitoring and Maintenance

Monitoring of hardware and applications helps to support a sound ITSM practice. Monitoring allows an organization to track the usage, error status, availability and even location of various network assets. This information can help an organization to be sure that it meets its SLAs with clients (see Chapter 3) and also improve security measures. The following types of monitoring technologies may be employed to improve security:

- Logging or auditing of successful or failed access attempts to files, applications, devices and other network resources. If reviews of this type of log indicate that malicious activity might e occurring, additional security measures may be implemented to deal with the problem proactively.
- Location of network assets and/or product shipments: This can be accomplished in several ways, depending on the method of shipment used. Scans of bar-codes printed on shipping labels or even newer RFID (Radio Frequency Identification tags may used to provide regular reports about the status of any given shipment. RFID may also be used to track the movement of key resources within an organization's infrastructure. RFID detectors may be used to provide warnings if monitors, PCs, printers or other assets are removed from the premises.
- The following may aid in maintenance efforts by influencing what type of upgrade or improvements should be made to the infrastructure during emergency or regular maintenance windows:
    - Hardware Utilization reports: The amount of data sent or received by a server, CPU processing statistics, number of transaction completed in a given timeframe and hard disk reads and writes are several examples of the types of utilization that may be monitored and evaluated. Note that this type of monitoring is also heavily used in **Capacity Management**, which involves planning to ensure that any promised availability of resources is delivered to both internal and external users of network resources.
    - Server/Website/Application Uptime figures

Computer Operating Systems and Architecture

Individual servers and workstations must be able to process data in order to be effective. The architecture of a computer system includes the various layers or stages of I/O (Input/Output) activity that goes on during this internal processing of data. This processing involves the operating system's handling of requests initiated by a user via one or more applications. Although many analogies might be used to describe what happens during this processing, it might be useful to view the entire process as a type of relay race.

Using this analogy, any request made by a user or application generates one or more instructions that must be processed by the CPU. The generation of these requests by applications is an output from the applications, but the request is an input to the operating system's CPU scheduling algorithms. In modern computer engineering, no request for access or data transfer to or from I/O devices such as keyboards, mice, trackballs, printers, hard disks, network interface cards (NICs) or any other peripheral device can take place without some sort of instruction processing approved by the OS and by the performed by the CPU. From a very high-level vantage point, every one of these requests for some kind of time is an output from something and an input to something else. The handoff of the baton in a relay race illustrates what must take place as each participant in the chain receives an input (instruction), processes it, and then passes it off to the next participant in the chain.

Since modern CPUs can handle billions of individual instructions (or cycles in GHz) per second, the perception of multiple actions taking place at once is created. However, because the CPU can only process one instruction at a time, the fact is that only one action may occur at single point in time. A single request may require thousands of cycles to complete. A user may initiate several such requests at once. The number of instructions involved is of no concern to the average computer user. However, the job of assigning the order of access to the CPU and the cycles allocated to a given thread or application at any time is the job of the operating system.

Although this may be debated, it is likely that supercomputers and mainframes offer the most efficient and comprehensive scheduling of CPU time and I/O requests. These devices often utilize proprietary ASICs (Application Specific Integrated Circuits) built onto their motherboards to help in caching of requests, caching of data needed to properly handle those requests and perform the calculations needed to determine CPU allocations. Some will contend that UNIX based systems on non-Intel hardware are the next best and that Linux and Windows OSes on Intel platforms follow in that order. When planning the development of an IS infrastructure, the Network and Systems administrators should carefully consider the requirements supplied by the client or organization to determine the best mix of devices and software to meet the stated needs.

Operating System and Application Integrity

Developers that create operating systems should have a high level of familiarity with the hardware platform's requirements. For example, Intel/AMD-based systems do not process instructions the same way that Motorola-based systems do. In addition, application developers must have a high-level of familiarity with an operating system's APIs (Application Programming Interfaces) to ensure that the I/O requests made can be understood by the operating system and that they do not cause conflicts in processing or memory usage. Since the OS controls I/O requests, it must also contain controls that verify the requests made by applications to ensure that conflicts do not occur.

When operating systems and/or applications do not precisely allocate memory and control access to devices, security holes may exist. These holes or **vulnerabilities** may be exploited by people that intend to gain unauthorized access to the operating system and the resources it controls. If the developers of these systems are made aware of the vulnerabilities, they may be able to create one or more patches or security updates that address the vulnerability or remove access to the vulnerability in some way.

A comprehensive logging /auditing program that includes monitoring and review of access attempts to key resources is a vital detective control when vulnerabilities are considered. It may not be possible to the average administrator to re-code an OS or an essential application. However, if successful or failed access attempts to key files show any uncharacteristic increases, an administrator might be concerned enough to begin to trace the source of these attempts. This could allow the administrator to locate any unauthorized accounts or software that may have been added to the network as the result of a successful exploit of some vulnerability.

This type of logging or auditing may be implemented by other areas of the OS, an application or even third-party **access control software**. Note that a sound network design will include plans for auditing or monitoring accesses of resources and data transfers and communications. Provisions for layered or overlapping preventive, detective and corrective security measures are usually less expensive to implement if their implementation is part of the initial design.

Database Management System (DBMS) Software

DBMSs are applications whose function is to manage the storage, organization, sorting, filtering and presentation of the data requested by users via other application programs. It also allows for optimization techniques such as normalization and indexing which may decrease search times and other access speeds, reduce redundancy in storage, and possibly improve security.

Modern DBMSs also include or allow integration with modules that facilitate reporting, data mining, various business intelligence applications and dashboard construction. The management controls often allow for creation of multiple groups and views that may be distributed to different user groups depending on their job functions. Customized DBMSs are at the heart of every CRM, SCM and ERP system available on the market. Current enterprise-level DBMSs offer highly granular access control options that apply to every level of database interaction. Some of the access levels include:

- Database to transaction, application or user
- Transaction to application or user
- User, program or transaction to data records (rows or tuples) or fields (columns)

Metadata

Metadata may be defined as "data about the data". It is used to configure and or describe the architecture and contents of a database. In general, there are three types of metadata, namely, conceptual, external and internal schema. A **data dictionary** or **directory system** (DD/DS) is an organizational system used to store and provide an ordered structure to the various types of metadata. A DD or DS usually offers a control application or interface that allows a database designer or administrator to interact with the database and implement security, develop queries or searches and create mappings between the different schemas and creating database structures.

SQL (Structured Query Language) is a programming language that includes **data definition language** (DDL) commands. DDL commands such as ALTER, CREATE, DROP and TRUNCATE facilitate this aspect of database management. SQL has been standardized by groups such as ANSI (American National Standards Institute) and ISO (International Organization for Standardization). However, in recent years, vendors of DBMS products have been called upon to certify their own products for conformity to the accepted standards. This means that industry giants such as IBM, Oracle and Microsoft may offer products that use different syntax to accomplish various functions, as long as those functions are in line with the standard.

A newcomer to the DDL arena is XML (Extensible Markup Language), which is a standard supported by the W3C (World Wide Web Consortium).[4] XML is being developed as a more robust DDL that allows greater flexibility in the creation of data structures and definition of new data types. This flexibility is being used to facilitate many of the new internet-based transaction and security technologies. Since XML is platform-independent, developers can write applications that use XML to publish and access **Web Services**, which are essentially resources or applications that an organization wants to offer via Internet connectivity.

Database Models

Several database models have been developed over the past few decades. Each model has strengths and weaknesses. The following is a brief description of the most common types:

- **Hierarchical:** This is the earliest model. It uses a tree structure and is fairly efficient at describing simple relationships between two types of data or nested data such as a table of contents. It is weaker when a relationship needs to be defined between data elements on different branches of the tree structure. XML is based on a hierarchical structure.
- **Network:** This model is derived from the hierarchical model. It facilitates the creation of multiple branches from a single point or node in a tree. A **navigation system** of some type is used to keep track of the location of data records and the relationships between them. This can speed access between data elements that might otherwise be on entirely different branches in a pure hierarchical system.
- **Object:** This model is distinguished by the ways in which developers enhanced the navigational systems in network models to allow for greater functionality and faster searches within and across multiple databases.
- **Relational:** This is the most common model offered by DBMS vendors today. The most basic structure in this model is a **table**, which contains rows and columns that define the elements and attributes of a type of entity or conceptual structure. A database may contain multiple tables. The strength of this model is in the way that "relations" between different tables may be created or modified. SQL contains statements that allow users to **query** or manipulate the data in tables to form new logical relationships. The new relationships may be arranged on a user's screen in a format called a **view**. Views are arrangements of data from one or more tables that allow data to be examined in a more efficient or meaningful form.
- **Hybrid:** Some vendors offer DBMS systems that are advertised as **Object-Relational** or some other variation on the models described above. Any of the variations or combinations that might be implemented are attempts to get the best possible balance of functionality, performance and security that may be had from a single system. Even systems that are described as relational may include features drawn from other models, so there is no standard method for categorizing them.

Storage Management

Data storage is a critical function in modern organizations. An in-depth discussion of storage techniques is well beyond the scope of this text. However, given the current trends in data management, it may be helpful to divide data storage into two broad categories based on the need for access to that data. The first type would be low or infrequent access and the second would be high or frequent access. The following is a brief description of these storage types:

- **Infrequent Access:** This type of access is the type that most non-technical users are familiar with. It includes all long-term backups or archived data and code. This type of data is usually stored on high density tape, optical or CD media that offer relatively slow access times. The types of media and devices used for this storage must be carefully considered and monitored since this type of storage is most often used to facilitate **disaster recovery** (DR) efforts. Business continuity and Disaster Recovery are the subjects of chapter 6, so further discussion of this type of storage will found there.
- **Frequent Access:** The development and implementation of **data warehouses** and **Storage Area Networks** (SANs) have facilitated the creation of many types of business intelligence (BI) applications. In general, BI is a method by which an organization can obtain more precise information about its processes and day-to-day operations. This is accomplished by the use of one or more **data mining** or analysis techniques. The applications that perform this type of analysis must be able to read the data stored in one or more DBMSs and perform various searches and calculations on this data. The objective is that some type of meaningful information may be obtained that will allow key decision makers to improve on or create new opportunities or processes.

The distinction between infrequent and frequent access is becoming blurred over time as the amount of data included in BI queries is increased. The capabilities of modern DBMSs and the introduction of Gigabit Ethernet connections for modern storage networks allows data that would normally be archived to be included in data mining efforts. Some believe that the larger the overall set of data is, the better the chances are that accurate results of analyses may be obtained. The following are some of the BI application types that are facilitated by advances in data warehousing and SANs:

- OLAP (Online Analytical Processing)
- BPR (Business Process Re-engineering)
- Project Management Forecasts (Cost, Time, Personnel and Material estimates)
- Executive Information Systems
- Decision Support Systems
- Generalized Dashboard Applications
- Knowledge Management
- Artificial Intelligence/Neural Networks

Network Infrastructures

The concept of the "infrastructure" has seen radical change in the last five to ten years. The availability of the Internet has forced many organizations to re-think their business models and their product and service offerings. Remaining competitive often requires implementing new hardware and software technologies that allow the following:

- Increased access for "internal" employees to network resources
- Access to network resources for mobile or remote employees that travel or work from branch offices or from their homes.
- Access to network resources via extranets for business to business (B2B) customers.
- Access to online catalogs and ordering for individual customers
- Access via wireless technology within the infrastructure for employees that don't have access to wired connections or to minimize wiring costs and construction-related inconveniences

Network Architectures

Some of the category distinctions below may be considered obsolete by individual network design personnel. However, the provisioning of telecommunications connections remains an important factor in the definitions of these architectures. Therefore, the list will mention as many types as possible, in spite of the fact that each type may be facilitated by more than one telecommunications method.

- **Wide Area Network (WAN):** These networks normally include multiple physical structures that span multiple states or countries. The connections at each site are usually made with a single carrier (or multiple carriers for redundancy) and the designers of the network choose one or more media types to enable data transfers.
- **Metropolitan Area Network (MAN):** This kind of architecture would be implemented by an organization that operated two or more sites within or very close to a single municipality. A university or a local public transportation system would use this type of architecture. Multiple carriers (or service providers) and media types may still be chosen as this level.
- **Local Area Network (LAN):** This architecture is normally included within a single physical structure, whether it is an office building, factory or some other facility. This type of architecture is experiencing the greatest amount of change in its definition because many of the new technologies offer changes to the way organizations work within single structures. Multiple carriers and media may be chosen to provide connectivity to these networks.

- **Wireless Local Area Networks (WLANs):** WLANs rely upon an existing LAN or at least an Internet connection to function. They use a device capable of converting an incoming Ethernet signal to a radio signal or vice-versa. They enable PCs laptops, PDAs or other Internet capable devices with the appropriate wireless receiver, to use the LAN's network and Internet connections. As wireless technologies are maturing in both the capacity and security areas, they are becoming increasing attractive for organizations that have the following needs:
    - They share space with other organizations in office buildings
    - They want to offer greater mobility to employees that must work at multiple locations within the same facility
    - They want to minimize the costs of hiring electricians or other contractors to install new wiring in an existing structure.

- **VoWLANs** (Voice over WLANs): Traditional phone systems require some kind of wiring to connect each user's phone to a PBX or other system that will, in turn, be connected to a phone service provider. VoIP (Voice over Internet Protocol) technology exists, but has been offered primarily over wired media such as Ethernet cables. Wireless connections may also carry IP traffic and can be configured to allow VoIP phones to be connected to an external carrier without the need to ad additional wiring to a facility.
- **Storage Area Network (SAN):** These are subsets of a LAN used to implement a fairly complex data storage and retrieval system.
- **Personal Area Network (PAN):** This term has been used to describe the set of Internet-connected devices assigned to or owned by a single person. A PAN may include one or more PCs, laptops, printers, PDAs, phones, etc that use a single internet connection. A PAN may be set up in a home, an apartment, an office, a cubicle or even in a hotel room.

The Internet

It is not feasible to include a detailed history of the Internet in this publication. Several online sites offer historical information about the Internet, but one of the most authoritative is maintained by the Internet Society (ISOC).[5] The Internet as we know it began in the early 1960s as research projects on packet switching theory that began at several universities and was eventually funded by the ARPA (Advanced Research Projects Agency), which was a branch of the DoD (Department of Defense) that funded defense related scientific efforts. The first WAN environment was named the ARPANET after the government agency that funded the development. The issue they needed to address was one of enabling redundant or alternative communications channels for the military in the event that some disaster, man-made or otherwise rendered the primary communications channels inoperable.

The initial ARPANET did not have all the protocols and standards we know of today. The first computer officially connected to the ARPANET in 1969 and email wasn't invented until 1972. Over a decade of research and development passed before the OSI published their seven layer reference model. The first Internet browser (Mosaic) was not developed until 1993. The DoD (or TCP/IP model) four layer model was drawn from the OSI model. Both models of these provide broad, high-level views of the way devices that used this network should communicate. The OSI's seven layer model is the more famous of the two but it is not necessarily better. Because each is a **reference model**, neither actually imposes a standard on software or hardware developers. The DoD model simply divides the same area into four groups instead of seven.

TCP/IP DOD Model	vs.	OSI Model
Process/Application		Application (7)
		Presentation (6)
		Session (5)
Host-to-host		Transport (4)
Internet		Network (3)
Network Access		Data Link (2)
		Physical (1)

Exam Tip: Concentrate most of your efforts on the **OSI model** and its way of representing network traffic and communication. It is the more popular of the two models. *Most* text books, study or certification guides and vendor materials describe network devices accessories and communications in terms of their relationship to the OSI model.

A more detailed and less abstract view of network traffic based on the OSI model:

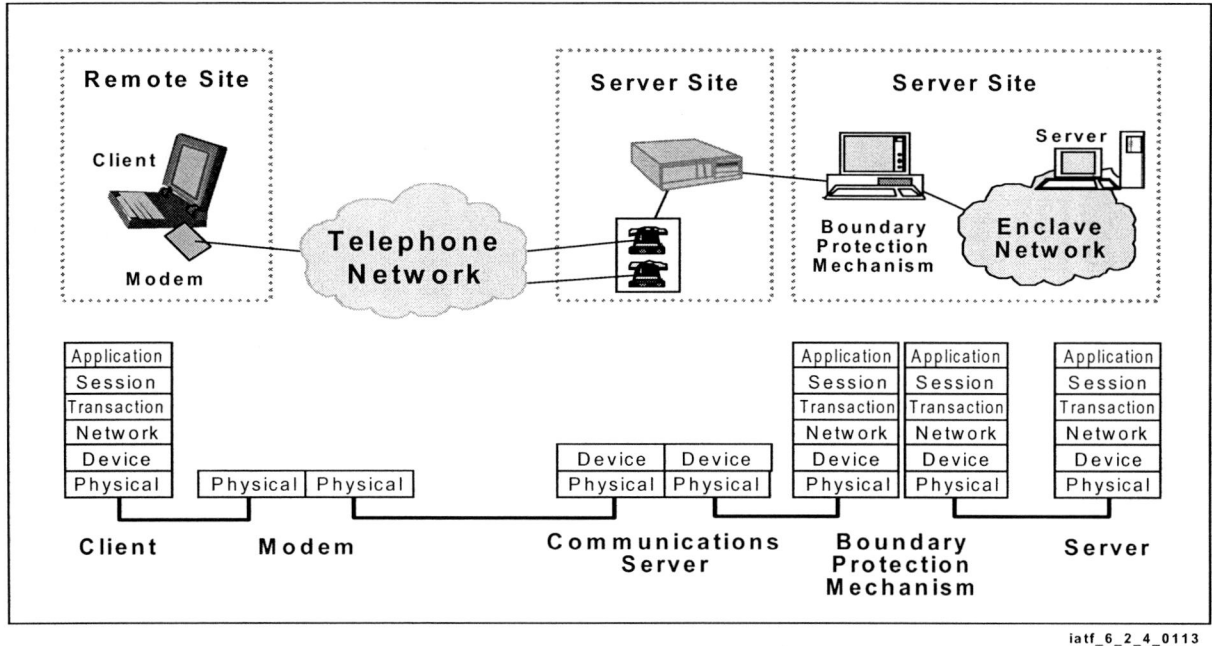

Application Layer – Provides services to the users of the OSI environment such as transaction server, file transfer protocol, network management, information validation. This is the application dialog (running an EDI application). Also provides application access security checking and information validation.

Presentation Layer – Performs transformations on data to provide a standardized application interface and to provide common communications services such as encryption, text compression, reformatting. This layer provides representation of information: formats, codes, transformation and encryption.

Session Layer – Provides the control structure for communication between applications. Establishes, manages and terminates connections (sessions) between cooperating applications -- Performs access security checking.

Transport Layer – Provides reliable, transparent transfer of data between end points; provides end-to-end error recovery and flow control. Instructions include breaking down a message into packets, addressing the packets, forwarding them across the network and acknowledging and reassembling them into the original message. (This identifies how you get between points, i.e. traffic within transmission).

Network Layer – Sends packets or streams. It also provides network management (routing, switching, traffic monitoring and congestion control) and initiates an end-to-end pathway. The network layer controls the packet routing and switching within the network as well as to any other network, if applicable. Controls over network connections, logical channels, segmenting, sequencing and data flow can be placed in this layer.

Data Link Layer – Provides for the reliable transfer of data across the physical link. It sends blocks of data (frames) with the necessary synchronization, bit error detection/correction error control and flow control. This node-to-node control of data flow across the circuit controls approximately 70 percent of all error handling. Encryption can be used to protect the message as it flows between each network node. Each node then decrypts the message received and re-encrypts it for transmission to the next node.

Physical Layer – Transmits bits over this channel to establish maintain and deactivate the physical link.

The protocols within the TCP/IP suite were developed over the past three decades. The table below describes the activities expected (but not mandated) at each layer of the OSI model:

Layer	Function	Protocols	Network Component
Application (Layer 7) Gets **DATA** from **Applications** via **USER INPUT**	User Interface • Used for applications specifically written to run over the network • Allows access to network services that support applications; • Directly represents the services that directly support user applications • Handles network access, flow control and error recovery • Example apps are file transfer, e-mail, NetBIOS-based applications	DNS; FTP; TFTP; BOOTP; SNMP;RLOGIN; SMTP; MIME; NFS; FINGER; TELNET; NCP; APPC; AFP; SMB	Gateway
Presentation (Layer 6) Gets **DATA** from **Applications** via **USER INPUT**	Translation • Translates from application to network format and vice-versa • All formats from any source are converted to a common format that the rest of the OSI model can understand • Responsible for protocol conversion, character conversion, data encryption / decryption, expanding graphics commands, data compression • Sets standards for different systems to provide seamless communication from multiple protocol stacks • Not always implemented in a network protocol	MIME, XML ASCII, EBCDIC	Gateway Redirector
Session (Layer 5) Gets **DATA** from **Applications** via **USER INPUT**	"Syncing and sessions" • Establishes, maintains and ends sessions across the network • Responsible for name recognition (identification) so only the designated parties can participate in the session • Provides synchronization services by planning check points in the data stream => if session fails, only data after the most recent checkpoint need be transmitted • Manages who can transmit data at a certain time and for how long • Examples are interactive login and file transfer connections, the session would connect and re-connect if there was an interruption; recognize names in sessions and register names in history	NetBIOS Names Pipes Mail Slots RPC	Gateway

Layer	Function	Protocols	Network Component
Transport (Layer 4) Takes **DATA** from the upper three layers and converts it to **SEGMENTS**	Packets; flow control & error-handling • Additional connection below the session layer • Manages the flow control of data between parties across the network • Divides streams of data into chunks or packets; the transport layer of the receiving computer reassembles the message from packets • A "train" is a good analogy => the data is divided into identical units • Provides error-checking to guarantee error-free data delivery, with on losses or duplications • Provides acknowledgment of successful transmissions; requests retransmission if some packets don't arrive error-free • Provides flow control and error-handling	TCP, ARP, RARP; SPX NWLink NetBIOS / NetBEUI ATP	Gateway Advanced Cable Tester Brouter
Network (Layer 3) Takes **SEGMENTS** from Transport layer and converts them **PACKETS**	Addressing; routing • Translates logical network address and names to their physical address (e.g. computername ==> MAC address) • Responsible for addressing, determining routes for sending, managing network problems such as packet switching, data congestion and routing if router can't send data frame as large as the source computer sends, the network layer compensates by breaking the data into smaller units. At the receiving end, the network layer reassembles the data. Think of this layer stamping the addresses on each train car	IP; ARP; RARP, ICMP; RIP; OSFP; IGMP;IPX, NWLink NetBEUI OSI DDP DECnet	Brouter Router Advanced Cable Tester
Data Link (Layer 2) Takes **PACKETS** from the Network layer and converts them to **FRAMES**	Turns packets into raw bits (0s and 1s) and at the receiving end turns bits into packets. • Handles data frames between the Network and Physical layers • The receiving end packages raw data from the Physical layer into data frames for delivery to the Network layer • Responsible for error-free transfer of frames to other computer via the Physical Layer • This layer defines the methods used to transmit and receive data on the network. It consists of the wiring, the devices use to connect the NIC to the wiring, the signaling involved to transmit / receive data and the ability to detect signaling errors on the network media	802.2 Logical Link Control LLC)/ Media Access Control (MAC) Error correction and flow control 802.1 OSI Model Communicates with the adapter card Controls the type of media being used: 802.3 CSMA/CD (Ethernet) 802.4 Token Bus (ARCnet) 802.5 Token Ring 802.12 Demand Priority	Bridge Switch ISDN Router Intelligent Hub NIC Frame Relay Device ATM Switch Advanced Cable Tester

Layer	Function	Protocols	Network Component
Physical (Layer 1) Takes **FRAMES** from the **DATA LINK** layer and converts them to **BITS**	Transmits raw bit stream over physical cable • Defines cables, cards, and physical aspects • Defines NIC attachments to hardware, how cable is attached to NIC • Defines techniques to transfer bit stream to cable	IEEE 802 IEEE 802.2 ISO 2110 ISDN	Repeater Multiplexer Hubs Passive Active TDR Oscilloscope Amplifier

Network Devices
Physical Layer (Layer 1)

Hubs and repeaters are physical-layer devices. Functionally, hubs and repeaters do the same thing; however hubs tend to have more ports than repeaters. As a result hubs are sometimes called multi-port repeaters. Neither hubs nor repeaters have software installed that is capable of distinguishing differing types of network traffic. Neither device can perform specialized actions on network traffic. They may be considered "dumb" devices.

The primary function of these devices is to receive and/or amplify a signal and repeat the signal out of all ports. Hubs cannot check the integrity of the data, so if the data contains an error, the hub will simply pass the error around. Hubs do nothing to reduce contention on the network; in fact, hubs increase contention because they pass any and all data coming in from any single port to every other port on the device. Every device that is connected to a hub "sees" every bit of traffic sent to or from every other device. Neither hubs nor repeaters are capable of being configured to provide security, therefore the IS auditor should recommend that these devices be removed from the network whenever they are found. Inexpensive unmanaged switches reduce contention, improving network performance and are better choices for low-end group connectivity than hubs in every way.

Exam Tip: A Mnemonic (memory aid) for the OSI model layers (Top-Down; Layer 7 to Layer 1) is: **A**ll **P**eople **S**eem to **N**eed **D**ata **P**rocessing

Datalink Layer (Layer 2)

Bridges and switches are datalink-layer devices. Bridges are usually implemented via software and provide only two "interfaces" linking two parts of a single segment to each other. Switches are hardware devices with more than two physical ports. Both bridges and switches can distinguish between each connected network device by the unique MAC (Media Access Control) address hard-coded into the NIC (Network Interface Card) found on each network device. The **MAC address** is also known as the **physical address**. Both bridges and switches use a table or database to store MAC address information on each connected device and the default gateway (the port leading out of the switch into a different switch or a router).Both switches and bridges can use the information in the database to forward traffic only to the device that is intended to see it or out of the default gateway. The switch has its software installed onto ASICs via firmware. This usually enables switches to forward traffic at higher rates than bridges or routers can.

Both bridges and switches can control **collision domains**. This means that their ability to segregate the traffic coming to and from each device by the MAC address in the frame keeps Ethernet packets from bumping into each other. When a "bump" or collision occurs, both devices that were trying to send and/or receive data must wait for a random time period, and then attempt to resend the same data again. The need to resend data is most common in dumb devices like hubs and repeaters and it can be a huge drain on performance. Preventing collisions is one way that low-end switches can improve network performance.

If a stream of traffic is forwarded to the subnet's broadcast address, the switch will not filter or distinguish anything, but will send the traffic to each connected device. The traffic within and intended for an entire subnet is known as **broadcast traffic** and the subnet is the **broadcast domain**. Switches do not have the capability to distinguish this traffic, so each device will get it. **Broadcast storms** are situations when the amount of traffic aimed at the entire subnet is so great that the switch cannot effectively forward frames. This can slow or even stop all traffic on the subnet.

VLANs

A VLAN is a **Virtual LAN**. This means that is is the equivalent of a Network layer subnet, but it is implemented in a switch. Many inexpensive switches have the ability to create VLANs. This does *not* mean that the switch can function as a router, which can distinguish traffic by Layer 3 information contained in the packet headers. Instead, a VLAN-capable switch has additional software that enables its owner to configure "subnets" by specifying ports on the switch that should be grouped together. Again, since the switch *cannot* function as a router, there is no way for traffic originating on one VLAN to get to devices on another VLAN unless the switch is configured to connect to a router. The router may be configured with mappings of IP addresses to VLAN numbers. The traffic from one VLAN destined for another VLAN would be forwarded out of the switch to a router. The router would then forward the traffic back to the switch to the other VLAN based on the IP address to VLAN number mapping configured on it.

Network Layer (Layer 3)
Routers

Routers continue to build on the technologies that we have previously discussed. Routers function at the Network layer, and are often referred to as a layer-3 device. Routers are able to further optimize network traffic by utilizing the logical addressing information available from the Network layer. Routers are considered "network aware" which means that routers can differentiate between different networks. Routers use this information to build routing tables, which are tables that list the following basic information:
- All the networks the router knows about:
- The remote router to use to connect to those networks (Next Hop address)
- The paths or routes to remote networks
- The cost, or metric of sending data over the paths

With this information, the router can make intelligent determinations of the most efficient, or at least what the router deems most efficient, path to the specified network. Routers may be used to segment large networks into smaller ones, as well as to reduce broadcasts on a network. Routers recognize that most broadcasts are specific to the network that they originated, so instead of forwarding the broadcasts as a hub or switch does, the router will stop the broadcast. Because routers function at a higher layer in the OSI model than switches, they are also able to provide more granular or specific traffic management and security capabilities than switches or hubs can. Routers are able to examine logical addresses (IP addresses) and the rest of the layer-3 header information to determine what application ports are being used and use the information for traffic filtering and blocking purposes.

Gateways and Proxies

The term "gateway" has a number of meanings. In some cases a gateway is just a router. A gateway can also refer to a device that provides proxy-type functionality. In its most basic definition, a gateway provides connectivity between two or more distinct or dissimilar networks. Proxies are used as intermediaries between a client and a server, or a client and the Internet. They can provide the client transparent access to the resources on the server or on the Internet without allowing the client to access those resources directly. As a result, proxies can be used as a security device (for example, an application proxy/firewall). Because the traffic between the client and remote server must go through the proxy, the administrator can restrict and control traffic at the proxy. A common use for proxies is to provide Internet access to an organization's internal workstations. Proxies may allow administrators to examine all incoming traffic and block inappropriate content. Monitoring and logging of repeated attempts to access blocked sites can allow administrators to locate users that could be violating acceptable use policies. Proxy servers may also be able to cache data, so they can provide better network performance by servicing requests with cached data as opposed to sending a new request to a remote host for the response.

Media Types

Each type of network architecture utilizes one or more types of transmission media to allow data transfer. Each media type has limits in terms of maximum speeds, bandwidth, security, and the distance over which the transmissions may travel before augmentation may be required. The following are media types used for different architectures:

- **WAN and MAN Connections:** In general, these connections involve the use of technology offered by long distance carriers. They are normally limited to layers 1 through 3 of the OSI model. These may include one or more of the following: Satellite, Microwave or Radio Technology (The medium is the atmosphere), Fiber-optic Cable, Copper Cable, Coaxial Cable, Wireless Broadband (This is a very new offering and not yet widely available)
- **LAN Connections:** Fiber-Optic Cable, Coaxial Cable, Copper, Wireless

Access Methods

There are protocols that are commonly used to facilitate data transfer over each media type. The access methods available depend on the service provider chosen, the media used and the funds available for provisioning and monthly service fees. Each access method/protocol type has different functionality in terms of maximum speeds, bandwidth, security methods, QoS (Quality of Service) options and even the distance over which the transmissions may travel. The protocols and standards governing these technologies operate at layers 1 through 3 of the OSI model. The job of the network design team is to balance the needs of the organization against the service available:

- WAN and MAN Links: T-1 thru T-3 (DS series), OC1 through OC192 (Optical Carrier/SONET {Synchronous Optical Network}), ATM (Asynchronous Transfer Mode), Frame-Relay, PPPoE (Point-to-Point Protocol over Ethernet), X.25, ISDN (Integrates Services Digital Network), DSL Variants.
- LAN links: Ethernet, Token Ring, Wireless

Exam Tip: It is recommended that CISA candidates research these technologies to gain additional familiarity with them. Audit of telecommunications and/or network edge configurations requires significant familiarity with the lower end of the OSI model and the capabilities and limitations of these methods.

Remote Access

Remote access enables traveling or telecommuting users to securely access resources on their organization's Local Area Network (LAN), local enclaves, or local enterprise-computing environments via telephone or high speed commercial data networks. Securing remote access may require the use of VPN (virtual private network), SSL (Secure Sockets Layer) or some other technology that will enable I&A (identification and authentication) of remote users. In general, the remote access user connects by a public or shared commercial path such as the Internet that is provided by a telecommunications carrier. Users can maintain privacy on their connections using encrypting modems, low-end routers with VPN capability or VPN client software installed on their computers. Because the user entry point into the enterprise-computing environment could be used or monitored by malicious parties, the organization must use strong protections at the edge of its network..

Traveling users and telecommuters are both treated as remote users. Virtual teams or enterprises have privacy challenges at each location from which collaborators or employees operate. However, the environments in which these groups normally function in provide different levels of vulnerability that should be taken into consideration by network administrators and security auditors. The remote user's computing assets are physically vulnerable, meaning they are probably more prone to theft or direct physical tampering than similar devices within the organization's infrastructure. These risks are increased for overseas travelers. The telecommuter's computer is also vulnerable to theft and tampering, but to a much lesser extent if the physical location of the hardware is within a home or apartment. In addition, because the telecommuter's remote location is relatively fixed, additional steps can be taken for physical protection that are not feasible for users that are constantly traveling. On the other hand, a telecommuter's fixed remote location makes it easier for a potential hacker to target his systems, while a mobile user may be at different locations each day.

Remote users access their enterprise-computing environments by communication paths shared with others. Many remote users employ the Public Switched Telephone Network (PSTN) for access or use the PSTN to connect to a data network such as an Internet Service Provider (ISP) that connects users to their enterprise-computing environment. Other remote users employ broadband communications technologies, including DSL, digital wireless service, coaxial cable modems, Integrated Services Digital Network (ISDN), and other high-data-rate media. Some providers are implementing fiber connections direct to users homes or businesses. Remote access of any kind via these networks increases the level of threat and adds additional security and administrative burdens to the IS management team.

Securing Remote Connections
Physical Layer Mechanisms

Secure modems offer a built-in means of boundary protection: the identity of the remote user's modem is established by strong authentication before any network connections are initialized, preventing unauthorized modems from attempting an active attack. Secure modems can implement encryption by use of hardware within the modem. This provides a high level of assurance provided that the encryption function is properly invoked and is protected from tampering. However, the implementation of additional features, such as plaintext bypass, can reduce some of that assurance. For instance, a secure modem needs a means of bypassing the encryption engine if it is also to interoperate with a nonsecure modem. Any bypass feature in a secure modem must be carefully implemented so it is not possible to bypass the cryptography accidentally or maliciously.

Strong encryption requires a significant cryptographic processing capability both in the calculations required to validate a signature and in the verification of the identity contained in a certificate (e.g., checking against a list of authorized users). The identity that is established by modem authentication may not necessarily be made available to the network. This requires the remote user to log into the network separately.

Data Link Layer Mechanisms
Data link layer protocols such as Point-to-Point Protocol (PPP) and Serial Line Internet Protocol (SLIP) encapsulate network layer packets for transmission via modems. Security services can be applied to these protocols to allow authentication and protect the connection between the remote user and the home enclave's communication server. Unlike the large bandwidth data links discussed in the VPN section, the remote user's link is connection-oriented (TCP), so authentication of individual users is possible. Data link mechanisms allow users to choose their own modem hardware and upgrade or change it at their convenience, provided that the hardware can interoperate with the enclave's boundary communications hardware.

A server implementing a data link mechanism could use the results of cryptographic authentication as a basis for access to the LAN. Data link security mechanisms are likely to be implemented in workstation software, where processing power and memory are more readily available than in the case of special-purpose security hardware. This makes implementation functions such as continuous authentication and certificate path validation more practical. However, it also makes these functions dependent on the integrity of the workstation on which they are running and more vulnerable to implementation errors and subversion. At the data link layer, no information is available about the network resources or services the remote user is attempting to access. Any filtering or access control mechanisms must be implemented at a higher layer of the protocol stack.

Network Layer Mechanisms
Network layer protocols assign addresses to devices and pass data packets between them. ISPs (Internet Service Providers) assign an IP address to the remote user and pass IP packets for the remote user. Since the ISP's equipment is on a different logical and physical network than a home user's equipment would be, the network layer is the lowest or earliest point at which an ISP can implement security unless some kind of dedicated line is used.

VPN technology works with IP connections across public networks. Internet Protocol Security (IPSec) with both Encapsulated Security Protocol (ESP) and Authentication Headers (AH) should be used to enable the greatest level of security. IPSec is incompatible with many versions of NAT and PAT (Network Address Translation and Port Address Translation) applied in low end routers. These "translations" change the IP address information in the headers. In a properly configured IPSec setup, packets that have their addresses altered by NAT or PAT will be dropped by the receiving router. This creates some very interesting troubleshooting scenarios for those that are unaware of the problem. NAT traversal methods for IPSec allow IPSec encrypted traffic to successfully pass through NAT routers. These solutions must be researched and tested by the organziation before this technology is deployed to telecommuting or travleing users.

IPSec technology may also be implemented via encryption hardware built into NICs (Network Interface Cards), modems, and in software on the user's computer. In cases where a software solution is implemented, security of the remote connection depends on the integrity of the remote user's computer. If this computer has been compromised by a hacker, any network asset the remote user is authorized to access may also be accessed by the hacker.

Network layer mechanisms allow strong encryption directly from the remote user's computer to the edge device. This allows the edge device to base access control decisions on the user's identity. Network layer information allows the boundary protection mechanism to filter access to individual machines in the LAN. Remote users attempting to connect to an organization's internal resources may have to connect to and be authenticated by a NAS (Network Access Servers) to gain access. If the NAS is properly configured and controlled, the potential for successful attacks against internal resources such as databases or email servers is decreased. Denial of Service (DoS) attacks are not handled by NASs; instead, edge routers or other network devices must be configured to deal with this kind of attck.

Transport and Session Layer Mechanisms

The transport layer helps form a reliable (connection-oriented) channel between devices. The session layer establishes and synchronizes a communication session between two devices. The transport or socket layer is the lowest layer with information on the service being accessed so that security services can be called on a per application basis. Although solutions at these layers provide greater flexibility, they may also provide lower throughput since they can do more complete checks of packet header information. For the remote access scenario, these layers share many of the advantages and disadvantages of network layer mechanisms—they can allow continuous authentication directly to the boundary protection mechanism and allow further access control decisions based on the cryptographically authenticated identity. Transport and session layer mechanisms may not be hardware-based (meaning a dedicated "appliance" type of device), making them vulnerable to tampering and dependent on the integrity of the user's computer.

Application Layer Mechanisms

Application layer security, supports the highest level and granularity of filtering options. Again, increased functionality often comes at a price, namely, slower throughput. Individual commands within applications, as well as access to specific machines and services, can be permitted or denied. One of the major shortcomings of application layer mechanisms is that they rely on platforms with minimal trust mechanisms and that connections must be established at a lower level in the protocol stack (network and transport layer) before the application mechanisms are applied. This leaves the machine vulnerable to network attacks that are unaffected by higher-layer security mechanisms. This means that an administrator must either:

- Be capable of configuring hardened servers for the installation of this type of security, or
- Recommend and implement dedicated "appliance" type machines to serve in this capacity.

LAN Topologies

There are four common LAN topologies. The four described below are the "pure" forms. However, few modern networks are built using only a single topology. Most networks are hybrids, containing at least one section based on a star topology and perhaps having one or more sections that are full mesh for redundancy and/or failover solutions. Ring topologies are rapidly disappearing from current LAN designs and the bus is almost never used in LANs.

Note that rings are an integral part of FDDI (Fiber Distributed Data Interface) topologies which are expensive and more commonly used for MAN or WAN designs. Dual rings are used to help build redundancy into the basic network design. Many broadband systems installed by cable companies use a bus topology for wire runs into certain housing areas.

- **Bus Configuration** – all stations are linked along one transmission medium.
    - **Advantages**
        - Reliable in very small networks as well as easy to use and understand.
        - Requires the least amount of cable to connect the computers together and therefore is less expensive than other cabling arrangements.
        - Is easy to extend. Two cables can be easily joined with a connector, making a longer cable for more computers to join the network.
        - A repeater can also be used to extend a Bus configuration
    - **Disadvantages**
        - Heavy network traffic can slow a Bus considerably. Because any computer can transmit at any time, Bus networks do not coordinate when information is sent. Computers interrupting each other can use a lot of bandwidth.
        - Each connection between two cables weakens the electrical signal
        - The Bus configuration can be difficult to troubleshoot. A cable break or malfunctioning computer can be difficult to find and can cause the whole network to stop functioning.

- **Ring Configuration** – the transmission medium forms a logical circle and all stations are attached to a point on the circle.
    - Advantages:
        - Every computer is given equal access to the network since a token is passed around the ring indicating authorization to transmit.
        - The network degrades gracefully.
    - Disadvantages:
        - Failure of one computer on the network can affect the whole network.
        - It is difficult to troubleshoot a ring network.
        - Adding or removing computers can disrupt the network.

- **Star Configuration** – each station is linked to a main hub (usually a switch or some other multi-port device). The main hub establishes the connection between stations by message or line switching.
    - Advantages:
        - It is easy to modify and add new computers.
        - The center of the Star is a good place to diagnose network problems.
        - Single computer failures do not bring down the network.
        - Several cable types can be used in the configuration.
    - Disadvantages:
        - If the central hub fails the whole network ceases to function.
        - Many star configurations require a device at the center to rebroadcast or switch network traffic.
        - It costs more to cable a star configuration (more cable is required than a Bus or Ring configuration).

- **Completely Connected (Mesh Configuration)** – there is a direct link between any two host machines.
    - Advantages:
        - It is fault tolerant.
        - It is easy to diagnose.
        - There is guaranteed communication channel capacity.
    - Disadvantages
        - It is difficult to install and reconfigure since there are multiple connections with every machine on the network.
        - The cost of installation is extremely high (more cable is required than any other configuration).

Wireless Technology

Current wireless LAN technologies utilize one or more of the 802.11 series of standards for communication. This standard specifies how certain radio frequency bands should be used to permit data traffic between an access point (AP) and one or more client devices. 802.11a and 802.11b are the older and slower standards. 802.11g, i and n are newer, faster and are capable of wider transmission ranges and increased security features.

Wireless setups offer the following potential advantages:
- Increased mobility for internal clients that must move their PCs from place to place within the infrastructure
- Decreased costs related to wiring
- Decreased downtime and fewer safety issues due to construction-related events
- Reasonable to excellent connection speeds depending on the distance of clients from an AP and any interference from the structure.

Wireless subnets have proven to be fairly problematic when security issues are considered. Many implementers of wireless access points, including many home broadband users, fail to implement security on these connections properly. As a result:
- Unauthorized access to network resources is common where APs are installed.
- A significant amount of bandwidth may be used by "war drivers" or people who bring laptops close enough to the wireless networks of others so that they can obtain free Internet access.
- Both WEP (Wired Equivalent Privacy) and its successor WPA (Wi-Fi Protected Access) are used as encryption protocols on many WAPs. However, both of these protocols, especially WEP, have been compromised by hackers. If these protocols must be used, long encryption keys should be the only choice accepted.
- Rogue or unauthorized APs may be installed by employees that want to increase their own mobility or allow connectivity for unapproved network devices.

Basic Wireless Security Methods

At the present time, Wireless technology used for home networks is very similar to that sold for use in corporate settings. Recently, several vendors have supplied additional controls for wireless connections, but use of these controls often requires use of their wireless hardware as well. In general, wireless systems at any price level offer at least three configuration settings that may be used to help secure the connections they allow. Auditors need to be aware of each of these settings and confirm that they are all properly configured:

- **SSID Hiding:** The SSID (Service Set Identifier) is a codename configured on a wireless router or access point. Any PC or other wireless device that must use a given wireless router must be configured with the same SSID as the one set on that router. In many cases, the default setting of wireless routers causes the router to broadcast its own SSID as long as it is powered up. Turning off this SSID broadcast makes it harder for unauthorized personnel to locate and connect to a wireless router.
- **MAC Address Filtering:** The MAC (Media Access Control) address is a data link layer address that is hard-coded into all types of NICs (Network Interface Cards) and Wireless Cards (built-in or otherwise). These layer-2 devices enable PCs. PDAs and other devices to be able to connect to the Internet and local networks. Wireless routers usually offer users the ability to type in the MAC addresses of the wireless cards within each of their devices. After these addresses have been entered, the router can be configured to deny access to any device with a different MAC address. This setting should help most home users ensure that their neighbors are not able to use the bandwidth they are paying for.
- **Encryption:** Communications between a PC and a wireless router may be captured and examined by those that have software capable of doing this. If information such as email or banking usernames and passwords are entered on a wireless PC and sent to a wireless router, these transmissions could eventually be deciphered and used by malicious parties. Encryption of the wireless communications may prevent low-level hackers and script kiddies from snooping on the information sent through the air. WEP, WPA and WPA2 are common choices for encryption on home wireless routers. As mentioned earlier, it is possible to compromise these encryption schemes. To decrease the possibility that the chosen encryption method will be broken by a third party:
    o Only use WPA or WPA2 encryption
    o If the wireless cards and routers currently available in the home or organization are not all WPA or WPA2 compatible:
        - Check with the vendor to see if a firmware upgrade for those devices is available
        - An upgrade to newer devices is strongly advised if no if no firmware upgrade is available. Note that the same encryption schemes must be available on both the router and on the wireless card for the newer encryption types to work.
    o Choose long encryption keys whenever possible (20 characters or more)

Wireless Setups in corporate settings should offer additional safeguards. These will often be vendor-specific; therefore, some amount of familiarity with vendor implementations will be necessary for audits of wireless configurations within a business setting.

Network Management
Management of a network infrastructure generally involves two core activities, namely, monitoring and control.

Network monitoring uses tools that enable administrators to log, audit and report on any given set of activities occurring on a given resource. As described in an earlier section, these tools may be implemented from operating systems, within applications or from third party security software. Monitoring can be implemented on access attempts, device utilization, bandwidth statistics, traffic or protocol types and many other metrics that may be of concern to an administrator.

The logging function can require a significant amount of storage space, depending on the size of the network, the number of resources monitored the extent of logging configured and the amount of traffic normally found on that network. Log data is normally not easy to read and it is impractical to pay people to devote entire work shifts to log reviews unless an investigation is occurring. Therefore, the best monitoring systems offer highly granular filtering functions for the data received by a logging server. Administrators want to be able to decide in advance what type of events warrant attention and they want to be sure that any monitoring solution will be able to isolate these events from huge streams of incoming data.

The flip side of the monitoring coin is reporting. Although some software may be good at catching certain items in logs, the same software may be lacking in functionality when it comes to the notification of relevant parties. If an event is determined to be important enough to warrant a filter, it follows that a quick response to its occurrence may be called for. If the reporting features are weak, log alerts may go unnoticed for hours or even days in a busy environment. Some reporting methods built into monitoring software include:
- Generation of emails or IMs (Instant Messages) to one or more staff members
- Opening of pop-up windows in running email or monitoring client software that highlights the target event.
- Sending automated voice or text messages to selected phones or PDAs of key personnel

Network control involves the use of various tools to implement policies regarding security and performance improvement measures. Devices such as routers, switches, firewalls, IPSs (Intrusion Protection Systems) and content filtering/proxy servers are able to manage or block traffic flows based on predefined rules. These are prime examples of network control measures. Network control may also include blocking or allowing access to certain resources based on job function. Even physical controls such as doors, biometric locks, closed circuit cameras and security personnel may be used to implement control over access to and movement of physical resources such as servers, laptops and monitors.

Infrastructure Development/Acquisition Practices
One of the most important and difficult tasks allotted to the IT department concerns the installation and maintenance of the organization's IS infrastructure. In most cases, no other department in the organization has enough SMEs (Subject Matter Experts) and technicians to substitute for the IT department in this area. The IT department must be able to perform accurate analyses of network traffic, server capacity, routing and switching issues and many other computer-related data. This knowledge helps them manage the day to day tasks of network maintenance and also prepares them to respond appropriately to changes in the needs of the organization.

When developing a new system or new enterprise solution, the physical architecture analysis must begin at the same time the requirements phase is being conducted in the software development process. The potential for an adverse impact to occur as a result of a poorly planned upgrade or rollout may not be restricted to financial loss. A negative impact may also have a domino effect on the technologies and procedures that the infrastructure supports; such as operational procedures, training needs, installation issues and poor network and/or application performance.

An organization functioning in today's business climate must accept that one of the few constants in the IT world is change. As an organization grows and/or refocuses its efforts, different departments within the company may develop needs for IT services that conflict with each other. Examples of possible conflicting needs are:
- An overall change in emphasis toward a services-based architecture
- Legacy hardware considerations
- Remote access/VPN/encryption issues
- Zero data loss targets
- 24*7 availability

If the effort needed to handle day to day support issues and all other projects is objectively assessed, the management of many organizations might learn that their IT staff is actually overtaxed. Since IT personnel are not immune from the adverse effects of BPR (Business Process Re-engineering) they may also suffer layoffs as a result of the rollout of systems management applications such as HP's OpenView, IBM's Tivoli or Computer Associates' Unicenter. When this type of software is purchased, one benefit often touted is that many software monitoring and control functions can be automated. A "successful" implementation should allow the organization to downsize the IT department.

A potential downside to this approach is that a disaster or other serious event might cause a diminished IT staff to be unable to handle incoming requests and deal with incident management. Therefore, when any network architecture is being planned, desired service levels, staffing requirements and possibility for growth must be factored into the expected capacity levels. A formal, reasoned choice must be made. To ensure the quality of results, it is necessary to use a phased approach to fit the whole puzzle together. It is also extremely important to build into an IT program a means by which communication may take place across project teams. An auditor assisting in this process should attempt to provide a balanced opinion about all aspects of the design and support any recommendations with the results of a risk assessment, if necessary.

As the project team progresses through each of the phases listed below, the various infrastructure components are made to work together. It is necessary to understand the scope of key business and technical requirements to prepare the next steps, which include the development of the delivery, installation and test plans. Moreover, to increase the likelihood of a successful conclusion to an infrastructure project, the project team must have access to the most skilled people available. The team must use a phased approach in its implementation plan. Within the timeframe allotted to each of four distinct phases, all the components of the project must be made to work together in order that the stage might be set for other projects, such as data migration.

Phase 1

The steps that follow map fairly well to the requirements phase and the initial part of the design phase of the traditional SDLC. Ideally, the accumulation and analysis of this set of requirements should enable the IT department to arrive at the most cost-effective, yet functional choice(s) for infrastructure upgrades. In addition, a road map for the migration of users and devices from one system to the other should be decided upon during this phase. Some of the objectives of Phase 1 should be:
- To design a new architecture which takes into account the existing architecture as well as a company's particular constraints such as
- Reduced costs
- Increased functionality
- Minimize impact on daily work
- Elimination of potential security and confidentiality issues
- Progressive migration to the new architecture
- Outlining the functional requirements of this new architecture
- Development a proof of concept based on these functional requirements:
- Clear delineation of price, functionality, and performance
- Identification of possible additional requirements

The results obtained at this phase will include documents and drawings describing the new infrastructure and upgrades that will be used by all projects downstream. When these documents are made available, other project teams may begin either:
- Implementing the proposed changes, or
- Developing other projects whose requirements phases could not be completed without this information

Phase 2

The primary objective of this second phase is to plan the implementation of the required infrastructure. In this phase, procurement activities such as contracting partners, setting up the service level agreements and developing installation plans and installation test plans are performed. A well-designed selection process must be devised and implemented. This plan should include deliverables, delivery times, test plans, etc. During the procurement process, communication is established with the analysis team to get an overview of the chosen solution and determine the nature, quantity and deadlines for each of the deliverables. Also, contracts and service level agreements may be signed.

It is also necessary to plan the exact method(s) that will be used to bring any new system online while phasing out the old system. A means by which any part of a new installation might be rolled back or reverted to its previous state should also be devised to ensure that a rapid recovery of functionality might take place if problems ariise. The suggested solution must:
- Ensure alignment of the IT systems with the corporate standards
- Provide appropriate levels of security
- Integrate with the current IT systems
- Consider IT industry trends
- Provide future operational flexibility to support business processes
- Allow for projected growth in infrastructure without major upgrades
- Include technical architecture considerations for information security, secure storage, etc.
- Allow the usage of standardized hardware and software
- Maximize ROI, cost transparency and operational efficiency

Phase 3

This phase may start with a review of the latest information on test results, deliverables and timetables. Specialists from any affected or relevant areas of the IT department should participate in this review. Special care must be taken to clarify and address all the operational constraints that impact physical architecture, such as:
- Ground issues
- Size limits
- Weight limits
- Current supply
- Physical security issues

The output of this initial review/workshop should include a list of the components of the current infrastructure and constraints defining the target physical architecture. After reviewing the existing architecture, the design of the actual physical architecture has to be analyzed and compared against best practices and business requirements. With the design of the current architecture in hand, the first draft of functional requirements for the new architecture/upgrades is composed. This set of requirements is the input for the next step and the vendor selection process. While the draft of the functional requirements is being written, the vendor selection process is started in parallel. This process is described in detail later in this section. After finishing the draft functional requirements, the initial functional requirements document is finalized. The results of this effort should be introduced at the second architecture workshop with staff from all affected parties.

The results will be discussed and a list of the requirements that need to be refined or added will be composed. This is the last checkpoint before the sizing and the proof of concept (POC) starts; the planning of the POC should begin starts after this workshop. With the finished functional requirements, the proof of concept phase begins. The **proof of concept** (or prototype) is a test-bed implementation of the physical architecture. It can save money because it may allow many potential problems to be detected and corrected early, when they are cheaper to correct and have little or no impact on the daily business functions. Success with the proof of concept testing gives confidence to the project teams regarding the results of their functional requirements. The assumption is that the success proves the validity of the requirements as they have been laid out. Therefore, the procurement team can focus on making sure that the vendor chosen will be able to meet or exceed the levels of service or functionality as they are currently defined.

Establishing a POC is highly recommended as a proof that the selected hardware and software is able to meet all expectations, including security requirements. To start, the POC should be based on the results of the procurement phase/Phase 2 discussed earlier. For this purpose, a subset of the target hardware is used. The software utilized for the POC can be either test versions or software already supplied by the vendor; so additional costs in that area should be minimal. To keep costs low, most elements of the framework are implemented in a simplified form. They will be extended to their final form later.

The design and implementation of a POC that adequately represents the proposed architecture requires an above-average level of expertise on the part of the design team. It must contain working versions of every type of technology, current or proposed, that will be supported or affected by the infrastructure changes. Although a complete POC or test bed setup may save money in the long run, it may require a significant initial investment in funds, equipment and time to create. This is especially true if the organization wants to migrate from or add onto proprietary or legacy systems and needs to duplicate their functionality within the test bed. The project management team must also prepare for the costs of the personnel needed to implement the POC. The POC implementation team will have to include some IT staff of fairly high skill to ensure proper functionality of the miniature network.

If the creation of a miniature, working model of the proposed network enables the organization to avoid losses in any or all areas of CIA (Confidentiality, Integrity, Availability), then the cost of the testing may be justified. At a minimum, the design team must be able to simulate the following:
- The basic step of the core security infrastructure
- Correct functionality of auditing components
- Basic, but functional implementation of security measures as defined
- Secured transactions and data protections such as encryption, access controls, etc
- Characteristics in terms of installation constraints and limits (server size, server current consumption, server weight, server room physical security)
    - Performance
    - Resiliency
    - Funding and costing model

If a POC is feasible and approved, the IS auditor should recommend that the team build in or provide for the means to properly stress test any proposed upgrades. In addition, the auditor should request that some means by which test data may be generated and logged be built into the POC. In addition, the designers should include a method by which test data may be compiled into meaningful reports that can be generated on a daily or even hourly basis. If the reports show that the POC test bed is incapable of handling the traffic anticipated, plus an approved percentage which allows for growth or unusual circumstances, the requirements document should be reviewed and all relevant improvements should be added to the document. Any related projects, which prepare the ground for deployment, should also be represented within the POC testing. They will be used in exactly the same way as in the production physical architecture. The deliverable of the POC should be a running prototype, plus the associated document and test protocols describing the tests and their results. The POC may be considered an iterative test; it should be run until an accurate set of requirements has been determined.

Phase 4

This phase is also called the delivery phase; at this stage, the delivery plan is developed. This phase overlaps in some parts with the procurement phase. The delivery plan should include topics such as priorities, goals and non-goals, key facts, principles, communication strategies, key indicators, progress on key tasks and responsibilities. The installation plan should be developed in cooperation with all affected parties. An additional review of the plan should be scheduled. This review should include those responsible for the integration projects and any other parties or vendor representatives that might be necessary. Planning the delivery of the upgrade is also an iterative process. Based on the known dependencies of the installation plan, the test plan is developed. The test plan includes test cases, basic requirements specifications, definition of the processes and-as far as possible-measurement information for the applications and infrastructure. Factors which are critical for the success of the implementation planning include:

- Key IT SMEs and implementation staff must attend workshops and participate for the whole project duration to avoid delays.
- Documentation that is both accurate and understandable by all relevant parties must always be available beginning at the start of the project.
- Key decision makers, either stakeholders or some other delegated parties, with the authority to compel behavior of company staff and sign agreements with vendors and suppliers must be involved at all steps, to ensure that all necessary decisions can be made quickly.
- Phase 1 of the project (Analysis of Physical Architecture) must be completed and the needed infrastructure decisions must be made.

Auditing the Acquisition Plan

In the procurement phase, a company initiates a search for one or more vendors of hardware or software solutions. The company should all ready have a stable set of requirements. The procurement team then arranges these requirements into a format for distribution to potential vendors. One possible format is known as an "Invitation to Tender" (ITT). This ITT process would normally be identified after Phase 1 of the infrastructure development process. An IS auditor should recommend that this invitation include the following:[6]

- Organization description indicating whether the computer facilities are centralized or decentralized
- Data processing requirements such as:
    - Major existing application systems and future application systems
    - Workloads and performance requirements
    - Processing approaches to be used (for example, online/batch, real time databases, continuous operation)
- Hardware requirements such as:
    - CPU processing speed
    - Peripheral devices (sequential devices such as tape drives, direct access devices such as magnetic disk drive, printers, CD-ROM drives, WORM-drives, etc.)
    - Data preparation/input devices that convert and accept data for machine processing (such as optical character readers [OCR], scanners, magnetic tape, cassette and diskette, magnetic ink character readers [MICR], magnetic card readers, optical mark sensing devices, etc.)
    - Direct entry devices (terminals, point-of-sale terminals, automatic teller machines, etc.)
    - Networking capability (such as Ethernet connections, modems, ISDN connections, etc.)
- System software requirements such as:
    - Operating system software (current version and any upgrades required)
    - Compilers
    - Program library packages
    - Database management packages and programs
    - Communications software
- Security/access control software and/or "appliances"

- Support requirements such as:
  - System Maintenance
  - Training
  - Backup
- Adaptability requirements such as:
  - Hardware/software upgrade capabilities
  - Compatibility with existing hardware/software platforms
  - Changeover to other equipment capabilities
- Constraints such as:
  - Manpower/operations
  - Existing hardware capacity
  - Delivery dates
- Conversion requirements such as:
  - Test time for the hardware/software
  - System conversion facilities
  - Cost/pricing schedule

Acquisition Steps

When purchasing hardware/software from a vendor, there are certain steps that should be evaluated for inclusion in the acquisition process:

• Testimonials/visits to other users • Provision for competitive bidding • Analysis of bids against requirements • Comparison of bids against each other • Analysis of vendor financial condition • Analysis of capability of vendors to provide maintenance and support (including training) • Review of delivery schedules against requirements • Analysis of hardware/software upgrade capability	• Analysis of security and control facilities • Evaluation of performance against requirements • Review and negotiation of price • Review of contract terms (including right to audit clauses) • Preparation of a formal written report summarizing the analysis for each of the alternatives and justification for the selection based on benefits and cost.

Criteria and data used for evaluating vendor proposals should be properly planned. The following are some of the criteria that should be considered in the evaluation process:

• Turnaround time • Response time • System reaction time – how the operating system processes information (usually measured in Millions of Instructions Per Second [MIPS])	• Throughput • Workload • Compatibility • Capacity • Utilization

Auditing the IT Infrastructure

Auditing an entire IT infrastructure can be a daunting task, especially for those whose technology expertise is weak or for those that lack experience in audit procedures. Depending on the size and complexity of an organization, even seasoned IT audit professionals may encounter one or more technologies or in-house proprietary implementations that fall outside of their areas of expertise. Fortunately, the audit process described in Chapter 1 offers a useful set of high-level audit objectives that may be adapted to nearly any technology. In addition, there are several sites on the Internet that offer audit programs aimed at specific technologies. Access to these programs may require a free membership or require some kind of membership fee or per-program charge. These audit programs may include checklists, templates and even specific suggestions for tests and/or configuration examples.

Vendors of audit software (CAATs) may also offer whitepapers, templates or other recommendations regarding the audit of specific technologies. When faced with unknown commercial software packages, auditors may research the vendor's web sites or user forums for information about the availability and configuration of any monitoring, auditing or logging functionality. Auditors that must review applications that are the result of in-house development and/or highly customized commercial applications may need to obtain documentation from the development teams or consultants involved in the creation and implementation of those products.

Given the huge number of application types, operating systems, hardware platforms and the variety of vendor implementations within each of these areas, it is impossible to offer any detailed set of audit activities for every technology. However, there are certain activities that are common to audits of technology in general. Drawing on material found in Chapter 1, the following may be used as a core set of audit steps that can be applied to any hardware or software review. Note that additional research and adaptation/modification of these steps will be necessary to provide accurate assessments of each organization's unique IS infrastructure.

Initial Steps
- Contract
    - Ensure agreement and meeting of the minds on all aspects of the audit charter
    - Review any relevant industry standards, best practices and regulatory requirements related to items included in the audit scope
- Documentation
    - Schedule a meeting with appropriate parties to determine the nature and amount of documentation available for review.
    - Set up a time or method during which all relevant documentation may be acquired or gathered for review
    - If the scope of the audit includes reviews of logical access controls, request a network account with read-only access to network assets
    - Perform the review of all documentation provided; note any items requiring further investigation.
    - Ensure that audit personnel with appropriate skill sets are available to conduct interviews, walk-throughs and system checks or tests

Intermediate Steps
- Interviews and walk-throughs
    - Schedule a meeting with appropriate parties to discover the identities of individuals performing key job functions or functions of interest to the audit process.
    - Arrange interviews with these personnel if necessary
    - Schedule opportunities to view employees during their work shifts if necessary
    - Schedule tours or walkthroughs of client sites as necessary
    - Ensure that a basic understanding of the organization's long-term goals and objectives is obtained
    - Ensure that the needs of the business are not unduly disrupted by the scheduling of interviews or walk-throughs, since these require the re-allocation of staff members to participate in these functions.
- System Checks and Testing
    - Based on documentation and interviews, decide on the types of checks and tests necessary to provide accurate results
    - Determine if use of CAATs is necessary.
    - If the use of hardware, CAATs or other software owned by the auditor is necessary to perform testing, determine the need for any special network access rights such as changes to ports on network devices, additional username and passwords, etc.
    - Acquire any additional permissions for vulnerability and/or penetration testing in writing **before** beginning tests of that type
    - Schedule checks and tests with appropriate personnel so that business processing needs are not disrupted by audit activities
    - Ensure that appropriate test inputs and/or recording methods for test results and analysis are properly configured and functional.
    - Perform compliance tests if necessary and determine if substantive testing is required.

- Evaluation
    - Make determinations about the effectiveness of existing controls
    - Ensure that any material findings are validated and relevant evidence is preserved
    - Inform appropriate parties about any issues requiring immediate attention or remediation (such as viruses, Trojans, rootkits, etc.)
    - Perform risk analysis based on findings about control effectiveness and stated values or criticality of resources obtained via interviews.

Closing steps
- Prepare report(s) according to agreed upon standards or formats.
- Schedule delivery of report(s) and/or presentation(s) to all appropriate parties
- Ensure or perform delivery of reports and presentations
- If applicable, schedule follow-up review to determine status of remediation efforts on material findings

Auditing Software

In common use, the term "**software**" refers to any type of computer program that may be installed by an administrator or end user on a network device, server or workstation. The terms "**program**" and "**application**" are synonymous with "software". Applications offer users the ability to initiate and control the performance of one or more activities that benefit from the speed, storage and connectivity provided by individual computer systems or networks. The term "**systems software**" usually refers to applications that are designed primarily to allow or control the operation of one or more hardware devices.

Firmware is a special type of software. It is usually loaded onto microprocessors (chips) that have been installed on computer motherboards, cell phones, microwave ovens or any other type of device that relies on internal electronic circuitry to function. Firmware is a limited-purpose type of software that can only be used to operate the type of devices for which it has been tailored. The BIOS (Basic Input Output System) is the firmware that handles the boot process on a computer. The average computer end-user does not usually change firmware or deal with it directly in any way.

The following list offers several broad categories of software:
- Operating systems
- Access control software
- Data communications software
- Database management software (DBMS)
- Program library management systems
- Tape and disk management systems
- Online programming facilities
- Network management software
- Job scheduling software
- Utility programs
- Middleware

Operating Systems

The architecture of most computers can be viewed as a number of layers in a hierarchical structure. At the base is the chipset. The chipset is at the heart of the **hardware platform**. Motorola and Intel chipsets (or motherboards and chipsets from other vendors that are compatible with one of these) are the most widely used. Intel has focused most of its efforts on the IBM/Windows compatible operating systems and Motorola has supplied Sun Microsystems and Apple with chips. In general, software developers plan in advance to write code for one or the other of these platforms because the CPUs (Central Processing Units) in each do not execute commands in the same ways.

Both the CPU and the BIOS (Basic Input Output System) chips are on the motherboard. Each contains a set of hard coded instructions (firmware) that controls the operation of the computer primarily during normal operations and at boot up, respectively. This "operation of the computer" includes the initial hardware/device setup and all subsequent interactions between the operating system and the memory and other hardware installed within or attached to the computer. After the BIOS performs its primary work at boot time, it hands off control of the machine to the OS (operating system) software that is stored on a hard disk, CD or other device. The OS is at the heart of the next layer in the hierarchy.

The **operating system** of a server or workstation (OS) is software that functions as the intermediary between application requests and the hardware and peripherals built into or connected to that device. Well designed OS software does not allow any access to any hardware or peripherals that is does not monitor and control. OS software offers one or more APIs (**Application Programming Interfaces**) that allow developers to write programs that request access to hardware resources in a standardized format. Applications that do not follow the conventions of the APIs may fail to work properly when installed on a device.

Most modern operating systems include applications that are not strictly designed to manage the system devices. These applications may include games, text editors, calculators, web browsers and many others. These inclusions can enable end users to achieve a reasonable level of productivity without the purchase of additional, specialized applications.

Application software functions at the top level in this hierarchy. It is usually not possible to install application software on a server or workstation that does not all ready have an operating system installed on it. Recent exceptions to this include OSes that may be run from CD-ROMs, Flash drives, DVD-ROMs or other devices that the BIOS may be configured to allow to "boot" the system. Popular end user applications include games, educational software and "office" suites that include word processing, drawing, spreadsheet and other functions.

Operating systems perform many functions. They include:
- Process management such as scheduling of tasks
- Handling system interrupts, issuing commands to the input/output devices and handling errors
- Communications between the operating system and application programs, allocating memory to processors and making the memory available upon the completion of a process
- System file management
- System accounting management
- Resource management: Some of these resources include:
    - Input and output devices: printers, disk drives, keyboards, monitors, external hard drives, USB devices
    - Memory: RAM (Random Access Memory), RAM and CPU caches, hard drives, CD-ROMs, DVD-ROMs
    - CPU time: the available time for instructional processing in the CPU
    - Network access: the communication devices and channels connecting a PC to a switch, router or other device that allows access to an internal network and/or the Internet

Users of the "system" (the OS) may include:
   - Computer operators
   - Application programmers
   - System programmers
   - Users
   - Security Administrators
   - Hardware/computer system equipment
   - Other system software programs and operating systems

Operating systems vary in the resources managed, comprehensiveness of management and techniques used to manage resources. Operating systems exist for devices ranging from PDAs up to proprietary supercomputer installations. The average computer user only interacts with an operating system such as the MAC OS or Windows, which can run PCs, high-end workstations and may offer some server capability, depending on the version purchased.

Minicomputers have a longer history than the PC. They may allow hundreds of users to interact with one or more applications that have been specially designed to run on this type of hardware. The type of OS suited to this hardware must be very efficient at allocating and segregating memory, disk space (files) and CPU time among several users, as well as manage the network connections to terminals. Various UNIX operating systems that have been developed over the last 30 years have been popular in this type of environment.

Mainframe computers are the oldest of the multi-user computing platforms. They can handle large numbers of transactions and user connections with ease. They are usually deployed to run a single application, but they can offer more. Over the decades since their introduction, these devices have been exposed to the highest number of work environments and have the most robust sets of security controls. The MVS (Multiple Virtual Storage) operating system from IBM has been specifically engineered to complement this environment.

CHAPTER 4 PRACTICE QUESTIONS

1) In a TCP/IP-based network, an IP address specifies a:
    A. network connection.
    B. router/gateway.
    C. computer in the network.
    D. device on the network.

2) Which of the following is a strength of a client-server security system?
    A. Change control and change management procedures are inherently strong.
    B. Users can manipulate data without controlling resources on the mainframe.
    C. Network components seldom become obsolete.
    D. Access to confidential data or data manipulation is controlled tightly.

3) To check the performance of flow and error control, an IS auditor should focus the use of a protocol analyzer on which of the following layers?
    A. Network
    B. Transport
    C. Data link
    D. Application

4) Which of the following is a network architecture configuration that links each station directly to a main hub?
    A. Bus
    B. Ring
    C. Star
    D. Completely Connected

5) Which of the following is a telecommunication device that translates data from digital form to analog form and back to digital?
    A. Multiplexer
    B. Modem
    C. Protocol converter
    D. Concentrator

6) A hub is a device that connects:
    A. two LANs using different protocols.
    B. a LAN with a WAN.
    C. a LAN with a metropolitan area network (MAN).
    D. two segments of a single LAN.

CHAPTER 4 PRACTICE QUESTIONS (CONT.)

7) Which of the following hardware devices relieves the central computer from performing network control, format conversion and message handling tasks?
    A. Spool
    B. Cluster controller
    C. Protocol converter
    D. Front end processor

8) Which of the following methods of providing telecommunication continuity involves routing traffic through split- or duplicate-cable facilities?
    A. Diverse routing
    B. Alternative routing
    C. Redundancy
    D. Long haul network diversity

9) In a client-server architecture, a domain name service (DNS) is MOST important because it provides the:
    A. address of the domain server.
    B. resolution service for the name/address.
    C. IP addresses for the Internet.
    D. domain name system

10) Which of the following types of transmission media provide the BEST security against unauthorized access?
    A. Copper wire
    B. Twisted pair
    C. Fiber-optic cables
    D. Coaxial cables

CHAPTER 4 ANSWERS TO PRACTICE QUESTIONS

1) Answer: A

   An IP address, specifies a network connection. An IP address encodes both a network and a host on that network, it does not specify an individual computer, but a connection to a network. A router/gateway connects two networks and will have two IP addresses. Hence, an IP address cannot specify a router. A computer in the network can be connected to other networks as well. It will then use many IP addresses. Such computers are called multi-homed hosts. Here again an IP address cannot refer to the computer. IP addresses do not refer to individual devices on the network, but refer to the connections by which they are connected to the network.

2) Answer: B

   Among the choices the only strength associated with a client-server system is that users can manipulate and change data without controlling resources on the mainframe. All other answers are false and are disadvantages of a client-server system.

3) Answer: B

   Although a protocol analyzer would work at all layers of the OSI model, the only layer that handles both flow and error control is the transport layer.

4) Answer: C

   A star network architecture configuration links each station directly to a main hub. Bus configurations link all stations along one transmission medium, ring configurations attach all stations to a point on a circle and completely connected configurations provide a direct link between two host machines.

5) Answer: B

   A modem is a device that translates data from digital to analog and back to digital.

6) Answer: D

   A hub is a device that connects two segments of a single LAN. A hub is a repeater. It provides transparent connectivity to users on all segments of the same LAN. It is a level 1 device. A bridge operates at level 2 of the OS1 layer and may be used to connect two LANs using the same or different protocols (e.g., joining an Ethemet LAN to a token-ring LAN) to form a logical network. A gateway, which functions at layer 3 or above, is used to connect either similar or dissimilar networks to each other based on logical (IP) address information. This may also include connecting LANs to a WAN or the Internet. A LAN is connected with a MAN using a router, which operates in the network layer.

CHAPTER 4 ANSWERS TO PRACTICE QUESTIONS

7) **Answer: D**
   A front-end processor is a hardware device that connects all communication lines to a central computer to relieve the central computer.

8) **Answer: A**
   Diverse routing is a method of providing telecommunication continuity that involves routing traffic through split or duplicate cable facilities. Alternative routing is accomplished via alternative media such as copper cable or wire optics, redundancy involves the use of excess capacity and long haul network diversity is a service provided by vendors to allow access to diverse long distance networks.

9) **Answer: C**
   DNS is utilized primarily on the Internet for resolution of the name/address of the web site. It is an Internet service that translates domain names into **IP** addresses. As names are alphabetic, they are easier to remember. However, the Internet is based on **IP** addresses. Every time a domain name is used, a DNS service must translate the name into the corresponding **IP** address. The DNS system has its own network. If one DNS server does not know how to translate a particular domain name, it asks another one, and so on, until the correct **IP** address is returned.

10) **Answer: C**
    Fiber-optic cables have proven to be more secure than the other media. Satellite transmission and copper wire can be violated with inexpensive equipment. Coaxial cable also can be violated more easily than other transmission media.

Chapter 5 Protection of Information Assets

Information Systems Integrity, Confidentiality and Availability

The objective of this chapter is to introduce the knowledge that an IS Auditor must have in order to analyze and evaluate:
- General Information Security Practices and Logical Access controls
- Network Infrastructure security
- Environmental exposures and controls
- Physical Access controls.
- Policies and Procedures regarding the storage, handling and disposal of sensitive data

This chapter represents approximately 31 percent of the CISA examination (approximately 62 questions).

There are five tasks within this area that the CISA candidate must understand and be able to perform:
- Evaluate the design, implementation, and monitoring of logical access controls to ensure the confidentiality, integrity, availability and authorized use of information assets.
- Evaluate network infrastructure security to ensure confidentiality, integrity, availability and authorized use of the network and the information transmitted.
- Evaluate the design, implementation, and monitoring of environmental controls to prevent or minimize loss.
- Evaluate the design, implementation, and monitoring of physical access controls to ensure that information assets are adequately safeguarded.
- Evaluate the processes and procedures used to store, retrieve, transport, and dispose of confidential information assets.

Knowledge Statements
The following statements describe specific topics a CISA candidate should be familiar with and use as guidance in the fulfillment of the tasks outlined above:

- Knowledge of the techniques for the design, implementation and monitoring of security (e.g., threat and risk assessment, sensitivity analysis, privacy impact assessment)
- Knowledge of logical access controls for the identification, authentication, and restriction of users to authorized functions and data (e.g., dynamic passwords, challenge/response, menus, profiles)
- Knowledge of logical access security architectures (e.g., single sign-on, user identification strategies, identity management)
- Knowledge of attack methods and techniques (e.g., hacking, spoofing, Trojan horses, denial of service, spamming)
- Knowledge of processes related to monitoring and responding to security incidents (e.g., escalation procedures, emergency incident response team)
- Knowledge of network and Internet security devices, protocols, and techniques (e.g., SSL, SET, VPN, NAT)
- Knowledge of intrusion detection systems and firewall configuration, implementation, operation, and maintenance
- Knowledge of encryption algorithm techniques (e.g., AES, RSA, etc.)
- Knowledge of public key infrastructure (PKI) components (e.g., certification authorities, registration authorities) and digital signature techniques
- Knowledge of virus detection tools and control techniques
- Knowledge of security testing and assessment tools (e.g., penetration testing, vulnerability scanning)

- Knowledge of environmental protection practices and devices (e.g., fire suppression, cooling systems, water sensors)
- Knowledge of physical security systems and practices (e.g., biometrics, access cards, cipher locks, tokens)
- Knowledge of data classification schemes (e.g., public, confidential, private, and sensitive data)
- Knowledge of voice communications security (e.g., voice over IP)
- Knowledge of the processes and procedures used to store, retrieve, transport, and dispose of confidential information assets
- Knowledge of controls and risks associated with the use of portable and wireless devices (e.g., PDAs, USB devices, Bluetooth devices)

Protection of Information Assets

Information assets may be the most vital assets a company possesses. These assets include any data that pertains to or identifies its clients, customers, employees or business processes. In addition, there may be information about strategic goals, high-level policies, procedures or tactics that may be of enormous value to interested third parties. In recent years, technological advances have enabled organizations to shift their record keeping to digital formats. This shift provides the necessary foundation for other techniques such as data mining, which may give forecasters greater insight into a company's successes and failures.

Why is Information Security Important?

Information Security involves the protection of these and any other data owned or controlled by an organization. A loss in any of the administrative areas mentioned above could seriously impact an organization's ability to maintain a competitive advantage. This could be disastrous in the Internet-powered global marketplace.

The "external" information is information that can only be obtained from clients or customers. Even employees bring their personal information with them from the outside. All of this information should be carefully guarded because its exposure may result in loss or damages to people or other organizations. Due to recent legislation, all of this information is considered to be privacy-related and organizations are required to take certain steps to protect it from unauthorized access. The loss of any of this information could also result in a loss of a competitive edge. For example, if a Company A obtains Company B's customer mailing list and the records of products they recently purchased, Company A can target a marketing campaign and discounts directly at the Company B's highest volume customers.

The objectives of a sound information security program are often described with the acronym CIA, which stands for Confidentiality, Integrity and Availability. Confidentiality refers to those actions which ensure that information assets can only be read by those people that are authorized to do so. Integrity refers to the trustworthiness, reliability and accuracy of the data being accessed. Availability refers to the amount of time that a given system or asset is "up" or accessible to authorized persons. These three attributes, and/or the means by which they are implemented, form the foundation of most standardized security frameworks.

The Increasing Importance of Privacy

The proliferation of identity theft and hacking attempts and recent corporate scandals have brought two additional issues into the minds of security personnel. The first of these issues is privacy. Legislation recently enacted in California, which requires businesses to notify customers about the loss or compromise of their personal data, has been duplicated in nearly a dozen other states. Some of these laws also mandate shredding of paper documents and adoption of best practices for securing customer PII. Organizations that fail to comply with local law may be subject to fines. Of course, any mandatory public disclosure regarding the compromise of PII can result in class action suits by any clients, customers or employees that claim to have suffered damages. In addition, the loss of PII (Personally Identifiable Information) may result in decreased sales due to a loss of confidence from both current and potential customers. HIPAA (Health Insurance Portability and Accountability Act) is privacy-related legislation that covers an individual's medical records. Health care providers, insurance companies, pharmacies and any other organization that maintains medical records are affected by this legislation.

The second new issue is related to the first. The Sarbanes-Oxley (SOX) act is a wide-ranging set of Federal rules that includes new and enhanced rules affecting all publicly held companies, their corporate-level managers, their boards of directors and any accounting firms or other businesses that may audit them. Implementing and/or auditing Sarbanes-Oxley controls within organizations have become very hot areas for those with the appropriate accounting and IT skill sets. Key issues for corporate-level executives are the following:

- New rules requiring CEOs and CFOs to certify financial reports
- Increased fines and jail terms for executives that knowingly misstate corporate financial information.
- New rules requiring an annual "internal control report" that includes a review of the organization's controls implemented for financial *and* IT assets.
- The new, mandatory rules have forced many businesses to examine and re-evaluate their accounting practices. In addition, the required reporting on IT controls has also caused businesses to think of security controls whenever they implement a major IT project. Security concerns are now being considered in the planning stages of these projects. This new emphasis increases the importance of the Audit, IT and Security functions of the organization.

Types of Information Assets	
Administrative Assets: <ul><li>Documents outlining long-term strategies</li><li>Documents that describe internal policies and/or procedures</li><li>Employee training manuals</li><li>Results of Research and Development for new product or service offerings.</li><li>Results of cost-benefit analyses</li><li>Results of research based on past sales and expenditures.</li><li>Any accounting and tax information held in the database used by an accounting software program.</li><li>Payroll/Salary information.</li><li>Inventory records.</li><li>Access to corporate bank account information and/or live bank transaction records</li></ul>	**External (Privacy-related) Assets:** <ul><li>Client/Customer email/mailing lists.</li><li>Client/Customer PII (Personally Identifiable Information). This can include contact information such as phone numbers or home addresses, but may include social security, credit card or bank account numbers if these items are kept on file.</li><li>Employee PII. This may include all of the above information and salary, health care, life insurance, performance evaluations and possibly PII about dependents and other family members.</li><li>Client/Customer purchase records. This can show what has been purchased, how and when it was purchased, who made the purchase and what payment method was used.</li></ul>

Prerequisites for a Successful Information Security Program

A sound security function has several key components that combine to form its foundation:

- A long-term commitment from senior (Corporate level) management.
- The creation of a comprehensive security policy and the adoption of any procedures necessary to make the policy work.
- An analysis of the current organizational structure, its classification of data and its management of security roles. This process should include an inventory of all relevant assets and controls. BCP (Business Continuity Planning) and DR (Disaster Recovery) should also be assessed.
- An understanding that security and privacy-related issues and controls should be considered and built into all projects in the planning stages.
- A commitment to the consistent use of professional risk analysis techniques to identify and assess any threats and risks that may exist.
- Information and training about security related issues tailored to each level of the organization (including any executive stakeholders) is a must.
- Periodic testing and reassessment of security measures must be performed by qualified managers, internal auditors and/or third party security analysts. A strong change and configuration management procedure should exist to allow for the testing, documentation and implementation of security updates.

Incident management involves the policies and procedures related to handling of occurrences that are considered detrimental or adverse to any area of the information security function. This may involve events ranging from issuing new passwords to authorizing an investigation or disclosure regarding the compromise of client information.

It is impossible to overstate the importance of the role executive management must play in ensuring the protection of information assets. First of all, without a strong commitment from the executives, information security cannot be implemented using a solid project management approach. This means that there will be no centralized planning or goals for information security. As a result, whatever measures that are implemented may be redundant or counterproductive, since each department will implement security as its managers see fit. In fact, without a mandate from executive management, some departments may implement little or no security because comprehensive security measures can increase costs significantly.

Due to the unique nature of each corporate environment, it is impossible to provide a list of job titles and descriptions that conform exactly to every situation. Many government agencies avoid the use of these designations. Also, in some federal organizations, military personnel perform these functions. To further complicate matters, in smaller organizations, one person or group may perform several functions, or there will be some overlap in the duties listed below. However, this listing is useful because it delineates the roles seen most often in all organizations. It is safe to conclude that a comprehensive information security policy should be adapted to take into account the current organizational structure. This means assigning the roles below to existing officers or groups when possible and/or creating new security-related positions when necessary.

Job titles, descriptions, roles and their impact on the Information Security Function

ROLE	RESPONSIBILITY
CEO, COO or other Corporate level operations officer (C-Level):	This person or group is ultimately responsible of for creating policies for the organization. New legislation makes them stakeholders and makes them liable for any financial misconduct It is important that the C-Level management team set the tone and precedence for the types of logical security controls that should be implemented in the organization.
IS/IT Steering Committee:	This group should always be led by a senior corporate level official. It should be comprised of managers from each department including HR and legal. This group may not have the expertise to create an effective security policy; it is probably best to utilize the expertise of qualified security and IT personnel to draft the policy that senior management will approve. If an organization is large enough to support it, a Security Advisory Committee with a similar mix of personnel can be established to handle any reviews of security plans. In general, it should be the Steering Committee's responsibility to approve, establish and enforce security procedures across the organization.
CIO (Chief Information Officer); CISO (Chief Information Security Officer); CSO (Chief Security Officer); CTO (Chief Technical Officer); CPO (Chief Privacy Officer):	It is difficult to predict the level at which each of these job titles will appear in an organizational chart. One or more of these titles may not exist in an organization at all. However, the functions performed by people in these roles may be summarized as follows: • Act as head of the Information Systems and/or Information Technology functions. • Act as bridge or liaison between the business and technology functions of the organization • Creates or oversees the creation of information security, acceptable use, business continuity and disaster recovery plans • Ensures that the technology chosen and implemented was selected in order to support known business goals and objectives. • Ensures that an adequate documentation procedure for all IS functions exists.

ROLE	RESPONSIBILITY
Data Owners:	The term "Data Owner" defines a function or role that an individual plays within an Information Security framework. They are usually people that manage or oversee a department, division or some other significant combination of organizational resources. These people may be Corporate–level executives. Regardless of the official title they hold, they are the people that determine the access rights and privileges that should be assigned to any party that needs access to the information assets they manage. In addition, they are responsible for the review and update of the access rules they have defined. People who perform in this role may also be known as Process owners. The task of a process owner is to guarantee that the controls and tools used to implement security are in compliance with the overall security policy and that those controls and tools are properly maintained.
Data Custodians:	Those that perform this security function are usually people within the IT department. They may have titles such as database administrator, network administrator, console operator or other similar positions. Their task is to ensure that important data is properly collected, cached and stored. They are also responsible for keeping the data safe. Within this category, several subgroups may exist: • **Security specialists:** These individuals have expert-level knowledge in the design and implementation of security measures. • **IT Developers:** These individual may assist in the implementation of various security measures. • **IS Auditors:** The job of the auditor is to review security policies, objectives and controls and provide management with a bias-free examination of their relevance and efficacy.
Data Users:	This group is comprised of those people that use the data and other IT assets that the organization maintains. These people may be accessing these assets as internal employees, external users or customers. The data user is required to know and comply with any established policies regarding security and privacy. In all of these cases, it is the data owners that decide the level of access that will be allowed. The data custodians are responsible for implementing the access policies and preventing unauthorized access.
Security Administrators:	Those performing in this role have the responsibility for the design and management of the logical security for all the assets within an information system. These people may also be responsible for the design and management of the physical security measures used to protect those assets.

IS/IT Auditors	The role of the auditor in the protection of information assets includes five key tasks:
	
	• Understanding, testing and evaluating the logical access controls utilized to protect information assets
	   o Understanding, testing and evaluating the controls related to the network security infrastructure.
	   o Assessing the status of all relevant environmental safeguards and controls.
	   o Assessing the status and effectiveness of all physical access controls.
	   o Evaluating all controls related to the organization's data storage, retrieval, and backup and recovery methods.

Components of a Good Security Policy

Key Elements of Information Security Management

For security to be successfully implemented and maintained, the framework and intent of each security policy and procedure must be clearly established and communicated to all appropriate parties. The key is a written security policy that serves to heighten security awareness throughout the organization. Key components of such a policy include the following:

- **Management Support and Commitment:** Management must demonstrate a commitment to security. Management shows this commitment by clearly approving and supporting formal security awareness and training. This may require special management-level training since security is not necessarily a part of management expertise.

- **Policies and Procedures:** The creation of an Information Security Policy is an essential step for any organization desiring to implement a sound and consistent approach to managing the security of its IS assets. This document should set forth clear and specific goals or objectives for the organization's Information Security efforts.

- **Organization**: It should be expected that upper management defines the high-level policies, and then a Security or IS Steering Committee will oversee the implementation of the procedures that enact the policies. These committees should be composed of at least one Corporate-level officer and representatives from the various departments and SMEs (Subject Matter Experts). The initial risk assessment should be reviewed by the members of these committees and the organization's assets should be prioritized according to their importance, criticality or value. The choice to mitigate, transfer or accept risk should be made here.

- **Security Design and Implementation**: The Security and/or Steering committees should consult with the appropriate SMEs to ensure that an adequate design for the overall security infrastructure is created. Depending on the size and resources of the organization, a security program may be established that will oversee all of the individual projects involved in implementing the design. The committees involved should ensure that sound systems development and project management principles are used throughout the process.

- **Security Awareness:** All employees, including management, need to be made aware of the importance of security on a regular basis. Security awareness training should teach employees how to spot security issues and avoid disclosing sensitive information. Security training modules should be tailored to each of the various groups or levels within the organization. The information provided to each group should be limited to only that set of items that they need to know in order to improve security at their level. Security policies provided to the employees should teach them not to disclose information such as: password file names, technical security configurations, and methods by which physical or logical security for the system may be bypassed. A number of different mechanisms are available for raising security awareness including:

    o Distribution of a written security policy
    o Training
    o Non-disclosure statements signed by the employee
    o Company newsletter
    o Visible enforcement of security rules
    o Periodic audits

Examples of employee responsibilities include the following:
- Keeping Logon-IDs and passwords secret
- Reporting suspected violations of security to the Security Administrator
- Reading the Security Policy
- Maintaining good physical security by keeping doors locked, safeguarding access keys, not disclosing access door lock combinations and questioning unfamiliar people.
- Non-employees with access to company systems also should be held accountable for security policies and responsibilities. This includes contract employees, vendor programmers/analysts, maintenance personnel and clients.

Monitoring and Compliance: No security design is perfect. Operating systems, applications and/or the periodic updates to these software assets may contain vulnerabilities. In addition, through ignorance or carelessness, either the OS or the applications being run on it might be misconfigured. The Committees in charge of managing the security effort should insist that appropriate tools to aid in monitoring and testing be added to the system. Also, a schedule for regular testing of the controls in place should be adopted.

Incident Handling and Response: No security plan is complete unless it provides a detailed set of procedures regarding the way incidents will be handled. When some kind of security issue has occurred, there should be no confusion within the organization about who has the authority to make decisions, who should be contacted to address the issue, what actions should be taken, and what type of reporting and/or postmortem should be performed.

Security Program Details

Security Lifecycle
The Security Lifecycle is structured around strong Security Policies, Standards, Procedures and Metrics, and provides the framework and measurement criteria for proper security management.

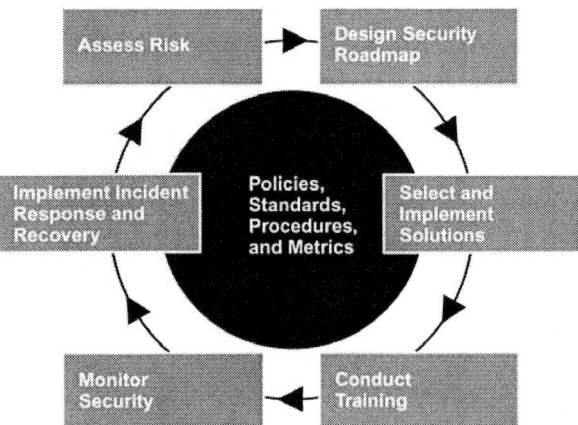

The overall security program is made up of components that are created around the organization's key data elements. Senior management should have defined these elements and it is the ISMs (Information Security Manager's) responsibility to create a security architecture or security program to match and meet management's expectation of protecting the organization's assets. The ISM should address all of the components identified below:

Security Program Components

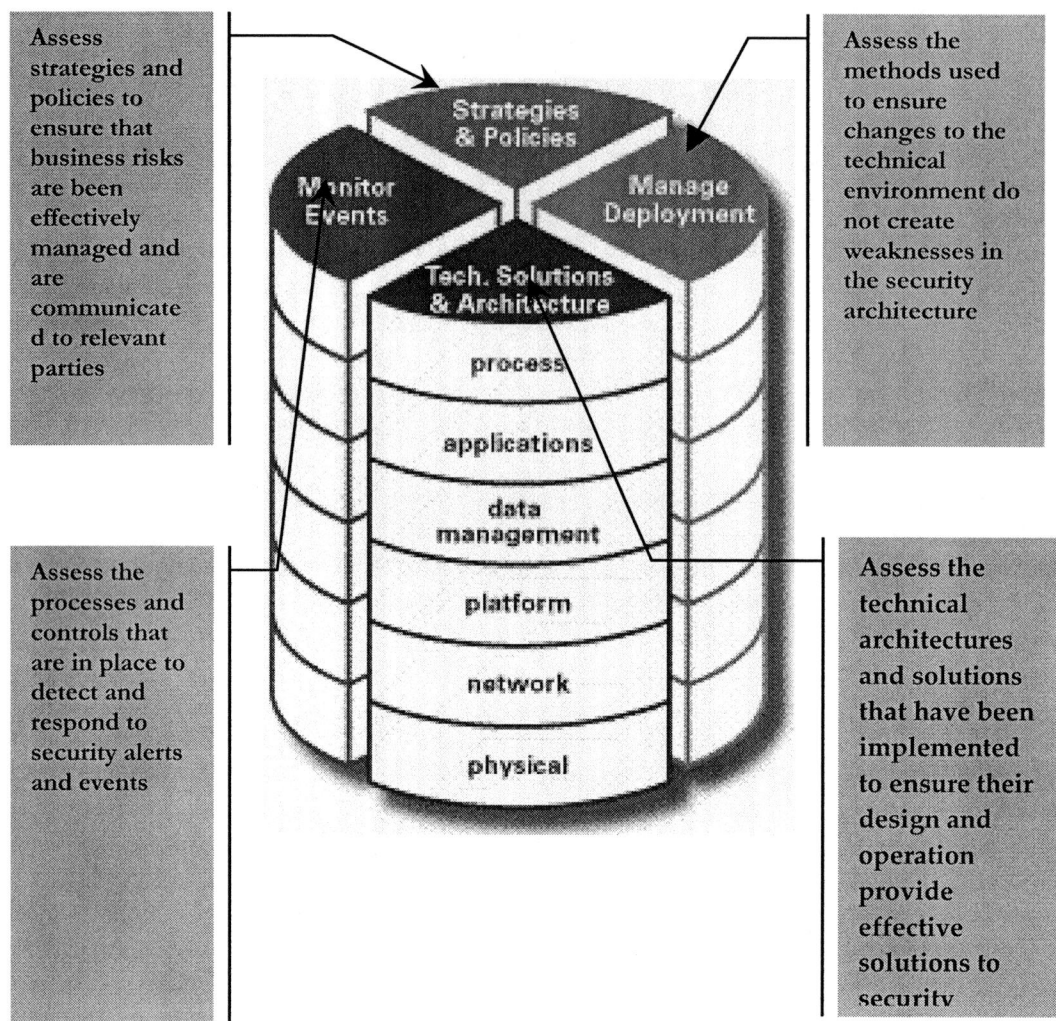

Assess strategies and policies to ensure that business risks are been effectively managed and are communicated to relevant parties

Assess the methods used to ensure changes to the technical environment do not create weaknesses in the security architecture

Assess the processes and controls that are in place to detect and respond to security alerts and events

Assess the technical architectures and solutions that have been implemented to ensure their design and operation provide effective solutions to security

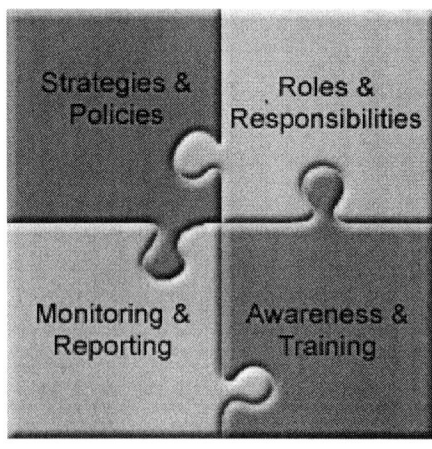

One perspective on the overall Information Security effort divides the process into four distinct areas of concentration, namely:

- Strategies and Policies
- Roles and Responsibilities
- Awareness and Training
- Monitoring and Reporting

Strategies & Policies

- Existence of documentation for a Corporate Security Strategy and Policy
- Approach to security and overall scope of security services
- Prioritization of security objectives
- Definition of the acceptable level of security risk management is willing to accept
- Establishment of a security plan providing an overview of the security requirements of the organization
- Existence of documentation outlining security process flows and operational procedures
- Periodic review for updating security policies and procedures

Roles and Responsibilities

- Identification and communication of roles, responsibilities and accountability for all critical information assets
- Documentation of information security roles, responsibilities and reporting structures
- Delineation in the security plan of responsibilities and expected behavior of all individuals who access information systems
- Establishment of security oversight groups (e.g. security advisory council, security review board)
- Assessment of organizational structure for appropriate separation of duties and consistency with the organization's strategy towards risk management
- Definition of skills requirements for the security function and skill and competency of personnel who administer security

Awareness & Training

- Communication plan used to inform personnel of the security policy
- Priority of security organization's initiatives
- Occurrence of meetings to explain the effectiveness and control of security measures
- User involvement in the security management process (e.g. contributions to self-assessments, reporting security incidents, etc.)
- Definition of training program to match skills to requirements needed for the security function
- New employee training related to security awareness
- Establishment of an ongoing security awareness training program to educate users on roles and responsibilities

Monitoring & Reporting
- Performance of independent and objective assessments of security controls such as provided by security audits
- Establishment of measures to detect and ensure correction of security breaches in real-time
- Measures to monitor system use (e.g. warnings alarm appropriate personnel when established limits on system use are exceeded)
- Performance of compliance testing to assess compliance with policy, standards, and minimum acceptable security practices
- Enforcement of policies and procedures
- Establishment of preventative measures such as vulnerability tests
- Effective reporting, audit trails, and violation reports that inform the security team of anomalies

Every organization is unique. On the other hand, organizations that offer competing products or services, or operate within the same industry may have very similar needs in regard to security implementations. Given the wide variety of circumstances in the marketplace, there is no single "right" way to implement each of the components listed below. However, any attempt at establishing a sound Information Security program should include all of these components or substitute processes that provide similar results. In summary, these components are:

- Senior management commitment and support
- Policies and procedures
- Organization
- Security Design
- Security Implementation
- Security awareness and education
- Monitoring and compliance
- Incident handling and response

Risk Assessment

The topic of Risk Assessment was covered in detail in Chapter 2. However, the risk assessment process itself must have a beginning. There are different approaches and theories about the optimal methods for performing risk assessment. Two distinct procedures are common to all approaches:

- Every asset must be identified
- Every asset must be evaluated and ranked based on some measure of value, importance or criticality.

Hardware and Software Inventory Control

Asset Inventory
Computer hardware and software should be cataloged and indexed to ensure the organization can determine computer resource availability, usage and need. It is essential that data owners, systems administrators and security personnel create a highly detailed inventory of all the technology and information assets the organization maintains. The compilation of this type of list is the first step in classifying the assets and determining the level of protection to be provided to each asset. Policies should require regular updating of the inventory, review for sufficient licenses and documentation of the individual responsible for this control. Effective control requires a detailed inventory of information assets. The information about hardware and software that should be included in an asset inventory includes the following:

- Determining which individual owns the data.
- Verifying the asset's location.
- Creating a naming convention that provides a simple and unique identification for every asset.
- Assigning each asset to a security group based on its role within the organization.
- Determining the value and risk classification of each asset.

Asset Classification

The determination of the value or criticality of an asset is a crucial part of a sound information security process. Every asset, including all hardware, software and data should be classified based on its importance or value to the organization. When this is done in a systematic way, the classifications can be used as a security control. It is best to use established risk analysis techniques so that a clear and defensible valuation is obtained. After all the assets have been assigned a value, they may be classified by type, security group, location, criticality or some other relevant system. Whatever convention is used, it should produce a simple and unique identification tag for every asset, including data files and folders. The classification of data should also specify the following:

- Who owns the data
- Who chooses the access levels and permissions granted to each user or group. (The data owner is usually responsible for this selection)
- What types of approval(s) are needed to add, modify or delete access rights or access levels.
- Which individuals or groups will be authorized to access each asset.
- What level of access will be granted to each individual or group.

There are three additional issues that should be addressed during the classification process:

- **Data classification may be used as a security control.** Classification can aid in enforcing the separation of duties. For example, within an organization's service department, the person responsible for the distribution of rebate checks should not be the person in charge of authorizing the issuance of those checks. In a case like this, the data owner and systems administrator might consider the following actions:
    - Ensure that the job titles and descriptions of those that authorize checks are clearly distinct from those of the people that distribute the checks.
    - Ensure that the systems administrator create two distinct user groups into which the authorization employees and distribution employees can be placed. When the groups are created, the systems administrator should grant to each group only those rights necessary to fulfill its day-to-day responsibilities.
    - Utilize any functionality within the check application (s) to guarantee that the people who authorize checks cannot implement and verify distribution.
    - A company's employees are also considered to be resources or assets. By establishing clear and unique identifiers for each job title/description and for the data required by each one, the process of separation of duties can be simplified.

- **The organization's legal and/or internal responsibilities** regarding the confidentiality of user/employee PII (Personally Identifiable Information) and other types of critical data. Since the classification process should include a stage in which assets are valued, those in charge of implementing security can clearly identify those assets that require the most protection. This will enable the organization to focus its security investments in the areas where they are needed most.

- **The organization's BCP/DR (Business Continuity Plan/Disaster Recovery Plan) function.** An organization may opt to use a consultant on a temporary basis or it may hire someone full-time to handle its BCP/DR function. In such cases, assets that are clearly necessary for the organization to run are identified, risk analyses are performed and solutions based on the organization's needs and means are discussed. This approach, while quite common, does not guarantee that all of the organization's assets are properly classified. In addition, this approach may cause the organization to adopt multiple sets of classifications and naming conventions if the assets included in the BCP/DR planning are not evaluated along with the remaining assets. On the other hand, if the organization adopts a comprehensive classification process, the same information used to determine the value or criticality of assets may be used directly by the BCP/DR team. This will save the organization both time and money in the long run.

Logical Access Controls

Access to network assets is normally governed by two types of controls, physical and logical. Physical controls include any means by which direct contact with network assets may be controlled or restricted. Examples of physical controls are: doors requiring a key, swipe card or the entry of a specific sequence of numbers to be entered; fences, biometric systems and floor-to-ceiling wall construction.

Logical access controls are built into the system itself. They may be implemented by options within the operating system, options in applications installed on the system or both. These controls are defined by policies and procedures in accordance with the objectives stated within the information security policy. This type of control is usually implemented by configuration settings within operating systems, applications or firmware. The process of I&A (Identification and Authentication) is used as the means by which a user gains access to the system. When the user has been authenticated, the permissions granted by the data owners and systems administrators immediately become active. Now that the user has access to the system, the access permissions control the actions a user can initiate upon any given asset or resource. In many cases, a user will have to go through multiple logins in order to become productive. This means that in addition to the first login to the system, the user may have to login to one or more applications in order to work.

It is useful to think of applying logical security in a layered format. There are four layers at which logical controls may be implemented. These layers are: networks, platforms, databases and applications. It is common to find that the user's initial login to some kind of Domain controller allows the user a broad access to the network and the platform layers. Many critical applications and all enterprise-level databases have a built-in set of logical controls designed specifically for that software package. In many cases the logical controls within applications and databases offer a higher degree of granularity than the OS the application is running on. This allows administrators to manage access permissions for the data that will be manipulated by the application with great precision.

Access Permissions

Access permissions are the means by which authority to utilize an asset or resource is granted to users or groups. It is important to remember that temporary employees, consultants, audit personnel and even the cleaning staff are responsible for maintaining the security of the systems or areas they have contact with. Any sound information security program should allow for the presence of those that are not company employees and procedures should be in place to handle the types of access they require.

Access rights or permissions are normally granted via logical (software) controls such as add, delete, modify or read permissions. Access to system assets should be assigned using the principle of least privilege. According to the principle of least privilege, any user of the system or network should only be granted those permissions that are immediately necessary in order for the user to accomplish authorized tasks. Need to know is another principle that should be employed when creating access permissions. With need-to-know, even a user that has the permission to access data at a given level is not granted the right to view every file or asset at that level. For example, a systems administrator may have full access to all of the network's assets. However, that administrator is not authorized to view payroll or medical information of other employees within that organization. In a need-to-know environment, access controls of some kind would have to be created to ensure that even a superuser or root cannot access data that must be kept private. Separation of duties should also be considered when access privileges are being assigned.

In general, data owners decide what assets can be viewed or manipulated and by whom. It is the responsibility of the highest level information security officer or person performing that role to ensure that data owners are clearly identified. The information security lead or director should also be involved in the creation of a process by which data owners classify all their assets according to a single standard. When this is done, the data owners must have a clear procedure by which they document the access permissions they have granted. The exact procedures chosen will vary by organization. However, there are three principles that are highly recommended for data owners or any other personnel that must decide and/or assign access privileges:

Access Philosophy: As mentioned previously, the person or group deciding the access privileges should only grant access to resources based on a "need-to-know, need-to-do" basis. Also, it is a better practice overall to create groups based on job roles and access needs and then add the employees to each group as needed. This approach provides the following benefits:
- It decreases the workload of administrators that have to add and delete users on a regular basis
- Fewer errors will occur when permissions are assigned to user groups than in instances where each user gets permissions assigned individually.
- It is easier to implement changes to permissions on a small number of groups than it is to make the same changes to hundreds of user accounts individually.
- It is easier to monitor, test and audit permissions on groups for compliance than it is to do the same for hundreds of user accounts.

Access Authorization: The data owner or manager who is responsible for the accurate use and reporting of the information should provide written authorization for users to gain access to computerized information. The manager should give this documentation directly to the Security Administrator so mishandling or alteration of the authorization does not occur. This step is an added control

Reviews of Access Authorization: Like any other control, access controls should be evaluated regularly to ensure they are still effective. Personnel and departmental changes, malicious efforts and human error or carelessness can impact the effectiveness of access controls. For this reason, the Security Administrator with the assistance of the managers who provide access authorization should review access controls. Any access exceeding the "need-to-know, need-to-do" philosophy should be changed accordingly.

Access Control Methods

Logical access controls generally fall into one of two categories:

Mandatory Access Controls (MACs): These controls are normally implemented by the use of one or more logical access control mechanisms. These mechanisms may be coded into the operating system, a user application, commercial access control software or some combination of these. This type of control is normally set by the administrator of the system or application that will be utilized. These controls are considered mandatory because they are not user-configurable. Once Mandatory Access Controls are configured, they remain in place until an administrator alters them. These controls act as default settings and they take effect at the time the user logs into the network or the application. Applications that provide SSO (Single Sign On) functionality are examples of a MAC.

Discretionary Access Controls (DACs):- As the name implies, Discretionary Access Controls refer to any type of control that can be used to grant, deny or modify access permissions whenever the need arises. These controls are most commonly available only to data owners or security personnel, but users may be allowed to use this type of control in certain applications or in directories and files they have created. The principle of need-to-know is one type of DAC implementation.

Paths of Logical Access
Logical access into the computer can be gained through several avenues. Each should be subject to appropriate levels of access security. These methods of access include the following:

Operator Console: These privileged computer terminals control most computer operations and functions. To provide security, these terminals should be located in the computer room or another suitably controlled facility so that physical access can only be gained by authorized personnel. Most operator consoles do not have strong logical access controls and provide a high level of computer system access; therefore, the terminal must be located in a physically secured area in order to secure the console.

Online Terminals: Online access to computer systems through terminals typically requires entry of at least a logon-ID and password to gain access to the host computer system and may also require further entry of authentication of identification data for access to application specific systems. Separate security and access control software may be employed on larger systems to improve the security provided by the operating system or application system.

Batch Job Processing: This mode of access is indirect since access is achieved via processing of transactions. It generally involves accumulating input transactions and processing them as batch only after a given interval of time or after a certain number of transactions has been accumulated. Security is achieved by restricting who can accumulate transactions (data entry clerks) and who can initiate batch processing (computer operators or the automatic job scheduling system). Additionally, procedures and/or authorization to manipulate accumulated transactions prior to processing the batch should be carefully controlled.

Dial-up Ports: Use of dial-up ports involves hooking a remote terminal or PC to a telephone line and gaining access to the computer by dialing a telephone number that is directly or indirectly connected to the computer. Often a modem must interface between the remote terminal and the telephone line to encode and decode transmissions. Security is achieved by providing a means of identifying the remote user to determine authorization to access. This may be a dial-back line, use of logon-ID and access control software or may involve a computer operator to verify the identity of the caller and then provide the connection to the computer.

Telecommunications Network: Telecommunications networks link a number of computer terminals or PCs to the host computer through a network of telecommunications lines. The telecommunications lines can be private (i.e., dedicated to one user) or public, such as a nation's telephone system. Security should be provided in the same manner as that applied to online terminals. See 3.3, IS Network and Telecommunication Infrastructure, for further information about the components of telecommunications systems.

Computer Crimes and Criminals

In the current business environment, information assets are increasing in value. Many organizations have converted most or all of their records into digital formats. As a result, database systems are increasing in importance because they provide a means by which vast amounts of information can be stored, accessed and analyzed. Unfortunately, items that have significant value are the targets of those that are capable of stealing them. Depending on the nature of the data or system involved, a malicious person can commit illegal acts by doing any of the following:

- Copying proprietary information for sale to a competing organization (Corporate espionage)
- Computer equipment can have significant resale value and it may be the target for some individuals
- Unauthorized access to routers, switches, domain or web servers, etc can be used to sabotage the organization by altering critical information, destroying that information or a combination of both
- Unauthorized access to payroll or banking applications may allow criminals to steal funds by electronic transfer.
- Copying customer transaction records:
    - These can be sold to competitors
    - These can be sold to spammers and telemarketers.
    - Stolen credit card information can be used to make purchases illegally
    - Stolen personal information can be used to create new identities.
    - Someone may do all of the above.
- The consequences of these actions can be devastating to the organization. Any or all of the following may occur as the result of a security breach that results in the loss of customer's personal information or any other valuable data:

- A computer criminal may blackmail a corporation into paying a large sum of money for the return of lost data. Since many states are creating laws that require organizations to report the loss of PII, some organizations might choose to pay rather than face any of the consequences that follow…
- A company that reports the loss of customer PII may find it difficult to maintain its credibility in the marketplace. Potential customers may not trust that company to safeguard its data.
- New laws allow individuals that can prove some kind of loss or damages due to the theft of their PII can sue the organization for failing to protect that information.
- The organization may be subject to significant fines under the new laws.
- The organization's credit rating may be adversely affected.
- If a competitor can create similar products or services due to receipt of stolen information, the victimized organization may lose its competitive edge.

Types of Computer Criminals

The list of potential criminals is quite extensive. They include the following:

Hackers and Crackers: There are a few different groups of people that are currently called "hackers". The one thing they have in common is that they possess above average to expert-level knowledge of several key computing skills. These skills include, but are not limited to the following: the ability to write code in C and C++, The ability to write scripts in Perl, VBScript and for the bash and korn shells; knowledge of the TCP/IP protocol stack and its workings. Finally, these people have knowledge of one or more operating systems, their associated file systems and the various ways in which one can gain root or administrator privileges.

The thing that separates one group of hackers from another is the motive driving their actions. The original use of the term hacker referred to an individual with the skills listed above who enjoyed the study of systems and applications. Normally, these people had no intention of performing any illegal activity. Their pursuit was mastery of a given technology. In more recent years, the media has applied the term "hacker" to people with significant computing skills and evil motives. This is the probably the most common use of the term today. This newer use of the term hacker has replaced the term "cracker" in usage.

The "**crackers**" of the 1970s and early 1980s were the original bad guys of computing. Today, this term is seldom used. The final type of hacker has been dubbed "hacktivist" by the media. This group of people uses advanced computing skills to further one or more social or political agendas. They can be classified as a subset of the bad hacker group, because their actions usually result in some kind of harm, monetary or otherwise, to their victims. However, some may view their activities as a type of guerrilla warfare on a digital battlefield.

Script Kiddies: The actions of this group are usually quite similar to those of the bad "black hat" hackers. However, script kiddies usually lack any advanced computing skills. To accomplish their goals, script kiddies rely upon the availability of pre-written scripts or blocks of code that have been written by a hacker and posted on a web site or message board. These scripts are designed to search for and exploit one or more vulnerabilities in an application or operating system. What makes script kiddies dangerous is they have usually learned how to gain root or administrator access to a device if the script is successful. After that, nearly every file on the system is available.

Insiders: A large percentage of the all computer crime is committed by people on the inside of the organization. In general, the insider group can be divided into two categories. The first is the IT staff. These employees usually have above average to expert-level knowledge of all the applications and devices deployed by the organization. In addition they also have direct physical access to the devices that control critical functions or store valuable data. Whenever possible, special care should be taken to ensure that a separation of duties exists within the IT function. In addition, logging and auditing of all network access by the IT staff is strongly recommended.

The other group of insiders is the end users. Whether these individuals are full or part-time, permanent or temporary, they are usually granted only the permissions that they need in order to perform their tasks. However, logical access controls can't stop an end user from making illegal copies of software that are not properly secured. Also, this will not stop end users from literally carrying one or more pieces of equipment such as monitors or entire PCs out of a building. In addition to the logical access controls, physical controls must be implemented and utilized in order to prevent end users from doing harm.

Outsiders: This group encompasses hackers, crackers and script kiddies regardless of their motivation. In addition, the following types of personnel should be added to this group: former employees (disgruntled or otherwise), product vendors, consultants and even the building's maintenance and cleaning staff. Steps should be taken to ensure that no one from these groups can get unauthorized access to the network, whether they have physical access to the machines or not.

Computer systems can be used by criminals to steal money, goods, software or corporate information such as customer lists. Crimes also can be committed when the computer application process or dates are manipulated to accept false or unauthorized transactions. There also is the simple, non-technical method of computer crime-stealing computer equipment. Computer crime can be performed with absolutely nothing physically being taken or stolen. Simply viewing computerized data can provide an offender with enough intelligence to steal ideas or confidential information (intellectual property). Committing crimes that exploit the computer and the information it contains can be damaging to the reputation, morale and very existence of an organization. Loss of customers, embarrassment to management and legal actions against the organization can be a result. Threats to business include the following:

- **Financial Loss** – These losses can be direct, through loss of electronic funds or indirect, through the costs of correcting the exposure.
- **Legal Repercussions** – There are numerous privacy and human rights laws the organization should consider when developing security policies and procedures. These laws can protect the organization but can also protect the perpetrator from prosecution. In addition, not having proper security measures could expose the organization to lawsuits from investors and/or insurers should a significant loss occur from a security violation. Most companies also have industry-specific regulatory agencies with whose regulations the company must comply. The IS Auditor should obtain legal assistance when reviewing the legal issues associated with computer security.
- **Loss of Credibility or Competitive Edge** – Many organizations, especially service firms such as banks, savings and loans and investment firms, need credibility and public trust to maintain a competitive edge. A security violation can severely damage this credibility, resulting in loss of business and prestige.
- **Blackmail/Industrial Espionage** – By gaining access to confidential information or the means to adversely impact computer operations, a perpetrator can extort payments or services from an organization by threatening to exploit the security breach.
- **Disclosure of Confidential, Sensitive or Embarrassing Information** – As noted previously, such events can damage an organization's credibility and its means of conducting business. Legal or regulatory actions against the company may also be the result of disclosure.
- **Sabotage** – Some perpetrators are not looking for financial gain. They merely want to cause damage due to some dislike of the organization or for self-gratification.

Logical Access Exposures

Based on the above types of computer criminals and crimes, many types of exposures can exist from accidental or intentional exploitation of logical access control weaknesses. These exposures include hidden program code and direct or indirect modification of data and programs. There are many names for these kinds of exposures, including the following:

- **Data Diddling:** This involves changing data before or as they are entered into the computer. This is one of the most common abuses because it requires limited technical knowledge and occurs before computer security can protect data.
- **Trojan Horse:** This involves hiding malicious, fraudulent code in an authorized computer program. This hidden code will be executed whenever the authorized program is executed. A classic example is the Trojan horse in the payroll calculating program that shaves a penny off each paycheck and credits it to the perpetrator's payroll account.
- **Rounding Down:** This involves drawing off small amounts of money from a computerized transaction or account and rerouting this amount to the perpetrator's account. The term "rounding down" refers to rounding small fractions of a denomination down and transferring these small fractions into the unauthorized account. Since the amounts are so small, they are rarely noticed.

- **Salami Technique:** This technique involves the slicing of small amounts of money from a computerized transaction or account and is similar to the rounding down technique. The difference between the rounding down technique and the salami technique is that in rounding down the program rounds off by the penny. For example, if a transaction amount were $1,235,954.39 the rounding down technique may round the transaction to $1,235,954.35. The salami technique truncates the last few digits from the transaction amount from $1,235,954.39 to $1,235,954.30 or $1,235,854.00 depending on the calculation built into the program.
- **Viruses:** Computer viruses are malicious programs that can self-replicate and spread from computer-to-computer, via sharing of computer diskettes, transfer of logic over telecommunication lines or direct contact with an infected machine/code. A virus can harmlessly display cute messages on computer terminals, dangerously erase or alter computer files or simply fill computer memory with junk to a point where the computer can no longer function. An added danger is that a virus may lie dormant for some time until triggered by a certain event or occurrence, such as date (January 1- Happy New Year!) or being copied a pre-specified number of times; however, during this time the virus has silently been spreading.
- **Worms:** Destructive programs that may destroy data or utilize tremendous computer and communication resources but do not replicate like viruses.
- **Logic Bomb:** Logic bombs are similar to computer viruses, but they do not self-replicate. The creation of logic bombs requires some specialized knowledge, as it involves programming the destruction or modification of data at a specific time in the future. However, unlike viruses or worms, logic bombs are very difficult to detect before they blow up; thus, of all the computer crime schemes, they have the greatest potential for damage. Detonation can be timed to cause maximum damage and to take place long after the departure of the perpetrator. The logic bomb may also be used as a tool of extortion, with a ransom being demanded in exchange for disclosure of the location of the bomb. A good example of a logic bomb that is not related to computer fraud is the Year 2000 problem. In this case a computer program or a whole data center may stop due to a logic error in the coding of the year month date format.
- **Trap Doors:** Trap doors are exits out of an authorized program that permit insertion of specific logic, such as program interrupts to permit a review of data during the middle of processing. These holes also permit insertion of unauthorized logic.
- **Asynchronous Attack:** In multiprocessing environments, data moves asynchronously (one character sent at a time with a start and stop signal) across telecommunications lines. As a result, numerous data transmissions must wait for the line to be free (and flowing in the proper direction) before being transmitted. Data that are waiting are susceptible to unauthorized accesses called asynchronous attacks. These attacks may be committed via hardware which are usually very small pin-like insertions into cables and are extremely difficult to detect. There are many forms of asynchronous attack. This is a very complex and technical exposure that the IS Auditor will require the assistance of a network manager and/or a system software analyst to evaluate.
- **Data Leakage:** Data leakage involves siphoning out or leaking information out of the computer. This can involve dumping disk files to paper or can be as simple as stealing computer reports and tapes.
- **Wire-Tapping:** This technique involves eavesdropping on information being transmitted over telecommunications lines.
- **Piggybacking:** This process can be non-technical, following an authorized person through a secured door or technical, attaching via an authorized telecommunications line to the computer to intercept and possibly alter transmissions.
- **Shutting Down or Overwhelming the Computer/Denial of Service:** A computer shut down can be initiated through terminals or microcomputers connected directly (online) or indirectly (dial-up lines) to the computer. Only individuals knowing a high-level systems logon-ID usually can initiate the shut down process. This security measure is effective only if proper security access controls are in place for the high-level logon-ID and the telecommunications connections into the computer. Some systems have shown to be vulnerable to shutting themselves down under certain conditions of overload. This technique has been particularly used by hackers to shut down computer systems over the Internet.

Controls against Viruses

Some of the controls that should be listed as policies and procedures and should be put in place are:

- Build any system from original, clean master copies. Boot only from original diskettes whose write protection has always been in place.
- Allow no disk to be used until it has been scanned on a stand-alone machine that is used for no other purpose and not connected to the network.
- Update scanning software frequently.
- Write-protect all diskettes with .EXE or .COM extensions.
- Have vendors run demonstrations on their machines, not yours.
- Enforce a rule of not using shareware without first scanning the shareware thoroughly for a virus.
- Commercial software is occasionally supplied with a Trojan Horse (viruses or worms). Scan before any new software is installed.
- Insist that field technicians scan their disks on a test machine before they use any of their disks on the system.
- Ensure that the network administrator uses workstation and server anti-virus software.
- Create a special master boot record that makes the hard disk inaccessible when booting from a diskette. This ensures that the hard disk cannot be contaminated by the floppy disk.
- Consider encrypting files and then decrypt them before execution.
- Ensure that bridge, router and gateway updates are authentic. This is a very easy way to place and hide a Trojan Horse.
- Backups are a vital element of anti-virus strategy. Be sure that you have a sound and effective backup plan in place.
- Educate users so they will heed these policies and procedures.
- Review anti-virus policies and procedures at least once a year.

Technical methods of preventing viruses can be implemented through hardware and software means. There are four hardware tactics that can reduce the risk of infection:

- Use workstations without floppy disks
- Use remote booting
- Use a hardware-based password
- Use write-protected tabs on floppy disks

Software is by far the most common anti-virus tool. Anti-virus software should primarily be used as a preventative control. Unless updated periodically anti-virus software will not be an effective tool against viruses. There are three different types of anti-virus software:

- **Scanners** look for sequences of bits called signatures that are typical of virus programs. Scanners examine memory, disk boot sectors, executables and command files for bit patterns that match a known virus. Scanners therefore need to be updated periodically to remain effective.
- **Active Monitors** interpret DOS and ROM basic input-output system (BIOS) calls, looking for virus like actions. Active monitors can be annoying because they cannot distinguish between a user request and a program or virus request. As a result, users are asked to confirm actions like formatting a disk or deleting a file or set of files.
- **Integrity Checkers** compute a binary number on a known virus-free program that is then stored in a database file. The number is called a cyclical redundancy check or CRC. When that program is called to execute, the checker computes the CRC on the program about to be executed and compares it to the number in the database. A match means no infection; a mismatch means that a change in the program has occurred. A change in the program could mean a virus within it. Integrity checkers take advantage of the fact that executable programs and boot sectors do not change very often if at all.

Specific Logical Controls

Computer files should be protected from unauthorized and unnecessary access by controls that reduce the risk of intentional or unintentional misuse, theft, alteration or destruction. In a batch processing environment, restricting and monitoring computer operator activities can provide this control. In an online system the avenues of access are more complex and direct; thus, the level of control must be more complex. These access controls need to be applied not only to computer operators but also to end users, programmers, security administrators, management and anyone authorized to use the computer (including outsiders).

Access to PC Data

Access control to PCs involves both physical and logical controls. Physical access controls reduce exposure to theft or destruction of data and hardware. Logical access controls reduce exposure to unauthorized alteration and manipulation of data and programs recorded on microcomputer storage media. Sensitive data should not be stored in a microcomputer. If business critical or sensitive data are being downloaded from the host computer to a disk, access to microcomputer equipment is an important control issue. The simplest and most effective way to secure data and software in a microcomputer is to remove the storage medium (such as the disk, cassette or tape) from the machine when it is not in use and lock it in a safe.

Microcomputers with fixed disk systems may require additional security procedures for theft protection. Vendors offer lockable enclosures, clamping devices and cable fastening devices that help prevent equipment theft. The computer can also be connected to a security system that sounds an alarm if equipment is moved. This is most effective when the alarm is tied into a building security network monitored by a guard station.

A clever thief may remove only memory chips or circuit boards; however, vendors offer devices to secure the hardware cabinet to prevent this problem. Preventing the theft of data is virtually impossible. The medium itself is inexpensive, but the data residing on disks may be vital to the company. An employee could slip a disk into a briefcase, make a copy on a home microcomputer and return the disk the next day. Placing signaling devices in disk jackets prevents the removal of important disks; however, it would not stop someone from using an unprotected disk to copy the data at the office. The following are more practical solutions:

- Record all sensitive data on removable hard drives, which are more easily secured than fixed or floppy disks.
- Begin the use of FDE (Full Disk Encryption) on:
    o Any internal computer used to store sensitive information
    o Any Laptops, PDAs, Blackberrys or other devices issued to employees that might be used to store sensitive information
- Configure internal computers to block installation of any removable media such as floppy disks, CD-ROMs, USB Flash Drives, etc. to prevent copying of sensitive data inside the organization.

Software can also be used to control access to microcomputer data. The basic software approach restricts access to program and data files with a password system. The password facility, which is usually a feature of the microcomputer operating system, uses a hashing algorithm to store the scrambled passwords with the operating system files. To provide even stronger controls microcomputer software vendors offer a variety of products, including hardware devices that contain access security software. Physical access to these devices must be restricted for them to effectively limit data access. The best security in any event is to encrypt the data.

Files and Facilities to be Protected by Logical Access Controls
The following is a list of files and IT assets that should be protected by logical access controls:

Data	Access Control Software
Logging Files	Procedure Libraries
Utilities	Bypass Label Processing Feature
Telecommunications Lines	Operator System Exits
Libraries	Dial-Up Lines
Password Library	Data Dictionary/Directory
Temporary Disk Files	Tape Files
Application Software: Test or Production	System Software

Logon-IDs and Passwords to Limit Access
A two-phase user identification/authentication process can be used to restrict access to computerized information, transactions, programs and system software. The computer can maintain an internal list of valid logon-IDs and a corresponding set of access rules for each logon-ID. These access rules identify the computer resources the user of the logon-ID can access and constitute the user's authorization. Access rules can usually be specified at the operating system level (controlling access to files) or within individual application systems (controlling access to menu functions and types of data).

The logon-ID provides individual identification. Each user gets a unique logon-ID that can be identified by the system. The format of logon-IDs is typically standardized. The password prevents unauthorized use because the user generally assigns it.

The password provides individual authentication. Identification/authentication is a two step process by which the computer system first verifies that the user has a valid logon-ID and then requires the user to substantiate his/her validity via a password.

Access rules (authorization) specify who can access what. Access should be on a "need-to-know, need-to-do" basis by type of access.

Having computer access does not always mean unrestricted access. Access privileges can be set to many different levels. By restricting access to the appropriate levels, an added layer of security can be provided. When the IS Auditor reviews computer accessibility, he/she will want to know what can be done with the access and what is restricted. Access restrictions at the file level generally include the following:

- Read, inquiry or copy only
- Write, create, update or delete only
- Execute

The least dangerous type of access is "inquiry" or "read", as long as the information being accessed is not sensitive or confidential. This is because the user cannot alter or use the computerized file beyond basic viewing or printing of the screen. It should be noted that in most client/server environments, read access permits copying of files or folders. Therefore, even read access should be granted only to those that truly need to see the information.

Logging Computer Access
With most security packages today, computer access and attempted access violations can be automatically logged by the computer and reported. The frequency of the security administrator's review of computer access reports should be commensurate with the sensitivity of the computerized information being protected. The IS Auditor should ensure that the logs can not be tampered with or altered without leaving an audit trail. When reviewing or performing security access follow-up, the IS Auditor should look for:

- Patterns or trends that indicate abuse of access privileges, such as concentration on a sensitive application.
- Violations (such as attempting computer file access that is not authorized) and/or use of incorrect passwords.

What to do about reports of violation attempts:

- The person who identified the violator should refer the problem to the Security Administrator for investigation.
- The security administrator and responsible management should work together to investigate and determine the severity of the violation. Generally, most violations are accidental.
- If the violation attempt is serious, executive management should generally be notified, not law enforcement officials. It is usual for executive management to be responsible for notifying law enforcement officials since involvement of external agencies may result in adverse publicity that is ultimately more damaging than the original violation. The decision to involve external agencies should be left to executive management.
- To facilitate proper handling of access violations, written guidelines should exist that identify various types and levels of violations and how they should be addressed. This effectively provides direction for judging the seriousness of a violation.
- Disciplinary action should be a formal process that is consistently applied. This may involve a reprimand probation or immediate termination; therefore, the procedures should be legally and ethically sound to reduce the risk of legal action against the company.
- Corrective measures should include a review of the computer access rules, not only for the perpetrator but for interested parties. Excessive or inappropriate access rules should be eliminated.

Features of Passwords
- A password should be easy for the user to remember but difficult for a perpetrator to guess.
- Initial password assignment should be done discretely by the security administrator. When the user logs on for the first time, the system should force a password change to improve confidentiality.
- "Three strikes, you're out!" If the wrong password is entered a predefined number of times, typically three, the logon-ID should be automatically and permanently deactivated (or at least for a significant period of time).
- If a logon-ID has been deactivated because of a forgotten password, the user should notify the security administrator. The security administrator should then reactivate the logon-ID only after verifying the user's identification, much like a bank verifies an account holder's ID before giving information over the phone (such as mother's maiden name), by returning the phone call after verifying the user's extension or calling the user's supervisor for verification.
- Internally, passwords should be one-way encrypted. Encryption is a means of encoding data stored in the computer. This reduces the risk that a perpetrator will gain access to other users' passwords (if the perpetrator cannot read and understand it, he cannot use it). Passwords should not be displayed in any form - either on a computer screen when entered, on computer reports, in index or card files or written on pieces of paper taped inside a person's desk. These are the first places a potential perpetrator will look.
- Passwords should be changed periodically. On a regular basis (for example, every 30 days), the user should change his/her password. The best method is for the computer system to force the change by notifying the user prior to the password expiration date. Voluntary changing is just that, voluntary; so it probably will not be done.

Password Syntax (format) Rules

- Ideally, passwords should be a minimum of eight characters in length. Anything shorter is too easy to guess. Anything longer becomes harder to remember.
- Should allow for a combination of alpha and numeric characters.
- Should not be particularly identifiable with the user (such as first name, last name, spouse name, pet's name, etc.). Some organizations prohibit the use of vowels, making word association/guessing of passwords more difficult.
- The system should not permit previous password(s) to be used after being changed.
- Logon-IDs not used after a number of days should be deactivated to prevent possible misuse. This can be done automatically by the system or be manually performed by the security administrator.

Automatic Log-Off

The system should automatically disconnect a logon session if no activity has occurred for a period of time (one hour). This reduces the risk of misuse of an active logon session left unattended because the user went to lunch, left home, went to a meeting, etc. or forgot to logoff.

Data Classification

Computer files, like documents, have varying degrees of sensitivity. By assigning classes or levels of sensitivity to these computer files, management can establish guidelines for the degree of access controls that should be assigned. Classifications should be simple, such as high, medium and low. The information used to determine these classifications should come from the risk assessment, as opposed to purely subjective judgments. End user managers and the security administrator can then use these classifications to assist with determining who should be able to access what.

Data classification also reduces the risk and cost of overprotecting computer resources. Data classification is extremely important when identifying who should have access to production versus test data and programs. Production data are live or historical data used to run the business. The owner must grant access to that data or program.

Safeguards for Confidential Data on a PC

In today's environment, it is not unusual to keep sensitive data on PCs and diskettes where it is more difficult to implement logical and physical access controls. Preventative controls such as encryption become more important for protecting sensitive data in the event that a PC or laptop is lost, stolen or sold. The most commonly used encryption schemes are DES and RSA. If encryption is not used then the owner of the data or security officer should create procedures for securing sensitive data. Such procedures may require that no data be stored on the hard drive of a PC or laptop. Other procedures may require that the PC or laptop may only be used in a physically secured area and must not be taken from that location.

Naming Convention for Access Controls

Access capabilities are implemented by security administration in a set of access rules that stipulate which users (or groups of users) are authorized to access a resource (such as a data set or file) and at which level (such as read or update). The access control mechanism applies these rules whenever a user attempts to access or use a protected resource. On larger mainframe and midrange systems access control naming conventions are structures used to govern user's access to the system and user authority to access or use computer resources such as files, programs and terminals. These general naming conventions and associated files are required in a computer environment to establish and maintain personal accountability and segregation of duties in the access of data. The owners of the data or application, with the help of the security officer, usually set up naming conventions.

Exam Tip: Naming Conventions are *not* a variation of Data Classification. Naming Conventions are a standardized format developed by data owners and/or IT staff that is used to uniquely identify or label each asset or resource within the organization. On the other hand, Data Classification is a measure of the sensitivity (security level or value) assigned to a given asset or resource.

The need for sophisticated naming conventions over access controls depends on the importance and level of security that is needed to ensure no unauthorized access has been granted. It is important to establish naming conventions that both promote the implementation of efficient access rules and simplify security administration. Naming conventions for system resources (datasets, volumes, programs, terminals, etc.) are an important prerequisite for efficient administration of security controls. Naming conventions can be structured so that resources beginning with the same high-level qualifier can be governed by one or more generic rules. This reduces the number of rules required to adequately protect resources, which in turn facilitates security administration and maintenance efforts.

Auditing Logical Access Controls

The auditor's work is valuable, but it should not be thought of as the foundation of an effective security management effort. The IS Auditor should be able to analyze and evaluate the policies pertaining to organizational structures, operating procedures and access controls that are used to protect computer software and data files from unauthorized access, disclosure, manipulation or destruction. The auditor may be called upon to examine one or several types of technology deployed within an organization. Ideally, the individual(s) performing the IT audit should have several years of IT work experience. It is unlikely that an auditor will have expert-level knowledge of every technology currently in use. This is especially true if the organization in question is large, if it has a significant amount of legacy hardware and software or if it uses any proprietary or highly customized applications. If a particular IT environment is comprised of a wide variety of IT assets, it may be necessary to use more than one person to perform the audit. If the audit team does not have personnel with sufficient expertise to review a given organization, additional personnel should be either hired or brought in on a temporary basis to achieve the best possible results. In every case, the goal of the auditor should be to gather information about the following:

- The individuals or groups that should have access to these assets.
- The categories into which each relevant application or device has been classified.
- The types of controls that should be present (under ideal conditions) when assets within these categories are deployed.
- The controls (including compensating controls) actually in place.
- The data owners and system administrators that are implementing security policy.

When evaluating logical access controls the IS Auditor should:

- Obtain a general understanding of the security risks facing information processing through a review of relevant documentation, inquiry, observation, risk assessment and evaluation techniques.
- Document and evaluate controls over potential access paths into the system to assess their adequacy, efficiency and effectiveness by reviewing appropriate hardware and software security features and identifying any deficiencies or redundancies.
- Test controls over access paths to determine that they are functioning and effective by applying appropriate audit techniques.
- Evaluate the access control environment to determine if the control objectives were achieved by analyzing test results and other audit evidence.
- Evaluate the security environment to assess its adequacy by reviewing written policies, observing practices and procedures and comparing them with appropriate security standards or practices and procedures used by other organizations using benchmarking techniques.

Network Infrastructure Security

Communication networks (wide area or local area networks) generally include devices connected to the network as well as programs and files supporting the network operations. Control is accomplished through a network control terminal and specialized communications software. The following are controls over the communication network:

- Network control functions should be performed by technically qualified operators.
- Network control functions should be separated, and the duties should be rotated on a regular basis, where possible.
- Network control software must restrict operator access from performing certain functions (e.g., as, the ability to amend/delete operator activity logs).
- Network control software should maintain an audit trail of all operator activities.
- Audit trails should be periodically reviewed by operations management to detect any unauthorized network operations activities.
- Network operation standards and protocols should be documented and made available to the operators and should be periodically reviewed to ensure compliance.
- Network access by the system engineers should be closely monitored and reviewed to detect unauthorized access to the network.
- Analysis should be performed to ensure workload balance, fast response time and system efficiency.
- A terminal identification file should be maintained by the communications software to check the authentication of a terminal when it tries to send or receive messages.
- Data encryption should be used, where appropriate, to protect messages from disclosure during transmission.

To improve the control and maintenance of the infrastructure and its use, besides the direct management of the network devices, consolidate the logs of these devices with the firewall's logs and the client-server operating system's logs.

LANS (Local Area Networks

Local area networks facilitate the storage and retrieval of programs and data used by a group of people. LAN software and practices also need to provide for the security of these programs and data. Unfortunately, most LAN software provides a low level of security. The emphasis has been on providing capability and functionality rather than security. As a result, risks associated with use of LANs include:

- Loss of data and program integrity through unauthorized changes
- Lack of current data protection through inability to maintain version control
- Exposure to external activity through limited user verification and potential public network access from dial-in connections
- Virus infection
- Improper disclosure of data because of general access rather than need-to-know access provisions
- Violating software licenses by using unlicensed or excessive numbers of software copies
- Illegal access by impersonating or masquerading as a legitimate LAN user
- Internal user's sniffing (obtaining seemingly unimportant information from the network that can be used to launch an attack, such as network address information)
- Internal user's spoofing (reconfiguring a network address to pretend to be a different address)
- Destruction of the logging and auditing data.
- The IT Auditor must be familiar with the commonly available network security administrative capabilities.

LAN Risks and Issues

The administrative and control functions available with network software might be limited. Software vendors and network users have recognized the need to provide diagnostic capabilities to identify the cause of problems when the network goes down or functions in an unusual manner. The use of logon IDs and passwords with associated administration facilities is only becoming standard now. Read, write and execute permission capabilities for files and programs are options available with some network operating system versions, but detailed automated logs of activity (audit trails) are seldom found on LANs. Fortunately, newer versions of network software have significantly more control and administration capabilities.

Dial-up Access Controls

It is possible to break LAN security through the dial-in route. Without dial-up access controls, a caller can dial in and try passwords until they gain access. Once in, they can hide pieces of software anywhere, pass through WAN links to other systems and generally create as much or as little havoc as they like. To minimize the risk of unauthorized dial-in access, remote users should never store their passwords in plain text login scripts on notebooks and desktops. Furthermore, portable PCs should be protected by physical keys and/or basic input/output system (BIOS) based passwords to limit access to data if stolen.

Client-server Security

A client-server system typically contains numerous access points. Security procedures for these server environments are usually not as well understood or as protected as a mainframe-based processing environment. Client-server systems utilize distributed techniques, creating increased risk of access to data and processing. To effectively secure the client-server environment, all access points should be identified. In mainframe-based applications, centralized processing techniques require the user to go through one predefined route to access all resources. In a client-server environment, several access routes exist, as application data may exist on the server or on the client. Therefore, each of these routes must be examined individually and in relation to each other to determine that no exposures are left unchecked. To increase the security in a client-server environment, an IS auditor may want to see that the following control techniques are in place:

- Securing access to the data or application on the client-server may be performed by disabling the floppy disk drive, much like a keyless workstation that has access to a mainframe. Diskless workstations prevent access control software from being bypassed and rendering the workstation vulnerable to unauthorized access. By securing the automatic boot or startup batch files, unauthorized users may be prevented from overriding login scripts and access.
- Network monitoring devices may be used to inspect activity from known or unknown users. These devices may identify client addresses, allowing proactive session termination as well as finding evidence of unauthorized access for later investigation. However, the method of securing the client-server environment may be only as good as the administrator who monitors it. Since this is a detective control, if the network administrator does not monitor or maintain these devices, the tool becomes useless against unauthorized intruders.
- Data encryption techniques (symmetric or asymmetric encryption) can help protect sensitive or proprietary data from unauthorized access.
- Authentication systems may provide environment-wide, logical facilities that can differentiate among users. Another method, system smart cards, uses intelligent handheld devices and encryption techniques to decipher random codes provided by client-server systems. A smart card displays a temporary password that is provided by an algorithm on the system and must be reentered by the user during the login session for access into the client-server system.
- The use of application-level access control programs and the organization of end users into functional groups is a management control that restricts access by limiting users to only those functions needed to perform their duties.

Client-server Risks and Issues

Traditionally, information technology in organizations employed a large central computer system. Since the early 1990s, client/server technology has become one of the most common ways many organizations have processed production data and developed and delivered mission critical products and services. Client/server technology enables business units to develop and deliver products and services to market much faster than those who use legacy methods. The trade-off is that logical controls within these systems are usually weaker than those associated with traditional mainframe systems. There are threats that can severely impact a company's business, if controls are not in place to prevent or detect them. The areas of risk and concern in a client-server environment are listed below:

- Access controls may be weak in a client-server environment, if network administrators do not set up password change controls or access rules properly.
- Change control and change management procedures, whether they are automated or manual, may be inherently weak. The primary reason for this weakness is due to the relatively high level of sophistication of client-server change control tools together with inexperienced IS staff, which is reluctant to introduce such tools for fear of introducing limitations on their capability.
- The loss of network availability may have a serious impact on the business or service.
- Obsolescence of the network components, including hardware, software and communications
- The use of synchronous and asynchronous modems to connect the network to other networks may be unauthorized and indiscriminate.

Internet Threats and Security

The very nature of the Internet makes it vulnerable to attack. The Internet was originally designed to allow for the freest possible exchange of information; it is widely used today for commercial purposes. This poses significant security problems for organizations when protecting their information assets. For example, hackers and virus writers try to attack the Internet and computers connected to the Internet. Some want to invade others' privacy and attempt to crack into databases containing sensitive information or sniff information as it travels across Internet routes. Consequently, it becomes more important for IS auditors to understand the risks and security factors that are needed to ensure proper controls are in place when a company connects to the Internet.

Network Security Threats

One class of network attacks involves probing for network information. These passive attacks can lead to active attacks or intrusions/penetrations into an organization's network. By probing for network information, the intruder obtains network information that can be used to target a particular system or set of systems during an actual attack.

Passive Attacks

Examples of passive attacks that gather network information include the following:

- **Network analysis:** The intruder applies a systematic and methodical approach known as **footprinting** to create a complete profile or map of an organization's network security infrastructure.

- **Eavesdropping:** The intruder gathers the information flowing through the network with the intent of acquiring and releasing the message contents for either personal analysis or for third parties who might have commissioned such eavesdropping.

- **Traffic analysis:** The intruder determines the nature of traffic flow between defined hosts, and through an analysis of session length, frequency and message length, he/she is able to guess the type of communication taking place.

Active Attacks

Once enough network information has been gathered, the intruder will launch an actual attack against a targeted system to either gain complete control over that system or enough control to allow other attacks to succeed. This may include obtaining unauthorized access to modify data or programs, causing a denial of service, escalating privileges, accessing other systems, and obtaining sensitive information for personal gain. These types of penetrations or intrusions are known as active attacks. They affect the integrity, availability and authentication attributes of network security. Common forms of active attacks may include any of the following:

- **Brute-force attack:** In this type of attack, the intruder uses software to make repeated attempts at guessing a password to gain unauthorized access to a system. This is also known by some as a "dictionary" attack since the software used may actually include dictionaries from one or more languages in a compressed form.

- **Masquerading:** Identical to "Spoofing". It involves altering the information in the header of a packet so that the source information appears to be from a trusted network

- **Packet replay:** Similar to a "man in the middle" attack, an intruder captures some data sent from one party to another. The intruder then tries to send the same data again, hoping that the device receiving the transmission will grant the access

- **Phishing:** In this attack, a malicious person or group crafts fake email messages, web sites, etc. pretending to be a legitimate service provider. The goal is to get the victim to enter login and/or other identifying information that can be used fraudulently to obtain goods and services

- **Message modification:** Similar to "replay". A captured message is altered and forwarded onto the intended recipient, but the information it contains is false.

- **Denial of service:** In this attack, a continuous series of packets is sent to a router or server in the hope that the resources of that device will be used up. If this happens, legitimate users will not be able to access the services of that device. **Dial-in penetration attacks**: Involve an attacker attempting to compromise the security of a dial up connection by guessing usernames and/or password.

- **E-mail bombing and spamming:** Email bombing involves sending the same unsolicited email to the same address repeatedly. Spamming is sending the same email to many different addresses

- **E-mail spoofing:** This involves configuring an email so that the information about the sender is fake. This is a favorite tactic of spammers.

Firewalls

A firewall is device running software that allows a user to control the types of traffic that can move between different security domains. All traffic between the security domains must pass through the firewall, regardless of the direction of the flow. Since the firewall serves as a choke point for traffic between security domains, they are ideally situated to inspect and block traffic and coordinate activities with network IDS (Intrusion Detection and Response) systems, proxies, content filtering devices and logging servers. There are four primary firewall types from which to choose: packet filtering, stateful inspection, proxy servers, and application-level firewalls.

Many current firewall products have characteristics of two or more firewall types. For example, every firewall on the market is capable of performing packet filtering of some kind. Packet filtering is the earliest type of firewall technology. Firewall vendors now distinguish their products by the additional technologies they have added to the packet filtering. The selection of firewall type is dependent on many characteristics of the security zone, such as the amount of traffic, the sensitivity of the systems and data, and applications. In most cases, a firewall of the type used to defend business networks comes in two forms: the dedicated appliance and the "software" firewall.

In general, a dedicated appliance is a computing device that serves only a single purpose. In the case of a firewall appliance, this is a machine that has had its operating system configured so that it does not expose any of the vulnerabilities that might be known for that OS platform. The vendor will then install a software package on this device and market it. In theory, the end user will only need to configure the firewall software, because the operating system has been taken care of. End users have to get updates from the vendor, so the choice of a vendor is a very important consideration.

A "software" firewall refers to a software package that must be installed by the end user directly. In addition, the end user must configure the computer on which the firewall software will run. Software firewalls exist for home users at the low end of the scale or for installation in clusters and examination of corporate traffic on the high end. Software firewalls for home users often install with many preconfigured rules for common applications. This allows non-technical users to add protection to their devices without needing to study basic networking principles.

The corporate level software firewall requires personnel with above average OS administration skills to properly set up the base computer, and then properly install the firewall on top of that. Most software firewall implementations are built on bastion hosts. A bastion host is a computer whose operating system has been installed and configured to minimize the number of services and applications that run on it. Only those services necessary to allow a firewall, IDS, IPS (Intrusion Prevention System) or other chosen applications to function are allowed to operate. A system set up this way is considered to be "hardened" or "locked down" because it has few or no vulnerabilities that are known and subject to attack.

When bastion hosts are configured, they are usually placed in the DMZ (**Demilitarized Zone**). Although some definitions for the term "DMZ" vary regarding the placement of the firewall, all agree that this area is used to allow an organization to place servers in area where the public can contact them. Public-facing, "front-end" or "proxy" email, web, chat and game servers are all examples of devices that should be placed in a DMZ.

Packet Filtering Firewalls

Packet filtering firewalls evaluate the headers of each incoming and outgoing packet to ensure that they have valid internal addresses, originate from a permitted external address, connect to an authorized protocol or service, and contains valid basic header instructions. If the packet does not match one of the pre-defined policies for allowed traffic, then the firewall drops the packet. The automatic dropping or discarding of packets that do not match any rules configured on the firewall is also known as an "Implicit Deny Rule". Packet filters generally do not analyze the packet contents beyond the header information. Dynamic packet filtering incorporates stateful inspection primarily for performance benefits. Before re-examining every packet, the firewall checks each packet as it arrives to determine whether it is part of an existing connection. If it verifies that the packet belongs to an established connection, then it forwards the packet without subjecting it to the firewall ruleset. Basic packet filtering does not include stateful inspection.

Weaknesses associated with packet filtering firewalls include the following:

- The system is unable to prevent attacks that employ application specific vulnerabilities and functions because the packet filter cannot examine packet contents.
- Logging functionality is limited to the same information used to make access control decisions.
- Most do not support advanced user authentication schemes such as RADIUS and 802.1X.
- Basic Packet filters are more vulnerable to attacks and exploitation that take advantage of problems in the TCP/IP specification.
- The firewalls are easy to misconfigure, which allows traffic to pass that should be blocked.

Packet filtering offers less security, but faster performance than any other firewall type. They are still useful in internal, high-speed environments where logging and user authentication with network resources are not as important as they are at the network edge. Packet filter firewalls are also commonly used in small office/home office (SOHO) systems and default operating system firewalls. Institutions internally hosting Internet accessible services should consider implementing additional firewall components that include application-level screening.

Stateful Inspection Firewalls
Stateful inspection firewalls are packet filters that monitor the state of the TCP connection. Each TCP session starts with an initial three-way handshake communicated through TCP flags (SYN; SYN-ACK; ACK) in the header information. When a connection is established the firewall adds the connection information to a table. The firewall can then compare future packets to the connection or state table. This essentially verifies that inbound traffic is in response to requests initiated from inside the firewall.

Proxy Server Firewalls
Proxy servers act as intermediaries between internal and external IP addresses and block direct access to the internal network. Essentially, they rewrite the headers on outbound packets, substituting the IP address of the proxy server for the IP of the internal machine. They are used to control what type of packets move to and from the internal machines. Proxy servers are commonly deployed in conjunction with other firewall devices. In that type of scenario, the primary firewall receives all traffic, determines which application is being targeted, and hands off the traffic to the appropriate proxy server. Common proxy servers are the domain name server (DNS), Web server (HTTP), and mail (SMTP, POP3, IMAP4) server. Proxy servers frequently cache requests and responses, providing potential performance benefits. Additionally, proxy servers provide another layer of access control by segregating the flow of Internet traffic to support additional authentication and logging capability, as well as content filtering. Web and e-mail proxy servers, for example, are capable of filtering for potential malicious code and application-specific commands.

Application-Layer Firewalls
Application-level firewalls perform application-layer screening, typically including the filtering capabilities of packet filter firewalls with additional validation of the data content in each packet. In common usage, this type of "application–layer" screening is related to the Application layer in the TCP model which maps to the Session, Presentation and Application layers of the OSI model. They can check the data part of a packet and determine what type of traffic is being forwarded. Application-layer firewalls capture and compare packets to state information in the connection tables. Unlike a packet filter firewall, an application level firewall continues to examine each packet after the initial connection is established for specific application or services such as telnet, FTP, HTTP, SMTP, etc. Many application-layer firewalls are highly configurable and can provide additional screening of the packet payload for commands, protocols, packet length, authorization, content, or invalid headers. Application layer firewalls provide the strongest level of security, but the trade off for added functionality is that they are slower and require greater expertise to administer properly. The primary disadvantages of application-level firewalls are:

- The time required to read and interpret each packet slows network traffic. Traffic of certain types may have to be split off before the application level firewall and passed through different access controls.
- Any particular firewall may provide only limited support for new network applications and protocols. They also simply may allow traffic from those applications and protocols to go through the firewall.

Dual-homed and Multi-homed Firewalls

Dual/Multi-homed firewalls: These are firewall devices that have two or more network interfaces, respectively, each of which is connected to a different network. In a firewall configuration, a dual-homed firewall usually acts to block or filter some or all of the traffic trying to pass between the networks. A dual-homed firewall system is a more restrictive form of a screened-host firewall system, when a dual-homed bastion host may be configured with one interface established for information servers and another for private network host computers.

Screened-subnet Firewall

Demilitarized zone (DMZ) or screened-subnet firewall—Utilizing (at a minimum) two packet filtering routers and a bastion host, this approach creates the most secure firewall system, since it supports both network and application-level security while defining a separate demilitarized zone network. The DMZ functions as a small isolated network for an organization's public servers, bastion host information servers and modem pools. DMZs are usually configured to limit access from the Internet headed inbound to the organization's private network. Incoming traffic access is restricted into the DMZ network by the outside router and protects the organization against certain attacks by limiting the services available for use.

As a result, external systems can access only the bastion host (and its proxy service capabilities to internal systems) and possibly information servers in the DMZ. The inside router provides a second line of defense, managing DMZ access to the private network, while accepting only traffic originating from the bastion host. For outbound traffic, the inside router manages private network access to the DMZ network. It permits internal systems to access only the proxy/bastion host and information servers in the DMZ. The filtering rules on the outside router require the use of proxy services by accepting only that outbound traffic that originates from the proxy/bastion host. The key benefits of this configuration are:

- An intruder must penetrate three separate devices
- Private network addresses are not disclosed to the Internet
- Internal systems do not have direct access to the Internet

A comparison of the firewalls can be seen below.

Firewall Type	PROS	CONS
Packet Filters (1st Generation)	<ul><li>Application Independent</li><li>High Performance</li><li>Scalable</li></ul>	<ul><li>Low Security</li><li>No Protection Above Network Layer</li></ul>
Stateful Inspection (2nd Generation)	<ul><li>Good Security</li><li>High Performance</li><li>Scalable</li><li>Partly Aware of Application Layer</li><li>Extensible</li></ul>	<ul><li>More Expensive</li></ul>
Proxy/Application Gateways (3rd – 4thGeneration)	<ul><li>Good Security</li><li>Fully Aware of Application Layer</li></ul>	<ul><li>Limited Application Support</li><li>Poor Scalability</li><li>Poor Performance</li><li>Very Expensive</li></ul>

Firewall Services and Configuration
Firewalls may provide additional preventative controls:

- **Network address translation (NAT):** NAT changes the source addresses on outbound packets to mask the internal IP addresses of the network. Untrusted networks see a different host IP address from the actual internal address. NAT allows an institution to hide the topology and address schemes of its trusted network from untrusted networks.
    o Although many low-end home routers cite NAT as a firewall technology, NAT is not a firewall. The translation of a routable, public IP address to a non-routable private IP address is not the same as firewall functionality. Basic packet filtering is more secure than NAT.
    o Many home-use routers actually include firewall functionality, but most home users do not learn to use this feature if it is available.
- **Dynamic host configuration protocol (DHCP):** DHCP assigns IP addresses to machines that will be subject to the security controls of the firewall.
- **Virtual Private Network (VPN) gateways:** A VPN gateway provides an encrypted tunnel between a remote external gateway and the internal network. Placing VPN capability on the firewall and the remote gateway protects information from disclosure between the gateways but not from the gateway to the terminating machines. Placement on the firewall, however, allows the firewall to inspect the traffic and perform access control, logging, and malicious code scanning.
    o One common firewall implementation in organizations hosting Internet applications is a DMZ, which is a neutral Internet accessible zone typically separated by two firewalls. One firewall is between the institution's private network and the DMZ and then another firewall is between the DMZ and the outside public network.
    o The DMZ constitutes one logical security domain, the outside public network is another security domain, and the institution's internal network may be composed of one or more additional logical security domains. An adequate and effectively managed firewall can help ensure that an organization's computer systems are not directly accessible to any direct contact from the Internet.

There are many types of firewalls and options available to the public. Due to the large number of products available, cost considerations are often the primary factor involved in purchase decisions. Additional considerations include the ease of firewall administration, degree of firewall monitoring support through automated logging and log analysis, and the capability to provide alerts for abnormal activity. Firewall configurations should be unique to each organization and carefully guarded from external parties. An extended discussion of secure firewall configuration is beyond the scope of this text. However, the following basic configuration concepts merit a brief mention here:

- **Traffic Quarantine and Default (Implicit) Deny Principle:** Firewall administrators must use extreme caution when creating rulesets or ACLs (Access Control Lists) on firewall devices. Rulesets should manage the flow of traffic from areas of low security (Internet or external) to any areas of higher security (DMZs or internal networks). For example, traffic from an extranet web server application or extranet subnet should not be allowed into the internal network unless a specific rule for this type of traffic is defined. Similarly, no traffic should be permitted onto the database subnet except that which originated from the extranet application subnet. Without these restrictions, the funds spent of building up the edge of the network will be wasted.

- **Explicit Denial of Traffic to Firewall:** While most firewalls have a default (albeit often hidden) deny-all rule at the bottom of their ruleset, an explicit denial rule should be defined toward the top of the firewall ruleset to prevent traffic with a destination IP address of the firewall (unless of course the firewall is acting in the capacity of an application proxy or as a VPN termination peer). Above this rule could be a permit statement permitting firewall management traffic to the firewall from the specified addresses of the firewall management console, if appropriate.

- **Permission of Management Traffic into Network:** The use of the Simple Network Management Protocol (SNMP) or other connectionless protocols to manage external routers from an internal management host carries some amount of risk. Connectionless protocols such as SNMP are easily spoofed, so the conduit created to permit these protocols into the network may represent an access vehicle for a malicious user. Caution should be taken when permitting these protocols into the network, and the convenience offered by these protocols should be considered in light of the associated risk.

- **Permission of VPN Traffic:** Consideration should be given to the placement of VPN termination in relation to the firewall and permission of that traffic through the firewall. A VPN tunnel that connects a completely trusted and secure network with the local network is not problematic, but VPNs that connect semi-trusted networks should not be permitted through a firewall without some form of filtering at its termination. The encryption of VPN traffic precludes the inspection process of the firewall. Permitting VPN traffic, such as IP protocol 50 and 51 (IPSec), through a firewall should be done only with caution. This is true particularly in instances where the VPN is being used to give access to hosts such as laptops, which are subject to a higher risk of compromise than those physically on the LAN.

Firewall Policies

A firewall policy states management's expectations for how the firewall should function and is a component of the overall security policy. It should establish rules for traffic coming into and going out of the security domain and how the firewall will be managed and updated. Therefore, it is a type of security policy for the firewall, and forms the basis for the firewall rules. The firewall selection and the firewall policy should stem from the ongoing security risk assessment process. Accordingly, management needs to update the firewall policy as the institution's security needs and the risks change. At a minimum, the policy should address:

- Firewall topology and architecture,
- Type of firewall(s) being utilized,
- Physical placement of the firewall components,
- Monitoring firewall traffic,
- Permissible traffic (generally based on the premise that all traffic not expressly allowed is denied, detailing which applications can traverse the firewall and under what exact circumstances such activities can take place),
- Firewall updating,
- Coordination with intrusion detection and response mechanisms,
- Responsibility for monitoring and enforcing the firewall policy,
- Protocols and applications permitted,
- Regular auditing of a firewall's configuration and testing of the firewall's effectiveness, and
- Contingency planning.

Organizations should also appropriately train and manage their staffs to ensure the firewall policies are implemented properly. Alternatively, organizations can outsource the firewall management, while ensuring that the outsourcer complies with the organization's specific firewall policy. Firewalls are an essential control for companies with an Internet connection and provide a means of protection against a variety of attacks. These attacks include:

- Spoofing trusted IP addresses;
- Denial of service by overloading the firewall with excessive requests or malformed packets;
- Sniffing of data that is being transmitted outside the network;
- Hostile code embedded in legitimate HTTP, SMTP, or other traffic that meet all firewall rules;
- Attacks on unpatched vulnerabilities in the firewall hardware or software;
- Attacks through flaws in the firewall design providing relatively easy access to data or services residing on firewall or proxy servers; and
- Attacks against machines and communications used for remote administration.

Companies can reduce their vulnerability to these attacks somewhat through network configuration and design, sound implementation of its firewall architecture that includes multiple filter points, active firewall monitoring and management, and integrated intrusion detection. In most cases, additional access controls within the operating system or application will provide an additional means of defense. Given the importance of firewalls as a means of access control, good practices include:

- Hardening the firewall by removing all unnecessary services and appropriately patching, enhancing, and maintaining all software on the firewall unit
- Restricting network mapping capabilities through the firewall, primarily by blocking inbound ICMP traffic;
- Using a ruleset that disallows all traffic that is not specifically allowed;
- Using NAT and split DNS (domain name service) to hide internal system names and addresses from external networks (split DNS uses two domain name servers, one to communicate outside the network, and the other to offer services inside the network);
- Using proxy connections for outbound HTTP connections;
- Filtering malicious code;
- Backing up firewalls to internal media, and not backing up the firewall to servers on protected networks;
- Logging activity, with daily administrator review;
- Using intrusion detection devices to monitor actions on the firewall and to monitor communications allowed through the firewall (see "Intrusion Detection and Response");
- Administering the firewall using encrypted communications and strong authentication, only accessing the firewall from secure devices, and monitoring all administrative access;
- Limiting administrative access to few individuals; and
- Making changes only through well-administered change control procedures.

As an example of how firewall policies might be proposed and implemented in an organization, please review the sample firewall policy request form below. In the form, the Information Security Manager and the Data Owner perform a risk assessment of the potential impact of adding a specific IP address into the organization. If the potential impact is negligible and the policy addition is approved, then the policy must conform to the remainder of the criteria established by senior management regarding firewall policies.

Firewall and Gateway Architecture
The positioning of the firewall in the gateway is an extremely important decision. The firewall is one of the most critical design elements of the gateway. Decisions about the level of control, the options that should be purchased, etc. must be made in the context of the business risk and available budget. Complex, multi-layered architecture solutions usually will be more expensive than single-layered gateways. Other issues that must be considered here are:

- **Configurability:** A consistent, multi-tiered gateway will require more time to configure and to maintain, and therefore will not only have a higher implementation cost, but also a far higher total cost of ownership. Of more concern is that configuration complexity may result in a gateway on which older or obsolete rule sets are not purged regularly and logs not reviewed consistently.
- **Performance:** Increasing WAN bandwidth has made firewall performance a key criterion in assessing firewall vendors and types and determining the gateway architecture. In high throughput environments, firewalls may have to be implemented in parallel and configured for load balancing.
- **Availability:** Some business models deem the availability of inter-network connectivity to be mission critical, so the uptime of the gateway devices is crucial. While a firewall cluster must be implemented to fail-closed, firewalls within the cluster may be configured in either a standby or load-balancing configuration to ensure continued inter-network connectivity.
- **Adaptability and scalability:** The business needs that must be supported by the gateway and the throughput demanded by those needs, are likely to change within the life span of the gateway. Consideration must be given to the extent to which the chosen architecture and firewall type is scalable (to accommodate increased throughput) and adaptable (to accommodate new networking technologies such as video streaming).

Firewall Rule Request / Update Form

Firewall Risk Assessment Section			
How confidential is your data?	☐ Low	☒ Medium	☐ High
How severe would the impact be if an external source saw your data?	☒ Low	☐ Medium	☐ High
Explain the risk to your business unit if an external source saw your data?			
No Risk			
Explain the risk to the enterprise if an external source saw your data?			
No Risk Public Website			
Is this connection across a dedicated line?	☐ Yes	☒ No	
Is this connection through the internet?	☒ Yes	☐ No	
I understand the risk to my business' data.		Information Security Section	
Business unit manager name:		Reviewed by Information Security Manager:	
Signature:			
Date:			

Is this an Incoming, Outgoing or Both firewall rule request? ☒ Incoming ☐ Outgoing   ☐ Both

Reason for Rule:
Company XYZ is moving their services to a new location is requesting a different IP address and ports
Application Access needed:
Application ZED access to the mainframe. Do not close current IP address this will be closed when migration is successful
Requested date of completion: Before or on June x, xxxx

Source IP Address (es)	Destination IP Address (es)	Application or Port Number(s)
12.313.3.2	34.2.3.45	7555

Requestor:	Signature	Business Unit:	Date:
Data Owner			Xx/yy/dd

To be filled in by an ITS employee:

Firewall Rule Request #		
Rule added by:	Signature:	Date Completed:

Exam Tip: Candidates should be aware of the various firewall and IDS types and the differences between them.

There are many variations on the placement of firewalls near the edge of the network. A few of the most common are identified below:

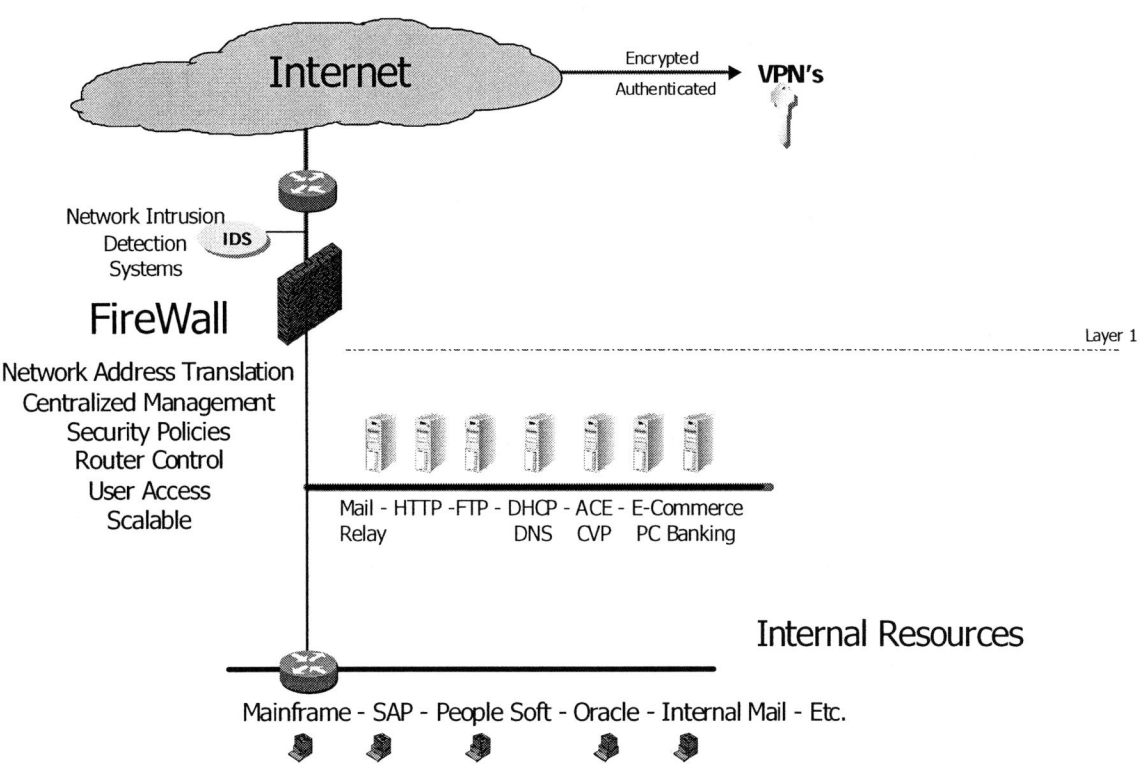

Border firewall without a screened subnet (figure I)

Unless all permitted protocols are proxied for on the firewall, this is not a secure configuration and should not be deployed. Hosts to which direct connections from the untrusted network are permitted are not quarantined. Any breach or compromise of these hosts will expose the remainder of the internal network to the unfettered probes of a malicious user. This architecture also will increase the work involved in any clean-up following the discovery of a security breach. Since the compromise of a given host cannot be presumed to have been contained within a scope of hosts, all critical internal hosts will have to be restored from an untainted backup.

Security & Subnets

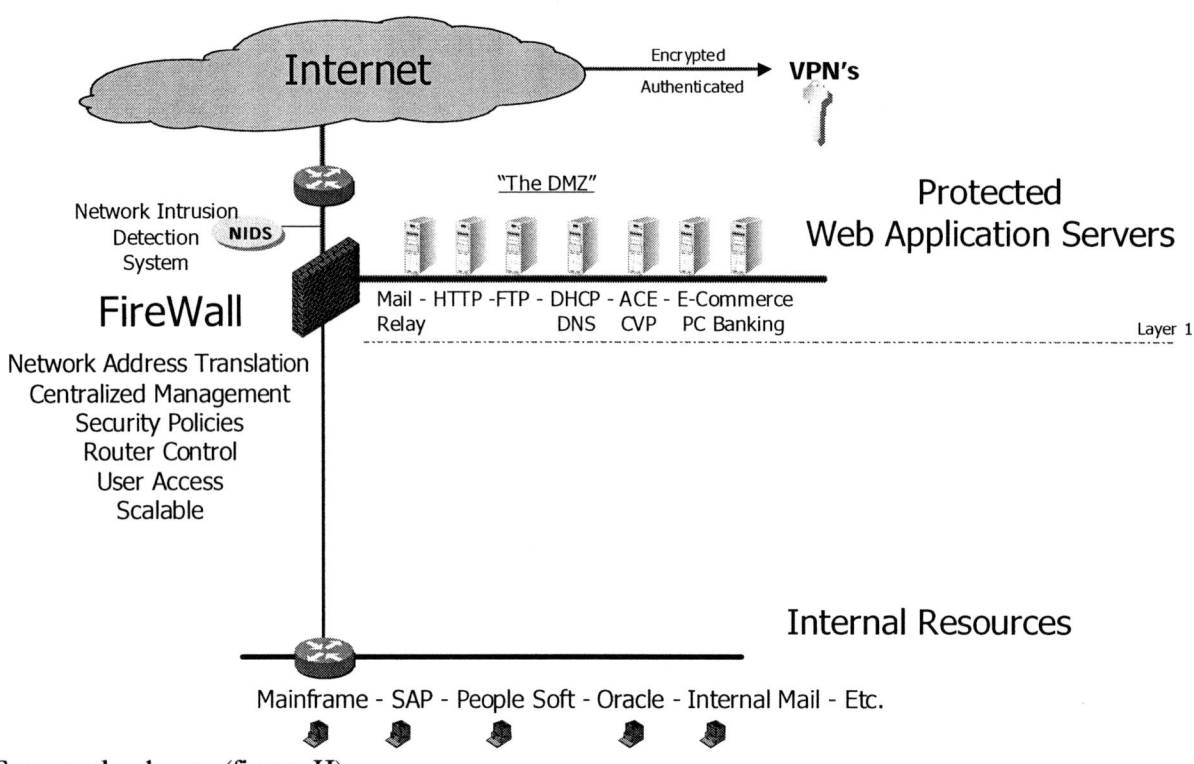

Screened subnets (figure II)

Here, the single firewall device has at least three network interfaces of varying trust/security levels. The untrusted network is connected to one interface, the internal network to another, and the hosts, to which Internet or untrusted connectivity is required, are placed in a third screened subnet. Any compromise of a host on this screened subnet will be quarantined on that subnet, and so this represents a significant advance on the security shown in **figure I**.

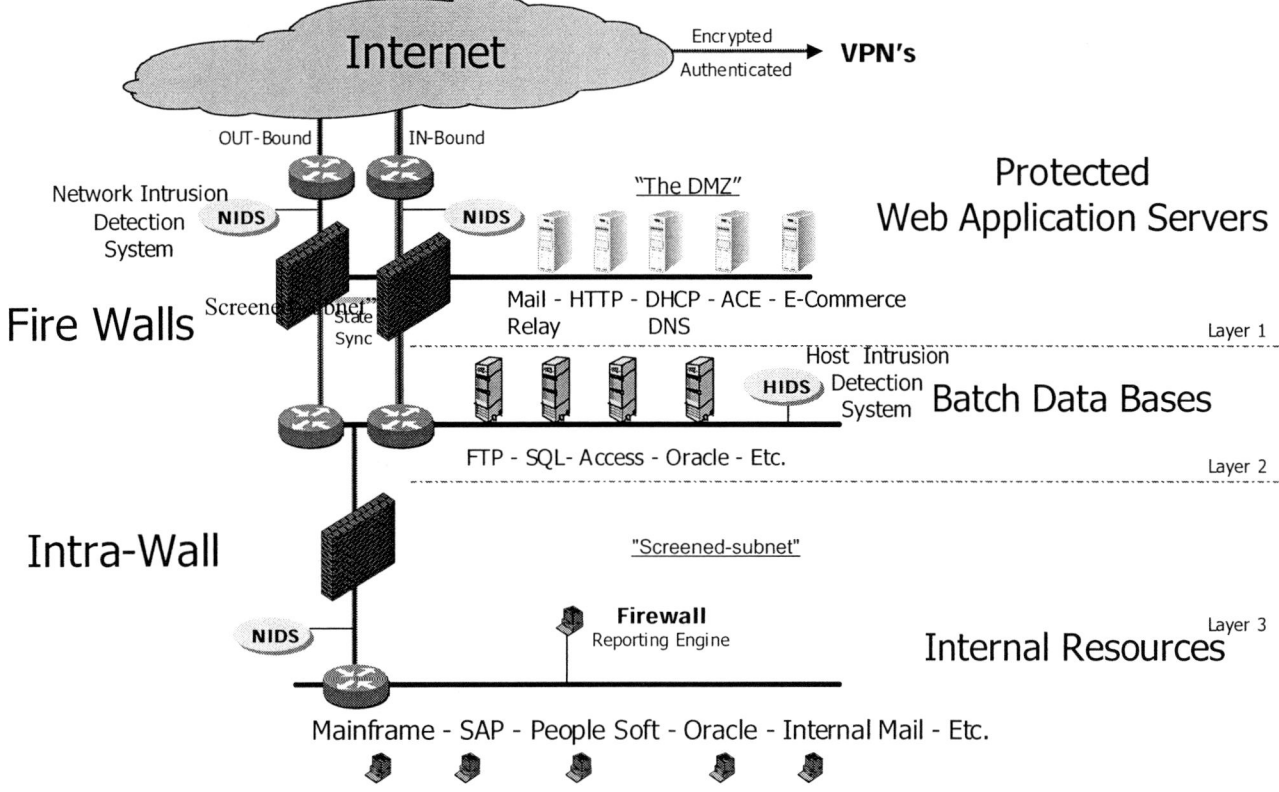

Multiple firewalls and DMZ (figure III)

A variant of this model, displayed in **figure II**, involves the use of multiple screened subnets, reducing the number of hosts on each subnet to which direct Internet connections are made and, hence, reducing the number of hosts exposed to the compromised host. Multiple-screened subnets are particularly useful in a distributed application architecture where direct Internet connections are made to application servers, which in turn reference database servers. Since no Internet direct connection need be permitted to the database servers, they should be quarantined in their own subnet to which the firewall permits no traffic except from the application subnet. Efforts also should be made to quarantine particularly high-risk servers, such as DNS servers, which historically have been the target of malicious attacks. Firewalls of different types are placed in a serial configuration. The higher throughput of the stateful packet filter makes it most appropriate as the front member of the serial array, while the more secure application proxy is best suited to protecting the sensitive internal LAN. As in **figure II**, hosts with common risk profiles and connectivity requirements are grouped together on subnets, quarantining them from hosts of different risk profiles. The core difference between **figures II and III** is the use of more than a single firewall, protecting the internal network against exploitation or misconfiguration of one of these firewalls.

A network architect also might consider implementing redundant exterior routers, connecting to different ISPs, as well as alternately patched cabling into the facility. Redundancy also can be implemented in respect to each firewall by teaming a second firewall of the same type and configuration to each firewall in the configuration above. Depending on the type of firewall, these may be configured as load-balancing or fail-over firewall clusters. Network redundancy also can be improved by implementing teamed interfaces, where two interfaces are assigned a single IP address and used in either load-balancing or fail-over mode. Of course, these redundant interfaces should be connected to the subnet via separate switches to ensure the redundancy of the interfaces is not defeated by switch failure. The placement of intrusion detection agents also should be considered in this context. This issue will be discussed in detail in the Intrusion Detection section. After deciding upon an architecture, a decision must be made regarding the firewall type. The order of these decisions is important, since a firewall type cannot be determined without understanding the architecture into which it will be placed.

Remote Access—Virtual Private Network (VPN)

For organizations that use branch offices and/or allow network access to employees working at remote locations, a VPN solution is probably the best choice for network security. Protection of information in transit in remote access sessions, branch network connections or internal networks is essential. For organizations that have remote users, there are several cost-effective solutions for remote access, including dial-up access and VPN connections. The aim of both of these is to provide the remote user with a simple means of becoming accessing the corporate network. Once connected, the remote user can use network resources as if physically connected to the corporate network.

The traditional method has been to maintain a modem pool and have users dial into these local modems to gain access to the corporate network. When properly configured and maintained, this can offer a solution that is quite secure; dial-up is limited in its scalability. With the growth of the Internet and the decreased cost of these connections, there has been an increase in the use of VPNs. This type of connection can allow users to connect through the Internet with a dial-up modem or a high-speed solution, such as cable or asymmetric digital subscriber line (ADSL). As with any network, the VPN solution can be a security risk if not properly configured and maintained; however it is far more scalable than the traditional dial-up connection.

The primary reason why an organization would consider implementation of a VPN over the Internet is the potential to realize significant cost savings over time. While the initial installation cost of a traditional solution such as dedicated or leased lines for communicating with remote locations or branches would be roughly the same as a VPN solution, the difference dissipates quickly. The real advantage with VPN solutions is gained in savings over long-distance communication costs. Instead of requiring the enterprise's offsite workers or business partners to install long-haul dedicated links or dial-in long distance to the corporate modem bank, a VPN is installed. The VPN enables remote users to connect to the enterprise's network, simply by placing a local call to their Internet service provider (ISP) or by using existing broadband connections. In either case, the remote users then can connect to the corporate network via the ISP and the Internet. Additional cost savings may be possible with the potential elimination of modem pools and remote access servers. Organizations also are realizing significant cost savings by carrying other traffic, such as voice, over the VPN links, by exploiting the ubiquitous nature of the Internet. While many organizations deploying VPN technology install and maintain their own infrastructure, it is becoming increasingly common to use a packaged managed service, usually provided by large telecommunication providers. The facilities provided in such cases vary, but they can include:

- The provision of the dedicated data lines linking each of the organization's sites to the telecommunication provider's points of presence
- Network equipment, such as routers, managed firewalls, VPN hardware and client software
- Dial-up facilities for mobile users
- Secure links to the Internet
- A managed site for infrastructure common across the organization's sites. It is not uncommon for such arrangements to span multiple regions or countries. The periodic outlay for such outsourced networks may seem excessive, but should be viewed with regard to the associated costs of deploying and maintaining the entire infrastructure, and the accompanying personnel costs.

One of the biggest benefits of VPN technology is its flexibility. Secure channels can be used for an hour, a day or as long as required. Once the components are in place, the creation of another VPN is achieved by simple software configuration changes. This makes the technology far more flexible than legacy dedicated circuits, which must be wired and possibly require additional hardware. It would not be likely that employees of a company would have dedicated integrated services digital network (ISDN) or leased lines to their homes to access the corporate LAN using a high-speed connection; however, it is feasible that a VPN connection could be configured easily using their cable or ADSL Internet connection.

Because the VPN solution is based mainly upon the existing infrastructure of the Internet and they use virtually the same technologies, the solution offers the enterprise unparalleled scalability. First, geographically, organizations are able to offer their business partners and mobile workers continued growth in the number and availability of points of presence (POP). This dynamic scalability can be very useful to enterprises as the path to globalization continues to expand rapidly. Another way that a VPN can offer the advantage of scalability is through continued expansion of bandwidth.

Virtual Private Network Technology

A virtual private network is essentially a private or secure communication channel between two parties or end points that occurs across an insecure medium. These parties can be either a client or a network. Typically, the connections between the two parties can be network-to-network or client-to-network. Each of these parties can be protected using specific security measures, such as firewalls, and there is a participating component at the network end called a security gateway, where the VPN connection is terminated. If the VPN connection is terminated at the firewall, then it also serves as the security gateway. The actual configurations vary depending on the business need. A term used often when referring to VPNs is tunnel. A tunnel is essentially a virtual connection between two computers, usually across the Internet. To say that a packet was "sent through the tunnel" means that the packet was encrypted, placed inside of another packet compatible with another network, sent over that network, extracted from the encapsulating packet at the receiving end, decrypted and then put on the wire of the remote LAN as though the packet originated there in the first place. A tunnel is like an encrypting pipe connecting two networks or computers, protecting the data in the pipe from the outside network and protecting the outside network from the addressing used within packets in the pipe.

Virtual Private Network Protocols
VPN protocols include:
- Internet Protocol Security (IPSec)—An architecture and protocol; also used to refer to related key exchange protocols
- Layer 2 forwarding (L2F)
- Point-to-point tunneling protocol (PPTP)
- Layer 2 tunneling protocol (L2TP)—A combination of PPTP and L2F

Of the protocols identified above, IPSec, L2TP and PPTP are the most commonly implemented. While they are viewed by many as competing technologies, each offers different capabilities that could be appropriate in differing circumstances.

IPSec Overview
IPSec is a standard for security at the network layer of data communication layer. Its primary advantage is that it needs minimal changes to existing client or server configuration for implementation. IPSec provides integrity protection, authentication, and (optional) privacy and replay protection services for IP traffic. IPSec packets are of two types:

- IP protocol 50, the **Encapsulating Security Payload** (ESP) format, which provides privacy, authentication and integrity
- IP protocol 51, the Authentication Header (AH) format, which provides only integrity and authentication for packets, not privacy IPSec can be used in two modes: **transport mode,** which secures an existing IP packet from source to destination, and **tunnel mode,** which puts an existing IP packet inside a new IP packet that is then sent to a tunnel end point in the IPSec format. Both transport and tunnel modes can use the ESP and AH packet formats. IPSec transport mode was designed to provide security for IP traffic, end-to-end between two communicating systems, for example, to secure a TCP connection or a UDP datagram. IPSec tunnel mode was designed primarily for network midpoints, routers or gateways—to secure IP traffic inside an IPSec tunnel connecting one private IP network to another, over a public or untrusted IP network (e.g., the Internet).

PPTP Overview

Point-to-point tunneling protocol (PPTP) was designed to provide authenticated and encrypted communications between a client and a gateway or between two gateways. It does not require a public key infrastructure, and instead uses a user ID and password model. It is the oldest of the three common VPN protocols. The design goal was simplicity, multi-protocol support and the ability to traverse a broad range of IP networks. Point-to-point protocol (PPP) frames also are encapsulated in the tunnel. The use of PPP provides the ability to negotiate authentication, encryption and IP address assignment services.

L2TP Overview

Layer 2 tunneling protocol (L2TP) is an extension of PPTP. It is a mature protocol that has been implemented widely. L2TP encapsulates point-to-point protocol frames to be sent over IP, X.25, frame relay or asynchronous transfer mode (ATM) networks. When configured to use IP as its transport, L2TP can be used as a VPN tunneling protocol over the Internet. In this form, L2TP tunnels take advantage of standard IPSec security and interoperability, and use IPSec transport mode for strong integrity, privacy and replay protection, and authentication.

VPN Architecture

The design of a VPN architecture is dependent mainly on the topology that needs to be adopted. This is based on the business needs driving the implementation. There are two common VPN topologies:

- **Security gateway to security gateway**: This topology essentially defines a network-to-network connection. It extends corporate network connectivity to a remote office and between business partners and/or suppliers.
- **Security gateway to client:** A remote user needs to access a resource that is inside the organization's corporate network, behind a firewall. In this type of topology the client will run software that allows a secure connection to the internal network.

Another important consideration is the placement of the security gateways. This is network- and site-dependent, and this design aspect has to take into account issues of network routing and security. As network traffic makes a transition from a private to a public network, or the reverse, differences in IP addressing schemes make it difficult for the transparent routing of packets. Most organizations use internal or private IP addresses in their protected network segments and cannot, or will not, expose these addresses to public networks. A common technique used to overcome this is Network Address Translation (NAT). However, when used with VPNs, where packets typically transit a tunnel, usage of NAT often can complicate the resultant architecture and this issue, along with security, often determines the placement of the security gateways, or specific VPN hardware. Some of the common security gateway placement solutions are:

- Outside the firewall,
- Within a screened subnet,
- Inside the firewall,
- Integrated with the firewall,
- Bypassing the firewall,
- Mixed implementation.

Firewall-based VPNs are probably the most common form of VPN implementation. There are many vendors offering this type of configuration. Most organizations use some kind of firewall to connect to the Internet. Since they already are connected to the Internet, all they usually need is to add encryption software. This can allow for great cost savings. Also, most firewall products come with the ability to implement VPN encryption technology, available on different platforms and hardware. One important security concern is the underlying operating system and its inherent vulnerabilities. Availability concerns are the main reasons why many organizations shy away from this architecture, as the firewall then becomes a single point of failure. Failure of the firewall also would cause VPN services to fail. Conversely, utilization of dedicated VPN hardware leaves the organization free to carry the VPN traffic via multiple routes and firewalls. Additionally, locating the VPN function on the firewall subjects it to a large processor overhead due to the computational requirements of most encryption techniques. This could have a great impact on the performance of the firewall itself and may limit its connection or packet throughput.

VPN Client Risks
As previously discussed, organizations can benefit greatly by deploying VPN services. However, along with these benefits, they should be aware of the security risks involved. These risks can arise at both the client end, and the network or server end. The main risks at the client end will be considered here, as they could result in additional security exposure for the organization.

Client Connection
The most common way for a client to connect to the corporate network via a VPN is to utilize local ISP services and traverse the Internet over the encrypted VPN links. However, this very configuration could provide significant exposure. Once the client computer is connected via a VPN to the corporate network, there is an authorized tunnel to predefined network resources. The client computer is connected simultaneously to the Internet, the corporate network and perhaps also to a local client-end network. It is very difficult to effectively secure the client computer and its immediate environment in this situation. If this client computer were to be compromised, it is possible that unauthorized parties could access easily the visible corporate resources. To minimize this risk, appropriate steps must be taken to ensure the security of the client computer. These computers should be secured by effectively hardening them as much as possible in the circumstances. For example, unnecessary services running on them could be exploited, as there are often many known vulnerabilities in them. The hardening process could limit these services, including FTP or web servers, which in some cases are turned on in default installations of client operating systems. An additional step to mitigate the risk associated with personal computers connected to the Internet is to use personal firewall software. This software acts as a firewall for the local computer and ensures that only services that have been defined are viewable from the public or Internet side of the computer.

Remote Access Security Risks
War Dialing
War dialers are software tools that iterate through a set of telephone numbers, dialing each and checking for the characteristics of an unsecured "listening" modem. Once the tool generates a list of discovered modems, the attacker can subsequently dial those systems to find an unprotected login or easily guessed password. One of the most sought-after items in a war dial attack is PC remote control software without strong authentication controls, typically installed by an end user to gain remote access to organization systems. These PC remote control programs are devastatingly vulnerable when improperly secured and accessible via insecure modem connections.

Modems Attached to Internal Workstations

Unauthorized or uncontrolled desktop modems can be a significant threat to the security of an organization's network. Official modem banks usually have been secured reasonably and often are segregated from the main corporate network by security measures such as firewalls. Modems connected by end users to their desktop machines, however, are likely to be vulnerable to attack. Poor security controls coupled with an active connection to the corporate network can provide an attacker with an unprotected back door from where unauthorized information access can occur or further attacks can be launched on multiple network resources. This is relevant particularly due to the extensive use of war dialers by malicious parties, specifically to locate such unsecured modems.

Unauthorized Access

Dial-up network access can be vulnerable to misuse or attack if the underlying authentication and authorization measures are weak. An example of this is when modem access authentication is through trivial, well-known or no passwords. Even strong passwords offer limited protection from a suitably motivated attacker if the authentication process does not have further controls such as account lockout, log monitoring or intrusion detection.

Remote Access Security Risk Countermeasures

- **Grant access to only specific users**: Dial-up access should not be open to all users and should not be granted by default. Only users who require access should be provided the facility.

- **Server/application access:** Appropriate dial-up server features or firewall filters should be used to restrict users to specific devices, computers or applications.

- **Encrypted authentication:** A form of authentication that is encrypted should be used. There are three common authentication protocols: PAP, CHAP and SPAP. Password authentication protocol (PAP) uses clear text passwords and is the least sophisticated authentication protocol. It is negotiated typically if the remote workstation and server cannot negotiate a more secure form of validation. Challenge handshake authentication protocol (CHAP) will negotiate the most secure form of encrypted authentication supported by both server and client. CHAP uses a challenge-response mechanism with one-way encryption on the response. The Shiva password authentication protocol (SPAP) is a two-way (reversible) encryption mechanism employed by some vendors.

- **Call-back:** Remote access call-back adds a further measure of security, which ensures that only users from specific locations can access the remote access server. It also can save call charges for the user, especially when the call is long distance. When using call-back, the user initiates a call and connects with the server. The server then drops the call and calls back a moment later to the predefined call-back number for the user. While call diversion can eliminate the benefit provided by this mechanism, it requires a highly motivated attacker to break into the premises to enable the call diversion to be set up.

- **Strong authentication:** A security host is used to provide this authentication method, which is a third-party authentication device that verifies whether a caller from a remote client is authorized to connect to the dial-up server. The security host generally provides an extra layer of security by requiring a stronger means of authentication than a user ID and password. This could involve the use of hardware tokens, smart cards, biometric methods or digital certificates, usually after providing traditional credentials such as user ID and password. This is sometimes referred to as strong authentication with multifactor identification. Verification that the remote user is in possession of the physical device takes place before access to the network is granted.

- **Restrict remote access time:** Inappropriate usage of remote access can be limited by restricting access to specific times of the day, when normal access would not be required.

- **Separate dial-up usernames and passwords:** Although this can be troublesome and a potential area of increased maintenance, the use of dial-up usernames and passwords separate from user's network access credentials can increase security across the corporate network.

- **Eliminate unauthorized modems:** Unauthorized modems can provide attackers with back doors to the corporate network. Their usage should be prevented through corporate policy, physical inspection and the internal use of tools like war dialers.

- **Monitor remote access:** All remote access logs should be monitored regularly by manual or automated means to detect unauthorized access attempts or intrusion patterns.

- **Review dial-up security:** The security and configuration of dial-up infrastructure should be reviewed regularly, and exceptions dealt with without delay.

Intrusion Detection

Corporate networks are subject to electronic attack, whether the attacks are initiated from an internal or external source. For this reason, IDSs are important components of the defense-in-depth approach to security architecture. Intrusion detection systems provide a further layer of security by attempting to identify and isolate intrusions such as unauthorized access or misuse of computer and network systems. These systems complement other security technologies to provide an added level of assurance that systems are being protected from unauthorized access.

Selection and Implementation of IDS Architecture
Host-based Intrusion Detection Systems

Host-based IDSs operate on the protected host system and use local system and log files to detect intrusive activity. As host-based systems are concerned only with intrusive activity on the host itself, host-based systems can monitor specific applications for anomalies and can detect specific host system activity that would be impossible to monitor using any other type of intrusion system. As the host-based intrusion system must reside on the host itself, one issue that must be taken into account is the amount of host system CPU and memory resources used to detect intrusive behavior. A second issue for consideration is the possibility that if an intruder gains privileged access to the host, the intruder may be able to disable the host-based intrusion system or modify the system such that all traces of activity are removed. "Rootkits" are examples of the type of software that can allow intruders to completely control the host on which the rootkit has been installed. Some examples of common host-based intrusion systems used today are:

- Tripwire
- Symantec Intruder Alert
- ISS RealSecure
- Intrusion Inc. SecureHost

Host-based IDSs are a mature technology. Implementation issues for IDSs typically surround the network-based systems; therefore much of the remainder of this discussion is focused on network-based IDSs.

Network-based Intrusion Detection Systems

Network-based IDSs (NIDS) monitor and evaluate data packets on a network segment to identify network anomalies and/or intrusive network activity. Network based intrusion systems are good at identifying attacks that involve manipulation of network traffic and are excellent at correlating attacks against multiple hosts on the network. One of the key advantages of network-based intrusion systems is that they benefit from utilizing "promiscuous mode" network access. This allows the network intrusion detection system to obtain copies of all data packets directly from the network, regardless of their destination. In the case of a shared network, this is as easy as connecting the NIDS sensor to the network hub. For a switched network, the promiscuous mode network access must be accomplished by using techniques such as taps, hubs and spanning ports.

This type of monitoring, commonly known as passive monitoring or network sniffing, is unobtrusive and difficult to evade and detect. In addition, there is usually little degradation to network performance. It must be noted that the use of spanning ports on heavily loaded switches may in fact impact performance. Network intrusion detection systems are commonly placed on the external perimeter as an additional layer of security defense in an attempt to identify unauthorized, intrusive behavior. Though this is the most common use of network based IDSs today, network intrusion detection systems slowly are becoming implemented within the internal network infrastructure in an attempt to monitor and control internal network security threats. Some examples of common network-based intrusion systems used today are:

- Symantec NetProwler
- ISS RealSecure
- Cisco Secure IDS
- Network Flight Recorder
- Snort

Network Architecture
A network-based IDS may be broken down into four elements:

- **Event module (E):** Also called the sensor, it is the "eyes and ears" of the IDS and is responsible for recording passing traffic.
- **Analysis module (A):** It performs traffic analysis based on the traffic detected by the sensor; in most implementations, the analysis and sensor modules core side on the same network device.
- **Response module (R):** It generates the configured response upon detection of an attack by the analysis module.
- **Database module (D):** It stores recorded traffic to which reference is made in subsequent correlation analysis.

This modular conception of an IDS was defined by the CIDF (Common Intrusion Detection Framework), whose efforts have been supplemented by the Intrusion Detection Working Group and its Intrusion Alert Protocol. This modular definition is raised here since it facilitates a more precise discussion on IDS positioning and architecture. The positioning of these IDS elements is critical to the success of the implementation. Issues worthy of consideration include:

- **Protection of the analysis, event and database modules:** If these can be compromised, the configured signatures and responses may be identified, and the IDS circumvented by careful selection of attack traffic.
- **Positioning of the event module:** If the sensor is positioned in front of the foremost firewall, maximum visibility will be afforded to the network administrator, but much of the logged activity will be meaningless since most will be blocked by the firewall. Alternatively, if the sensor is positioned behind the firewall, responses may be configured more aggressively since traffic seen by the sensor is more likely to represent a threat, but an accurate profile of attack traffic to which the network is subjected is difficult to compile.

- **Adequacy of event module population:** The difficulties of where to place the sensor is best responded to by implementation of several sensors, each serving different purposes. When deciding on the number of sensors needed, consideration must be given to the extent of coverage that a single sensor will have—pattern bearing traffic which never reaches a subnet cannot be detected, and will pass unmolested or unidentified into the network.

The appropriate IDS architecture, of course, depends on the network context into which it will be implemented, and the IDS type. Some IDS types consolidate the E, A and R modules and so their separation may not be feasible. Alternatively, some IDS implementations allow the E and A modules to be separated, allowing the network architect to remove the signature patterns on the analysis module into the protected LAN.

IDS Errors in Attack Identification
The three main approaches used by IDSs are:

- **Signature-based Approach**: An attack signature is defined based on network traffic
- **Statistical Approach:** Attacks are detected by observing specific variations in the trend of traffic flow
- **Heuristic/Anomaly-based approach**: A characterization of known network traffic is provided and anomalies are detected.

Although there are strengths and weaknesses to each of these approaches, three fundamental challenges exist that must be seriously considered when implementing an IDS. These challenges are:
- How are normal and abnormal (attack) traffic distinguished?
- How should the IDS should respond to each type of network traffic patterns.
- Minimizing or eliminating attack identification errors, which may be divided into fundamental types:

    o **False negatives**, whereby abnormal data traffic entering the network (a real intrusion) is not detected by the IDS
    o **False positives**, whereby normal and authorized data traffic entering the network is falsely reported as an attack

To reduce the attack identification error rate, it is critical to identify normal and authorized data traffic patterns and to, therefore, deduce the traffic patterns and protocols that are abnormal for the network being monitored. An important factor to consider when identifying abnormal data traffic and defining attack signatures for the IDS is to ensure that while eliminating false positives, discussed above, false negatives are not introduced. For example, assume an organization allows external web traffic to its public web server. This network traffic would be considered normal network traffic as it represents an external system sending HTTP request traffic to a web server hosted within the network. In this example, an IDS would be expected to allow the HTTP request traffic through without any concern. What is of concern though, is whether the HTTP request contained known malicious code within it. There are three options available:

- Do not create an attack signature for HTTP requests—a false negative (in the case of a HTTP request with malicious code inserted.
- Create an attack signature for all HTTP requests—a false positive (in the case of any HTTP request).
- Create an attack signature specifically to capture the malicious code within the HTTP request (allow normal HTTP requests through, while identifying HTTP requests with known malicious code inserted).

These examples only touch on the complexity of defining attack signatures for detecting intrusions. Systems that detect only widely known attack behaviors will produce large numbers of false negatives. Therefore, defining normal and abnormal network traffic for a given network is a very important issue. It should be noted that attacks identified by IDSs should not necessarily be taken on face value. They should be investigated further to ensure the validity of the attack.

Denial-of-service
Unlike well-configured firewalls, which are fail-closed, the passive nature of intrusion detection systems make them fail-open without compromising the availability of the networks they seek to protect. The processing load of an IDS is determined more by the number of packets and the computational complexity invoked by each packet than the amount of data passed onto a network. Accordingly, a malicious user can consume disproportionately large amounts of the IDS's memory and CPU resources relative to the bandwidth of the link connecting the target network to the Internet. Since IDSs are fail-open, an exhaustion of the IDS's resources will void its effectiveness and will allow a malicious user to pass traffic into the network that would otherwise be identified and perhaps reacted to by the IDS.

IDS Limitations—Impact of Traffic Volumes

The effectiveness of an NIDS is highly dependent on the efficiency of the sensor in capturing all the network packets on the monitored network segment, as well as the ability of the analysis module to correctly analyze these packets. As networks get faster, the volume of packets transmitted over a network segment can overwhelm any intrusion detection system. The NIDS is then likely to portray an inaccurate picture, as the analysis of intrusions would be incomplete. This factor of error will be higher as the traffic volume and complexity of analysis increases. There is no easy answer to correctly determine the threshold at which performance of the NIDS will start to decrease. This would be highly dependent on the intrusion detection product, infrastructure configuration and actual traffic volumes. However, it is usually evident from the product displays or monitors when this occurs, and they would manifest as sensor or analysis errors.

There are many ways in which this problem can be tackled. One possible solution is to deploy multiple sensors and/or analysis modules on each network segment being monitored. This is a statistical solution and is dependent on packets that are dropped at one location being processed at another. Of course, the processed output then may include multiple notifications for a single event, and it may be possible to compensate for this at the analysis or inspection engine. Another solution is to have sensors at network locations where the traffic volumes are not likely to be very high. Inter-network connection points such as routers and firewalls usually are points of traffic concentration, and if sensors are kept away from these locations, they are less likely to suffer from the effects of traffic overdose. However, the deployment strategy is usually highly site-dependent as it may well be that the location the network administrator would like to monitor is one of these points of concentration.

With some intrusion detection products, it is possible to deploy multiple sensors and/or analysis modules, and tune each to process only a subset of the traffic or event types. The detection and analysis load then can be divided among the many NIDS modules, thus keeping the effective load on each under strict check. It may be necessary to use a combination of these techniques to find an optimum solution for a site. The problem is likely to be exacerbated with the increasing use of gigabit or multi-gigabit networks. It is possible that there may be a multitude of solutions from the product vendors themselves as the NIDS technologies mature further.

Response to Intrusion

The implementation of an IDS will be of little consequence if the IDS is not configured to properly alert administrators and if the organization has not established adequate incident response procedures. The automated response capabilities of modern IDSs are quite extensive, but should be used with caution. The focus should be on alerting the appropriate administration staff rather than activating modifications to filter rulesets or even more extreme hack-back countermeasures. The activation of reactive measures, such as ruleset modifications or reverse penetration attempts, presumes signature identification accuracy and ignores the possibility of spoofed source addresses. Given the propensity of even sophisticated and well-configured IDSs to report false positives and of the prevalence of spoofed source address attacks, these reactive measures are clearly inappropriate and potentially damaging to commercial relationships. A more appropriate and measured response is for the IDS to alert the administrator and log the event. The fidelity and integrity of these logs should be guarded closely, since they may form the basis of subsequent forensic investigation and possible litigation.

Incident Management

Within the Information Security function, incident management refers to the entire process used to handle security-related events of any size. Incident management procedures should be built into every area of the organization, including those that do not relay upon computers. As usual, to ensure that a sound and comprehensive incident management policy is implemented, the executive management must be committed to the process. When support for the process has been assured at this level, it will be possible to create a viable incident management framework.

- The first step that should be taken is the identification or appointment of those parties that will be accountable for the incident management process. All the people mentioned will form a committee that will contribute to each stage of the process. The first person chosen should be a coordinator or manager of the committee. This person should have as high a rank as possible in order to ensure that the group can function properly when it is needed. A corporate-level officer such as a CIO, CSO, or CISO would be appropriate for this role.
- The next step would be to have each department appoint one or more people to act as coordinators or liaisons to the group. In addition, the IT department should have someone to act in a similar role. These people will work to make sure that all of the needs of the organization and of each department are understood and met.
- The organization may also have individuals with relevant non-technical SME (Subject Matter Expertise), such as the legal team; take part in the planning of the process.
- The IT department may utilize technical people with relevant SME to help develop and implement the process.
- Finally, the organization may appoint people to oversee the handling of each incident. These people may be drawn from the technical/security areas or they may be appointed from within each department.

Once the group has been assembled, they will have to consider how each of the following may occur or be handled within each department:

- Spyware, viruses or Trojan programs.
- Identification of valuable assets.
- Misuse of computers or violations of the Acceptable Use policy.
- Unauthorized personnel within the office, especially in secure areas.
- Successful DoS attacks and/or unauthorized alteration of the organization's web site.
- Alerts stemming from the logging and auditing of network access attempts.
- Theft of software or equipment.
- Alerts from the IDS (Intrusion Detection System)
- Compromised systems/computer forensics
- Known loss of data including PII

In general, the Incident Management process should utilize project management principles as a guide for its actions. In particular, this means that planning should be done first and should be done comprehensively. Since each department has different assets and these assets are in different locations, the plan will have to take all of these issues into account. If a systematic classification of assets has all ready been performed by the data owners and systems administrators, this information can be used to speed up the planning process. In addition, any risk analyses that have been performed may also be used. The next steps should be as follows:

1. Means by which incidents may be detected.
2. Steps necessary to initiate an investigation
3. Procedures used to evaluate the nature and extent of the incident.
4. Procedures to be used in order to contain or restrict any further spread of the incident.
5. Response: methods used to remove or eliminate unauthorized code or access privileges from the network.
6. Recovery: steps taken to restore the network and any compromised systems to a functional state.
7. Steps to be taken to close the official investigation.
8. Review of the findings, lessons learned and suggestions for the change management process.

An essential part of the process will involve training of the end users. As part of an ongoing security training function, documentation regarding acceptable use of the company's information assets should be developed and distributed. Employees should be advised about various types of suspicious behavior and be encouraged to report these events. Employees should also know that there are penalties for violations of the security policy. In addition, employees should be taught what actions they should take in the event of an investigation. Procedures should also be established that specify the types of access and training about the network that will be given to vendors, consultants and any other parties that might be authorized to access the network.

If it is possible, the organization should create a single CERT (Computer Emergency Response Team) with the expertise to handle all necessary investigations and corrections. It is possible that the creation of a single team will be more cost effective in the long run. This team will be able to focus on any posted security bulletins regarding applications and systems deployed within the organization and ensure that the required fixes are implemented. This team can also manage the IDSs and handle the review of access logs. This group may even be tasked to create the documentation for the end user security training.

Technology Overview
Wireless Networking
Traditional networks, such as the ones that have been discussed so far, have always been connected physically or wired into a network before being allowed to access other resources. This requirement has allowed organizations to apply physical restrictions on devices permitted to access the network. Wireless networks, on the other hand, cannot rely on wired physical restrictions.

The inherently open nature of wireless networks makes it very difficult to secure them effectively, as current standards or implementations do not go far enough to provide such controls. Additionally, as the medium for these networks is wireless, their range cannot be restricted to physical property boundaries. This makes it very easy for outsiders to anonymously access these networks in the absence of stronger controls and even attempt to gain access to wired networks via this back door. This important weakness makes the discussion of wireless networks pertinent to perimeter security. Indeed, by itself, the deployment of wireless networking technology in an organization breaks through the traditional network perimeter.

The ease of deployment of wireless networks has made them very popular, not only in the home and small business market, but also in large-scale corporate networks. As its implementation can be as simple as installing a base station and a wireless card in one or more devices, it provides a cheaper and more convenient method of network rollout than the installation of cables, switches, patch panels and other components of a wired network. The problem with this approach is that security is compromised, and coupled with the common finding that implementers do not even enable the weak built-in security features of the current standards, can often lead to significant security weaknesses in organizations' network defenses. Many security professionals have demonstrated this by a technique called "wardriving," where just driving through city streets with a mobile computer using a wireless networking card has highlighted a huge number of unprotected wireless networks.

As the name suggests, Wireless LANs (WLAN) use wireless means of communication, in this case, radio transmissions. Other applications of radio communication, such as AM-FM, emergency services and ham radio, often are designed to reach a large number of people where privacy is not a major concern. WLANs, on the other hand, are deployed to connect a specific set of users with privacy and confidentiality being a primary concern. Additionally, WLANs usually are interconnected to other traditional or wired networks containing data that usually must be protected from unauthorized access or modification. The Institute of Electrical and Electronic Engineers (IEEE) has developed the 802.11 standard to specify the requirements for the implementation of wireless LANs. The IEEE 802.11 standard is a networking technology consisting of clients, who are called stations (STA), and servers, which are called access points (AP). The STA can operate in a peer-to-peer configuration or through APs in a client server model. Both STA and AP include radio transceivers and cooperate actively to associate themselves into a WLAN. Stations connecting directly with each other are said to form a unit called an independent basic service set (IBSS). A service set identifier (SSID) identifies each AP. A network consisting of stations and a single AP is a basic service set (BSS), while a network connecting stations through several APs is an extended service set (ESS).

The 802.11 specifications include services for wireless authentication and an optional confidentiality service named wired equivalent privacy (WEP). WEP was designed to protect the privacy of the wireless leg of the traffic. The authentication service is specified to contain two basic levels of security—the mandatory open system authentication (OSA) and the shared-key authentication service, which uses WEP. OSA provides no inherent security, while shared-key authentication provides virtually the only security available in current implementations. There are a few approved IEEE 802.11 specifications and more are being developed. For example, the 802.11 specification supports a data rate of 2Mbits/second. It has not been implemented widely because of the low speed and the availability of faster alternatives. IEEE 802.11b specifies rates up to 11 Mbits/second and has proved to be very popular.

The later 802.11a and 802.11g specifications also are being used in products, providing mainly increases in speed, and are prone to the same inherent security limitations of the base standard. Other standards may provide some improvements. The 802.11i Task Group has been set up to develop standards that will increase the security of 802.11 networks. It is working on improvements to WEP, including the provision of different encryption algorithms. Another emerging standard is 802.1x. This is not specific to wireless networks, but also applies to wired Ethernet. It provides a centralized, port-based framework for authentication of connected devices, and includes provisions for the usage of authentication servers, such as those using the RADIUS protocol.

Wireless Risks

The popularity of wireless LANs has ensured rapid growth of this market. Unfortunately, this means that the security problems with the implementations usually have been overlooked. Even without considering the problems with the 802.11 specifications, it must be conceded that wireless networks are inherently less secure than wired networks, and must be treated with extra care as a consequence. The technology is changing fast but current implementations, mainly 802.11b and 802.11a, have drawbacks that must be considered during the design stage to avoid later security implications. Some of these threats are as follows:

- WLAN traffic easily can be monitored or sniffed. As there are no physical boundaries to limit eavesdroppers, any party with the right equipment potentially can see all the WLAN traffic, with no fear of detection. If the data are not encrypted, they can be read, presenting significant privacy and confidentiality issues. Depending on the information sniffed, it subsequently could be used to masquerade as a legitimate corporate user to perform a network intrusion.
- In a wired LAN, the members of the network can be identified easily as they are connected to the same segment. On a WLAN, however, the SSID identifies the devices that are intended to be connected in a network. The problem with this mechanism is that even when encryption is used, the SSID is always visible in the clear. By manually configuring the SSID into their equipment, malicious parties can make themselves "part" of the WLAN.

All access points transmit a beacon management frame (sometimes called an ESS beacon) at fixed intervals. To associate with an access point (AP) and join a BSS, a station listens for beacon messages to identify the APs within range. Unfortunately, many WLAN attack tools use this feature to locate target wireless networks. Some wireless base stations or AP have the provision of restricting access by media access control (MAC) addresses. Every wireless network card is expected to have a unique MAC address. However, publicly available software can allow this address to be changed or spoofed.

The nature of a WLAN also presents problems in the shape of IP address spoofing. In a wired LAN, routing issues dictate the usage and allocation of IP addresses. This can be difficult to overcome for an attacker, as network access requires physical connection to the specific LAN. In a WLAN, however, attackers can choose an IP address after making themselves part of the network, as shown above, and thus gain access to the devices on the same WLAN. In fact, in cases where DHCP servers have been implemented for wireless devices, an attacker may be able to automatically obtain a valid IP address.

The WEP specification provides for device authentication on WLANs by using pre-shared keys. The problem with this specification is that keys are not changed frequently, as the specification does not include the frequency or method of key distribution. This gives potential malicious parties more time to isolate the pre-shared keys or brute-force them from network traffic.

It has been demonstrated that a large number of installations do not even enable the WEP features of their wireless networks. Even when used, the WEP encryption protocol has some inherent design failings that can permit attackers to decrypt the encrypted data. These weaknesses are not in the RC4 algorithm used or in the length of the keys used, but in the implementation of the algorithm. Indeed, it has been shown that decryption is possible for even longer key lengths because of these implementation issues. Researchers have demonstrated some simple means of decrypting WEP traffic, and also have shown that after a relatively small number of encrypted traffic frames, the WEP key itself can be uncovered. As mentioned in Chapter 4, use of the WPA and WPA2 encryption protocols is recommended.

Controls for Wireless Networking

The solutions to WLAN security are not very different from a traditional security approach. It requires that multiple layers of security should be used so a single point of compromise does not result in the complete exposure of a network. The deployment of the wireless components thus should be done as part of the corporate perimeter defense policy. The following list outlines some of the countermeasures that organizations can adopt to reduce the risk due to current wireless network weaknesses:

- WPA features should be enabled, and the maximum key size allowable should be selected.
- Factory defaults for administrator user ID, password, WEP key and SSID should be changed. The AP's response to ESS beacons should be disabled.
- The wireless network should be not be placed on the internal or trusted side of an organization's perimeter firewall; it should be treated as another untrusted network.
- A virtual private network (VPN) should be used to secure access between mobile devices and systems inside the perimeter firewall. This should be done to add protection in addition to the WLAN encryption features, and can be done by using protocols, such as tunnel-mode IPSEC, that implement strong authentication, confidentiality and integrity.
- The perimeter firewall should limit traffic from the wireless network to only allow the IPSEC tunneled traffic to enter the internal network.
- As much as possible, the wireless network should be protected from public networks like the Internet to limit the possibility of attacks from those networks. This should be done by using appropriate perimeter protection, such as firewalls, router filters and intrusion detection systems (IDSs), usually already deployed in most organizations.
- The problems in WLAN key management can be minimized by assigning separate keys to each wireless device and by changing these keys at frequent intervals. The changed keys should be distributed safely and encrypted within the VPN tunnel.
- Access point level protection by using MAC address filters for wireless devices cannot be trusted and should not be used as a single authentication countermeasure.
- A comprehensive WLAN architecture and security policy should be developed and integrated into the organization's governance framework.

Wireless Security Threats and Risk Mitigation

The classification of security threats may be segmented into nine categories. All of these represent potential threats in wireless networks as well. However, the more immediate concerns for wireless communications are device theft, denial of service, malicious hackers, malicious code, theft of service, and industrial and foreign espionage. Theft is likely to occur with wireless devices because of their portability. Authorized and unauthorized users of the system may commit fraud and theft; however, authorized users are more likely to carry out such acts. Since users of a system may know what resources a system has and the system's security flaws, it is easier for them to commit fraud and theft.

Malicious hackers, sometimes called crackers, are individuals who break into a system without authorization, usually for personal gain or to do harm. Such hackers may gain access to the wireless network access point by eavesdropping on wireless device communications. Malicious code involves viruses, worms, Trojan horses, logic bombs or other unwanted software that is intended to damage files or bring down a system. Theft of service occurs when an unauthorized user gains access to the network and consumes network resources. In wireless networks, the unauthorized access threat stems from the relative ease with which eavesdropping can occur on radio transmissions. Ensuring confidentiality, integrity, authenticity and availability are the prime objectives in wireless networks. Security requirements include the following:

- **Integrity**—A third party must be able to verify that the content of a message has not been changed in transit.
- **Authenticity**—A third party must be able to prove that a given message was actually sent by the party named in the message as the sender.
- **Accountability**—The actions of an entity must be uniquely traceable to that entity.
- **Network availability**—The information technology resource must be available on a timely basis to meet mission requirements or to avoid substantial losses. Availability also includes ensuring that resources are used only for intended purposes.

Risks in wireless networks are equal to the sum of the risk of operating a wired network plus the new risks introduced by weaknesses in wireless protocols. To mitigate these risks, an organization must adopt security measures and practices that help bring their risks to a manageable level.

Threats and vulnerabilities of Wireless systems:

- All the vulnerabilities that exist in a conventional wired network apply to wireless technologies.
- Malicious entities may gain unauthorized access to an agency's computer or voice (IP telephony) network through wireless connections, potentially bypassing any firewall protections.
- Sensitive information that is not encrypted (or that is encrypted with poor cryptographic techniques) and that is transmitted between two wireless devices may be intercepted and disclosed.
- Denial-of-service (DoS) attacks may be directed at wireless connections or devices.
- Malicious entities may steal the identity of legitimate users and masquerade as them on internal or external corporate networks.
- Sensitive data may be corrupted during improper synchronization.

Currently, there are many ways that malicious entities may gain access to wireless devices. Those related to WLANs include, but are not limited to, war driving, war walking and warchalking. War driving and war walking involve bringing a wireless device close to a wireless signal that has not been secured. Warchalking is making a mark on the ground that allows others to identify the location of open APs

Security for Voice Over Internet Protocol (VoIP)

Although Voice Over Internet Protocol (VoIP) has been around for many years, it has only recently gained widespread interest and implementation. Because it is a fairly new technology, it has not undergone the same level of scrutiny and use as more established technologies. Although many of the risks associated with VoIP are known, there is still much to be learned. In some ways, we are still at the point in the learning curve where we don't know how much we do not know.

Some of the risks and vulnerabilities related to VoIP will be remedied as the technology evolves, but there inevitably will be some residual risk that cannot be ameliorated. It is still difficult to determine what portion of the current security issues fall into the "fixable" category, and which must be classified as "managed residual risk." Because VoIP is still, to a large extent, an unknown quantity, this section will discuss the related security issues at a conceptual level. Thus, we will not indicate a particular setting of a particular field in a given protocol as a problem but will discuss the issues in generic terms. For example, we may discuss crypto as a source of delay, which may affect voice quality, but we will not suggest a particular crypto algorithm or piece of crypto equipment. In addition, because the technology is still in the "early adopter" phase, this section takes a somewhat cautionary tone: Prudence dictates that security practitioners take care when faced with technologies that have not yet established a strong foundation of security analysis and experience.

Although this section focuses on Voice Over Internet Protocol, many of the same general concepts may be equally valid for similar technologies that move digitized voice over digital networks using protocols that may have been originally designed for data networking rather than voice.

Such technologies include, but are not limited to, Voice over Frame Relay (VoFR), Voice over Asynchronous Transfer Mode (VoATM), and Voice over Digital Subscriber Link (VoDSL). The key feature of all of these related technologies is the migration of voice from its historic technological underpinnings of analog signals on a synchronous, connection-based architecture to a digital signal moving over a packet-switched architecture. The latter means of transit is asynchronous, although it is perceived by the end user as being "real time." This migration has created several complications and necessitated the revisiting of some of the underlying design assumptions of traditional phone networks. A critical feature of this technology shift is the culture shock that occurs when technical personnel who have worked with telephone networks and those with a network background must work together. The tendency is for each group to view the problem of a converged network encompassing data and voice in the context of its own experience and history.

Telephony engineers tend to think of the system as a phone network that is using new technology and expanding to include data, while data network engineers view voice on their digital networks as just another type of bits. In reality, both groups must undergo a significant learning process as they become familiar with problems and concerns that those from the other camp view as common knowledge. Each group must familiarize itself with the basic concepts and knowledge of the other group and fill in the gaps in its own knowledge. Only when this initial acclimatization has occurred can the two groups effectively consider the complications that arise from the interactions of these formerly separate realms. To assume that installing VoIP is "…just like hooking up a familiar product or piece of equipment" seriously understates the system-level implications. Like any new technology, there are nuances that may not be initially recognized, since the transition involves new architectural assumptions not just a direct replacement of an old technology with a newer one.

An additional area in which the transition from one set of assumptions to another will prove critical is the realm of law, regulation, and policy. With VoIP, any new technology, it will take some time for the rules to catch up with the technology. A tangential issue that may have an indirect impact on security is the perception that significant cost savings will be generated by switching to VoIP. The argument is that moving from two separate infrastructures to a single infrastructure, will naturally produce a great reduction in cost. There have now been many cost analyses of the short-term expenses incurred for equipment, wiring, personnel (retraining, hiring, or replacement), and the transition of telephony bandwidth to network bandwidth, but these cost figures do not include security expenses. It remains to be seen whether security considerations will increase costs, or even mitigate against converging into a single network. There may be both security and reliability arguments for moving voice to a separate packet-switched network.

Poor cost planning can have hidden implications for security. If cost estimates for switching to VoIP are not carefully performed, resources originally allocated for security might instead be tapped to achieve basic functionality. Estimates of the costs of security for the new technology may also be inaccurate, due to VoIP's brief history and the new assumptions and interrelationships it brings with it. Conservative budgeting is called for to avoid shortfalls caused by imprecise understanding of the costs of implementing the core technology and applying security functionality on top of it.

In one sense, attackers are in the same situation as defenders with respect to VoIP. They are also facing a new technology and will probably need time to develop the theories, tools, and techniques to maximally exploit it. Although some VoIP attack tools are available and other tools and exploits from the data network realm can be adapted for use against VoIP, the threat is still in a ramp-up mode. It is hard to predict how long this stage will last. At least one factor will be the market penetration of VoIP in the coming months and years. As potential targets increase in number and attractiveness, the likelihood that the technology will draw adversary attention increases. This may result in a race between attackers and defenders as to who will turn their attention to any particular vulnerability first. This second stage will introduce a now familiar cycle, with advantage swinging back and forth between attackers and defenders as new vulnerabilities are found and techniques to minimize or exploit the vulnerabilities are deployed by the respective sides.

VoIP is potentially a functional replacement for both regular and secure phones and can, at least hypothetically, be used in any location where more traditional phones have been used in the past. That said, the transition to VoIP is not simply a matter of unplugging the old handset and plugging in the new one. In VoIP, the majority of the changes are hidden from the end user, involving replacement of telephone cabling, private branch exchanges (PBX), and other equipment with network cable, routers, and other such elements. The target environment is in some ways very familiar, since there is broad user experience with data networks and basic phone usage. At the same time, use of a phone over a data network and its implications from an administrative perspective are very new. The technology and issues are understandable, though complex. What is unclear is how best to adapt the historically connection-based synchronous phone system model to a packet switching–based asynchronous infrastructure, and the implications of that transition.

Another set of issues concerning the new environment is the policy, legal, and regulatory framework that covers the phone system and the data network. Numerous laws, policies, and regulations, on issues ranging from wiretaps to Emergency 911 functionality, have been developed over the years with the traditional telephone system in mind and with the assumption that the telephone network is a fairly homogeneous and isolated environment. Similarly, some existing laws, regulations, and policies governing the operation of data networks may not cover the concept of content other than traditional data.

Although there have already been attempts to adapt regulation and law to the new technological landscape, it may be many years before the legal and regulatory picture stabilizes. There are numerous questions about how the combined environment will be treated. For example, there are now specific rules on the treatment of information that flows over government networks, such as e-mail and file transfers. Some of this information is designated as "official government records" based on its presence on a government network, how it was generated, how it is stored, and so on. Once telephone conversations are converted to data packets on a government network, do those same rules apply? On the other hand, does a network sniffer become an illegal wiretap if it sniffs VoIP packets (as it would if the same content were intercepted on the public switched telephone network [PSTN])? For legal purposes, what makes a phone call a phone call as opposed to data?

The general requirements for VoIP can be stated simply: VoIP is to provide a functional replacement for a traditional telephone infrastructure in a given context. However, in meeting user expectations, more detailed requirements emerge, some of which may be optional in some circumstances. These more specific requirements include, but are not limited to, the following items:

- Acceptable voice quality in real time (<150 ms delay).
- An acceptable addressing scheme, which may or may not map directly to existing phone number schemes, but which must be translatable to existing phone networks and legacy systems.
- Access control to allow one to limit calls into or out of the organization's telephone infrastructure from either a public system or another enclave on the basis of such factors as calling number, called number, time of day, and others. This type of access control is what one would expect from a conventional private branch exchange (PBX), and this functionality should not be lost in a VoIP implementation. Indeed, this capability may prove to be more crucial in the VoIP realm than it was in traditional telephony.
- Sufficient auditing and billing functionality to meet mission, regulatory, and statutory requirements.
- Cost which is equivalent to, or an improvement over, existing phone technology, when all factors are added in.
- Ability to interface and interoperate with existing secure telephone technology, such as secure telephone unit (STU) III and secure telephone equipment (STE).
- Quality of service, including reliability and availability, that is comparable to that of existing telephone technology.
- Call prioritization and preemption capabilities, including both prioritization of telephone calls (e.g., "the General's call always goes through") and prioritization of telephone traffic versus data traffic on the network to maintain acceptable service levels.
- Emergency 911 geo-location information, as required by law and/or regulation (and perhaps the ability to disable it for some applications).
- Robustness. A converged network is a single point of failure; therefore, it must be designed for redundancy, fault tolerance, and graceful degradation.
- Confidentiality. Sniffing a network is easier than tapping a traditional phone network, in large part because it requires less precise physical access. Therefore, some sort of confidentiality mechanism may be needed to achieve functionality (even basic functionality) equivalent to that of the traditional phone network.
- Legality. All pertinent legal and regulatory requirements applicable to the traditional phone network must be met in a VoIP environment. However, as noted in the previous section, it should not be assumed that the same rules automatically apply in the same ways in the new environment. Therefore, there should be a conscious effort to determine the ground rules when using the new technology.
- Connection to the PSTN must not introduce errors or vulnerabilities to the PSTN, lest the PSTN decline to allow the connection.
- Feature set (conferencing, call waiting, call forwarding, voice mail, Caller ID, automatic dial-back, etc.) similar to the standard feature suite one expects from PSTN service.
- Traffic management and load monitoring capabilities similar to what one would expect from a typical PBX installation.

Potential Attacks

Research regarding potential attacks on VoIP systems is still in its early stages. The technology has not been around long enough for truly creative or detailed exploits to be developed or hypothesized. Nevertheless, many aspects of these systems are likely to provide fertile ground for those interested in exploiting VoIP. Some of these attacks will involve simple exploitation of "beginner's mistakes" that will be rapidly corrected as the technology matures. Other forms of attacks will focus on flaws that are much more deeply rooted, and will be more difficult to prevent or mitigate. The following list of attack types should not be viewed as complete. This technology is still too new for practitioners to fully understand the threat situation and its nuances.

- **Direct Access Over the Network.** If the phone is on the network, it is likely that some of its functions (speaker phone, room monitor, etc.) will be remotely accessible over the network. Limiting such access to authorized usage may be tricky.
- **Network Sniffing.** The original telephone infrastructure was designed to create a point-to-point link between caller and recipient, with the assumption that there would be no other parties on the line. Switched-packet networks are designed to send data over commonly accessible paths. Any signal that is not protected by encryption or other means must be assumed to be accessible to an adversary, possibly without the direct physical access that was generally necessary to tap the PSTN.
- **Manipulation of Traffic Flow.** Data networks are inherently asynchronous, in that the data packets do not flow over a dedicated connection for the duration of a session. By manipulating the routing of packets, an adversary could cause dropouts, insert latency (time delay between transmission and reception), or insert jitter (variation in the latency). Although such attacks make little sense in a data network, except in very specialized cases, they would have significant effect on the perceived quality of a connection to a voice user. It remains to be seen how difficult such attacks would be to implement, or how prevalent they will become.
- **Data Exfiltration.** VoIP traffic will require what is essentially a high-bandwidth breach of guards and firewalls, so as not to incur too much delay. It is also a given that VoIP packets, unlike data packets in known formats, will be very difficult (perhaps impossible) to scan for legitimate content or hidden data without introducing unacceptable delay. Unless effective means are found to isolate VoIP traffic from data traffic, VoIP will prove to be an attractive vehicle for data exfiltration, either by malicious Trojan horse code, or by an insider with bad intentions.
- **Denial of Service (DoS).** While a DoS attack could take many forms, the most obvious would be taking down or flooding the network, or some portion thereof. In the traditional system, if the network were rendered inoperable, an organization could still maintain some communications functionality over the phone. In a commingled "converged network," one would have both (i.e., network and phone service), or neither. This situation creates an attractive target. Obviously, if the VoIP portion of the network were isolated from the data portion, or if there were a fall back to traditional telephone infrastructure, this type of attack could be less effective.
- **Routing Delay Attacks.** An attacker might attempt to artificially induce delay to ensure that particular phone conversations were routed through particular network paths. In this way, an adversary could potentially choose a location for a packet sniffer or other monitoring equipment, and then maneuver the desired traffic past that point.
- **Control/Signaling Attacks.** As noted, modern data networks often run control and data signals over common links. Hypothetically, this is also possible on conventional phone networks, but given the limited access to the switching systems, the phone network is less vulnerable.
- **Bandwidth Attacks.** If an attacker could tie up sufficient bandwidth on a given link, there might not be sufficient throughput to support VoIP voice encoding schemes, which assume a certain minimum bandwidth to function properly.
- **Protocol-Based Attacks.** Because VoIP is still new, it remains to be seen what might occur if an adversary manipulated the various protocols in unanticipated ways. More analysis of the protocols and the implementations is needed to determine what protocol-based vulnerabilities to buffer overflows, man-in-the-middle attacks, traffic analysis, content-based attacks, or other mischief may exist in VoIP systems.

- **IP Spoofing.** IP spoofing is a well-known class of data networking attacks, in which an adversary hijacks a session, assuming the identity of the intended recipient. It is not hard to imagine the use of these same techniques to reroute or intercept VoIP phone traffic, allowing either masquerade or man-in-the-middle attacks.
- **Domain Name Server (DNS).** DNS system is a sort of distributed repository of network address information. It is roughly analogous to a phone book; it allows one to query based on an identifier such as a name, and get a corresponding address, usually expressed as a series of numbers in a particular format. At present, there is little security or authentication in the DNS system. As phone traffic moves to Internet Protocol (IP), the DNS system will become an even more critical piece of the infrastructure.
- **Brute Force Password/Personal Identification Number (PIN) Attacks.** Because a telephone handset (the entry mechanism in the VoIP environment) has only a numeric keypad, the possible symbol search space for passwords and PIN is greatly reduced. The limitations of human memory limit the useful length of a PIN or password even further. The result is that passwords and PINs are likely to be less secure. Alternative forms of identification and authentication (I&A) may be needed in some applications.

Potential Countermeasures:
- **Encryption.** Various efforts to use high-speed links or end-to-end encryption have been made in early VoIP installations. The critical concerns are latency, jitter, bit error rate, error propagation, and bandwidth. As is often the case with encryption, the implementation details are crucial to success. One should also be aware of the various levels at which encryption can be applied. Application layer encryption can provide end-to-end coverage but increase covert channel problems at firewalls and guards because of the traffics being encrypted. Virtual Private Networks (VPNs) and link encryptors may be used at the network layer but may require decryption and re-encryption at various points, leaving the message exposed briefly at some nodes. Encryption can also introduce delay, either during call setup or as latency during the session. If the encryption is not sufficiently fast, some form of voice compression may be required for effective use.
- **Firewalls/Guards.** The use of VoIP requires the adaptation of the firewalls in the network to allow access to ports used by VoIP and to allow out the various protocols VoIP use. Because an adversary could use these paths as well, configurations must be chosen carefully. Note that in this instance the concern is not so much about the impact on VoIP, as about the effect of the introduction of VoIP equipment and traffic on the security of the preexisting data network. In a similar vein, it is unclear how VoIP can be incorporated across a network boundary protected by a guard. The very concept of a guard, or other secure downgrading mechanism, implies a degree of delay that would be unacceptable for VoIP. In such cases, another solution for the voice traffic must be found, whether this entails putting VoIP only on networks (whether unclassified or "system high") that do not require the downgrade function or reverting to traditional telephony solutions.
- **Covert Channel and Steganography Detection.** Whereas the preceding item addressed the need for adaptation of existing firewalls and guards and the effects on the preexisting data network, this item assumes that additional filtering or monitoring will be necessary to detect modulation or other misuse of legitimate VoIP traffic flows to carry covert data either in or out. Historically, identification and prevention of covert channels have constituted one of the knottiest problems in computer security, even when confined to the data realm. The additional need to detect covert channels in the underlying analog signal increases this protection challenge significantly. This problem may require isolation of the VoIP system to prevent introduction of modulating signals. This is another area in which combining digital signal processing and the sharing of a single network between voice and data create a class of risk that was not present (or was far less likely) in separate voice or data systems.
- **Traffic Flow Tools.** Given the relative accessibility of network traffic information, protection against traffic analysis may be more crucial in a VoIP realm than in the more closed environment of a traditional telephone network. As a result, there may be a need to create a means of disguising traffic flow patterns, either by covering or masking routing information or by generating bogus traffic to disguise the flow of the real calls.
- **TEMPEST.** Given the high bandwidth of a VoIP channel, we may need to be conscious of potential modulation of the signal by other equipment in the operational environment. TEMPEST analysis of relevant equipment may be necessary in some environments.

- **Anti-Tamper.** The VoIP channel's high bandwidth and the ability to remotely access the VoIP equipment over the network make the VoIP handset an attractive target for such basic tampering as modifying the switch that disconnects the handset microphone when the phone is on the hook. There are many other tampering possibilities, but most can be addressed by a standardized program of inspection and analysis of the equipment, combined with simple tamper-detection mechanisms.

Voice over ATM

- Asynchronous Transfer Mode or ATM is a multi-service, high-speed, scalable technology. It is a dominant switching fabric in carrier backbones, supporting services with different transfer characteristics. ATM simultaneously transports voice, data, graphics, and video at very high speeds. Large enterprises continue to increase their spending on broadband connectivity to the wide area network (WAN) for headquarters and main offices. ATM is one way to provide a broadband connection to accommodate these enterprises' vast amounts of voice and data transmissions, such as heavy graphics, payroll information, and voice and video conferencing.

- ATM networks have the ability to negotiate a traffic contract at connection establishment. For a voice connection, a traffic contract can be negotiated to meet the specific requirements of the connection. In addition, ATM protocols include an ATM adaptation layer (AAL 2) specific to voice. These characteristics make ATM an ideal network for carrying voice traffic. On the down side, ATM services are expensive and are not universally available. Most networks today do not have ATM protocols running from end terminal to end terminal. Instead, ATM is usually used as a backbone or technology to transport IP packets or other network traffic. For voice communications, QoS must be provided end to end. This means that the protocol running over ATM, as well as the ATM network, must establish a traffic contract that can support the voice connection.

Voice over Frame Relay

Of the three packet/cell technologies (frame relay, IP and ATM), frame relay is the most widely deployed. Frame relay is commonly used in corporate data networks because of its flexible bandwidth, widespread accessibility, support of a diverse traffic mix, and technological maturity. Initially, frame relay gained acceptance as a means of providing end users with a solution for LAN-to-LAN connections and other data connectivity requirements. In addition to providing a flexible and efficient data transport mechanism, frame relay lowered the cost of bandwidth for tying together multiprotocol networks and devices. Often, it is used as a transport protocol linking two or more IP networks. Although frame relay does specify a minimum throughput for each connection, it does not support a rich QoS scheme. However, it has better QoS characteristics than IP networks and is used to carry both voice and data connections today.

Frame relay service is based on permanent virtual connections (PVC). The technology is appropriate for closed user groups and is also recommended for star topologies and situations in which performance must be predictable. VoFR is a logical progression for organizations that already use frame relay for data. If congestion occurs in frame relay networks; some data frames may be dropped. Voice connections are less tolerant of dropped frames than are data connections, so too many dropped frames will create choppy or distorted audio. There are mechanisms for traffic management in frame relay networks to mitigate congestion conditions. With the ratification of the frame relay forum's (FRF) FRF.11, a standard was established for frame relay voice transport. The Frame Relay Forum Technical Committee developed the Implementation Agreement FRF.11 to define standards for how vendor equipment interoperates to transport of voice across a carrier's public frame relay network.

Encryption

Encryption is a process by which a given message is obscured or rearranged so that the end result is illegible. The purpose of encryption is to allow individuals and groups to share confidential communications with each other. The assumption made by those sending and receiving encrypted messages is that they are the only ones that have the means to decrypt or restore the original message from the illegible version.

Modern encryption schemes rely on the use of mathematical problems that tend to be difficult, if not impossible to solve. The **plaintext** or original message is subjected to multiple mathematical procedures that are based on difficult equations. The difficulty in solving a math single problem of that type is compounded many times over by the variations that the designer of the **encryption algorithm** built into the scheme. The end result is called **ciphertext**, which cannot be understood.

Technology is used to send messages across a fairly unsafe space known as the Internet. If a message is intercepted somewhere along its path, and it had not been encrypted, then a third party, perhaps one with malicious intent, may know the details of the message. The ability of computers to process mathematical instructions much faster than humans can enables people to send and receive secure messages across an insecure network. The study of creating secret messages is known as cryptography. There are basically two types of cryptography, namely private key and public key.

Private Key Cryptography

The advantages of using private (also known as "secret key" or "symmetric key") key systems are as follows:

- Both the sender and the receiver of the message use the same key
- The algorithms are difficult to break if a large key size is used.
- The mathematical processes for both encrypting and decrypting symmetric key messages are much faster than the alternative, asymmetric cryptography.

The disadvantages of using private key are these:

- Since the parties at both ends have the same key, there is no way to verify who sent a message
- The key can open any messages that were sent using it. Therefore, the way the keys are distributed the both parties must be very secure.
- Managing an organization in which every two parties must have a unique key can become an administrative nightmare.

A few examples of private key systems are:

- AES (Advanced Encryption System)
- IDEA (International Data Encryption Algorithm)
- DES (Data Encryption Standard) and 3DES (Triple DES)

Public Key Cryptography

In Public Key, or asymmetric cryptography, multiple algorithms exist and are used in conjunction with each other to provide security. In this system, each user gets two keys; one is called a private key and the other is called a public key. The "private" key here is not a symmetric key. Instead it is an asymmetric key that is called "private" because its owner never shares it with anyone else. On the other hand, each user also gets a public key, which can be shared only with certain people or made open to the world for use. The private and public keys are generated using the same mathematical system. They are related numbers, but it is virtually impossible to guess one simply by looking at the other one. There are other algorithms or functions that are generated during this process and they have some important uses in public key cryptography.

Encryption in a Public Key System
- Let's assume Joe wants to send an encrypted message to Mary.
- Joe and Mary have two different keys each, for a total of 4 different keys.
- Both Joe and Mary have made their public keys available for use via the CA (Certificate Authority) that issued the keys.
- Joe types in the message "I'll see you at noon", and **encrypts it using Mary's public key**.
    - Joe does not perform the encryption himself. His web browser or email client will do this for him.
- Mary can **decrypt the message using her own private key**, since her public and private keys are mathematically linked.
    - Mary does not do any decrypting on her own, her email client or browser will handle it automatically.
- The end result from a security standpoint is that they were able to share a secret message over the Internet. They had confidentiality, but not authenticity. There was no authenticity because there was no way that Mary could prove the message came from Joe. Her public key was used, and that key is openly available for free on the web. Anyone could download that key and try to trick her; she can't be sure the message came from Joe.
    - Note that Mary never has to reveal her private key to Joe or anyone else in order for them to be able to send her an encrypted message.

Authentication in a Public Key System
Joe and Mary didn't meet that day because Mary could not be sure Joe sent the message. Now Joe wants to send a message to Mary that includes proof of who sent it.
- Joe types in his email client the message: "Lets' meet after work".
- Joe **encrypts the message with Mary's public key**, just as before.
- However, this time he **signs the message with his own private key.**
    - Joe's email client will do the work of adding this digital signature to his message
- Mary sees another email that is allegedly from Joe.
- She uses **her own private key, as before, to decrypt** the message.
- Mary now sees that *someone* wants to meet her after work, but can she be sure that it is Joe?
- Mary uses her email client to **verify the signature using Joe's openly available public key**
    - Mary can verify the signature with Joe's ***public*** key, because Joe's private and public keys are mathematically linked. As long as Mary has the software that can run the algorithm installed in her email client, she can prove that the signature must have been generated by the person that has access to the private key.
    - Joe does not have to reveal his private key to Mary in order for her to be able to verify his signature.
- The end result is that Mary can safely assume that Joe was indeed the originator of the message.

Non-Repudiation in a Public Key System
- Joe never showed up after work that day.
- When Mary confronted him about it, he denied sending the email.
- Mary showed Joe a copy of the email and the fact that she was able to verify the signature on it. Since Joe is not claiming that someone stole his computer, only he could have used it to send the email.
- The end result? Joe cannot deny being the originator of the email **since his signature, which could only have been generated by his private key**, was successfully verified by Mary.

Integrity in a Public Key System (Part 1)
- Joe was in trouble; he had to think fast.
- He asked Mary if she was also able to **verify the message digest that he attached to the message**.
- Mary admits that she couldn't because she didn't see one.
- Joe tells her that **the message must have been intercepted during transit and changed**. He claims that in *his* message, he asked her to meet him on Saturday, not after work.
- Mary can prove Joe sent a message, but she cannot prove that the message she received was an unaltered original. The keys she had used so far do not prove the integrity of the email.

Integrity in a Public Key System (Part 2)
- Mary knows how one-way hashing works, so she tells Joe to resend the email while she watches him do it.
- Joe is in a tough spot, but if he says he deleted it, Mary will simply send a copy of it back to him anyway so that he can resend it.
- Joe reluctantly sends the original email. The **one-way hash function** (yet another mathematical function) is applied to the message using a symmetric key. A **message digest** is created and sent along with the message.
- Mary receives the email and applies the same symmetric key to the message.
- Now Mary applies a hashing algorithm to the result and receives her own MAC (message authentication code)
- The code she generates is exactly the same as the one included in the email Joe sent.
- Mary is now furious because she has proof that:
    - Joe sent the message; the signature is his.
    - Joe's message could not have been altered; otherwise, the MACs would not be the same.
    - She now believes Joe must have been dishonest with her and she is beginning to wonder if he has been dishonest about anything else…

The strengths of Public Key (Asymmetric) Cryptography are as follows:

- It adds both non-repudiation and authentication to the confidentiality of an encrypted message
- A user only needs one public and one private key to securely communicate with all other users. Symmetric Key systems, require a shared key for each unique pair of people that are communicating (It scales better)
- The key distribution process is safer; no party ever needs to reveal the private key they were issued

The weaknesses of Public Key are:

- It requires a lot of computing power as opposed to symmetric systems.
- It is slower because of the extra work that has to be done.

To sum up the public key process:

Encryption:
- Uses only the receiver's keys
- Initiated by the sender, who encrypts with the receiver's public key
- The message is decrypted by the receiver using the private key

Digital Signatures
- Use only the sender's keys
- A hashing algorithm is run against the message, which produces a separate hash value
- Then the sender signs (encrypts the hash value) with a private key and adds that to the message.
- The signature (encrypted hash) is verified by the receiver using the sender's public key

Hashing/Message Digest
- The sender adds a symmetric key to the message
- The sender runs a hashing algorithm against the new, concatenated (original message + symmetric key) result.
- The hashing algorithm produces a MAC. (message authentication code)
- The MAC is added to the message and sent to the receiver
- The receiver adds a symmetric key to the message
- The receiver runs the result through a hashing algorithm and generates another MAC.
- If the result is the same as the MAC received in the email, the message is unaltered.

Public Key Infrastructure (PKI)

PKI is **not** the same as Public Key Cryptography. ***PKI uses Public Key Cryptography as an enabler of a trust relationship***. The trust relationship is a three-way relationship. The following is an example of one way that this relationship might develop

- First, a company wants to begin selling its widgets online. The company has a great IT guy who can set them up on the web with no problem, but
- There is no way that smart people will enter credit card or any other personal information on that site. Their browsers keep telling them that **the site is not trusted**; People can't see the **small lock on the bottom of the page or https:// in the address bar**, so they go elsewhere to shop.
- The IT guy tells Management that they need to go to a CA (Certificate Authority), buy a **SSL (**Secure Sockets Layer) Certificate, and then they might be able to generate some sales.
- The CIO of the widgets company gets online and finds a vendor for these certificates.
- The CIO sees that he needs to **register** by supplying quite a bit of information about the business and he even needs to send the company some information generated by the servers that Widgets Inc. is running.
- Within a week, Widgets has their SSLError! Bookmark not defined. certificates and the IT guy installs them.
- Shortly after that, Widgets gets its first Internet sale.

Digital Certificate: A Digital Certificate is (the public key of the person or group) + (Additional identifying information about that person or group) and all of this is digitally signed by the CA. Therefore:

- The group applying for the certificate proves its identity to an RA (Registration Authority), which is often a separate division of the company that offers the CA.
- After verifying the information provided, the CA "trusts" the group while it uses that server for its web pages.
- Your browser "trusts the CA, so if it can verify the digital signature in the certificate, the browser will proceed with allowing the server to authenticate and open a session.

SSL (Secure Sockets Layer): This use of Public Key Cryptography enables a secure connection to be established between a host and a server. If the server cannot send a digital certificate to the host's browser to be verified, no secure connection can be established via SSL.

SET (Secure Electronic Transaction): A standard proposed by Visa and MasterCard that would enable the secure transmission of credit card information. This standard utilizes a digital "wallet" that may be stored on a computer or coded onto a smart card.

A few examples of public key systems are:

- RSA
- ECC
- El Gamal

A few examples of hashing algorithms are:

- SHA
- MD5
- HAVAL

Auditing Applications

There are thousands of software applications in existence. These applications are deployed in organizations ranging in size from home-based businesses to multi-national corporations. No single book can document all of the applications in use and provide an audit program tailored to each one. However, there are some general guidelines that apply to the audit of every application type.

These guidelines can be separated into two phases. In the first phase, the groundwork for the audit is performed. First of all, it is vital that the auditor work with the data owners and system administrators to identify the assets or the data within the assets that is deemed to be highest value. It is fair to assume that the most valuable assets will be the targets of attack. The auditor should devote a majority of the total time allotted for the audit to assessing the controls related to these assets. The final step in the first phase is to create an audit program based on the information obtained. At a minimum, the audit program should include a summary of the assets that will be reviewed, the methods that will be used to perform the review and the resources that will be needed from the organization in order to expedite the process.

The second phase of the audit begins after the organization has agreed to the proposed audit program. If possible, the first thing the auditor should do is conduct interviews. During the interviews, the auditor should identify the access rights for privileges for groups and individuals. In addition, the data owners should define the access paths they intended for each authorized party. The organization should be able to produce documentation that clearly delineates all of the access rights granted to each group or individual for the assets in question. This documentation should be detailed enough that it identifies even file and folder permissions. During the interviews, the auditor should document the controls currently implemented by the data owners and systems administrators. The auditor should also review all relevant job titles and roles to ensure that access to various resources is only allowed for those that the data owner intended. The auditor can later compare the actual permissions granted with the permissions intended to identify any discrepancies. The second part of this phase involves testing of the controls that have been identified. Since most of this testing is done within the organization's network, this is often referred to as a vulnerability analysis. This analysis can be performed by making direct attempts to bypass security methods, by the use of CAATs (Computer Assisted Auditing Techniques) or both. If any of the applications are accessible from the Internet, such as E-Commerce and mail servers, then these access paths should also be tested.

The most secure of applications is only as secure as the platform it runs on. Therefore, any vulnerability test of an application should also include testing of the operating system that underlies it. Data owners have the right to decide who can access a given asset, but often, data owners are not the people that implement the access controls. As operating systems become more complex, the probability that they will be issued with vulnerabilities increases. In fact, there are several websites devoted to the documentation and discussion of software vulnerabilities and the fixes designed for them. An IT auditor should have some understanding of the operating systems used within the organization. Any vulnerability that allows an unauthorized person to obtain root or administrator rights to the network or system running an application puts any of that application's data at risk.

The third part of this phase calls for the auditor to compare the findings obtained with any industry guidelines or legal obligations that may be relevant to this organization. There may be no harm done if an organization fails to measure up to an industry standard; in fact, this may unavoidable in many cases. On the other hand, it is not acceptable for that organization to be in violation of any relevant laws regarding its operations. The auditor may or may not report a failure to meet industry guidelines based on the needs and means of the organization in question. However, due professional care requires an auditor to report any condition that amounts to a violation of relevant law.

The order of events listed for the second phase may not be practical in live environments. The auditor must be flexible enough to accommodate the business needs of the organization. Scheduling issues may force the auditor to change plans significantly during the time allotted for the process. In any case, the results obtained from the interviews, comparisons, tests and any other material observations must now be compiled into a final document. The auditor has an obligation to be honest and above reproach in the final report. On the other hand, an auditor should be sensitive to the status and means of the organization when defining recommendations. For example, a small not-for-profit may accept donations via its Internet site. In another case, a brick and mortar retail store with hundreds of locations in the U.S. may allow customers to buy products via its Internet site. Although both of the Web sites mentioned require security and adequate controls, it is unlikely that the not-for-profit would be capable of purchasing and maintaining the same amount of security that the retail chain can afford. Therefore, the auditor must tailor each report to the organization at hand; a cookie-cutter approach will not work.

Auditing Devices
All hardware devices require some kind of operating system to perform its basic tasks. Many devices, especially servers and workstations, require both an operating system and additional applications to be installed in order that they may provide some useful service. Other devices, such as routers and switches, require only an operating system in order to be functional. Several software and security companies are now selling dedicated "appliances". These are hardware devices that are pre-installed with a custom or hardened operating system and some kind of application. From an administrator's point of view, there is still a learning curve associated with the device. However, since the device has (allegedly) had all unnecessary services turned off or removed altogether, the system is far less vulnerable to attack.

The audit of a device is often much easier than the audit of an application. Either a penetration scan, which is launched externally or vulnerability scan may reveal one or more weaknesses in the operating systems in use on a given device. As stated earlier, the auditor should obtain documents which provide every detail concerning the access rights to every file, folder, feature and application running on a given machine. This is an excellent way to check the way that servers and workstations have been configured. In the case of routers and switches, firewalls, IDS devices, VPN and access servers, etc. the situation is quite different. Although these devices may allow hundreds or thousands of people to access the Internet or devices on different parts of the network simultaneously, very few people are allowed to access these devices directly or change the way they are configured. In such cases, the auditor should also request documents which show the configuration settings of these devices. An examination of the device's configuration settings is the only way that an auditor can determine whether the policies intended by the organization for that device are being properly implemented.

Privacy in the Organization

Within an organization, privacy may be defined as the commitment to uphold any type of obligation or agreement that might exist in regard to protecting information relating directly to an individual. Privacy has become an issue that organizations may no longer ignore. Many government and private concerns have begun the task of collecting and converting all their transactions and other information into digital formats. When this trend is considered along with the rapid growth of the Internet, it is not surprising that some will question the safety of PII (Personally Identifiable Information). Many states have implemented laws regarding privacy. In addition, many organizations have crafted their own privacy policies. Due to the complexity of the issues relating to privacy it is essential that organizations consider and build privacy controls into their system at the very beginning. The process of including privacy controls into the organization begins with a privacy assessment. In the same way that risk analysis may be performed in regard to other information assets, a privacy analysis can be performed in order to quantify the potential impact a breach of privacy might cause. In general a privacy analysis should include the following steps:

1. Identification of all of the assets that contain PII or any other information that might be construed as private.
2. Identification of any individuals that are owners of this data and/or those that will be held accountable for its protection.
3. Examine the access paths related to the assets in question. Determine if existing controls regarding the ways this data is obtained, viewed or disposed of are sufficient.
4. Development of a document that will be used to create privacy policy and aid in the creation of design modifications aimed at minimizing any risk or exposure due to privacy concerns

This type of analysis requires expert-level advice on legal, technical and operations-related issues. The legal and operations concerns would reveal the extent of the organization's privacy risk. Any necessary policies should be generated from these analyses. The technical part can focus on the means by which security controls may be implemented. Changes in an organization's PPT (People, Processes and Technology) can affect privacy risk. Some examples of the assets and processes that are subject to change are:

- People
    - Consultants and Vendors
    - Business partners
    - Temporary and permanent employees
    - Outsourcers Service Providers

- Processes
    - New Operations or systems
    - Legacy systems and new system rollouts
    - BPR (Business Process Reengineering)
    - Capacity, Continuity and Change Management
    - Increased Website functionality or Extranet

- Technology
    - New Product or Service offerings
    - Data Mining /Warehousing
    - Modifications to existing applications or systems.

An IT auditor may be tasked to review a privacy policy and implementation for compliance to relevant laws, security requirements and data protection. This review should also cover any OECD (Organization for Economic Co-operation and Development) or Safe Harbor rules governing data transfer situations. In such cases, the auditor may require expert assistance in order to ensure that the review covers all necessary areas.

The goals of a privacy impact assessment

- Pinpoint the nature of personally identifiable information associated with business processes
- Document the collection, use, disclosure and destruction of personally identifiable information
- Ensure that accountability for privacy issues exists
- Be the foundation for informed policy, operations and system design decisions based on an understanding of privacy risk and the options available for mitigating that risk.

Disposal or Destruction of PII

Individuals and organizations store data on a wide variety of media. The disposal of these assets can jeopardize the confidentiality of that data. In general, there are three levels of effort or care that may be used in the disposal of data:

- **Clearing:** This level of effort primarily involves:
    - Media that was not used to hold sensitive data
    - Magnetic Media
    - The use of software overwrites as the method of choice

- **Purging:** This level of effort involves:
    - Media that held sensitive data or any media whose contents are in doubt
    - Magnetic Media
    - The use of degaussing tools, drilling holes in hard disks, use of Secure Erase software as methods of choice

- **Destruction:**
    - Media that held sensitive data or any media whose contents are in doubt
    - All non-magnetic media or magnetic media whose contents are so sensitive that destruction is imperative
    - Incineration, shredding pulverizing, bending and breaking, disintegration.

Physical Access Security

Physical Security, in its broadest sense, deals with controls in three different areas:

- Barriers or restrictions preventing access to certain areas
- Methods by which approach or access to restricted areas is recorded
- Technology used to protect assets and/or stabilize the physical environment

Barriers to Access

Barriers to access are primarily preventive controls. They are normally implemented as a means by which unauthorized personnel ma be kept from obtaining direct access to an organization's assets and resources. The following is a list of some widely used barriers:

- **Fences:** Fences can be an effective deterrent to intruders if they are high enough to discourage climbers. The minimum recommended height for this purpose is 8 feet. Adding 3 or more rows of barbed wire along the top of the fence increases the overall deterrent effect.
- **Gates:** Strong fences should have gates that are equally strong. Deterrents to unauthorized entry through gates include:
    - Guard posts
    - Swipe cards
    - Electronic locking mechanism with camera/intercom

- **Walls:**
  - Exterior Walls and Roofing: The strength of exterior walls, particularly those at the street level should be determined by the nature of the assets stored inside the structure. For example, a fast food establishment probably needs much less security on its walls and roof than a store that sells jewelry or high end electronics.
  - Interior Walls: The same principle applies for interior and exterior walls. The materials used should be chosen based on the value of the assts that will be housed within. For example, it would be better to use cinderblocks and reinforced steel than drywall on a room housing a safe or valuable computer equipment.
- **Drop Ceilings:** The use of drop ceilings should be avoided in and near rooms that house valuables. These ceilings provide a way for an intruder to bypass expensive locks and sturdy walls by simply climbing over them. This means that walls must extend from floor to ceiling to provide adequate security for sensitive materials.
- **Doors, Locks and Entryways:** This combination is usually the last line of defense in many organizations. Once an intruder has bypassed interior doors and locking mechanisms, direct access to company resources is available. The following suggestions should add considerably to the effectiveness of this deterrent:
  - Situate a guard station at the outside of the door. Ensure that identification must be supplied before entry may be attempted.
  - Install adequate lighting and cameras at all entryways. Ensure that no one may enter or leave without being recorded. Keep backups of the recordings for at least 60 -90 days.
  - Set up a man-trap or secure turnstile/revolving door entry: These methods are intended to deter piggybacking. An unauthorized person that follows an authorized person in through an open door is said to be "piggybacking" his way into that area.
    - A man-trap uses a corridor set up between two secure doors as a barrier. A guard post is inside the interior door. If set up properly, only one person should enter the corridor at a time, and the guard should only open the interior door if only one person is present.
    - A secure turnstile or revolving door requires a swipe card or some other authentication token. Once used, the turnstile or revolving door only turns once, and only turns 90 degrees. In addition, this device is usually constructed to be too small to allow two average adults to move through it at once. A guard post here would definitely add to the security provided.

Two- Factor Authentication

I&A (Identification and Authentication) are usually the means by which an individual gains access to a secure area, building or network resources.

- **Identification** involves supplying a username or other label by which the individual might be uniquely known to the system.
- **Authentication** may be supplied by one of three methods: something known by the person, something possessed by the person or something that person is.
  - Something known might include: passwords, place of birth, PIN numbers, etc
  - Something possessed by the person might be an ID card, a magnetic swipe card or a smart card.
  - Something that person is has to do with biometrics, including hand or fingerprint recognition, retina scans, signature matching, etc

When two-factor authentication is employed, a person must use two of the three methods to be properly authenticated. The use of two factor authentication in conjunction with any of the physical barriers mentioned above is becoming very common. Some consider this a compensating control when a guard is not posted at a door or entryway.

Methods by which access is recorded
Recording devices are a deterrent to many intruders. In particular, cameras placed at angles that guarantee clear views of faces will keep most unauthorized people away from secure entryways. Good lighting is also necessary for proper use of cameras and to allow authorized personnel to clearly see if anyone is simply waiting around outside the entryway.

If a magnetic swipe card, smart card or biometric system is installed, logging of access to buildings or secure rooms within buildings may be implemented. Although it is possible that these cards might be lost or stolen, the use of two-factor authentication should prevent the average intruder from gaining access. If a biometric method is employed, the use of the swipe card by an unauthorized person will usually fail.

Biometric systems have weaknesses:
- The data obtained from a voice-print, fingerprint, retina scan or signature may undergo some change as it is translated into a digital format. This translation is called "**enrollment**"
- The person from whom the data was obtained may also change over time or even on a temporary basis. Medications, illness, stress and even temperature can affect voice, retina and signature methods.
- The three most significant figures in the measurement of biometric systems are:

    - **Type 1 - False Rejection Rate (FRR)**: This is the probability that a biometric system will fail to identify an enrollee, or verify the legitimate claimed identity of an enrollee. The lower this number is, the better the system is.
    - **Type 2 – False Acceptance Rate (FAR)**: This is the probability that a biometric system will incorrectly identify an individual or will fail to reject an imposter. The lower this number is, the better the system is.
    - **Crossover error rate (CER)**: This is the point at which the FRR equals the FAR and it is stated as a percentage. Again, the lower the number, the better the system's performance is.

Environmental Controls and Protection of Assets
One of the most popular reasons that organizations outsource part of their IT departments is the need to save on the costs associated with the care and security that their servers require.
- Computer equipment functions best in areas where the temperature can be kept fairly low and the humidity is carefully controlled.
- Computer equipment is vulnerable to changes in the power supplied to it.
- Any structure is subject to damage resulting from fire, floods or other natural occurrences.

Some precautions that may be taken to control these potential problems are as follows:

Heat and humidity: Hot air rises and cold air sinks. As computer equipment generates heat, that heat will tend to rise up toward the ceiling. Air conditioning vents placed under the floors will have to work very hard to provide adequate cooling to the equipment at the top of racks. The best location for AC units is directly above the racks forcing cool air down onto the equipment. In this way, the cooler air will sink naturally and require less power to provide the same effect. In general, temperatures should range between 70 and 75 degrees and humidity should be kept between 45 and 60%.

Electrical issues: Devices such as toasters, refrigerators and even air conditioners are fairly tolerant of changes in current. Their circuitry is not as delicate as that within computer equipment. There are several types of power issues that may occur and cause damage to computers:

- **Blackout:** This is a sudden and complete loss of power. If the computer equipment is not damaged, there is certain to be some data loss as a result. A UPS (Uninterruptible Power Supply) is the best solution.
- **Brownout:** This is an action deliberately taken by power companies to reduce power output to certain areas during periods of high utilization. A transformer capable of supplying constant voltage must be used to keep the power levels up and stable.
- **Surge:** This is a situation where the voltage is increased for a relatively long period. Surge protectors should help with this problem.
- **Fault:** This is a very brief loss of power; the UPS should handle this.
- **Sag:** A short-term brownout. This is another job for a transformer.
- **Spike:** This is a brief jump in power. The surge protector should protect your equipment.

Flood: To keep computer equipment from water damage due to flooding, it is best that they be housed in rooms with raised flooring. Also, whenever possible, computer equipment should not be housed at or below ground level to avoid flood damage. Since roofs may become damaged and leak water, computers should not be housed on the top floor.

Fire: *In case of fire or any other dangerous situation, the first responsibility of any organization is the protection of human life.*
This statement is also applicable to any BCP (Business Continuity Plan) or DR (Disaster Recovery) plan. When seeking to implement controls against fire, there are several things to keep in mind:

- Classes of fire:
    - **Wood, paper and laminates:** Class A - Use water or soda acid.
    - **Oil, petroleum and coolants:** Class B – Use Gas extinguishers: Halon, FM200, CO_2 or soda acid.
    - **Electrical equipment:** Class C - Use Gas extinguishers: Halon, FM200 or CO_2.
    - **Combustible metals** (Potassium, Sodium, Magnesium) – Use Dry powder.

- Sprinkler Types:
    - **Dry pipe:** Water is held out of the pipes until fire is detected
    - **Wet pipe:** Water is in the pipes at all times
    - **Deluge:** Similar to Dry pipe, except the sprinkler heads are wide open. More water comes out faster and this is not suited for electrical equipment.
    - **Preaction:** Hybrid Wet and Dry system – Water is held outside of the pipes until a certain temperature is achieved. Then the water fills the pipes, but a certain substance (thin metal) must melt before the water can be released.

Note that Halon may no longer be installed in new fire suppression systems. FM200 and CO_2 are the primary options for gas extinguishers now.

CHAPTER 5 PRACTICE QUESTIONS

1) Which of the following can identify attacks and penetration attempts to a network?
   A. Firewall
   B. Packet filters
   C. Stateful inspection
   D. Intrusion detection system (IDs)

2) An organization is considering connecting a critical PC-based system to the Internet. Which of the following would provide the BEST protection against hacking?
   A. An application-level gateway
   B. A remote access server
   C. A proxy server
   D. Port scanning

3) Which of the following applet intrusion issues poses the GREATEST risk of disruption to an organization?
   A. A program that deposits a virus on a client machine
   B. Applets recording keystrokes and, therefore, passwords
   C. Downloaded code that reads files on a client's hard drive
   D. Applets opening connections from the client machine

4) Which of the following is a feature of an intrusion detection system (IDS)?
   A. Gathering evidence on attack attempts
   B. Identifying weakness in the policy definition
   C. Blocking access to particular sites on the Internet
   D. Preventing certain users from accessing specific servers

5) The feature of a digital signature that ensures the sender cannot later deny generating and sending the message is:
   A. data integrity.
   B. authentication.
   C. non-repudiation.
   D. replay protection.

6) Which of the following physical access controls would provide the highest degree of security over unauthorized access?
   A. Bolting door lock
   B. Cipher lock
   C. Electronic door lock
   D. Fingerprint scanner

CHAPTER 5 PRACTICE QUESTIONS (CONT.)

7) A single digitally signed instruction was given to a financial institution to credit a customer's account. The financial institution received the instruction three times and credited the account three times. Which of the following would be the MOST appropriate control against such multiple credits?
   A. Encrypting the hash of the payment instruction with the public key of the financial institution.
   B. Affixing a time stamp to the instruction and using it to check for duplicate payments.
   C. Encrypting the hash of the payment instruction with the private key of the instructor.
   D. Affixing a time stamp to the hash of the instruction before being digitally signed by the instruction.

8) An IS auditor reviewing operating system access discovers that the system is not secured properly. In this situation, the IS auditor is LEAST likely to be concerned that the user might:
   A. create new users.
   B. delete database and log files.
   C. access the system utility tools.
   D. access the system writeable directories.

9) Which of the following functions is performed by a virtual private network (VPN)?
   A. Hiding information from sniffers on the net
   B. Enforcing security policies
   C. Detecting misuse or mistakes
   D. Regulating access

10) A programmer included a routine into a payroll application to search for his/her own payroll number. As a result, if this payroll number does not appear during the payroll run, a routine will generate and place random numbers onto every paycheck. This routine is known as:
    A. scavenging.
    B. data leakage.
    C. piggybacking.
    D. a trojan horse.

CHAPTER 5 ANSWERS TO PRACTICE QUESTIONS

1) Answer: D

An IDS has a large database of attack signatures, which is used to ward off attacks. Packet filter and stateful inspection are types 0f firewalls. A firewall is a fence around a network designed to block certain types of communications routed or passing through specific ports. It is not designed to discover someone bypassing or going under the firewall.

2) Answer: A

"An application-level gateway is the best way to protect against hacking because it can define with detail rules that describe the type of user or connection that is, or is not permitted. It analyzes in detail each package, not only in layers one through four of the OSI model but also layers five through seven, which means that it reviews the commands of each higher level protocol (HTTP, FTP, SNMP, etc.) For a remote access server there is a device (server) asking for username and passwords before entering the network. This is good when accessing private networks, but it can be mapped or scanned from the Internet creating security exposure. Proxy servers can provide protection based on the IP address and ports. However, an individual is needed who really knows how to do this, and second applications can use different ports for the different sections of their program. Port scanning works when there is a very specific task to do, but not when trying to control what comes from the Internet (or when all the ports available need to be controlled somehow). For example, the port for Ping (echo request) could be blocked and the **IP** addresses would be available for the application and browsing, but would not respond to Ping.

3) Answer: D

An applet is a program downloaded from a web server to the client, usually through a web browser that provides functionality for database access, interactive web pages and communications with other users. Applets opening connections from the client machine to other machines on the network and damaging those machines as a denial-of-service attack pose the greatest threat to an organization and could disrupt business continuity. A program that deposits a virus on a client machine is referred to as a malicious attack (specifically meant to cause harm to a client machine), but may not necessarily result in a disruption of service. Applets recording keystrokes and, therefore, passwords and downloaded code that reads files on a client's hard drive relate more to organizational privacy issues, and although significant, are less likely to cause a significant disruption of service.

4) Answer: A

An IDS can gather evidence on intrusive activity like an attack or penetration attempt. Identifying weaknesses in the policy definition is a limitation of an IDS. Choices C and D are features of firewalls, and choice B requires a manual review and is, therefore, outside the functionality of IDS.

CHAPTER 5 ANSWERS TO PRACTICE QUESTIONS (CONT.)

5) Answer: C

All of the above are features of a digital signature. Non-repudiation ensures that the claimed sender cannot later deny generating and sending the message. Data integrity refers to changes in the plaintext message that would result in the recipient failing to compute the same message hash. Since only the claimed sender has the key, authentication ensures that the message has been sent by the claimed sender. Replay protection is a method that a recipient can use to check that the message was not intercepted and replayed.

6) Answer: D

All are physical access controls designed to protect the organization from unauthorized access. However, biometric door locks, such as a fingerprint scanner, provide advantages since they are harder to duplicate, easier to deactivate and individually identified. Biometric door locks, using an individual's unique body features are used for access when extremely sensitive facilities must be protected.

7) Answer: B

Affixing a time stamp to the instruction and using it to check for duplicate payments makes the instruction unique. The financial institution can check that the instruction was not intercepted and replayed and thus it could prevent crediting the account three times. Encrypting the hash of the payment instruction with the public key of the financial institution does not protect replay, it only protects confidentiality and integrity of the instruction. Encrypting the hash of the payment instruction with the private key of the instruction ensures integrity of the instruction and non-repudiation of the issued instruction. The process of creating a message digest requires applying a cryptographic hashing algorithm to the entire message. The receiver, upon decrypting the message digest, will re-compute the hash using the same hashing algorithm and compare the result with what was sent. Hence, affixing a time stamp into the hash of the instruction before being digitally signed by the instructor would violate the integrity requirements of digital signature.

8) Answer: A

Access to the operating system does not result necessarily in granting access to creating new users. Hence, it is not a likely concern. The other choices are likely concerns if the operating system is not defined properly. In this case, users can access the system writeable directories, delete database and log files, and access system utility tools.

9) Answer: A

A VPN hides information from sniffers on the net. Using encryption, a VPN hides information. It works based on tunneling. A VPN does not analyze information packets and therefore cannot enforce security policies, nor does it check the content of packets and so cannot detect misuse or mistakes, and it does not perform an authentication function, and hence cannot regulate access.

10) Answer: D

A trojan horse is malicious code hidden in an authorized computer program. The hidden code will be executed whenever the authorized program is executed. In this case, as long as the perpetrator's payroll number is part of the payroll process nothing happens, but as soon as the payroll number is gone havoc occurs.

Chapter 6 Business Continuity and Disaster Recovery

Business Continuity Planning
Business Continuity Planning (BC or BCP) and its technical component Disaster Recovery (DR) include strategies and tactics related to enabling business operations to continue in spite of any disruptive events. This process also includes risk management and project management techniques as applied to creating and maintaining an alternate processing site. This process includes planning, implementation, testing and revision or the plan to compensate for changes in the business, its technology and operating environment.

This chapter represents approximately 14 percent of the CISA examination (approximately 28 questions).

There are three tasks in this area that the CISA candidate must understand and be able to perform:

- Evaluate the adequacy of backup and restore provisions to ensure the availability of information required to resume processing.
- Evaluate the organization's disaster recovery plan to ensure that it enables the recovery of IT processing capabilities in the event of a disaster.
- Evaluate the organization's business continuity plan to ensure its ability to continue essential business operations during the period of an IT disruption.

Knowledge Statements
The following statements describe specific topics a CISA candidate should be familiar with and use as guidance in the fulfillment of the tasks outlined above:

- Knowledge of data backup, storage, maintenance, retention and restoration processes, and practices
- Knowledge of regulatory, legal, contractual, and insurance issues related to business continuity and disaster recovery
- Knowledge of business impact analysis (BIA)
- Knowledge of the development and maintenance of the business continuity and disaster recovery plans
- Knowledge of business continuity and disaster recovery testing approaches and methods
- Knowledge of human resources management practices as related to business continuity and disaster recovery (e.g., evacuation planning, response teams)
- Knowledge of processes used to invoke the business continuity and disaster recovery plans
- Knowledge of types of alternate processing sites and methods used to monitor the contractual agreements (e.g., hot sites, warm sites, cold sites)

Components of an Effective BCP
Senior IS and end user management must choose critical business functions to be protected and fund and deploy all resources necessary to ensure that a viable business continuity plan is designed and functional. This means they must also assign responsibility for plan development, testing, implementation, documentation, review and update and set target dates for each of these phases. Management also must insist on adequate feedback to assure itself that the business continuity plans are indeed workable and that procedures are kept current.

The personnel assigned to respond to disaster scenarios are the most critical resource in the DR (Disaster Recovery) plan. Therefore, both management and user involvement is vital to the success of any planning and testing efforts. The involvement of data or process owners is essential to the identification and analysis of critical systems, their associated critical recovery times and the specification of needed resources. The three major divisions that require involvement in the formulation of the business continuity plan are support services, business operations and data processing support. The seven major steps in completing and having a successful BCP are described in the graphic below.

Exam Tip: The protection of human life should always be the first concern in any BCP/DR plan. Candidates for the CISA exam should be aware of this priority for the exam and for real-world scenarios as well.

The figure above outlines the contingency planning activities involved in all phases of the system development life cycle (SDLC). During the **Initiation phase**, the capability to recover data should be built into the design. During the **Development phase**, recovery strategies should be added. During the **Implementation phase**; Contingency processes should be tested and maintained. During the **Operations/Maintenance phase**, Contingency plans should be exercised and maintained. The legacy system should be prepared to function as a backup to the new information system when the information system has reached the **Disposal phase**.

It should be noted that the steps outlined above are generally better suited to the recovery of technology-based operations. The IT aspect of recovery or business continuity planning usually falls under the heading of Disaster Recovery. However, not all business continuity planning is focused on technology.

There are many business functions that do not rely directly on IT, meaning that a disruption in one of these functions cannot be alleviated by any type of hardware or software implementation. One example of this would be the loss of a key researcher in a pharmaceutical company. The reasons behind the loss may be injury, death or even voluntary resignation of the employee. However, if the skill and knowledge supplied by that employee cannot be easily replaced, one or more vital projects may experience delays. The types of controls or backup plans that might be implemented to mitigate the risks in this situation are very different than those applied when IT resources are lost. Other non-IT losses or disruptions might include:

- Loss of reputation: This may occur due to published notifications of hacking, a product recall, a major financial scandal or any other event that causes present or future customers to avoid doing business with the organization.
- Change in economic climate: A competitor may develop a product or service that is far more attractive due to features sets, pricing or quality.
- Change in regulatory climate: Federal, State or local legislators may create laws, including those regarding taxation, environmental issues, etc. that have a major impact on the way the organization operates.

It has been stated previously that IS/IT audit professionals should be risk and control experts. In the examples given above, an IT auditor reviewing the documentation provided by an organization would attempt to identify critical processes and key or critical personnel. In addition, if the auditor performs reviews of the organization's business and regulatory environment as discussed in chapter 1, then it is possible that one or more issues that could create problems for the organization would be detected early. Hopefully, the auditor will be able to spot any serious omissions in the organization's BCP/DR planning and suggest appropriate methods to remediate the problems.

Develop Contingency Planning Policy Statement

When developing an IT contingency plan, the first step is to establish a contingency planning policy within the organization. Organizations are not required to establish contingency or continuity plans. However, if an organization wants to have certified, accredited departments and systems, then it must implement IT contingency plans for those systems and adopt an organizational **Continuity of Operations** (COOP) plan. The statement should define the organization's overall contingency objectives; identify leadership, roles and responsibilities, resource requirements, test, training, and exercise schedules; and develop maintenance schedules and determine the minimum required backup frequency.

The Business Impact Analysis

A **business impact analysis** (BIA) should be performed prior to the start of business continuity planning. The BIA allows an organization to assess the overall importance and value of each component of its information system. Completing the BIA process also gives the organization the ability to analyze the interdependencies between these components and the potential impact that any downtime might produce. The impact might occur immediately or be something that materializes over time. An adverse impact might be tracked across related resources and dependent systems (e.g., cascading domino effect).

A BIA should address the following issues:
- What people, processes and technology (PPT) are critical to the organization?
- What data assets are critical to normal business operations?
- How long can the organization survive the loss of any of its critical assets before a major loss (financial or otherwise) is certain?

Risk Ranking

Risk ranking is one way that organizations can perform an adequate BIA. Risk ranking involves the prioritization of critical systems according to the time sensitivity and criticality that are necessary for business resumption following a disaster. The identification of critical systems is usually the result of a formal exercise in risk analysis. Another result of this analysis is a determination of **systems tolerance**; that is, a measure of the organization's ability to cope with systems interruption. Tolerance may be expressed as a dollar value, or loss of revenues. Low tolerance is expressed as a high dollar value or cost. Varying levels of tolerance lead into the classification of systems. The risk ranking procedure should be performed in coordination with both information systems processing and end user personnel. A typical risk ranking system may contain the following classifications:

- **Critical:** These functions cannot be performed unless they are replaced by identical capabilities. Critical applications cannot be replaced by manual methods. Tolerance to interruption is very low; therefore, cost of interruption is very high.
- **Vital:** These functions can be performed manually but only for a brief period of time. There is higher tolerance to interruption than with critical systems and therefore, somewhat lower costs of interruption provided that functions are restored within a certain time frame (usually 5 days or less).
- **Sensitive:** These functions can be performed manually, at tolerable cost, for an extended period of time. While they can be performed manually, it usually is a difficult process and requires additional staff to perform.
- **Non-Critical:** These functions may be interrupted for an extended period of time, at little or no cost to the company and require little or no catching up when restored.

Once the BIA has been completed, the organization can prioritize the steps prescribed during a recovery effort. The priority assigned to each resource will be determined based on the length of time the organization can function without the resource. The period of time that the organization can reasonably function without the resource is called the **maximum allowable outage** (MAO). From the perspective of those that would have to perform the actual recovery effort, this time period is also known as the RTO (Recovery Time Objective).

Recovery Point Objective and Recovery Time Objective

The RPO (Recovery Point Objective) and RTO are metrics used to help managers and IT implementers properly evaluate and select recovery methods and technologies. The RPO is primarily concerned with:
- The flow of data or number of transactions occurring within a given time frame
- A specific period of time just prior to a disruptive event

RPO is a measure of the amount of data or transactions that might normally flow or occur over a given time period during normal business processing. In practice, data or process owners should determine what amount of data (based on a time measurement) that could be lost without hampering recovery efforts.

For example, if a particular application can manage the loss of three hours worth of data due to transaction logging or some similar functionality, then backups need to be scheduled so that the end of last valid set of data to be backed up would have been saved sometime within three hours prior to any possible disruption. If the end of the last backup somehow took place four hours prior to such an event, that one hour gap between the RPO and the actual data available for recovery could be costly to the organization.

The RTO is a measurement that is only concerned with the time immediately following a disruptive event. This time calculation is an estimate of how long the organization can survive without access to its critical IT functions before a major loss of some kind occurs. Many graphical representations of these two concepts utilize a variation of a number line to show the key points in time in a very simple way.

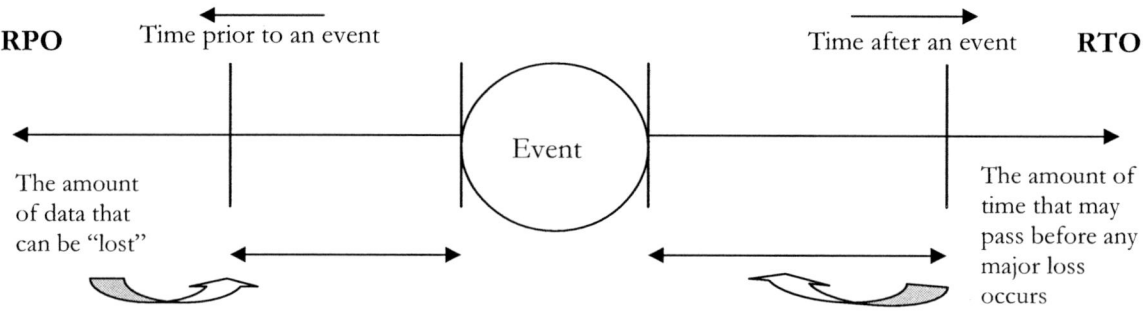

Other Important Metrics

The following represent additional estimates that may be of interest to planners of business continuity or disaster recovery efforts:

Interruption Window: This is the amount of time between the disruption and the restoration of some level of service at an alternate site.
Maximum Tolerable Outage: The amount of time an organization can function using a backup site.
Service Delivery Objective: This is the minimum level of functionality or processing that the backup site should provide to enable the organization to survive. If the backup site cannot sustain this level until regular processing is restored or this level is too low for some other reason, the organization could suffer major losses in spite of the presence of the backup site.
Critical Recovery Time Period: is that window of time in which business processing must be resumed before the suffering significant or unrecoverable losses (Synonymous with RTO).

Develop an IT contingency plan.
The contingency plan should contain detailed guidance and procedures for restoring a damaged system. The plan contains the roles, responsibilities, teams, and procedures associated with restoring the IT system following a disruption. The contingency plan should document the technical capabilities needed to support contingency operations. A generic contingency plan will not be effective; contingency plans should be tailored to each organization and its requirements. The plan devised needs to balance detail with flexibility; usually the more detailed the plan is, the less scalable and versatile the approach. Templates, forms and checklists regarding BCP can be very helpful. They may enable the BCP project team to ensure that they basics are not overlooked. However, any guide or template has to be modified using specific information from the BIA. The combination of the general to-do lists plus the specific needs of the organization into a single new document would give the organization a viable place to begin planning. The table below contains a list of different BCP approaches.

Types of Contingency Plans

Plan	Purpose	Scope
Business Continuity Plan (BCP)	Provide procedures for sustaining essential business operations while recovering from a significant disruption	Addresses business processes; IT addressed based only on its support for business process
Business Recovery (or Resumption) Plan (BRP)	Provide procedures for recovering business operations immediately following a disaster	Addresses business processes; not IT-focused; IT addressed based only on its support for business process
Continuity of Operations Plan (COOP)	Provide procedures and capabilities to sustain an organization's essential, strategic functions at an alternate site for up to 30 days	Addresses the subset of an organization's missions that are deemed most critical; usually written at headquarters level; not IT-focused
Continuity of Support Plan/IT Contingency Plan	Provide procedures and capabilities for recovering a major application or general support system	Same as IT contingency plan; addresses IT system disruptions; not business process focused
Crisis Communications Plan	Provides procedures for disseminating status reports to personnel and the public	Addresses communications with personnel and the public; not IT focused
Cyber Incident Response Plan	Provide strategies to detect, respond to, and limit consequences of malicious cyber incident	Focuses on information security responses to incidents affecting systems and/or networks
Disaster Recovery Plan (DRP)	Provide detailed procedures to facilitate recovery of capabilities at an alternate site	Often IT-focused; limited to major disruptions with long-term effects
Occupant Emergency Plan (OEP)	Provide coordinated procedures for minimizing loss of life or injury and protecting property damage in response to a physical threat	Focuses on personnel and property particular to the specific facility; not business process or IT system functionality based

Varying Levels of Disaster

Many disruptions in service or business operations do not qualify as disasters. Therefore, a well-defined classification system must be in effect so that a decision to initialize business continuity efforts might be made in a timely manner, if it is necessary at all.

- **Non-Disasters:** Sometimes disruption in service stems from system malfunctions or other failures. Action is required to recover operational status in order to resume service that may necessitate restoration of hardware, software or data files. There is a relatively short period of downtime.
- **Disasters:** Disasters are disruptions causing the entire facility to be inoperative for a lengthy period of time, usually more than one day. They require action to recover operational status, usually through the use of an alternate processing facility. Restoration of software and data files from off-site copies may be required. It is necessary that the alternate facility be available until the original information processing facility is restored.
- **Catastrophes:** Catastrophes are major disruptions resulting from the destruction of the processing facility. Short-term and long-term fallback strategies are required. An alternate processing facility is needed to satisfy immediate operational needs, as in the case of a disaster. In addition, a new, permanent facility must be identified and equipped to provide for continuation of information systems processing service on a regular basis.

Alternate/Backup Processing Facilities

If a disaster or catastrophe occurs, the organization's main processing area could be severely damages or completely destroyed. The following types of arrangements for backup facilities are commonly used:

- **Hot Sites**
    - This type of site is one of the more expensive types of backup facility. All necessary equipment is present, tested and ready for the installation of software and data as soon as the recovery team arrives. The increased costs usually come from two sets of fees:
        - The rental of the space used to keep all of the equipment at full readiness.
        - The additional costs associated with going live at the new site, including power, network access, any special daily or hourly fees for live processing, etc.
    - In general, the costs associated with this type of backup can only be justified by the potential losses that might occur from the loss of the most critical of processes, such as the e-commerce site of an online-only vendor. Since the costs associated with the use of maintenance of a hot site are so high, many organizations cannot maintain the site in an operational status for extended periods. This type of arrangement is usually made only to limit losses while a cheaper, long-term, solution such as a cold site, is prepared.

- **Warm Sites**
    - These sites have some equipment including one or more computers, network connections, drives to accept backup media such as tapes or optical disks all ready installed and ready to accept the loading of software, backup data or both. It is possible that additional computers may be needed to allow full functionality for the site. In theory, money can be saved by acquiring any other necessary devices or computers only when they are needed. This adds to the recovery time, but costs less to maintain than a hot site.

- **Cold Sites**
    - These sites have the bare minimum setup required to allow backup equipment to function. This would include only power and environmental concerns (raised floors, air conditioning/humidity controls access to wiring, etc.) A cold site usually has no computers, software or other IT resources available, but it is completely ready to accept equipment when delivered. This type of arrangement is the least expensive, but it takes much longer to bring up to a functional state than the other methods.

- **Duplicate Information Processing Facility**
    - These are dedicated, self-developed recovery sites that can backup critical applications. They can range in form from a standby hot site to a reciprocal agreement with another company installation. The assumption is that there are fewer problems in coordinating compatibility and availability in the case of duplicate information processing facility sites. However, larger organizations may experience problems similar to those encountered by reciprocal agreements between unrelated companies. This is particularly true whenever departmental or divisional information processing facilities are managed separately or when hostilities exist between in-house employee groups. Several principles must be in place in order to ensure the viability of this approach:

        - **The hardware and software recovery strategies must be a well coordinated**. A reasonable degree of compatibility must exist to serve as a basis for backup.
        - **Resource availability must be assured**. The workloads of the sites must be monitored to ensure that availability for emergency backup use would not be impaired.
        - **Regular testing is necessary**. Even though duplicate sites are under common ownership and even if the sites are under the same management, testing of the backup operation is necessary.

- **Reciprocal Agreements**
    - Reciprocal Agreements are agreements between two or more organizations with similar equipment or applications. Under the typical agreement, participants promise to provide time to each other when an emergency arises.

    - Advantages
        - Low cost
        - May be the only option available because of unavailable hot sites due to unique vendor equipment

    - Disadvantages
        - Agreements may be difficult to enforce, especially when one party needs to restore operations ASAP
        - Updates to software or hardware may be difficult to implement.
        - Implementing a regular schedule for testing of the plan at the site of another organization may be difficult.
        - Contracts require very specific language and understanding (a meeting of the minds) to improve the odds of enforcement. Regular changes to one or more aspects of a contract can invalidate contract provisions, endangering the organization that might need the use of a facility.

    - Managers and Auditors need to be aware that reciprocal agreements require the same level of effort and care as any other outsourcing agreement. Given the critical nature of the outsourced service, (a backup processing site) the vendor or third party should be researched thoroughly and audited regularly. Some of the audit concerns might be:

- Security for any equipment, software and data stored at the site.
- Confidentiality (VPN or other secure methods) for transactions or other communication types if the site must go live.
- Exact specifications of equipment, space, power, networking, environmental conditions, etc.
- Contact lists for emergency access and onsite support options
- Additional fees, conditions and other concerns related to going live
- What options are available for the amount of time that the backup site can remain operational
- Specific contract language should address:
    - The circumstances that validate allowing the backup site to go live
    - The maximum amount of time allowed for the third party's personnel to respond to requests for physical access to the backup facility, equipment support, network connectivity, etc.
    - Limitations on the number of other organizations/subscribers that may share space at the same site in case of a large scale catastrophe.
    - SLAs regarding: equipment types, software types and versions, preference lists for access to space at the site, redundancy, reliability, sufficiency of network bandwidth and power allocated to the organization's equipment
    - Insurance, Certifications and Warranties maintained by the third party vendor.

The table below offers a side-by-side comparison of the various plans' strengths and weaknesses. This listings in the table have been prioritized by the cost of the arrangements:

Site	Cost	Hardware Equipment	Telecommunications	Setup Time	Location
Reciprocal Agreement	Zero	None	None	Long	Fixed
Cold Site	Low	None	None	Long	Fixed
Warm Site	Medium	Partial	Partial/Full	Medium	Fixed
Hot Site	Medium/High	Full	Full	Short	Fixed
Mobile Site	High	Dependent	Dependent	Dependent	Not Fixed
Mirrored	High	Full	Full	None	Fixed

Preventive controls

Whenever possible, it is preferable to avoid the need to utilize any type of alternate processing facility. Therefore, it is recommended that BC/DR planning include preventive, detective and corrective measures that may be employed by trained staff. These measures may limit the adverse effects of some types of disruption. If the consequences of some events, such as fires and floods can be offset by planning, training and testing of corrective or other emergency measures, then it may be possible for an organization to avoid the need to use a backup site.

As an example, planning to limit the effects of a flood might include:
- Locating critical IT equipment on the third floor or higher in the primary facility
- Purchasing and testing the use of industrial-size UPS devices and gas powered generators at the same level as the IT equipment.
- Ensuring that an alternate and secure means for communications (possibly satellite or point-to-point microwave) exists
- Scheduling regular tests of evacuation and other contingency plans and rotating the personnel involved in these tests to obtain a larger group of capable staff.

The following list includes other possible preparations:
- Installation of smoke, fire and water sensors in key areas around critical equipment and work locations
- Fire, water and heat-resistant storage for important documents, backup media, etc.
- Waterproof coverings installed in areas where critical equipment is located
- Temperature and humidity control equipment that can function on backup power and whose effects can be isolated to critical areas of the facility if necessary.
- Water pumps and fire suppression systems

Development of Recovery Strategies

It is responsibility of management and the board of directors to provide plans for the continuation of operations in the event of any disaster. Risk management is a key part of this effort, as is the use of a project management approach to the planning, implementation and testing of any strategies developed. Any audit of a BCP/DR plan should include a review of the methodologies used by management in the creation of the plan.

The Risk Assessment Process

The risk assessment process was discussed at length in chapters 1 and 2. However, the nature of the planning effort for the BCP/DR warrants a review of the basic steps:
- Physical Inventory
- Naming conventions/classifications for all data and other resources (Data and process owners)
- Value assessment (Data and process owners)
- Vulnerability assessment
- Threat Assessment
- Risk Evaluation: Use of qualitative and/or quantitative methods and assignment of risk rating

As stated earlier in the description of the BIA, management must identify the critical processes and the equipment, applications and data needed to allow those processes to continue. If a thorough risk assessment has been performed recently within the organization, then the majority of this work has already been done. The risk assessment process actually requires the same type of information, but this information is used for a different purpose.

Assuming the information is current, the results of each of the basic steps of the risk assessment process may be used to facilitate the BCP/DR planning effort. In particular, the outputs of the risk assessment process may be safely reused to complete the BIA. This allows the organization to save time and effort retracing the steps all ready taken. The new emphasis for the BIA will require the following changes in perspective on the steps listed above:
- The most critical processes in the organization should have all ready received the highest ranking in the "Value Assessment" step.
- The exact locations of the equipment and data used by these processes would have been identified in the Physical Inventory
- A consistent approach to the naming and logical security of the equipment, applications and data should have been applied during and after the "Naming Conventions" step
- Any known vulnerabilities and threats should have been identified during the Vulnerability and Threat Assessments. The issues identified in these steps may also need to be addressed by the management of the backup facility in order to ensure secure processing for the organization's data.

An adequate BCP/DR effort will require more planning. However, the possibility that the process could be expedited by the reuse of the risk-related data should be explored by those in charge of the project.

Development of a Contingency Plan

The use of the PPT (People, Processes and Technology) framework is one way that planning can be organized. If some disruptive event causes the loss of its primary processing facility, the organization must ensure that some group of people is available to set up and restore processing capability at another location. This setup will include the hardware, software and data necessary to achieve the minimum amount of processing needed to keep the organization functional.

The BIA should have provided very concrete results about all of the people and items required. In addition, the BIA will produce time-related metrics concerning the amount of data that may be lost and the amount of time that all processing can be offline before serious consequences occur. Management must choose a plan that will allow it to meet all of the requirements stated within the time periods supplied. The following is an abbreviated list of the various items or activities that management must be able to duplicate at one or more alternate sites:

- Equipment:
    - Servers and workstations
    - Backup devices/Readers for backup media
    - Specialized security, load balancing, clustering and any other "appliance" type devices
    - Networking devices
    - Phones, faxes or other communications devices
- Software:
    - Any applications, operating system software and utilities needed to run the equipment selected
- Data:
    - Any needed backup/archived data must be available to the recovery team in some form. The possibilities include:
    - Physical backup media obtained from another offsite storage location or from media in use at the backup site.
    - Network/Internet connection to an offsite backup provider
- Documentation
    - Records, instructions and workflows for the employees that must continue the processing operations once the backup site is operational
    - Contact lists for high-level organization staff
    - Contact lists for alternate processing personnel. It should not be assumed that the recovery team will also be able to handle all of the steps related to processing. If the backup site in question is focused on the IT component of the BCP, then services such as Customer Support, Shipping, Payroll and others will almost certainly need to be performed at another location. Contact with these parties will have to be established via a VPN or other secure means.
    - Recovery procedures or scripts to be used by the recovery team
    - Emergency chain of command information
    - Contact lists, contract info, SLAs applicable to the supplier of the backup site
- Communications and Environment
    - Power
    - Network/Internet Connectivity
    - Temperature and Humidity controls
    - Security measures, including control of physical access to the organization's contracted processing area

Acquisition of Equipment

It is accurate to say that the type of facility arrangement selected (duplicate, hot, warm, etc) has much to do with the choice of equipment to be stored at the site and the manner in which this equipment will be obtained. Since cost savings is always a priority, some organizations wait until the last minute to purchase needed equipment. The availability of the Internet, a wide selection of vendors and the possibility of overnight delivery (at an extra cost), make the decision to delay purchasing even more attractive. The following describes some equipment provisioning options:

Advance purchase: This method works well with those arrangements that require all or some of the equipment to be ready at the site, such as Duplicate Information Processing Facilities, hot and warm sites. An advantage to having the equipment placed in advance is that there is less setup time needed to reach operational status. A disadvantage is that once purchased and placed, it is likely that this equipment will simply sit unused and unproductive unless the backup site must be brought online.

Off the shelf: This works best with sites such as warm or cold sites that may allow longer delays before operational status is achieved. One or more recovery team members simply makes the purchase of the needed equipment from whichever store or vendor meets some pre-established criteria for price and functionality. A disadvantage may be that the cost of a retail purchase is usually higher than that of a purchase made via a purchase order (PO) from an approved vendor.

Third-party vendor: This is very similar to the "off the shelf" method above. However, it adds the disadvantage of being the slowest of the acquisition types because an approved vendor is used. This may lower costs, but also increase the time necessary for actual delivery of the items. In general, this type of acquisition is only suited for cold sites, which may have a window of one week or more for full operational status to be achieved.

Other concerns

It should also be noted that the criticality of the processes to be replaced should have been factored into the decision regarding the type of facility to contract. If vital processing needs must be delayed while the recovery team waits for one or more crucial pieces of equipment, the organization may suffer unnecessary losses. It is also possible to use the methods listed above for software purchases.

Documentation

The BCP/DR planning process should be thoroughly and carefully documented. Clear and accurate documentation can facilitate recovery efforts in a time of crisis that maybe affecting the business and the personal lives of those employees that live nearby and may be directly affected by the same event that disrupted the business. The following types of documentation should be kept and updated regularly:

- Contact lists that include the names and phone numbers of equipment vendors, facility employees, organizational and managerial contacts, insurance providers and recovery team members.
- Test plan results
- Recovery procedures, including any checklists and scripts
- Usernames and passwords (if the usernames and passwords at a backup site are never used until a disruption, administrators and other recovery personnel may not have memorized them
- Procedures for end users at any other locations
- Copies of any contracts and SLAs established with the provider of the backup facility
- Any other important documents including emergency credit cards, equipment, software and data lists and instructions for operating or security procedures.
- Continuity plans for support, processing and other end user operations (COOP – Continuity of operations)
- Locations of any other alternate facilities that may be used by end users, shipping or other organizational functions.

It is likely that some documentation will include sensitive material. Care should be taken when selecting the staff members that will do the initial contacts or callout of staff members for a recovery effort. If the effects of a disruptive event are spread over a large geographic area, one or more staff members may not respond to a callout. Therefore, updated copies of planning material that include the procedures, passwords must be in the possession of several staff members at all times. Hopefully, this will ensure that at least one copy of the entire plan is available if the effects of a disaster or catastrophe are widespread.

Testing of BCP/DR plans

After the site has been acquired and any equipment has been placed, the recovery plans must be tested. The type of tests that can be run at the backup site depend on the nature of the site. For example, it is possible to schedule any type of testing at a duplicate processing facility, since everything is always live there. On the other hand, a cold site has no equipment in place. Therefore, any testing of that plan must be done:

- Without the use of the equipment, or
- At the primary location in a test bed designed for this type of test or on production equipment.

If possible, tests of the entire plan should be done on an annual basis at a minimum. Costs of testing and the nature of the facilities chosen are factors that affect the frequency and extent of testing. The following are types of tests that may be run against a BCP/DR plan:

- Full Operational Test: As the name implies, this test is the most comprehensive. The test is run at the backup site, on the backup equipment with the assumption that a real disruption has taken place. This kind of testing is not suited for use at cold or warm sites or any arrangement where days or weeks must pass before operational status may be achieved (Functional testing)
- Preparedness Test: This test type is normally done locally, at the primary facility. Production or carefully configured test equipment is used in the simulation of a disaster. The test may be run against the entire plan or against one or more segments of the plan. (Functional testing)
- Paper test: This is a walkthrough of the plan performed without equipment. In practice, it is very similar to a brainstorming session. Key personnel meet and discuss the plan, and come up with various problems and scenarios that should be tested. This kind of test can be done against the entire plan or any part of the plan at any time (Classroom testing)

Testing may be divided into three basic phases which are:

- Pre-test: This phase includes everything that must be done to set up an area for the particular type of test that will be run.
- Test: Depending on the nature of the test chosen, this will include simulations of processing, phone calls, equipment and software installation and configuration and any other activities relevant to that test type.
- Post-test: This phase includes a review or post-mortem of the test, including grading or evaluation of the actions performed. This pahse also includes any cleanup activities such as wiping hard drives of sensitive data, replacing equipment and allowing personnel to return to their regular duties.

Plan Updates and Evaluation

BCP/DR plans may require periodic updates for the following reasons:

- Changes to the hardware or software used at the primary site
- Changes to the processes considered critical to the organization
- Changes in the staffing and funding levels at the business
- Test results show that certain procedures cannot work as expected

In order to ensure that the plan is adequate for the needs of the business, regular reviews of the business' operations should be performed. Any changes that warrant a review of the BCP plan should be noted and additional risk assessments performed as needed. Since the testing of the plan can highlight problems in the plan or in the equipment, software or facilities used in the test, those that evaluate the plan should be able to analyze the test results carefully and provide meaningful results to the coordinator of the plan or any group of personnel designated to oversee the development of the plan. Any proposed changes to the BCP/DR plan should be subject to an established change management process.

Any test performed should have a well-defined scope and clear objectives. Any metrics used should be decided upon in advance if possible to ensure that methods for the capture and recording of the necessary data can be implemented during the pre-test phase. The ability of the plan's coordinator, other management personnel or an auditor to make accurate assessments regarding the effectiveness of the plan depends heavily on careful planning before the test is conducted.

Recovery Teams

As shown below, ISACA lists over a dozen possible teams that might be created to take part in a recovery effort[1]. The number of teams, team types and staffing levels of each team are management decisions. Organizations are not required to set up, train and run tests with all of the types of teams listed below. However, the responsibilities listed for each type of team may be quite useful to plan implementers. These descriptions may function as a guide and help those that create the plans to ensure that important tasks are handled by some group of people, if not a team devoted to that purpose alone.

- **Emergency Action Team:** This is the first response team. They are the designated fire wardens and "bucket crew" whose function is to deal with fires or other emergency response scenarios. Their primary responsibility is the orderly evacuation of personnel and the securing of human life.

- **Damage Assessment Team:** The function of this team is to assess the extent of damage following the disaster. The team should be comprised of individuals who have the ability to assess damage and estimate the time required to recover operations at the affected site. This team should include staff skilled in the use of testing equipment, knowledgeable about systems and networks and trained in applicable safety regulations and procedures. In addition, they have the responsibility of identifying possible causes of the disaster and its impact on damage and predictable downtime.

- **Emergency Management Team:** This group is responsible for coordinating the activities of all other recovery teams and handles key decision-making. They determine activation of the business continuity plan. Other functions entail arranging the finances of the recovery, handling legal matters evolving from the disaster and handling public relations and media inquiries. This team functions as "disaster overseers" and therefore, is required to coordinate the following activities:
    - Retrieving critical and vital data from off-site storage
    - Installing and testing systems software and applications at the systems recovery site (hot site, cold site, service bureau, etc.)
    - Identifying, purchasing and installing hardware at the system recovery site
    - Operating from the system recovery site
    - Rerouting network communications traffic
    - Reestablishing the user/system network
    - Transporting users to the recovery facility
    - Reconstructing databases
    - Supplying necessary office goods, i.e., special forms, checks, stock, paper, etc.
    - Coordinating systems use and employee work schedules

- **Off-Site Storage Team:** Responsible for obtaining, packaging and shipping media and records to the recovery facilities as well as establishing and overseeing an off-site storage schedule for information created during operations at the recovery site.

- **Software Team:** Responsible for restoring system packs, loading and testing operating systems software and resolving system level problems.

- **Administrative Support Team:** This team provides clerical support to the other teams and serves as a message center for the user recovery site. They may control accounting and payroll functions as well as on-going facilities management.

- **Supplies Team:** This team supports the efforts of the user hardware team by contacting vendors and coordinating logistics for an on-going supply of necessary office and computer supplies.

- **Communications Team:** This team travels to the recovery site where they work in conjunction with the remote network recovery team to establish a user/system network. Also responsible for soliciting and installing communications hardware at the recovery site and working with local exchange carriers and gateway vendors in the rerouting of local service and gateway access.

- **Transportation Team:** This team serves as a facilities team to locate a recovery site if one has not been predetermined and is responsible for coordinating the transport of company employees to a distant recovery site. They also may assist in contacting employees to inform them of new work locations and scheduling and arranging employee lodgings.

- **Applications Team:** Travels to the system recovery site and restores user packs and application programs on the backup system. As the recovery progresses, this team may have the responsibility of monitoring application performance and database integrity.

- **Security Team:** Continually monitors the security of system and communication links, also resolves any security conflicts that impede the expeditious recovery of the system. They may also assure the proper installation and functioning of any necessary security hardware or software packages.

- **Emergency Operations Team:** This team consists of shift operators and shift supervisors who will reside at the systems recovery site and manage system operations during the entirety of the disaster and recovery projects. Another responsibility might detail coordinating hardware installation if a hot site or other equipment-ready facility has not been designated as the recovery center.

- **Network Recovery Team:** This team is responsible for rerouting wide area voice and data communications traffic and reestablishing host network control and access at the system recovery site. Provides on-going support for data communications and oversees communications integrity.

- **Transportation Team:** This team serves as a facilities team to locate a recovery site if one has not been predetermined and is responsible for coordinating the transport of company employees to a distant recovery site. They also may assist in contacting employees to inform them of new work locations and scheduling and arranging employee lodgings.

- **User Hardware Team:** This team locates and coordinates the delivery and installation of user terminals, printers, typewriters, photocopiers and other necessary equipment. Offers support to the communications team and to any hardware and facilities salvage efforts.

- **Data Preparation and Records Team:** This team updates the applications database working from terminals installed at the user recovery site. Oversees contract data-entry personnel and assists record salvage efforts in acquiring primary documents and other input information sources.

- **Salvage Team:** This team manages the relocation project. They make a more detailed assessment of the damage to the facilities and equipment at some point the initial assessment has been completed. They provide the emergency management team with the information required to determine whether planning should be directed toward reconstruction or relocation. Provides information necessary for filing insurance claims (insurance is the primary source of funding for the recovery efforts). They coordinate the efforts necessary for immediate records salvage, such as restoring paper documents, electronic media, etc.

- **Relocation Team:** This team coordinates the process of moving from the hot site to a new location or to the restored original location. This involves relocating the information systems processing operations, communications traffic and user operations. This team also monitors the transition to normal service levels.

Crisis Management

It is the responsibility of management to provide leadership in the event of an emergency. The Emergency Management Team mentioned above should get its mandate from executives and the board of directors. Ultimately, the survival of the firm will relay in part upon its ability to respond appropriately to events that take place during a crisis. Therefore, part of the BC process is advance planning regarding:

- Creation of policy regarding the goals and objectives of the company if it should become subject to a disastrous event.
- The delegation of authority to appropriate personnel
- Creation of an emergency command structure
- Design of redundancy into any command structures that are created
- Training and testing of these personnel in BC/DR scenarios

Training

Testing of a plan can also reveal areas that need improvement within the skills sets of the staff members that must implement the plan. Both speed and accuracy in execution are important in these tests. In general, management should consider training as many staff members as possible to participate in BCP/DR testing. In the event of a real disaster, the effects of the problem may be so widespread that some recovery team members cannot get to their assigned emergency locations. In such a case, the contact lists utilized by the first responders to the event should include second tier and possibly third tier backup personnel. This will enable the company to ensure that all key functions are properly staffed.

The types and extent of training required are controlled by the same sets of variables that govern the testing. These include:
- The nature of the backup facility chosen
- The types of equipment, software, etc. that needs to be installed and configured
- The types of non-IT related work that needs to be done, such as customer support, shipping, etc.

Whenever feasible, staff members should receive training in multiple areas of the continuity/recovery effort. This cross-training will allow the coordinator of the recovery effort to reassign staff to different locations as needed to provide adequate coverage for all essential business functions. In the event that a disaster affects a large geographic area, it is likely that a significant percentage of the staff available to report for work will be unable to do so because they have been directly affected by the same disaster that rendered the primary facility unusable.

It will be more expensive to provide the training for many employees. The costs are primarily due to lost work time and may be summarized as follows:
- Employees are being paid to attend training for their primary recovery roles instead of performing their regular duties.
- The same set of employees must also attend cross-training in one or more other areas so they can function in those capacities as well. Again, the employees are not performing their regular duties.
- Employees must now take part in different training scenarios throughout the year and demonstrate their performance in each of the roles they were trained for. They cannot perform their regular duties while taking part in these tests.

ISACA has also identified a core set of functions that should be restored in the event of a disaster. Their list is shown below.
- **Emergency Action** - Procedures for reacting to crises, ranging from Halon activation procedures to emergency evacuations
- **Notification** - Procedures for notifying relevant managers in the event of a disaster. A contact list of home and emergency telephone numbers is typically provided.
- **Disaster Declaration** - Procedures pertaining to the assessment of damage following a disaster, criteria for determining whether the situation is a disaster and procedures for declaring a disaster and invoking the plan
- **Systems Recovery** - Procedures to be followed to restore critical and vital systems at emergency service levels within a specified time frame in accordance with the systems recovery strategy defined in the plan
- **Network Recovery** - Procedures to reinstate voice and data communications at emergency service levels within a specified time in accordance with the network recovery strategy defined in the plan
- **User Recovery** - Procedures for recovering critical and vital user functions within a specified time frame in accordance with the planned strategy. This includes the documentation of instructions for processing data manually that might have been previously processed via an automated system. Even if the manual procedure were the standard at one time, knowledge of such should not be assumed. This is especially true as tenured employees who may have once performed manual procedures leave via attrition and manual documentation and forms are destroyed or misplaced.
- **Salvage Operations** - Procedures for salvaging facilities, records and hardware, often including the filing of insurance claims and the determination of the feasibility of reoccupying the disaster site
- **Relocation** - Procedures for relocating emergency operations (system, network and user) to the original or a new facility and their restoration to normal service levels

If the PPT framework is considered unattractive, it may be useful for the BCP/DR coordinator and other planners to focus the design of their plan on these core areas as they related to the unique needs of their organization. Whatever teams are created and whatever skill sets they may possess, it is very likely that they will have to perform one or more of the tasks listed above.

Additional Considerations for Recovery Efforts
There are several areas identified by ISACA as worthy of extended consideration during a recovery effort. These areas include:
- Supply and Data Backups
- Hard Disk Redundancy
- Insurance Coverage
- Telecommunications

Backups
Backup of Required Supplies
All supplies necessary for the continuation of normal business activities should be provided for in the recovery effort. Depending on the recovery facility type chosen, some or all of the supplies may be purchased in advance, off the shelf or acquired through a vendor. If the organization uses special forms in the performance of normal processing, then these should be printed in advance and stored in one or more locations where they might be obtained by staff during the disruptive event. Software licensing is also an issue that should be considered. Precautions should be taken to ensure that any software stored for use during a disaster is authorized for use, especially if the software is some type of server.

Data and Documentation Backups
Backups of data and documentation are vital to any recovery effort. Although it is common to think of documentation as hard copy only, it is often created in word processing or other software, meaning that it exists in digital format prior to the generation of hard copy. Therefore, application data and documentation can be considered for inclusion in a backup scheme. If data relevant to the critical processes is not available, it will not be possible to restore operational status, regardless of how well trained the staff is. Backups should be done on a regular basis and the timing and content of the backups should be dictated by the results of the BIA. The backups available should enable the recovery team to restore data that falls outside of the RPO. Transaction logging should have been enabled, but if the disaster was widespread, it may not be possible to recover all of these logs. In such cases, the data is known as orphan data.

There are several common backup schemes that may be deployed by an organization. In general, the purpose of these schemes is to provide backups of changes in cumulative and/or overlapping methods to allow for greater redundancy and efficiency in backup operations. Backups are usually automated, but they often require media changes or rotation to enable the best overall coverage. The following is a brief list of backup schemes.

- Full Backup: This is a backup of all files regardless of what the last backup was.
- Differential: This is a full backup of all data changed since the last full backup. Depending on when it occurs, it may be more comprehensive than an incremental backup. Often, Differential backups span multiple incremental backups.
- Incremental: This is a backup of the data that has been changed since the last backup, whether the last backup was Full, Differential or Incremental. This backup is usually shorter and faster than a differential type.
- Towers of Hanoi: This is a more comprehensive scheme usually designed to span a week or a month of data backups. Under the umbrella of a Towers of Hanoi scheme, full, incremental and differential backups are scheduled at specific intervals to ensure that both cumulative (incremental) and overlapping (differential) backups are combined with regular full backups. These schemes are more complicated to manage, but they provide the greatest overall assurance that the data needed in backups will be available.

Transaction Logging

Transaction Logging is not strictly a backup scheme. It allows an operating system, database software or other application to recover from abends that may be caused by power outages or other disruptive events. If possible, the contents of these logs should be used to restore the data that was in use when a disruptive event occurred. If this data is added to the data backed up by other means, the organization has a greater chance of recovering everything. If the log files and checkpoint information are mirrored to a remote site in real time, this can help to ensure the availability of this data.

Storage Locations

The data backed up should be stored in a secure facility that is a reasonable distance from the primary site. The objective is to store the backups in a place that is unlikely to be affected by the same event that could cripple the primary site. For the purposes of BCP/DR, offsite backups may be grouped into two categories, manual and automated. The distinction is not in the way the backups are initiated, but in how the data is acquired and restored in case of an emergency.

- Manual backups: Most backups are scheduled to run automatically. In a manual backup scheme, some employee must go to the offsite backup storage facility, submit to a verification process, obtain the correct media and return with that media to the recovery site. This data is then loaded onto the servers via the use of various media readers and backup software or import features built into applications or operating systems.
- Automated backups: This is a newer feature that has been facilitated by higher bandwidth availability and greater coverage of broadband services by telecommunications carriers. In this scenario, the data needed is stored on a hard drive or other media in a facility with high-speed links. When the recovery team has completed all the preliminary steps, it can then contact the remote backup facility, verify identities and initiate a download of the needed data from the backup storage provider. The benefits of this approach are as follows:
  - It allows the organization to store backups at greater distances from the primary site than would be feasible in a manual pickup and delivery scheme.
  - The organization can use the person that would have been assigned to obtain the media to other recovery-related tasks.
  - If the telecommunications links at the recovery site are available before all of the equipment is ready, some of the equipment may be devoted to receiving the download from the remote provider. This allows the team to work on the hardware setup and configuration in parallel with the download of data which should save time.

ISACA has identified the following items as important in determining the frequency of rotation for data/documentation backups:[2]

- Frequency of backup cycle and depth of retention generations must be determined for each data file
- Backup strategy must anticipate failure at any step of the processing cycle
- Master files should be retained at appropriate intervals, such as the end of an updating procedure, to provide synchronization between files and systems
- Transaction files should be presented to coincide with master files, so that a prior generation of a master file can be brought completely up to date to recreate a current master file
- Real-time files require special backup techniques, such as duplicate logging of transactions, use of before and/or after images of master records, time stamping of transactions, communication simulation, etc.
- Database Management Systems (DBMS) require specialized backup, usually provided as an integral feature of the DBMS
- File descriptions need to be maintained so as to coincide with each version of a file that is retained; for DBMS systems this may entail keeping separate versions of data dictionaries
- It may be necessary to secure the license to use certain vendor software at an alternate site; this should be arranged in advance of the need
- Backup for software must include both object code and source code libraries and must include provisions for maintaining program patches on a current basis at all backup locations

Additional Backups

Operating Systems, application software, utility software and others are often purchased and stored on some type of removable media such as CDs and DVDs. Copies of this software must be available to the recovery team. In addition any hard copies of documentation, including contact lists, must be safely stored as well. Fire, heat and waterproof safes, cabinets or lock boxes should be employed for this purpose. The following is a list of some of the documentation that should be available to recovery teams:

- **Operating Procedures** - Application run books, job stream control instructions, operating system manuals and special procedures
- **System and Program Documentation** - Flowcharts, program source code listings, program logic descriptions, special job control language statements, error conditions and other descriptions
- **Special Procedures** - Any procedures or instructions that are out of the ordinary such as exception processing, variations in processing and emergency processing
- **Input Source Documents** - Duplicate copies, photocopies, microfiche, microfilm
- **Output Documents** - Reports or summaries required for the purpose of auditing, historical analysis, performance of vital work, satisfaction of legal requirements, expediting insurance claims
- **Copy of the current business continuity plan**

Hard Drive Redundancy

Hard Drives remain the primary storage media used in servers and workstations. Over the years, their reliability, storage capacity and speed have increased while the price for a gigabyte of storage has decreased. However, hard drives can fail. One technology that allows for the recovery of data written to hard drives is called RAID (Redundant Array of Independent Disks). RAID is usually offered as a combination of hardware controller and software that allow data to be written across multiple hard drives according to different schemes. In general these schemes implement the following four methods:

Disk Striping: In this case, a single stream of data is written across multiple disks. No single disk holds an entire data stream.

Disk Mirroring: With this method, an entire data stream is written to two or more disks simultaneously. The full data stream appears in both locations.

Error Correction: there are several error correction methods available for RAID. They differ in functionality and enable recovery from the failure of a single hard drive in a RAID array.

Nested RAID: In this method, two RAID technologies are combined to obtain the benefits of both.

The following list includes some of the more common RAID implementations:

RAID 0: Disk Striping with no parity information
RAID 1: Disk Mirroring without parity
RAID 3 and RAID 4: Disk Striping with a single disk devoted to storing parity information
RAID 5 and RAID 6: Disk Striping with parity information spread across each disk in the array once or twice, respectively
RAID 0+1: A Striped set is mirrored by another striped set.
RAID 10 (1+0): A striped set is generated form a mirrored set

Exam Tip: The benefits and disadvantages associated with each RAID implementation are fairly intricate and deserve further attention. Candidate may have to describe which RAID implementation offers which features.

Insurance Coverage

As explained in Chapters 1 and 2, risk management is an important area for several reasons. The mitigation of risk involves the organization's attempts to lower risk themselves. The transfer of risk involves the agency employing a third-party at some cost, to accept some or all of the risk. Insurance coverage is a means by which the financial consequences of one or more risks may be transferred to another party, namely an insurance company.

Insurance coverage takes many forms. Insurance may be purchased that is targeted to provide coverage for a given type of risk. ISACA provides the following list of coverage types[3] but auditors and management personnel should also understand that each insurance type is also a risk category.

- **IS Equipment and Facilities** - Provides coverage of physical damage to the information processing facility and owned equipment. (Insurance of leased equipment should be obtained when the lessee is responsible for hazard coverage.) The auditor is cautioned to review these policies since many policies are only obligated to replace non-restorable equipment with "like kind and quality" not necessarily with new equipment by the same vendor as the damaged equipment.

- **Media (software) Reconstruction** - Covers damage to IS media which is the property of the insured and for which the insured may be liable. Insurance is available for on-premises, off-premises or in-transit situations and covers the actual reproduction cost of the property. Consideration in determining the amount of coverage needed are programming costs to reproduce the media damaged, backup expenses and physical replacement of media devices, such as tapes, cartridges, disks, etc.

- **Extra Expense** - Designed to cover the extra costs of continuing operations following damage or destruction at the information processing facility. The amount of extra expense insurance needed is based on the availability and cost of backup facilities and operations. (This insurance should be adequate enough to cover the total cost of the business continuity efforts.)

- **Business Interruption** - Covers the loss of net profits caused by computer media damage. This provides reimbursement for monetary losses resulting from suspension of operations because of physical loss of equipment or media. An example of a situation requiring this type of coverage would be if the information processing facilities were on the sixth floor and the first five floors were burned out, operations would be interrupted even though the information processing facility remained unaffected.

- **Valuable Papers and Records** - Covers actual cash value of valuable papers and records (not defined as media) on the insured's premises against direct physical loss or damage.

- **Errors and Omissions** - Provides legal liability protection in the event that the professional practitioner commits an act, error or omission that results in financial loss to a client. This insurance was originally designed for service bureaus but is now available from several insurance companies for protecting systems analysts, software designers, programmers, consultants and other IS personnel.

- **Fidelity Coverage** - Usually takes the form of bankers blanket bonds, excess fidelity insurance and commercial blanket bonds. This also covers loss from dishonest or fraudulent acts by employees. This type of coverage is prevalent in financial institutions operating their own information processing facility.

- **Media Transportation** - Provides coverage for potential loss or damage to media in transit to off-premises information processing facilities. Transit coverage wording in the policy usually specifies that all documents must be filmed or otherwise copied. When the policy does not specifically state that data be filmed prior to being transported and the work is not filmed, management should obtain from the insurance carrier a letter that specifically describes the carrier's position and coverage in the event data are destroyed.

Telecommunications

Modern telecommunications links may include services such as POTS (Plain Old Telephone Service), ISDN lines (Integrated Services Digital Network), Broadband connections such as DSL/Fractional T-1 variants and even higher speed connections such as T-3 and OC-1 through OC-768 (Optical Carrier). Internet connections must have some type of media whether it is some kind of metal wire, optical fiber cable or even the atmosphere in the case of satellite and microwave connections.

Redundancy of these connections should be implemented at the primary site, but if the primary site is lost, then the redundant links are useless. It is best for planners of BCP/DR efforts to choose backup facility providers that also have redundant telecommunications links. There are 4 basic types of telecommunications links and redundancy. The following list describes each:

- **Alternate Routing:** This method of implementing redundancy requires the use of two or more different telecommunications providers and two or more media types such as Ethernet and Coaxial cable if the local phone company and the local cable company are used.
- **Diverse Routing:** In this method, a single carrier provides multiple links, usually of the same media type, through multiple entry points into a facility. A weakness of the method is that anything that affects the single carrier is likely to disable all of that carrier's links into the facility.
- **Last-Mile Circuit Protection:** This a variation of Alternate Routing that uses several different carriers and/or media types to enable redundancy
- **Long-haul Network Diversity:** This is usually transparent to the end user or organization that benefits from it. It involves agreements between telecommunications carriers to offer routing services to each other in the event that some disturbance in service occurs. It may be possible for a carrier suffering from a loss of service to have its traffic re-routed via another carrier's circuits until the problem is solved.

Disposal or Destruction of PII

Individuals and organizations store data on a wide variety of media. The disposal of these assets can jeopardize the confidentiality of that data. In general, there are three levels of effort or care that may be used in the disposal of data:

- **Clearing:** This level of effort primarily involves:
    - Media that was not used to hold sensitive data
    - Magnetic Media
    - The use of software overwrites as the method of choice

- **Purging:** This level of effort involves:
    - Media that held sensitive data or any media whose contents are in doubt
    - Magnetic Media
    - The use of degaussing tools, drilling holes in hard disks, use of Secure Erase software as methods of choice

- **Destruction:**
    - Media that held sensitive data or any media whose contents are in doubt
    - All non-magnetic media or magnetic media whose contents are so sensitive that destruction is imperative
    - Incineration, shredding pulverizing, bending and breaking, disintegration.

Auditing Business Continuity and Disaster Recovery

Much of what an auditor would need to look for in these arrangements has been discussed in previous chapters. However, for the sake of clarity, several key items will be repeated here.

The Audit Process: Chapter 1 supplies a great deal of information about the audit process including descriptions of the following activities:

- Understand the businesses' goals and objectives
- Reviewing all relevant documentation from the organization.
- Researching the legal and business/industry environments
- Interviewing key personnel
- Verifying the use of appropriate Risk and Project Management techniques in the decision making and implementation processes. Performing reviews of the calculations performed and judgments made.
- Review of the dependencies (peripheral or supporting hardware, software and processes) of the organization's critical processes.
- Reviewing prior audit/test results
- Insurance is mentioned in Chapters 1, 2 and 6.

Chapters 2, 3 and 4 have discussions about the audit of third-party or outsourced products and services. The activities involved here include:

- Review of any and all contractual agreements
- Review and monitoring of SLAs and the service levels at given intervals
- Visits to the third-party provider's site
- Analysis of security, environmental and other relevant processes and controls. This is also covered in Chapter 5
- Survey of past and present client of the provider if possible
- Quality, Performance and Change Management

Finally, chapters 4, 5 and 6 all provide more detailed information about individual technologies that might be worthy of review if the organization uses them. These technologies may include:

- VPNs
- Types and redundancy of telecommunications links
- Logical and physical security controls

The auditor is expected to be able to combine the techniques described in earlier chapters in order to fulfill any review obligations. A review of a BCP/DR plan and implementation is a prime example of the need to synthesize these techniques.

CHAPTER 6 PRACTICE QUESTIONS

1) Which of the following is MOST likely to result from a business process reengineering (BPR) project?
    A. An increased number of people using technology
    B. Significant cost savings, through a reduction in the complexity of information technology
    C. A weaker organizational structures and less accountability
    D. Increased information protection (IP) risk will increase

2) An offsite information processing facility having electrical wiring, air conditioning and flooring, but no computer or communications equipment is a:
    A. cold site.
    B. warm site.
    C. dial-up site.
    D. duplicate processing facility.

3) The MOST significant level of effort for business continuity planning (BCP) generally is required during the:
    A. testing stage.
    B. evaluation stage.
    C. maintenance stage.
    D. early stages of planning.

4) Which of the following is a continuity plan test that uses actual resources to simulate a system crash to cost-effectively obtain evidence about the plan's effectiveness?
    A. Paper test
    B. Post test
    C. Preparedness test
    D. Walk-through

5) An organization having a number of offices across a wide geographical area has developed a disaster recovery plan (DRP). Using actual resources, which of the following is the MOST cost-effective test of the DRP?
    A. Full operational test
    B. Preparedness test
    C. Paper test
    D. Regression test

6) For which of the following applications would rapid recovery be MOST crucial?
    A. Point-of-sale system
    B. Corporate planning
    C. Regulatory reporting
    D. Departmental chargeback

7) During the review of an organization's disaster recovery and business continuity plan, the IS auditor found that a paper test was performed to verify the existence of all necessary procedures and actions within the recovery plan. This is a:
    A. preparedness test.
    E. module test.
    C. full test.
    D. walk-through test.

CHAPTER 6 PRACTICE QUESTIONS (CONT.)

8) While reviewing the business continuity plan of an organization, the IS auditor observed that the organization's data and software files are backed up on a periodic basis. Which characteristic of an effective plan does this demonstrate?
   A. Deterrence
   B. Mitigation
   C. Recovery
   D. Response

9) Which of the following would BEST ensure continuity of a wide area network (WAN) across the organization?
   A. Built-in alternative routing
   B. Full system backup taken daily
   C. A repair contract with a service provider
   D. A duplicate machine alongside each server

10) Which of the following processes is the FIRST step in developing a business continuity and disaster recovery plan for an organization?
   A. Alternate site selection
   B. Business impact analysis
   C. Test procedures and frequency
   D. Information classification

CHAPTER 6 ANSWERS TO PRACTICE QUESTIONS

1) Answer: A

   A BPR project more often leads to an increased number of people using technology, and this would be a cause for concern. As BPR is often technology oriented, and this technology is usually more complex and volatile than in the past, cost savings do not often materialize in this area. There is no reason for IP to conflict with a BPR project, unless the project is not run properly.

2) Answer: A

   A cold site is ready to receive equipment but does not offer any components at the site in advance of the need. A warm site is an offsite backup facility that is configured partially with network connections and selected peripheral equipment, such as disk and tape units, controllers and CPUs, to operate an information processing facility. A duplicate information processing facility is a dedicated, self-developed recovery site that can back up critical applications.

3) Answer: D

   A company in the early stages of a BCP will incur the most significant level of program development effort, which will level out as the BCP moves into maintenance, testing and evaluation stages. It is during the planning stage that an IS auditor will play an important role in obtaining senior management's commitment to resources and assignment of BCP responsibilities.

4) Answer: C

   A preparedness test is a localized version of a full test, wherein resources are expended in the simulation of a system crash. This test is performed regularly on different aspects of the plan and can be a cost-effective way to gradually obtain evidence about the plan's effectiveness. It also provides a means to improve the plan in increments. A paper test is a walkthrough of the plan, involving major players in the plan's execution who attempt to determine what might happen in a particular type of service disruption. A paper test usually precedes the preparedness test. A post-test is actually a test phase and is comprised of a group of activities, such as returning all resources to their proper place, disconnecting equipment, returning personnel and deleting all company data from third party systems. A walk-through is a test involving a simulated disaster situation that tests the preparedness and understanding of management and staff, rather than the actual resources.

5) Answer: A

   A point-of-sale system is a critical online system that when inoperable will jeopardize the ability of a company to generate revenue and track inventory properly.

6) Answer: B

   A preparedness test is performed by each local office/area to test the adequacy of the preparedness of local operations for the disaster recovery. A paper test is a structured walkthrough of the DRP and should be conducted before a preparedness test. A full operational test is conducted after the paper and preparedness test. A regression test is not a DRP test and is used in software maintenance.

CHAPTER 6 ANSWERS TO PRACTICE QUESTIONS (CONT.)

7) Answer: B

An effective business continuity plan includes steps to mitigate the effects of a disaster. Files must be restored on a timely basis for a backup plan to be effective. An example of deterrence is when a plan includes installation of firewalls for information systems. An example of recovery is when a plan includes an organization's hot site to restore normal business operations.

8) Answer: A

Alternative routing would ensure the network would continue if a server is lost or if a link is severed as message rerouting could be automatic. System backup will not afford immediate protection. The repair contract is not as effective as permanent alternative routing. Standby servers will not provide continuity if a link is severed.

10) Answer: B

All four processes are essential for developing the business continuity plan; however, a business impact analysis is the first process. It allows the organization to estimate the potential impact a disaster could have on business operations. Information classification helps to determine the priorities of application recovery, while recovering from a disaster event. Alternate site requirements are decided and the site is selected based on the business impact analysis and recovery priorities. The testing of the plan is done after the above processes are complete.

Glossary

abend	An abnormal end to a computer job; termination of a task prior to its completion because of an error condition that cannot be resolved by recovery facilities while the task is executing
absorbed overhead	(Financial Management) Indirect cost of providing a Service, which can be fairly allocated to specific Customers. This can be based on usage or some other fair measurement. For example cost of providing network bandwidth or shared servers. See also Direct Cost, Indirect Cost, Unabsorbed Overhead.
acceptance	Synonym for Assurance.
access control	The process that limits and controls access to resources of a computer system; a logical or physical control designed to protect against unauthorized entry or use. Access control can be defined by the system (mandatory access control, or MAC) or defined by the user who owns the object (discretionary access control, or DAC).
access control table	An internal computerized table of access rules regarding the levels of computer access permitted to logon IDs and computer terminals
access method	The technique used for selecting records in a file, one at a time, for processing, retrieval or storage. The access method is related to, but distinct from, the file organization that determines how the records are stored.
access path	The logical route an end user takes to access computerized information. Typically, it includes a route through the operating system, telecommunications software, selected application software and the access control system.
access rights	Also called permissions or privileges, these are the rights granted to users by the administrator or supervisor. Access rights determine the actions users can perform (e.g., read, write, execute, create and delete) on files in shared volumes or file shares on the server.
account manager	(Business Relationship Management) A Role that is very similar to Business Relationship Manager, but includes more commercial aspects. Most commonly used when dealing with External Customers.
accountability	The ability to map a given activity or event back to the responsible party
accounting	In the context of ITSM, this is a synonym for IT Accounting.
accounting period	(Financial Management) A period of time for which Budgets, Charges, Depreciation and other financial calculations are made. Usually one year. See Financial Year.
accredited	Officially authorized to carry out a Role. For example an Accredited body may be authorized to provide training or to conduct Audits. See Registered Certification Body (RCB). (Security Management) Official authorization for a Certified Configuration to be used for a specific purpose.
ack (acknowledgement)	A flag set in a packet to indicate to the sender that the previous packet sent was accepted correctly by the receiver without errors, or that the receiver is now ready to accept a transmission
active recovery site (mirrored)	Recovery strategy that involves two active sites, each capable of taking over the other's workload in the event of a disaster. Each site will have enough idle processing power to restore data from the other site and to accommodate the excess workload in the event of a disaster.
active response	A response, in which the system (automatically or in concert with the user) blocks or otherwise affects the progress of a detected attack. The response takes one of three forms—amending the environment, collecting more information or striking back against the user.
activity	A set of actions designed to achieve a particular result. Activities are usually defined as part of Processes or Plans, and are documented in Procedures.

address	The code used to designate the location of a specific piece of data within computer storage
address space	The number of distinct locations that may be referred to with the machine address. For most binary machines, it is equal to 2n, where n is the number of bits in the machine address.
addressing	The method used to identify the location of a participant in a network. Ideally, addressing specifies where the participant is located rather than who they are (name) or how to get there (routing).
adjusting period	The calendar can contain "real" accounting periods and/or adjusting accounting periods. The "real" accounting periods must not overlap, and cannot have any gaps between "real" accounting periods. Adjusting accounting periods can overlap with other accounting periods. For example, a period called DEC-93 can be defined that includes 01-DEC-1993 through 31-DEC-1993. An adjusting period called DEC31-93 can also be defined that includes only one day: 31-DEC-1993 through 31-DEC-1993.
administrative controls	The actions/controls dealing with operational effectiveness, efficiency and adherence to regulations and management policies
agreed service time	(Availability Management) A synonym for Service Hours, commonly used in formal calculations of Availability. See Downtime.
agreement	A Document that describes a formal understanding between two or more parties. An Agreement is not legally binding, unless it forms part of a Contract. See Service Level Agreement, Operational Level Agreement.
alert	A warning that a threshold has been reached, something has changed, or a Failure has occurred. Alerts are often created and managed by System Management tools and are managed by the Event Management Process.
allocation entry	A recurring journal entry used to allocate revenues or costs. For example, an allocation entry could be defined to allocate costs to each department based on headcount.
alpha	The use of alphabetic characters or an alphabetic character string
analog	A transmission signal that varies continuously in amplitude and time and is generated in wave formation. Analog signals are used in telecommunications.
analytical modeling	A technique that uses mathematical models to predict the behavior of a Configuration Item or IT Service. Analytical Models are commonly used in Capacity Management and Availability Management. See Modeling.
anomaly	Unusual or statistically rare
anomaly detection	Detection on the basis of whether the system activity matched that defined as abnormal
anonymity	The quality or state of not being named or identified
anonymous file transfer protocol (ftp)	A method for downloading public files using the File Transfer Protocol (FTP). Anonymous FTP is called anonymous because users do not need to identify themselves before accessing files from a particular server. In general, users enter the word anonymous when the host prompts for a username; anything can be entered for the password, such as the user's e-mail address or simply the word guest. In many cases, an anonymous FTP site will not even prompt users for a name and password.
antivirus software	Applications that detect, prevent and possibly remove all known viruses from files located in a microcomputer hard drive
appearance	The act of giving the idea or impression of being or doing something
appearance of independence	Behavior adequate to meet the situations occurring during audit work (interviews, meetings, reporting, etc.). The IS auditor should be aware that appearance of independence depends upon the perceptions of others and can be influenced by improper actions or associations.
applet	A program written in a portable, platform independent computer language, such as Java. It is usually embedded in an HTML page and then executed by a browser. Applets can only perform a restricted set of operations, thus preventing, or at least minimizing, the possible security compromise of the host computers.

application	A computer program or set of programs that perform the processing of records for a specific function Software that provides functions required by an IT Service. Each Application may be part of more than one IT Service. An Application runs on one or more Servers or Clients. See Application Management, Application Portfolio.
application acquisition review	An evaluation of an application system being acquired or evaluated, which considers such matters as: appropriate controls are designed into the system; the application will process information in a complete, accurate and reliable manner; the application will function as intended; the application will function in compliance with any applicable statutory provisions; the system is acquired in compliance with the established system acquisition process.
application controls	Refer to the transactions and data relating to each computer-based application system and are therefore specific to each such application. The objectives of application controls, which may be manual, or programmed, are to ensure the completeness and accuracy of the records and the validity of the entries made therein resulting from both manual and programmed processing. Examples of application controls include data input validation, agreement of batch totals and encryption of data transmitted.
application development review	An evaluation of an application system under development which considers matters such as: appropriate controls are designed into the system; the application will process information in a complete, accurate and reliable manner; the application will function as intended; the application will function in compliance with any applicable statutory provisions; the system is developed in compliance with the established systems development life cycle process
application implementation review	An evaluation of any part of an implementation project (e.g., project management, test plans, user acceptance testing procedures)
application layer	A layer within the International Organization for Standardization (ISO)/Open Systems Interconnection (OSI) model. It is used in information transfers between users through application programs and other devices. In this layer various protocols are needed. Some of them are specific to certain applications and others are more general for network services.
application maintenance review	An evaluation of any part of a project to perform maintenance on an application system (e.g., project management, test plans, user acceptance testing procedures)
application management	The Process responsible for managing Applications throughout their Lifecycle. See Application Portfolio.
application portfolio	A Database used to manage Applications throughout their Lifecycle. An Application Portfolio contains key Attributes of all Applications deployed in the Business. See Portfolio of Services.
application program	A program that processes actions upon business data, such as data entry, update or query. It contrasts with systems program, such as an operating system or network control program, and with utility programs, such as copy or sort.
application programming	The act or function of developing and maintaining applications programs in production
application programming interface (API)	A set of routines, protocols and tools referred to as "building blocks" used in business application software development. A good API makes it easier to develop a program by providing all the building blocks related to functional characteristics of an operating system, which applications need to specify when, for example, interfacing with an operating system (e.g., provided by MS-Windows, different versions of UNIX). A programmer would utilize these APIs in developing applications that can operate effectively and efficiently on the platform chosen.
application proxy	A proxy service that connects programs running on internal networks to services on exterior networks by creating two connections, one from the requesting client and another to the destination service
application security	Refers to the security aspects supported by the ERP, primarily with regard to the roles or responsibilities and audit trails within the applications

application service provider (ASP)	An External Service Provider that provides IT Services using Applications running at the Service Provider's premises. Users access the Applications by network connections to the Service Provider.
application sizing	(Capacity Management) The Activity responsible for understanding the Resource Requirements needed to support a new Application, or a major Change to an existing Application. Application Sizing helps to ensure that the IT Service can meet its agreed Service Level Targets for Capacity and Performance.
application software tracing and mapping	Specialized tools that can be used to analyze the flow of data, through the processing logic of the application software, and document the logic, paths, control conditions and processing sequences. Both the command language or job control statements and programming language can be analyzed. This technique includes program/system: mapping, tracing, snapshots, parallel simulations and code comparisons.
application system	An integrated set of computer programs designed to serve a particular function that has specific input, processing and output activities (e.g., general ledger, manufacturing resource planning, human resource management)
arithmetic-logic unit (ALU)	The area of the central processing unit that performs mathematical and analytical operations
artificial intelligence	Advanced computer systems that can simulate human capabilities, such as analysis, based on a predetermined set of rules
ASCII	(American Standard Code for Information Interchange) An eight-digit/seven-bit code representing 128 characters; used in most small computers
ASP/MSP (application or managed service provider)	A third party that delivers and manages applications and computer services, including security services to multiple users via the Internet or a private network
assembler	A program that takes as input a program written in assembly language and translates it into machine code or relocatable code
assembly CI	(Configuration Management) A Configuration Item that is made up from a number of other CIs. For example a Server CI may contain CIs for CPUs, Disks, Memory etc.; an IT Service CI may contain many Hardware, Software and other CIs. See Component CI, Build.
assembly language	A low-level computer programming language which uses symbolic code and produces machine instructions
asset	Something that contributes to an IT Service. Assets can include people, accommodation, Servers, software, data, networks, paper Records, telephones etc. Assets that need to be individually managed are also Configuration Items. For example the door lock on a computer room, or a consumable item would not be a Configuration Item. In the context of Financial Management, items below a specific value are not considered to be Assets as it would not be Cost Effective to track and manage them. See Asset Management, Depreciation, Risk Assessment.
asset management	(Financial Management) Asset Management is the Business Process responsible for tracking and reporting the value and ownership of financial Assets throughout their Lifecycle. See Asset Register.
asset register	(Financial Management) A list of Assets, which includes their ownership and value. The Asset Register is maintained by Asset Management.
assurance	The Activity that obtains management agreement that a Process, Plan, or other Deliverable is complete, accurate, reliable and meets its specified Requirements. Assurance is different from Audit, which is more concerned with Compliance to a formal Standard.
asymmetric key (public key)	A cipher technique whereby different cryptographic keys are used to encrypt and decrypt a message (see public key cryptosystems)

asynchronous transfer mode (ATM)	ATM is a high-bandwidth low-delay switching and multiplexing technology. It is a data link layer protocol. This means that it is a protocol-independent transport mechanism. ATM allows integration of real-time voice and video as well as data. ATM allows very high speed data transfer rates at up to 155 Mbit/s.
asynchronous transmission	Character-at-a-time transmission
attest reporting engagement	An engagement where an IS auditor is engaged to either examine management's assertion regarding particular a subject matter or the subject matter directly. The IS auditor's report consists of an opinion on one of the following: * The subject matter. These reports relate directly to the subject matter itself rather than an assertion. In certain situations management will not be able to make an assertion over the subject of the engagement. An example of this situation is when IT services are out-sourced to third party. Management will not ordinarily be able to make an assertion over the controls that the third-party is responsible for. Hence, an IS auditor would have to report directly on the subject matter rather than an assertion * Management's assertion about the effectiveness of the control procedures * Examination reporting engagement where the IS auditor is engaged to issue an opinion on particular subject matter. These engagements can include reports on controls implemented by management and on their operating effectiveness
attitude	Way of thinking, behaving, feeling, etc.
attribute	(Configuration Management) A piece of information about a Configuration Item. Examples are name, location, Version number, and Cost. Attributes of CIs are recorded in the Configuration Management Database (CMDB). See Relationship.
attribute sampling	An audit technique used to select items from a population for audit testing purposes based on selecting all those items that have certain attributes or characteristics (such as all items over a certain size)
audit (definition)	1) The process of generating, recording and reviewing a chronological record of system events to ascertain their accuracy 2) Formal inspection and verification to check whether a Standard or set of Guidelines is being followed, that Records are accurate, or that Efficiency and Effectiveness targets are being met. An Audit may be carried out by internal or external groups. See Certification, Assurance.
audit accountability	Performance measurement of service delivery including cost, timeliness and quality against agreed service levels
audit authority	A statement of the position within the organization, including lines of reporting and the rights of access
audit charter	A document which defines the IS audit function's responsibility, authority and accountability
audit evidence	The information systems auditor (IS auditor) gathers information in the course of performing an IS audit. The information used by the IS auditor to meet audit objectives is referred to as audit evidence (evidence). Also used to describe the level of risk that an auditor is prepared to accept during an audit engagement.
audit expert systems	Expert or decision support systems that can be used to assist IS auditors in the decision-making process by automating the knowledge of experts in the field. This technique includes automated risk analysis, systems software and control objectives software packages.
audit objective	The specific goal(s) of an audit. These often center on substantiating the existence of internal controls to minimize business risk.

audit plan	A high level description of the audit work to be performed in a certain period of time (ordinarily a year). It includes the areas to be audited, the type of work planned, the high level objectives and scope of the work, and topics such as budget, resource allocation, schedule dates, type of report and its intended audience and other general aspects of the work.
audit program	A series of steps to complete an audit objective
audit responsibility	The roles, scope and objectives documented in the service level agreement between management and audit
audit risk	The risk of giving an incorrect audit opinion
audit sampling	The application of audit procedures to less than 100 percent of the items within a population to obtain audit evidence about a particular characteristic of the population
audit trail	A visible trail of evidence enabling one to trace information contained in statements or reports back to the original input source
auditability	The level to which transactions can be traced and audited through a system
authentication	The act of verifying the identity of a system entity (e.g., a user, a system, a network node) and the entity's eligibility to access computerized information. Designed to protect against fraudulent logon activity. Authentication can also refer to the verification of the correctness of a piece of data.
authorized examination center	A body authorized by an Examination Board to host examinations. The Authorized Examination Center provides a place where examinations may be taken, and may also provide exam supervision and automated marking.
authorization	The process of determining what types of activities are permitted. Ordinarily, authorization is in the context of authentication: once you have authenticated a user, he/she may be authorized to perform different types of access or activity
automated teller machine (atm)	A 24-hour, stand-alone mini-bank, located outside branch bank offices or in public places like shopping malls. Through ATMs, clients can make deposits, withdrawals, account inquiries and transfers. Typically, the ATM network is comprised of two spheres: a proprietary sphere, in which the bank manages the transactions of its clients, and the public or shared domain, in which a client of one financial institution can use another's ATMs.
automatic call distribution (ACD)	(Service Desk) Use of Information Technology to direct an incoming telephone call to the most appropriate person in the shortest possible time. ACD is sometimes called Automated Call Distribution.
availability (definition)	1) Availability relates to information being available when required by the business process now and in the future. It also concerns the safeguarding of necessary resources and associated capabilities. (Availability Management) (Security Management) (C-I-A) 2) Ability of a Configuration Item or IT Service to perform its agreed Function when required. Availability is determined by Reliability, Maintainability, Serviceability, Performance, and Security. Availability is usually calculated as a percentage. This calculation is often based on Agreed Service Time and Downtime. It is Best Practice to calculate Availability using measurements of the Business output of the IT Service. See Security Principle.
availability management	(Availability Management) The Process responsible for defining, analyzing, Planning, measuring and improving all aspects of the Availability of IT services. Availability Management is responsible for ensuring that all IT Infrastructure, Processes, Tools, Roles etc are appropriate for the agreed Service Level Targets for Availability.
availability management database (AMDB)	(Availability Management) A Database containing all data needed to support Availability Management. The AMDB may be part of the Configuration Management Database.
availability plan	(Availability Management) A Plan to ensure that existing and future Availability Requirements for IT Services can be provided Cost Effectively.
back-out plan	(Change Management) (Release Management) A Plan that documents the steps required to recover to a known working state if a Change or Release fails.

backup	1) Files, equipment, data and procedures available for use in the event of a failure or loss, if the originals are destroyed or out of service (Availability management) (IT Service Continuity Management) 2) Copying data to protect against loss of Integrity or Availability of the original.
balance check	(Financial Management) A calculation to verify that the sum of all individual Costs or Charges equals the total Cost or Charge. Used to check that all amounts have been fully accounted for.
balanced scorecard	A management tool developed by Drs. Robert Kaplan (Harvard Business School) and David Norton. A Balanced Scorecard enables a Strategy to be broken down into Key Performance Indicators. Performance against the KPIs is used to demonstrate how well the Strategy is being achieved. A Balanced Scorecard has 4 major areas, each of which has a small number of KPIs. The same 4 areas are considered at different levels of detail throughout the Organization.
bandwidth	The range between the highest and lowest transmittable frequencies. It equates to the transmission capacity of an electronic line and is expressed in bytes per second or Hertz (cycles per second).
bar case	A standardized body of data created for testing purposes. Users normally establish the data. Base case validates production application systems and tests the ongoing accurate operation of the system.
bar code	A printed machine-readable code that consists of parallel bars of varied width and spacing
base case	A standardized body of data created for testing purposes. Users normally establish the data. Base cases validate production application systems and test the ongoing accurate operation of the system.
baseband	A form of modulation in which data signals are pulsed directly on the transmission medium without frequency division and usually utilize a transceiver. In baseband the entire bandwidth of the transmission medium (e.g., coaxial cable) is utilized for a single channel.
baseline	The recorded state of something at a specific point in time. A Baseline can be created for a Configuration, a Process, or any other set of data. For example, a baseline can be used in: - Continuous Service Improvement, to establish a starting point for Planning improvements. - Capacity Management, to document performance characteristics during normal operations. - Configuration Management, to enable the IT Infrastructure to be restored to a known configuration if a Change fails. Also used to specify a standard Configuration for data capture, release or Audit purposes.
baseline security	(Security Management) The minimum level of security required throughout an Organization.
batch control	Correctness checks built into data processing systems and applied to batches of input data, particularly in the data preparation stage. There are two main forms of batch controls: 1) sequence control, which involves numbering the records in a batch consecutively so that the presence of each record can be confirmed, and 2) control total, which is a total of the values in selected fields within the transactions.
batch processing	The processing of a group of transactions at the same time. Transactions are collected and processed against the master files at a specified time.
baud rate	The rate of transmission for telecommunication data. It is expressed in bits per second (bps).

benchmark	1) A test that has been designed to evaluate the performance of a system. In a benchmark test, a system is subjected to a known workload and the performance of the system against this workload is measured. Typically, the purpose is to compare the measured performance with that of other systems that have been subject to the same benchmark test. 2) A Baseline used as a reference point. For example: • An ITSM Benchmark can be used to compare one Organization's ITSM Processes with another • A Performance Benchmark may be established by taking measurements of a simulated environment. • See Simulation Modeling.
best practice	A proven Activity or Process that has been successfully used by multiple Organizations. ITIL is an example of Best Practice.
billing	(Financial Management) Part of the Charging Process. Billing is the Activity responsible for producing an invoice or a bill and recovering the money from Customers. See Pricing.
binary code	A code whose representation is limited to 0 and 1
biometric locks	Door and entry locks that are activated by such biometric features as voice, eye retina, fingerprint or signature
biometrics	A security technique that verifies an individual's identity by analyzing a unique physical attribute, such as a handprint
black box testing	A testing approach which focuses on the functionality of the application or product and does not require knowledge of the code intervals.
border router	See external router.
brainstorming	A technique that helps a team to generate ideas. Ideas are not reviewed during the Brainstorming session, but at a later stage. Brainstorming is often used by Problem Management to identify possible causes.
bridge	A device that connects two similar networks together
british standards institution (bsi)	The UK National Standards body, responsible for creating and maintaining British Standards. See http://www.bsi-global.com for more information. See ISO.
broadband	In broadband, multiple channels are formed by dividing the transmission medium into discrete frequency segments. It generally requires the use of a modem.
brouters	Devices that perform the functions of both bridges and routers, are called brouters. Naturally, they operate at both the data link and the network layers. A brouter connects same data link type LAN segments as well as different data link ones, which is a significant advantage. Like a bridge it forwards packets based on the data link layer address to a different network of the same type. Also, whenever required, it processes and forwards messages to a different data link type network based on the network protocol address. When connecting same data link type networks, they are as fast as bridges besides being able to connect different data link type networks.
browser	A computer program that enables the user to retrieve information that has been made publicly available on the Internet; also, that permits multimedia (graphics) applications on the World Wide Web
brute force	The name given to a class of algorithms that repeatedly try all possible combinations until a solution is found
BS 15000	British Standards Institution Specification and Code of Practice for IT Service Management. BS 15000 is based on ITIL Best Practice, and has been superseded by ISO/IEC 20000.
BS 7799	British Standards Institution Specification and Code of Practice for Information Security Management. BS 7799 has been superseded by ISO/IEC 17799 and ISO/IEC 27001.
BSP (business service provider)	An ASP that also provides outsourcing of business processes such as payment processing, sales order processing and application development

budget (definition)	1) (Financial Management) A list of all the money an Organization or Business Unit plans to receive, and plans to pay out, over a specified period of time. 2) Estimated cost and revenue amounts for a given range of periods and set of books. There can be multiple budget versions for the same set of books.
budget formula	A mathematical expression used to calculate budget amounts based on actual results, other budget amounts and statistics. With budget formulas, budgets using complex equations, calculations and allocations can be automatically created.
budget hierarchy	A group of budgets linked together at different levels such that the budgeting authority of a lower-level budget is controlled by an upper-level budget.
budget organization	An entity (department, cost center, division or other group) responsible for entering and maintaining budget data.
budgeting	(Financial Management) The Activity of predicting and controlling the spending of money. Consists of a periodic negotiation cycle to set future Budgets (usually annual) and the day-to-day monitoring and adjusting of current Budgets. See Accounting Period.
buffer	Memory reserved to temporarily hold data. Buffers are used to offset differences between the operating speeds of different devices, such as a printer and a computer. In a program, buffers are reserved areas of RAM that hold data while they are being processed.
build (definition)	1) (Release Management) The Activity of assembling a number of Configuration Items to create part of an IT Service. 2) The term Build is also used to refer to a Release that is authorized for distribution. For example Server Build or laptop Build. See Assembly CI.
build environment	(Release Management) A controlled Environment where Applications, IT Services and other Builds are assembled prior to being moved into a Test or Live Environment.
bulk data transfer	A data recovery strategy that includes a recovery from complete backups that are physically shipped off site once a week. Specifically, logs are batched electronically several times daily, and then loaded into a tape library located at the same facility as the planned recovery.
bus	Common path or channel between hardware devices. It can be between components internal to a computer or between external computers in a communications network.
bus topology	A type of local area network (LAN) architecture in which each station is directly attached to a common communication channel. Signals transmitted over the channel take the form of messages. As each message passes along the channel, each station receives it. Each station then determines, based on an address contained in the message, whether to accept and process the message or simply to ignore it.
business	An overall corporate entity or Organization formed of a number of Business Units. In the context of ITSM, the term Business includes public sector and not-for-profit Organizations, as well as companies. An IT Service Provider provides IT Services to a Customer within a Business. The IT Service Provider may be part of the same Business as their Customer (Internal Service Provider), or part of another Business (External Service Provider).
business capacity management (bcm)	(Capacity Management) In the context of ITSM, Business Capacity Management is the Activity responsible for understanding future Business Requirements for use in the Capacity Plan. See Service Capacity Management.
business case	Justification for a significant item of expenditure. Includes information about Costs, benefits, options, issues, Risks, and possible problems. See Cost Benefit Analysis, Investment Appraisal.
business continuity management (bcm)	(IT Service Continuity Management) Business Continuity Management is the Business Process which sets the Objectives, Scope and Requirements for IT Service Continuity Management. BCM is responsible for managing Risks that could seriously impact the Business. BCM ensures that the Business can always Operate to a minimum agreed level, by reducing the Risk to an acceptable level and Planning to Restore Business Processes.

business continuity plan (BCP)	(IT Service Continuity Management) A Plan defining the steps required to Restore Business Processes following a disruption. The Plan will also identify the triggers for Invocation, people to be involved, communications etc. IT Service Continuity Plans form a significant part of Business Continuity Plans.
business continuity team	(IT Service Continuity Management) The team of people responsible for carrying out Activities defined in a Business Continuity Plan.
business customer	A recipient of a product or a Service from the Business. For example if the Business is a car manufacturer then the Business Customer is someone who buys a car.
business driver	Something that influences the definition of Business Objectives and Strategy. For example new legislation or the actions of competitors. The term Business Driver is sometimes used as a synonym for Business Objective or Strategy.
business impact analysis (BIA)	1) (IT Service Continuity Management) BIA is the Activity in Business Continuity Management that identifies Vital Business Functions and their dependencies. These dependencies may include Suppliers, people, other Business Processes, IT Services etc. BIA defines the recovery requirements for IT Services. These requirements include Recovery Time Objectives, Recovery Point Objectives and minimum Service Level Targets for each IT Service. 2) An exercise that determines the impact of losing the support of any resource to an organization and establishes the escalation of that loss over time, identifies the minimum resources needed to recover and prioritizes the recovery of processes and supporting systems
business alignment or business it alignment (BITA)	Understanding how the IT Service Provider provides value to the Business, and ensuring that IT Strategy, Plans, and Services support the Business Objectives, and Vision. See Service Culture.
business objective	The Objective of a Business Process, or of the Business as a whole. Business Objectives support the Business Vision, provide guidance for the IT Strategy, and are often supported by IT Services.
business operations	The day-to-day execution, monitoring and management of Business Processes. See Operate.
business perspective	An understanding of the Service Provider and IT Services from the point of view of the Business, and an understanding of the Business from the point of view of the Service Provider. See Business IT Alignment.
business process (definition)	A Process that is owned and carried out by the Business. A Business Process contributes to the delivery of a product or Service to a Business Customer. For example, a retailer may have a purchasing Process which helps to deliver Services to their Business Customers. Many Business Processes rely on IT Services. See Vital Business Function, Value Chain.
business process integrity	Controls over the business processes that are supported by the ERP
business process reengineering (BPR)	Modern expression for organizational development stemming from IS/IT impacts. The ultimate goal of BPR is to yield a better performing structure, more responsive to the customer base and market conditions, while yielding material cost savings. To reengineer means to redesign a structure and procedures with intelligence and skills, while being well informed about all of the attendant factors of a given situation, so as to obtain the maximum benefits from mechanization as basic rationale.
business relationship management (BRM)	(Business Relationship Management) The Process responsible for maintaining a Relationship with the Business. This Process usually includes: • Managing personal Relationships with Business managers • Portfolio Management • Ensuring that the IT Service Provider is satisfying the Business needs of the Customers This Process has strong links with Service Level Management. See Account Manager.

business relationship manager	(Business Relationship Management) A Role responsible for maintaining the Relationship with one or more Customers. This Role is often combined with the Service Level Manager Role. See Account Manager.
business risk	Risks that could impact the organization's ability to perform business or provide a service. They can be financial, regulatory or control oriented.
business service	A Service that is delivered to Business Customers by Business Units. For example delivery of financial services to Customers of a bank, or goods to the Customers of a retail store. Successful delivery of Business Services often depends on one or more IT Services.
business unit	A segment of the Business which has its own Plans, Metrics, income and Costs.
business-to-consumer e-commerce (B2C)	Refers to the processes by which Organizations conduct business electronically with their customers and or public at large using the Internet as the enabling technology.
bypass label processing (blp)	A technique of reading a computer file while bypassing the internal file/data set label. This process could result in bypassing of the security access control system.
CAATs	See computer-assisted audit techniques
Cadbury	The Committee on the Financial Aspects of Corporate Governance, set up in May 1991 by the UK Financial Reporting Council, the London Stock Exchange and the UK accountancy profession, was chaired by Sir Adrian Cadbury and produced a report on the subject commonly known, in the UK, as the Cadbury Report.
call	(Service Desk) (Incident Management) A telephone call to the Service Desk from a User. A Call could result in an Incident or a Service Request being logged.
call center	(Service Desk) An Organization or Business Unit which handles large numbers of incoming and outgoing telephone calls. See Service Desk.
call type	(Service Desk) A Category that is used to distinguish incoming requests to a Service Desk. Common call types are Incident, Service Request and Complaint.
capability maturity model (CMM)	The Capability Maturity Model for Software (also known as the CMM and SW-CMM) is a model used to identify Best Practices to help increase Process Maturity. CMM was developed at the Software Engineering Institute (SEI) of Carnegie Mellon University. In 2000, the SW-CMM was upgraded to CMMI® (Capability Maturity Model Integration). The SEI no longer maintains the SW-CMM model, its associated appraisal methods, or training materials.
capability maturity model integration (CMMI)	Capability Maturity Model® Integration (CMMI) is a process improvement approach developed by the Software Engineering Institute (SEI) of Carnegie Melon University. CMMI provides organizations with the essential elements of effective processes. It can be used to guide process improvement across a project, a division, or an entire organization. CMMI helps integrate traditionally separate organizational functions, set process improvement goals and priorities, provide guidance for quality processes, and provide a point of reference for appraising current processes. See http://www.sei.cmu.edu/cmmi/ for more information. See Continuous Improvement, Process Maturity.
Capacity (definition)	(Capacity Management) The maximum Throughput that a Configuration Item or IT Service can deliver whilst meeting agreed Service Level Targets. For some types of CI, Capacity may be the size or volume, for example a disk drive.
capacity management	(Capacity Management) The Process responsible for ensuring that the Capacity of IT Services and the IT Infrastructure is able to deliver agreed Service Level Targets in a Cost Effective and timely manner. Capacity Management considers all Resources required to deliver the IT Service, and plans for short, medium and long term Business Requirements.
capacity management database (CMDB)	(Capacity Management) A Database containing all data needed to support Capacity Management. The Capacity Management Database is usually separate from the Configuration Management Database (CMDB) because it contains large amounts of rapidly changing data.

capacity plan	(Capacity Management) A Capacity Plan is used to manage the Resources required to deliver IT Services. The Plan contains scenarios for different predictions of Business demand, and costed options to deliver the agreed Service Level Targets.
capacity stress testing	Testing an application with large quantities of data to evaluate its performance during peak periods. It also is called volume testing.
capital cost	(Financial Management) The cost of purchasing something that will become a financial Asset, for example computer equipment and buildings. The value of the Asset is Depreciated over multiple Accounting Periods. See Operational Cost
capital expenditure (CAPEX)	Synonym for Capital Cost.
capital item	(Financial Management) Synonym for an Asset that is of interest to Financial Management because it is above an agreed financial value.
capitalization	(Financial Management) Identifying major Cost as Capital, even though no Asset is purchased. This is done to spread the impact of the Cost over multiple Accounting Periods. The most common example of this is software development, or purchase of a software license.
card swipe	A physical control technique that uses a secured card or ID to gain access to a highly sensitive location. Card swipes, if built correctly, act as a preventative control over physical access to those sensitive locations. After a card has been swiped, the application attached to the physical card swipe device logs all card users that try to access the secured location. The card swipe device prevents unauthorized access and logs all attempts to enter the secured location.
category (definition)	A named group of things that have something in common. Categories are used to group similar things together. For example Cost Types are used to group similar types of Cost. Incident Categories are used to group similar types of Incident, CI Types are used to group similar types of Configuration Item.
cathode ray tube (crt)	A vacuum tube that displays data by means of an electron beam striking the screen, which is coated with suitable phosphor material or a device similar to a television screen upon which data can be displayed
cause / effect diagram	(Problem Management) A technique that helps a team to identify all the possible causes of an effect, such as a Problem. Originally devised by Kaoru Ishikawa and often called an Ishikawa Diagram, The output of this technique is a diagram that looks like a fishbone.
CCTA	The UK Government "Central Communications and Telecommunications Agency" was the original author of ITIL. This Organization no longer exists and its functions are now carried out by of the Office of Government Commerce (OGC).
CCTA risk analysis & management method (CRAMM).	See CRAMM
central office (CO)	A telecommunications carrier's facilities in a local area in which service is provided where local service is switched to long distance
central processing unit (CPU)	Computer hardware that houses the electronic circuits that control/direct all operations of the computer system
centralized data processing	Identified by one central processor and databases that form a distributed processing configuration
certificate authority (ca)	A trusted third party that serves authentication infrastructures or organizations and registers entities and issues them certificates
certificate revocation list	A list of retracted certificates
certification	1) Issuing a certificate to confirm Compliance to a Standard. Certification includes a formal Audit by an independent and Accredited body. 2) Certification is also used to mean awarding a certificate to verify that a person has achieved a qualification.

challenge/response token	A method of user authentication. Challenge response authentication is carried out through use of the Challenge Handshake Authentication Protocol (CHAP). When a user tries to log into the server, the server sends the user a "challenge," which is a random value. The user enters a password, which is used as an encryption key to encrypt the "challenge" and return it to the server. The server is aware of the password. It, therefore, encrypts the "challenge" value and compares it with the value received from the user. If the values match, the user is authenticated. The challenge/response activity continues throughout the session and this protects the session from password sniffing attacks. In addition, CHAP is not vulnerable to "man in the middle" attacks as the challenge value is a random value that changes on each access attempt.
change (definition)	(Change Management) The addition, modification or removal of anything that could have an effect on IT Services. The Scope should include all Configuration Items, Processes, Documentation etc.
change advisory board (CAB)	(Change Management) A group of people that assists the Change Manager in the assessment, prioritization and scheduling of Changes. This board is usually made up of representatives from all areas within the IT Service Provider, representatives from the Business, and Third Parties such as Suppliers.
change advisory board / emergency committee (CAB/EC)	(Change Management) A sub-set of the Change Advisory Board who make decisions about Emergency Changes. Membership of the CAB/EC may be decided at the time a meeting is called, and depends on the nature of the Emergency Change.
change history	(Change Management) Information about all changes made to a Configuration Item during its life. Change History consists of all those Change Records that apply to the CI.
change management	(Change Management) The Process responsible for controlling the Lifecycle of all Changes. The primary objective of Change Management is to enable beneficial Changes to be made, with minimum disruption to IT Services.
change model	A repeatable way of dealing with a particular Category of Change. A Change Model defines specific pre-defined steps that will be followed for a change of this Category. Change Models may be very simple, with no requirement for approval (e.g. Password Reset) or may be very complex with many steps that require approval (e.g. major software release). See Standard Change, Change Advisory Board.
change record	(Change Management) A Record containing the details of a Change. Each Change Record documents the Lifecycle of a single Change. A Change Record is created for every Request for Change that is received, even those that are subsequently rejected. Change Records should reference the Configuration Items that are affected by the Change. Change Records are often stored in a Configuration Management Database.
change request	Synonym for Request for Change.
change schedule	(Change Management) A Document that lists all approved Changes and their planned implementation dates. A Change Schedule is sometimes called a Forward Schedule of Change. See Projected Service Availability (PSA).
change slot	(Change Management) A regular, agreed time when Changes may be implemented with minimal impact on Services. Change Slots are usually documented in SLAs. See Planned Downtime.
chargeable item	A Deliverable of an IT Service that is used in calculating Charges to Customers. For example, number of Transactions, number of desktop PCs.
charging	(Financial Management) Requiring payment for IT Services. Charging for IT Services is optional, and many Organizations choose to treat their IT Service Provider as a Cost Centre. See Charging Process, Charging Policy

charging policy	(Financial Management) A Policy specifying the Objective of the Charging Process, and the way in which charges will be calculated. See Cost, Cost Plus, Going Rate, Market Rate.
charging process	(Financial Management) The Process responsible for deciding how much Customers should pay (Pricing) and recovering money from them (Billing).
check digit	A numeric value, which has been calculated mathematically, is added to data to ensure that original data have not been altered or that an incorrect, but valid match has occurred. This control is effective in detecting transposition and transcription errors.
check digit verification (self-checking digit)	A programmed edit or routine that detects transposition and transcription errors by calculating and checking the check digit
checkpoint restart procedures	A point in a routine at which sufficient information can be stored to permit restarting the computation from that point
CI type	(Configuration Management) A Category that is used to Classify CIs. The CI Type identifies the required Attributes and Relationships for a Configuration Record. Common CI Types include: hardware, Document, User etc.
ciphertext	Information generated by an encryption algorithm to protect the plaintext. The ciphertext is unintelligible to the unauthorized reader.
circuit-switched network	A data transmission service requiring the establishment of a circuit-switched connection before data can be transferred from source data terminal equipment (DTE) to a sink DTE. A circuit-switched data transmission service uses a connection network.
circular routing	In open systems architecture, circular routing is the logical path of a message in a communications network based on a series of gates at the physical network layer in the open systems interconnection (OSI) model.
classification	The act of assigning a Category to something. Classification is used to ensure consistent management and reporting. CIs, Incidents, Problems, Changes etc. are usually classified.
cleartext	Data that is not encrypted. Also known as plaintext.
client (definition)	A computer that is used directly by a User, for example a PC, Handheld Computer, or Workstation. The term Client is also used to mean the part of a Client-Server Application that the user directly interfaces with. For example an email Client. The term Client is also used to mean Customers or the Business in a general sense. For example Client Manager may be used as a synonym for Account Manager.
client access license (CAL)	A software license that permits one Client to make use of resources on a Server.
client-server	A group of computers connected by a communications network, where the client is the requesting machine and the server is the supplying machine. Software is specialized at both ends. Processing may take place on either the client or the server but it is transparent to the user.
closed (definition)	The final Status in the Lifecycle of an Incident, Problem, Change etc. When the Status is Closed, no further action is taken.
closure (definition)	The act of changing the Status of an Incident, Problem, Change etc. to Closed.
closure code	A Category that is assigned to an Incident or Problem before it is Closed. This code identifies the cause, and is intended for use in reporting and Trend Analysis. For example "Customer training required", "Documentation error", "Software bug".
cluster controller	A communications terminal control hardware unit that controls a number of computer terminals. All messages are buffered by the controller and then transmitted to the receiver.
coaxial cable	It is composed of an insulated wire that runs through the middle of each cable, a second wire that surrounds the insulation of the inner wire like a sheath, and the outer insulation which wraps the second wire. Coaxial cable has a greater transmission capacity than standard twisted-pair cables but has a limited range of effective distance.
COBIT	Control Objectives for Information and related Technology (COBIT) provides guidance and Best Practice for the management of IT Processes. COBIT is published by the IT Governance Institute. See http://www.isaca.org/ for more information.
COCO	Criteria Of Control, published by the Canadian Institute of Chartered Accountants in 1995

code of practice (COP)	A Guideline published by a public body or a Standards Organization, such as ISO or BSI. Many Standards consist of a Code of Practice and a Specification. The Code of Practice describes recommended Best Practice.
cohesion	The extent to which a system unit--subroutine, program, module, component, subsystem--performs a single dedicated function. Generally, the more cohesive are units, the easier it is to maintain and enhance a system, since it is easier to determine where and how to apply a change.
cold site	An IS backup facility that has the necessary electrical and physical components of a computer facility, but does not have the computer equipment in place. The site is ready to receive the necessary replacement computer equipment in the event the users have to move from their main computing location to the alternative computer facility.
cold standby	Synonym for Gradual Recovery.
combined code on corporate governance	The consolidation in 1998 of the "Cadbury," "Greenbury" and "Hampel" Reports. Named after the Committee Chairs, these reports were sponsored by the UK Financial Reporting Council, the London Stock Exchange, the Confederation of British Industry, the Institute of Directors, the Consultative Committee of Accountancy Bodies, the National Association of Pension Funds and the Association of British Insurers to address the Financial Aspects of Corporate Governance, Directors' Remuneration and the implementation of the Cadbury and Greenbury recommendations.
command, control and communications (C3I)	The Processes and infrastructure that enable an Organization to effectively pass instructions and information. This enables management control of Resources. This term is typically used in the management of Major Incidents, Business Continuity and IT Service Continuity.
communications controller	Small computers used to connect and coordinate communication links between distributed or remote devices and the main computer, thus freeing the main computer from this overhead function
comparison program	A program for the examination of data, using logical or conditional tests to determine or to identify similarities or differences
compensating control	An internal control that reduces the risk of an existing or potential control weakness resulting in errors and omissions
compiler	A program that translates programming language (source code) into machine executable instructions (object code)
completeness check	A procedure designed to ensure that no fields are missing from a record
compliance (definition)	Ensuring that a Standard or set of Guidelines is followed. See Audit.
compliance testing	Tests of control designed to obtain audit evidence on both the effectiveness of the controls and their operation during the audit period
component (definition)	A general term that is used to mean one part of something more complex. For example, a computer System may be a component of an IT Service, an Application may be a Component of a Release Unit. Components that need to be managed should be Configuration Items.
component ci	(Configuration Management) A Configuration Item that is part of an Assembly CI. For example, a CPU or Memory CI may be part of a Server CI.
component failure impact analysis (CFIA)	(Problem Management) (Availability Management) A technique that helps to identify the impact of CI failure on IT Services. A matrix is created with IT Services on one edge and CIs on the other. This enables the identification of critical CIs (that could cause the failure of multiple IT Services) and of fragile IT Services (that have multiple Single Points of Failure).

components (as in component-based development)	Cooperating packages of executable software that make their services available through defined interfaces. Components used in developing systems may be commercial off-the-shelf software (COTS) or may be purposely built. However, the goal of component-based development is to ultimately use as much pre-developed, pre-tested components as possible.
comprehensive audit	An audit designed to determine the accuracy of financial records, as well as evaluate the internal controls of a function or department
computationally greedy	Requiring a great deal of computing power; processor intensive
computer sequence checking	Verifies that the control number follows sequentially and any control numbers out of sequence are rejected or noted on an exception report for further research
computer server	1) A computer dedicated to servicing requests for resources from other computers on a network. Servers typically run network operating systems. 2) A computer that provides services to another computer (the client).
computer telephony integration (CTI)	(Service Desk) CTI is a general term covering any kind of integration between computers and telephone Systems. It is most commonly used to refer to Systems where an Application displays detailed screens relating to incoming or outgoing telephone calls. See Automatic Call Distribution, Interactive Voice Response.
computer-aided software engineering (case)	The use of software packages that aid in the development of all phases of an information system. System analysis, design programming and documentation are provided. Changes introduced in one CASE chart will update all other related charts automatically. CASE can be installed on a microcomputer for easy access.
computer-assisted audit technique (CAATs)	CAATs - Any automated audit technique, such as generalized audit software, test data generators, computerized audit programs and specialized audit utilities
concurrency	A measure of the number of Users engaged in the same Operation at the same time. Used in Capacity Management and License Management.
concurrent access	A fail-over process, in which all nodes run the same resource group (there can be no IP or MAC addresses in a concurrent resource group) and access the external storage concurrently
confidentiality (definition)	1) (Security Management) (C-I-A) A Security Principle that requires that data should only be accessed by authorized people. 2) Confidentiality concerns the protection of sensitive information from unauthorized disclosure
configuration (definition)	1) A "configuration" describes the parameter settings for one or more CIs (ie. devices, applications or systems). 2) A generic term, used to describe a group of Configuration Items (CIs) that work together to deliver an IT Service, or a recognizable part of an IT Service.
configuration management (C&CM)	An integrated approach to Planning, implementing and operating Configuration Management, Change Management and Release Management.
configuration control	(Configuration Management) The Activity responsible for ensuring that adding, modifying or removing a CI is properly managed, for example by submitting a Request for Change or Service Request.
configuration identification	(Configuration Management) The Activity responsible for collecting information about Configuration Items and their Relationships, and loading this information into the CMDB. Configuration Identification is also responsible for labeling the CIs themselves, so that the corresponding Configuration Records can be found.

configuration item (CI)	(Configuration Management) Any Component that needs to be managed in order to deliver an IT Service. Information about each CI is recorded in a Configuration Record within the CMDB and is maintained throughout its Lifecycle by Configuration Management. CIs are under the control of Change Management. CIs typically include hardware, software, buildings, people, and formal documentation such as Process documentation and SLAs.
configuration management	(Configuration Management) The Process responsible for maintaining information about Configuration Items required to deliver an IT Service, including their Relationships. This information is managed throughout the Lifecycle of the CI. The primary objective of Configuration Management is to underpin the delivery of IT Services by providing accurate data to all IT Service Management Processes when and where it is needed.
configuration management database (CMDB)	(Configuration Management) A Database used to manage Configuration Records throughout their Lifecycle. The CMDB records the Attributes of each CI, and Relationships with other CIs. A CMDB may also contain other information linked to CIs, for example Incident, Problem or Change Records. The CMDB is maintained by Configuration Management and is used by all IT Service Management Processes.
configuration record	(Configuration Management) A Record containing the details of a Configuration Item. Each Configuration Record documents the Lifecycle of a single CI. Configuration Records are stored in a Configuration Management Database.
configuration status accounting	(Configuration Management) The Activity responsible for recording and reporting the Lifecycle of each Configuration Item.
configuration structure	(Configuration Management) The hierarchy and other Relationships between all the Configuration Items that comprise a Configuration.
configuration verification and audit	(Configuration Management) The Activities responsible for ensuring that information in the CMDB is accurate and that all Configuration Items have been identified and recorded in the CMDB. Configuration Verification includes routine checks that are part of other processes. For example, verifying the serial number of a desktop PC when a User logs an Incident. Configuration Audit is a periodic, formal check.
console log	An automated detail report of computer system activity
content filtering	Controlling access to a network by analyzing the contents of the incoming and outgoing packets and either letting them pass or denying them based on a list of rules. Differs from packet filtering in that it is the data in the packet that are analyzed instead of the attributes of the packet itself (e.g., source/target IP address, TCP flags).
continuity (definition)	The acts preventing, mitigating and recovering from disruption. The terms business resumption planning, disaster recovery planning and contingency planning also may be used in this context; they all concentrate on the recovery aspects of continuity.
continuous auditing approach	This approach allows IS auditors to monitor system reliability on a continuous basis and to gather selective audit evidence through the computer.
continuous availability	(Availability Management) An approach or design to achieve 100% Availability. A Continuously Available IT Service has no planned or unplanned Downtime.
continuous improvement	The Process responsible for managing improvements to IT Service Management Processes and IT Services. Continuous Improvement continually measures achievement and modifies Processes and the IT Infrastructure to improve Efficiency, Effectiveness, and Cost Effectiveness. See CSIP, SIP, Deming Cycle, Optimize.
continuous operation	(Availability Management) An approach or design to eliminate planned Downtime of an IT Service. Note that individual Configuration Items may be down even though the IT Service is Available.
continuous service improvement program (CSIP)	A formal Program to implement and manage a Continuous Improvement Process.
contract	A legally binding Agreement between two or more parties.

contract manager	(Supplier Management) A Role responsible for managing Contracts with one or more Suppliers. Contract Managers usually work closely with Service Level Managers to ensure that Supplier Contracts support agreed Service Level Targets for IT Services.
control (definition)	A means of managing a Risk, or ensuring that a Business Objective is achieved. Example Controls include Policies, Procedures, Roles, software configurations, passwords, RAID, fences, door-locks etc. A control is sometimes called a Countermeasure or safeguard. Control is also used as a generic term meaning to manage something.
control group	Members of the operations area that are responsible for the collection, logging and submission of input for the various user groups
control objective	The objectives of management that are used as the framework for developing and implementing controls (control procedures).
control objectives for enterprise governance	A discussion document which sets out an "Enterprise Governance Model" focusing strongly on both the enterprise business goals and the information technology enablers which facilitate good enterprise governance, published by the Information Systems Audit and Control Foundation in 1999
control objectives for information and related technology (COBIT)	See COBIT.
control perimeter	The boundary defining the scope of control authority for an entity. For example, if a system is within the control perimeter, the right and ability exists to control it in response to an attack.
control processes	The ISO/IEC 20000 Process group that includes Change Management and Configuration Management.
control risk	The risk that an error which could occur in an audit area, and which could be material, individually or in combination with other errors, will not be prevented or detected and corrected on a timely basis by the internal control system
control risk self-assessment	An empowering method/process by which management and staff of all levels collectively identify and evaluate IS related risks and controls under the guidance of a facilitator who could be an IS auditor. The IS auditor can utilize CRSA for gathering relevant information about risks and controls and to forge greater collaboration with management and staff. CRSA provides a framework and tools for management and employees to: *Identify and prioritize their business objectives. *Assess and manage high risk areas of business processes. *Self-evaluate the adequacy of controls. *Develop risk treatment recommendations
control section	The area of the central processing unit (CPU) that executes software, allocates internal memory and transfers operations between the arithmetic-logic, internal storage and output sections of the computer
control weakness	A deficiency in the design or operation of a control procedure. Control weaknesses can potentially result in risks relevant to the area of activity not being reduced to an acceptable level (relevant risks are those that threaten achievement of the objectives relevant to the area of activity being examined). Control weaknesses can be material when the design or operation of one or more control procedures does not reduce to a relatively low level the risk that misstatements caused by illegal acts or irregularities may occur and not be detected by the related control procedures.
corporate governance	"...the structure through which the objectives of an organization are set, and the means of attaining those objectives, and determines monitoring performance guidelines. Good corporate governance should provide proper incentives for board and management to pursue objectives that are in the interests of the company and stakeholders and should facilitate effective monitoring, thereby encouraging firms to use resources more efficiently." (Source: Principles of Corporate Governance, 1999 issued by the Organization for Economic Cooperation and Development (OECD))

corrective control	These controls are designed to correct errors, omissions and unauthorized uses and intrusions, once they are detected.
COSO	A report on "Internal Control--An Integrated Framework" sponsored by the Committee of Sponsoring Organizations of the Treadway Commission in 1992. It provides guidance and a comprehensive framework of internal control for all organizations.
cost (definition)	(Financial Management) The amount of money spent on a specific Activity, IT Service, or Business Unit. Costs consist of real cost (money), notional cost such as people's time, and Depreciation. Cost is also used as the name of a Charging Policy that recovers the exact cost of providing the service. See Opportunity Cost, Full Cost, Marginal Cost.
cost benefit analysis	An Activity that analyses and compares the costs and the benefits involved in one or more alternative courses of action. See Business Case, Cost Effectiveness, Investment Appraisal.
cost center	(Financial Management) A Business Unit or Project to which costs are assigned. A Cost Centre does not charge for Services provided. An IT Service Provider can be run as a Cost Centre or a Profit Centre.
cost effectiveness	A measure of the balance between the Effectiveness and Cost of a Service, Process or activity, A Cost Effective Process is one which achieves its Objectives at minimum Cost. See KPI, Return on Investment, Value for Money.
cost element	(Financial Management) The middle level of category to which Costs are assigned in Budgeting and Accounting. The highest level category is Cost Type. For example a Cost Type of "people" could have cost elements of payroll, staff benefits, expenses, training, overtime etc. Cost Elements can be further broken down to give Cost Units. For example the Cost Element "expenses" could include Cost Units of Hotels, Transport, Meals etc.
cost management	(Financial Management) A general term that is used to refer to Budgeting and Accounting, sometimes used as a synonym for Financial Management for IT Services.
cost model	(Financial Management) A framework used in Budgeting and Accounting in which all known Costs can be recorded, categorized, and allocated to specific Customers, Business Units or Projects. Cost-by-Customer and Cost-by-Service are common types of Cost Model. See Cost Type, Cost Element, Cost Unit.
cost plus	(Financial Management) A Charging Policy in which Charges are calculated by adding a percentage to the Cost of providing the IT Service. The additional money is often used for future investment.
cost type	(Financial Management) The highest level of category to which Costs are assigned in Budgeting and Accounting. For example hardware, software, people, accommodation, external and Transfer. See Cost Element, Cost Unit, Cost Model.
cost unit	(Financial Management) The lowest level of category to which Costs are assigned, Cost Units are usually things that can be easily counted (e.g. staff numbers, software licences) or things easily measured (e.g. CPU usage, Electricity consumed). Cost Units are included within Cost Elements. For example a Cost Element of "expenses" could include Cost Units of Hotels, Transport, Meals etc.
cost-by-customer cost model	(Financial Management) A type of Cost Model in which Costs are identified and allocated to Customers.
cost-by-service cost model	(Financial Management) A type of Cost Model in which Costs are identified and allocated to IT Services.
countermeasure	A synonym for Control. The term Countermeasure can be used to refer to any type of Control, but it is most often used when referring to measures that increase Resilience, Fault Tolerance or Reliability of an IT Service.

coupling	Measure of interconnectivity among software program modules' structure. Coupling depends on the interface complexity between modules. This can be defined as the point at which entry or reference is made to a module, and what data passes across the interface. In application software design, it is preferable to strive for the lowest possible coupling between modules. Simple connectivity among modules results in software that is easier to understand, maintain and less prone to a ripple or domino effect caused when errors occur at one location and propagate through the system.
coverage	The proportion of known attacks detected by an intrusion detection system
CRAMM	(Security Management) (Availability Management) (IT Service Continuity Management) CCTA Risk Analysis & Management Method (CRAMM). A methodology and tool for analyzing and managing Risks. CRAMM was developed by the UK Government, but is now privately owned. Further information is available from http://www.cramm.com/
credentialed analysis	In vulnerability analysis, passive monitoring approaches in which passwords or other access credentials are required. This sort of check usually involves accessing a system data object.
credit risk	The risk to earnings or capital arising from an obligor's failure to meet the terms of any contract with the bank or otherwise to perform as agreed. Internet banking provides the opportunity for banks to expand their geographic range. Customers can reach a given bank from literally anywhere in the world. In dealing with customers over the Internet, absent any personal contact, it is challenging for banks to verify the good faith of their customers, which is an important element in making sound credit decisions.
crisis management	(IT Service Continuity Management) Crisis Management is the Process responsible for managing the wider implications of Business Continuity. A Crisis Management team is responsible for Strategic issues such as managing media relations and shareholder confidence, and decides when to invoke Business Continuity Plans.
criteria (definition)	The standards and benchmarks used to measure and present the subject matter and against which the IS auditor evaluates the subject matter. Criteria should be: Objective—free from bias Measurable—provide for consistent measurement Complete—include all relevant factors to reach a conclusion Relevant—relate to the subject matter
critical success factor (CSF)	Something that must happen if a Process, Project, Plan, or IT Service is to succeed. KPIs are used to measure the achievement of each CSF. For example a CSF of "protect IT Services when making Changes" could be measured by KPIs such as "percentage reduction of unsuccessful Changes", "percentage reduction in Changes causing Incidents" etc.
cross-certification	A certificate issued by one certification authority to a second certification authority so that users of the first certification authority are able to obtain the public key of the second certification authority and verify the certificates it has created. Often cross certification refers specifically to certificates issued to each other by two CAs at the same level in a hierarchy.
cryptography (definition)	The art of designing, analyzing and attacking cryptographic schemes
culture	A set of values that is shared by a group of people, including expectations about how people should behave, ideas, beliefs, and practices. See Vision.
customer focus	Understanding and meeting the real needs of Customers and Users. This is done to maximize Customer satisfaction and thus to obtain long term benefits for the IT Service Provider. Customer Focus can be displayed by the entire Organization (see Service Culture) or by specific people or Processes.
customer-managed use	(Software Asset Management) The management of licenses by the Customer or IT Service Provider. Licenses may also be managed by the Supplier of the software (Vendor Managed Use).

data analysis	Typically in large Organizations where the quantum of data processed by the ERPs is extremely voluminous, analysis of patterns and trends prove to be extremely useful in ascertaining the efficiency and effectiveness of operations. Most ERPs provide opportunities for extraction and analysis of data, some with built-in tools through the use of third-party developed tools that interface with the ERP systems
data communications	The transfer of data between separate computer processing sites/devices using telephone lines, microwave and/or satellite links
data custodian	Individuals and departments responsible for the storage and safeguarding of computerized information. This typically is within the IS organization.
data dictionary	A data dictionary is a database that contains the name, type, range of values, source and authorization for access for each data element in a database. It also indicates which application programs use that data so that when a data structure is contemplated, a list of the affected programs can be generated. The data dictionary may be a stand-alone information system used for management or documentation purposes, or it may control the operation of a database.
data diddling	Changing data with malicious intent before or during input into the system
data encryption standard (DES)	A private key cryptosystem published by the National Bureau of Standards (NBS), the predecessor of the US National Institute of Standards and Technology (NIST). DES has been used commonly for data encryption in the forms of software and hardware implementation (also see private key cryptosystems).
data flow (definition)	The flow of data from the input (in Internet banking, ordinarily user input at his/her desktop) to output (in Internet banking, ordinarily data in a bank's central database). Data flow includes traveling through the communication lines, routers, switches and firewalls as well as processing through various applications on servers which process the data from user fingers to storage in bank central database.
data integrity (definition)	The property that data meet with a priority expectation of quality and that the data can be relied upon
data leakage	Siphoning out or leaking information by dumping computer files or stealing computer reports and tapes
data owner	Individuals, normally managers or directors, who have responsibility for the integrity, accurate reporting and use of computerized data
data security	Those controls that seek to maintain confidentiality, integrity and availability of information
data structure	The relationships among files in a database and among data items within each file
database (definition)	1) A stored collection of related data needed by organizations and individuals to meet their information processing and retrieval requirements 2) In IT Service Management, a Database is a structured collection of data, used to support one or more Processes. A Database of this sort does not need to be a single physical Database, but may consist of various data sources and tools that together meet the requirements. For example, Configuration Management Database, Capacity Database, Availability Database, Application Portfolio.
database administrator (DBA)	An individual or department responsible for the security and information classification of the shared data stored on a database system. This responsibility includes the design, definition and maintenance of the database.
database management system (BBMS)	A complex set of software programs that control the organization, storage and retrieval of data in a database. It also controls the security and integrity of the database.
database replication	The process of creating and managing duplicate versions of a database. Replication not only copies a database but also synchronizes a set of replicas so that changes made to one replica are reflected in all the others. The beauty of replication is that it enables many users to work with their own local copy of a database but have the database updated as if they were working on a single centralized database. For database applications where geographically users are distributed widely, replication is often the most efficient method of database access.

database specifications	These are the requirements for establishing a database application. They include field definitions, field requirements and reporting requirements for the individual information in the database.
datagram	A packet (encapsulated with a frame containing information), which is transmitted in a packet-switching network from source to destination
data oriented systems development	The purpose is to provide usable data rather than a function. The focus of the development is to provide ad hoc reporting for users by developing a suitable accessible database of information.
DDoS (distributed denial-of-service) attack	A denial-of-service (DoS) assault from multiple sources; see DoS
decentralization	The process of distributing computer processing to different locations within an organization
decision support system (DSS)	An interactive system that provides the user with easy access to decision models and data, to support semi-structured decision-making tasks
decoy server	See honey pot.
decryption (definition)	A technique used to recover the original plaintext from the ciphertext such that it is intelligible to the reader. The decryption is a reverse process of the encryption.
decryption key	A piece of information, in a digitized form, used to recover the plaintext from the corresponding ciphertext by decryption
default deny policy	A policy whereby access is denied unless it is specifically allowed. The inverse of default allow.
default password	The password used to gain access when a system is first installed on a computer or network device. There is a large list published on the Internet and maintained at several locations. Failure to change these after the installation leaves the system vulnerable.
definitive hardware store (DHS)	(Release Management) One or more physical locations in which hardware Configuration Items are securely stored when not in use. All hardware in the DHS is under the control of Change and Release Management and is recorded in the CMDB. The DHS contains spare parts, maintained at suitable revision levels, and may also include hardware that is part of a future Release.
definitive software library (dsl)	(Release Management) One or more locations in which the definitive and approved versions of all software Configuration Items are securely stored. The DSL may also contain associated CIs such as licenses and documentation. The DSL is a single logical storage area even if there are multiple locations. All software in the DSL is under the control of Change and Release Management and is recorded in the CMDB. Only software from the DSL is acceptable for use in a Release.
degauss	To apply a variable, alternating current (AC) field for the purpose of demagnetizing magnetic recording media. The process involves increasing the AC field gradually from zero to some maximum value and back to zero, which leaves a very low residue of magnetic induction on the media. Degauss loosely means to erase.
deliverables	Something that must be provided to meet a commitment in a Service Level Agreement or a Contract. Deliverable is also used in a more informal way to mean a planned output of any Process.
delta release	(Release Management) A Release that includes only those Components of a Release Unit that have actually changed since the last Release. A Delta Release is also referred to as a partial Release. See Release Type.
demand management	(Capacity Management) Optimizing the use of Capacity by moving Workload to less utilized times, Servers, or places. Demand Management often uses Differential Charging to encourage Customers to use IT Services at less busy times. Demand Management also makes use of other techniques such as limiting the number of concurrent Users.
Deming cycle	Synonym for Plan Do Check Act.
demodulation	The process of converting an analog telecommunications signal into a digital computer signal

dependency	The direct or indirect reliance of one Process or Activity upon another.
deployment	(Release Management) The Activity responsible for movement of new or changed hardware, software, documentation, Process, etc to the Live Environment. See Rollout.
depreciation	(Financial Management) A measure of the reduction in value of an Asset over its life. This is based on wearing out, consumption or other reduction in the useful economic value.
detailed IS/IT controls	Controls over the acquisition, implementation, delivery and support of IS systems and services. They are made up of application controls plus those general controls not included in pervasive controls.
detection (definition)	(Incident Management) A stage in the Incident Lifecycle. Detection results in the Incident becoming known to the Service Provider. Detection can be automatic, or can be the result of a user logging an Incident.
detection risk	The risk that the IS auditor's substantive procedures will not detect an error which could be material, individually or in combination with other errors
detective controls	These controls exist to detect and report when errors, omissions and unauthorized uses or entries occur.
development (definition)	The Process responsible for creating or modifying an IT Service or Application. Also used to mean the Role or group that carries out Development work.
development report environment	An Environment used to create or modify IT Services or Applications. Development Environments are not typically subjected to the same degree of control as Test Environments or Live Environments. See Development.
diagnosis	(Incident Management) (Problem Management) A stage in the Incident and Problem Lifecycles. The purpose of Diagnosis is to identify a Workaround for an Incident or the Root Cause of a Problem.
diagnostic script	(Service Desk) A structured set of questions used by Service Desk staff to ensure they ask the correct questions, and to help them Classify, Resolve and assign Incidents. Diagnostic Scripts may also be made available to Users to help them diagnose and resolve their own Incidents.
dial-back	Used as a control over dial-up telecommunications lines. The telecommunications link established through dial-up into the computer from a remote location is interrupted so the computer can dial back to the caller. The link is permitted only if the caller is from a valid phone number or telecommunications channel.
dial-in access controls	Controls that prevent unauthorized access from remote users that attempt to access a secured environment. These controls range from dial-back controls to remote user authentication.
differential charging	(Financial Management) A technique used in Charging to support Demand Management by charging different amounts for the same IT Service Function at different times.
digital certificate	A certificate identifying a public key to its subscriber, corresponding to a private key held by that subscriber. It is a unique code that typically is used to allow the authenticity and integrity of communicated data to be verified.
digital certification	A process to authenticate (or certify) a party's digital signature, carried out by trusted third parties.
digital signature	A piece of information, a digitized form of signature, that provides sender authenticity, message integrity and nonrepudiation. A digital signature is generated using the sender's private key or applying a one-way hash function.
direct cost	(Financial Management) A cost of providing an IT Service which can be allocated in full to a specific Customer, Cost Centre, Project etc. For example cost of providing non-shared servers or software licenses. See also Indirect Cost.
direct reporting engagement	An engagement where management does not make a written assertion about the effectiveness of their control procedures, and the IS auditor provides an opinion about subject matter directly, such as the effectiveness of the control procedures

discovery sampling	A form of attribute sampling that is used to determine a specified probability of finding at least one example of an occurrence (attribute) in a population
diskless workstations	A workstation or PC on a network that does not have its own disk. Instead, it stores files on a network file server.
distributed data processing network	A system of computers connected together by a communications network. Each computer processes its data and the network supports the system as a whole. Such a network enhances communication among the linked computers and allows access to shared files.
DMZ (demilitarized zone)	Commonly it is the network segment between the Internet and a private network. It allows access to services from the Internet and the internal private network, while denying access from the Internet directly to the private network.
DNS (domain name system)	A hierarchical database that is distributed across the Internet that allows names to be resolved into IP addresses (and vice versa) to locate services such as web and e-mail servers
do nothing	(IT Service Continuity) A Recovery Option. The Service Provider formally agrees with the Customer that Recovery of this IT Service will not be performed.
document (definition)	Information in readable form. A Document may be paper or electronic. For example a Policy statement, Service Level Agreement, Incident Record, diagram of computer room layout. See Record.
dormant contract	(IT Service Continuity) A Recovery Option. The Service Provider takes out a Contract with a Supplier to provide required products or Services within agreed times for an agreed price. The Contract is invoked as part of a Recovery Plan, at which time an additional payment is made and the goods or Service are provided.
DoS (denial-of-service) attack	An assault on a service from a single source that floods it with so many requests that it becomes overwhelmed and is either stopped completely or operates at a significantly reduced rate
downloading	The act of transferring computerized information from one computer to another computer
downtime (definition)	(Availability Management) The time when a Configuration Item or IT Service is not Available during its Agreed Service Time. The Availability of an IT Service is often calculated from Agreed Service Time and Downtime.
downtime report	A report that identifies the elapsed time when a computer is not operating correctly because of machine failure
dry-pipe fire extinguisher system	Refers to a sprinkler system that does not have water in the pipes during idle usage, unlike a fully charged fire extinguisher system that has water in the pipes at all times. The dry-pipe system is activated at the time of the fire alarm, and water is emitted to the pipes from a water reservoir for discharge to the location of the fire.
due care	Diligence which a person would exercise under a given set of circumstances
due professional care	Diligence which a person, who possesses a special skill, would exercise under a given set of circumstances
dumb terminal	A display terminal without processing capability. Dumb terminals are dependent upon the main computer for processing. All entered data are accepted without further editing or validation.
duplex routing	The method or communication mode of routing data over the communication network (also see half duplex and full duplex)
dynamic analysis	Analysis that is performed in real time or in continuous form
echo checks	Detects line errors by retransmitting data back to the sending device for comparison with the original transmission
e-commerce	Defined by ISACA as the processes by which Organizations conduct business electronically with their customers, suppliers and other external business partners, using the Internet as an enabling technology. It therefore encompasses both business-to-business (B2B) and business-to-consumer (B2C) e-Commerce models, but does not include existing non-Internet e-Commerce methods based on private networks such as EDI and SWIFT.

edit controls	Detects errors in the input portion of information that is sent to the computer for processing. The controls may be manual or automated and allow the user to edit data errors before processing.
editing	Editing ensures that data conform to predetermined criteria and enable early identification of potential errors.
effectiveness	A measure of whether the Objectives of a Process, Service or Activity have been achieved. An Effective Process or activity is one that achieves its agreed Objectives. See KPI.
efficiency	A measure of whether the right amount of resources have been used to deliver a Process, Service or Activity. An Efficient Process achieves its Objectives with the minimum amount of time, money, people or other resources. See KPI.
electronic cash	An electronic form functionally equivalent to cash in order to make and receive payments in cyber-banking
electronic data interchange (EDI)	The electronic transmission of transactions (information) between two organizations. EDI promotes a more efficient paperless environment. EDI transmissions can replace the use of standard documents, including invoices or purchase orders.
electronic funds transfer (EFT)	The exchange of money via telecommunications. EFT refers to any financial transaction that originates at a terminal and transfers a sum of money from one account to another.
electronic signature	Any technique designed to provide the electronic equivalent of a handwritten signature to demonstrate the origin and integrity of specific data. Digital signatures are an example of electronic signatures.
electronic vaulting	A data recovery strategy that allows organizations to recover data within hours after a disaster. It includes recovery of data from an offsite storage media that mirrors data via a communication link. Typically used for batch/journal updates to critical files to supplement full backups taken periodically.
e-mail/interpersonal messaging	An individual using a terminal, PC or an application can access a network to send an unstructured message to another individual or group of people.
embedded audit module	Integral part of an application system that is designed to identify and report specific transactions or other information based on pre-determined criteria. Identification of reportable items occurs as part of real-time processing. Reporting may be real-time online, or may use store and forward methods. Also known as integrated test facility or continuous auditing module.
emergency change	(Change Management) A Change that must be introduced as soon as possible. For example to resolve a Major Incident or implement a Security patch. The Change Management Process will normally have a specific Procedure for handling Emergency Changes. See Change Advisory Board / Emergency Committee (CAB/EC).
encapsulation (objects)	Encapsulation is the technique used by layered protocols in which a lower layer protocol accepts a message from a higher layer protocol and places it in the data portion of a frame in the lower layer.
encryption (definition)	The process of taking an unencrypted message (plaintext), applying a mathematical function to it (encryption algorithm with a key) and producing an encrypted message (ciphertext)
encryption key	A piece of information, in a digitized form, used by an encryption algorithm to convert the plaintext to the ciphertext
end-user computing	The ability of end users to design and implement their own information system utilizing computer software products
engagement letter	Formal document which defines the IS auditor's responsibility, authority and accountability for a specific assignment

enterprise governance	A broad and wide-ranging concept of corporate governance, covering associated organizations such as global strategic alliance partners. (Source: Control Objectives for Enterprise Governance Discussion Document, published by the Information Systems Audit and Control Foundation in 1999)
enterprise resource planning (ERP)	1) It denotes the planning and management of resources in an enterprise. 2) It denotes a software system that can be used to manage whole business processes, integrating purchasing, inventory, personnel, customer service, shipping, financial management and other aspects of the business. An ERP system typically is based on a common database, various integrated business process application modules and business analysis tools
environment (definition)	1) A subset of the IT Infrastructure that is used for a particular purpose. For Example: Live Environment, Test Environment, Build Environment. It is possible for multiple Environments to share a Configuration Item, for example Test and Live Environments may use different partitions on a single mainframe computer. 2) Also used in the term Physical Environment to mean the accommodation, air conditioning, power system etc.
error (definition)	1) A design flaw or malfunction that causes a Failure of one or more Configuration Items or IT Services. 2) A mistake made by a person or a faulty Process that impacts a CI or IT Service is also an Error.
error control	(Problem Management) The Activity responsible for managing Known Errors until they are Resolved by the successful implementation of Changes. See Problem Control.
error risk	The risk of errors occurring in the area being audited
escalation	An Activity that obtains additional Resources when these are needed to meet Service Level Targets or Customer expectations. Escalation may be needed within any IT Service Management Process, but is most commonly associated with Incident Management, Problem Management and the management of Customer complaints. There are two types of Escalation, Functional Escalation and Hierarchical Escalation.
estimation	The use of experience to provide an approximate value for a Metric or Cost. Estimation is also used in Capacity and Availability Management as the cheapest and least accurate Modeling method,
Ethernet	A popular network protocol and cabling scheme that uses a bus topology and CSMA/CD (carrier sense multiple access/collision detection) to prevent network failures or collisions when two devices try to access the network at the same time
European foundation for quality management (EFQM)	The EFQM Excellence Model was introduced at the beginning of 1992 as the framework for assessing Organizations for the European Quality Award. It is now the most widely used Organizational framework in Europe and it has become the basis for the majority of national and regional Quality Awards. See http://www.efqm.org/ for more information.
event (definition)	An Alert or notification created by any IT Service, Configuration Item or monitoring tool. For example a notification that a batch job has completed. Events typically require IT Operations personnel to take actions, and often lead to Incidents being logged. See Event Management.
event management	The Process responsible for managing Events throughout their Lifecycle. Event Management is one of the main Activities of IT Operations.
evidence	The information an auditor gathers in the course of performing an IS audit. Evidence is relevant if it pertains to the audit objectives and has a logical relationship to the findings and conclusions it is used to support.
examination board	An Organization Accredited to develop and manage examinations. IT Service Management Examination Boards are accredited by ICMB to develop ITIL examinations, based on a common syllabus, to Accredit training Organizations, and to award Certificates. See ISEB, EXIN.

examination institute for information science (EXIN)	The Examination Institute for Information Science, is accredited by the ICMB as an Examination Board. See http://www.exin-exams.com/ for more information.
exception report	An exception report is generated by a program that identifies transactions or data that appear to be incorrect. These items may be outside a predetermined range or may not conform to specified criteria. Examples include SLA targets being missed or about to be missed, and a Performance Metric indicating a potential Capacity problem.
executable code	The machine language code that is generally referred to as the object or load module
expert systems	Expert systems are the most prevalent type of computer systems that arise from the research of artificial intelligence. An expert system has a built in hierarchy of rules, which are acquired from human experts in the appropriate field. Once input is provided, the system should be able to define the nature of the problem and provide recommendations to solve the problem.
exposure	The potential loss to an area due to the occurrence of an adverse event
extended binary-coded decimal interchange code (EBCDIC)	An eight-bit code representing 256 characters; used in most large computer systems
extensible markup language (XML)	Promulgated through the World Wide Web Consortium, XML is a web-based application development technique that allows designers to create their own customized tags, thus, enabling the definition, transmission, validation and interpretation of data between applications and organizations.
external customer	A Customer who works for a different Business to the IT Service Provider. See External Service Provider, Internal Customer.
external router	The router at the extreme edge of the network under control, usually connected to an ISP or other service provider; also known as border router
external service provider	An IT Service Provider which is part of a different Business to their Customer. An IT Service Provider may have both Internal Customers and External Customers. See Internal Service Provider, Application Service Provider, Internet Service Provider.
fail-over	The transfer of service from an incapacitated primary component to its backup component
fail-safe	Describes the design properties of a computer system that allow it to resist active attempts to attack or bypass it
failure (definition)	Loss of ability to Operate to Specification, or to deliver the required output. The term Failure may be used when referring to IT Services, Processes, Activities, Configuration Items etc. A Failure often causes an Incident. See Error.
false negative	In intrusion detection, an error that occurs when an attack is misdiagnosed as a normal activity
false positive	In intrusion detection, an error that occurs when a normal activity is misdiagnosed as an attack
fault	Synonym for Error.
fault tolerance	The ability of an IT Service or Configuration Item to continue to Operate correctly after Failure of a Component part (ie. hardware and/or software). See Resilience, Countermeasure.
fault tree analysis	(Problem Management) (Availability Management) A technique that can be used to determine the chain of events that leads to a Problem. Fault Tree Analysis represents a chain of events using Boolean notation in a diagram.
feasibility study	A phase of an SDLC methodology that researches the feasibility and adequacy of resources for the development or acquisition of a system solution to a user need
fiber optic cable	Glass fibers that transmit binary signals over a telecommunications network. Fiber optic systems have low transmission losses as compared to twisted-pair cables. They do not radiate energy or conduct electricity. They are free from corruption and lightning-induced interference, and they reduce the risk of wiretaps.

field	An individual data element in a computer record. Examples include employee name, customer address, account number, product unit price and product quantity in stock.
file	A named collection of related records
file layout	Specifies the length of the file's record and the sequence and size of its fields. A file layout also will specify the type of data contained within each field. For example, alphanumeric, zoned decimal, packed and binary are types of data.
file server	A high-capacity disk storage device or a computer that stores data centrally for network users and manages access to that data. File servers can be dedicated so that no process other than network management can be executed while the network is available; file servers can be non-dedicated so that standard user applications can run while the network is available.
filtering router	A router that is configured to control network access by comparing the attributes of the incoming or outgoing packets to a set of rules
FIN (final)	A flag set in a packet to indicate that this packet is the final data packet of the transmission
financial audit	An audit designed to determine the accuracy of financial records and information
financial management	A common abbreviation of Financial Management for IT Services
financial management for it services	(Financial Management) The Process responsible for managing an IT Service Provider's Budgeting, Accounting and Charging requirements.
financial year	(Financial Management) An Accounting Period covering 12 consecutive months. A Financial Year may start on any date, for example 1 April to 31 March.
finger	A protocol and program that allows the remote identification of users logged into a system
firewall	A device that forms a barrier between a secure and an open environment. Usually, the open environment is considered hostile. The most notable hostile environment is the Internet. In other words, a firewall enforces a boundary between two or more networks.
firmware	Memory chips with embedded program code that hold their content when power is turned off
first time fix rate	(Service Desk) (Incident Management) A Metric that measures the percentage of Incidents resolved by First-line Support without delay or Escalation. Other definitions of this Metric are possible, for example some IT Service Providers define it as the percentage of Incidents that are Resolved during the initial User phone call.
first-line support	(Service Desk) (Incident Management) The first level in a hierarchy of Support Groups involved in the resolution of Incidents. Each level contains more specialist skills, or has more time or other resources. See Escalation.
fiscal year	Any yearly accounting period without regard to its relationship to a calendar year.
fishbone diagram	Synonym for Cause / Effect Diagram.
fit for purpose	An informal term used to describe a Process, Configuration Item, IT Service etc. that is capable of meeting its objectives or Service Levels. Being Fit for Purpose requires suitable design, implementation, control and maintenance.
fixed cost	(Financial Management) A Cost that does not vary with IT Service usage. For example the cost of Server hardware. See Variable Cost.
fixed facility	(IT Service Continuity Management) A permanent building, available for use when needed by an IT Service Continuity Plan. See Recovery Option, Portable Facility.
fixed price	(Financial Management) A Cost or Charge agreed with a Supplier or Customer. This Cost or Charge remains the same, even if Resource usage or time to deliver a Project changes.
follow the sun support	(Service Desk) A methodology for using Service Desks and Support Groups around the world to provide seamless 24 * 7 Service. Calls, Incidents, Problems and Service Requests are passed between groups in different time zones.

foreign exchange risk	Is present when a financial asset or liability is denominated in a foreign currency or is funded by borrowings in another currency
format checking	The application of an edit, using a predefined field definition to a submitted information stream; a test to ensure that data conform to a predefined format
fourth generation language (4GL)	English-like, user friendly, nonprocedural computer languages used to program and/or read and process computer files
frame relay	A packet-switched wide-area-network technology that provides faster performance than older packet-switched WAN technologies such as X.25 networks, because it was designed for today's reliable circuits and performs less rigorous error detection. Frame relay is best suited for data and image transfers. Because of its variable-length packet architecture, it is not the most efficient technology for real-time voice and video. In a frame-relay network, end nodes establish a connection via a permanent virtual circuit (PVC).
fraud risk	The risk that activities will include deliberate circumvention of controls with the intent to conceal the perpetuation of irregularities. The unauthorized use of assets or services and abetting or helping to conceal.
FTP (file transfer protocol)	A protocol used to transfer files over a TCP/IP network (Internet, UNIX, etc.)
full cost	(Financial Management) The total Cost of all the resources used in supplying an IT Service, i.e., the sum of the Direct Costs of producing the output, a proportional share of Indirect Costs, and any selling and distribution expenses. See Total Cost of Ownership, Marginal Cost.
full duplex	A communications channel over which data can be sent and received simultaneously
full release	(Release Management) A Release that includes all Components of a Release Unit, including those that have not changed. See Release Type.
function (definition)	1) An intended purpose of a Configuration Item, Person, Team, Process, or IT Service. For example one Function of an Email Service may be to store and forward outgoing mails, one Function of a Business Process may be to dispatch goods to Customers. 2) Perform the intended purpose correctly, "The computer is Functioning" 3) team or group of people, "The Change Management Function".
function point analysis	A technique used to determine the size of a development task, based on the number of function points. Function points are factors such as inputs, outputs, inquiries and logical internal sites.
functional escalation	Transferring an Incident, Problem or Change to a technical team with a higher level of expertise to assist in an Escalation.
gateway	A hardware/software package that is used to connect networks with different protocols. The gateway has its own processor and memory and can perform protocol and bandwidth conversions.
general controls	Controls, other than application controls, which relate to the environment within which computer-based application systems are developed, maintained and operated, and which are therefore applicable to all applications. The objectives of general controls are to ensure the proper development and implementation of applications, the integrity of program and data files and of computer operations. Like application controls, general controls may be either manual or programmed. Examples of general controls include the development and implementation of an IS strategy and an IS security policy, the organization of IS staff to separate conflicting duties and planning for disaster prevention and recovery.

generalized audit software	A computer program or series of programs designed to perform certain automated functions. These functions include reading computer files, selecting data, manipulating data, sorting data, summarizing data, performing calculations, selecting samples and printing reports or letters in a format specified by the IS auditor. This technique includes software acquired or written for audit purposes and software embedded in production systems.
geographic disk mirroring	A data recovery strategy that takes a set of physically disparate disks and synchronously mirrors them over high performance communication lines. Any write to a disk on one side will result in a write on the other. The local write will not return until the acknowledgement of the remote write is successful.
going rate	(Financial Management) A Charging Policy in which Charges are the same as those charged by other internal departments or internal departments of similar Organizations.
gradual recovery	(IT Service Continuity Management) A Recovery Option which is also known as Cold Standby. Provision is made to Recover the IT Service in a period of time greater than 72 hours. Gradual Recovery typically uses a Portable or Fixed Facility that has environmental support and network cabling, but no computer Systems. The hardware and software are installed as part of the IT Service Continuity Plan.
guideline (definition)	A Document describing Best Practice, that recommends what should be done. Compliance to a guideline is not normally enforced. See Standard.
hacker	An individual who attempts to gain unauthorized access to a computer system
half duplex	A communications channel that can handle only one signal at a time. The two stations must alternate their transmissions.
handprint scanner	A biometric device that is used to authenticate a user through palm scans
harden	To configure a computer or other network device to resist attacks
hardware (definition)	Relates to the physical features of the computer
hash function	An algorithm that maps or translates one set of bits into another (generally smaller) so that a message yields the same result every time the algorithm is executed using the same message as input. It is computationally infeasible for a message to be derived or reconstituted from the result produced by the algorithm. It is computationally infeasible to find two different messages that produce the same hash result using the same algorithm.
hash total	The total of any numeric data field on a document or computer file. This total is checked against a control total of the same field to facilitate accuracy of processing.
help desk (definition)	(Service Desk) A point of contact for Users to log Incidents. A Help Desk is usually more technically focused than a Service Desk and does not provide a Single Point of Contact for all interaction. The term Help Desk is often used as a synonym for Service Desk.
hexadecimal	A numbering system that uses a base of 16 and uses 16 digits: 0, 1, 2, 3, 4, 5, 6, 7, 8, 9, A, B, C, D, E and F. Programmers use hexadecimal numbers as a convenient way of representing binary numbers.
hierarchical database	A database structured in a tree/root or parent/child relationship. Each parent can have many children, but each child may have only one parent.
hierarchical escalation	Informing or involving more senior levels of management to assist in an Escalation.
honey pot	A specially configured server, designed to attract intruders so that their actions do not affect production systems; also known as a decoy server
hot site	A fully operational offsite data processing facility equipped with both hardware and system software to be used in the event of a disaster
hot standby	Synonym for Immediate Recovery
HTTP (hyper text transfer protocol)	A communication protocol used to connect to servers on the World Wide Web. Its primary function is to establish a connection with a web server and transmit HTML pages to the client browser.

HTTPS (hyper text transfer protocol secure)	A protocol for accessing a secure web server, whereby all data transferred is encrypted
hub	A common connection point for devices in a network. Hubs commonly are used to connect segments of a LAN. A hub contains multiple ports. When a packet arrives at one port, it is copied to the other ports so that all segments of the LAN can see all packets.
hyperlink	Is an electronic pathway that may be displayed in the form of highlighted text, graphics or a button that connects one web page with another web page address.
hypertext (definition)	A language, which enables electronic documents that present information that can be connected together by links instead of being presented sequentially, as is the case with normal text.
ICMP (internet control message protocol)	A set of protocols that allow systems to communicate information about the state of services on other systems. It is used, for example, in determining whether systems are up, maximum packet sizes on links, whether a destination host/network/port is available. Hackers typically (abuse) use ICMP to determine information about the remote site.
idle standby	A fail-over process in which the primary node owns the resource group. The backup node runs idle, only supervising the primary node. In case of a primary node outage, the backup node takes over. The nodes are prioritized, which means the surviving node with the highest priority will acquire the resource group. A higher priority node joining the cluster will thus cause a short service interruption.
IDS (intrusion detection system)	An intrusion detection system (IDS) inspects network activity to identify suspicious patterns that may indicate a network or system attack from someone attempting to break into or compromise a system
IEEE	(Institute of Electrical and Electronics Engineers)--Pronounced I-triple-E, IEEE is an organization composed of engineers, scientists and students. The IEEE is best known for developing standards for the computer and electronics industry.
image processing	The process of electronically inputting source documents by taking an image of the document, thereby eliminating the need for key entry
immediate recovery	(IT Service Continuity Management) A Recovery Option which is also known as Hot Standby. Provision is made to Recover the IT Service in a short period of time, typically less than 2 hours but could be up to 24 hours. Immediate Recovery typically uses a dedicated Fixed Facility with computer Systems, and software configured ready to run the IT Services. Immediate Recovery may take up to 24 hours if there is a need to Restore data from Backups.
impact (definition)	A measure of the effect of an Incident, Problem or Change on Business Processes. Impact is often based on how Service Levels will be affected. Impact and Urgency are used to assign Priority. See Impact Code.
impact code	A Category used to represent Impact. For example Major, Minor, Catastrophic. See Priority.
implementation life cycle review	Refers to the controls that support the process of transformation of the Organization's legacy information systems into the ERP applications. This would largely cover all aspects of systems implementation and configuration, such as change management
incident (definition)	1) (Incident Management) An unplanned interruption to an IT Service or reduction in the Quality of an IT Service. See Incident Management, Incident Record. 2) Any event which could affect an IT Service in the future is also an Incident. For example Failure of one disk from a mirror set.
incident management	(Incident Management) The Process responsible for managing the Lifecycle of all Incidents. The primary Objective of Incident Management is to return the IT Service to Customers as quickly as possible.
incident record	(Incident Management) A Record containing the details of an Incident. Each Incident record documents the Lifecycle of a single Incident.
incremental testing	Deliberately testing only the value-added functionality of a software component

independence	Self-governance and freedom from conflict of interest and undue influence. The IS auditor should be free to make his/her own decisions, not influenced by the organization being audited and its people (managers and employers).
independent appearance	The outward impression of being self-governing and free from conflict of interest and undue influence
independent attitude	Impartial point of view which allows the IS auditor to act objectively and with fairness
indexed sequential access method (ISAM)	A disk access method that stores data sequentially, while also maintaining an index of key fields to all the records in the file for direct access capability
indexed sequential file	A file format in which records are organized and can be accessed, according to a pre-established key that is part of the record
indirect cost	(Financial Management) A Cost of providing an IT Service which cannot be allocated in full to a specific customer. For example Cost of providing shared Servers or software licenses. Also known as Overhead. Indirect costs are divided into Absorbed Overhead and Unabsorbed Overhead. See Direct Cost.
information engineering	Data-oriented development techniques that work on the premise that data are at the center of information processing and that certain data relationships are significant to a business and must be represented in the data structure of its systems
information processing facility (IPF)	The computer room and support areas
information security management	(Security Management) The Process that ensures the Confidentiality, Integrity and Availability of an Organizations Assets, information, data and IT Services. Information Security Management usually has a wider scope than the Service Provider. It normally includes handling of paper, building access, phone calls etc., for the entire Organization.
information security manager	(Security Management) The Information Security Manager is the Role responsible for the Information Security Management Process in the IT Service Provider. The Information Security Manager is responsible for fulfilling the security demands as specified in the Information Security Policy and SLAs. The Information Security Manager typically delegates the actual implementation to other personnel in the IT Service Provider. The Information Security Officer and the Information Security Manager work closely together.
information security officer	(Security Management) The Information Security Officer is responsible for assessing the business Risks and setting the Information Security Policy. This Role is the counterpart of the Information Security Manager and resides in the Customer Organization. The Information Security Officer and the Information Security Manager work closely together.
information security policy	(Security Management) The Policy that governs the Organizations approach to Information Security Management.
information systems examination board (iseb)	The British Computer Society Information Systems Examination Board is accredited by the ICMB as an Examination Board. See http://www.bcs.org/bcs/products/qualifications/iseb for more information.
information technology (IT) (definition)	The use of technology for the storage, communication or processing of information. The technology typically includes computers, telecommunications, Applications and other software. The information may include Business data, voice, images, video, etc. Information Technology is often used to support Business Processes through IT Services.
informed customer	A manager who works for the Customer, and is a specialist in dealing with and managing IT Service Providers. The Informed Customer is responsible for all aspects of managing the relationship with Service Providers.
infrastructure service	An IT Service that is not directly used by the Business, but is required by the IT Service Provider so they can provide other IT Services. For example directory services, naming services, or communication services.
inherent risk	The susceptibility of an audit area to error which could be material, individually or in combination with other errors, assuming that there are no related internal controls

inheritance (objects)	1) Inheritance refers to database structures that have a strict hierarchy (no multiple inheritance). 2) Inheritance can initiate other objects irrespective of the class hierarchy, thus there is no strict hierarchy of objects.
initial program load (IPL)	The initialization procedure that causes an operating system to be loaded into storage at the beginning of a workday or after a system malfunction
input controls	Techniques and procedures used to verify, validate and edit data, to ensure that only correct data are entered into the computer
insource	Transferring the provision of IT Services from an External Service Provider to an Internal Service Provider. The term Insourcing is used to mean running or managing IT Services as an Internal Service Provider. See Outsource.
integrated services digital network (ISDN)	A public end-to-end digital telecommunications network with signaling, switching and transport capabilities supporting a wide range of service accessed by standardized interfaces with integrated customer control. The standard allows transmission of digital voice, video and data over 64 Kbps lines.
integrated test facilities (ITF)	Test data are processed in production systems. The data usually represent a set of fictitious entities such as departments, customers and products. Output reports are verified to confirm the correctness of the processing.
integration testing	Testing of a Build or Release to ensure that the parts work correctly together.
integrity (definition)	1) The accuracy and completeness of information as well as to its validity in accordance with business values and expectations 2) (Security Management) A Security Principle that ensures data and Configuration Items are only modified by authorized personnel and Activities. Integrity considers all possible causes of modification, including software and hardware Failure, environmental Events, and human intervention. (C-I-A)
intelligent terminal	A terminal with built-in processing capability. It has no disk or tape storage but has memory. The terminal interacts with the user by editing and validating data as they are entered prior to final processing.
interactive voice response (IVR)	(Service Desk) A form of Automatic Call Distribution that accepts User input, such as key presses and spoken commands, to identify the correct destination for incoming Calls.
interest rate risk	Is the risk to earnings or capital arising from movements in interest rates. From an economic perspective, a bank focuses on the sensitivity of the value of its assets, liabilities and revenues to changes in interest rates. Internet banking may attract deposits, loans and other relationships from a larger pool of possible customers than other forms of marketing. Greater access to customers who primarily seek the best rate or term reinforces the need for managers to maintain appropriate asset/liability management systems, which should include the ability to react quickly to changing market conditions.
interface testing	A testing technique that is used to evaluate output from one application, while the information is sent as input to another application
intermediate recovery	(IT Service Continuity Management) A Recovery Option which is also known as Warm Standby. Provision is made to Recover the IT Service in a period of time between 24 and 72 hours. Intermediate Recovery typically uses a shared Portable or Fixed Facility that has Computer Systems and Network Components. The hardware and software will need to be configured, and data will need to be restored, as part of the IT Service Continuity Plan.
internal controls	The policies, procedures, practices and organizational structures designed to provide reasonable assurance that business objectives will be achieved and that undesired events will be prevented or detected and corrected.

internal control structure	The dynamic, integrated processes, effected by the governing body, management and all other staff, that are designed to provide reasonable assurance regarding the achievement of the following general objectives:
	    -Effectiveness, efficiency and economy of operations
	    -Reliability of management
	    -Compliance with applicable laws, regulations and internal policies
	
	Management's strategies for achieving these general objectives are affected by the design and operation of the following components:
	    -Control environment
	    -Information system
	    -Control procedures

internal customer	A Customer who works for the same Business as the IT Service Provider. See Internal Service Provider, External Customer.
internal penetrators	Authorized users of a computer system who overstep their legitimate access rights. This category is divided into masqueraders and clandestine users.
internal service provider	An IT Service Provider which is part of the same Business as their Customer. An IT Service Provider may have both Internal Customers and External Customers. See External Service Provider.
internal storage	The main memory of the computer's central processing unit
international organization for standardization (ISO)	The International Organization for Standardization (ISO) is the world's largest developer of Standards. ISO is a non-governmental organization which is a network of the national standards institutes of 156 countries. Further information about ISO is available from http://www.iso.org/
Internet (definition)	1) Two or more networks connected by a router 2) The world's largest network using TCP/IP protocols to link government, university and commercial institutions
internet banking	Use of the Internet as a remote delivery channel for banking services. Services include the traditional ones, such as opening an account or transferring funds to different accounts, and new banking services, such as electronic bill presentment and payment (allowing customers to receive and pay bills on a bank's web site).
internet engineering task force (IETF)	The Internet standards setting organization with affiliates internationally from network industry representatives. This includes all network industry developers and researchers concerned with evolution and planned growth of the Internet.
internet inter-orb protocol (IIOP)	A protocol developed by the object management group (OMG) to implement Common Object Request Broker Architecture (CORBA) solutions over the World Wide Web. CORBA enables modules of network-based programs to communicate with one another. These modules or program parts, such as tables, arrays, and more complex program sub-elements, are referred to as objects. Use of IIOP in this process enables browsers and servers to exchange both simple and complex objects. This significantly differs from HTTP, which only supports the transmission of text.
internet packet (IP) spoofing	An attack using packets with the spoofed source Internet packet (IP) addresses. This technique exploits applications that use authentication based on IP addresses. This technique also may enable an unauthorized user to gain root access on the target system.
internet service provider (ISP)	An External Service Provider that provides access to the Internet. Most ISPs also provide other IT Services such as web hosting.
intranet	A private network that uses the infrastructure and standards of the Internet and World Wide Web, but is isolated from the public Internet by firewall barriers.
intrusion (definition)	Any intentional violation of the security policy of a system
intrusion detection (definition)	The process of monitoring the events occurring in a computer system or network, detecting signs of security problems
intrusive monitoring	In vulnerability analysis, gaining information by performing checks that affects the normal operation of the system, even crashing the system

investment appraisal	(Financial Management) The Activity responsible for carrying out a Cost Benefit Analysis to justify Capital Expenditure for a new or changed IT Services. See Business Case, Cost Effectiveness, Return on Investment, Return on Capital Employed.
invocation	(IT Service Continuity Management) Initiation of the steps defined in a plan. For example initiating the IT Service Continuity Plan for one or more IT Services.
IP (internet protocol)	Specifies the format of packets and the addressing scheme
IPSEC (internet protocol security)	A set of protocols developed by the IETF to support the secure exchange of packets
irregularities	Intentional violations of established management policy or regulatory requirements. Deliberate misstatements or omissions of information concerning the area under audit or the organization as a whole; gross negligence or unintentional illegal acts.
Ishikawa diagram	Synonym for Cause / Effect diagram.
ISO 9000	A generic term that refers to a number of international Standards and Guidelines for Quality Management Systems. See http://www.iso.org/ for more information. See ISO.
ISO 9001	An international Standard for Quality Management Systems. See ISO 9000.
ISO/IEC 17799	(Security Management) ISO Code of Practice for Information Security Management, based on BS 7799 Part 1. It defines information confidentiality, integrity and availability controls
ISO/IEC 20000	ISO Specification and Code of Practice for IT Service Management. ISO/IEC 20000 is aligned with ITIL Best Practice, and supersedes BS 15000. See Standard.
ISO/IEC 27001	(Security Management) ISO Specification for Information Security Management. The corresponding Code of Practice is ISO/IEC 17799. ISO/IEC 27001 supersedes BS7799 Part 2. See Standard.
IT Accounting	(Financial Management) The Process responsible for identifying actual Costs of delivering IT Services, comparing these with budgeted costs, and managing variance from the Budget. See also Charging.
IT availability metrics model (ITAMM)	(Availability Management) A model that helps to ensure all aspects of Availability are considered when defining Availability Metrics and reports.
IT directorate	Senior Management within a Service Provider, charged with developing and delivering IT services. Most commonly used in UK Government departments.
IT governance (definition)	A structure of relationships and processes to direct and control the enterprise in order to achieve the enterprise's goals by adding value while balancing risk versus return over IT and its processes
IT infrastructure (definition)	All of the hardware, software, networks, facilities etc. that are required to develop, test, deliver or support IT Services. The term IT Infrastructure includes all of the Information Technology but not the associated people, Processes and documentation.
IT infrastructure library (ITIL)	A set of Best Practice guidance for IT Service Management. ITIL is owned by the OGC and is developed in conjunction with the itSMF. ITIL consists of a series of publications giving guidance on the provision of Quality IT Services, and on the Processes and facilities needed to support them. See http://www.ogc.gov.uk/index.asp?id=2261 for more information.
IT operations	The Process responsible for the day-to-day monitoring and management of one or more IT Services and the IT Infrastructure they depend on. The term IT Operations is also used to refer to the group or department within an IT Service Provider responsible for IT Operations. See Operations Bridge, Event Management.

IT service (definition)	A Service provided to one or more Customers by an IT Service Provider. An IT Service is based on the use of Information Technology and supports the Customer's Business Processes. An IT Service is made up from a combination of people, Processes and technology and should be defined in a Service Level Agreement.
IT service continuity management (ITSCM)	(IT Service Continuity Management) The Process responsible for managing Risks that could seriously impact IT Services. ITSCM ensures that the IT Service Provider can always provide minimum agreed Service Levels, by reducing the Risk to an acceptable level and Planning for the Recovery of IT Services. ITSCM should be designed to support Business Continuity Management.
IT service continuity plan	(IT Service Continuity Management) A Plan defining the steps required to Recover one or more IT Services. The Plan will also identify the triggers for Invocation, people to be involved, communications etc. The IT Service Continuity Plan should be part of a Business Continuity Plan.
IT service management forum (ITSMF)	The IT Service Management Forum is an independent Organization dedicated to promoting a professional approach to IT Service Management. The itSMF is a not-for-profit membership Organization with representation in many countries around the world (itSMF Chapters). The itSMF and its membership contribute to the development of ITIL and associated IT Service Management Standards. See http://www.itsmf.com/ for more information.
IT service provider (definition)	A Service Provider that provides IT Services to Internal Customers or External Customers.
IT steering group	A formal group that is responsible for ensuring that Business and IT Service Provider Strategies and Plans are closely aligned. An IT Steering Group includes senior representatives from the Business and the IT Service Provider.
ITIL certification management board (ICMB)	The body responsible for the maintenance and ongoing development of the ITIL qualification scheme. See http://www.itil.co.uk/icmb.htm for further information.
job control language (JCL)	A language used to control run routines in connection with performing tasks on a computer
job description	A Document which defines the Roles, responsibilities, skills and knowledge required by a particular person. One Job Description can include multiple Roles, for example the Roles of Configuration Manager and Change Manager may be carried out by one person.
journal entry	A debit or credit to a general ledger account. See also manual journal entry.
judgment sampling	Any sample that is selected subjectively or in such a manner that the sample selection process is not random or the sampling results are not evaluated mathematically
Kepner-Tregoe analysis	(Problem Management) A structured approach to Problem solving. The Problem is analyzed in terms of what, where, when and extent. Possible causes are identified. The most probable cause is tested. The true cause is verified.
key performance indicator (KPI)	A Metric that is used to help manage a Process, IT Service or Activity. Many Metrics may be measured, but only the most important of these are defined as KPIs and used to actively manage and report on the Process, IT Service or Activity. KPIs should be selected to ensure that Efficiency, Effectiveness, and Cost Effectiveness are all managed. See Critical Success Factor.
knowledge base	(Service Desk) (Incident Management) A Database containing information about Incidents, Problems and Known Errors. The Knowledge Base is used to match new Incidents with historical information, improving Resolution times and First Time Fix Rates.
knowledge management	The Process responsible for gathering, analyzing, storing and sharing knowledge information within an Organization. The primary purpose of Knowledge Management is to improve Efficiency by reducing the need to rediscover knowledge.
known error (KE)	(Problem Management) A Problem that has a documented Root Cause and a Workaround. Known Errors are created by Problem Control and are managed throughout their Lifecycle by Error Control. Known Errors may also be identified by Development or Suppliers. See Known Error Record, Knowledge Base.

known error database	(Service Desk) (Incident Management) (Problem Management) A Database containing all Known Error Records. This Database is created by Problem Management and used by Incident and Problem Management. See Knowledge Base.
known error record	(Problem Management) A Record containing the details of a Known Error. Each Known Error Record documents the Lifecycle of a Known Error, including the Status, Root Cause and Workaround. In some implementations a Known Error is documented using additional fields in a Problem Record.
L2F (layer 2 forwarding)	A tunneling protocol developed by Cisco Systems to support the creation of VPNs
L2TP (layer 2 tunneling protocol)	An extension to PPP to facilitate the creation of VPNs. L2TP merges the best features of PPTP (from Microsoft) and L2F (from Cisco).
latency	The time it takes a system and network delay to respond. System latency is the time a system takes to retrieve data. Network latency is the time it takes for a packet to travel from source to the final destination.
LDAP (lightweight directory access protocol)	A set of protocols for accessing information directories. It is based on the X.500 standard, but is significantly simpler.
leased lines	A communication line permanently assigned to connect two points, as opposed to a dial-up line that is only available and open when a connection is made by dialing the target machine or network. Also known as a dedicated line.
legal risk	Is the risk to earnings or capital arising from violations of, or nonconformance with, laws, rules, regulations, prescribed practices or ethical standards. Banks are subject to various forms of legal risk. This can include the risk that assets will turn out to be worth less or liabilities will turn out to be greater than expected because of inadequate or incorrect legal advice or documentation. In addition, existing laws may fail to resolve legal issues involving a bank; a court case involving a particular bank may have wider implications for banking business and involve costs to it and many or all other banks; and, laws affecting banks or other commercial enterprises may change. Banks are particularly susceptible to legal risks when entering new types of transactions and when the legal right of a counter-party to enter into transactions is not established.
librarian	The individual responsible for the safeguard and maintenance of all program and data files
license management	The Process responsible for the management of software licenses throughout their Lifecycle.
lifecycle (definition)	The various stages in the life of a Configuration Item, Incident, Problem, Change etc. The Lifecycle defines the Categories for Status and the Status transitions that are permitted. For example: • The Lifecycle of an Application includes Design, Build, Test, Deploy, Operate etc. • The lifecycle of an Incident includes Detect, Respond, Diagnose, Repair, Recover, Restore. • The lifecycle of a Server may include: Ordered, Received, In Test, Live, Disposed etc.
limit check	Tests of specified amount fields against stipulated high or low limits of acceptability. When both high and low values are used, the test may be called a range check.
link editor (linkage editor)	A utility program that combines several separately compiled modules into one, resolving internal references between them
liquidity risk	Is the risk to earnings or capital arising from a bank's inability to meet its obligations when they come due, without incurring unacceptable losses. Internet banking may increase deposit volatility from customers who maintain accounts solely on the basis of rate or terms.
live environment	A controlled Environment containing Live Configuration Items used to deliver IT Services to Customers.

local area network (LAN)	A communication network that serves several users within a specified geographic area. It is made up of servers, workstations, a network operating system and a communications link. Personal computer LANs function as distributed processing systems in which each computer in the network does its own processing and manages some of its data. Shared data are stored in a file server that acts as a remote disk drive to all users in the network.
local loop	The communication lines that provide connectivity between the telecommunications carrier's central office and the subscriber's facilities
log (definition)	To record details of information or events in an organized record-keeping system, usually sequenced in the order they occurred
logical access controls	The policies, procedures, organizational structure and electronic access controls designed to restrict access to computer software and data files
logoff	Disconnecting from the computer
logon	The act of connecting to the computer. It typically requires entry of a user ID and password into a computer terminal.
logs/log file	Files created specifically to record various actions occurring on the system to be monitored, such as failed login attempts, full disk drives and e-mail delivery failures
machine language	The logical language a computer understands
magnetic card reader	A card reader that reads cards with a magnetized surface on which data can be stored and retrieved
magnetic ink character recognition (MICR)	Used to electronically input, read and interpret information directly from a source document; requires the source document to have specially-coded magnetic ink typeset
maintainability	(Availability Management) A measure of how quickly and Effectively a Configuration Item or IT Service can be restored to normal working after a Failure. Maintainability is often measured and reported as MTTR. See Availability.
major incident	(Incident Management) The highest Category of Impact for an Incident. A Major Incident results in significant disruption to the Business. See Escalation.
managed object (mo)	An abstract representation of a Resource that is used for Operational management of that Resource. An MO is defined in terms of the attributes of the Resource, operations that may be performed on it, notifications it may issue and relationships with other MOs. MOs differ from Configuration Items as their status is dynamic, and Changes to their Operational state do not need to be approved by the Change Management Process.
managed services	Synonym for Outsourced IT Services. Also used in ISO/IEC 20000 as a Synonym for IT Services, whether Outsourced or not.
management information (definition)	Information that is used to support decision making by managers. Management Information is often generated automatically by tools supporting the various IT Service Management Processes. Management Information often includes the values of KPIs such as "Percentage of Changes leading to Incidents", or "First Time Fix Rate".
management information system (mis)	1) An organized assembly of resources and procedures required to collect, process and distribute data for use in decision making 2) The term MIS is also informally used to mean the output of MIS, including data and reports.
management system	The framework of Policy and Processes that ensures an Organization can achieve its Objectives.
man-in-the-middle attack	An attack strategy in which the attacker intercepts the communications stream between two parts of the victim system and then replaces the traffic between the two components with the intruder's own, eventually assuming control of the communication
manual journal entry	A journal entry entered at a computer terminal. Manual journal entries can include regular, statistical, inter-company and foreign currency entries
manual workaround	(Incident Management) (Problem Management) A Workaround that requires manual intervention. (IT Service Continuity Management) A Recovery Option. The Business Process Operates without the use of IT Services. This is a temporary measure and is usually combined with another Recovery Option.

mapping	Diagramming data that are to be exchanged electronically, including how it is to be used and what business management systems need it. It is a preliminary step for developing an applications link. (Also see application tracing and mapping.)
marginal cost	(Financial Management) The Cost of continuing to providing the IT Service. Marginal Cost does not include investment already made, for example the cost of developing new software and delivering training. See Full Cost, Opportunity Cost
market price	(Financial Management) A Charging Policy in which Charges are the same as those an external Supplier would charge.
masking	A computerized technique of blocking out the display of sensitive information, such as passwords, on a computer terminal or report
masqueraders	Attackers that penetrate systems by using user identifiers and passwords taken from legitimate users
master file	A file of semi-permanent information that is used frequently for processing data or for more than one purpose
materiality	An auditing concept regarding the importance of an item of information with regard to its impact or effect on the functioning of the entity being audited. An expression of the relative significance or importance of a particular matter in the context of the organization as a whole.
maturity level	A named level in a maturity model such as the Carnegie Mellon Capability Maturity Model Integration. See Process Maturity.
mean time between failures (MBTF)	(Availability Management) A Metric for measuring and reporting Reliability. MTBF is the average time that a Configuration Item or IT Service can perform its agreed Function without interruption. This is measured from when the CI or IT Service starts working, until it next fails.
mean time between service incidents (MTBSI)	(Availability Management) A Metric used for measuring and reporting Reliability. MTBSI is the mean time from when a System or IT Service fails, until it next fails. MTBSI is equal to MTBF + MTTR.
mean time to repair (MTTR)	(Availability Management) A Metric for measuring and reporting Maintainability. MTTR is the average time taken to restore a Configuration Item or IT Service after a Failure. MTTR is measured from when the CI or IT Service fails until it is fully restored and delivering its normal functionality.
memory dump	The act of copying raw data from one place to another with little or no formatting for readability. Usually, dump refers to copying data from main memory to a display screen or a printer. Dumps are useful for diagnosing bugs. After a program fails, one can study the dump and analyze the contents of memory at the time of the failure. Dumps are usually output in a difficult-to-read form (that is, binary, octal or hexadecimal), so a memory dump will not help unless each person knows exactly for what to look.
message switching	A telecommunications traffic controlling methodology in which a complete message is sent to a concentration point and stored until the communications path is established
metric (definition)	Something that is measured and reported to help manage a Process, IT Service or Activity. See KPI.
microwave transmission	A high-capacity line-of-sight transmission of data signals through the atmosphere which often requires relay stations
middleware	Another term for an application programmer interface (API). It refers to the interfaces that allow programmers to access lower- or higher-level services by providing an intermediary layer that includes function calls to the services.
mission statement	The Mission Statement of an Organization is a short but complete description of the overall purpose and intentions of that Organization. It states what is to be achieved, but not how this should be done.

misuse detection	Detection on the basis of whether the system activity matches that defined as bad
modeling	Any technique used to predict the future behavior of an IT Service, Configuration Item or Business Process. Models are commonly used in Financial Management, Capacity Management and Availability Management. See Estimation, Analytical Modeling, Simulation Modeling.
modem (modulator-demodulator)	Connects a terminal or computer to a communications network via a telephone line. Modems turn digital pulses from the computer into frequencies within the audio range of the telephone system. When acting in the receiver capacity, a modem decodes incoming frequencies.
modulation	The process of converting a digital computer signal into an analog telecommunications signal
monetary unit sampling	A sampling technique that estimates the amount of overstatement in an account balance
monitor (definition)	Any information collection mechanism utilized by an intrusion detection system
monitoring policy	The rules outlining the way in which information is captured and interpreted
multiplexing	The transmission of more than one signal across a physical channel
multiplexer	A device used for combining several lower-speed channels into a higher-speed channel
mutual takeover	A fail-over process; which is basically a two-way idle standby: two servers are configured so that both can take over the other node's resource group. Both must have enough CPU power to run both applications with sufficient speed, or performance losses must be taken into account expected until the failed node reintegrates. This also works nicely in three or more node configurations.
NAT (network address translation)	An Internet standard that allows a network to use one set of IP addresses for internal traffic and a second set of addresses for external traffic. The server, providing the NAT service, changes the source address of outgoing packets from the internal to the external address and reverses it for packets returning.
Netware	A popular local area network operating system developed by the Novell Corp.
network (definition)	A system of interconnected computers and the communications equipment used to connect them
network administrator	The person responsible for maintaining a LAN and assisting end users
network hop	1) An attack strategy in which the attacker successively hacks into a series of connected systems, obscuring his/her identify from the victim of the attack 2) The link or connection between two routers, a metric used in calculations of network distance
n-line support	(Service Desk) (Incident Management) (Problem Management) A generic term for any level of Support Group. See First-line Support, Second-line Support, Third-line Support.
node	Point at which terminals are given access to a network
noise	Disturbances, such as static, in data transmissions that cause messages to be misinterpreted by the receiver
non-intrusive monitoring	In vulnerability analysis, gaining information by performing standard system status queries and inspecting system attributes
Non-repudiable transactions	Transactions that cannot be denied after the fact
Non-repudiation	The assurance that a party cannot later deny originating data, that it is the provision of proof of the integrity and origin of the data which can be verified by a third party. Non-repudiation may be provided by a digital signature.
normalization	The elimination of redundant data
notional charging	(Financial Management) A Charging Policy where Customers are sent Bills for the IT Services they have used, but money is not actually transferred. This is sometimes introduced to ensure that Customers are aware of the Costs they incur, or as a stage during the introduction of Real Charging.
numeric check	An edit check designed to ensure the data in a particular field is numeric

object code	Machine-readable instructions produced from a compiler or assembler program that has accepted and translated the source code
object management group (OMG)	A consortium with more than 700 affiliates from the software industry. Its purpose is to provide a common framework for developing applications using object-oriented programming techniques. For example, OMG is known principally for promulgating the CORBA specification.
object orientation	An approach to system development where the basic unit of attention is an object, which represents an encapsulation of both data (an object's attributes) and functionality (an object's methods). Objects usually are created using a general template called a class. Classes are the basis for most design work in objects. Classes and their objects communicate in defined ways. Aggregate classes interact through messages, which are directed requests for services from one class (the client) to another class (the server). A class may share the structure or methods defined in one or more other classes--a relationship known as inheritance.
objective (definition)	The defined purpose or aim of a Process, an Activity or an Organization as a whole. Objectives are usually expressed as measurable targets. The term Objective is also informally used to mean a Requirement.
objectivity	The ability to exercise judgment, express opinions and present recommendations with impartiality
object-oriented system development	A system development methodology that is organized around "objects" rather than "actions" and "data" rather than "logic." Object-oriented analysis is an assessment of a physical system to determine which objects in the real world need to be represented as objects in a software system. Any object-oriented design is software design that is centered around designing the objects that will make up a program. Any object-oriented program is one that is composed of objects or software parts.
office of government commerce (OGC)	OGC own the copyright to the ITIL publications. They are a UK Government department that works with public sector Organizations to help them improve their Efficiency, gain better Value for Money from their commercial Activities, and deliver improved success from Programs and Projects.
office of public sector information (OPSI)	OPSI are the publishers of the ITIL publications. They are a UK Government department who provide online access to UK legislation, license the re-use of Crown copyright material, manage the Information Fair Trader Scheme, maintain the Government's Information Asset Register and provide advice and guidance on official publishing and Crown copyright
offline files	Computer file storage media not physically connected to the computer; typically tapes or tape cartridges used for backup purposes
offsite storage	A storage facility located away from the building housing the primary information processing facility (IPF), used for storage of computer media such as offline backup data and storage files
online data processing	Processing is achieved by entering information into the computer via a video display terminal. The computer immediately accepts or rejects the information, as it is entered.
open systems	Systems for which detailed specifications of their components composition are published in a nonproprietary environment, thereby enabling competing organizations to use these standard components to build competitive systems. The advantages of using open systems include portability, interoperability and integration.
operate (definition)	To perform as expected. A Process or Configuration Item is said to Operate if it is delivering the Required outputs. Operate also means to perform one or more Operations. For example, to Operate a computer is to do the day-to-day Operations needed for it to perform as expected. See Operation, IT Operations, Business Operations.
object code	

operating system (definition)	A master control program that runs the computer and acts as a scheduler and traffic controller. It is the first program copied into the computer's memory after the computer is turned on and must reside in memory at all times. It is the software that interfaces between the computer hardware (disk, keyboard, mouse, network, modem, printer) and the application software (word processor, spreadsheet, e-mail), which also controls access to the devices and is partially responsible for security components and sets the standards for the application programs that run in it.
operating system audit trails	Records of system events generated by a specialized operating system mechanism
operation (definition)	A pre-defined Activity or Transaction. For example loading a magnetic tape, accepting money at a point of sale, or reading data from a disk drive. See Operate, IT Operations, Business Operations.
operational (definition)	1) The lowest of three levels of Planning and delivery (Strategic, Tactical, Operational). Operational Activities include the day-to-day or short term Planning or delivery of a Business Process or IT Service Management Process. 2) The term Operational is also used to refer to a Configuration Item or IT Service being ready for use.
operational acceptance	(Release Management) Part of the Release Acceptance Activity, responsible for ensuring that everything needed for IT Operations is in place before the Release is deployed. Operational Acceptance often uses a checklist to ensure that all required documentation, IT Operations Processes, tools and training are in place.
operational audit	An audit designed to evaluate the various internal controls, economy and efficiency of a function or department
operational control	These controls deal with the everyday operation of a company or organization to ensure all objectives are achieved.
operational cost	(Financial Management) Cost resulting from running the IT Services. Often repeating payments. For example staff costs, hardware maintenance and electricity (also known as "current expenditure" or "revenue expenditure") See Capital Costs
operational expenditure (OPEX)	Synonym for Operational Cost.
operational level agreement (OLA)	(Service Level Management) An Agreement between an IT Service Provider and another part of the same Business that provides Services to them. For example there could be an OLA with a facilities department to provide air conditioning, or with the procurement department to obtain hardware in agreed times. An OLA may also be between two parts of the same IT Service Provider, for example between the Service Desk and a Support Group. See Service Level Agreement.
operational risk	The most important types of operational risk involve breakdowns in internal controls and corporate governance. Such breakdowns can lead to financial losses through error, fraud or failure to perform in a timely manner or cause the interests of the bank to be compromised in some other way, for example, by its dealers, lending officers or other staff exceeding their authority or conducting business in an unethical or risky manner. Other aspects of operational risk include major failure of information technology systems or events such as security problems or other disasters
operations bridge	A physical location where IT Services and IT Infrastructure are monitored and managed. See IT Operations, Event Management.
operator console	A special terminal used by computer operations personnel to control computer and systems operations functions. These terminals typically provide a high level of computer access and should be properly secured.
opportunity cost	(Financial Management) A Cost that is used in deciding between investment choices. Opportunity Cost represents the revenue that would have been generated by using the Resources in a different way. For example the Opportunity Cost of purchasing a new Server may include the loss of interest that the money would otherwise have earned in the bank. See Full Cost, Marginal Cost

optical character recognition (OCR)	Used to electronically scan and input written information from a source document
optical scanner	An input device that reads characters and images that are printed or painted on a paper form into the computer.
optimize (definition)	Review, Plan and request Changes, in order to obtain the maximum Efficiency and Effectiveness from a Process, Configuration Item, Application etc. See Continuous Improvement.
organization (definition)	A company, legal entity or other institution. Examples of Organizations that are not companies include International Standards Organization, itSMF. The term Organization is sometimes used to refer to any entity which has People, Resources and Budgets. For example a Project or Business Unit.
output analyzer	Checks the accuracy of the results produced by a test run. There are three types of checks that an output analyzer can perform. First, if a standard set of test data and test results exists for a program, the output of a test run after program maintenance can be compared with the set of results that should be produced. Second, as programmers prepare test data and calculate the expected results, these results can be stored on a file and the output analyzer compares the actual results of a test run with the expected results. Third, the output analyzer can act as a query language; it accepts queries about whether certain relationships exist in the file of output results and reports compliance or noncompliance.
outsource	Transferring the provision of IT Services from an Internal Service Provider to an External Service Provider. The term Outsourcing is used to mean making use of an External Service Provider to manage IT Services, or acting as an External Service Provider to manage IT Services. See Insource.
overhead	See Indirect cost
package release	(Release Management) A single Release that includes a number of Full or Delta Releases. See Release Type
packet (definition)	Data unit that is routed from source to destination in a packet-switched network. A packet contains both routing information and data. Transmission control protocol/Internet protocol (TCP/IP) is such a packet-switched network.
packet filtering	Controlling access to a network by analyzing the attributes of the incoming and outgoing packets and either letting them pass, or denying them, based on a list of rules
packet switching	The process of transmitting messages in convenient pieces that can be reassembled at the destination
parallel simulation	Parallel simulation involves the IS auditor writing a program to replicate those application processes that are critical to an audit opinion and using this program to reprocess application system data. The results produced are compared with the results generated by the application system and any discrepancies identified.
parallel testing	The process of feeding test data into two systems, the modified system and an alternative system (possibly the original system) and comparing results
pareto principle	A technique used to prioritise Activities. The Pareto Principle says that 80% of the value of any activity is created with 20% of the effort.
parity check	A general hardware control, which helps to detect data errors when data are read from memory or communicated from one computer to another. A 1-bit digit (either 0 or 1) is added to a data item to indicate whether the sum of that data item's bit is odd or even. When the parity bit disagrees with the sum of the other bits, the computer reports an error. The probability of a parity check detecting an error is 50 percent.
partitioned file	A file format in which the file is divided into multiple sub-files and a directory is established to locate each sub-file
partnership	A relationship between two Organizations which involves working closely together for common goals or mutual benefit. The IT Service Provider should have a Partnership with the Business, and with Third Parties who are critical to the delivery of IT Services.

passive attack/assault	In a passive assault, intruders attempt to learn some characteristic of the data being transmitted. They may be able to read the contents of the data so the privacy of the data is violated. Alternatively, although the content of the data itself may remain secure, intruders may read and analyze the plaintext source and destination identifiers attached to a message for routing purposes, or they may examine the lengths and frequency of messages being transmitted.
passive response	A response option in intrusion detection in which the system simply reports and records the problem detected, relying on the user to take subsequent action
password (definition)	A protected, generally computer-encrypted string of characters that authenticate a computer user to the computer system
password cracker	Specialized security checker that tests user's passwords, searching for passwords that are easy to guess by repeatedly trying words from specially crafted dictionaries. Failing that, many password crackers can brute force all possible combinations in a relatively short period of time with current desktop computer hardware.
payment system	A financial system that establishes the means for transferring money between suppliers and users of funds, ordinarily by exchanging debits or credits between banks or financial institutions.
penetration testing	A live test of the effectiveness of security defenses through mimicking the actions of real-life attackers
percentage utilization	(Capacity Management) The amount of time that a Component is busy over a given period of time. For example, if a CPU is busy for 1800 seconds in a one hour period, its utilization is 50%
performance (definition)	A measure of what is achieved or delivered by a person, team or Process. See KPI. (Capacity Management) A measure of the overall time taken to carry out one or more Transactions. See Response Time, Throughput.
performance indicators	A set of metrics designed to measure the extent to which performance objectives are being achieved on an on-going basis. They can include service level agreements, critical success factors, customer satisfaction ratings, internal or external benchmarks, industry best practices and international standards.
performance management	(Capacity Management) The Process responsible for day-to-day Capacity Management Activities. These include monitoring, threshold detection, Performance analysis and Tuning, and implementing changes related to Performance and Capacity.
performance testing	Comparing the system's performance to other equivalent systems using well defined benchmarks
peripherals (definition)	Auxiliary computer hardware equipment used for input, output and data storage. Examples include disk drives and printers.
permanent virtual circuit (PVC)	A permanent connection between hosts in a packet switched network
personal identification number (PIN)	A type of password (i.e., a secret number assigned to an individual) that, in conjunction with some means of identifying the individual, serves to verify the authenticity of the individual. PINs have been adopted by financial institutions as the primary means of verifying customers in an electronic funds transfer system (EFTS).
pervasive is controls	General controls which are designed to manage and monitor the IS environment and which, therefore, affect all IS-related activities
piggy backing	1) Following an authorized person into a restricted access area; 2) electronically attaching to an authorized telecommunications link to intercept and possibly alter transmissions.
plaintext	Digital information, such as cleartext, that is intelligible to the reader

plan (definition)	A Document which identifies a series of Activities and the Resources required to achieve an Objective. For example a Plan to implement a new IT Service or Process. ISO/IEC 20000 requires a Plan for the management of each IT Service Management Process. See Project.
plan-do-check-act (PDCA)	A four stage cycle for Process management, devised by Edward Deming. Plan-Do-Check-Act is also called the Deming Cycle. PLAN: Design or revise Processes that support the IT Services. DO: Implement the Plan and manage the Processes. CHECK: Measure the Processes and IT Services, compare with objectives and produce reports ACT: Plan and implement changes to improve the Processes.
planned downtime	(Availability Management) Agreed time when an IT Service will not be available. Planned Downtime is often used for maintenance, upgrades and testing. See Change Slot, Downtime.
planning (definition)	An Activity responsible for creating one or more Plans. For example, Capacity Planning.
point-of-presence (POP)	A phone number that represents the area in which the communications provider or Internet service provider (ISP) provides service
point-of-sale systems (POS)	Point-of-sale systems enable capture of data at the time and place of transaction. POS terminals may include use of optical scanners for use with bar codes or magnetic card readers for use with credit cards. POS systems may be online to a central computer or may use stand-alone terminals or microcomputers that hold the transactions until the end of a specified period when they are sent to the main computer for batch processing.
policy (definition)	Formally documented management expectations and intentions. Policies are used to direct decisions, and to ensure consistent and appropriate development and implementation of Processes, Standards, Roles, Activities, IT Infrastructure etc.
polymorphism (objects)	Polymorphism refers to database structures that send the same command to different child objects that can produce different results depending on their family hierarchical tree structure.
population	The entire set of data from which a sample is selected and about which the IS auditor wishes to draw conclusions
port (definition)	1) An interface point between the CPU and a peripheral device 2) An address point for applications running on a workstation or server, normally associated with the Transport Layer of the OSI model
portable facility	(IT Service Continuity Management) A prefabricated building, or a large vehicle, provided by a Third Party and moved to a site when needed by an IT Service Continuity Plan. See Recovery Option, Fixed Facility.
portfolio management	(Business Relationship Management) The Process responsible for managing the Portfolio of Services. Portfolio Management includes maximizing the value to the Business of existing and proposed new IT Services, and identifying the need to create new IT Services and retire IT Services that are no longer of value. The detailed Planning and implementation work is carried out as part of the Service Planning Process.
portfolio of services	(Business Relationship Management) A published description of all IT services. The Portfolio is maintained by the Service Provider and includes all IT Services whether they are Live, in Development, or proposed new Services. See Service Catalogue, Application Portfolio.
post implementation review (PIR)	A Review that takes place after a Change or a Project has been implemented. A PIR determines if the Change or Project was successful, and identifies opportunities for improvement.
posting	The process of actually entering transactions into computerized or manual files. Such transactions might immediately update the master files or may result in memo posting, in which the transactions are accumulated over a period of time, then applied to master file updating.
PPP (point-to-point protocol)	A protocol used for transmitting data between two ends of a connection

PPTP (point-to-point tunneling protocol)	A protocol used to transmit data securely between two end points to create a VPN
preventive controls	These controls are designed to prevent or restrict an error, omission or unauthorized intrusion.
price risk	Is the risk to earnings or capital arising from changes in the value of portfolios of financial instruments. Price risk arises from market making, dealing and position taking in interest rate, foreign exchange, equity and commodities markets. Banks may be exposed to price risk if they create or expand deposit brokering, loan sales or securitization programs as a result of Internet banking activities.
pricing	(Financial Management) Pricing is the Activity for establishing how much Customers will be Charged. See Billing, Charging Process.
PRINCE2	The standard UK government methodology for Project management. See http://www.ogc.gov.uk/prince2/ for more information.
priority (definition)	A Category used to identify the relative importance of an Incident, Problem or Change. Priority is based on Impact and Urgency, and is used to identify required times for actions to be taken. For example the SLA may state that Priority2 Incidents must be resolved within 12 hours.
privacy (definition)	Freedom from unauthorized intrusion
private key (definition)	A mathematical key (kept secret by the holder) used to create digital signatures and, depending upon the algorithm, to decrypt messages or files encrypted (for confidentiality) with the corresponding public key
private key cryptosystems	Used in data encryption, it uses a secret key to encrypt the plaintext to the ciphertext. It also uses the same key to decrypt the ciphertext to the corresponding plaintext. In this case, the key is symmetric such that the encryption key is equivalent to the decryption key.
privilege (definition)	The level of trust with which a system user or object is imbued
proactive problem management	(Problem Management) Part of the Problem Management Process. The Objective of Proactive Problem Management is to identify Problems that might otherwise be missed. Proactive Problem Management analyses Incident Records, and uses data collected by other IT Service Management Processes to identify trends or significant problems.
problem (definition)	The root cause of one or more incidents. See Problem Management, Problem Record.
problem control	(Problem Management) Part of the Problem Management Process. Problem Control is the Activity responsible for identifying the Root Cause and developing a Workaround or Structural Solution for a Problem. See Error Control.
problem management	(Problem Management) The Process responsible for managing the Lifecycle of all Problems. The primary objectives of Problem Management are to prevent Incidents from happening, and to minimise the Impact of Incidents that cannot be prevented. Problem Management includes Problem Control, Error Control and Proactive Problem Management.
problem record	(Problem Management) A Record containing the details of a Problem. Each Problem Record documents the Lifecycle of a single Problem.
procedure (definition)	1) The portion of a security policy that states the general process that will be performed to accomplish a security goal 2) A Document containing steps that specify how to achieve an Activity. Procedures are defined as part of Processes. See Work Instruction.
process (definition)	A structured set of Activities designed to accomplish a specific Objective. A Process takes one or more defined inputs and turns them into defined outputs. A Process may include any of the Roles, responsibilities, tools and management Controls required to reliably deliver the outputs. A Process may define Policies, Standards, Guidelines, Activities, and Work Instructions if they are needed. See Business Process.

process control	The Activity of planning and regulating a Process, with the Objective of performing it in an Effective, Efficient, and consistent manner.
process manager	A Role responsible for Operational management of a Process. The Process Manager's responsibilities include Planning and co-ordination of all Activities required to carry out, monitor and report on the Process. There may be several Process Managers for one Process, for example regional Change Managers or IT Service Continuity Managers for each data centre. The Process Manager Role is often assigned to the person who carries out the Process Owner Role, but the two Roles may be separate in larger Organizations.
process maturity	A measure of how reliable, Efficient and Effective a Process is, and of how well it is integrated with other processes. The most mature processes are formally aligned to Business Objectives and Strategy, and are supported by a framework for Continuous Improvement.
process owner	A Role responsible for ensuring that a Process is Fit for Purpose. The Process Owner's responsibilities include sponsorship, design, and change management of the Process and its Metrics. This Role is often assigned to the same person who carries out the Process Manager Role, but the two Roles may be separate in larger Organizations.
production programs/software	Programs that are used to process live or actual data that were received as input into the production environment. Such software is to be distinguished from test software, which is being developed or modified, but has not yet been authorized for use by management.
professional competence	Proven level of ability, often linked to qualifications issued by relevant professional bodies and compliance with their codes of practice and standards
profit center	(Financial Management) A Business Unit which charges for Services provided. A Profit Center can be created with the objective of making a profit, recovering Costs, or running at a loss. An IT Service Provider can be run as a Cost Center or a Profit Center.
program evaluation and review technique (PERT)	A project management technique used in the planning and control of system projects
program flowcharts	Program flowcharts show the sequence of instructions in a single program or subroutine. The symbols used should be the internationally accepted standard. Program flowcharts should be updated when necessary.
program narratives	Program narratives provide a detailed explanation of program flowcharts, including control points and any external input.
program (definition)	A number of Projects that are planned and managed together to achieve an overall Objective.
project (definition)	A temporary Organization, with people and other Resources required to achieve an Objective. Each Project has a Lifecycle that typically includes initiation, Planning, execution, Closure etc. Projects are usually managed using a formal methodology such as PRINCE2.
project sponsor	Considered for acquisition the person responsible for high-level decisions, such as changes to the scope and/or budget of the project, and whether or not to implement
project team	Group of people responsible for a project, whose terms of reference may include the development, acquisition, implementation or maintenance of an application system. The team members may include line management, operational line staff, external contractors and IS auditors.
projected service availability (PSA)	(Change Management) A Document that identifies the effect of planned Changes on agreed Service Levels, based on the Forward Schedule of Change (FSC).
promiscuous mode	Allows the network interface to capture all network traffic irrespective of the hardware device to which the packet is addressed
protection domain	The area of the system that the intrusion detection system is meant to monitor and protect
protocol (definition)	The rules by which a network operates and controls the flow and priority of transmissions
protocol converter	Hardware devices, such as asynchronous and synchronous transmissions, that convert between two different types of transmission

protocol stack	A set of utilities that implement a particular network protocol. For instance, in Windows machines a TCP/IP stack consists of TCP/IP software, sockets software and hardware driver software.
prototyping	A system development technique that enables users and developers to reach agreement on system requirements. Prototyping uses programmed simulation techniques to represent a model of the final system to the user for advisement and critique. The emphasis is on end-user screens and reports. Internal controls are not a priority item since this is only a model.
proxy server	A server that acts on behalf of a user. Typical proxies accept a connection from a user, make a decision as to whether or not the user or client IP address is permitted to use the proxy, perhaps perform additional authentication, and complete a connection to a remote destination on behalf of the user.
public key (definition)	In an asymmetric cryptographic scheme, the key that may be widely published to enable the operation of the scheme
public key cryptosystem	Used in data encryption, it uses an encryption key, as a public key, to encrypt the plaintext to the ciphertext. It uses the different decryption key, as a secret key, to decrypt the ciphertext to the corresponding plaintext. In contrast to a private key cryptosystem, the decryption key should be secret; however, the encryption key can be known to everyone. In a public key cryptosystem, two keys are asymmetric, such that the encryption key is not equivalent to the decryption key.
public key infrastructure (PKI)	A system that authentically distributes users' public keys using certificates
quality (definition)	The ability of a product, Service, or Process to provide the intended value. For example, a hardware Component can be considered to be of high quality if it performs as expected and delivers the required Reliability. Process Quality also requires an ability to monitor Effectiveness and Efficiency, and to improve them if necessary. See Quality Management System.
quality assurance (QA)	The Process responsible for gaining Assurance that the Quality of a product, Service or Process will provide its intended Value.
quality management system (QMS)	The set of Processes responsible for ensuring that all work carried out by an Organization is of a suitable Quality to reliably meet Business Objectives or Service Levels. See ISO 9000.
queue	A group of items that is waiting to be serviced or processed
quick ship	A recovery solution provided by recovery and/or hardware vendors and includes a pre-established contract to deliver hardware resources within a specified number amount of hours after a disaster occurs. This solution usually provides organizations with the ability to recover within 72 hours or greater.
quick win	An improvement Activity which is expected to provide a Return on Investment in a short period of time with relatively small Cost and effort. See Pareto Principle.
RADIUS	(remote authentication dial-in user service) A type of service providing an authentication and accounting system often used for dial-up and remote access security
random access memory (RAM)	The computer's primary working memory. Each byte of memory can be accessed randomly regardless of adjacent bytes.
range check	Range checks ensure that data fall within a predetermined range (also see limit checks).
rapid application development	A methodology that enables Organizations to develop strategically important systems faster, while reducing development costs and maintaining quality by using a series of proven application development techniques, within a well-defined methodology.
real charging	(Financial Management) A Charging Policy where actual money is transferred from the Customer to the IT Service Provider in payment for the delivery of IT Services. See Notional Charging
real-time analysis	Analysis that is performed on a continuous basis, with results gained in time to alter the run-time system

real-time processing	An interactive online system capability that immediately updates computer files when transactions are initiated through a terminal
reasonable assurance	A level of comfort short of a guarantee but considered adequate given the costs of the control and the likely benefits achieved
reasonableness check	Compares data to predefined reasonability limits or occurrence rates established for the data.
reciprocal agreement	Emergency processing agreements between two or more organizations with similar equipment or applications. Typically, participants promise to provide processing time to each other when an emergency arises.
record (definition)	1) A collection of related information treated as a unit. Separate fields within the record are used for processing of the information. 2) A Document containing the results or other output from a Process or Activity. Records are evidence of the fact that an activity took place and may be paper or electronic. For example, an Audit report, an Incident Record, or the minutes of a meeting.
record, screen and report layouts	Record layouts provide information regarding the type of record, its size and the type of data contained in the record. Screen and report layouts describe what information is provided and necessary for input.
recovery (definition)	(Incident Management) (IT Service Continuity Management) Returning a Configuration Item or an IT Service to a working state. Recovery of an IT Service often includes recovering data to a known consistent state. After Recovery, further steps may be needed before the IT Service can be made available to the Users (Restoration).
recovery center	(IT Service Continuity Management) Third Party provision of a shared Fixed Facility for use in Recovery. See Recovery Options.
recovery option	(IT Service Continuity Management) A Strategy for responding to an interruption to Service. Commonly used Strategies are Do Nothing, Manual Workaround, Reciprocal Agreement, Gradual Recovery, Intermediate Recovery, Immediate Recovery. Recovery Options may make use of dedicated facilities, or Third Party facilities shared by multiple Businesses.
recovery point objective (RPO)	(IT Service Continuity Management) The point in time to which data will be restored after recovery of an IT Service. This may involve loss of data. For example a Recovery Point Objective of one day may be supported by daily Backups, and up to 24 hours of data may be lost. Recovery Point Objectives for each IT Service should be negotiated, agreed and documented. See Business Impact Analysis.
recovery testing	A test to check the system's ability to recover after a software or hardware failure
recovery time objective (RTO)	(IT Service Continuity Management) The maximum time allowed for recovery of an IT Service following an interruption. The Service Level to be provided may be less than normal Service Level Targets. Recovery Time Objectives for each IT Service should be negotiated, agreed and documented. See Business Impact Analysis.
redo logs	Files maintained by a system, primarily a database management system, for the purposed of reapplying changes following an error or outage recovery (transaction logs)
redundancy (definition)	Synonym for Fault Tolerance. The term Redundant also has a generic meaning of obsolete, or no longer needed.
redundancy check	Detects transmission errors by appending calculated bits onto the end of each segment of data
reengineering	A process involving the extraction of components from existing systems and restructuring these components to develop new systems or to enhance the efficiency of existing systems. Existing software systems thus can be modernized to prolong their functionality. An example of this is a software code translator that can take an existing hierarchical database system and transpose it to a relational database system. CASE includes a source code reengineering feature.

registered certification body (RCB)	An Organization that has been Accredited to perform Certification against a published Standard such as ISO/IEC 17799 or ISO/IEC 20000.
registration authority (RA)	An entity that may be given responsibility for performing some of the administrative tasks necessary in the registration of subjects, such as confirming the subject's identity, validating that the subject is entitled to have the attributes requested in a certificate and verifying that the subject has possession of the private key associated with the public key requested for a certificate.
regression testing	A testing technique used to retest earlier program abends or logical errors that occurred during the initial testing phase
relationship (definition)	A connection or interaction between two people or things. In Business Relationship Management it is the interaction between the IT Service Provider and the Business. In Configuration Management it is a link between two Configuration Items that identifies a dependency or connection between them. For example Applications may be linked to the Servers they run on, IT Services have many links to all the CIs that contribute to that IT Service.
relationship processes	The ISO/IEC 20000 Process group that includes Business Relationship Management and Supplier Management.
release (definition)	(Release Management) A collection of hardware, software, documentation, Processes or other Components required to implement one or more approved Changes to IT Services. The contents of each Release are managed, tested, and deployed as a single entity. See Full Release, Delta Release, Package Release, Release Identification
release acceptance	(Release Management) The Activity responsible for testing a Release, and its implementation and Back-out Plans, to ensure they meet the agreed Business and IT Operations Requirements.
release identification	(Release Management) A naming convention used to uniquely identify a Release. The Release Identification typically includes a reference to the Configuration Item and a version number. For example Microsoft Office 2003 SR2.
release management	(Release Management) The Process responsible for Planning, scheduling and controlling the movement of Releases to Test and Live Environments. The primary objective of Release Management is to ensure that the integrity of the Live Environment is protected and that the correct Components are released. Release Management works closely with Configuration Management and Change Management.
release mechanism	(Release Management) The methodology for deploying a Release to its target Environment. A Release Mechanism may include hardware and software tools as well as Procedures.
release process	The name used by ISO/IEC 20000 for the Process group that includes Release Management. This group does not include any other Processes.
release record	A Record in the CMDB that defines the content of a Release. A Release Record has Relationships with all Configuration Items that are affected by the Release.
release type	(Release Management) A Category that is used to classify Releases. A Release Type may be one of Full, Delta or Package Release.
release unit	(Release Management) Components of an IT Service that are normally Released together. A Release Unit typically includes sufficient components to perform a useful Function. For example one Release Unit could be a Desktop PC, including Hardware, Software, Licenses, Documentation etc.; a different Release Unit may be the complete Payroll Application, including IT Operations Procedures and user training. See Release Type.
relevant audit evidence	Audit evidence is relevant if it pertains to the audit objectives and has a logical relationship to the findings and conclusions it is used to support.
reliability	(Availability Management) A measure of how long a Configuration Item or IT Service can perform its agreed Function without interruption. Usually measured as MTBF or MTBSI. See Availability.

reliable audit evidence	Audit evidence is reliable if, in the IS auditor's opinion, it is valid, factual, objective and supportable.
remote job entry (RJE)	The transmission of job control language (JCL) and batches of transactions from a remote terminal location
remote procedure call (RPC)	The traditional Internet service protocol widely used for many years on UNIX-based operating systems and supported by the Internet Engineering Task Force (IETF) that allows a program on one computer to execute a program on another (e.g., server). The primary benefit derived from its use is that a system developer need not develop specific procedures for the targeted computer system. For example, in a client-server arrangement, the client program sends a message to the server with appropriate arguments, and the server returns a message containing the results of the program executed. (See also CORBA and DCOM, as two newer object-oriented methods for related RPC functionality.)
repository	The central database that stores and organizes data
repudiation	The denial by one of the parties to a transaction or participation in all or part of that transaction or of the content of communications related to that transaction.
reputational risk	The current and prospective effect on earnings and capital arising from negative public opinion. This affects the bank's ability to establish new relationships or services or continue servicing existing relationships. Reputation risk may expose the bank to litigation, financial loss or a decline in its customer base. A bank's reputation can be damaged by Internet banking services that are poorly executed or otherwise alienate customers and the public. An Internet bank has a greater reputation risk as compared to a traditional brick-and-mortar bank since it is easier for its customers to leave and go to a different Internet bank and since it cannot discuss any problems with the customer in person
request for change (RFC)	(Change Management) A formal proposal for a Change to be made. An RFC includes details of the proposed Change, and may be recorded on paper or electronically. The term RFC is often misused to mean a Change Record, or the Change itself.
request for proposal (RFP)	A document distributed to software vendors requesting them to submit a proposal to develop or provide a software product
requirement (definition)	A formal statement of what is needed. For example a Service Level Requirement, a Project Requirement or the required Deliverables for a Process. See Statement of Requirements.
requirements definition	A phase of an SDLC methodology where the affected user groups define the requirements of the system for meeting the defined needs
residual risk	The risk associated with an event when the control is in place to reduce the effect or likelihood of that event being taken into account
resilience	The ability of a Configuration Item or IT Service to resist Failure or to Recover quickly following a Failure. For example, an armored cable will resist failure when put under stress. See Fault Tolerance.
resolution (definition)	(Incident Management) (Problem Management) Action taken to repair the Root Cause of an Incident or Problem, or to implement a Workaround. In ISO/IEC 20000, Resolution Processes is the Process group that includes Incident and Problem Management. See Workaround.
resolution processes	The ISO/IEC 20000 Process group that includes Incident Management and Problem Management.
resource (definition)	A generic term that includes IT Infrastructure, people, money or anything else that might help to deliver an IT Service. See Asset.
resource capacity management (RCM)	(Capacity Management) The Process responsible for understanding the Capacity, Utilization, and Performance of Configuration Items. Data is collected, recorded and analyzed for use in the Capacity Plan. See Service Capacity Management.

response time	A measure of the time taken to complete an Operation or Transaction. Used in Capacity Management as a measure of IT Infrastructure Performance, and in Incident Management as a measure of the time taken to answer the phone, or to start Diagnosis.
responsiveness	A measurement of the time taken to respond to something. This could be Response Time of a Transaction, or the speed with which an IT Service Provider responds to an Incident or Request for Change etc.
restore/ restoration of service	(Incident Management) Taking action to return an IT Service to the Users after Repair and Recovery from an Incident. This is the primary Objective of Incident Management.
retire	Withdraw an Application, IT Service etc. from use in the Live Environment.
return on capital employed (ROCE)	(Financial Management) A measurement of the expected benefit of an investment. Calculated by dividing (Net Profit Before Tax and Interest) by (Total assets minus current liabilities). This ratio is used by business analysts to judge the Effectiveness of the Organization as a whole. Any changes to IT Services or products are expected to improve this figure. See Cost Effectiveness, Investment Appraisal, Return on Investment.
return on investment (ROI)	(Financial Management) A measurement of the expected benefit of an investment. Calculated by dividing the average increase in financial benefit (taken over an agreed number of years) by the investment. See Cost Effectiveness, Return on Capital Employed.
return to normal	(IT Service Continuity Management) The phase of an IT Service Continuity Plan during which full normal operations are resumed. For example, if an alternate data centre has been in use, then this phase will bring the primary data centre back into operation, and restore the ability to invoke IT Service Continuity Plans again.
reverse engineering	A software engineering technique whereby an existing application system code can be redesigned and coded using computer-aided software engineering (CASE) technology
review (definition)	An evaluation of a Change, Problem, Process, Project etc. Reviews are typically carried out at predefined points in the Lifecycle, and especially after Closure. The purpose of a Review is to ensure that all Deliverables have been provided, and to identify opportunities for improvement. See Post Implementation Review.
RFC (request for comments)	A document that has been approved by the IETF becomes an RFC and is assigned a unique number once published. If it gains enough interest, it may evolve into an Internet standard.
ring topology	A type of LAN architecture in which the cable forms a loop, with stations attached at intervals around the loop. Signals transmitted around the ring take the form of messages. Each station receives the messages and each station determines, on the basis of an address, whether to accept or process a given message. However, after receiving a message, each station acts as a repeater, retransmitting the message at its original signal strength
risk (definition)	The possibility of suffering harm or loss. In quantitative Risk Management this is calculated as how likely it is that a specific Threat will exploit a particular Vulnerability.
risk assessment	1) A process used to identify and evaluate risks and their potential effects 2) The initial steps of Risk Management. Analyzing the value of Assets to the business, identifying Threats to those Assets, and evaluating how Vulnerable each Asset is to those Threats. See CRAMM.
risk management (definition)	The Process responsible for identifying, assessing and managing Risks. Risk Management can be quantitative (based on numerical data) or qualitative. See Risk Assessment, Risk Treatment, CRAMM.
risk reduction measure	Synonym for Control. See Countermeasure.

risk treatment	The part of Risk Management responsible for choosing and implementing an option for managing a Risk. Options for Risk Treatments include: • Applying Cost Effective Controls to reduce the Risk • Deciding to accept the Risk • Avoiding the Risk, by preventing the situation that could lead to it • Transferring the Risk to a Third Party, for example by taking out insurance.
role (definition)	A set of responsibilities defined in a Process and assigned to a person or team. One person or team may have multiple Roles, for example the Roles of Configuration Manager and Change Manager be carried out by a single person. See Job Description.
rollout	(Release Management) Synonym for Deployment. Most often used to refer to complex or phased Deployments.
root cause (definition)	(Problem Management) The underlying or original cause of an Incident or Problem.
root cause analysis (RCA)	(Problem Management) An Activity that identifies the Root Cause of an Incident or Problem. RCA typically concentrates on IT Infrastructure failures. See Service Outage Analysis.
rootkit	A software suite designed to aid an intruder in gaining unauthorized administrative access to a computer system
rotating standby	A fail-over process in which there are two nodes (as in idle standby but without priority). The node that enters the cluster first owns the resource group, and the second will join as a standby node.
rounding down	A method of computer fraud involving a computer code that instructs the computer to remove small amounts of money from an authorized computer transaction by rounding down to the nearest whole value denomination and rerouting the rounded off amount to the perpetrator's account
router (definition)	A networking device that can send (route) data packets from one local area network (LAN) or wide area network (WAN) to another, based on "IP" or "logical" addressing at the network layer (Layer 3) in the OSI model. Networks connected by routers can use different or similar networking protocols. Routers usually are capable of filtering packets based on parameters, such as source addresses, destination addresses, protocol and network applications (ports).
RS-232 interface	Interface between data terminal equipment and data communications equipment employing serial binary data interchange
RSA	A public key cryptosystem developed by R. Rivest, A. Shamir and L. Adleman. The RSA has two different keys, the public encryption key and the secret decryption key. The strength of the RSA depends on the difficulty of the prime number factorization. For applications with high-level security, the number of the decryption key bits should be greater than 512 bits. RSA is used for both encryption and digital signatures.
rulebase	The list of rules and/or guidance that is used to analyze event data (ACL - access control list)
run instructions	Computer operating instructions which detail the step-by-step processes that are to occur so an application system can be properly executed. It also identifies how to address problems that occur during processing.
running costs	Synonym for Operational Costs
run-to-run totals	Provide verification that all transmitted data are read and processed
salami technique	A method of computer fraud involving a computer code that instructs the computer to slice off small amounts of money from an authorized computer transaction and reroute this amount to the perpetrator's account
SAM database	(Software Asset Management) A Database containing all data needed to support Software Asset Management. The SAM Database could be part of the CMDB.

sampling risk	The probability that the IS auditor has reached an incorrect conclusion because an audit sample, rather than the whole population, was tested. While sampling risk can be reduced to an acceptably low level by using an appropriate sample size and selection method, it can never be eliminated.
scalability	The ability of an IT Service, Process, Configuration Item etc. to perform its agreed Function when the Workload or Scope changes.
scheduling (definition)	1) A method used in the information processing facility (IPF) to determine and establish the sequence of computer job processing 2) A function of Project Management processes
scope	The boundary, or extent, to which a Audit, Process, Procedure, Certification, Contract etc. applies. For example the Scope of Change Management may include all Live IT Services and related Configuration Items, the Scope of an ISO/IEC 20000 Certificate may include all IT Services delivered out of a named data centre.
screening routers	A router configured to permit or deny traffic based on a set of permission rules installed by the administrator
second-line support	(Service Desk) (Incident Management) (Problem Management) The second level in a hierarchy of Support Groups involved in the resolution of Incidents and investigation of Problems. Each level contains more specialist skills, or has more time or other resources. See Escalation.
secure socket layer (SSL)	A protocol originally developed by Netscape Communications to provide a high level of security for its browser software. It has become accepted widely as a means of securing Internet message exchanges. It ensures confidentiality of the data in transmission using encryption.
security administrator (definition)	The person responsible for implementing, monitoring and enforcing security rules established and authorized by management
security management (definition)	1) The process of establishing and maintaining security in a computer or network system. The stages of this process include prevention of security problems, detection of intrusions, investigation of intrusions and resolution. 2) In network management, controlling access to the network and resources, finding intrusions, identifying entry points for intruders and repairing or otherwise closing those avenues of access.
security perimeter	The boundary that defines the area of security concern and security policy coverage
security policy (definition)	1) The set of management statements that documents an organization's philosophy of protecting its computing and information assets 2) The set of security rules enforced by the system's security features 3) Synonym for Information Security Policy
security principle	(Security Management) A Strategic Objective in an Information Security Policy. Common Security Principles include Confidentiality, Integrity and Availability. Other Objectives such as Non-Repudiation and Accountability can also be Security Principles.
security software	Software used to administer logical security. It usually includes authentication of users, access granting according to predefined rules, monitoring and reporting functions.
security testing	Making sure the modified/new system includes appropriate access controls and does not introduce any security holes that might compromise other systems
security/transaction risk	The current and prospective risk to earnings and capital arising from fraud, error and the inability to deliver products or services, maintain a competitive position and manage information. Security risk is evident in each product and service offered and encompasses product development and delivery, transaction processing, systems development, computing systems, complexity of products and services and the internal control environment. A high level of security risk may exist with Internet banking products, particularly if those lines of business are not adequately planned, implemented and monitored

segregation/separation of duties	A basic control that prevents or detects errors and irregularities by assigning responsibility for initiating transactions, recording transactions and custody of assets to separate individuals. Commonly used in large IT organizations so that no single person is in a position to introduce fraudulent or malicious code without detection.
sequence check	Verifies that the control number follows sequentially and any control numbers out of sequence are rejected or noted on an exception report for further research (can be alpha or numeric and usually utilizes a key field)
sequential file	A computer file storage format in which one record follows another. Records can be accessed sequentially only. It is required with magnetic tape.
server (definition)	A computer that is connected to a network and provides software Functions that are used by other Computers.
service (definition)	1) Providing something of value to a customer that is not goods (physical things with material value). Examples of services include banking and legal support. Service is also used as a Synonym for IT Service. See Business Service, Service Request. 2) Daemons or smaller applications that run within an OS or or application, providing additional functionality
service bureau	A computer facility that provides data processing services to clients on a continual basis
service capacity management (scm)	(Capacity Management) The Activity responsible for understanding the Performance and Capacity of IT Services. The Resources used by each IT Service and the pattern of usage over time are collected, recorded, and analysed for use in the Capacity Plan. See Business Capacity Management, Resource Capacity Management.
service catalog	A Document listing all IT Services, with summary information about their SLAs and Customers. The Service Catalog is created and maintained by the IT Service Provider and is used by all IT Service Management Processes. See Portfolio of Services.
service culture	A Customer oriented Culture. The major Objectives of a Service Culture are Customer satisfaction and helping the Customer to achieve their Business Objectives. See Business IT Alignment, Customer Focus.
service delivery	The core IT Service Management Processes that have a Tactical or Strategic focus. In ITIL these are Service Level Management, Capacity Management, IT Service Continuity Management, Availability Management, and Financial Management for IT Services. Service Delivery is also used to mean the delivery of IT Services to Customers. See Service Support.
service dependency modelling	A technique that is used to graphically represent the dependency of IT services on Configuration Items.
service desk	(Service Desk) The Single Point of Contact between the Service Provider and the Users. A typical Service Desk manages Incidents and Service Requests, and also handles communication with the Users. See Call Center.
service hours	(Service Level Management) An agreed time period when a particular IT Service should be Available. For example, "Monday-Friday 08:00 to 17:00 except public holidays". Service Hours should be defined in a Service Level Agreement.
service improvement plan (SIP)	A formal Plan to implement improvements to a Process or IT Service. A SIP is managed as part of a Continuous Improvement Process
service level (definition)	Measured and reported achievement against one or more Service Level Targets. Service Level is sometimes used as an informal term to mean Service Level Target.
service level agreement (SLA)	1) Defined minimum performance measures at or above which the service delivered is considered acceptable 2) (Service Level Management) An Agreement between an IT Service Provider and a Customer. The SLA describes the IT Service, documents Service Level Targets, and specifies the responsibilities of the IT Service Provider and the Customer. A single SLA may cover multiple IT Services or multiple customers. See Operational Level Agreement.

service level management (SLM)	(Service Level Management) The Process responsible for negotiating Service Level Agreements, and ensuring that these are met. SLM is responsible for ensuring that all IT Service Management Processes, Operational Level Agreements, and Underpinning Contracts, are appropriate for the agreed Service Level Targets. SLM monitors and reports on Service Levels, and holds regular Customer reviews. See Service Reporting.
service level requirement (SLR)	A Customer Requirement for an aspect of an IT Service. SLRs are based on Business Objectives and are used to negotiate agreed Service Level Targets. See Service Level Agreement.
service level target	A commitment that is documented in a Service Level Agreement. Service Level Targets are based on Service Level Requirements, and are needed to ensure that the IT Service design is Fit for Purpose. Service Level Targets should be measurable, and are usually based on KPIs. See Service Level, SMART.
service maintenance objective (SMO)	(Availability Management) The expected time that a Configuration Item will be unavailable due to planned maintenance Activity. See Planned Downtime.
service manager	A generic term that can be used to mean any manager within the IT Service Provider. Most commonly used to refer to a Business Relationship Manager, a Process Manager, an Account Manager or a senior manager with responsibility for IT Services overall.
service outage analysis (SOA)	(Problem Management) (Availability Management) An Activity that identifies underlying causes of an IT Service interruption. SOA identifies opportunities to improve the IT Service Provider's Processes and tools, and not just the IT Infrastructure. SOA is a time constrained, project-like activity, rather than an ongoing process of analysis. See Root Cause Analysis.
service planning	The Process responsible for implementing and retiring IT Services. Service Planning includes understanding Customer Requirements and Planning the Lifecycle of an IT Service. ISO/IEC 20000 calls this Process "Planning and implementing new or changed services". See Portfolio Management.
service provider (definition)	1) An Organization supplying Services to one or more Customers. Service Provider is often used as an abbreviation for IT Service Provider. 2) The organization providing the outsourced service
service reporting	(Service Level Management) The Process responsible for producing and delivering reports of achievement and trends against Service Levels. Service Reporting should agree the format, content and frequency of reports with Customers.
service request	(Service Desk) A request from a User for information or advice, or for a Standard Change. For example to reset a password, or to provide standard IT Services for a new User. Service Requests are usually handled by a Service Desk, and do not require an RFC to be submitted.
service support	The core IT Service Management Processes that have an Operational focus. These are Incident Management, Problem Management, Configuration Management, Change Management and Release Management. Service Support also includes the Service Desk. See Service Delivery.
service user	The organization using the outsourced service
serviceability	(Availability Management) The ability of a Third Party Supplier to meet the terms of their Contract. This Contract will include agreed levels of Reliability, Maintainability or Availability for a Configuration Item.
shell	The interface between the user and the system
signatures	Patterns indicating misuse of a system
simple fail-over	A fail-over process in which the primary node owns the resource group. The backup node runs a non-critical application (e.g., a development or test environment) and takes over the critical resource group but not vice versa.

simple object access protocol (SOAP)	A platform-independent XML-based formatted protocol enabling applications to communicate with each other over the Internet. Use of this protocol may provide a significant security risk to web application operations, since use of SOAP piggybacks onto a web-based document object model and is transmitted via the web's HTTP service protocol (port 80) to penetrate server firewalls, which are usually configured to accept port 80 and port 21 (FTP) requests. Web-based document models define how objects on a web page are associated with each other, and how they can be manipulated while being sent from a server to a client browser. SOAP typically relies on XML for presentation formatting and also adds appropriate HTTP-based headers to send it.
simulation modeling	A technique that creates a detailed model to predict the behavior of a Configuration Item or IT Service. Simulation Models can be very accurate but are expensive and time consuming to create. A Simulation Model is often created by using the actual Configuration Items that are being modeled, with artificial Workloads or Transactions. They are used in Capacity Management when accurate results are important. A simulation model is sometimes called a Performance Benchmark.
single point of contact (SPOC)	Providing a single consistent way to communicate with an Organization or Business Unit. For example, a Single Point of Contact for an IT Service Provider is usually called a Service Desk.
single point of failure (SPOF)	1) A resource whose loss will result in the loss of service or production 2) Any Configuration Item that can cause an Incident when it fails, and for which a Countermeasure has not been implemented. A SPOF may be a person, or a step in a Process or Activity, as well as a Component of the IT Infrastructure. See Failure.
slam chart	(Service Level Management) A Service Level Agreement Monitoring Chart is used to help monitor and report achievements against Service Level Targets. A SLAM Chart is typically color coded to show whether each agreed Service Level Target has been met, missed, or nearly missed during each of the previous 12 months.
SMART (acronym)	An acronym for helping to remember that targets in Service Level Agreements and Project Plans should be Specific, Measurable, Achievable, Relevant and Time based.
smart card	A small electronic device that contains electronic memory, and possibly an embedded integrated circuit. It can be used for a number of purposes including the storage of digital certificates or digital cash, or it can be used as a token to authenticate users.
SMTP (simple mail transport protocol)	The standard outbound e-mail protocol on the Internet
sniff	The act of capturing network packets, including those not necessarily destined for the computer running the sniffing software
software (definition)	Programs and supporting documentation that enable and facilitate use of the computer. Software controls the operation of the hardware.
software asset management	(Software Asset Management) The Process responsible for management, control and protection of software Assets throughout their Lifecycle.
software process improvement and capability determination (SPICE)	An independent, international Quality Management System for software Development. See http://www.sqi.gu.edu.au/spice/ for more information. See Capability Maturity Model Integration.
source code	Source code is the language in which a program is written. Source code is translated into object code by assemblers and compilers. In some cases, source code may be converted automatically into another language by a conversion program. Source code is not executable by the computer directly. It must first be converted into a machine language.
source code compare programs	Programs that provide assurance that the software being audited is the correct version of the software, by providing a meaningful listing of any discrepancies between the two versions of the program
source documents	The forms used to record data that have been captured. A source document may be a piece of paper, a turnaround document or an image displayed for online data input.
source lines of code (SLOC)	Source lines of code are often used in deriving single-point software-size estimations.

spanning port	A port configured on a network switch to receive copies of traffic from one or more other ports on the switch
specification	A formal definition of Requirements. A Specification may be used to define technical or Operational Requirements, and may be internal or external. Many public Standards consist of a Code of Practice and a Specification. The Specification defines the Standard against which an Organization can be Audited.
split data systems	A condition in which each of an organization's regional locations maintains its own financial and operational data while sharing processing with an organizationwide, centralized database. This permits easy sharing of data while maintaining a certain level of autonomy.
split DNS	An implementation of DNS intended to secure responses provided by the server such that different responses are given to internal vs. external users
spoofing	Faking the sending address of a transmission in order to gain illegal entry into a secure system
spool (simultaneous peripheral operations online)	An automated function that can be operating system or application based in which electronic data being transmitted between storage areas are spooled or stored until the receiving device or storage area is prepared and able to receive the information. This operation allows more efficient electronic data transfers from one device to another by permitting higher speed sending functions, such as internal memory, to continue on with other operations instead of waiting on the slower speed receiving device, such as a printer.
stakeholder	All people who have an interest in an Organization, Project, IT Service etc. Stakeholders may be interested in the Activities, targets, Resources, or Deliverables. Stakeholders may include Customers, Partners, employees, shareholders, owners, etc.
standard (definition)	A mandatory Requirement. Examples include ISO/IEC 20000 (an international Standard), an internal security standard for Unix configuration, or a government standard for how financial Records should be maintained. The term Standard is also used to refer to a Code of Practice or Specification published by a Standards Organization such as ISO or BSI. See Guideline.
standard change	A pre-approved Change that is low Risk, relatively common and follows a Procedure or Work Instruction. For example password reset or provision of standard equipment to a new employee. RFCs are not required to implement a Standard Change, and they are logged and tracked using a different mechanism, such as a Service Request. See Change Model.
standard cost	(Financial Management) A pre-determined calculation of the Cost of carrying out a common operation. For example a Standard Cost per desktop may be used, rather than calculating the exact Cost each time a desktop PC is provided to a User.
standby	(IT Service Continuity Management) Used to refer to Resources that are not required to deliver the Live IT Services, but are available to support IT Service Continuity Plans. For example a Standby data centre may be maintained to support Hot Standby, Warm Standby or Cold Standby arrangements.
standing data	Permanent reference data used in transaction processing. These data are changed infrequently, such as a product price file or a name and address file.
star topology	A type of LAN architecture that utilizes a central controller to which all nodes are directly connected. All transmissions from one station to another pass through the central controller, which is responsible for managing and controlling all communication. The central controller often acts as a switching device.
statement of requirements (SOR)	A Document containing all Requirements for a product purchase, or a new or changed IT Service. See Terms of Reference.
static analysis	Analysis of information that occurs on a non-continuous basis; also known as interval-based analysis
statistical sampling	A method of selecting a portion of a population, by means of mathematical calculations and probabilities, for the purpose of making scientifically and mathematically sound inferences regarding the characteristics of the entire population

status (definition)	The name of a required field in many types of Record. It shows the current stage in the Lifecycle of the associated Configuration Item, Incident, Problem etc.
status accounting	Synonym for Configuration Status Accounting.
storage management	The Process responsible for managing the storage and maintenance of data throughout its Lifecycle.
strategic (definition)	The highest of three levels of Planning and delivery (Strategic, Tactical, Operational). Strategic Activities include Objective setting and long term Planning to achieve the overall Vision.
strategic alignment objectives model (SAOM)	A diagram showing the Relationships between Deliverables and Requirements. For example IT Services supporting Business Requirements, IT Infrastructure supporting Technical Requirements.
strategic risk	The current and prospective effect on earnings or capital arising from adverse business decisions, improper implementation of decisions or lack of responsiveness to industry changes.
strategy (definition)	A Strategic Plan designed to achieve defined Objectives.
structured programming	A top-down technique of designing programs and systems. It makes programs more readable, more reliable and more easily maintained.
structured query language (SQL)	The primary language used by both application programmers and end users in accessing relational databases
subject matter	(Area of activity) The specific information subject to the IS auditor's report and related procedures which can include things such as the design or operation of internal controls and compliance with privacy practices or standards or specified laws and regulations.
substantive testing	Tests of detailed activities and transactions, or analytical review tests, designed to obtain audit evidence on the completeness, accuracy or existence of those activities or transactions during the audit period
sufficient audit evidence	Audit evidence is sufficient if it is adequate, convincing and would lead another IS auditor to form the same conclusions.
supplier (definition)	A Third Party responsible for supplying goods or Services that are required to deliver IT services. Examples of suppliers include commodity hardware and software vendors, network and telecom providers, and outsourcing Organizations. See Underpinning Contract, Supply Chain.
supplier management	Supplier Management is one of the ISO/IEC 20000 Relationship Management Processes. It is responsible for ensuring that all Contracts with Suppliers support the needs of the Business, and that all Suppliers meet their contractual commitments. Supplier Management is also responsible for understanding the entire Supply Chain, which includes Suppliers to the IT Service Provider's own major Suppliers. See Supply Chain.
supply chain	The Activities in a Value Chain carried out by Suppliers. A Supply Chain typically involves multiple Suppliers, each adding value to the product or Service.
support group	A group of people with technical skills. Support Groups provide the Technical Support needed by all of the IT Service Management Processes. See n-line Support, Technical Support.
support hours	The times or hours when support is available to the Users. Typically this is the hours when the Service Desk is available. Support Hours should be defined in a Service Level Agreement, and may be different from Service Hours. For example, Service Hours may be 24 hours a day, but the Support Hours may be 07:00 to 19:00.
surge suppressor	Filters out electrical surges and spikes

SWIFT (acronym)	Founded in Brussels in 1973, the Society for the Worldwide Interbank Financial Telecommunication (SWIFT) is a co-operative Organization dedicated to the promotion and development of standardized global interactivity for financial transactions. SWIFT's original mandate was to establish a global communications link for data processing and a common language for international financial transactions. The Society operates a messaging service for financial messages, such as letters of credit, payments, and securities transactions, between member banks worldwide. SWIFT's essential function is to deliver these messages quickly and securely—both of which are prime considerations for financial matters. Member Organizations create formatted messages that are then forwarded to SWIFT for delivery to the recipient member Organization. SWIFT operates out of its Brussels headquarters and processes data at centers in Belgium and the United States
switch (definition)	A device that forwards packets between LAN devices or segments based on Layer 2 (datalink) information. LANs that use switches are called switched LANs.
symmetric key encryption	Two trading partners both share one or more secrets. No one else can read their messages. A different key (or set of keys) is needed for each pair of trading partners. Same key is used for encryption and decryption. (Also see Private Key Cryptosystems).
SYN (synchronize)	A flag set in the initial setup packets to indicate that the communicating parties are synchronizing the sequence numbers used for the data transmission
synchronous transmission	Block-at-a-time data transmission
system (definition)	A number of related things that work together to achieve an overall Objective. For example: • A computer System including hardware, software and Applications. • A management System, including multiple Processes that are planned and managed together. For example a Quality Management System. • A Database Management System or Operating System that includes many software modules that are designed to perform a set of related Functions.
system exit	Special system software features and utilities that allow the user to perform complex system maintenance. Use of these exits often permits the user to operate outside of the security access control system.
system flowcharts	System flowcharts are graphical representations of the sequence of operations in an information system or program. Information system flowcharts show how data from source documents flow through the computer to final distribution to users. Symbols used should be the internationally accepted standard. System flowcharts should be updated when necessary.
system management	The part of IT Service Management that focuses on the management of IT Infrastructure rather than Process.
system narratives	System narratives provide an overview explanation of system flowcharts, with explanation of key control points and system interfaces.
system software	A collection of computer programs used in the design, processing and control of all applications. The programs and processing routines that control the computer hardware, including the operating system and utility programs.
system testing	A series of tests designed to ensure that the modified program interacts correctly with other system components. These test procedures typically are performed by the system maintenance staff in their development library.
systems acquisition process	The procedures established to purchase application software, or an upgrade, including evaluation of the supplier's financial stability, track record, resources and references from existing customers
systems analysis	The systems development phase in which systems specifications and conceptual designs are developed, based on end-user needs and requirements
systems development life cycle (SDLC)	An approach used to plan, design, develop, test and implement an application system or a major modification to an application system. Typical phases include the feasibility study, requirements study, requirements definition, detailed design, programming, testing, installation and post-implementation review.

table look-ups	Used to ensure that input data agree with predetermined criteria stored in a table
TACACS+	(terminal access controller access control system plus)-- An authentication protocol, often used by remote-access servers
tactical	The middle of three levels of Planning and delivery (Strategic, Tactical, Operational). Tactical Activities include the medium term Plans required to achieve specific Objectives, typically over a period of weeks to months.
tape management system (TMS)	A system software tool that logs, monitors and directs computer tape usage
taps	Wiring devices that may be inserted into communication links for use with analysis probes, LAN analyzers and intrusion detection security systems
TCP (transmission control protocol)	A layer 4 connection-based Internet protocol that supports reliable data transfer connections. Packet data is verified using checksums and retransmitted if it is missing or corrupted. The application plays no part in validating the transfer.
TCP/IP protocol	(Transmission Control Protocol/Internet Protocol) A set of communications protocols that encompasses media access, packet transport, session communications, file transfer, electronic mail, terminal emulation, remote file access and network management. TCP/IP provides the basis for the Internet.
tcpdump	A network monitoring and data acquisition tool that performs filter translation, packet acquisition and packet display
technical infrastructure security	Refers to the security of the infrastructure that supports the ERP networking and telecommunications, operating systems and databases.
technical observation post (TOP)	A technique used in Service Improvement, Problem investigation and Availability Management. Technical support staff meet to monitor the behavior and Performance of an IT Service and make recommendations for improvement.
technical support	The Process responsible for the technical aspects of supporting IT Services. Technical Support defines the Roles of Support Groups, as well as the tools, Processes and Procedures required. See Support Group.
telecommunications	Electronic communications by special devices over distances or around devices that preclude direct interpersonal exchange
teleprocessing	Using telecommunications facilities for handling and processing of computerized information
telnet	Used to enable remote access to a server computer. Commands typed are run on the remote server.
terminal	A device for sending and receiving computerized data over transmission lines
terms of reference (TOR)	1) A document that confirms the client's and the IS auditor's acceptance of a review assignment 2) A Document specifying the Requirements, Scope, Deliverables, Resources and schedule for a Project or Activity. See Statement of Requirements.
test	A Test is used to verify that a Configuration Item, IT Service, Process etc. meets its Specification, and is able to correctly deliver specific Functional or Service Level Requirements. There should be no negative effects on other Processes or IT Services.
test data	Simulated transactions that can be used to test processing logic, computations and controls actually programmed in computer applications. Individual programs or an entire system can be tested. This technique includes Integrated Test Facilities (ITFs) and Base Case System Evaluations (BCSEs).
test environment	A controlled Environment used to Test Configuration Items, Builds, IT Services, Processes etc.
test generators	Software used to create data to be used in the testing of computer programs

test programs	Programs that are tested and evaluated before approval into the production environment. Test programs, through a series of change control moves, migrate from the test environment to the production environment and become production programs.
third party (definition)	A person, group, or Business who is not part of the Service Level Agreement for an IT Service, but is required to ensure successful delivery of that IT Service. For example a software Supplier, a hardware maintenance company, or a facilities department. Requirements for Third Parties are typically specified in Underpinning Contracts or Operational Level Agreements. See Partnership.
third-line support	(Service Desk) (Incident Management) (Problem Management) The third level in a hierarchy of Support Groups involved in the resolution of Incidents and investigation of Problems. Each level contains more specialist skills, or has more time or other resources. See Escalation.
third-party review	An independent audit of the control structure of a service organization, such as a service bureau, with the objective of providing assurances to the users of the service organization that the internal control structure is adequate, effective and sound
threat (definition)	1) Any situation or event that has the potential to harm a system 2) A threat is any thing that might exploit a Vulnerability. Any potential cause of an Incident can be considered to be a Threat. For example a fire is a Threat that could exploit the Vulnerability of flammable floor coverings. This term is commonly used in Information Security Management and IT Service Continuity Management, but also applies to other areas such as Problem and Availability Management.
threshold	The value of a Metric which should cause an Alert to be generated, or management action to be taken. For example "Priority1 Incident not solved within 4 hours", "more than 5 soft disk errors in an hour", or "more than 10 failed changes in a month".
throughput	(Capacity Management) A measure of the number of Transactions, or other Operations, performed in a fixed time. For example 5000 emails sent per hour, or 200 disk I/Os per second.
tied users	(Financial Management) Users who have no choice about whether to use the IT Services provided by their Internal Service Provider. See Untied Users
token	A device that is used to authenticate a user, typically in addition to a username and password. It is usually a credit card-sized device that displays a pseudo random number that changes every few minutes.
token ring topology	A type of LAN ring topology in which a frame containing a specific format, called the token, is passed from one station to the next around the ring. When a station receives the token, it is allowed to transmit. The station can send as many frames as desired until a predefined time limit is reached. When a station either has no more frames to send or reaches the time limit, it transmits the token. Token passing prevents data collisions that can occur when two computers begin transmitting at the same time.
top-level management	The highest level of management in the organization, responsible for direction and control of the organization as a whole (such as director, general manager, partner, chief officer and executive manager).
topology	The physical layout of how computers are linked together. Examples include ring, star and bus.
total cost of ownership (TCO)	(Financial Management) A methodology used to make investment decisions. TCO assesses the full Lifecycle Costs of a Configuration Item, not just the initial cost or purchase price. See Full Cost.
total quality management (TQM)	A methodology for managing Continuous Improvement by using a Quality Management System. TQM establishes a Culture involving all people in the Organization in a Process of continuous monitoring and improvement.

transaction (definition)	1) Business events or information grouped together because they have a single or similar purpose. Typically, a transaction is applied to a calculation or event that then results in the updating of a holding or master file. 2) A discrete Function performed by an IT Service. For example transferring money from one bank account to another. A single Transaction may involve numerous additions, deletions and modifications of data. Either all of these complete successfully or none of them is carried out.
transaction log	A manual or automated log of all updates to data files and databases
transaction protection	Also known as "automated remote journaling of redo logs." A data recovery strategy that is similar to electronic vaulting, except that instead of transmitting several transaction batches daily, the archive logs are shipped as they are created.
transfer cost	(Financial Management) Transfer Cost is a Cost Type, which records expenditure made on behalf of another part of the Organization. For example the IT Service Provider may pay for an external consultant to be used by the Finance department and transfer the Cost to them. The IT Service Provider would record this as a Transfer Cost.
trap door	Unauthorized electronic exits, or doorways, out of an authorized computer program into a set of malicious instructions or programs
trend analysis	Analysis of data to identify time related patterns. Trend Analysis is used in Problem Management to identify common Failures or fragile Configuration Items, and in Capacity Management as a Modeling tool to predict future behavior. It is also used as a management tool for identifying deficiencies in IT Service Management Processes.
Trojan horse	Purposefully hidden malicious or damaging code within an authorized computer program. Unlike viruses, they do not replicate themselves, but they can be just as destructive to a single computer.
trust (definition)	1) Generally, the assumption that an entity will behave substantially as expected. Trust may apply only for a specific function. The key role of this term in an authentication framework is to describe the relationship between an authenticating entity and a certificate authority (CA). An authenticating entity must be certain that it can trust the CA to create only valid and reliable certificates, and users of those certificates rely upon the authenticating entity's determination of trust. 2) A level of access privilege granted to a specific domain or managed group pf computers
trusted processes	Processes certified as supporting a security goal
trusted systems	Systems that employ sufficient hardware and software assurance measures to allow their use for processing of a range of sensitive or classified information
tuning	(Capacity Management) The Activity responsible for Planning changes to make the most efficient use of Resources. Tuning is part of Performance Management, which also includes Performance monitoring and implementation of the required Changes.
tuples	A row or record consisting of a set of attribute value pairs (column or field) in a relational data structure
twisted pairs	A pair of small, insulated wires that are twisted around each other to minimize interference from other wires in the cable. Ethernet is a type of twisted-pair cable.
UDP (user datagram protocol)	A connectionless Internet protocol that is designed for network efficiency and speed at the expense of reliability. A data request by the client is served by sending packets without testing to verify if they actually arrive at the destination, not if they were corrupted in transit. It is up to the application to determine these factors and request retransmissions.
unabsorbed overhead	(Financial Management) Indirect cost of providing an IT Service, which cannot be fairly allocated to specific Customers. For example Cost of providing an IT Service manager, or other shared Resource which is not measured. Unabsorbed overhead is normally recovered by applying a percentage uplift to the Cost of all IT Services. See also Direct cost, Indirect cost, Absorbed Overhead.

underpinning contract (UC)	A Contract with an external Third Party that supports delivery of an IT Service by the IT Service Provider to a Customer. The Third Party provides goods or Services that are required by the IT Service Provider to meet agreed Service Level Targets in the SLA with their Customer.
uninterruptible power supply (UPS)	Provides short-term backup power from batteries for a computer system when the electrical power fails or drops to an unacceptable voltage level
unit cost	(Financial Management) The Cost of providing a single item. For example, if a box of paper with 1,000 sheets costs £10, then each sheet costs 1p. Similarly if a CPU costs £1m a year and performs 1,000 jobs in a year, the Unit Cost for each job is £1,000.
unit testing	A testing technique that is used to test program logic within a particular program or module. The purpose of the test is to ensure that the program meets system development guidelines and does not abnormally end during processing.
universal description, discovery and integration (UDDI)	A web-based version of the traditional phone book's yellow and white pages enabling businesses to be publicly listed in promoting greater e-commerce activities.
UNIX	A multi-user, multitasking operating system that is used widely as the master control program in workstations and especially servers
untied users	(Financial Management) Users who can choose whether to use the Services provided by an Internal Service Provider or to purchase services from another source. See Tied Users.
untrustworthy host	To the basic border firewall, add a host that resides on an untrusted network where the firewall cannot protect it. That host is minimally configured and carefully managed to be as secure as possible. The firewall is configured to require incoming and outgoing traffic to go through the untrustworthy host. The host is referred to as untrustworthy because it cannot be protected by the firewall; therefore, hosts on the trusted networks can place only limited trust in it.
uploading	The process of electronically sending computerized information from one computer to another computer. Most often, the transfer is from a smaller computer to a larger one.
urgency	A measure of how long it will be until an Incident, Problem or Change has a significant Impact on the Business. For example a high Impact Incident may have low Urgency, if the Impact will not affect the Business until the end of the Financial Year. Impact and Urgency are used to assign Priority.
usability	The ease with which an Application, product, or IT Service can be used. Usability Requirements are often included in a Statement of Requirements.
useful audit evidence	Audit evidence is useful if it assists the IS auditors in meeting their audit objectives.
user	A person who uses the IT Service on a day-to-day basis. Users are distinct from Customers, as some Customers do not use the IT Service directly.
utility software/program	1) Specialized system software used to perform particular computerized functions and routines that are frequently required during normal processing. Examples include sorting, backing up and erasing data. 2) Computer programs provided by a computer hardware manufacturer or software vendor and used in running the system. This technique can be used to examine processing activities; to test programs, system activities and operational procedures; to evaluate data file activity; and, to analyze job accounting data.
vaccine	A program designed to remove computer viruses
validity check	Programmed checking of data validity in accordance with predetermined criteria
value chain	A sequence of Processes that creates a product or Service that is of value to a Customer. Each step of the sequence builds on the previous steps and contributes to the overall product or Service. See Business IT Alignment.
value for money	An informal measure of Cost Effectiveness. Value for Money is often based on a comparison with the Cost of alternatives. See Cost Benefit Analysis.

value-added network (VAN)	A data communication network that adds processing services such as error correction, data translation and/or storage to the basic function of transporting data
variable cost	(Financial Management) A Cost that depends on how much the IT Service is used, how many products are produced, or something else that cannot be fixed in advance. See Fixed Cost.
variable sampling	A sampling technique used to estimate the average or total value of a population based on a sample; a statistical model used to project a quantitative characteristic, such as a dollar amount
variance	The difference between a planned value and the actual measured value. Commonly used in Financial Management, Capacity Management and Service Level Management, but could apply in any area where Plans are in place.
variant	(Configuration Management) A Configuration Item that is identical to another CI except for specific Attributes. Variants are used to group similar CIs together for analysis. For example it may be necessary to identify all Users with a particular model of laptop, even though that laptop has a number of Variants.
vendor-managed use	(Software Asset Management) The management of licenses by the Supplier of the software. Licenses may also be managed by the Customer or the IT Service Provider (Customer Managed Use).
verification	Checks that data are entered correctly
version	A Version is used to identify a specific Baseline of a Configuration Item. Versions typically use a naming convention that enables the sequence or date of each Baseline to be identified. For example Payroll Application Version 3 contains updated functionality from Version 2.
virtual organizations	Organizations that have no official physical site presence and are made up of diverse geographically dispersed or mobile employees.
virtual private network (VPN)	A private network that is configured within a public network. For years, common carriers have built VPNs that appear as private national or international networks to the customer, but physically share backbone trunks with other customers. VPNs enjoy the security of a private network via access control and encryption, while taking advantage of the economies of scale and built-in management facilities of large public networks.
virus	A destructive computer program that spreads from computer to computer using a range of methods, including infecting floppy disks and other programs. Viruses typically attach themselves to a program and modify it so that the virus code runs when the program is first started. The infected program typically runs normally, but the virus code then infects other programs whenever it can. (Also see worm.)
vision	A description of what the Organization intends to become in the future. A Vision is created by senior management and is used to help influence Culture and Strategic Planning.
vital business function (VBF)	A Function of a Business Process which is critical to the success of the Business. Vital Business Functions are an important consideration of Business Continuity Management, IT Service Continuity Management and Availability Management.
voice mail	A system of storing messages in a private recording medium where the called party can later retrieve the messages
vulnerability (definition)	A weakness that could be exploited by a Threat. For example an open firewall port, a password that is never changed, or a flammable carpet. A missing Control is also considered to be a weakness or vulnerability.
vulnerability analysis	Analysis of the security state of a system or its compromise on the basis of information collected at intervals
war dialer	Software packages that sequentially dial telephone numbers, recording any numbers that answer
warm standby	Synonym for Intermediate Recovery.
warm-site	A warm-site is similar to a hot-site; however, it is not fully equipped with all necessary hardware needed for recovery.

waterfall development	Also known as traditional development, it is a very procedure-focused development cycle with formal sign-off at the completion of each level.
web page	A viewable screen displaying information, presented through a web browser in a single view sometimes requiring the user to scroll to review the entire page. A bank web page may display the bank's logo, provide information about bank products and services, or allow a customer to interact with the bank or third parties that have contracted with the bank.
web services description language (WSDL)	An XML-formatted language used to describe a web service's capabilities as collections of communication endpoints capable of exchanging messages. WSDL is the language that UDDI uses. (Also see Universal Description, Discovery and Integration (UDDI))
web site	Consists of one or more web pages that may originate at one or more web server computers. A person can view the pages of a website in any order, as he or she would a magazine.
white box testing	A testing approach that uses knowledge of a program/module's underlying implementation and code intervals to verify its expected behavior.
wide area network (WAN)	A computer network connecting different remote locations that may range from short distances, such as a floor or building, to extremely long transmissions that encompass a large region or several countries
Windows NT	A version of the Windows operating system that supports preemptive multitasking
wiretapping	The practice of eavesdropping on information being transmitted over telecommunications links
work in progress (WIP)	A Status that means Activities have started but are not yet complete. It is commonly used as a Status for Incidents, Problems, Changes etc.
work instruction	A Document containing detailed instructions that specify exactly what steps to follow to carry out an Activity. A Work Instruction contains much more detail than a Procedure and is only created if very detailed instructions are needed.
workaround	(Incident Management) (Problem Management) Reducing or eliminating the Impact of an Incident or Problem for which a full Resolution is not yet available. For example by restarting a failed Configuration Item. Workarounds for Problems are documented in Known Error Records. Workarounds for Incidents that do not have associated Problem Records are documented in the Incident Record.
workload	(Capacity Management) The Resources required to deliver an identifiable part of an IT Service. Workloads may be Categorized by Users, groups of Users, or Functions within the IT Service. This is used to assist in analyzing and managing the Capacity, Performance and Utilization of Configuration Items and IT Services. The term Workload is sometimes used as a synonym for Throughput.
world wide web (WWW)	A sub-network of the Internet through which information is exchanged by text, graphics, audio and video.
world wide web consortium (W3C)	An international consortium founded in 1994 of affiliates from public and private organizations involved with the Internet and the web. The W3C's primary mission is to promulgate open standards to further enhance the economic growth of Internet web services globally.
worm	With respect to security, a special type of virus that does not attach itself to programs, but rather spreads via other methods such as e-mail (also see virus)
X.25	A protocol for packet-switching networks
X.25 interface	An interface between data terminal equipment (DTE) and data circuit-terminating equipment (DCE) for terminals operating in the packet mode on some public data networks
X.500	Standard that defines a particular hierarchical structure for global directories. Different levels may be created for each category such as country, state and city.

Index

4
4GL 102, 115, 116, 177, 353

A

abend 325
absorbed overhead 325
acceptance 2, 89, 90, 91, 96, 99, 100, 107, 109, 110, 112, 125, 129, 146, 148, 173, 183, 185, 283, 325, 327, 366, 385
access control 44, 173, 197, 208, 209, 216, 239, 240, 242, 248, 249, 251, 255, 257, 259, 275, 280, 325, 335, 384, 385, 389
access method 206, 325, 356
access path 325
access rights 218, 231, 237, 288, 289, 325, 358
account manager 325
accountability ... 11, 22, 90, 91, 102, 110, 152, 168, 235, 248, 291, 320, 325, 329, 349
accounting 2, 15, 16, 17, 45, 66, 112, 149, 160, 173, 189, 220, 229, 311, 325, 326, 341, 352, 359, 372, 388
accredited 110, 301, 325, 350, 351, 356
acknowledgement 325, 354
active recovery site 325
active response 325
activity.... 1, 4, 11, 15, 17, 23, 45, 51, 56, 65, 69, 79, 88, 113, 114, 120, 134, 135, 138, 140, 149, 158, 164, 174, 191, 195, 196, 241, 248, 250, 251, 257, 259, 269, 270, 297, 325, 326, 330, 337, 341, 342, 343, 349, 351, 355, 364, 367, 373, 380, 383, 388
address.... 11, 19, 23, 24, 28, 32, 43, 49, 53, 57, 84, 88, 91, 96, 98, 105, 121, 154, 161, 166, 168, 172, 191, 196, 200, 203, 205, 208, 211, 214, 222, 223, 224, 225, 233, 250, 253, 254, 255, 257, 258, 259, 260, 264, 266, 272, 275, 276, 282, 287, 297, 301, 306, 326, 332, 333, 339, 341, 352, 355, 364, 372, 376, 377, 382
addressing 90, 95, 97, 101, 201, 203, 205, 265, 266, 280, 326, 359, 377
adjusting period 326
administrative controls 16, 188, 189, 326
agreed service time 326
agreement 10, 67, 99, 100, 125, 153, 164, 170, 175, 189, 218, 290, 305, 326, 327, 328, 330, 366, 372, 373
alert 189, 272, 326
allocation entry 326
alpha 74, 108, 113, 248, 326, 379
analog 222, 224, 278, 282, 326, 346, 364
analytical modeling 326
anomaly 326
anonymity 326
anonymous file transfer protocol 326
antivirus software 326
appearance 11, 83, 326, 356
applet 295, 297, 326
application.... 2, 3, 4, 15, 19, 22, 23, 24, 30, 32, 35, 36, 37, 42, 45, 47, 52, 68, 69, 70, 74, 75, 77, 79, 83, 85, 88, 89, 90, 92, 93, 96, 97, 99, 101, 103, 105, 106, 107, 108, 109, 110, 113, 114, 116, 118, 119, 120, 139, 142, 146, 147, 148, 150, 151, 155, 156, 158, 159, 160, 162, 163, 164, 165, 166, 167, 169, 172, 177, 179, 180, 186, 189, 190, 191, 193, 194, 196, 197, 198, 201, 202, 206, 209, 212, 216, 218, 219, 220, 221, 237, 238, 239, 240, 241, 242, 246, 247, 248, 249, 251, 254, 255, 256, 257, 259, 263, 268, 288, 289, 295, 296, 297, 302, 303, 312, 314, 315, 316, 323, 325, 327, 328, 330, 331, 332, 336, 344, 345, 346, 347, 349, 350, 351, 353, 357, 363, 366, 367, 371, 372, 376, 377, 380, 381, 382, 383, 384, 385, 387
arithmetic-logic unit 328
artificial intelligence 118, 139, 173, 177, 328, 351
ascii 328
asp 328, 359
assembler 328, 365
assembly ci 328
assembly language 328
asset.... 28, 39, 56, 72, 75, 208, 228, 236, 237, 238, 248, 289, 328, 353, 357
assurance 11, 16, 27, 28, 31, 42, 43, 49, 51, 52, 79, 83, 85, 92, 93, 102, 107, 110, 115, 148, 150, 151, 155, 156, 158, 161, 179, 181, 184, 185, 186, 207, 269, 314, 328, 357, 358, 364, 372, 373, 381, 387
asymmetric key 284, 328
asynchronous transfer mode 266, 329
asynchronous transmission 329
attest reporting engagement 329
attitude 11, 12, 329, 356
attribute 35, 36, 70, 173, 175, 329, 332, 348, 387
audit (definition) 329
audit authority 329
audit charter 10, 11, 19, 44, 45, 46, 47, 218, 329
audit evidence.11, 12, 13, 23, 24, 32, 34, 37, 38, 41, 50, 147, 159, 249, 329, 330, 339, 341, 383
audit expert systems 24, 329
audit objective 329, 330
audit plan 11, 13, 15, 19, 24, 33, 43, 44, 46, 47, 330
audit program 10, 11, 20, 21, 22, 38, 68, 288, 330
audit responsibility 330
audit risk 12, 13, 27, 37, 47, 330
audit sampling 35, 36, 330
audit trail 16, 42, 47, 149, 154, 155, 158, 163, 168, 170, 181, 184, 186, 246, 250, 330
auditability 330
authentication 1, 163, 164, 167, 168, 207, 208, 209, 227, 240, 246, 250, 253, 255, 259, 265, 266, 267, 268, 275, 276, 282, 286, 287, 292, 293, 295, 298, 330, 336, 337, 347, 358, 372, 378, 385, 387
authorization 16, 31, 79, 85, 151, 152, 156, 157, 158, 164, 165, 168, 169, 170, 210, 237, 239, 240, 246, 255, 268, 277, 330, 345
authorized examination center 330
automated teller machine 170, 330
automatic call distribution 330
availability (definition) 330
availability management 330
availability plan 330

B

back-out plan 330
backup .. 26, 77, 148, 170, 171, 172, 231, 244, 261, 299, 300, 301, 302, 304, 305, 306, 307, 308, 309, 310, 312, 313, 314, 315, 317, 318, 321, 322, 323, 331, 339, 351, 355, 365, 380, 388
balance check 331
balanced scorecard 331
bandwidth...80, 206, 208, 209, 211, 212, 259, 265, 271, 279, 281, 282, 283, 306, 315, 325, 329, 331, 353
bar case 331

bar code 331
base case 331
baseband 331
baseline 1, 90, 101, 117, 127, 128, 149, 331
batch control 152, 331
batch processing 240, 245, 331, 369
baud rate 331
benchmark 82, 332
best practice 114, 150, 332
billing 189, 280, 332
binary code 332
biometric locks 150, 212, 332
biometrics 228, 292, 332
black box testing 332
border router 332, 351
brainstorming 59, 60, 310, 332
bridge 52, 224, 230, 244, 332, 366
british standards institution 332
broadband 207, 209, 211, 264, 283, 315, 332
brouters 332
browser 119, 159, 176, 200, 285, 287, 288, 297, 326, 332, 354, 378, 381, 390
brute force 332, 368
bs 15000 332
bs 7799 332
bsp 332
budget (definition) 333
budget formula 333
budget hierarchy 333
budget organization 333
budgeting 104, 134, 333
buffer 156, 281, 333
build (definition) 333
build environment 333
bulk data transfer 333
bus topology 209, 333, 350
business 333
business alignment 51, 69, 95, 334
business capacity management .... *See* capacity management
business case 61, 85, 88, 89, 95, 97, 116, 125, 333
business continuity management 333
business continuity plan 299, 311, 316, 320, 321, 323, 334
business continuity team 334
business customer 334
business driver 334
business impact analysis 299, 301, 323, 334
business objective 88, 334
business operations 177, 299, 301, 303, 304, 323, 334
business perspective 334
business process (definition) 334
business process integrity 334
business process reengineering 320, 334
business relationship management 334
business relationship manager 335
business risk 28, 89, 259, 329, 335
business service 335
business unit 335
business-to-consumer e-commerce 335
bypass label processing 335

C

caats 335
CAATs 9, 23, 24, 37, 38, 42, 151, 218, 288, 340
cadbury 335
call 335
call center 335
call type 335
capability maturity model 335

capability maturity model integration 335
Capacity (definition) 335
capacity management 335, 379
capacity plan 336
capital cost 336
capital expenditure 336
capital item 336
capitalization 336
card swipe 336
CASE 34, 340, 373, 376
category (definition) 336
cathode ray tube 336
cause / effect diagram 336
ccta 336
central office 336, 362
centralized data processing 336
certificate authority 161, 336, 387
certificate revocation list 336
certification 1, 2, 3, 4, 6, 25, 86, 104, 109, 110, 200, 227, 336, 344, 347, 360, 374
Certified Information Systems Auditor (CISA) 1, 9
challenge/response 227, 337
change (definition) 337
change advisory board 337
change history 337
change management 40, 86, 101, 127, 139, 142, 143, 149, 151, 170, 192, 222, 252, 273, 310, 337, 355, 371
change model 337
change record 337
change request 337
change schedule 337
change slot 337
CHAP 268, 337
chargeable item 337
charging 337, 338, 347, 364, 372
check digit 185, 338
checkpoint restart procedures 338
ci type 338
ciphertext 284, 338, 346, 349, 370, 372
circuit-switched network 338
circular routing 338
CISM (Certified Information Systems Manager) 3
classification . 77, 92, 177, 228, 229, 237, 238, 248, 273, 277, 301, 304, 321, 323, 338, 345
cleartext 338, 368
client (definition) 338
client access license 338
client-server 222, 223, 224, 250, 251, 252, 338, 375
closed (definition) 338
closure (definition) 338
closure code 338
cluster controller 338
CMMI 51, 70, 181, 182, 335
coaxial cable 207, 331, 338
COBIT 6, 9, 10, 25, 26, 50, 51, 52, 95, 96, 181, 338, 342, 401
COCO 338
code of practice 339
cohesion 103, 339
cold site 304, 310, 311, 320, 322, 339
cold standby 339
combined code on corporate governance 339
command, control and communications 339
communications controller 339
comparison program 339
compensating control 38, 39, 142, 292, 339
compiler 102, 339, 365
completeness check 339
compliance (definition) 339
compliance testing 35, 36, 236, 339

component (definition)	339
component ci	339
component failure impact analysis	339
components	34, 39, 43, 53, 57, 100, 103, 104, 106, 110, 119, 120, 128, 129, 159, 162, 163, 174, 175, 185, 187, 213, 214, 215, 222, 227, 229, 232, 233, 236, 240, 252, 255, 258, 265, 269, 274, 276, 301, 322, 333, 339, 340, 358, 362, 365, 366, 373, 374, 384
comprehensive audit	32, 340
computationally greedy	340
computer sequence checking	340
computer server	340
computer telephony integration	340
concurrency	340
concurrent access	340
confidentiality (definition)	340
configuration (definition)	340
configuration control	149, 340
configuration identification	340
configuration item	341
configuration management	16, 101, 103, 141, 149, 188, 229, 340, 341
configuration record	341
configuration structure	341
configuration verification and audit	341
console log	341
content filtering	193, 212, 254, 255, 341
continuity (definition)	341
continuous audit techniques	9, 42, 181
continuous auditing approach	341
continuous availability	341
continuous improvement	69, 341
continuous operation	341
continuous service improvement program	341
contract	19, 49, 50, 67, 68, 85, 98, 99, 123, 125, 127, 128, 129, 139, 169, 217, 233, 283, 305, 306, 308, 309, 312, 321, 323, 341, 342, 344, 348, 372
control (definition)	342
control group	342
control objective	16, 17, 25, 27, 39, 342
control objectives for enterprise governance	342
control perimeter	342
control processes	342
control risk	26, 342
control section	342
control self-assessment	9
control weakness	38, 39, 79, 339, 342
corporate governance	14, 50, 51, 342, 350, 366
corrective control	343
COSO	43, 50, 343, 401
cost (definition)	343
cost benefit analysis	343
cost center	333, 343
cost effectiveness	343
cost element	343
cost management	343
cost model	343
cost plus	343
cost type	343
cost unit	343
cost-by-customer cost model	343
cost-by-service cost model	343
countermeasure	276, 343
coupling	103, 161, 344
coverage	344
cpu	336
CRAMM	336, 344, 376
credentialed analysis	344
credit risk	344
crisis management	344
criteria (definition)	344
critical success factor	344
cryptography (definition)	344
culture	67, 69, 86, 88, 122, 278, 344, 379
customer focus	344
customer-managed use	344

D

data analysis	176, 345
data communications	312, 313, 345, 377
data custodian	345
data dictionary	81, 197, 345
data diddling	345
data encryption standard	345
data flow (definition)	345
data integrity (definition)	345
data leakage	296, 345
data oriented systems development	346
data owner	96, 237, 239, 288, 345
data security	345
data structure	175, 176, 345, 356, 387
database (definition)	345
database administrator	81, 83, 231, 345
database management system	345, 373
database replication	345
database specifications	346
datagram	266, 346
decentralization	346
decision support system	177, 346
decoy server	346
decryption (definition)	346
decryption key	346
default deny policy	346
default password	346
definitive hardware store	346
definitive software library	346
degauss	346
deliverables	85, 86, 87, 91, 92, 93, 98, 99, 107, 123, 125, 127, 128, 129, 130, 133, 138, 139, 140, 214, 346
delta release	346
demand management	346
demilitarized zone	256, 348
Deming cycle	346
demodulation	346
dependency	26, 347, 374, 379
deployment	86, 88, 99, 101, 110, 115, 116, 148, 149, 167, 215, 272, 274, 276, 347
depreciation	347
detailed IS/IT controls	347
detection (definition)	347
detection risk	26, 27, 347
detective controls	16, 190, 347
development (definition)	347
development environment	347
diagnosis	347
diagnostic script	347
dial-back	240, 280, 347
dial-in access controls	347
digital certificate	288, 347
digital signature	161, 167, 227, 285, 287, 295, 298, 347, 364
direct cost	347
direct reporting engagement	347
discovery sampling	348
diskless workstations	348
distributed data processing network	348
distributed denial-of-service	346
dmz	348

DNS..................................202, 223, 225, 255, 259, 263, 282, 348, 382
do nothing 348
document (definition) 348
downloading 326, 348
downtime (definition) 348
downtime report 348
dry-pipe 348
due care 69, 348
due professional care 11, 24, 67, 289, 348
dumb terminal 348
duplex routing 348
dynamic analysis 183, 185, 348

E

EBCDIC 202, 351
echo checks 348
e-commerce 50, 102, 120, 159, 160, 161, 162, 164, 167, 304, 348, 388
EDI 120, 159, 162, 163, 164, 165, 194, 201, 348, 349
edit controls 349
editing 349
effectiveness 349
efficiency 349
EFQM 70, 350
EFT 169, 170, 349
electronic cash 349
electronic signature 349
electronic vaulting 349, 387
e-mail 166, 167, 202, 255, 280, 326, 348, 349, 362, 366, 381, 390
embedded audit module 47, 349
emergency change 349
encapsulation 349, 365
encryption (definition) 349
encryption key 170, 337, 349, 370, 372, 377
end-user computing 34, 349
engagement letter 11, 349
enterprise governance 342, 350
environment (definition) 350
ERP 19, 86, 97, 160, 174, 197, 327, 334, 345, 350, 355, 385
error (definition) 350
error control 201, 222, 224, 350
error risk 350
escalation 64, 82, 84, 187, 189, 227, 334, 350, 353, 354
estimation 36, 62, 104, 130, 140, 350
Ethernet 198, 199, 200, 203, 205, 206, 216, 275, 318, 350
event (definition) 350
event management 350
evidence 2, 9, 10, 11, 13, 19, 20, 23, 24, 31, 32, 34, 38, 39, 41, 79, 100, 109, 152, 154, 156, 180, 219, 251, 295, 297, 320, 322, 329, 330, 350, 373, 374, 375, 383, 388
examination board 350, 356
exception report 155, 157, 340, 351, 379
executable code 147, 351
EXIN 350, 351
expert systems 173, 179, 351
external customer 351
external router 332, 351
external service provider 351

F

fail-over 264, 340, 351, 355, 364, 377, 380
fail-safe 351
failure (definition) 351
false negative 271, 351
false positive 271, 351
fault 351

fault tolerance 280, 351
fault tree analysis 351
feasibility study 88, 89, 95, 96, 97, 99, 111, 351, 384
fiber optic 351
field 352
file 352
file layout 352
file server 348, 352, 362
filtering router 352
fin 352
financial audit 32, 352
financial management 350, 352
financial year 352
finger 352
firewall 161, 162, 206, 227, 250, 254, 255, 256, 257, 258, 259, 260, 261, 262, 263, 264, 265, 266, 267, 268, 270, 276, 277, 297, 352, 358, 388, 389
firmware 205, 211, 219, 220, 238, 352
first time fix rate 352
first-line support 352
fiscal year 352
fishbone diagram 352
fit for purpose 352
fixed cost 352
fixed facility 352
fixed price 352
follow the sun support 352
foreign exchange risk 353
format checking 353
frame relay 266, 283, 353
fraud risk 353
FTP 202, 255, 267, 297, 326, 353, 381
full cost 353
full duplex 348, 353
full release 353
function (definition) 353
function point analysis 105, 353

G

gateway 163, 205, 206, 222, 224, 244, 257, 259, 265, 266, 295, 297, 311, 353
general controls 24, 83, 164, 347, 353
generalized audit software 24, 30, 37, 340, 354
geographic disk mirroring 354
going rate 354
gradual recovery 354
guideline (definition) 354

H

hacker 166, 193, 207, 208, 241, 354
half duplex 348, 354
handprint scanner 354
harden 354
hardware (definition) 354
hash function 286, 347, 354
hash total 354
help desk (definition) 354
hexadecimal 354
hierarchical database 348, 354, 373
honey pot 346, 354
hot site 304, 305, 311, 312, 323, 354
hot standby 354
HTTP 255, 258, 259, 271, 297, 354, 358, 381
HTTPS 355
hub 204, 206, 210, 222, 224, 269, 355
hyperlink 355

hypertext (definition) 355

I

ICMP 203, 259, 355
idle standby 355, 364, 377
IDS ... 161, 193, 194, 254, 260, 269, 270, 271, 272, 273, 289, 295, 297, 355
IEEE 204, 274, 275, 355
IETF 358, 359, 375, 376
IIOP 358
image processing 171, 355
immediate recovery 355
impact (definition) 355
impact code 355
implementation life cycle review 355
incident (definition) 355
incident management 16, 87, 187, 213, 272, 273, 355
incident record 355
incremental testing 355
independence ... 9, 13, 37, 40, 79, 81, 82, 83, 84, 87, 103, 326, 356
indexed sequential file 356
indirect cost 356
information engineering 356
information processing facility .. 75, 304, 305, 317, 320, 322, 356, 365, 378
information security management 3, 356
information security manager 356
information security officer 239, 356
information security policy 44, 53, 230, 238, 356
information technology (IT) (definition) 356
informed customer 356
infrastructure service 356
inherent risk 26, 356
inheritance 173, 357, 365
initial program load 357
input controls 151, 357
insource 357
integrated test facilities 357
integration testing 107, 357
integrity (definition) 357
intelligent terminal 357
interactive voice response 357
interest rate risk 357
interface testing 357
intermediate recovery 357
internal control structure 358
internal controls 357
internal customer 358
internal penetrators 358
internal service provider 358
internal storage 342, 358
Internet (definition) 358
internet banking 358
internet protocol
    IP 359
internet service provider 358
intranet 176, 358
intrusion (definition) 358
intrusion detection (definition) 358
intrusive monitoring 358, 364
investment appraisal 359
invocation 359
IPSEC 276, 359
irregularities 12, 35, 41, 45, 106, 342, 353, 359, 379
ISACA .. 1, 3, 4, 5, 6, 7, 8, 9, 10, 11, 13, 23, 25, 26, 28, 33, 52, 65, 83, 192, 311, 313, 314, 315, 317, 348, 401
ISDN 203, 204, 206, 207, 216, 265, 318, 357
ishikawa diagram 359

ISO 50, 51, 70, 81, 83, 181, 182, 184, 186, 197, 204, 327, 332, 339, 342, 358, 359, 362, 369, 372, 374, 375, 378, 380, 382, 383
ISO 9000 359
ISO 9001 359
IT Accounting 359
IT availability metrics model 359
IT directorate 359
IT governance 1, 4, 5
IT governance (definition) 359
IT infrastructure (definition) 359
IT operations 359
IT service (definition) 360
IT service continuity management 360
IT service continuity plan 360
IT service management forum 360
IT service provider (definition) 360
IT steering group 360
ITIL 51, 188, 332, 336, 350, 359, 360, 365, 379

J

job control language 316, 360, 375
job description 360
journal entry 326, 360, 362
judgment sampling 360

K

kepner-tregoe analysis 360
key performance indicator
    KPI 360
knowledge base 173, 174, 360
knowledge management 360
known error 360
known error database 361
known error record 361

L

latency 281, 282, 361
layer 2 forwarding
    L2F 361
layer 2 tunneling protocol
    L2TP 361
LDAP 361
leased lines 69, 264, 265, 361
legal risk 361
librarian 74, 361
license management 361
lifecycle (definition) 361
limit check 361
link editor 361
liquidity risk 361
live environment 98, 361
local area network 77, 333, 362, 364, 377
local loop 362
log (definition) 362
logical access controls .15, 218, 227, 231, 240, 241, 246, 249, 362
logoff 362
logon 362
logs/log file 362

M

machine language 351, 362, 381
magnetic card reader 362
magnetic ink character recognition 362

maintainability 362
major incident 362
managed object 362
managed services 362
management information (definition) 362
management information system 362
management system 38, 74, 167, 177, 182, 362, 372
man-in-the-middle attack 362
manual workaround 362
mapping 24, 81, 83, 163, 205, 259, 328, 363
marginal cost 363
market price 363
masking 282, 363
masqueraders 358, 363
master file 153, 163, 165, 315, 363, 369, 387
materiality 13, 19, 27, 39, 40, 363
maturity level 93, 181, 363
mean time between failures 363
mean time between service incidents 363
mean time to repair 363
memory dump 363
message switching 163, 363
metric (definition) 363
microwave transmission 363
middleware 114, 115, 119, 159, 160, 161, 363
mission statement 125, 363
misuse detection 364
modeling 118, 139, 179, 364
modem 207, 208, 224, 240, 256, 264, 267, 268, 332, 364, 366
modulation 282, 331, 364
monetary unit sampling 364
monitor (definition) 364
monitoring policy 364
multiplexing 329, 364
multiplexor 364
mutual takeover 364

N

NAT 208, 227, 257, 259, 266, 364
Netware 364
network (definition) 364
network administrator 231, 244, 251, 270, 272, 364
network hop 364
n-line support 364
node 198, 201, 330, 355, 364, 377, 380
noise 364
nonrepudiable transactions 364
nonrepudiation 347, 364
normalization 197, 364
numeric check 364

O

object code 102, 148, 315, 339, 365, 381
object management group 358, 365
object orientation 365
objective (definition) 365
objectivity 17, 25, 57, 87, 98, 102, 130, 365
object-oriented system development 365
office of government commerce 365
office of public sector information 365
offline files 365
offsite storage 308, 349, 365
OLA
    operational level agreement 366
online data processing 365
open systems 338, 365

operate (definition) 365
operating system (definition) 366
operating system audit trails 366
operation (definition) 366
operational (definition) 366
operational audit 17, 26, 32, 366
operational control 54, 72, 366
operational cost 366
operational expenditure 366
operational risk 366
operator console 366
opportunity cost 366
optical character recognition 367
optical scanner 367
optimize (definition) 367
organization (definition) 367
output analyzer 367
outsource 67, 189, 258, 293, 367
overhead 41, 267, 339, 367, 387

P

package release 367
packet (definition) 367
packet filtering 254, 255, 256, 257, 341, 367
packet switching 200, 203, 279, 367
parallel simulation 367
parallel testing 109, 146, 367
pareto principle 367
parity check 158, 367
partitioned file 367
partnership 367
passive attack 368
passive response 368
password (definition) 368
password cracker 368
payment system 368
penetration testing 107, 218, 227, 368
percentage utilization 368
performance (definition) 368
performance indicators 43, 50, 52, 109, 174, 368
performance management 13, 368
performance testing 368
peripherals (definition) 368
permanent virtual circuit 353, 368
personal identification number 169, 368
PERT 134, 138, 371
pervasive is controls 368
piggy backing 368
PKI 161, 227, 287, 372
plaintext 207, 284, 298, 338, 346, 349, 368, 370, 372
plan (definition) 369
plan-do-check-act 369
planned downtime 369
planning (definition) 369
point-of-presence 369
point-of-sale systems 369
policy (definition) 369
polymorphism 118, 369
population 27, 35, 36, 270, 329, 330, 348, 369, 378, 382, 389
port (definition) 369
portable facility 369
portfolio management 50, 86, 87, 369
portfolio of services 369
post implementation review 369
posting 17, 191, 369
PPP 208, 266, 361, 369
PPTP 265, 266, 361, 370
preventive controls 16, 156, 291, 370

price risk	370
pricing	217, 300, 370
PRINCE2	123, 370, 371
priority (definition)	370
privacy (definition)	370
private key (definition)	370
private key cryptosystems	345, 370
privilege (definition)	370
proactive problem management	370
problem (definition)	370
problem control	370
problem management	139, 140, 187, 190, 191, 370
problem record	370
procedure (definition)	370
process (definition)	370
process control	105, 371
process manager	371
process maturity	93, 181, 371
process owner	231, 371
production programs	78, 371, 386
professional competence	11, 25, 371
profit center	371
program (definition)	371
program flowcharts	371
program narratives	148, 371
project (definition)	371
project sponsor	91, 92, 125, 371
project team	59, 72, 91, 92, 96, 97, 98, 100, 112, 123, 128, 129, 133, 213, 303, 371
projected service availability	371
promiscuous mode	269, 371
protection domain	371
protocol (definition)	371
protocol converter	371
protocol stack	208, 209, 241, 372
prototyping	34, 85, 101, 102, 115, 117, 118, 178, 372
proxy server	255, 295, 372
public key (definition)	372
public key cryptosystem	372, 377

Q

quality (definition)	372
queue	372
quick ship	372
quick win	372

R

RA	161, 287, 374
RADIUS	255, 275, 372
random access memory	372
range check	185, 361, 372
real-time analysis	372
real-time processing	349, 373
reasonableness check	373
reciprocal	106, 305, 373
record (definition)	373
record, screen and report layouts	373
recovery (definition)	373
recovery center	312, 373
recovery option	373
recovery testing	3, 299, 373
recovery time objective	373
redo logs	373, 387
redundancy (definition)	373
redundancy check	244, 373
reengineering	120, 183, 185, 373

regression testing	108, 374
relationship (definition)	374
relationship processes	374
release (definition)	374
release acceptance	374
release identification	374
release management	85, 149, 187, 192, 374
release mechanism	374
release process	374
release record	374
release type	374
release unit	374
relevant audit evidence	374
reliability	1, 16, 32, 35, 36, 41, 42, 43, 83, 96, 105, 115, 117, 163, 172, 180, 186, 228, 279, 280, 306, 316, 341, 374, 387
reliable audit evidence	375
remote job entry	375
remote procedure call	375
repository	116, 176, 282, 375
repudiation	163, 168, 286, 295, 298, 375
reputational risk	164, 169, 375
request for change	375
requirement (definition)	375
requirements definition	89, 91, 96, 100, 375, 384
residual risk	56, 278, 375
resilience	375
resolution (definition)	375
resolution processes	375
resource (definition)	375
resource capacity management	375
response time	103, 250, 376
responsiveness	376, 383
restore	273, 284, 299, 305, 308, 313, 314, 315, 323, 325, 363, 376
return on capital employed	376
return to normal	376
reverse engineering	376
review (definition)	376
RFC	375, 376, 380
RFP	97, 99, 100, 125, 140, 375
ring topology	376, 386
risk (definition)	376
risk assessment	9, 12, 13, 26, 27, 28, 30, 44, 46, 54, 56, 59, 60, 61, 69, 81, 126, 213, 227, 232, 236, 248, 249, 258, 259, 307, 376
risk management (definition)	376
risk reduction measure	376
risk treatment	342, 377
ROI	50, 52, 90, 95, 214, 376
role (definition)	377
rollout	70, 108, 111, 116, 142, 192, 212, 213, 274, 377
root cause (definition)	377
root cause analysis	377
rootkit	269, 377
rotating standby	377
rounding down	242, 243, 377
router (definition)	377
RPO	302, 314, 373
RS-232	377
RSA	167, 227, 248, 288, 377
RTO	302, 373
rulebase	377
run instructions	377
running costs	377
run-to-run totals	377

S

salami technique	243, 377
SAM database	377

sampling risk 27, 35, 378
scalability 168, 259, 264, 265, 378
scheduling (definition) 378
scope .. 9, 10, 11, 13, 14, 17, 18, 19, 22, 32, 40, 41, 44, 46, 56, 66, 67, 70, 86, 88, 96, 101, 102, 115, 116, 117, 121, 122, 123, 125, 126, 127, 129, 130, 131, 133, 138, 139, 151, 176, 182, 192, 198, 213, 218, 235, 257, 261, 310, 330, 342, 356, 371, 378
screening routers 378
second-line support 378
security administrator (definition) 378
security management 188, 233, 235, 249
security management (definition) 378
security perimeter 378
security policy (definition) 378
security principle 378
security software 212, 245, 378
security testing 227, 378
security/transaction risk 378
segregation/separation of duties 379
sequence check 379
sequential file 379
server (definition) 379
service (definition) 379
service bureau 311, 379, 386
service catalog 379
service delivery 49, 329, 379
service desk 379
service hours 379
service improvement plan 379
service level (definition) 379
service level agreement 379
service level management 380
service level requirement 380
service level target 380
service maintenance objective 380
service manager 380
service outage analysis 380
service provider (definition) 380
service reporting 380
service request 380
service support 380
service user 380
serviceability 380
shell 195, 380
signatures ... 35, 148, 151, 156, 161, 164, 166, 167, 244, 270, 271, 297, 349, 370, 377, 380
simple fail-over 380
simulation modeling 381
single point of contact 381
single point of failure 187, 267, 280, 381
slam chart 381
SMART (acronym) 381
smart card 251, 288, 292, 293, 381
SMTP 381
sniff 252, 381
SOAP 120, 381
software (definition) 381
software asset management 381
source code 381
source code compare programs 381
source documents 38, 74, 79, 152, 154, 355, 381, 384
spanning port 382
specification 382
SPICE 182, 381
split data systems 382
split DNS 259, 382
spoofing 227, 250, 253, 275, 282, 358, 382
spool 156, 382

SSL 162, 207, 227, 287, 288, 378
stakeholder 382
standard (definition) 382
standard change 382
standard cost 382
standby 382
standing data 382
star topology 209, 382
statement of requirements 382
static analysis 382
statistical sampling 27, 35, 36, 382
status (definition) 383
status accounting 383
storage management 383
strategic (definition) 383
strategic alignment objectives model 383
strategic risk 383
strategy (definition) 383
stress testing 336
structured programming 103, 383
subject matter 383
substantive testing 26, 31, 32, 35, 36, 218, 383
sufficient audit evidence 383
supplier (definition) 383
supplier management 383
supply chain 97, 174, 383
support group 179, 383
support hours 383
surge suppressor 383
SWIFT (acronym) 384
switch (definition) 384
symmetric key encryption 384
SYN 384
synchronous transmission 384
system (definition) 384
system exit 384
system flowcharts 101, 102, 148, 384
system management 384
system narratives 384
system software 384
system testing 384
systems acquisition process 384
systems analysis 384
systems development life cycle 93, 327, 384

T

table look-ups 385
TACACS+ 385
tactical 385
tape management system 385
taps 385
TCP 385
TCP/IP 385
tcpdump 385
technical infrastructure security 385
technical observation post 385
technical support 385
telecommunications 385
teleprocessing 385
telnet 255, 385
terminal 385
terms of reference 371, 385
test 385
test data 24, 37, 47, 150, 151, 181, 215, 248, 340, 367, 385
test environment 75, 104, 146, 380, 385, 386
test generators 385
test programs 386, 388
third party (definition) 386

third-line support ... 386
third-party review ... 386
threat (definition) ... 386
threshold ... 272, 326, 368, 386
throughput ... 386
tied users ... 386
token ... 386
top-level management ... 386
topology ... 386
total cost of ownership ... 386
TQM ... 70, 386
transaction (definition) ... 387
transaction log ... 79, 154, 387
transaction protection ... 387
transfer cost ... 387
trap door ... 387
trend analysis ... 387
trojan horse ... 296, 298, 387
trust (definition) ... 387
trusted processes ... 387
trusted systems ... 387
tuning ... 77, 104, 194, 387
tuple ... 387
twisted pairs ... 387

U

UDP ... 266, 387
unabsorbed overhead ... 387
underpinning contract ... 388
unit cost ... 388
unit testing ... 108, 112, 388
universal description, discovery and integration ... 388
UNIX ... 388
untied users ... 388
untrustworthy host ... 388
uploading ... 388
UPS ... 180, 294, 306, 388
urgency ... 111, 142, 388
usability ... 388
useful audit evidence ... 388
user ... 16, 17, 34, 69, 74, 75, 76, 77, 79, 82, 83, 84, 89, 90, 91, 92, 96, 98, 99, 100, 101, 102, 105, 107, 108, 109, 110, 111, 113, 116, 139, 146, 147, 148, 149, 150, 154, 158, 160, 161, 166, 167, 173, 175, 176, 177, 178, 179, 182, 185, 186, 193, 194, 196, 197, 198, 200, 202, 207, 208, 209, 218, 219, 220, 221, 227, 231, 237, 238, 239, 240, 241, 244, 246, 247, 248, 250, 251, 254, 255, 258, 261, 264, 266, 267, 268, 269, 271, 274, 275, 276, 277, 278, 279, 280, 281, 283, 284, 286, 388
utility software ... 24, 316, 388

V

vaccine ... 388
validity check ... 388
value chain ... 388
value for money ... 388
value-added network ... 389
variable cost ... 389
variable sampling ... 35, 36, 389
variance ... 36, 134, 359, 389
variant ... 104, 175, 263, 389
vendor-managed use ... 389
verification ... 389
version ... 389
virtual organizations ... 389
virtual private network ... 69, 207, 265, 276, 296, 389
virus ... 389
vision ... 389
vital business function ... 389
voice mail ... 280, 389
vulnerability (definition) ... 389
vulnerability analysis ... 288, 344, 358, 364, 389

W

war dialer ... 389
warm standby ... 389
warm-site ... 389
waterfall development ... 390
web page ... 160, 355, 381, 390
web site ... 390
whitebox testing ... 390
wide area network ... 283, 321, 377, 390
Windows NT ... 390
wiretapping ... 390
work in progress ... 390
work instruction ... 390
workaround ... 390
workload ... 187, 239, 250, 325, 332, 390
world wide web ... 390
world wide web consortium ... 390
worm ... 389, 390
WSDL ... 120, 390

X

X.25 ... 390
X.25 interface ... 390
X.500 ... 361, 390
XML ... 120, 160, 161, 197, 198, 202, 351, 381, 390

References

Introduction

[1] ISACA. 2007. "ISACA Overview and History". http://www.isaca.org/Content/NavigationMenu/About_ISACA/Overview_and_History/Overview_and_History.htm.

[2] Anonymous. 2007. IT Security Certifications Pay Breaking out of the Pack As Customer Discontent Rises. http://www.footepartners.com/FooteNewsrelease_1Q2007skillspay_053007.pdf.

[3] ISACA. 2007. 2007 Candidate's Guide to the CISA Exam. http://www.isaca.org/AMTemplate.cfm?Section=CISA_Exam_Info&Template=/ContentManagement/ContentDisplay.cfm&ContentID=24364

[4] ISACA. 2007. "2007 Candidate's Guide to the CISM Exam". http://www.isaca.org/Content/ContentGroups/Certification3/CISM_Exam_Info/2007CISMCandidatesGuide.pdf

Chapter 1

[1] ISACA. 2007. IS Standards, Guidelines and Procedures for Auditing and Control Professionals. (ISSGP) (June 2007). Rolling Meadows. Information Systems Audit and Control Association. http://www.isaca.org/AMTemplate.cfm?Section=Standards2&Template=/ContentManagement/ContentDisplay.cfm&ContentID=33307. Pg. 6.

[2] Ibid. Pgs. 8 – 17.

[3] Ibid. Pgs. 10-17.

[4] Peace and Simitian. SB 1386 CHAPTERED. (July 2007) http://info.sen.ca.gov/pub/01-02/bill/sen/sb_1351-1400/sb_1386_bill_20020926_chaptered.html

[5] Ibid. ISACA. ISSGP. Pg. 4.

[6] Warren, J. Donald, Jr. *Handbook of It Auditing*. (Handbook) Boston: Warren Gorham & Lamont, 1998. Chapters A2 and C3.

[7] ITGI. 2007. COBIT 4.1. (COBIT) (July 2007). http://www.COBITonline4.info/Pages/Public/Browse/PdfDownload.aspx. Section ME3, "Ensure Compliance With External Requirements".

[8] ISACA. 2007. "CISA Review Manual 2007". (CISA Manual) Rolling Meadows. Information Systems Audit and Control Association. Pg. 27.

[9] Ibid. Warren. Handbook. Chapter A.

[10] Ibid. Chapter D1.

[11] Ibid. ISACA CISA Manual. Pg. 29.

[12] Ibid. Warren. Handbook. Chapters A5 and A6.

[13] Ibid. ISACA CISA Manual. Pg. 31.

[14] Ibid. Warren. Handbook. Chapter B4.

[15] Weber, Ron. *EDP Auditing: Conceptual Foundations and Practice*. (EDP) New York. McGraw-Hill. 1988. Chapter 4.

[16] Ibid. Warren. Handbook. Chapter B2.

[17] Ibid. Weber. EDP. Chapter 20.

[18] Ibid. Warren. Handbook. Chapter A4.

[19] Ibid. Chapter A5.

[20] Ibid. Chapters A5 and E1.

[21] Ibid. Weber. EDP.

[22] Ibid. Warren. Handbook. Chapter A7.

[23] Ibid.

[24] The Committee of Sponsoring Organizations of the Treadway Commission. 1992. Internal Control — Integrated Framework. (COSO). http://www.cpa2biz.com/AST/Main/CPA2BIZ_Primary/InternalControls/COSO/PRDOVR~PC-990009/PC-990009.jsp

[25] The Committee of Sponsoring Organizations of the Treadway Commission. (July 2007) http://www.coso.org/key.htm

[26] The Committee of Sponsoring Organizations of the Treadway Commission. (July 2007) http://www.coso.org/publications/executive_summary_integrated_framework.htm

References (cont.)

Chapter 2

[1] ISACA. 2007. *"CISA Review Manual 2007"*. (CISA Manual) Rolling Meadows. Information Systems Audit and Control Association. Pg. 63.
[2] ZIFA. 2007. Zachman Framework. The Zachman Institute for Framework Advancement. (June 2007). http://www.zifa.com/
[3] Office of Management and Budget. 2007. FEA Reference Models. (June 2007). http://www.whitehouse.gov/omb/egov/a-2-EAModelsNEW2.html
[4] The Open Group Architecture Framework. 2007. Welcome to TOGAF. (August 2007) http://www.opengroup.org/architecture/togaf8-doc/arch/
[5] Information Society Technologies. 2007. IST Project Fact Sheet. (August 2007). http://cordis.europa.eu/fetch?ACTION=D&CALLER=PROJ_IST&RCN=54837.
[6] InnoVisions Canada. 2007. The Canadian Telework Association. (August 2007). http://www.ivc.ca/cta/
[7] Free Management Library, 2007. Virtual Teams. (August 2007). http://www.acm.org/crossroads/xrds4-1/organ.html.
[8] ITGI. 2007. COBIT 4.1. (COBIT) (July 2007). http://www.cobitonline4.info/Pages/Public/Browse/PdfDownload.aspx. Section PO4, "Define the IT Processes Organization and Relationships".
[9] Warren, J. Donald, Jr. *Handbook of It Auditing*. (Handbook) Boston: Warren Gorham & Lamont, 1998. Chapter B2.
[10] Ibid. ISACA. 2007. (CISA Manual). Pg. 99.

Chapter 3

[1] ITGI. 2007. COBIT 4.1. (COBIT) (July 2007). http://www.cobitonline4.info/Pages/Public/Browse/PdfDownload.aspx. "Executive Overview". Pg. 8.
[2] BUNDESREPUBLIK DEUTSCHLAND 2004. "V-Modell XT. Part 1: Fundamentals of the V-Modell" http://ftp.uni-kl.de/pub/v-modell-xt/Release-1.1-eng/Dokumentation/pdf/V-Modell-XT-eng-Teil1.pdf
[3] ISACA. 2007. *"CISA Review Manual 2007"*. (CISA Manual) Rolling Meadows. Information Systems Audit and Control Association. Pg. 140.
[4] Warren, J. Donald, Jr. *Handbook of IT Auditing*. (Handbook) Boston: Warren Gorham & Lamont, 1998. Chapter B1.
[5] ITGI. 2007. COBIT 4.1. (COBIT) (July 2007). http://www.cobitonline4.info/Pages/Public/Browse/PdfDownload.aspx. Section AI7, "Install and Accredit Solutions and Changes".
[6] ISACA. 2007. *"CISA Review Manual 2007"*. (CISA Manual) Rolling Meadows. Information Systems Audit and Control Association. Pg. 152.
[7] Ibid. Pg. 161.
[8] Ibid. Section AI6, "Manage Changes".
[9] Ibid.
[10] Ibid. Section AI4, "Enable Operation and Use".
[11] Anonymous. 2007. SORBS Retest FAQ. (July 2007). http://www.au.sorbs.net/faq/retest.shtml
[12] G. Gorry, M.S. Morton. A framework for management information systems. (July 2007). Sloan Management Review 12(2). 1971. Pgs. 55-70.
[13] Anonymous. 2007. Lewin's Freeze Phases. ChangingMinds.org. Syque. (July 2007) http://changingminds.org/disciplines/change_management/lewin_change/lewin_change.htm
[14] International Organization for Standardization. 2005. (ISO). Software Engineering -- Software product Quality Requirements and Evaluation (SQuaRE) -- Guide to SQuaRE. (July 2007). http://www.iso.org/iso/en/CatalogueDetailPage.CatalogueDetail?CSNUMBER=35683&ICS1=35&ICS2=80&ICS3=
[15] Carnegie Mellon University and Software Engineering Institute. 2006. CMMI® for Development, Version 1.2. (July 2007). http://www.sei.cmu.edu/cmmi/models/model-v12-components-word.html. Pgs 31-40.
[16] Ibid. COBIT. Appendix III. Maturity Model for Internal Control.
[17] Ibid. ISO. 2003. Information technology -- Process assessment -- Part 2: Performing an assessment. http://www.iso.org/iso/en/CatalogueDetailPage.CatalogueDetail?CSNUMBER=37458&ICS1=35&ICS2=80&ICS3=

References (cont.)

Chapter 4

[1] ITGI. 2007. COBIT 4.1. (COBIT) (July 2007). http://www.cobitonline4.info/Pages/Public/Browse/PdfDownload.aspx. Section AI1 "Identify Automated Solutions".

[2] Office of Government Procurement. 2007. Service Management - ITIL® (IT Infrastructure Library) (July 2007) http://www.best-management-practice.com/IT-Service-Management-ITIL/

[3] University of California. 2007. What is SETI@home? (July 2007). http://setiathome.berkeley.edu/

[4] World Wide Web Consortium. 2003. Extensible Markup Language. (July 2007). http://www.w3.org/XML/

[5] Internet Society. 2003. Histories of the Internet. (June 2007). http://www.isoc.org/internet/history/brief.shtml

[6] Ibid. COBIT. Section PO3, "Determining Technological Direction".

Chapter 5

Reference: COBIT Control Objectives, DS5, Ensuring Systems Security

References: Handbook of IT Auditing, Chapter D5; EDP Auditing: Conceptual Foundations and Practice, Chapter 9; COBIT Control Objectives, DS5, Ensuring Systems Security

References: Handbook of IT Auditing, Chapters B1, B6, D5 & E4; EDP Auditing: Conceptual Foundations and Practice, Chapter 9

Reference: IS Audit & Control Journal, Vol. 6, 1997 "How to Manage and Reduce Computer Crime," Vol. 1, 1998 "An Introduction to Computer Crime and Attendant IT Audit and Security Functions"

Reference: Handbook of IT Auditing, Chapters A5, B1, B6, B8, D4, D5, E4, & E5

References: Handbook of IT Auditing, Chapters C1, D4, D5 & E5; COBIT Control Objectives DS12 Managing Facilities

Reference: COBIT Control Objectives DS12, Managing Facilities References

Reference: Handbook of IT Auditor, Chapter B6, IS Audit & Control Journal, Vol. 3, Dynamic Handwritten Signature Verification System"

Elachi, Joanna. Standards Snapshot: The State of the Big 3 in VoIP Signaling Protocols. November 27, 2000.

Gil Biran. Voice over Frame Relay, IP and ATM: The Case for Cooperative Networking.
   http://www.protocols.com/papers/voe.htm

International Telecommunication Union ITU-T H.235 Version 2 (11/2000) Telecommunication Standardization Sector of ITU

Frame Relay Forum: Market Development & Education Committee and Technical Committee, White Paper: A Discussion of Voice over Frame Relay, August 2000.

http://www.frforum.com/, The Basic Guide to Frame Relay Networking

http://www.esoft.com.tw/product/mgcpo.htm

IAEC3186. Introduction to Information Systems Security Engineering (ISSE), Session 02-01, September 2001.

References (cont.)

Chapter 6

[1] ISACA. 2007. *"CISA Review Manual 2007"*. (CISA Manual) Rolling Meadows. Information Systems Audit and Control Association. Pgs. 457-459.
[2] Ibid. CISA Manual. Pg. 467.
[3] Ibid. CISA Manual. Pg. 463-464.
References: Handbook of IT Auditing, Chapter D6; EDP Auditing: Conceptual Foundations and Practice, Chapter 3, IS Audit & Control Journal, Vol. 4, 1998 "Point of Failure Recovery Plan", Vol. 5, 1998 "Auditors Add Value to the Business Continuity Program"
Reference: EDP Auditing: Conceptual Foundations and Practice, Chapter 7
References: COBIT Control Objectives DS4, Ensuring Continuous Service, IS Audit & Control Journal, Vol. V 1998, "Auditors Add Value to the Business Continuity Program"
Reference: National Institute of Standards and Technology (NIST), "Information Technology Security Practices & Checklist/Implementation Guides," USA, www.csrc.nist.gov/pcig/ppsp.html

Glossary

Reference: ISACA. 2007. Glossary. (June 2007). www.isaca.org/glossary.
Reference: Office of Government Commerce. 2007. ITIL Version 3. (July 2007). http://www.best-management-practice.com/gempdf/ITIL_Glossary_V3_1_24.pdf.
"ITIL ® is a Registered Trade Mark, and a Registered Community Trade Mark of the Office of Government Commerce, and is Registered in the U.S. Patent and Trademark Office".
"PRINCE ® is a Registered Trade Mark and a Registered Community Trade Mark of the Office of Government Commerce, and is Registered in the U.S. Patent and Trademark Office".